MASTERPLOTS II

CHRISTIAN LITERATURE

MASTERPLOTS II

CHRISTIAN LITERATURE

3

Lif–Sen

Edited by
JOHN K. ROTH
Claremont McKenna College

SALEM PRESS
Pasadena, California   Hackensack, New Jersey

Editor in Chief: Dawn P. Dawson
Editorial Director: Christina J. Moose
Acquisitions Editor: Mark Rehn
Research Supervisor: Jeffry Jensen
Research Assistant: Keli Trousdale

Manuscript Editor: Rowena Wildin Dehanke
Production Editor: Andrea E. Miller
Graphics and Design: James Hutson
Photo Editor: Cynthia Breslin Beres
Editorial Assistant: Dana Garey

Cover photo: Christ Pantocrator, 13th c. mosaic, Palatine Chapel, Palermo, Italy
(The Granger Collection, New York)

Library of Congress Cataloging-in-Publication Data
Masterplots II. Christian literature / edited by John K. Roth.
  p. cm.
  Includes bibliographical references and index.
  ISBN 978-1-58765-379-7 (set : alk. paper) — ISBN 978-1-58765-380-3 (vol. 1 : alk. paper) — ISBN 978-1-58765-381-0 (vol. 2 : alk. paper) — ISBN 978-1-58765-382-7 (vol. 3 : alk. paper) — ISBN 978-1-58765-383-4 (vol. 4 : alk. paper)
  1. Christian literature—History and criticism. 2. Christian literature—Stories, plots, etc. I. Roth, John K. II. Title: Masterplots 2. III. Title: Masterplots two.

BR117.M15 2007
230—dc22

2007024245

First Printing

LIST OF TITLES IN VOLUME

COMPLETE LIST OF TITLES IN ALL VOLUMES

Volume 1

Volume 2

COMPLETE LIST OF TITLES IN ALL VOLUMES

Volume 3

Volume 4

COMPLETE LIST OF TITLES IN ALL VOLUMES

THE LIFE OF JESUS

Author: Ernest Renan (1823-1892)
First published: Vie de Jésus, 1863 (English translation, 1864)
Edition used: The Life of Jesus, introduction by John Haynes Holmes. New York: Modern Library, 1927
Genre: Nonfiction
Subgenres: Biography; history
Core issues: Chastity; Gospels; Jesus Christ; works and deeds

Renan's The Life of Jesus *presented its subject, for the first time, as a completely human being, not as a supernatural being. As literature, Renan's account of Jesus' life is highly skillful and generally plausible, and even Renan's detractors conceded that his narrative possessed great charm, despite some factual and logical shortcomings.*

Overview

Ernest Renan names five main sources for his biography: the Gospels, the Old Testament Apocrypha, the works of Philo Judaeus, the works of Flavius Josephus, and the Talmud. Josephus barely mentions Jesus. Philo knew nothing of him but lived in a contemporary intellectual center, Alexandria, and this afforded a perspective on the dominant religious and philosophical ideas of the time.

In Renan's account, Jesus is born at Nazareth, a small, obscure and nondescript town in the region of Galilee, within a few years of what is now called the beginning of the Christian Era. His given name, Jesus, is a variation of Joshua. His parents, Joseph and Mary, are artisans and laborers. Renan reports that Jesus' family includes brothers and sisters.

Jesus learns to read and write as a boy, but because the Gospels show him speaking "Aramean" (Aramaic), Renan expresses doubt that he understood Hebrew or Greek texts. Renan gives thanks that Jesus did not learn the "scholasticism" of the type demonstrated in the Talmud. Renan believes that the scholars of the time tended to overinterpret the Pentateuch and the Prophets, hoping to justify the popular Messianic dream. Jesus undoubtedly shared that dream, but with his "grand genius," he sees the true meaning of the Old Testament, especially its truly poetic portions such as the lyrical Psalms. He is perhaps inspired by the apocryphal testaments as well, with their tales of the Messiah arriving to make the nations bow down. Jesus takes the marvels described in these books as a matter of course, though this does not entail visions such as that of the burning bush that had appeared to Moses; Renan states that Jesus understands God as distinguished from seeing him.

Jesus follows Joseph's profession of carpenter. Renan points out that Jewish custom of the time called for a man engaged in intellectual pursuit to take up a manual trade; Saint Paul, for example, worked as a tentmaker. Initially, Jesus sees himself as a "son of man" (like Ezekiel), convinced of the need to take action beyond the requirements of Mosaic law, but when he meets John the Baptist, his thinking undergoes a drastic development. According to Renan, Jesus and John were about the same age and, seeing each other as equals, became allies.

Jesus adopts John's watchword, "Repent, for the kingdom of heaven is at hand." To many Jews, the kingdom of heaven was the ancient theocracy, and its restoration would mean the overthrow of the Roman regime. The Messiah would be the king of David's restored dynasty. At first, Jesus does not claim to be this Messiah but seeks to prepare his people for the coming kingdom by preaching an ethic of love and righteousness. He adopts John's practice of baptizing his countrymen. However, John's work as a prophet is soon ended, for his censorious style in the ancient tradition brings him into conflict with Herod Antipas. This event actually opens the way for Jesus, who has previously deferred to John, to develop his own voice fully.

Jesus illustrates his teachings with parables and stories of everyday events. The mustard seed grows into a mighty tree that canopies the world; the shepherd leaves a flock of ninety-nine to search for one lost sheep; and the Samaritan helps the wounded stranger. Similarly, parables were often employed in the discourse of rabbis and in the Talmud. This practice endears Jesus to the common people, whose faith enables him to cure many illnesses. However, the Pharisees and Sadducees, guardians of the Jewish faith, resent his popularity, especially among Jews whose fidelity to orthodox principles is already uncertain.

His popularity, coupled with the disapproval of religious and political leaders, makes Jesus more self-assured. He begins to call himself the Messiah instead of a son of man. He also foretells his death at the hands of authority, his ascent to heaven, and his eventual triumphant return to establish the kingdom of righteousness on earth. His nature undergoes a decided change; he becomes an ardent revolutionary who believes not in the restoration but the destruction of the law. According to Renan, he even commits something akin to fraud by appearing miraculously to raise up Lazarus, or allowing the people to think he has done so.

Inevitably, he is brought down by a combination of a treacherous disciple, Judas Iscariot, who Jesus knew would betray him; a Jewish high priest; and Pontius Pilate, Roman procurator of Judea. Reluctantly, Pilate sentences Jesus to crucifixion only to prevent an uprising. Jesus is buried by Joseph of Arimathea, a sympathetic member of the Sanhedrin. After three days, a devotee, Mary of Magdalen, brings word that Jesus is gone from the tomb, and the disciples quickly spread the word that "He is risen!"

Renan carefully sticks to the "naturalistic" elements of the story, saying, "For the historian, the life of Jesus finishes with his last sigh." Still, tying up loose ends, he adds a chapter on the fate of Jesus' enemies, and another on the far-reaching effects of Jesus' work. He concludes by affirming that "all the ages will proclaim that among the sons of men, there is none born who is greater than Jesus."

Christian Themes

For centuries, Christians had revered Jesus as God incarnate. Renan, however, attempted to draw a realistic portrait of a man who could be loved, and his character was entirely human. Many readers praised the charming style and sympathetic portrayal of the man in *The Life of Jesus*, but this portrayal, without any semblance of the miraculous or of divine intercession, enraged the authorities of orthodox religion, just as Jesus himself was reported to have done.

Did Jesus perform miracles? Renan's nineteenth century readers had already been exposed to doubts about the supernatural. The Enlightenment of the previous century had gone so far as to declare that authentic miracles were not needed to support a natural religion based on common sense. One may ask whether Renan, in fact, throws new light on the question of the supernatural in Jesus' life. Intent on portraying a fully human figure, he omits detailed descriptions of miracles, suggesting only that the stories about them sprang from a "spontaneous conspiracy" among Jesus' devotees. Yet the Gospels are a primary source for Renan's story, and he concedes, rather equivocally, "That the Gospels are in part legendary, is evident, since they are full of miracles and of the supernatural; but legends have not all the same value." He debunks, however gently, the notion of a "supernatural birth" and the visit soon afterward from Chaldean astrologers.

At another point, Renan hints at a charge that can be neither proved nor disproved, namely that the raising up of Lazarus may have been a hoax. Not surprisingly, the Church found this suggestion offensive and unjustified. Understandably, this suggestion, along with Renan's treatment of the Bible as being subject to the same standards as other historical documents, infuriated some orthodox critics. There can be no doubt of Renan's devout Catholicism or his deep love for Jesus, but as a historian he presents some purported facts that, if authenticated, could render their subject unworthy of respect.

In addition, while generally plausible, Renan's biography is occasionally given to idle, even sentimental, speculation. Generally, in keeping with the most widely accepted image of Jesus, Renan portrays him as having no romantic impulses toward women. However, near the end of the narrative, Jesus is shown in the Garden of Gethsemane, possibly reflecting for a moment on the "young maidens who, perhaps, would have consented to love him." Reportedly, a young Frenchwoman of Renan's day, after reading *The Life of Jesus*, complained, "What a pity it does not end with a marriage!"

Sources for Further Study

Chadbourne, Richard. *Ernest Renan*. New York: Twayne, 1968. A biography of Renan that discusses his works as well.

Fredriksen, Paula. *Jesus of Nazareth, King of the Jews: A Jewish Life and the Emergence of Christianity*. New York: Vintage, 2000. A much later biography of Jesus, which traces the development of Christianity.

Lee, David C. J. *Ernest Renan: In the Shadow of Faith*. London: Duckworth, 1996. Looks at the religious beliefs of Renan; contains some biographical information.

Singley, Carol J. "Race, Culture, Nation: Edith Wharton and Ernest Renan." *Twentieth Century Literature* 49, no. 1 (Spring, 2003): 32. This discussion of Wharton's admiration for Renan and his works talks at length about Renan and his writings.

Thomas Rankin

THE LIFE OF JESUS CRITICALLY EXAMINED

Author: David Friedrich Strauss (1808-1874)
First published: Das Leben Jesu, 1835 (English translation, 1846)
Edition used: The Life of Jesus Critically Examined. Edited by Peter C. Hodgson and
   David Friedrich Strauss. Philadelphia: Fortress, 1972
Genre: Nonfiction
Subgenres: Biblical studies; critical analysis; hermeneutics
Core issues: Gospels; Jesus Christ; myths; reason

Strauss's The Life of Jesus Critically Examined *marks the dividing point in nineteenth century theology. Written by Strauss when he was a twenty-seven-year-old University of Tübingen professor, it would cost him positions both in the university and in the church, but it laid the groundwork for generations of scholarly study.*

Overview

When David Friedrich Strauss published *The Life of Jesus Critically Examined,* there were two ways in which the life of Jesus was commonly interpreted. The traditional approach, followed by many, including J. T. Beck at the University of Tübingen in Germany, was to simply take the Gospels at face value. Even though many of the events in the Gospels were contrary to modern understandings of the natural world, readers were called on to accept them through faith. Therefore the supernatural events in the Gospels, such as virgin birth, miracles, and the resurrection of the dead, were taken literally.

The second approach was a rationalist one that often led to an outright rejection of the Gospels. In 1778, Hermann Samuel Reimarus's *Von dem Zwecke Jesu und seiner Jünger* (*The Goal of Jesus and His Disciples,* 1970) began with the assumption that the supernatural events mentioned in the Gospels were simply incorrect perceptions or mistaken interpretations. Therefore the virgin birth must be explained by a young woman trying to cover up an unwanted pregnancy; the miracle of Jesus' walking on water by confusion caused by fog hiding the shoreline, and the resurrection by the disciples' removal of the body of Jesus. Reimarus sought to show that the aim of the disciples was a grand deception and that the role of Jesus was that of a deluded eschatological visionary. Heinrich Paulus followed in 1828 with his own rationalist life of Jesus, as did Karl Hase in 1829.

In *The Life of Jesus Critically Examined,* Strauss sought a middle ground between the traditional literalist view and the Enlightenment rationalist view. Four years earlier he had traveled to Berlin to study with the systematic theologian Friedrich Schleiermacher, who stressed that critical scholarship could be employed for the Church in a positive way. The key was to focus authority on the person of Jesus rather than on Scripture itself. As Schleiermacher's *Das Leben Jesu* (1864; *The Life of Jesus,* 1975) would not be published for another thirty years, Strauss was the first to publish a major work incorporating this approach.

Strauss had hoped to study with the philosopher Georg Wilhelm Friedrich Hegel, but he arrived in Berlin in 1831 to news that the philosopher was on his deathbed, and his goal was never fulfilled. One of Strauss's earlier teachers, Ferdinand Christian Bauer, had taken Hegel's dialectical approach to explain the progress of early church history. Bauer saw the thesis and antithesis of the early church in the Jewish Jesus and the Gentile Pauline church that synthesized in early Catholicism. In Bauer's view, the evangelists were not deceptive in their presentations of Jesus, as many of the rationalists had claimed. Rather they were simply passing on the truths of the eternal Christ as couched in the language of the first century worldview—a layer that needed to be stripped away through critical historical methodology.

Here Strauss introduces the idea of myth to Gospel studies. This was a concept relatively new to the scholarly world, attributed to Christian Gottlob Heyne, who in the late eighteenth century used "myth" to understand how preliterate people preserved their beliefs and ideas. Georg Lorenz Bauer in his "Entwurf einer Hermeneutik des Alten und Neuen Testamentes" (1799; hermeneutics of the Old and New Testaments) then introduced the concept to New Testament study, arguing that careful analysis can lead to a discovery of the truth beyond the plain meaning of words. For Strauss, myth was present in the Gospels in the messianic portrait that derived from the Old Testament and in the aspirations of the early Christian community. For Strauss, the recovery of the mythical level meant the truth of Christianity. Yet myth left historicity an open question.

The Life of Jesus Critically Examined is divided into five main parts. In the introduction, Strauss explains his understanding of myth, and in the conclusion, he turns to systematic theology to describe the importance of Jesus' life. The three main sections cover first the birth and childhood of Jesus, then his Galilean ministry, and finally his passion, death, and resurrection.

One by one, Strauss treats the various episodes of the Gospels, paying close attention to the details of the text. First, he gives the traditional supernatural interpretation, including his critique of various errors and contradictions that make such a view untenable. Then, he introduces the characteristic rationalistic explanations. In the same way that he discounts the supernatural interpretations, he ridicules the rationalist proposals as no better. He argues that only with the mythical interpretation, which he then presents, can one understand the meaning and purpose of the four evangelists. It becomes clear that, for Strauss, myth is rooted in the Old Testament story. The Gospels were written to show the fulfillment of the biblical message in the person and work of Jesus.

Strauss's treatment of the episode of Jesus' transfiguration on a hillside in Galilee illustrates his approach. Strauss sees the difficulties of taking the story literally because the episode presents supernatural elements, including the voice of God speaking from Heaven, a spectacular change in the appearance of Jesus, and the visitation of Elijah and Moses back from the dead. Such things simply do not happen in the modern worldview. However, the rationalists' explanation, that such details arose out of the confusion of newly awakened disciples who were fooled by the reflection of the early morning sun shining on Jesus' face, were perceived by Strauss as lacking in credibility. Rather Strauss argues that the meaning must be found in the Old Testament stories in which Moses had been transfigured on a mountaintop and that the evangelists were using this mythic language to proclaim that Jesus was indeed superior to Moses.

Albert Schweitzer was later to describe Strauss's contribution to biblical scholarship as "one of the most perfect things in the whole range of learned literature," noting that in spite of the size of his work—more than fourteen hundred pages—"he has not a superfluous phrase." With a simple and picturesque style, as Schweitzer noted, Strauss still was able to include the most minute details about the gospel texts.

Christian Themes

From the title, *The Life of Jesus Critically Examined*, the reader would expect a healthy historical skepticism about what one can know about the historical Jesus. Yet the contribution of Strauss to the study of the Gospels was that behind the words, there exists Jesus the Messiah. In his introduction, Strauss announced to the reader that no matter what the outcome of his critical examination, the significance of Jesus' life would remain inviolate—a claim not accepted by his contemporaries.

In his conclusion, Strauss demonstrated that he was very uncomfortable with the various rationalist descriptions of Jesus as merely a hero or a great teacher or the exemplary moral leader. Likewise, he was to reject his own teacher Schleiermacher's description of Jesus as a man possessing the highest God-consciousness. These were far from the orthodox confession of Jesus as true God and true man. Yet Strauss was not satisfied with the supernatural explanations of the incarnation.

The key to Christology for Strauss was in the nature of God. Strauss preferred to see God as the impersonal spirit manifested in the world and dwelling in humankind rather than as the transcendent creator figure. Christology then is not about a single individual, Jesus of Nazareth, but a universal idea. The divine spirit manifesting itself in Jesus also manifests itself in all humanity, negating the material and sensual side and freeing the spirit for a higher life. What happens in Jesus is not supernatural but natural. What the Gospels proclaim in Jesus, according to Strauss, is not unique but that which occurs in all humankind.

Sources for Further Study

Borg, Marcus. "David Friedrich Strauss: Miracle and Myth." *The Fourth R* 4, no. 3 (May/June 1991). Borg treats the miracle of the multiplication of loaves and fishes to illustrate Strauss's approach to miracle and myth.

Grant, Robert M., and David Tracy. *A Short History of the Interpretation of the Bible.* Rev. ed. London: SCM, 1996. Historical survey of approaches to biblical interpretation. Chapters 12 and 13 treat the nineteenth century.

Harris, Horton. *David Friedrich Strauss and His Theology.* Cambridge, England: Cambridge University Press, 1973. Described by the author as a theological biography with a survey of Strauss's career and an assessment of his theology. Includes numerous quotations from correspondence of Strauss's contemporaries.

Krentz, Edgar. *The Historical-Critical Method.* Philadelphia: Fortress Press, 1975. Discusses the roots of modern historical criticism in the Renaissance, Reformation, and Enlightenment. Strauss is treated briefly.

Schweitzer, Albert. *The Quest for the Historical Jesus.* Edited by John Bowden. Minneapolis, Minn.: Fortress, 2001. Originally published in 1906, this is considered the next significant work on the life of Jesus after that of Strauss, which is critiqued directly in chapters 7 and 8.

Fred Strickert

THE LILIES OF THE FIELD

Author: William E. Barrett (1900-1986)
First published: 1962
Edition used: The Lilies of the Field. New York: Warner Books, 1995
Genre: Novella
Subgenre: Legends
Core issues: African Americans; conscience; faith; humility; racism; trust in God

The Lilies of the Field *emphasizes that faith can accomplish seemingly impossible tasks. Five refugee nuns from Eastern Europe, living on a half-burnt-out farm in the Southwest, dream of building a chapel and a school for juveniles. Everyone around them is waiting for the nuns to give up, when an itinerant worker, Homer Smith, enters their lives. Initially reluctant, he is gradually drawn into their lives and helps bring their dream to reality.*

> *Principal characters*
> *Homer Smith,* a twenty-four-year-old African American
>   exploring the West in his station wagon after his discharge
>   from the army
> *Mother Maria Marthe,* a nun from East Germany, the mother
>   superior of a small community of nuns
> *Sister Albertine,*
> *Sister Elisabeth,*
> *Sister Gertrud,* and
> *Sister Agnes,* nuns under the supervision of Mother Maria Marthe
> *Gus Ritter,* the deceased owner of the farm bequeathed to Mother
>   Maria Marthe's religious order
> *Orville Livingston,* owner of the Livingston Construction
>   Company, the executor of Gus Ritter's estate

Overview

The Lilies of the Field is an account of the legendary accomplishments of Homer Smith, instrumental in helping five refugee nuns realize their dream. Legends often get embellished and assume a life of their own, so the narrator sets the record straight by re-creating the past—how Smith, a twenty-four-year-old African American from South Carolina, just released from the army, meets the nuns. An impetuous, kind but headstrong man, he equips a station wagon for travel on the West Coast. A skilled man, he travels around, living frugally and working only when he feels the need. One day in May as he is driving by a valley in the Rocky Mountains, his curiosity is aroused by the sight of four women, attired in bulky clothes and head scarves, putting up a fence. Wondering if they need his help, he stops to offer his services.

Smith finds that the women speak German and have a limited knowledge of English. He is greeted by an elderly woman, who introduces herself and her fellow nuns. Mother Maria Marthe thanks God for sending her a big, strong man to help. Smith refutes this by saying he was not sent by anyone but stopped of his own will, yet the mother superior remains firm in her conviction that he is the answer to her prayers.

Smith assumes he will be helping the nuns put up the fence, but the mother superior assigns him the task of repairing the roof. To his surprise, Smith finds that the nuns already possess the shingles and needed tools, suggesting that they had intended to fix the roof themselves. At midday, he is asked to join the nuns for their frugal meal of bread, cheese, and milk, and after the day ends, it is assumed that he will be staying for supper. Smith plans on leaving after repairing the roof, but the evening he spends with the nuns helping them learn English softens his heart toward them.

The next morning Mother Maria Marthe takes Smith to the foundation of the old burnt house, shows him a good drawing of a church, not very different from the Baptist churches Smith has attended and declares, "Ve build a shapel." When Smith realizes that "ve" includes him, he makes it clear once again that he has neither the expertise nor any desire to build a chapel. However, he offers to clear the foundation before leaving.

In the evening, as Smith is called to join the nuns for dinner, he asks the mother for his wages. Noticing her difficulty in understanding him, he turns to the Bible and points to Luke 10:7: "And in the same house remain, eating and drinking such things as they give: for the labourer is worthy of his hire." The nun, grasping his intent, points to Proverbs 1:14: "Cast in thy lot among us: let us all have one purse." When Smith insists that he be paid his wages, Mother Maria Marthe refers him to Matthew 6:28-29, "And why take ye thought for raiment? Consider the lilies of the field, how they grow; they toil not, neither do they spin. And yet I say unto you. That even Solomon in all his glory was not arrayed like one of these." Silenced, but by no means convinced, Smith is determined to go on his way.

Nevertheless, the next morning when the nuns expect Smith to drive the nuns to a nearby town to attend the Sunday Mass, he finds it difficult to decline. Being a Baptist himself, he has no interest in attending the Mass, so while the nuns are at the church, he enjoys a hearty breakfast and learns of the community's pessimistic attitude toward what they consider the futile efforts of the nuns. However, his nascent empathy vanishes when the priest reiterates the mother superior's belief that with the God-sent help, her chapel would be built. Smith resents being treated as God's gift to the nuns and retorts that he has no intention of fulfilling their expectations.

Despite his continuing resistance, Smith is moved by the faith of these simple nuns. He has always worked for others and has no idea of how to proceed. Yet the idea keeps him preoccupied, primarily for the challenge it offers him. However, in the absence of bricks and other materials, there is little to be done.

The events that follow lead to Smith's accepting the challenge. When he drives the mother superior to Orville Livingston to request bricks, Livingston not only is unwilling to help the nuns any further but also is even less inclined to change his mind when he finds that a black man is expected to build the chapel. This condescending, racist attitude fuels Smith's determination to prove his ability. He offers to work for Livingston for two days a week and uses the money earned to buy food and construction materials to begin his project. He builds the foundation on the days he is not working for Livingston, though the lack of resources limits his progress. In despair, he drives away from the farm.

Initially, Smith revels in the town life: working, sleeping, eating at his will, but he cannot get the mother superior's dream out of his mind. After a few weeks, he returns to the farm bearing the gift of an old tub for the nuns and some windows for the chapel, items recovered from a demolition job in the city.

The nuns express no surprise at his return. Once the work begins and people see his commitment, the entire community pitches in. Many obstacles impede progress on the chapel, yet Smith does not give up. Eventually, Livingston, impressed by Smith, sends a load of fine bricks, and soon the chapel is completed.

The night before the first Mass is to be held at the new chapel, Smith leaves with a sense of having completed his mission. The narrator provides the subsequent developments. The unique appearance of the chapel and the history of its construction draw a stream of visitors and the resulting fame brings money, allowing the nuns to realize their ambition to run a school for Spanish boys on the premises. The chapel, situated at the center of the buildings, honors Saint Benedict the Moor, and an oil painting of Smith by Sister Albertine hangs on the wall at the back.

Christian Themes

The Lilies of the Field is primarily about the power of prayer and faith and the need for humility in accomplishing one's goals. It was a daunting task for five German-speaking nuns to escape from communist Eastern Europe, come to a strange land, and dream of their own chapel and some day a school for poor Spanish boys. Not only did they lack material resources but also they had no one who believed in their dreams. Yet, Mother Maria Marthe never doubts that God will help them. Thus the power of faith is at the heart of the narrative.

Homer Smith also learns the lesson of humility. Initially, his attitude of self-sufficiency and independence, a defense mechanism for dealing with the racist attitudes prevalent during the period, makes him reject the help of the community. He has skills and is proud of his intellect and ability to survive. Even after he is certain that the nuns are totally oblivious to the color of his skin, he bristles at the slightest provocation. Gradually, he undergoes a spiritual regeneration, realizes that ignorance breeds superstitions and misunderstandings, and sees the importance of humility in his life. He accepts the fact that building God's house leaves no room for individual glorification but offers an opportunity to bring the community of worshipers closer. Smith's odyssey teaches him to be a better human being and accept his role of being an instrument of divine will.

Sources for Further Study

Kelly, M. E. Review of *The Lilies of the Field*. *Kirkus* (February 1, 1962): 128. Basically, a brief summary of the plot.

Levin, Martin. Review of *The Lilies of the Field*. *The New York Times Book Review*, April 22, 1962, 23. An explication of William Barrett's attempt to show "the basic goodness" in all people.

"William E. Barrett Dies at Eighty-Five: Author of *Lilies of the Field*." *The New York Times*, September 17, 1986, C22. This obituary of Barrett sums up his life and works.

"William E(dmund) Barrett." *Contemporary Authors Online*. Farmington Hills, Mich.: Thomson Gale, 2006. Biography of the author that lists his works and briefly describes his life.

Leela Kapai

THE LIST

Author: Robert Whitlow (1954-   )
First published: Nashville, Tenn.: Word, 2000
Genre: Novel
Subgenres: Evangelical fiction; thriller/suspense
Core issues: Conversion; good vs. evil; guidance; prayer

Whitlow's first suspense thriller explores the impact of spiritual warfare on human events. Operating within an evangelical worldview, Whitlow infuses common religious practices such as prayer and Bible study with cosmic significance as characters use these practices to combat evil occult forces. While the novel advances a theology of salvation through a born-again experience, it shifts the emphasis of the story to spiritual growth after rebirth. Whitlow uses the protagonist's quest for spiritual fulfillment to emphasize the necessity of continual prayer and worship in maintaining the Christian faith.

> *Principal characters*
> *Josiah "Renny" Jacobson*, the protagonist, a young lawyer
> *Jo Johnston*, a concerned Christian who becomes romantically
>   involved with Renny
> *Daisy Stokes*, Renny's landlady
> *Agnes Darlene "Mama A,"* a friend of Renny's mother
> *Desmond LaRochette*, president of the List
> *A. L. Jenkins*, a Christian lawyer

Overview

Robert Whitlow's *The List* describes the culmination of a spiritual battle between good and evil that has spanned generations. Set in South Carolina, it highlights the impact of supernatural elements in local and family history on events in the present time. The story centers on a young lawyer, Josiah "Renny" Jacobson, who simultaneously inherits two family legacies. His father was a member of the List, an occult secret society that passes membership from father to son, and his maternal grandfather was an evangelical Christian who prayed that the young man would have a special purpose in God's plan. As Renny learns more about his family's past, the List tries to seduce him with wealth and power while evangelical Christians come to his aid through ministry and prayer. These Christians serve to exemplify Whitlow's ideal of a dynamic prayer life centered on private conversation with God and fellowship with other Christians. With their support, Renny eventually learns how to become an instrument of God in the ongoing battle between good and evil.

Renny's father has died suddenly, leaving the young lawyer with assets in a company called Covenant List. The List, Renny learns, is an investment group that smuggled assets out of the country during the American Civil War and invested them overseas. When a member of the group dies, membership passes to his son, who must swear loyalty to the List in return for a share in the wealth generated by the investments. After the List contacts him, Renny meets Jo Johnston, the daughter and sole child of a List member who has recently inherited membership. Jo is an exemplary Christian who is not tempted by the promise of wealth or power. Though not religious himself, Renny becomes intensely attracted to Jo, and the two begin dating.

The List is wary of Jo's religiosity and lack of desire for wealth. Desmond LaRochette, the group's president, asks Jo to leave while they debate her eligibility. Once Jo is gone, they induct Renny into the List in a ceremony with occult overtones, complete with shedding a drop of his blood. Then they vote to reject Jo. One List member who argues against this decision suddenly falls down dead after the vote. The rest of the meeting is postponed. Jo becomes increasingly suspicious of the List's occultism, but Renny dismisses the possibility of danger.

As Renny and Jo continue to spend time together, Renny becomes more receptive to Jo's Christian beliefs. His quest to learn more about his family brings him into contact with old acquaintances, many of whom are Christian. Two of these characters are exemplary Christians like Jo: Mama A is a friend of the family who was close to Renny's mother, and Daisy Stokes is Renny's landlady and a former missionary. Their example kindles in him a desire for spiritual fulfillment, a desire that had been suppressed throughout his childhood by the emotional distance of his father and of his church. This desire leads to spiritual rebirth after Renny learns how to pray with sincerity and openness, accepting God's promise of salvation.

Despite his newfound faith, Renny remains vulnerable to spiritual assault, temptation, and error. He is still attracted to the List, refusing to believe that he is in any danger. When Renny is invited to LaRochette's home, Jo begs him not to go, but Renny dismisses her concerns. In LaRochette's library Renny is told that the List's ledger has magical power. Under LaRochette's instruction, Renny directs some of its power toward Jo, believing it will bless her in some way. Instead she becomes ill and is hospitalized. When Renny discovers what has happened, he decides to destroy the ledger. Renny tries to break into LaRochette's home, but is caught by a member of LaRochette's private security. LaRochette offers Renny a choice: He can go to prison or become LaRochette's student in the occult. Renny refuses to become the man's student, declaring his loyalty to God. Angered, LaRochette reveals that he murdered the fathers of Renny and Jo with the power of the List. Then he has Renny arrested for the break-in.

Mama A sends Renny a Christian lawyer, A. L. Jenkins, who agrees to help Renny destroy the List. Renny provides Jenkins with documented evidence of illegal financial activity by the List. Jenkins uses his sessions with Renny to teach him the principles of spiritual warfare, chief of which is submission to God's will before taking action. He also tells Renny that Mama A and Daisy Stokes are fasting and praying on his behalf. Renny is sentenced to three years of probation and released from jail.

Prepared by Jenkins and fortified by the prayers of Mama A and Daisy Stokes, Renny asks God for guidance. That evening, filled with the Holy Spirit, Renny walks into the hotel room where the List is meeting and declares that its members will face retribution for their sins. The members try to interrupt but find themselves unable to speak until Renny leaves. Renny's signature disappears from the ledger, and one of the members flees from the room. Soon after he leaves, officers from the Drug Enforcement Agency arrive to arrest the members of the List for involvement in illegal drug trafficking.

Jo's illness vanishes. Daisy Stokes, weakened from days of fasting, suffers a heart attack and dies in the hospital. Her will leaves her house to Renny and Jo, who have decided to get married. The book ends with a brief epilogue in which Renny's deceased friends and relatives comment on the importance of prayer and welcome Daisy Stokes into Heaven.

Christian Themes

Though *The List* is premised on an unequivocally evangelical worldview, Whitlow avoids references to specific denominational doctrines. (There is no mention of speaking in tongues or sanctification, for example.) Christianity's relevance to an individual's personal life is more important than denominational affiliation, to Whitlow, although he privileges more emotive styles of worship. Church congregations sway and clap their hands to contemporary music. Prayers are spontaneous and intimate, sometimes involving laughter or weeping. Renny's lackluster spiritual upbringing is tied directly to his emotional distance from his father as well as the half-hearted worship style of his church.

Whitlow's primary concern is the centrality of prayer and Christian fellowship in daily life. Though church attendance is important, Christian practice outside of church is crucial. In this respect the novel exemplifies the evangelical conviction that religion must be present in every aspect of life. For Whitlow, prayer is a supernatural act in that it allows Christians to communicate directly with God. It extends their awareness beyond the natural world, bringing them greater knowledge of God's will and strengthening their perception of the spiritual forces around them. Prayer also allows Christians to participate meaningfully in the supernatural struggle between good and evil, a struggle that affects people's lives whether they realize it or not. In *The List* prayer is often more effective than modern medicine, eliminating headaches, heart failure, and aplastic anemia after medicine has failed. Next to Scripture, it is the most powerful resource Christians have to effect change in the world.

The threat of supernatural evil lends urgency to the need for a prayer-centered spiritual life. Instead of focusing on the eventual reward of eternal salvation, Whitlow stresses the impact of religious life in the present. As a parody of Christianity, occult magic can also influence the physical world. Curses disrupt concentration, cause illness, or kill instantaneously. Individuals who do not believe in the supernatural are especially vulnerable, and Christians who have been strengthened by prayer are especially resistant. According to Whitlow, prayer is ultimately an act of total submission to God in which the individual becomes a vessel for the Holy Spirit. Human efforts are useless against supernatural evil. Only submission to God's will can empower human beings to succeed.

Sources for Further Study

Blodgett, Jan. *Protestant Evangelical Literary Culture and Contemporary Society.* Westport, Conn.: Greenwood Press, 1997. Reviews sixty evangelical novels from 1972 to 1994, with attention to how they are used to define, describe, and explore Christian themes in contemporary society.

Murphy, Edward. *The Handbook for Spiritual Warfare: Revised and Updated.* Nashville, Tenn.: Thomas Nelsen, 2003. An example of an articulated theology and method for spiritual warfare. Expands on the bifurcation between naturalistic and spiritualistic worldviews implied in *The List*.

Peretti, Frank. *This Present Darkness.* Wheaton, Ill.: Crossway Books, 1986. An influential best-selling novel about spiritual warfare in a small town. Whitlow's books have been compared to a cross between the works of Peretti and John Grisham.

Whitlow, Robert. *The Trial.* Nashville, Tenn.: Word, 2001. Whitlow's second novel and winner of the 2001 Christy award. As in *The List*, a lawyer is healed emotionally and spiritually while investigating a mystery.

Shaun Horton

THE LITTLE FLOWERS OF ST. FRANCIS

Author: Unknown

First transcribed: Fioretti di San Francesco d'Assisi, c. 1328 (English translation, 1864)

Edition used: The Little Flowers of St. Francis, translated and edited by Raphael Brown. Garden City, N.Y.: Image Books, 1958

Genre: Nonfiction

Subgenres: Legends; morality tales

Core issues: Humility; Jesus Christ; poverty; simplicity; trust in God

These tales and legends of Saint Francis and his companions in thirteenth century Italy were originally written down from the oral tradition by Brother Ugolino di Monte Santa Maria (1270-1340) and later were condensed and translated into Italian by a gifted anonymous author.

Overview

The spirit of simplicity, humility, and joyful obedience of Saint Francis of Assisi (c. 1181-1226) and his jubilant followers, who tramped the thirteenth century plains and hills of Italy winning the hearts and minds of countless citizens of their day, is wonderfully captured in *The Little Flowers of St. Francis.* Not a biography or even a historical chronology of Francis or his movement, *The Little Flowers* is a collection of incidents drawn together more than one hundred years after Francis's death. In a straightforward and moving style, the stories capture the buoyancy and childlike innocence of the early medieval spirit and bring one into the Christlike presence of the saint.

Born c. 1181 to a wealthy cloth merchant, Francis was an attractive and fun-loving youth given to revelry and worldly excitement. He dreamed of being a soldier and fighting in the Crusades but was captured following a local battle and spent a discouraging year in prison. There followed a long period of illness that led to his awakening to more serious questions about life and to a search for God. At about age twenty-five, following a trip to Rome and attempts to care for lepers, Francis heard God speak to him from the wooden crucifix of an abandoned church at San Damiano: "Francis, go repair my house, which is falling into ruins." Three times the voice spoke, and when Francis came to himself, he obeyed in the most literal way, by beginning the physical rebuilding of the church at San Damiano. Soon, the whole church was to feel the effects of his obedience as thousands followed after him in the most widespread spiritual awakening in the Catholic Church of the Middle Ages.

Francis understood his vocation in simple Gospel terms. *The Little Flowers* recounts how one day, after Mass at the Church of San Nicolo, Francis and Brother Bernard prayed to the Lord Christ that he reveal to them through the Scripture his path of obedience for them. Opening the text, their eyes fell on the words: "If you wish to be perfect, go, sell all you have, and give to the poor, and come, follow Me." They opened the Scripture a second time and read: "Take nothing for your journey, neither staff, nor wallet, nor bread, nor money." And then a third time: "If anyone wishes to come after Me, let him deny himself, and take up his cross, and follow Me." Closing the Bible, Francis exclaimed to Bernard that this was the counsel of Christ and that they should go and do perfectly what Christ commanded them. For Francis, Christ was enough. The renewal movement he founded was a return to the Gospel teachings of Jesus with such force that it shook the entire world.

Francis exerted a strange attraction on the people of his time. Brother Masseo asked him one day, "Why after you? Why after you? . . . Why does all the world seem to be running after you? . . . You are not a handsome man. You do not have great learning or wisdom. You are not a nobleman. So why is all the world running after you?" Francis, rejoicing in the Spirit, answered that it was perhaps because of all men he had the least to boast of in himself. No one was more vile or insufficient, and thus he had been chosen because God chooses what is foolish in order to shame the wise, so that all excellence and goodness may be seen to come from God and not from his creatures.

Such humility was evident in the way Francis sought guidance through the prayers of friends, in his willing acceptance of ridicule and public insult, and in his gentle and forgiving spirit toward all people. In one incident, some robbers came begging food from the brothers, and the one in charge drove them away. When Francis heard what had happened, he scolded the brother in charge, saying that sinners are led back to Christ by holy meekness rather than cruel scolding. Reminding him that Jesus came as a physician to be with the sick, he sent the brother to find the robbers and give them food and seek their pardon. All three robbers were in this way brought back to God.

This same quality of gentleness provides the secret of Francis's legendary influence over animals. He preached to the birds, who remained quiet and attentive before flying away in the pattern of a cross to the four corners of the earth; he calmed the fierce wolf of Gubbio and helped the people of that community to overcome their fears. He was an instrument of God's peace, both in the human world and in nature.

Francis's pure vision of Gospel life was rooted in poverty and the joy of simple living close to the earth. On one occasion, Francis and Brother Masseo went begging bread in a small village. Masseo, a tall, handsome, imposing figure, was more successful in his begging than the small and insignificant-looking Francis. The two brought their begged pieces of bread to a nearby spring with a flat rock that served as their table. When Francis saw the larger pieces of bread that Masseo had begged, he was filled with intense joy, and exclaimed over and over, louder each time, "Oh, Brother Masseo, we do not deserve such a great treasure as this!" Finally, Masseo protested that such poverty and lack of things could hardly be considered a treasure. They had no cloth, no knife, no dish, no bowl, no table, no house. Francis replied that what made it a great treasure was that nothing had been prepared by human labor, but everything had been given by God—the begged bread, the fine stone table, and the clear spring. "Therefore, I want us to pray to God that He may make us love with all our hearts the very noble treasure of holy poverty."

Poverty, for Francis, was not a romantic ideal. He wanted to be poor because Jesus was poor and the biblical promises were made to the poor. He thought the Gospel could be preached only to the poor because they alone had the freedom to hear it without distorting it for their own purposes. One could only see rightly from a place of weakness and poverty: "For poverty is that heavenly virtue by which all earthly things are trodden under foot . . . by which every obstacle is removed from the soul so that it may freely enter into union with the eternal Lord God." In contrast to the rest of the human race, Francis hurried in the direction of poverty, certain that he was following in the steps of Christ.

A joyous trust also characterized the simplicity of the early Franciscans. When the movement was only a few years old, Francis called all of the friars together, nearly five thousand brothers, to an open camp meeting on the plain at Saint Mary of the Angels. Several prominent people, including Saint Dominic, were present as observers. When everyone had assembled, Francis rose to preach, encouraging the brothers in love, prayer, praise to God, service to others, and patience in adversity. He concluded with the command that the brothers not have "any care or anxiety concerning anything to eat or drink or the other things necessary for the body, but to concentrate only on praying and praising God . . . because He takes special care of you." Saint Dominic was greatly surprised at Francis's command and thought he was proceeding in a impudent way. What would the friars eat? Who would care for them? Soon, however, from all the surrounding countryside, people arrived bringing food and drink. A great celebration followed as the friars praised God for his provision. Saint Dominic reproached himself and knelt before Francis, saying, "God is truly taking care of these holy little poor men, and I did not realize it. Therefore I promise henceforth to observe the holy poverty of the Gospel."

The dominant keynote in Francis's life was joy: joy in God, in poverty, in the wonders of creation, in the cross of Christ. One of the most delightful stories in *The Little Flowers* concerns how Francis taught Brother Leo the meaning of perfect joy. Walking together in the rain and bitter cold, Francis spoke to Leo of all the things that people believed would bring joy, such as having all knowledge, or healing the sick, or converting prominent people to the Franciscan order. After each recounting, Francis added: "Perfect joy is not in that." Brother Leo finally begged Francis to tell him where to find perfect joy. Francis then began an imagined account of how the two of them would be shabbily treated at the friary they were approaching, and how they would be humiliated, beaten, and left hungry in the cold and rain, and how that was the context of perfect joy. He concluded: "Above all the graces and gifts of the Holy Spirit which Christ gives to His friends is that of conquering oneself and willingly enduring sufferings, insults, humiliations, and hardships for the love of Christ."

Christian Themes

True joy, peace, and happiness are found only in loving, knowing, and serving God and one's neighbor with true humility, simplicity, compassion, meekness, patience, and obedience to Christ. To read *The Little Flowers* is to discover a man in love with

God, lost in the joy of relationship to Christ, the greatest of all lovers. Francis's life reveals what is happening in the heart of God: not omnipotence but humility; not cold omniscience but endless self-revelation; not detached judgment but relentless welcoming and giving. There seems no bottom to Francis's grateful happiness, no matter the amount of his suffering. Eyewitnesses tell us that he was so filled with gladness he would pick up a stick and place it across his arm like a bow on a violin and play, dance, and sing to the Lord in an ecstasy of joy. Bonaventure recounts that even on his deathbed, two years after mystically receiving the stigmata of Christ in his own body, Francis wanted to go forward again because he had still done so little to heed and obey the call of Christ. Such joyful obedience and humility, love and simplicity, shine through *The Little Flowers of St. Francis* so that to read it today is to be carried across time into the presence of Francis and his followers and to want to join them in a more faithful, less selfish, more joyful following after Christ.

Sources for Further Study

Fortini, Arnaldo. *Nova Vita di San Francisco*. 1959. Translated into English as *Francis of Assisi* by Helen Monk. New York: Crossroad, 1981. Fortini, one of the foremost Franciscan historians, moves beyond the spiritual portraits of the early biographies to give a critical reconstruction of the social, economic, political, and religious milieus during the time of Saint Francis.

Green, Julien. *God's Fool: The Life and Times of Francis of Assisi*. Translated by Peter Heinegg. San Francisco: Harper & Row, 1985. A lively, sensitive, and authoritative biography.

Habig, Marion A., ed. *St. Francis of Assisi, Writings and Early Biographies: English Omnibus of the Sources for the Life of St. Francis*. Chicago: Franciscan Herald Press, 1973. The complete sourcebook, including authentic writings of Saint Francis, the earliest biographies by Thomas Celano (1228) and Bonaventure (1263), and other material, along with extensive introductions, historical notes, and bibliography.

The Little Flowers of St. Francis of Assisi. Written by Ugolino di Monte Santa Maria, edited and adapted from a translation by W. Heywood. New York: Vintage Books, 1998. Madeleine L'Engle's preface appears in this widely available edition. Bibliography.

The Little Flowers of St. Francis of Assisi: A Modern English Translation from the Latin and the Italian. Translated by Raphael Brown. New York: Image Books, 1991. Brown offers useful notes, biographical sketches, and an introduction in this "entirely new version with twenty additional chapters." Bibliography.

Douglas H. Gregg

LOAVES AND FISHES

Author: Dorothy Day (1897-1980)
First published: New York: Harper & Row, 1963
Genre: Nonfiction
Subgenre: Autobiography
Core issues: The Beatitudes; capitalism; Catholics and Catholicism; discipleship; nonviolent resistance; poverty

The title, Loaves and Fishes, *suggests the book's interrelated themes: Christ's compassion toward all, belief in the miraculous, and two spiritual practices, feeding the hungry and practicing the "little way," or doing whatever one is able to and leaving the rest to God. Day's spirituality encompasses expressions of faith and charity and nonviolent direct action meant to achieve a revolution of the heart. This revolution has the potential to transform a divided, violent society into communities guided by the Christian law of love. Her* Catholic Worker *paper, houses of hospitality, farming communes, and community discussions are integral parts of her agenda.*

Overview

Dorothy Day's *Loaves and Fishes* tells the story of the movement that she cofounded in 1933, the Catholic Worker. She intended the book to be a sequel to *The Long Loneliness: The Autobiography of Dorothy Day* (1952), which focused on her conversion from secular radicalism to Catholicism grounded in Jesus' radical message of love. It also updates Day's *House of Hospitality* (1939), an account of the movement's first five years.

The book is divided into nineteen chapters and five thematic parts, each relating the values of her radical gospel Catholicism through her experiences and observations. A journalist rather than a philosopher, Day presents her radical gospel Catholic beliefs as an integral part of the movement's history, not as abstractions.

In part 1, Day recounts Catholic Worker history, emphasizing the role of Peter Maurin, originally a French peasant, whose ideas helped her live her Catholic faith while finding a vocation that allowed her to blend her radical activist past with a gospel faith nourished by Catholic worship, sacraments, and teaching. What begins as a journalist's attempt during the Depression to promote the radical implications of Catholic social teaching through the *Catholic Worker* (the paper where she was founder, publisher, editor, and often contributor), evolves into an urban movement that houses, feeds, and clothes the poor; an agrarian communal alternative to industrial capitalism; and a movement uncompromising in its pacifism and nonviolent resistance, an approach previously unfamiliar to Catholicism in the United States. Day believed that by living Christianity, she and others could start building a new society.

In part 2, chapters such as "Poverty and Precarity" offer reflections on such topics as the working poor, the racial and ethnic discrimination underlying poverty, the conditions of poverty, and Christian voluntary poverty. Many Americans were enjoying postwar economic prosperity, but Day exposes the poverty so easily hidden from the experience of large numbers of suburbanized Americans. Part 3 features the ideas of especially influential Catholic Workers. Maurin's personalism advocates individual responsibility for social ills. Ammon Hennacy, a lifelong opponent of war, uses voluntary poverty, manual labor, nonpayment of taxes, picketing, leafleting, and fasting as spiritual tools to resist nuclear weapons and war. The unadulterated gospel lived and preached by courageous priest advisors involves their personal challenges to luxury and social conservatism in the Church hierarchy. Although Day did not deliberately intend to bend gender roles, the work of the Catholic Worker required male and female volunteers to meet the responsibilities of Christian love. Women might write, edit, publish, and mail the paper. Men might tend to household tasks and meet the basic needs of guests in the hospices or on the food line.

In part 4 Day writes of some defining events among those whose paths cross hers at the Catholic Worker. She explains how it was possible to find dignity in guests even as they battled poverty, addiction, homelessness, and mental disorders. Day, who had committed civil disobedience against mandatory air raid drills and therefore had experienced incarceration, criticizes its degrading conditions.

Day's honest yet affectionate portrayal of guests and volunteers provides convincing examples of her spiritual practices in living the gospel of love. Without resorting to didacticism, Day promotes her message of radical transformation of self by example. She models continuing personal conversion and shows how society could be transformed through nonviolent direct action rooted in love and nourished by prayer and reception of the Eucharist.

In a powerful concluding section, "Love in Practice," Day explains the radical Christian spirituality underpinning the movement's sometimes controversial positions. She once rejected interest paid on money owed the movement as unearned by work and therefore unjust, and she returned an interest payment to puzzled city authorities. To public health officials who regarded the farming commune as a slum awaiting improvement or eradication, Day spoke of the freedom to invite a guest in need into one's home. Dedicated to living a communal life of voluntary poverty with the poor and working for a nonviolent revolution of the heart to challenge the social, economic, and political status quo, Day agrees with Teresa of Ávila's wry observation that life is like a night spent at an uncomfortable inn. Reliance on direct action, prayer, and the sacraments help meet every need.

Christian Themes

Central to the development of Dorothy Day's Catholic Worker movement was her reading of the Bible, youthful radical activism, conversion to Catholicism in 1927, and the gradual realization of her vocation in living and publicizing Catholic gospel radicalism after meeting Maurin in 1932. Her synthesis of renewed Catholicism involved a life that was nourished by Catholic sacraments and worship and the social encyclicals of modern popes, orthodox in the essentials of the faith, and allowed her to practice corporal and spiritual works of mercy, which originated in Christ's teaching to love one another. Day created a movement of lay initiative long before the reforms of Vatican II (1962-1965) legitimated lay leadership. She explained that no permission was needed to practice the corporal and spiritual works of mercy, such as feeding the hungry and visiting prisoners. Taught to every Catholic in the catechism, these works of mercy embodied specific ways to live the Beatitudes and Christ's teaching of love.

Day's earlier radicalism, aimed at a social, political, and economic revolution by whatever means necessary, contributed to her conversion to Catholicism and the establishment of the Catholic Worker. The young radical had experienced community and sacrifice on behalf of workers and the poor, something lacking in the mainstream Christianity she once discarded as hypocritical. Experience as a radical taught her to prefer uncompromising individual direct action to either indifference or overdependence on bureaucracies of church or state to address social problems. With Maurin's guidance and her own common sense, she synthesized ideas from a variety of sources into the beliefs of the Catholic Worker movement: Christ's gospel of love, Catholic social teachings, and countercultural views of American society influenced by mainstream Catholicism (critique of materialism) and secular radicalism (critique of capitalism and imperialism). Day grafted Gandhian nonviolent direct action to Christ's commandment to love one's neighbor not only as a path to revolutionary change but also as a means of resistance to all wars. In so doing, she created the Catholic Worker during the Depression, a movement unlike any other American Catholic movement of the time.

Thirty years after the founding of the movement, when Day published *Loaves and Fishes*, she and her movement continued to define what it meant to be a disciple of Christ in a modern urban industrial era. Her espousal of a life of voluntary poverty shared with the poor provided her most convincing critique of industrial capitalism. Although Day's uncompromising pacifism divided the movement during World War II, during the Cold War it attracted followers morally troubled by the development and use of weapons of mass destruction. Not only had she pointed out the incompatibility of war with Christian love and Catholic teachings on respect for God's creation, but also she underscored the futility of surviving nuclear war with her open defiance of a civil defense law, which resulted in a jail sentence. As a tribute to her profound and consistent example of living Christianity, in 2000 Cardinal John J. O'Connor of New York initiated the cause of Dorothy Day for sainthood.

Sources for Further Study
Coy, Patrick G., ed. *Revolution of the Heart: Essays on the Catholic Worker*. Philadelphia: Temple University Press, 1988. Some of the most accessible and incisive writings on such aspects of the movement as personalism, peace, advocacy journalism, free obedience, hospitality, and resistance.
Ellsberg, Robert, ed. *Dorothy Day: Selected Writings*. Maryknoll, N.Y.: Orbis Books, 1992. The introduction provides an excellent brief study of Day, her spirituality,

and the movement, with judiciously chosen selections from a wide range of her writings.

Klejment, Anne, and Nancy L. Roberts, eds. *American Catholic Pacifism: The Influence of Dorothy Day and the Catholic Worker Movement.* Westport, Conn.: Praeger, 1996. Highlights include Day's letters to Thomas Merton and essays on Day's preconversion pacifism, conscience and conscription, Cold War era peacemaking, and the movement's international influence.

Riegle, Rosemary, ed. *Dorothy Day: Portraits by Those Who Knew Her.* Maryknoll, N.Y.: Orbis Books, 2003. A collective biography of Day, thematically organized, based on interviews with family and friends. With contextual comments and photographs.

Thorn, William, et al., eds. *Dorothy Day and the Catholic Worker Movement: Centenary Essays.* Milwaukee, Wis.: Marquette University Press, 2001. Contributions by activists and scholars. The most valuable essays discuss the movement's significance, spiritual and philosophical roots, radical orthodoxy, and mystical body theology.

Zwick, Mark, and Louise Zwick. *The Catholic Worker Movement: Intellectual and Spiritual Origins.* New York: Paulist Press, 2005. A well-researched popular volume that analyzes such influences on the movement as the works of mercy, monasticism, voluntary poverty, pacifism, and the "little way."

Anne Klejment

THE LONG TRAIL HOME

Author: Stephen A. Bly (1944-   )
First published: Nashville, Tenn.: Broadman & Holman, 2001
Genre: Novel
Subgenres: Evangelical fiction; Western
Core issues: Acceptance; alienation from God; awakening; faith; redemption

Sam Fortune, a man of the Old West, has been an outlaw for years, but after his release from prison, he becomes attuned to a new force in his life. Several events cause him to feel the influence of God in his life, and he develops faith that God has a plan for him. His sets out on a new direction that brings both stability and peace to his life.

> *Principal characters*
> *Sam Fortune*, the protagonist
> *Kiowa Fox*, Sam's sidekick
> *Ladosa McKay*, a former girlfriend of Sam
> *Piney Burleson*, another former girlfriend of Sam
> *Rocklin*, Sam's employer
> *Brazos Fortune*, Sam's father
> *Abigail Gordon*, the woman Sam marries
> *Dacee June*, Sam's sister
> *Todd Fortune*, Sam's older brother

Overview

Awarded the Christy Award in 2002, *The Long Trail Home* is the third book in the Fortunes of the Black Hills series, which includes *Beneath a Dakota Cross* (1999), *Shadow of Legends* (2000), *Friends and Enemies* (2002), *Last of the Texas Camp* (2002), and *The Next Roundup* (2003). The book tells the story of Sam Fortune, a legendary outlaw just released from prison near Dry Fork, in Indian Territory, on June 17, 1885. When Sam tries to pick up where he left off, he discovers that he no longer has much in the way of family or friends. Sam has had little to do with his family since his mother died in Coreyell County, Texas, thirteen years earlier, and his father and siblings moved to the Black Hills of South Dakota. Sam's sidekick, Kiowa Fox, points out that aside from some former girlfriends, all Sam's old companions are either dead or in prison. This observation serves as an awakening for Sam, who longs to change directions. Despite a reputation as a gunslinger that accompanies him into every small town and saloon he enters, Sam manages to make choices that effect a transformation in his life.

The first opportunity presents itself when Sam connects with an old girlfriend, Ladosa McKay, in a dirty, dreary saloon near Dry Fork. When he knew her in more pleasant and profitable times, she was a popular hostess, but she is now stuck in this godforsaken place. She has suffered much abuse in her line of work, but she welcomes Sam because they once cared for each other. She provides Sam and Kiowa with the means to get out of town in exchange for their escorting her to Dodge City. With her mules and wagon, they have the means to head away from trouble and grief.

On the way to Dodge City, the travelers swing by Antelope Flats to get supplies and to pick up a mysterious package from another old girlfriend, Piney Burleson. When Sam finds Piney, he sees that she also has been injured by abusive men. Piney has been kicked in the head by two scoundrels, McDermitt and Burns, and she often wanders the streets, lost and confused. Her condition provokes Sam to pray for her, something he has not done in years. The package she has for him contains the .50 caliber Sharps carbine that belonged to Brazos Fortune, Sam's father. Piney had been sent this package to keep for Sam without a word of explanation. Receiving the carbine makes him determined to find his father and reconcile with him. Ladosa, who has been longing for meaning in her life, sees Piney's condition and concludes that caring for Piney is God's plan for her, and she decides to stay with Piney. All these events rekindle in Sam a faith that life can be different. He cannot leave before punishing the scoundrels who hurt Piney, but his mind is open to new possibilities.

The next indication that a better life awaits Sam comes in the form of an opportunity to do honest work. A decent man, Rocklin, offers him the job of breaking horses. Sam and Kiowa head to Rocklin's ranch on the San Francisco Creek in the public land along the Oklahoma panhandle. They work like the skilled cowboys they are. Rocklin joins them, confiding his dream of reconnecting with his estranged daughter and sharing this place with her. He elicits a promise from Sam to see that she inherits this place if something happens to him in this dangerous territory. This responsibility contributes to Sam's new destiny.

When both his new friend and his old sidekick die, he sets out to keep his promise. On the way, Sam resists the temptation to mete out vengeance, and once again he benefits from kindness shown to a woman from his former life. When he finds Rocklin's daughter, he arrives just in time to save her and her husband from bankruptcy and help her with the delivery of her baby. His charitable action, which benefits Rocklin's daughter and her husband, marks another step in the new direction Sam pursues.

Rocklin's daughter and her husband give Sam money in gratitude for his efforts, which have saved their home and livelihood, and they invite him to develop their innovative telephone business in South Dakota. Sam sets off for South Dakota with the mission of setting up a telephone line and finding out why he possesses his father's carbine.

Life seems charmed for Sam. He meets Amber Gordon and then her widowed mother, Abigail Gordon, a woman for whom he feels immediate attraction. Abigail is able to connect him with his family. Coincidentally, he has arrived just in time to attend the wedding of his beloved little sister, Dacee June. Her wedding becomes a double celebration as his father and his siblings welcome him back into the family as their beloved son and brother.

After he marries Abigail and successfully introduces the telephone business to town, his life still presents challenges. The two men he whipped for injuring Piney come to kill him. However, now he has help to face them. In addition to feeling the sense of love and belonging to family and community, he now has family and friends who help him overcome these enemies.

Christian Themes

The Long Trail Home explores evangelical Christian themes using the Western genre. In this work, Stephen A. Bly, a prolific author of Christian fiction in several genres and inspirational works, presents Sam as a person of kindness and potential goodness who rejects his Christian upbringing and lives his life as an outlaw. Then through the power of grace, he regains his faith, direction in life, home, and Christian community. The transformation is described as an awakening, clearly presented as the grace of God. Grace provokes Sam to open himself to new possibilities and put his trust in the life that God has planned for him. Through Sam, Bly presents the results of recognizing grace, accepting God's plan, and reconciling oneself with God and others.

While Sam is fully open to the grace acting in his life, he performs a good and kind act. He is repaid for this by developing an awareness that life can be different for him. An old girlfriend says she now believes that God has a plan for her. This observation and the mysterious and treasured gift to him from his father enable him to consider that God may be calling him as well.

Sam reinforces one good behavior with another, and he consciously refuses to act in the ways he once would have as a gunslinger and outlaw. He seeks out honest work, and he accepts the friendship and confidence of a good man, agreeing to fulfill his wishes if and when the opportunity presents itself. As he acts in these morally and socially responsible ways, he finds that he can pray as he once had. He longs to be reconciled with his father, a feeling that reflects a desire to be reconciled with his heavenly father as well.

Reconciliation with God and a determination to effect reconciliation with the parent and siblings he abandoned years earlier form the next steps in his transformation. With each action, the next step of a new life miraculously unfolds for him. When he returns to his family, he is received as was the prodigal son but with no resentful brothers. All members of his family welcome him. He is rewarded with the happiness of married love and a supportive community as well.

Sources for Further Study

Bly, Stephen A. *Help! My Adult Child Won't Leave Home*. Carol Stream, Ill.: Tyndale House, 2006. Nonfiction work by this prolific author examines the relationship between parents and adult children. Provides insights into his fiction.

_____. *Quality Living in a Complicated Age*. San Bernardino, Calif.: Here's Life, 1984. This nonfiction work describes Bly's views on how to live a Christian life and sheds light on the philosophy evident in his many works of fiction.

_____. *The Surprising Side of Grace: Appreciating God's Loving Anger*.

Grand Rapids, Mich.: Discovery House, 1994. This nonfiction work by this prolific author describes the author's view of grace, which is evident in *The Long Trail Home*.

"Bly Books." http://www.blybooks.com. Stephen A. Bly's official Web site describes his life, his current work, and his collaboration with his wife; site offers e-mail connection with the author.

"Stephen A(rthur) Bly." *Contemporary Authors Online*. Farmington Hills, Mich.: Thomson Gale, 2007. This overview of Bly's life and extensive writing includes a list of books he has published alone and with his wife, Janet Bly.

Bernadette Flynn Low

THE LORD

Author: Romano Guardini (1885-1968)
First published: Der Herr: Betrachtungen über die Person und das Leben Jesu Christi, 1937 (English translation, 1954)
Edition used: The Lord, translated by Elinor Castendyk Briefs. Gateway edition. Washington, D.C.: Regnery, 2000
Genre: Nonfiction
Subgenres: Biblical studies; critical analysis; exegesis; meditation and contemplation; theology
Core issues: Gospels; Jesus Christ; love; salvation; scriptures; sin and sinners

In The Lord, *written first as a series of meditations on the Gospels and shared with his congregation, Guardini hoped to instill a lively awareness of both the human and divine personality of Christ as the ultimate revelation of God's love for the world. A personal encounter with the person of Christ is the essence of Christianity, which produces conversion of the heart from sin and a desire for holiness and union with God.*

Overview

After several years of economic turmoil and hardship in Germany, many people were thirsting for a leader, a father figure who could save them from their economic and political ills. Adolf Hitler appealed to this popular thirst for a Führer (father). At the same time, with the explosion of comparative religion and the Nazi revival of neo-pagan ideology, many German Christians began to wonder what was so special about Christianity and Christ.

Romano Guardini's personal conversion, which took place in 1905, and his subsequent study of other great religious figures in comparison with Jesus, deepened his faith in Christ, convincing him that the person of Jesus was unique in that the Christ was fully human and thus approachable by people at all times and places but also fully divine. Unlike any other man in history, Jesus was "wholly Other" and therefore ultimately beyond complete human comprehension. Nonetheless as the most complete expression of God's love of human creation, the person of Jesus invites everyone into a deeply personal and individual encounter with him that teaches what it is to be fully human, fully alive, and fully loved.

Guardini hoped to introduce his students and parishioners to this living God-man as the only person worthy of complete trust. There could be only one Savior for all creation and times, and in the Germany of the 1930's, this savior was not Hitler, but Christ. *The Lord,* then, began as a series of meditations on the life of Christ as described in the Gospels. Drawing on his own and others' study of Jesus, including earlier historical critical literature, Guardini, a Roman Catholic priest, wrote his meditations as sermons and preached them to his students at Saint Benedict's Chapel in Berlin and to commoners who attended Mass at Burg Rothenfels from 1932 through

1936. He then collected the meditations and rewrote them, producing a single coherent narrative that became *The Lord*.

The book consists of eighty-six meditations on the Scriptures and is divided into seven parts, which examine the life of Christ in approximate chronological order, beginning with the entry of God's Son into human history, continuing with a reflection on his life and ministry on earth, and ending with his return to the Father, where he reigns in eternal glory. Part 1, "The Beginnings," examines the origins and ancestry of Jesus in the Hebrew Scripture, the role of his mother Mary, the mystery of the Incarnation, and the role of John the Baptist. Next, he addresses Christ's rejection at Nazareth, where those who knew him were scandalized by his claim to be the Messiah, followed by his healing miracles, his calling out of the apostles, and his preaching of the Beatitudes that reveal the interior mystery and nature of true love. On one level of organization, the rest of *The Lord* represents an extended meditation on the virtues preached in the Beatitudes, including humility, well-ordered love, justice, mercy, peace, and love of enemies.

In part 2, "Message and Promise," Guardini explores in depth the beatitudes of justice and mercy, the kindness of God, and the will of the Father to demonstrate through Jesus the Son the depth of his sacrificial love, which will overcome the spirit of evil and sin and restore eternal life in conquering death through a rebirth of the Holy Spirit. In part 3, "The Decision," Guardini explores Jesus' realization that his mission must embrace suffering and death because of human blindness to the fullness of God's love and human rejection of his own gospel message of divine forgiveness. Only by his free offering of his life for the forgiveness of sin can creation be renewed by God's spirit of love. Part 4, "On the Road to Jerusalem," explores the beatitudes of poverty of spirit and humility, as the God-man prepares to humble himself even to the point of suffering and death, as he establishes a church to succeed him in his work, and as he shows what a life of discipleship looks like. Part 5, "The Last Days," is a further meditation on God's humility and love for the world; it traces Jesus' entry into Jerusalem, his last encounters with the spiritual blindness of the Pharisees, his final night with his disciples in which he gives them the Eucharist as a gift by which he will remain with them until the end of time. At the Last Supper, he commissions the disciples to "do this" in his memory, and he demonstrates the nature of discipleship through service, by humbling himself to wash their feet. Then follows the road to the cross, the agony in the garden, the arrest, trial, crucifixion, and death, in which the betrayal of his disciples figures prominently.

Part 6 explores the post-Resurrection appearances of Jesus, his final teachings, the Ascension of Jesus into glory, the true nature of history, the role of God's spirit and of God's church in history, and the role of Christ the eternal high priest who returns as judge. Part 7 reflects on the passages of the book of Revelation, exploring the imagery and meaning of the Lamb, the final judgment, the woman clothed in the sun and the dragon, the final war between good and evil, the throne of judgment, and the bride of the Lamb in time and eternity.

Christian Themes

Guardini explores many Christian themes in these evocative meditations, including the reality of sin and evil in the world, which come not from God but from the darkened intellects, weak wills, and disordered hearts of human beings, made ultimately to know, love, and serve God. However, sin separates humans from God, and this wound festers under the temptation of Satan, who hates humans and tempts them to evil. Only God can repair humankind's estrangement from God, and this is the mission of Jesus, who enters human history to restore spiritual life to human souls and to reveal the fullness of God's love for humankind. Jesus reveals God as the true desire of every human heart.

For Guardini, this makes Jesus unique among religious figures. He is not just another human guide to truth and goodness like Buddha or Socrates, but rather he is truth and goodness personified. He is not a seeker of truth, but the truth, the way, and the life of every person. Nonetheless, he is mysteriously and fully human, more fully human than any other figure in history. All humanity, and each person individually, is called to conversion in Christ, and this conversion demands a decision to embrace the beatitudes he preached and the values of humility, well-ordered love, and justice fulfilled in mercy— which alone lead to purity and peace of heart—and the ability to love and bless enemies as wayward children of the Father desperately in need of redemption.

These are not, manifestly, the values of the world, nor of the Nazi system whose dark ideology was already threatening the world in which Guardini lived. Instead, Guardini says, they are the values that even in the midst of persecution and trial will sustain and nurture the heart in the midst of suffering, leading to a personal encounter with the God who willingly took on human flesh to suffer, to forgive in the midst of suffering, to die, and in so doing, to open the doors to eternal life and true bliss.

Sources for Further Study

Guardini, Romano. *Learning the Virtues That Lead You to God.* Manchester, N.H.: Sophia Institute Press, 1998. A book of meditations by Guardini on the virtues that lead to a mature moral life.

_____. *Power and Responsibility.* Translated by Elinor C. Brief. 1951. Reprint. Chicago: Henry Regnery, 1961. Guardini reflects on how humans must use the increasing knowledge of science not in the destructive ways of modern ideologies, but in recognition of the obligation to serve as stewards of God's creation.

_____. *The Spirit of the Liturgy.* Translated by Ada Lane. New York: Crossroad, 1998. One of Guardini's most influential books, apart from *The Lord.* Underscores Guardini's conviction that the encounter with Christ is made possible in time and history through the sacramental and liturgical life of the Church.

Krieg, Robert A. *Romano Guardini.* Notre Dame, Ind.: University of Notre Dame Press, 1997. This comprehensive biography of Guardini, one of the few available in English, offers assessments of his life and work, including an insightful summary of *The Lord* as a pivotal event in Guardini's life.

Robert F. Gorman

THE LORD OF THE RINGS

Author: J. R. R. Tolkien (1892-1973)
First published: The Fellowship of the Ring, 1954; *The Two Towers,* 1954; *The Return of the King,* 1955. London: Allen & Unwin
Genre: Novels
Subgenres: Adventure; fantasy
Core issues: Good vs. evil; grace; hope; nature; sacrifice

Hailed in several major British polls as "the novel of the century," Tolkien's The Lord of the Rings *became a modern Christian classic neither by proselytizing nor by allegorizing, but by demonstrating that Christian and classical virtues can be made attractive to the modern reader. The protagonist's resistance to the ultimate temptation, power, in the form of the One Ring and the Christlike self-sacrifice of characters such as Aragorn are illuminated by Tolkien's faith without being apologetic in the theological sense.*

> *Principal characters*
> *Frodo Baggins,* the protagonist
> *Samwise Gamgee,* Frodo's gardener and closest friend
> *Gandalf,* a wizard who guides Frodo
> *Sauron,* the Dark Lord, principal antagonist
> *Strider (also known as Aragorn),* the rightful king of Gondor, in exile
> *Gimli,* son of Gloin, a dwarf
> *Legolas,* an elf

Overview

J. R. R. Tolkien's modern fantasy classic *The Lord of the Rings* is a massive novel, often called epic both for its size and scope and for its heroic theme. At half a million words, balancing scores of main characters and hundreds of minor ones (the index lists more than seven hundred personal names) and interweaving several plot strands, *The Lord of the Rings* was too big for one volume in its first publication, resulting in a three-volume version that was (inaccurately) dubbed a trilogy. The setting is Middle-earth, conceived vaguely as Northern Europe before the recorded history of humankind and before geological forces changed the shape of the land.

The unlikely hero of the story is a little hobbit named Frodo Baggins, nephew of Bilbo Baggins, the hero of Tolkien's earlier and more child-oriented novel, *The Hobbit* (1937). The story opens with a party at which Bilbo hands over his estate to his nephew and leaves the Shire for good. With his estate, Bilbo leaves Frodo the magic ring that makes the wearer invisible. As Frodo receives it, however, the wizard Gandalf discovers this and reveals to Frodo, that the ring is in reality the One Ring that controls a host of other rings of power dispersed among the races of Middle-earth (three to the elves, seven to the dwarves, and nine to humans). Sauron, a mysterious power who has sought for millennia to control all people, now seeks the ring from his stronghold in Mordor. Holding the ring endangers Frodo and all around him: He must leave the Shire he loves.

Frodo attempts to sneak off alone, but his loyal hobbit friends—his gardener Sam Gamgee, and younger cousins Merry and Pippin—guess Frodo's secret and willingly share his danger. Pursued by the shadowy Black Riders—cloaked figures so shadowy that they seem to have no substance—the four hobbits are trapped between the Riders, menacing Barrow Wights, and malicious willows that enclose the hobbits until the kindly Tom Bombadil rescues them. Moving on, the hobbits seem lost without Gandalf until they fall in with a scruffy character, a Ranger named Strider, who looks disreputable, but whom Frodo decides to trust. Strider fends off the Black Riders, but not before Frodo is wounded by a Morgul Blade, a magic sword whose wound can be cured only by elvish healing. Strider rushes Frodo to the Halfelven King Elrond at Rivendell, while Gildor calls down a flood that vanquishes the Black Riders.

Recovering at Rivendell, Frodo is called to a council where the greatest minds— elf, dwarf, human, hobbit, and wizard—debate how to answer the threat of the ring. The inescapable conclusion is that the ring must be destroyed in the fires of Mount Doom, in the heart of Mordor where the evil power resides. Frodo agrees to the dangerous mission, supported by the Fellowship of the Ring: Gandalf, Strider, Sam, Pippin, Merry, an elf named Legolas, a dwarf named Gimli, and a man named Boromir.

Unable to cross the treacherous Mount Caradhras, the company goes beneath it, into the Mines of Moria, an underground city of the dwarves. There they are attacked by the monstrous orcs, and Gandalf is killed by a fiery monster known as a balrog. After a healing rest in the elvish retreat of Lórien, Frodo runs off when Boromir tries to seize the ring. Repentant, Boromir dies defending the hobbits, but the fellowship has been divided by his momentary treachery.

Searching for the scattered hobbits, Legolas, Gimli, and Strider meet the Riders of Rohan, fierce mounted warriors who defend the frontiers of Gondor. Meanwhile, Pippin and Merry narrowly escape the orcs and run into the kindly ents, giant treelike creatures who care for the forests. When they learn from the hobbits the danger they face from an evil white-clad wizard named Saruman, the peaceful ents go to war. Meanwhile, a mysterious white-robed figure appears to Gimli and Legolas; they poise to strike him down, only to discover it is the resurrected form of Gandalf, now in glistening white. He rides with them to Edoras, releases Théoden, king of Rohan, from the spell of Grima Wormtongue (who in turn serves Saruman), and leads the Riders of Rohan into battle against the army of orcs. The orcs prove too strong, and the Riders must retreat to their stronghold at Helm's Deep, where they hold off the orcs until the White Rider Gandalf appears, and the ents destroy Saruman's citadel at Isengard.

At the same time, Sam and Frodo are being pursued by Gollum, a creature who seems a wretched monster, but in reality is the remains of a hobbit who had once held Frodo's ring and is in its power. Frodo uses that power to bind Gollum to serve his quest, but Sam does not trust the creature. Wandering into domains patrolled by Faramir, Boromir's younger brother, Frodo learns of Boromir's death. As they continue toward Mordor, Sam and Frodo are betrayed again as Gollum leads them to the lair of a giant (and hungry) spider named Shelob.

Rescued from the flooded ruins of Isengard, Pippin rides with Gandalf to the fortified capital of Gondor, the splendid city of Minas Tirith. Meeting the steward of Gondor, and father of Boromir, Denethor (not "king"; the kings are in exile until the sword of their ancestor can be reforged), Pippin solemnly offers him service. Back in Rohan, Merry offers the same to King Théoden. Strider rides into the Paths of the Dead to summon the spirits who had broken an oath to Strider's ancestor, the king of Gondor—for Strider is the exiled king, his real name being Aragorn. The spirits join the fight. In Rohan, Théoden's niece Éowyn takes command while her uncle leads the armies; disguising herself in armor, she grabs Merry and rides into battle.

In the siege of Gondor, Pippin enlists Gandalf's aid when the steward despairs, seeking only suicide. The three armies (Aragorn's Dead Hosts, Denethor's army bolstered by Gandalf, and the Rohirrim under Théoden) converge on the Orcish Hosts at Pelennor Fields, where the least likely warriors—the woman Éowyn and the hobbit Merry—defeat the king of the Nazgûl (the resurrected Black Riders).

In Mordor, Sam rescues Frodo, gives him back the ring, and leads him to the summit of Mount Doom, an active volcano. Poised on the fiery brink, Frodo suddenly refuses to destroy the ring and announces his intention to use its power himself. However, Gollum jumps Frodo, bites off his ring finger, and dances in triumph with the ring—only to topple into the volcano and fulfill the quest by accident.

In Gondor, Aragorn reclaims his ancestral throne. The hobbits return to the Shire only to find it overrun by exploiters who oppressed the Shire folk. The Fellows of the Ring easily defeat the bullies, but the Shire is scorched by the war. The last of the elves depart for the Undying Lands, and Frodo and Bilbo join them, leaving the Shire forever. Sam, however, stays, marries Rosie Cotton, and becomes a prominent citizen of the Shire.

Christian Themes

The Lord of the Rings is virtually a test case for a definition of Christian Literature, since it contains not a single reference to religion in general, much less Christ or Christianity in particular—yet many critics (and Tolkien himself) have asserted that it is centrally Christian in conception and execution. Tolkien went even farther: in a December 2, 1953, letter to Father Robert Murray, he asserted that the Catholicism of *The Lord of the Rings* was unconscious at first, but then conscious in revision. As the setting of *The Lord of the Rings* preceded Christianity by several thousand years, Christian references would be anachronisms, and pagan references contrary to spiritual truth would also run counter to the vital truths Tolkien was trying to articulate in his novel.

In many ways this dilemma was exactly the one faced by Tolkien's favorite Old English writer, the *Beowulf* poet. Critics before Tolkien had seen that heroic classic as a clumsy and anachronistic mishmash of Christian and pagan ideas, or as a pagan masterpiece spoiled with Christian excrescences. Tolkien, in his famous monograph "*Beowulf*: The Monsters and the Critics" (1936), instead suggested that the Christian poet knew he was conveying pagan legend and that Beowulf's heroic morality resonated more with Christianity than later critics would think. The *Beowulf* poet's solution to the tension was Christian commentary on pagan values: Tolkien's solution was to explore those virtues common to pre-Christian and Christian cultures and allow them to shine through in the characters without comment.

Thus, for example, the moral contrast between Denethor, steward of Gondor, and Théoden, king of Rohan, not only illustrates the Christian virtue of hope (which for the Catholic Tolkien is a "theological virtue") but also a Germanic pagan virtue that Tolkien dubbed the "Northern theory of courage." Denethor (his name being almost an anagram of Théoden emphasizes the complementarity of the characters) sees no point in fighting impossible odds and seeks suicide. Théoden, on the contrary, relishes the battle precisely because of the impossible odds: It allows him to show his undaunted courage. Yet higher than both is Sam's transcendent hope in the face of the same impossible odds: He realizes, in singing an old song, that though Sauron has blotted out the sun, the sun is still there, if unseen (a clear image of transcendence). When the happy ending comes unlooked for, Sam feels the movement of what Christian theology calls grace (and Tolkien called "eucatastrophe").

Another spiritual theme of Tolkien's fiction that is strikingly Christian (and perhaps particularly Catholic) is what theologians call the "sacramental" view of nature. In many non-Western spiritual traditions and in some Christian denominations, nature presents a spiritual danger: The world we perceive through the senses and the sensual, the flesh, drag the spirit down. It is clear that for Tolkien, nature instead lifts the spirit up. This phenomenon is called "sacramental" because, like the sacraments, nature is a physical reality that points to a spiritual reality.

Perhaps the most striking result of Tolkien's faith informing his fiction is a favorite attack of hostile critics against *The Lord of the Rings*: the unabashed clarity of good versus evil in the book. The twentieth century mind, critics like Edwin Muir and Edmund Wilson asserted, rejects a moral vision that sees only black and white and instead demands shades of grey. The immense popularity of Tolkien's fiction would suggest otherwise.

Sources for Further Study

Birzer, Bradley. *Tolkien's Sanctifying Myth*. Wilmington, Del.: ISI Books, 2003. Argues that *The Lord of the Rings* is a "sublimely mystical Passion Play" in which myth is "sanctified" by expressing eternal (Christian) truths.

Caldecott, Stratford. *The Power of the Ring: The Spiritual Vision Behind "The Lord of the Rings."* New York: Crossroad, 2005. Suggests that Tolkien's Catholic spirituality "illuminates" his writing, and the Christian virtues of the heroes in *The Lord of the Rings* purify the reader without proselytizing.

Pearce, Joseph. *Tolkien: Man and Myth*. San Francisco: Ignatius Press, 1998. A biography of Tolkien emphasizing the role of his Catholic spirituality in developing his myth.

Wood, Ralph C. *The Gospel According to Tolkien.* Louisville, Ky.: Westminster John Knox Press, 2003. Explores Tolkien's fiction as an "embedded gospel" providing an answer to the moral dilemmas of the twentieth century.

John R. Holmes

THE LORD'S PRAYER AND THE BEATITUDES

Author: Saint Gregory of Nyssa (c. 335-c. 394 C.E.)

First published: De oratione dominica and *De beatitudinibus*, last quarter of the fourth century C.E. (English translation, 1954)

Edition used: The Lord's Prayer, The Beatitudes, translated and annotated by Hilda C. Graef. Westminster, Md.: Newman Press, 1954

Genre: Nonfiction

Subgenres: Exegesis; homilies; instructional manual; meditation and contemplation

Core issues: Asceticism; the Beatitudes; the Bible; contemplation; devotional life; peace; prayer; repentance

These five homilies on the Lord's Prayer and eight homilies on the Beatitudes are moral and practical exhortations for the Christian life, although they frequently employ allegorical and figurative interpretations of Scripture. In the homilies on the Lord's Prayer, Gregory of Nyssa admonishes his audience about the power and majesty of prayer and teaches how and for what one should pray. He then guides his audience through a meditation on the meaning of each of the various petitions contained in the prayer that Jesus himself taught to his disciples. The homilies on the Beatitudes of Jesus' Sermon on the Mount treat the eight individual blessings as steps leading toward spiritual perfection, meditation, humility, and love of God and neighbor.

Overview

Gregory of Nyssa, a bishop in Nyssa, Cappadocia (central Turkey), wrote five homilies on the Lord's Prayer and eight homilies on the Beatitudes to guide his readers to a deeper understanding of these biblical passages and make them aware of the importance of prayer and the value of striving to lead a better Christian life. In his homilies on the Lord's Prayer, he states that the soul is made in God's image and that image remains although it has lost its original beauty. Therefore, one should therefore pray in accordance with the dignity of that image. A prayer of request (*proseuche*) is proper only after making a vow (*euche*) of an acceptable spiritual gift. Christ, by instructing us to address God as Father, set a high standard.

In the Lord's Prayer, according to the homilies of Gregory of Nyssa, when "hallowed be Thy name" is said, the person praying is hallowed by affirming that God's name is not to be blasphemed. "Thy kingdom come" is said not because we think that God should become king. We say those words because as slaves to death and the impulses of the flesh, we need the Kingdom of God to come as our only means of escape from the power of corruption. "On earth as it is in heaven" asks that the peace, obedience, and freedom from evil enjoyed by the angels may also be on earth. "Our daily bread," asks for what we need and nothing that we do not need. "Give us this day" means that we should not be troubled about tomorrow, for God provides what is needed in its time. Forgiving our debtors allows us to imitate the divine nature.

In sum, Gregory of Nyssa says, the Lord's Prayer reminds us that we are made in God's image and can still call on God as Father. Just as we ask God to be good and just and merciful toward us, so too must we be toward our neighbor. We should not think like the Pharisee that we are personally free from sin. The corrupt world's effect on our corrupt nature makes our own sinning inevitable. Thus we pray, "Lead us not into temptation" and "Deliver us from evil." These words mean the same: We ask to be released from the corruption and temptation of the devil and this world.

The Beatitudes show a path upward, like the rungs of a spiritual ladder, according to Gregory of Nyssa. He explains that "poverty of spirit" is a lack of diabolical treasures and a voluntary humility, a standard that Jesus himself demonstrated. Poverty of spirit is also material poverty, for material riches are burdens in the striving for the holy life.

Why are the meek blessed, since the saints are fighters, and Saint Paul encourages running the good race and fighting the good fight? asks Gregory of Nyssa, Properly understood, meekness is a slowness in moving toward baseness. It is impossible not to be affected by the passions, but the Lord calls for meekness before the passions as a just and attainable standard.

Most would see mourning as misery, Gregory of Nyssa says, but the mourning of true repentance, although painful, is a blessing just as many medicines cause pain in their healing. This does not mean that a perpetual state of pain in healing is good. It must also be remembered that "they shall be comforted." Rather, mourning represents the painful awareness that something good is missing from life, just as one who has had a glimpse of true sunlight is not satisfied with the filtered light and shadow of a cave. Those who hunger and thirst are blessed if they hunger for salvation and thirst to do the will of God.

Gregory of Nyssa goes on to say that the obvious meaning of being merciful and obtaining mercy is practicing mutual charity, for mercy is a compassion toward those who suffer. When the Beatitudes say, "they shall obtain mercy," the future tense is significant, for it suggests that the reward for mercy is reserved for later times: God will be merciful toward us at the Last Judgment if we are merciful now. Further, because we have fallen into the slavery of sin, it would be right that we pity ourselves. If we do not, it is because we are insensitive to our own malaise.

The pure of heart shall see God, but "no one has seen God." How can both teachings be true? Gregory of Nyssa asks. The Word teaches that the pure of heart will see God, but who can be pure of heart? Does this not hold out a reward for what is impossible? The Lord does not command the impossible, he answers. Rather, saints do see God, but in his energies, not his essence. Also the Beatitudes point to what happens to the person who strives for purity of heart. In doing this, that individual strips away the sordidness from human nature and can thus see the God within the self.

Gregory of Nyssa notes that "sonship" itself is the reward for peacemaking. The reward is so profound because the virtue, peacemaking, is required for the enjoyment of all other goods. The peacemaker, who heals the infirmities of the soul, is superior to the healer of infirmities of the body. However, perhaps the greatest peacemaker is the one who pacifies not others but his own mind and body so that they are truly one.

Finally, those suffering persecution for justice's sake are blessed because they use the evil directed against them to get closer to God. The bishop asks us to compare what we lose with what we will gain.

Christian Themes

Gregory's homilies on the Lord's Prayer belong to the early Christian tradition of reflecting on the meaning, manner, and efficacy of prayer, especially the prayer that Jesus taught to his disciples. The homilies on the Beatitudes belong to the tradition of spiritual ascent and the ladder of perfection, which are featured prominently in the Christian ascetic tradition. Both sets are also important witnesses to the Christian patristic tradition of spiritual, allegorical, and often mystical interpretation of Scripture.

These homilies are products of the ongoing blending of Hellenic natural philosophy with biblical revelation in the early Christian centuries. Gregory exemplifies the ways that many Church Fathers, educated in the Greco-Roman intellectual tradition, made use of the concepts and language of secular culture to present Christianity not only as understandable within the Hellenic tradition as well as through Judaism but also as the solution to problems unsolved by Greek philosophy. Chief among these is the doctrine of the Incarnation, which gave humanity the means of recovering the glories of its own nature made in God's image but rendered useless by sin.

Also visible in Gregory are elements of the Christian tradition undistorted by the Augustinian determinism that had dominated the West. Gregory urges his audience, for example, to realize this latent dignity when approaching the Lord in prayer as Father and to act on that realization. Gregory also reminds his audience of the fundamental freedom of the human soul despite its entrapment in a corrupt world. For Gregory, the fires of Hell must be the result of one's own choice to separate oneself from God. They are not the result of anything God has done. Gregory's understanding of human excellence (*arete*) and his notion of the meaning of blessed (*makarios*) show the skillful blending of Greek and Hebraic concepts.

Sources for Further Study

Balthasar, Hans Urs von. *Presence and Thought: An Essay on the Religious Philosophy of Gregory of Nyssa.* Translated by Mark Sebanc. San Francisco: Ignatius Press, 1995. Works on the premise that Gregory is the most successful translator of ancient Hellenic philosophy and spirituality into the Christian context.

Drobner, Hubertus R., and Albert Viciano, eds. *Gregory of Nyssa: Homilies on the Beatitudes—An English Version with Commentary and Supporting Studies,* Supplements to Vigiliae Christianae 52. Leiden, the Netherlands: E. J. Brill, 2000. Provides a translation of homilies on the Beatitudes with commentary by many scholars on individual aspects of Gregory's perspective.

Laird, Martin. *Gregory of Nyssa and the Grasp of Faith.* Oxford Early Christian Studies series. New York: Oxford University Press, 2004. Related to the homilies on the Lord's Prayer and the Beatitudes as they both help their audience understand how God is and is not known by the human mind.

Meredith, Anthony. *Gregory of Nyssa*. Early Church Fathers series. New York: Routledge, 1999. Offers an accessible introduction to Gregory's environment and basic teachings. Includes representative passages from Gregory's theological, philosophical, and devotional writings.

Pelikan, Jaroslav. *Christianity and Classical Culture: The Metamorphosis of Natural Theology in the Christian Encounter with Hellenism*. New Haven, Conn.: Yale University Press, 1993. Gifford Lectures delivered at the University of Aberdeen, 1992-1993. Studies the presence of Greek philosophical concepts within the writings of the three Cappadocians (Saint Basil, Gregory of Nazianzus, and Gregory of Nyssa).

Daniel J. Nodes

LOVE COMES SOFTLY SERIES

Author: Janette Oke (1935-   )
First published: Love Comes Softly, 1979; *Love's Enduring Promise,* 1980; *Love's Long Journey,* 1982; *Love's Abiding Joy,* 1983; *Love's Unending Legacy,* 1984; *Love's Unfolding Dream,* 1987; *Love Takes Wing,* 1988; *Love Finds a Home,* 1989. Minneapolis, Minn.: Bethany House
Genre: Novels
Subgenres: Evangelical fiction; historical fiction (nineteenth century); romance
Core issues: Acceptance; daily living; love; salvation; trust in God

With this series of prairie romances, Oke combined plot with Christian faith to put a new slant on fiction about the era of westward expansion and the pioneers who settled the land. She opened the door to writing and publishing opportunities within Christian fiction that did not exist previously.

> *Principal characters*
> *Marty Claridge Davis,* widowed protagonist
> *Clark Davis,* protagonist who marries Marty
> *Missie Davis,* Clark's daughter
> *Willie LaHaye,* Missie's suitor
> *Nandry Larson,* neighbor girl taken in by the Davises
> *Clae Larson,* neighbor girl taken in by the Davises
> *Ellie Davis,* Clark and Marty's daughter
> *Lane Howard,* a ranch hand who is Ellie's suitor
> *Belinda Davis,* Clark and Marty's youngest daughter and a nurse
> *Luke Davis,* Clark and Marty's son and a doctor
> *Melissa LaHaye,* Willie and Missie's daughter
> *Amy Jo Davis,* Belinda's niece
> *Drew Simpson,* Belinda's suitor
> *Virginia Stafford-Smyth,* a wealthy patient of Luke and Belinda

Overview

The *Love Comes Softly* series, eight Christian novels about the lives of the Davis family, helped create a new genre known as prairie romances, historical romances involving the frontier. These books convey Christian values through the thoughts and actions of the characters.

In *Love Comes Softly,* the first novel in the series, one day in fall, the husband of youthful pioneer Marty Claridge dies. At the burial, Clark Davis proposes a marriage of convenience in which he will provide for Marty in exchange for her tending to his daughter Missie. He promises Marty the fare to go home on the spring wagon train. Everything goes wrong as Marty adjusts to her new life and tends Missie, but Clark patiently demonstrates kindness and prays for her. Marty does not know much about religion but figures the religious Clark will not drink or beat her. When Clark realizes Marty is expecting, he feels glad she will have a child to remember her husband by. Marty finally sees past her grief to notice Clark's goodness. On Christmas, they share a special day, and the nativity story strikes a chord with Marty. Marty and Clark experience joys and tragedy. Each evening they talk about the day's events and their feelings, dreams, hopes, and even faith. On Easter Sunday Marty attends her first church service and learns that Jesus Christ died for her sins. Clark's God becomes her God. Marty grows in her faith and draws closer to Clark. Marty and Clark realize that love grew slowly and came softly, and they choose to stay together.

In *Love's Enduring Promise*, Marty feels gratitude for God's provision through Clark as their family flourishes. When an ailing neighbor passes away, they take in Nandry and Clae Larson, the neighbor's daughters. The community builds a school and hires a teacher. Missie comes home with her daily report about classes and how much she hates Willie LaHaye, who torments her. Time passes, and eleven-year-old Missie still dislikes Willie but instead of fretting she ignores him. Clae trains to be a teacher. Nandry marries. The girls thank Marty and Clark for helping them succeed. Clae is hired to teach the same fall that the new preacher settles in. Missie finishes her schooling and trains for teaching. She returns and takes the position when Clae marries the parson. During Missie's second year of teaching, Willie declares his plans to move West and his interest in her. On her wedding day, Missie thanks Marty for raising her.

In *Love's Long Journey*, Missie and Willie travel West. They rely on the promises from Isaiah 41:10 that assure them of God's presence, strength, and help. The rigors of trail life drain Missie, who battles homesickness and fatigue from pregnancy. Missie values God's provision of a cautious and careful wagon master who leads them safely to Tettsford Junction. She remains alone in town, close to a doctor for three months, while Willie hires hands and establishes their land. When his son is nearly two weeks old, Willie moves his family to their ranch. Missie faces more disappointments at the desolate and isolated spread. The cramped sod house seems almost unbearable, but the baby brings her joy. Hardships, endless wind, blizzards, rustlers, and illness force Missie and Willie to draw strength from God's promises. As their lot improves, Missie reflects on how God kept his promise from Isaiah 41:10— their love journeyed a long way and found a home.

In *Love's Abiding Joy*, Clark gives Marty a birthday trip to visit Missie and Willie. After years apart, they relish a joyous reunion. During their stay, two boys are playing inside a mine when it collapses. Clark frees one boy and carries him out. When he retrieves the other boy's body, another cave-in crushes his leg. He regains consciousness and the concussion clears, but gangrene claims his leg, and the poison spreads through his system. Marty and Missie come to terms with letting God heal Clark or take him home. A doctor is found and Clark's leg is amputated to save his life. Clark sobs and prays but trusts God to help him cope. God heals him emotionally and physically. Clark and Marty stay until spring, and Clark preaches at church. On their trip home, a young boy mentions the "poor man." Clark and Marty both look around until they realize he is referring to Clark. They laugh, jubilant that Clark does not feel handicapped—God brought joy and blessing out of sorrow.

In *Love's Unending Legacy*, Marty and Clark return home and reunite with family and friends. Marty battles emotional fatigue. As her poor health continues, she realizes that she is pregnant. At forty-three, she dreads telling the family, but they surprise her with their joyful response. Lane, a Hanging W ranch hand, comes to run a neighboring farm and becomes interested in the Davises' daughter Ellie. Although Marty and Clark treat Lane like one of Ellie's brothers, Ellie senses Lane's attraction and returns his interest. At Christmas, Lane gives Ellie a locket. Because Marty needs help during her pregnancy, Ellie feels she cannot leave home and returns it. She pines over losing Lane. Clark assures her that Marty wants her happiness. Lane gives Ellie the locket again, and the couple plan to wed. Ellie helps Marty deliver Belinda. The whole family cherishes the baby girl. Clark and Marty discuss their legacy of faith, character, and love for others, evident through their grown children. They trust God to help them again as Belinda will also need that legacy.

In *Love's Unfolding Dream*, Clark and Marty's grown son Luke, who is a doctor, recognizes Belinda's desire to ease suffering. He takes her on routine medical calls to see if nursing suits her. By the time she reaches thirteen, she helps Luke regularly, though it cuts in on time spent with her niece Amy Jo, who is near her age. Melissa, Missie's fourteen-year-old daughter, comes to live with the Davis family because she wants more schooling to become a teacher. The three girls get along well. Belinda accompanies Luke to set a broken bone, but Drew Simpson's arm is crushed and requires amputation. She feels scared and ill but performs admirably. Belinda talks about the ordeal with Marty. Despite her fears and tears, she wants to continue nursing. Drew visits Clark to ask questions about his accident and phantom pain. When Drew sobs about his loss, Clark comforts him and talks about God's love. Drew prays for forgiveness and God's peace. The next time Belinda sees Drew, they talk of God and her prayer for him. Drew shares his dream of becoming a lawyer, and they discuss not being bitter.

In *Love Takes Wing*, Clark and Marty's granddaughter Melissa completes teacher training and returns to the West, taking Amy Jo with her. When both girls wed, Belinda rejoices for her nieces, but she also feels lonely and left behind. When Virginia Stafford-Smyth, a passenger on a train passing through, suffers a stroke and is brought to Luke for treatment, Belinda tends her. Virginia asks Belinda to move to Boston to nurse her there. Belinda bids her family farewell and accompanies Virginia to her mansion. Although she is not used to wealth and finery, Belinda enjoys touring Boston. She sets sail for Europe as Virginia's companion, savoring the sights and sensations of Spain, Italy, and France. In spring, they sail home. On board Belinda unearths her Bible and reacquaints herself with God and his joy. She has subtly let him slip out of her daily thoughts and habits. Repenting, she makes her heart right.

In *Love Finds a Home*, Belinda travels home to see her family. When Belinda returns to Boston, she and Virginia add daily Bible study to their routine. Virginia has become more open to spiritual things. At church, she asks God to forgive her sins then shares her new faith with her staff. Shortly after, Virginia dies in her sleep, and Belinda inherits much of the estate. She guarantees the staff their home and positions, but she also ponders a way to help others. Belinda devises a plan to provide housing for the elderly, and the staff agrees. On a visit to the lawyer, Belinda discovers that Drew works as a partner. They begin seeing each other, but Drew feels awkward about Belinda's wealth. However, they still attend events and church together. Belinda sets up a board to run the home, and the occupants arrive throughout the month of December. Belinda is now free to leave Boston—and, sadly, Drew. She finishes her tasks and says emotional farewells to her friends. Back home, when another legal matter arises, Belinda seeks the new lawyer in town and finds Drew. He had not wanted to ask Belinda to leave Boston, and she came home not knowing his plans to return. They admit their feelings for each other, and love finds a home.

Christian Themes

Janette Oke's historical novels helped launch Christian fiction and created a genre known as prairie romance. However, her books are more about love than romance. Romantic love, of course, exists between Marty and Clark and later between their grown children and their chosen life mates. However, the attraction for readers and what Oke said she wanted to convey was love.

Throughout the eight-book series, Oke shows love pervading the lives of the Davis family. God's love becomes evident in his provision for the widowed Marty. A less than ideal marriage blooms into a lifetime commitment and a legacy of love passed down through succeeding generations. As a result, the Davises develop married love that grows out of compassion. They demonstrate love between parents and children as Marty and Clark each raise the other's child from a former marriage as well as offspring conceived from their own union. They foster love for siblings despite hardships of life on the prairie and the age gap between some of their children. They encourage love for extended family by supporting the pursuit of dreams and God-given gifts. They nurture love in the form of compassion by helping neighbors and providing a home for two abandoned children.

Most important, in these books Oke bring to fiction the power of love between God and those who follow him. God demonstrates his unending love and faithfulness to members of this family, who in turn are faithful in loving him. When they face trials, they need not fear because he is with them. He keeps the promises in his word—the Bible. As the Davises place their trust in him, God brings blessings out of their sufferings and joy from their sorrows. The Davis family's lives abound with enduring love because of their deep trust in God and their determination to live out their faith on the prairie.

Sources for Further Study

DeLong, Janice, and Rachel Schwedt. *Contemporary Christian Authors: Lives and Works.* Lanham, Md.: Scarecrow Press, 2000. Biographical sketch details Oke's books and awards as well as her purpose and themes in writing.

Hedblad, Alan, ed. *Something About the Author: Facts and Pictures About Authors and Illustrators of Books for Young People*. Detroit, Mich.: Gale Research, 1998. Provides young adults an overview of Oke's writing career and accomplishments.

Johnson, Sarah. "Pioneering Efforts in Christian Historicals: Sarah Johnson profiles Bethany House." *Solander: The Magazine of the Historical Novel Society* 9, no.1 (May, 2005): 26-28. Profiles Bethany House's and Oke's impact on Christian historical fiction, starting with *Love Comes Softly*.

Logan, Laurel Oke. *Janette Oke: A Heart for the Prairie*. Minneapolis, Minn.: Bethany House, 1993. Biography of "best loved" novelist whose simple stories opened the door to Christian fiction.

"*Love Comes Softly*, Janette Oke's Message of Hope and Expectation." *Christian Literature Today* 1, no. 5 (March, 2002). Analyzes the themes of love and hope that characterize Oke's *Love Comes Softly* and her other successful novels.

Kimberly T. Peterson

MAGNIFICENT OBSESSION

Author: Lloyd C. Douglas (1877-1951)
First published: 1929
Edition used: Magnificent Obsession. New York: Houghton Mifflin, 1999
Genre: Novel
Subgenre: Evangelical fiction
Core issues: Awakening; charity; conversion; faith; responsibility; service

When the life of irresponsible playboy Bobby Merrick is saved at the expense of that of revered brain surgeon Wayne Hudson, Merrick determines to devote his own life to replacing Hudson's. He discovers among Hudson's papers the secret to achieving personal power through anonymous works of charity. After becoming a famous surgeon, Merrick marries Hudson's young widow and changes the lives of many by using the New Testament as an "actual textbook of a science relating to the expansion and development of the human personality."

> *Principal characters*
> *Robert Merrick*, protagonist, a young wastrel who becomes a
> famous surgeon
> *Dr. Wayne Hudson*, a legendary Detroit surgeon
> *Helen Hudson*, Hudson's beautiful young widow who reluctantly
> falls in love with Merrick
> *Joyce Hudson*, Dr. Hudson's dissolute daughter
> *Nancy Ashford*, hospital administrator devoted to Dr. Hudson

Overview

The protagonist of *Magnificent Obsession*, brilliant brain surgeon Dr. Wayne Hudson, has his own hospital in Detroit, a worrisome playgirl daughter, and a beautiful young bride. While on holiday, he drowns after a water accident because a respirator he kept handy was being used to resuscitate a drunken young man who was friends with his daughter, Joyce. The young man, Bobby Merrick, awakes in Hudson's hospital and is mystified by the coldness with which he is treated by the staff. He learns of Hudson's death through Nancy Ashford, the hospital superintendent who has devoted her life to Hudson. Nancy suggests that Bobby can assuage his guilt by using his wasted potential to take Hudson's place. While Bobby considers this proposition, he learns that Dr. Hudson has secretly given money, advice, and help to countless people, declining to be repaid by saying, "I've used it all up." Bobby decides to embark on the quest to replace Hudson and becomes friends with Nancy, who shares with him all Hudson's papers, including a secret journal written in code. Bobby accidentally meets Helen, Hudson's young widow, who becomes attracted to him without knowing who he is.

By decoding Hudson's journal and interviewing Hudson's devotees, Bobby learns that the surgeon achieved professional success through a series of clandestine good works, swearing his beneficiaries to secrecy. Bobby, who scorns churches and religion, is at first disillusioned to learn that Hudson's method was extracted from the teachings of Jesus. He is intrigued, however, with Hudson's assertion that one can do, be, or have anything one wants by following this secret formula, which Hudson claimed revolutionized his life. The key to power, according to Hudson's journal, is to project oneself into other personalities by helping them in secret, and then going to God, the Major Personality, in secret and requesting what one wants. First one must mend the wrongs in which one has been implicated, and then the process can begin. The success of this formula is attested to by one of Hudson's beneficiaries, a well-known sculptor, who tells Bobby his own success was gained by following the formula.

Bobby decides to put Hudson's method to the test and begins by rescuing Hudson's daughter, Joyce, from a drunken brawl. Although his actions are misconstrued by the lovely Helen, he declines to correct her blame or accept credit for the rescue. In another trial of the formula, Bobby gives a substantial loan to a needy medical student; afterward, he begins to excel in his studies and experiences a sense of opening doors. Meanwhile, Nancy, who is also experimenting with Hudson's formula, reports that although she cannot give particulars, amazing things are happening in her life as well.

After finishing medical school with top honors along with the student he aided, Bobby becomes a brilliant young resident with his own lab. He secretly supports Helen, whose finances have been depleted by an unscrupulous cousin. Bobby repays the debts and also rehabilitates the cousin, teaching him how to "project yourself through investments in other people" to earn additional personal power. Bobby goes on to tell his grandfather about the theory of the Major Personality, claiming that religion is sentimental, but this principle is scientific. Through performing these secret good works, Bobby obtains a vision of how to invent a new electric cauterizing scalpel, which quickly revolutionizes brain surgery. He becomes famous in his field. He makes friends with a minister, who joins him in his quest for a new religious vocabulary that uses modern terms and ideas. Says Bobby, "God's not a hypothesis; He's a source for power, energy, and dynamics . . . it's not ethics; it's science."

Meanwhile Helen, after discovering that Bobby has intervened in her financial affairs to become her secret benefactor, is humiliated and angry, and refuses to listen to his explanations or protests of love. She goes to Europe to become a tour guide. While there, she is in an automobile accident and requires brain surgery. Bobby, in Europe to address a medical conference, performs the surgery and saves her life. When she learns this, she attempts to flee, but Bobby intercepts her, whereupon she conquers her pride and admits her love for him, and the two are married.

Christian Themes

Douglas, a former minister, wrote *Magnificent Obsession* to update Christian principles for a generation that considers itself too objective, too scientific, and too modern to accept Christianity couched in traditional religious rites and observances. By selecting the medical profession for his setting, he brings the religious debate into an arena known for its practicality and usefulness to humanity, as well as into one in which scientific principles are recognized over superstitions or sentimental concerns. His protagonists are shown to be modern scientists, skeptical and grounded in common sense. Only after being shown evidence of the pragmatic results of applying Christian principles are the protagonists convinced that the teachings of Jesus have value. Moreover, these teachings are demonstrated to deliver substantial, tangible benefits to those who practice them to provide motivation for those who wonder what is in it for themselves.

The New Testament source for Hudson's "secret formula" is described in the novel but never actually quoted, obliging readers to find it themselves. The buildup of suspense is designed to bring readers to the Bible, where they must read and search for the "secret formula," thereby becoming more acquainted with the teachings of Christ as they discover the key to personal power. The secrecy emphasized in the novel adds excitement and a feeling of adventure for readers who might otherwise pass over admonitions to do alms in secret so that they may be rewarded openly.

The stories of Bobby Merrick and the others who change from ne'er-do-wells, drunks, and despairing failures to become admired, prosperous, and happy successes serve as anecdotal evidence to convince readers that following Christian principles of service, forgiveness, honesty, and charity will lead to real, earthly benefits not only for the recipients of good deeds but also for the doers.

A final theme of this novel is the change in religious vocabulary represented by Douglas's attempt to couch Christian doctrine in new, scientific terms that will attract modern readers. Those who reject the ideas of repentance and atonement for sin may want to "restore dissipated personality" or "recover energy" instead. Those eschewing traditional topics such as salvation, redemption, heaven, and hell may be interested instead in "personality projection," "having anything you want," "turning the key to personal power," and "the principles imperative to an expanded personality." This novel's popularity testifies to its readers' interest in updating Christian terminology and to its author's success in presenting Christian charity and service as not only relevant to the modern world but also essential in achieving a happy life within it.

Sources for Further Study

Bode, Carl. "Lloyd Douglas and America's Largest Parish." *Religion in Life* 19, no. 3 (Summer, 1950): 440-447. Discussion of the author and his works.

Bourget, Jean-Loup. "God Is Dead, or Through a Glass Darkly." *Bright Lights Film Journal* 48 (May, 2005). A film critic discusses film adaptations of the novel by John M. Stahl and by Douglas Sirk.

Carroll, Noel. "The Moral Ecology of Melodrama: The Family Plot and *Magnificent Obsession*." *New York Literary Forum* 7 (1980): 197-206. Relates the novel to literary concerns.

Goddard, O. E. Review of *Magnificent Obsession*. *Methodist Quarterly Review* 79, no. 2 (April, 1930): 317-318. A contemporary review from the novel's first publication.

Sally B. Palmer

A MAN FOR ALL SEASONS

Author: Robert Bolt (1924-1995)
First produced: pr. 1954 (radio play), pr. 1957 (televised), pr. 1960 (staged), pb. 1960
Edition used: The New Theatre of Europe: Five Contemporary Plays from the European Stage, edited with an introduction by Robert W. Corrigan. New York: Dell, 1962
Genre: Drama
Subgenre: Historical drama (sixteenth century)
Core issues: Conscience; responsibility; self-knowledge; silence

Using techniques drawn from his years of writing for radio, Bolt in this highly successful stage play depicts the conflict between King Henry VIII and his lord chancellor, Thomas More, in a drama that uses history to draw attention to one man's determination to remain true to himself.

> *Principal characters*
> *The Common Man*, the play's narrator and "central character"
> *Sir Thomas More*, the protagonist, lord chancellor of England
> *Cardinal Wolsey*, sitting lord chancellor
> *Lady Alice More*, More's wife
> *Margaret More*, the Mores' daughter
> *Duke of Norfolk*, More's closest friend
> *William Roper*, the Mores' son-in-law
> *Henry VIII*, king of England
> *Thomas Cromwell*, More's replacement as lord chancellor
> *Richard Rich*, More's betrayer
> *Thomas Cranmer*, the Church's representative

Overview

In 1533, King Henry VIII of England decided to divorce Queen Catherine in order to marry his mistress, Anne Boleyn. His reasons were simple: First, after years of trying, Queen Catherine had not provided him with a male heir; second, Mistress Boleyn was pregnant with his child; and third, Catherine had been his brother Arthur's wife and queen before died. To divest himself of Catherine, Henry was required by the Catholic Church to secure permission from the pope, the same individual who had granted him special permission to marry his brother's widow in the first place (such a marriage would otherwise have been viewed by the Church as incestuous). When it became clear that the pope would not grant his dispensation, Henry determined that he did not need the pope's approval, declared the pope to be nothing more than the bishop of Rome, and separated himself and his state from the Catholic Church, creating instead the Anglican Church, or the Church of England, with the king as its titular head. The clergy in England capitulated to Henry's wishes, the divorce occurred, and the marriage to Anne Boleyn followed.

This historical background forms the context for the action in Robert Bolt's play *A Man for All Seasons*. In order for Henry VIII to take his action, he felt compelled to secure the support of the Catholic leadership in England. This he managed as all except one swore an oath of obedience to the king. That one was Thomas More, lord chancellor of England and one of the most highly revered philosophers and lawyers of his day.

The play begins with the sociopolitical intrigues generated by a young and virile king finding satisfaction outside the realm of his castle. Thomas More is summoned to Cardinal Wolsey, the sitting lord chancellor of England, at which point More's understanding of the tenuous nature of the situation between the king's desires and the requirements of the church are made clear: When Wolsey asks More what he plans to do about the king's need for a son, More replies, "I pray for it daily." When requested to put his private conscience aside in favor of national needs, More states:

> [W]hen statesmen forsake their own private conscience for the sake of their public duties . . . they lead their country by a short route to chaos. And we shall have my prayers to fall back on.

Thus, from the outset, lines are drawn: The battle of wills (that of Henry VIII and of Thomas More) will commence with one (Henry) rebelling against Catholic strictures and the other (More) doing what he can to support them.

That which is safe becomes the matter as the rush toward a final English break with the Holy See in Rome becomes inevitable. To remain safe, More guards his words and measures every statement in such a way as to protect himself, his family, and his beloved church, while at the same time striving to vouchsafe his very being. He finds temporary refuge in silence, for, as he interprets the law, if anyone is to construe meaning from silence, that meaning must be one of assent. It is upon this interpretation that More resides, unwilling to take the oath of obedience to the King, for as he reasons, man might well lie to himself and others but not to God. An oath is a promise made before God. When swearing an oath, a man takes his soul in his own hands and risks losing it. Therefore, More instead remains silent even when imprisoned in the Tower of London.

It takes a lie to break him. Richard Rich, in the service of Thomas Cromwell, who has replaced More as lord chancellor, bears false witness against Thomas More in court, bringing a judgment of death by beheading against him. Even at his sentencing, More expounds upon his situation:

> I am the King's true subject, and pray for him and all the realm. . . . I do none harm, I say none harm, I think none harm. And if this be not enough to keep a man alive, in good faith, I long not to live.

Perhaps one of the more interesting aspects of *A Man for All Seasons* is the play's narrator, the Common Man, who throughout the play not only speaks directly to the audience from numerous points in time but also portrays such varied characters as More's head servant, an oarsman, a jailor, a member of the jury, and ultimately the executioner. He changes character simply by changing his hat. He manages the flow of the play, removes pieces of clothing that fall from above, and reads from a history text written several hundred years after the death of Henry VIII. He knows the past, the present, and the future—and he is delighted to still be breathing at the end.

When produced on Broadway in 1962, *A Man for All Seasons* surprised its critics with a successful run and a series of road companies playing to packed audiences. Judging from its success, Bolt's play apparently touched the right tone at a most appropriate time, and even today, *A Man for All Seasons* manages a to have a powerful impact on audiences.

Christian Themes

In his preface to the play, Bolt writes:

> More was a very orthodox Catholic and for him an oath was something perfectly specific; it was an invitation to God, an invitation God would not refuse, to act as a witness, and to judge; the consequence of perjury was damnation, for More another perfectly specific concept.

When More is confronted with the prospect of taking an oath that he does not accept, the oath of obedience to the king, it becomes a matter of his being true to himself. Thus at its heart, *A Man for All Seasons* is a treatise on the length to which one will go to preserve one's soul—the very core of one's being. Bolt is apologetic for "treating Thomas More, a Christian saint, as a hero of selfhood." After all, Bolt writes, "I am not a Catholic nor even in the meaningful sense of the word a Christian."

One of the more compelling moments in the play occurs between More and his future son-in-law, Will Roper. Roper, during his devout "reformation" stage, responds to More's statement of giving even the Devil benefit of law by remarking that he would "cut down every law in England to [get to the Devil]." More responds:

> And when the last law was down, and the Devil turned 'round on you—where would you hide, Roper, the laws all being flat? This country's planted thick with laws from coast to coast—man's laws, not God's! And if you cut them down—and you're just the man to do it—d'you really think you could stand upright in the winds that would blow then? Yes, I'd give the Devil benefit of law, for my own safety's sake.

Man, according to More, is an anomaly, a creature of complexity who has the capacity to delight God with occasional splendor, the natural product of angels.

The fact remains that Thomas More devoted himself to a lost cause: The Church was destined to change, and nothing he did could defer that change. He ultimately gave his life, not for the Church or his family or his country. He gave it for himself. That makes for compelling drama.

Sources for Further Study

Brown, John Russell. *A Short Guide to Modern British Drama*. London: Heinemann, 1983. A valuable overview of the works of Robert Bolt, including *A Man for All Seasons*.

Corrigan, Robert, ed. *The New Theatre of Europe: An Anthology*. New York: Dell, 1962. A collection of five European plays including Robert Bolt's *A Man for All Seasons* along with Bolt's preface to the play and an insightful introduction by the editor.

Harben, Niloufer. *Twentieth-Century English History Plays: From Shaw to Bond*. Totowa, N.J.: Barnes and Noble Books, 1988. The volume contains a useful chapter, "Three Plays of the 1960's: Robert Bolt, *A Man for All Seasons*; Peter Shaffer, *The Royal Hunt of the Sun*; John Osborne, *Luther*."

Nightingale, Benedict. *A Reader's Guide to Fifty Modern British Plays*. London: Heinemann, 1982. A brief statement on the life and writings of Robert Bolt followed by a useful analysis of his play, *A Man for All Seasons*.

Taylor, John Russell. *The Angry Theatre: New British Drama*. New York: Hill and Wang, 1969. In his epilogue, Russell places *A Man for All Seasons* in the context of other British writings of the time.

Kenneth Robbins

THE MAN NOBODY KNOWS
A Discovery of the Real Jesus

Author: Bruce Barton (1886-1967)
First published: Indianapolis, Ind.: Bobbs-Merrill, 1925
Genre: Nonfiction
Subgenre: Biography
Core issues: Capitalism; Jesus Christ

Barton believed that the image and personality of Jesus had been softened and distorted by organized religion. In this work, he attempted to set forth a more virile and modern portrait of the man, portraying him as a business executive (in fact "the founder of modern business"), a vigorous outdoorsman, and a popular dinner guest. The portrait that emerges is strongly connected to U.S. popular culture in the 1920's.

Overview

In the introduction, "How It Came to Be Written," Bruce Barton states that his chief goal in writing *The Man Nobody Knows* was to create a more popular, virile, and modern depiction of Jesus. In line with this, in the first chapter, "The Executive," he argues that Jesus demonstrated the self-confidence and forceful demeanor of a modern business executive. Jesus was audacious and self-assured, and his utterances commanded the attention of those who heard them. As examples of Jesus' inherent leadership ability, Barton cites his interactions with Nicodemus, an older man of considerable prominence in Jerusalem; with the Roman centurion, a man used to giving orders and being in command of people; and with Matthew, the tax collector. He also draws parallels with the leadership style of President Abraham Lincoln to argue his case.

In the second chapter, "The Outdoor Man," Jesus' virility is highlighted. Jesus grew up doing manual labor in his father's carpentry shop, enjoyed time spent in the "open air," and was popular among women. He drove the moneychangers out of the temple, and his cures and healings were performed forcefully and with a high degree of certainty and self-confidence.

The third chapter, "The Sociable Man," continues the process of correcting what the author sees as the theologians' dour view of Jesus. Barton challenges the statement that "nobody has ever seen him laugh," using a modernized retelling of the events at the wedding feast at Cana to demonstrate Jesus' sociability and citing his attacks on "the narrow code of the Pharisees" to give evidence of his overall enjoyment of life. The author again makes a comparison to Abraham Lincoln.

The fourth chapter, "His Method," begins with a highly simplified view of Jesus' place in the evolution of religious thought. Barton states that the teachings of Moses brought knowledge of one God, the writings of the prophet Amos brought the idea of a just God, and the writings of Hosea brought the idea of a good God. To this Jesus added the idea of democracy, that all human beings are equal before God. From there the author moves to a discussion of Jesus' "method" of getting his ideas across, primarily through simplicity, understatement, and the use of parables. Continuing to give his discussion a contemporary emphasis, Barton states, "Surely no one will consider us lacking in reverence if we say that every one of the 'principles of modern salesmanship' on which business men so much pride themselves, are brilliantly exemplified in Jesus' talk and work."

The contemporary 1920's business emphasis is given its strongest expression in the fifth and sixth chapters, entitled respectively "His Advertisements" and "The Founder of Modern Business." Barton, a highly successful advertising executive and cofounder of the well-known Barton, Durstine & Osborn advertising agency, here views Jesus specifically through the lens of the advertising profession. In the first of these two chapters, he states, "Every advertising man ought to study the parables of Jesus" as examples of the basic principles of modern advertising, and then he proceeds to give numerous examples. He also provides modern, newspaper-type headlines, such as the following (taken from an imaginary *Capernaum News*), to demonstrate Jesus' ability to gain "front page coverage" of his activities and ideas:

PROMINENT TAX COLLECTOR JOINS NAZARETH FORCES

MATTHEW ABANDONS BUSINESS TO PROMOTE NEW CULT

* * *

GIVES LARGE LUNCHEON

In "The Founder of Modern Business," he continues this theme, using the biblical quotation (which also serves as the book's epigraph): "Wist ye not that I must be about my father's *business*?" (italics added by Barton). Key aspects of modern business, such as service, hard work, and vision, are stressed, and to reinforce his discussion, Barton gives examples from the lives of such prominent figures as George W. Perkins (of New York Life Insurance), Theodore N. Vail (founder of American Telephone and Telegraph), J. P. Morgan, Henry Ford, and Thomas Jefferson.

In the book's final chapter, "The Master," Barton offers a more conventional, popular summation of Jesus' life, while still continuing to highlight the chief themes of the book set forth in the introduction. The work, overall, places Jesus within a highly modern, popular (especially 1920's) context, and its popularity during the period (it was one of the top-selling books of both 1925 and 1926) makes it of considerable significance as a cultural artifact and reflection of prevailing religious attitudes.

Christian Themes

Barton, who grew up in Tennessee and in Oak Park, Illinois, and whose father was a Congregational minister, shows many of the characteristics of twentieth century liberal Protestantism. He unashamedly stresses the humanity of Jesus, stating at one point that "If . . . we are criticized for overemphasizing the human side of his character we shall have the satisfaction of knowing that our overemphasis tends a little to offset the very great overemphasis which has been exerted on the other side." He likewise leaves the miracles of Jesus up to the choice of the reader. In regard to Jesus' calming of the storm at sea, he says, "Call it a miracle or not—the fact remains that it is one of the finest examples of self-control in all human history." This "human" interpretation of Jesus offers a sharp contrast to the literal, fundamentalist interpretation of the Bible expressed by William Jennings Bryan during the famous Scopes Trial in Dayton, Tennessee, the same year that Barton's book was published.

Barton's most unique Christian theme, of course, is his identification of Jesus with the twentieth century business executive. This seems to fit particularly well with the culture of the 1920's and with the often quoted statement of President Calvin Coolidge, "The business of America is business." In the midst of the economic boom of the decade and the prevailing faith in modern business, Barton's theme clearly hit a responsive chord with readers. The book's enormous popularity made him, along with evangelists Billy Sunday and Aimee Semple McPherson, one of the best-known religious figures of the era.

Coming at Barton (and his writings) from a somewhat different direction also serves to place him within the context of the American progressive generation as discussed, for example, in Robert M. Crunden's *Ministers of Reform: The Progressives' Achievement in American Civilization, 1889-1920* (1982). Crunden characterizes this group—broadly speaking, Americans born between 1854 and 1894—as marked by a number of common elements. Among them: coming from a devout Protestant background (Barton's father was a Congregational minister), adhering strongly to the Republican Party and admiring Abraham Lincoln (Barton was a lifelong Republican who served two terms in the U.S. Congress from 1937 to 1941, and the example of Lincoln appears numerous times in his book), and finding oneself in early life unable to pursue a religious calling and instead turning to a modern profession (in Barton's case, advertising) and investing it with a high degree of moral purpose and idealism. Although his book came out a few years after the Progressive era in the United States ended, the attempt Barton makes to link the life and teachings of Jesus to the principles of modern advertising nevertheless offers an interesting reflection of the Progressive ethos and its connections to popular religious thought.

Sources for Further Study

Fried, Richard M. *The Man Everybody Knew: Bruce Barton and the Making of Modern America*. Chicago: Ivan R. Dee, 2005. A full, well-researched biography of Barton.

Lippy, Charles H. *Do Real Men Pray? Images of the Christian Man and Male Spirituality in White Protestant America*. Knoxville: University of Tennessee Press, 2005. The author offers a summary of Barton's life and career as an example of one of the themes ("The Efficient Businessman") that he develops in this study.

Marchand, Roland. *Advertising the American Dream: Making Way for Modernity, 1920-1940*. Berkeley: University of California Press, 1985. Offers a good summary of the development of modern advertising in which Barton played a prominent role.

Ribuffo, Leo P. "Jesus Christ as Business Statesman: Bruce Barton and the Selling of Corporate Capitalism." *American Quarterly* 33, no. 2 (Summer, 1981): 206-231. Offers a solid overview of Barton's life and career. Of particular interest is the influence of Barton's father, William E. Barton, on his writing, as well as Barton's own particular reflection of the progressive worldview.

Scott Wright

THE MAN WHO DIED

Author: D. H. Lawrence (1885-1930)
First published: 1929 in France as *The Escaped Cock*, 1931 in England as *The Man Who Died*
Edition used: *"St. Mawr" and "The Man Who Died."* New York: Vintage, 1953
Genre: Novella
Subgenre: Literary fiction
Core issues: Awakening; healing; Jesus Christ; myths; regeneration

Lawrence's novella treats Jesus' resurrection with a focus on his physical self. Unlike most Christian statements on the resurrection, this story postulates Jesus as reevaluating and rejecting his mission on earth after becoming interested in the physical world rather than the next life. Lawrence situates Jesus' resurrection within the context of other myths of death and resurrection.

> *Principal characters*
> *The man who died*, the unnamed protagonist who is actually Jesus
> *An unnamed priestess of Isis*
> *Madeleine*, a former friend of the man who died and who is presumably the Mary Magdelene of the Bible
> *A peasant and his wife*

Overview

D. H. Lawrence's novella *The Man Who Died* was originally a story titled "The Escaped Cock." Later, Lawrence added a second part, and his publishers changed the title to *The Man Who Died*. Literary critics often refer to the novella by Lawrence's preferred title, *The Escaped Cock*, which focuses more on liberation than on death.

Part 1 opens with a description of peasants and their gamecock. The lively cock has been tied up to prevent its escape. The bird, described in detail, is a metaphor for the man who died. The cock, despite his depression at being tied up, still has life bubbling inside him, and one morning he manages to break the string. He flies to the top of the wall and crows loudly.

At that moment, the man who died walks by and helps the peasant catch the cock. Noticing the man's deathly pallor and wounds, the peasant is afraid; the man explains that he has not died at all, for his executioners unwittingly placed him in his tomb too early. The man remains unnamed throughout the story, but he is clearly Jesus. By leaving his protagonist nameless, Lawrence gives the character more freedom to deviate both from usual Christian interpretations and from Jesus' specific historical context.

The man who died has awakened at the exact moment that the escaping cock crowed loudly. He found himself in a tomb wrapped in bandages. Sick, sore, disillusioned, and not really ready to be alive, he emerged from the tomb slowly and reluctantly.

The peasant invites the man to hide in his house. Lying in the courtyard and drawing sustenance from the sun, the man slowly regains life and feeling. Watching the cock interact with the three hens, the man sees more than just a cock; he sees life in its persistence and brilliance.

The man revisits the tomb several times and encounters Madeleine, a friend from his former life. He rebuffs her sisterly embrace, for he wants a new kind of life. He does not wish to continue his former mission. She cannot understand this new attitude and spreads a story that he has arisen as a "pure God."

When the man's wounds heal, he decides to become a physician. He asks the peasant for the cock (a symbol of the Greek god of healing, Asclepius) and leaves with the bird. The man is still in awe of the lively, bubbling world, and he is amazed that he ever desired to conform to his former mission. The man remembers how crowds tried to influence him and nearly caused his death. He continues on, feeling sick at the thought of the world.

In part 2, the man continues his healing process at a temple of Isis. The temple is near the Mediterranean sea, surrounded by pines, oaks, and rocks. The scene is filled with sensuous imagery, from the splendid sunlight to the splashing water to slaves copulating. Inside the temple is a statue of the goddess in her incarnation as Iris Bereaved, the sad Isis who searches for the body parts of the god Osiris, who has been murdered and scattered by his brother Seth.

The temple is tended by a twenty-seven-year-old priestess. She asks the man to look at Isis, and he praises the goddess. The priestess wonders whether he might be Osiris and asks him to stay. He agrees, worrying about giving himself over to her touch. He remembers how men have tortured him, but he also knows that touch can be healing.

The priestess asks if he is Osiris, and he says yes, if she will heal him. The identification with Osiris links the man and his story with the death and revival of the fertility gods found in many cultures.

The man and the priestess experience a sexual consummation that takes place in the temple. The encounter is not simple lust, but a sacramental healing for both. He has feared touch; the priestess has been waiting, like Isis in search. She asks several times if he is Osiris and anoints the scar on his torso. Sexually aroused, he also feels renewed. This, he feels, is his real rising: warmth, life, and tenderness. Both are happy with their union: she, to have communed with Osiris; he, to feel whole. He is healed in both body and spirit. For days and nights they meet, neither knowing the other's name, but each filling a need for the other.

When the priestess becomes pregnant, both rejoice. Because they fear betrayal to the authorities, he leaves. However, he says he will return. The man rows out to sea, feeling good about his relationship with the priestess and looking forward to the next day.

Christian Themes

Many of D. H. Lawrence's works reflect his belief that contemporary Christianity was abstract and sterile—an altruistic ideal that ignored human feeling. *The Man Who Died* was written near the end of Lawrence's life (he died at the relatively young age of forty-four), after he had experienced an illness that nearly killed him.

Lawrence's unnamed protagonist is clearly and deliberately Jesus Christ, who in Lawrence's tale rejects his mission and accepts both his sexuality and the existence of other gods. Although this may be unsettling to some readers, in fact the story does not reject Christ or Christianity. Instead, it addresses themes important to Christian thinkers—such as the Resurrection, the humanity of Jesus, and the message of Jesus—from a nontraditional perspective that provokes fresh thought about the significance of Christ and Christianity.

Lawrence believed that contemporary Christianity ignored a basic tenet of faith, that Christ's body rose. Therefore, Lawrence presents a very human Jesus after the crucifixion. Focusing on physical sensations—the bandages, the feel of the wheat beneath the man's wounded feet, and the sexual union with the priestess—Lawrence suggests that it is natural for humans to be of the world; that is how they are truly alive. In this story, Jesus rejects his messianic mission, a mission he now feels was misdirected because it had allowed him to share only part of himself, his spirit and his thought.

Rather than depict Saint Paul's emphasis on Jesus' suffering and sacrifice (a teaching stressed by Lawrence's Congregationalist upbringing), Lawrence wanted to portray Jesus' love and affirmation of life. The man who died is initially afraid of life, but as he reawakens, he reveals himself to be gentle, caring, thoughtful, and perceptive. He chooses to engage positively with the world, first by his admiration of the cock, then by becoming a physician, and later by his relationship with the priestess. The reciprocal relationship with the priestess affirms the totality of life and connects him with a major aspect of the natural world, the female. Her consequent pregnancy is a positive symbol of the life force.

Lawrence's use of biblical imagery adds resonance to the story. One of many possible examples is the image of the cock: Lawrence's literary use of the cock is given more depth not only by the term's phallic meaning in English slang but also by its reference to the biblical cock that crowed three times when Simon Peter betrayed Christ (John 18:15-27). Although Peter is not mentioned in Lawrence's story, there are multiple allusions to him: in several instances of betrayal; when the priestess asks the man three times if he is Osiris; and when the man describes the priestess as "the rock" of his new life ("Peter" derives from the Latin word for "rock").

Sources for Further Study

Cowan, James C. "Allusions and Symbols in D. H. Lawrence's *The Escaped Cock*." In *Critical Essays on D. H. Lawrence*, edited by Dennis Jackson and Fleda Brown Jackson. Boston: G. K. Hall, 1988. Compares and contrasts dialogue and imagery in the story with specific biblical passages; also discusses Osirian myth.

Hough, Graham. "Lawrence's Quarrel with Christianity: *The Man Who Died.*" In *D. H. Lawrence: A Collection of Critical Essays*, edited by Mark Spilka. Englewood Cliffs, N.J.: Prentice-Hall, 1963. Discusses Lawrence's concern that modern Christianity is estranged from the deep sources of life. The collection includes a chronology and a bibliography.

Viinikka, Anja. *"The Man Who Died*: D. H. Lawrence's Phallic Vision of the Restored Body." *Journal of the D. H. Lawrence Society* (1994-1995): 39-46. Relates the story to Lawrence's life, late essays, and poetry. Footnotes suggest further useful bibliographic sources.

Walterscheid, Kathryn A. *The Resurrection of the Body: Touch in D. H. Lawrence.* New York: Peter Lang, 1993. Analyzes Lawrence's fiction using psychoanalytical, medical, and Lawrence's own theories. Includes bibliographic essay on touch and a bibliography.

Wright, T. R. *D. H. Lawrence and the Bible.* Cambridge, England: Cambridge University Press, 2000. Chapter 12 suggests sources for the original title and for various images, including Nietzschean philosophy and Osirian myths. Also discusses variants in the manuscript.

Kathryn A. Walterscheid

THE MARRIAGE OF HEAVEN AND HELL

Author: William Blake (1757-1827)
First published: 1790
Edition used: The Marriage of Heaven and Hell, copy C, in *The William Blake Archive*, edited by Morris Eaves, Robert N. Essick, and Joseph Viscomi. Charlottesville: University Institute for Advanced Technology in the Humanities at the University of Virginia, 1997
Genre: Poetry
Subgenres: Narrative poetry; parables and fables; proverbs; satire
Core issues: Gnosticism; good vs. evil; the Word

Blake's tour-de-force satire on the orthodox religion of his day presented Christianity as the deadening force of institutional and ideological tyranny. Using an amalgam of literary forms, Blake allows the "voice of the Devil" to offer a rebel's reaction to organized religion.

Overview

William Blake was born in London to a working-class family. His father, a hosier, provided for his training in drawing and engraving, practical skills which he would use to support himself and his wife Catherine for the rest of his life. One of six children, Blake claimed to have received angelic visitations and other visionary experience even as a child. After his brother Robert's death, William said that Robert often appeared to him, providing him with practical information such as an acid-wash engraving system that William used to produce his "illuminated," or illustrated, works, including *The Marriage of Heaven and Hell*. Never financially successful as an artist or writer, he was often reduced to drudge work, such as engraving drawings for the catalog of the Wedgwood China Company. From 1800 to 1803, Blake received the patronage of minor poet William Hayley; however, the experience proved bitter and demeaning to the independent-minded Blake. During this period, the fiery-tempered Blake was also accused of treason after evicting a drunken soldier from his garden with the epithet "God d—— the King!" Blake, who was eventually acquitted of the charge, transmuted the twin ordeal of patronage and accusation into his masterpieces *Vala: Or, The Four Zoas* (wr. 1795-1804, pb. 1963; best known as *The Four Zoas*) and *Jerusalem: The Emanation of the Giant Albion* (1804-1820).

Two concepts are key to understanding *The Marriage of Heaven and Hell* and Blake's idiosyncratic form of Christianity. First, as articulated in his classic *Songs of Innocence and of Experience* (1794), is the notion of "contraries," or opposing forces, similar to the Daoist notion of yin and yang. Blake saw all life as a necessary interplay of opposites. "The Argument" of *The Marriage of Heaven and Hell* applies this notion of the contraries to orthodox Christian dogma:

> As Without Contraries is no progression. Attraction and Repulsion, Reason and Energy,
> Love and Hate, are necessary to Human existence.

From these contraries spring what the religious call Good and Evil. Good is the passive that obeys Reason. Evil is the active springing from Energy: "Good is Heaven. Evil is Hell."

For Blake any system, religious or philosophical, which tries to give preference to one half of such a dichotomy does not admit the complexity and unity of human experience and is destined to failure. Such failure leads to oppression and tyranny by the "elect" half of the dichotomy, which turns its opposite, to use Calvinist jargon, into the "reprobate."

The second key concept springs from the first. In the personal mythology presented in his prophetic works, Blake satirizes the notion of the Old Testament Jehovah, as refracted through Enlightenment thought, as "Urizen" (often seen as homophone for "Your Reason"). Blake rejects the notion of God as a ruthless, rule-making punisher who is guided by an impersonal, stony rationalism. Blake excoriated the Christianity of his day, both Protestant and Catholic, as a form of primitive idol worship to this "Old Nobodaddy" with his rules and regulations, rewards and punishments. He considered the Church of England an arm of state tyranny, offering an ideological framework for un-Christian practices ranging from child labor to slavery. Even more than the physical abuses of which the Church washed its hand, Blake deemed the mental enslavement of its believers as its ultimate corrupting influence.

For Blake, imagination, and not rationality or intellect, is the central faculty of mind that unites the human with the creativity of the divine. Blake identified this creative imagination with the notion of the Logos, or Word made Flesh, in the divine humanity of Jesus Christ. Several of the "Proverbs of Hell" reinforce the primacy of imagination and energy: "What is now prov'd, was once only imagined" and "The road of excess leads to the palace of wisdom." The first indicates that the creative act begins with an imaginative concept; the second suggests that wisdom is not a matter of following the straight and narrow rationalistic guides but the impulses of creative energy.

Blake's faith in the creative imagination as the link between the divine and the human leads him to satirize what he perceived as the rational materialism underpinning Enlightenment Christianity. Five sections of *The Marriage of Heaven and Hell* are titled "A Memorable Fancy." Blake uses sarcastically the term "Fancy" (the term used by John Milton and eighteenth century poets for "imagination"). The first of these describes Blake as "walking among the fires of Hell, delighted with the enjoyments of Genius, which to Angels look like torment and insanity"; a "mighty Devil" appears and, just as Blake used corrosives in his engraving process, inscribes the following couplet on a plutonian mountainside:

> How do you know but ev'ry Bird that cuts the airy way,
> Is an immense World of Delight, clos'd by your senses five?

Unlike the biblical Jehovah who inscribes his Ten Commandments for Moses, Blake's Devil is more concerned about imagination than ethics. The "fires of hell" burn away the constricting limitations of the material world as perceived by the five senses.

Christian Themes

Blake, whose later works belie easy identification with any religious system, has been cautiously interpreted as a Gnostic Christian. However, *The Marriage of Heaven and Hell*, an early work, would seem to fit such a label. The very title indicates a quest for mystical unity capable of transcending the apparent dualism of the body and soul, physical and metaphysical worlds. Also, his identification with the devils in the work conforms to the Gnostic belief that a demiurge rather than the transcendent godhead was responsible for creating the material world.

In the work's second "Memorable Fancy," Blake "dines" with Ezekial and Isaiah, who sound more like Gnostic seekers than Old Testament prophets. When Blake asks them to explain how God spoke to them, the latter responds: "I saw no God, nor heard any, in a finite organical perception; but my senses discover'd the infinite in everything, and as I was then persuaded, and remain confirm'd, that the voice of honest indignation is the voice of God, I cared not for consequences, but wrote."

The section ends with a famous epigram later borrowed by Aldous Huxley for the title of his influential book on hallucinatory mescaline and then adopted by the 1960's rock group The Doors:

If the doors of perception were cleansed everything would appear to man as it is, infinite.
For man has closed himself up till he sees all things thro' narrow chinks of his cavern.

While Blake seems to undertake the Gnostic's quest for hidden knowledge, he does not assume the Gnostic denial of the reality of the body or physical world. Thus his search for the infinite comes not through denial of the senses but by an expansion of them.

The Marriage of Heaven and Hell also sketches Blake's unusual, if not heterodox, vision of Jesus Christ. Blake sees Christ as an incarnation of the eternal Logos or Word, but one that is at odds with a biblical literalism symbolized by the Ten Commandments. In the fifth "Memorable Fancy" Blake presents a dialogue between an angel and a devil regarding Jesus' adherence to Old Testament law. After a literalistic angel argues that God and Jesus are one in the law, a subtle devil responds that Jesus broke many of the Ten Commandments, including ignoring the Sabbath and protecting the woman caught in adultery. The devil concludes: "Jesus was all virtue, and acted from impulse, not from rules."

Sources for Further Study

Altizer, Thomas J. J. *The Genesis of God: A Theological Genealogy*. Louisville, Ky.: John Knox Press, 1993. "Death of God" religious thinker and Blake student Altizer incorporates Blakean ideas and language into his notion of the ultimate "contrary" of God and Nothingness.

Bentley, G. E., Jr. *The Stranger from Paradise: A Biography of William Blake*. New Haven, Conn.: Yale University Press, 2001. Bentley offers a detailed biography of Blake as artisan and visionary, providing practical information on Blake's work as painter and engraver as well as speculation on Blake's idiosyncratic Christianity.

Bindman, David, ed. *Blake's Illuminated Books*. 6 vols. Princeton, N.J.: William Blake Trust and Princeton University Press, 1991-1995. This herculean effort reproduces all of Blake's illustrated and engraved works, in color, in a single collection. Volume 3 includes *The Marriage of Heaven and Hell* among Blake's early illuminated books.

Frye, Northrop. *Fearful Symmetry*. Edited by Nicholas Halmi. Princeton, N.J.: Princeton University Press, 1947. Reprint. Buffalo: University of Toronto Press, 2004. Still the starting point for modern criticism of Blake, Frye's work analyzes Blake's use of contraries as the guiding principle for his personal mythology based upon Christianity.

Viscomi, Joseph. *Blake and the Idea of the Book*. Princeton, N.J.: Princeton University Press, 1993. Viscomi, an expert of Blake's innovative printing method, explores Blake's approach to the book as both physical object and metaphysical idea.

Luke A. Powers

MARY MAGDALENE

Author: Ellen Gunderson Traylor (1946-   )
First published: 1985
Edition used: Mary Magdalene. Polson, Mont.: Port Hole Publications, 2001
Genre: Novel
Subgenre: Historical fiction (first century)
Core issues: Healing; love; suffering; women

This historical novel imagines the life of Mary Magdalene from her childhood when she is sold into sexual slavery by her alcoholic father through her early years as a follower of Jesus. Jesus casts out the demons that have driven Mary to a state of madness, and the repentant prostitute embraces his ministry, his teachings, and his love. Although the novel has a historical setting, it confronts social issues pertinent to the modern age: the role of women in the Christian faith, the trafficking of children in the global sex trade, and the destruction addictions wreak on the family.

> *Principal characters*
> *Mary (Magdalene) Bar Michael*, the protagonist, a follower of
>   Jesus, known as Rahab during her years as a prostitute
> *Michael Bar Andreas*, Mary's widowed alcoholic father, who
>   sells his daughter into prostitution
> *Tobias*, Mary's younger brother
> *Tamara*, Mary's younger sister, Tobias's twin
> *Suzanna*, Mary's disabled childhood friend and liberator
> *Ezra*, a brothel owner
> *Judah Bar David*, Mary's lover
> *Jesus of Nazareth*, the savior who heals Mary

Overview

Ellen Gunderson Traylor's *Mary Magdalene* is a fictional account of the life of Mary Magdalene, Jesus of Nazareth's most significant female follower. The novel chronicles Mary's life from childhood through early adulthood. At the age of nine, Mary Bar Michael has many responsibilities, but she bears them with grace and resolve. She is a model Jewish girl, and the promise she made to her dying mother lingers: to keep the family together as long as she can. Young twins, a boy and a girl, are placed in Mary's care. Her widowed father, Michael Bar Andreas, once a fisherman of repute, allows alcoholism, fueled by despair over his wife's death, to engulf his life.

With her father no longer willing or able to provide for his children, Mary becomes her family's chief caretaker. The children scavenge outside the village of Magdala, searching for scraps along the shoreline of Galilee. When sympathetic fishermen leave a portion of their catch for the children, the bounty enrages Michael. He refuses to allow his children to feast on charity. Obedient offspring, they deposit the fish on the ash heap and deny their hunger. The memory of her mother's instruction in the domestic arts keeps Mary's attitude positive in the face of parental neglect. A pact of lifelong friendship made with Suzanna, a disabled friend, is another blessing. Mary contemplates working as a maid in neighboring homes to support her siblings, but her plans derail.

Without Mary's knowledge, Michael sells his daughter to the owner of a local brothel to secure funds for his addiction. In her own home, a terrified Mary endures a gang rape instigated by Ezra, manager of the brothel, and sanctioned by her father. It is a cruel initiation into the life that awaits her. For the next decade she will serve the pleasures of paying customers. However, before this transformation can occur, her identity as Mary must be expunged. Through a systematic brainwashing, Mary's memories of her family and her Jewish faith are erased until only Rahab remains, a child prostitute who cannot recall her prior existence.

Initially, life in the brothel is less harsh for Rahab than for the other women. Because Ezra can demand a high price based on her beauty and youth, Rahab's clientele are select and often from reputable society. Unlike other enslaved women, she does not have to ply her trade on the streets and suffer the dangers of the night. Rahab falls in love with a particularly handsome and loving client, Judah Bar David, who, as indicated by his name, is a descendent of the Old Testament house of David. Judah reciprocates her love. His family, shaken by the inappropriate attachment, sends a servant to Rahab to demand she end their affair. Ultimately Judah abandons Rahab; heartbroken, she despairs her lonely state. On the street fronting the brothel, another descendent of the house of David, Jesus of Nazareth, preaches. Rahab hears his voice, and his words intrigue her, but she is not free to leave and follow his teachings.

Rahab's incarceration as a prostitute living under an assumed name eventually leads to insanity. She hallucinates and breaks with reality at the same time that memories from her former life intrude. Quite possibly she has contracted a venereal disease, syphilis, the symptoms of which include mental derangement. Thrown into a dungeon beneath the brothel, unkempt and uncared for, she is left to writhe alone with her illness and her demons. Rowdy young boys, led by Ezra's illegitimate son, tease her through the bars of her prison. She exposes her diseased flesh to their view and screams like the madwoman she has become.

For years, Suzanna has been searching for her missing childhood friend. Rumors lead her to the brothel. When she locates the altered Mary in the dungeon, she initiates her escape from sexual slavery and reunites her with her younger sister and brother. A convert to the messiah's teachings and a recipient of his healing, Suzanna introduces Mary to Jesus. He casts demons from Mary's mind and body and purifies her spirit. Drawn to Jesus, she seeks to repay his kindness. At a dinner hosted by Suzanna's skeptical father, Jesus is invited to speak. In a scene that reenacts gospel accounts, Mary washes Jesus' feet with the expensive oils of her former trade and dries his feet with strands of her hair. While her actions scandalize the attendant Pharisees, Jesus declares himself pleased, reminding the crowd that her sins have been forgiven.

Mary leaves behind her old life and follows Jesus and his disciples. She is among a small band of women whose presence displeases the apostles. Jesus rebukes the forbidding men and welcomes the women into his discipleship. In an age when women were often excluded from religious practice, Jesus' act announces a central role for their gender in the new religion he will inspire. Loyal Mary is at the foot of his cross to witness Jesus' suffering and death, and it is to Mary that Jesus appears after leaving his tomb. She is the first to hear his good news of resurrection.

The novel concludes with Mary seeking Michael Bar Andreas, now aged and infirm and alone. She welcomes him back into the family fold. Her forgiveness of her father's sins extends the forgiveness she received from Jesus, and her commitment to a life of good acts in his name is evident.

Christian Themes

The primary theme of Traylor's novel is healing, whether the pain that needs remedy derives from physical or spiritual suffering. Mary's family is torn apart by her mother's death and her father's alcoholism. Her innocence is shattered by her induction into prostitution at a young age and by the knowledge of her father's complicity in her bondage. The pain inflicted on Mary's body is rife, but her spiritual suffering is more poignant. The sanctified and comforting rituals of Jewish faith were replaced by vulgar and defiling acts of physical and mental abuse in the brothel, particularly her harrowing sexual initiation. When Jesus drives the demons from Mary's mind and body, he heals both her flesh and her spirit. If Rahab is cast out of Mary's body, so too is the old Mary. Mary is cleansed of her afflictions and receives both revived health and a new identity. She is introduced through Jesus' teachings to a new kind of love, one that is the foundation of the Christian ethos: "Love one another as I have loved you."

A second theme critical to the novel is forgiveness. When Jesus casts out Mary's demons, he simultaneously forgives her sins. Mary, who has been more sinned against than sinning, must consider her own future course of action. Bitterness at the memory of what others have done to her is replaced by compassion for her former tormentors.

When a prostitute from the brothel visits Mary at Suzanna's home, Mary greets her and treats her with respect. When Mary locates her outcast father, she remains with him even after he tells her his children are dead to him. Their reunion is based on her ability to forgive his past behaviors and to love him unconditionally, behaviors she has learned from Jesus.

Sources for Further Study

Duncan, Melanie C. Review of *Mary Magdalene*. *Library Journal* 126, no. 14 (September, 2001): 158-159. Recommends the novel's intense depiction of the life of Mary Magdalene.

"Ellen Gunderson Traylor." *Contemporary Authors Online*. Farmington Hills, Mich.: Thomson Gale, 2006. A brief biography of Traylor that lists her works.

Haskins, Susan. *Mary Magdalene: Myth and Metaphor.* New York: Harper Collins, 1993. Account of the life of Mary Magdalene that offers facts about what scholars know of the historical Mary and insight into the myths that surround her legacy.

Dorothy Dodge Robbins

THE MASTER AND MARGARITA

Author: Mikhail Bulgakov (1891-1940)
First published: Master i Margarita, expurgated 1966-1967, unexpurgated 1973 (English translation, expurgated 1967, unexpurgated 1995)
Edition used: The Master and Margarita, translated by Michael Glenny. New York: New American Library, 1967
Genre: Novel
Subgenres: Biblical fiction; fantasy; mysticism; satire
Core issues: Atheism; faith; God; good vs. evil; Jesus Christ; love; truth

A strange-looking man appears in a Moscow park and amazes two writers with the prediction that one of them will die the same day. He is Woland, the devil, accompanied by a retinue of performers that includes a pistol-shooting tomcat. Woland forces writers, especially the Master, to think about good and evil and life and death. The impoverished Master tries to write a novel. He is supported only by the love of Margarita, who saves his novel from being burned. In a parallel story, Pontius Pilate converses with an itinerant Yeshua Ha-Notsri (Jesus Christ) about the meaning of truth, then he allows the Jerusalem elders to condemn Yeshua to crucifixion.

> *Principal characters*
> *The Master*, an aspiring writer
> *Woland*, the devil, who is visiting Moscow
> *Yeshua Ha-Notsri*, an itinerant, representing Jesus Christ
> *Pontius Pilate*, the procurator of Judea
> *Margarita*, who saves the Master and the novel from being
> burned

Overview

The Master and Margarita is a multilevel novel. It has been called a tale of two cities, Moscow and Jerusalem, and a novel-puzzle. It starts in Moscow and ends in Moscow; between, there is a fantastic tale containing several important happenings. When Woland (the devil) suddenly arrives in Moscow, he chastises the Muscovites for their immoral behavior; dazzles them with predictions of death and tricks performed by his retinue, especially by a pistol-packing tomcat; and organizes theater performances at which he brings to light the citizens' insincerity, avarice, selfishness, and other weaknesses. Mikhail Bulgakov is criticizing and satirizing how the Soviet system totally controls every aspect of life.

In the second chapter, the tale of the other city, Jerusalem, begins, introducing different problems with similar basic meanings. When Pontius Pilate faces an itinerant, Yeshua Ha-Notsri, who represents Jesus Christ, the confrontation brings out important moral and philosophical issues such as the nature of truth, matters of guilt and innocence, and the dichotomy of good and evil, the spiritual and the material, as well as the real and the imagined. The novel then tries to answer and solve these questions.

The main reason, however, for Bulgakov's connecting these apparent opposites is the oppressive life the citizens were forced to live in the Soviet Union in the first half of the twentieth century. The protagonist of the novel, known only as the Master, a budding young writer who is working on a novel about his difficult life, is led to despair and to thoughts of burning his manuscript and committing suicide. He and his novel are saved by the young woman Margarita, whose love for him overpowers his problems. Another victim of circumstance is Bulgakov himself, who for years had been forced by the regime to live under heavy restrictions because of his nonconformist writings. Therefore, the travails of the Master reflect those of Bulgakov, and Margarita recalls his own wife, who saved him from ruin.

Another similarity can be seen in the cowardice of many characters. Pontius Pilate cannot find enough courage to free Yeshua from the Jerusalem powers-that-be. The Master cannot finish his novel because he fears what censors would do. Bulgakov himself did not find enough strength to write the way his artistic creed demanded. He was joined by many writers in the Soviet Union who showed the same weakness, preferring to burn their manuscripts. When Margarita snatches the Master's manuscript from the fire, it proves Woland's assertion that "the manuscripts don't burn," in a clear reference to the Soviet situation. Thus, cowardice becomes the greatest sin in this novel. It is ironic that the manuscript of *The Master and Margarita*, which for all purposes was lost and "burned," was rescued and published fifty years later.

Love in *The Master and Margarita* is the only force that can overcome the dismal state of mind in which these characters find themselves. This is the message brought to them by none other than Woland. Margarita understands this best; moreover, she finds enough strength to support her lover even at the grave danger to herself. She also understands that one who loves must share the fate of the loved one.

The novel presents many explanations and solutions for the problems it sets forth. More obvious solutions include creativity in a totalitarian society, art as the revelation of the mysteries of life, and the personal courage of every citizen. Related issues are sanity and madness, reality and fantasy, and above all the question, What is truth? There are also issues that Bulgakov failed to clarify, perhaps because he died before giving the novel its final touch. The slogan What is truth? was especially important to Bulgakov because he had to live and create under the belief enforced by the regime that there is only one truth—that of the regime. Perhaps as compensation, Bulgakov was critical of many well-established beliefs such as those of Christianity.

Despite some shortcomings, *The Master and Margarita* contains many qualities that, in the opinion of critics like Andrew Barrat, make it one the great novels of all time. It offers "a vision of grace which, because of its stubborn resistance to intellectual explanations, must inevitably remain a mystery beyond the grasp of mere reason. That is what makes it the most deeply religious of books." Although Christian themes are not discussed per se, genuinely religious tones are exhibited enough to treat them as such.

Christian Themes

The main Christian theme in *The Master and Margarita* is presented in the three chapters of the so-called Jerusalem story, featuring the last days of Jesus Christ, his confrontation with Pontius Pilate, and the Crucifixion. Foremost is the question, What is truth? which Pontius Pilate poses to the itinerant Yeshua Ha-Notsri, when they face each other shortly before Pilate turns Yeshua over to the authorities, thus "washing his hands." Bulgakov uses this biblical mainstay because of the Bolshevik insistence on their "truth" being the only one. Without making a direct comparison between Christ's suffering and that of the Russian people in the Soviet period, he insinuates that the suffering arises for the same reason.

It should be kept in mind that Bulgakov changes many details found in the Gospels to suit his own purposes. Some examples of the differences: Pilate's intention to save Christ; Yeshua's denial that he had arrived in Jerusalem on foot rather than on a donkey or that he had tried to incite the populace; the nature of Judas's betrayal of Christ, meaning that without it there would be no Crucifixion or Resurrection; and the account of the Crucifixion by Matthew, the only disciple left with Yeshua. The differences stem partly from Bulgakov's agreement with one of the Gnostic beliefs that good and evil are of the same value, as illustrated by the motto to the novel, "That Power I serve Which wills forever evil yet does forever good," borrowed from Goethe's *Faust: Eine Tragödie* (1808; *The Tragedy of Faust*, 1823). Bulgakov is known to have studied Gnosticism during the writing of *The Master and Margarita*. Most important, by making Yeshua (Jesus) an itinerant and by changing many details from the Gospels, Bulgakov wants to make his points, the most important of which are bringing the Gospels and, indeed, Christianity down to earth, and making comparisons with, and satirizing, the Soviet reality of his time.

Sources for Further Study

Barrat, Andrew. *Between Two Worlds: A Critical Introduction to "The Master and Margarita."* Oxford, England: Oxford University Press, 1987. Astute examination of various interpretations dealing mainly with the Gnostic message and the appearance of the mysterious messenger Woland. Extensive select bibliography and index.

Curtis, J. A. E. *Bulgakov's Last Decade: The Writer as Hero.* Cambridge, England: Cambridge University Press, 1987. Study of Bulgakov's literary profile. Contains a discussion of *The Master and Margarita.* Good bibliography of primary and secondary sources. Useful index.

Erickson, Edward E. Lewiston. *Apocalyptic Vision of Mikhail Bulgakov's "The Master and Margarita."* New York: E. Mellen Press, 1991. Challenging interpretation of the apocalyptic aspect of the novel as its basic underpinning.

Milne, Lesley, ed. *Bulgakov: The Novelist-Playwright.* Luxembourg: Harwood Academic, 1995. Collection of background articles, including one on *The Master and Margarita.* Illustrated, bibliography and index.

Proffer, Ellendea. *Bulgakov: Life and Work.* Ann Arbor, Mich.: Ardis, 1984. Thorough biography covering all important aspects of Bulgakov's life and works. *The Master and Margarita* is discussed at length.

Weeks, Laura D., ed. *Master and Margarita: A Critical Companion.* Evanston, Ill.: Northwestern University Press, 1996. Collection of articles by various authors, covering recent criticism, problems of genre and motif, apocalyptic and mythic aspects, letters and diaries, and others.

Vasa D. Mihailovich

MATER ET MAGISTRA

Author: John XXIII (Angelo Giuseppe Roncalli; 1881-1963)
First published: 1961 (English translation, 1961)
Edition used: Mater et Magistra, Encyclical Letter of His Holiness Pope John XXIII; Christianity and Social Progress, edited by William Joseph Gibbons. Mahwah, N.J.: Paulist Press, 1961
Genre: Nonfiction
Subgenre: Encyclical
Core issues: Capitalism; charity; freedom and free will; justice; poverty; social action

On the seventieth anniversary of Rerum Novarum, *John XXIII addressed the socioeconomic issues of the early 1960's. The encyclical identifies the Catholic Church as "Mother and Teacher" of all nations, concerned for people's physical and spiritual well-being, and calls for societies to live in Christian brotherhood, honoring God's law and human dignity. It condemns communism, consumerism, and all systems that detach God from public life. It upholds the right to private property and the centrality of the family.*

Overview

In his encyclical *Mater et Magistra,* John XXIII declares that the Catholic Church is "Mother and Teacher of all Nations," responsible for the care and guidance of God's people. Just as Christ was concerned for both the spiritual and physical needs of people, so too is the Church.

John identifies Leo XIII's *Rerum Novarum* (1891; English translation, 1891) as the first major compendium of Catholic social teachings, noting how it opened new avenues for the Church's social mission. He summarizes the encyclical, its circumstances, and impact. Four key points are the dignity of work, just wages, the right to private property, and the importance of the family. John then discusses *Quadragesimo Anno* (1931; English translation, 1931), which Pope Pius XI issued to clarify some points of *Rerum Novarum* and address the circumstances of his day. Pius XII provided an update in a radio address on May 15, 1941.

Twenty years later, John XXIII finds that conditions have improved the dignity and security of the working classes. Nations have adopted many forms of economic regulation and redistribution, but these improvements are not evenly spread across all segments of the economy. Despite this progress, millions of people around the world live in abject poverty, while a few live in extreme luxury. A nation's greatness should not be measured by the size of its military or gross national product but on the redistribution of its prosperity. Both communist and capitalist economies are based on a self-destructive competition. In contrast, John calls for all societies to adopt a spirit of Christian brotherhood and cooperation.

John XXIII emphasizes subsidiarity, a belief that higher-level organizations should do only what cannot be accomplished at lower levels of society. Even though technology allows governments to have wider spheres of influence, the state must keep a balance between human rights and human liberty. One counterbalance to government power is the ability of individuals to form private associations to promote various causes.

John notes that there is nothing wrong with state ownership of productive goods, so long as it is guided by the concept of subsidiarity. Government officials should be appointed for their virtue and held to strict checks and balances. However, individuals and private groups are always better than governments at promoting spiritual goods.

The purpose of work is the fulfillment of the human person, John says. Work itself is more important than the profits earned, and there is no purpose in work that degrades the human person. Workers must not be treated like machines; management should listen to their input. They must be taught culture, religion, and morality. Companies can help build justice by paying fairer wages and giving their employees more authority, employing as many people as possible, and reducing class distinctions among their workers. Even the dividends paid to shareholders can work to balance out the economy.

The agricultural segment does not advance in pace with industry and service. John calls on agricultural workers to keep up to date with technology and efficiency. To do this, they need proper educational and economic support from society. He calls on governments to improve public works in rural areas. He asks for proportional taxes, special credit programs, insurance programs, and price protection to help farmers. Agriculture is family centered, provides for humanity's most basic needs, and involves direct participation with God's creation. It incorporates many scientific disciplines. Farming cooperatives and support organizations help farmers keep up with the latest knowledge and technology.

John asserts that population density and distribution of natural resources would not be problems if societies were willing to share their abundance with others. However, it is far more important to help impoverished nations develop and sustain their own economies. More developed nations must not use this aid or education as a tool for colonialism. Local cultures must be safeguarded. Economic and scientific progress must never come at the cost of human dignity or spiritual growth.

The pope argues that the various political ideologies in the world fail to achieve a proper social order because they fail to include God's role in society. When there is no transcendent morality, "justice" comes to mean whatever the speaker wants. Yet, many people in advanced societies are beginning to see the emptiness of a secular lifestyle. Related to this is modern disregard for the Sabbath, as human dignity demands a day for rest and prayer.

John observes that God has provided humanity with seemingly limitless resources and the mental capacity to use them. The real problem of poverty has to do the failure of people to live in solidarity. People's dominion over nature does not entitle them to abuse natural resources indiscriminately.

John establishes a hierarchy for Catholic social principles: the sanctity of life and dignity of the person, then mutual cooperation and brotherhood, and the importance of the family. He then lists three steps for addressing social problems: analysis of the situation, judgment according to moral principles, and practical application. Catholics of goodwill may disagree about the practical application, but they must do so respectfully. Arguments about what is theoretically best should never get in the way of what is possible.

John closes with the assertion that putting God's law first will not prevent, but enhance, human progress. It is impossible for those driven by the love of Christ to fail in charity to others.

Christian Themes

Because Catholic bishops are his main audience, John takes many Catholic principles for granted. For example, he declares that the Church is the "Mother and Teacher" of the entire world, and that he, as pope, is spiritual father to all people, not just Catholics. These ideas would be developed in later documents of Vatican II, including *Lumen Gentium* (1964; English translation, 1964) and *Gaudium et Spes* (1965; English translation, 1965).

The main themes are the principles of Catholic social teachings: human dignity, subsidiarity, and solidarity. Catholic social teachings are based on the idea that the human individual is made in the "image and likeness of God." A good government secures human dignity by balancing individual liberty (subsidiarity) with the common good (solidarity). Under the concept of subsidiarity, the government is to do only what lower level groups cannot. Therefore, the most important and active social group is the family, and giving too much power to the government endangers individual liberty. However, too much emphasis on property and liberty means that some individuals or groups deprive others of basic rights. John sees the main problem of modern societies as the competitive spirit as manifested in class warfare, corporate competition, and national rivalries. He calls people to trust one another and work together for the "common good." This is the principle of "solidarity," or "Christian brotherhood."

The Gospel is clear that people should use their gifts, whether spiritual, material, physical or intellectual, for the good of others. John emphasizes the importance of charity, as opposed to modern hedonism. He touches briefly on the question of environmental stewardship, noting that, while natural resources are virtually unlimited, it is wrong to abuse or simply destroy those resources.

The Church favors smaller social groups, such as families, small businesses, and farms. Therefore, John approves of modern grassroots organizations. Likewise, he calls for workers and managers to be given ownership stakes in their companies, something realized by contemporary profit-sharing and stock options. John also discusses Catholic morality in regard to marriage and family. He shows how Catholic teachings on divorce, artificial birth control, and parental rights are necessarily elements in both principles, subsidiarity and solidarity.

John talks about the importance of God in public life. He contends that morality is impossible without God, so that a religious component in education is necessary to protect human dignity. As his title would indicate, the teaching role of the Church in general and Christian laity in particular is emphasized throughout the document.

Sources for Further Study

Cronin, John Francis. *Christianity and Social Progress: A Commentary on "Mater et Magistra."* Baltimore: Helicon, 1965. A collection of articles that first appeared in *Our Sunday Visitor* and examined the pope's encyclical.

Masse, Benjamin L., ed. *The Church and Social Progress: Background Readings for Pope John's "Mater et Magistra."* Milwaukee, Wis.: Bruce, 1966. A collection of articles on the Church's social teachings.

Moody, Joseph N., and George Lawler, eds. *The Challenge of "Mater et Magistra."* New York: Herder and Herder, 1963. An anthology of articles by Catholic social thinkers responding to the encyclical's call for social reforms.

Pontifical Council for Justice and Peace. *Compendium of the Social Doctrine of the Church.* Washington, D.C.: United States Conference of Catholic Bishops, 2005. A recent document summarizing Catholic social teachings, drawing from a variety of official documents, including *Mater et Magistra.*

John C. Hathaway

THE MEANING OF PERSONS

Author: Paul Tournier (1898-1986)
First published: Le Personnage et la personne, 1955 (English translation, 1957)
Edition used: The Meaning of Persons, translated by Edwin Hudson. Cutchogue, N.Y.: Buccaneer Books, 1999
Genre: Nonfiction
Subgenres: Didactic treatise; handbook for living; spiritual treatise
Core issues: Confession; freedom and free will; grace; healing; psychology; responsibility

According to Tournier in The Meaning of Persons, *the practice of medicine needs to be conducted on the whole person. Therefore, doctors must enter into trusting dialogue with patients to ensure their healing. The principles involved in practicing medicine in this way are applicable to every area of life and are for everyone, because they involve the freeing of the person from outward forms or personages. Only in Christ is this fully possible, since he is the true person and is able to form a true personal relationship with people.*

Overview

Paul Tournier was a Swiss doctor in general practice in Geneva. He was brought up in a Calvinist church and experienced a conversion when he was about eleven years old. He was emotionally reserved, having been orphaned early in life. He was graduated in 1923 and by that time had gained confidence in his studies and in student affairs. Even so, his early medical practice was marked by great formality with patients. However, in 1932, after attending a small Christian group inspired by the Moral Re-Armament movement (MRA), he had a deep spiritual experience that gradually freed him emotionally and helped him enter a meditative dialogue with God. In this he was greatly helped by his first wife, Nelly. From 1937, his clinical practices changed dramatically as he moved more into the role of counselor.

Tournier became concerned with reconciling the scientific and spiritual practices of medicine, and this concern expressed itself in a series of books and essays, beginning with *Médecine de la personne* (1940; *The Healing of Persons*, 1965). At first, these circulated only in the French-speaking world and were met with a good deal of skepticism. With the translation of *The Meaning of Persons* in 1957 and its publication in the United Kingdom and the United States, his ideas began to gain some acceptance. Tournier's easily digested wisdom of European psychology and theology met a real need in the English-speaking world. While his psychological theories are eclectic, it is possible to see the influence of Emil Brunner, one of the Geneva group and a noted neo-Calvinist theologian, in his religious expression.

In the early 1960's, almost in fulfillment of Tournier's own theory, there was a growing desire to break out of current pietistic rigidities and to seek spiritual renewal, which included a concern for inner healing. His other books were translated, including *Bible et médecine* (1951; *A Doctor's Casebook in the Light of the Bible*, 1954); *Les Fort et les faibles* (1948; *The Strong and the Weak*, 1963); and *Vraie ou fausse culpabilité* (1958; *Guilt and Grace*, 1962). Often invited to speak and tour the United States, Tournier became a forerunner of many widely accepted counseling practices.

    The Meaning of Persons is constructed in Tournier's hallmark way. Twelve chapters of roughly equal length are divided into four parts, each having three chapters. The four parts are "The Personage," "Life," "The Person," and "Commitment." His argument is interspersed with many examples from his clinical practice, quotations from colleagues and mentors, and frequent summations of the argument so far. His Christian principles are gradually introduced at relevant moments, until the last part of the book is deeply religious. Tournier aims at a popular audience, not trying to rigorously back up his claims nor systematically using Scripture.

    Tournier's main thesis is that as humans, we all long for authenticity. We realize we put on masks and assume roles, which he calls our personages. Utopian humanists assume we can somehow dispense with these personages to reveal the true person and walk naked, as it were, outside inauthentic attitudes. By contrast, Tournier suggests that true freedom is found by practicing those things that are truly personal, such as relationships with others; creating dialogue with and making commitments to others; exercising choices that lead to freedom at whatever cost and taking responsibility for them; and respecting others' choices. He builds in various touchstones to mark our truth: our respect for others' secrets and our use of confession to restore relationships as well as trust and transparency.

    Tournier uses a number of instructive examples. One of his favorites is that of the orchestra. The composer is God, who has written the score of our lives and thus determined a purpose and direction for us. The conductor is the person interpreting the score and directing the orchestra, which is the various personages we have. If the person/conductor is in charge, then the personages will all harmonize, or be integrated, to use the psychological term. Another example is driving. For much of the time, our driving is automatic. However, at junctions, the driver, the person, has to make a choice. Thus, the person needs personages, but they should be true expressions of the person's purpose and direction in life.

    As a doctor, Tournier realizes that we cannot treat people as a set of outward personages. Illness is psychosomatic and can be effectively dealt with only by personal dialogue, physician to patient. He calls this "medicine of the person" and presents it in opposition to the growing trend toward the impersonal, objective practice of medicine in which a patient is merely a machine that has gone wrong. A doctor, thus, needs to learn to listen humbly to the patient.

Christian Themes
    Tournier also sees the Christian life in terms of person and personage. We have a spiritual encounter with God that reveals our true person and brings new life to it. However, our new person needs expression and forms of practice to maintain our new

spiritual life. Gradually these forms become our religious personage and can hedge us in, even killing our new life. Then we need a fresh experience of God through repentance and confession. Thus, he sees the spiritual life not as a steady flow, but as intermittent, with highs, plateaus, and valleys.

More significant, Tournier sees that a true dialogue, for instance, the dialogue of marriage, can be maintained only if there is a dialogue with God going on at the same time. God is only personal; he "calls us by name" (Isaiah 45:4) and seeks a relationship through dialogue with us. Such a dialogue can be conducted in various ways, but listening prayer is the most effective. Christ is the only human who has truly been a person and not a personage: It is through his authenticity that we can know God's commitment to us and our choices. It is only through him that our fallenness can be mended. Tournier's Calvinism is very strong here, in his stress on the inability of humans to ultimately heal themselves.

Tournier holds the Bible in high regard. He sees it as a book that demands authentic choices and as a record of people who have listened to God and heard him. It is a record of God's grace. Since Tournier, Christian theology has tended to emphasize the work of the Holy Spirit, and in hindsight, Tournier's lack of reference to the third person of the Trinity and his comparatively few references to supernatural healing through corporate prayer might make him seem dated and account for the difficulty in finding his books on any publisher's list. However, his insistence that life is relational and all medicine must be the same is profoundly urgent in contemporary society, as is his insistence that all life is spiritual, though there is a high price to be paid for making such choices to gain true freedom in the spirit.

Sources for Further Study

Collins, Gary R. *The Christian Psychology of Paul Tournier*. Grand Rapids, Mich.: Baker, 1973. Collins is an evangelical who was forced to study Tournier through the interests of his students. He went to Geneva and talked with him at length. He is not uncritical of Tournier's theology but tries to make a fair assessment.

Hacpille, Lucie. *Le Défi de l'âge: Se réconclier avec la vie—Hommage à Paul Tournier*. Paris: Éditions Frison-Roche, 1993. In the absence of recent English reassessments of Tournier, this French work is the best availaible.

Johnson, Paul E., ed. *Healer of the Mind: A Psychiatrist's Search for Faith*. Nashville, Tenn.: Abingdon, 1972. A collection of essays, including an autobiographical one by Tournier.

Peaston, Monroe. "Aspects of the Person: Some Themes in the Recent Writings of Paul Tournier." *Pastoral Psychology* 33, no. 1 (Fall, 1984): 35-43. Peaston updates his earlier book.

_____. *Personal Living: An Introduction to the Thought of Paul Tournier*. New York: Harper and Row, 1972. A good introduction to Tournier's thought and writings until 1970.

David Barratt

THE MEANING OF PRAYER

Author: Harry Emerson Fosdick (1878-1969)
First published: New York: Abingdon Press, 1915, with an introduction by John R. Mott
Genre: Nonfiction
Subgenres: Meditation and contemplation; prayer book; theology
Core issues: Daily living; God; prayer; union with God

Fosdick proposes that prayer is at the heart of the Christian life and is the most personal and intimate of actions that humans take toward God. He states that Christians who pray seek to emulate the example of Jesus Christ, who regularly turned to God for comfort, wisdom, and direction. All people of faith pray in the hope that their lives might be mysteriously connected to that of God. Far from being an abstract idea or unknowable reality, the God whom Fosdick writes about is one who cares deeply about each and every human being and is directly accessible through daily prayer.

Overview

How does one pray? How does prayer work? How can a believer create and cultivate a discipline of daily prayer to draw closer to God? These are the mysteries of faith that Harry Emerson Fosdick seeks to address in *The Meaning of Prayer*, a slim volume (194 pages) of daily devotions. Fosdick guides the reader through a ten-week cycle of everyday prayer, with each of the ten chapters addressing a different element of prayer. Each of the seventy devotions features a straightforward method for approaching God in prayer: an introductory Scripture passage, a theological reference or exposition by Fosdick on how prayer works, and a closing prayer to frame his daily theme. Fosdick's approach to teaching how to pray is eclectic and was modern for its time. He draws on a wide breadth of scriptural allusions, literature, theology, and historic events and figures. A daily devotion might include a quote from the New or Old Testament and several paragraphs about Fosdick's beliefs, interspersed with extended quotes from a wide array of spiritual thinkers, such as French theologian and mathematician Blaise Pascal, Saint Augustine, or the poet Robert Burns. Chapters then conclude with "A Comment for the Week" in which Fosdick digs more deeply into the prayer issue being presented and "Suggestions for Thoughts and Discussion," questions for the individual or group reading the book.

To understand the significance of Fosdick's treatise on prayer, it is important to recognize the context in which he preached, taught, and wrote. Born in 1878 in Buffalo, New York, Fosdick trained for ministry at Colgate University and New York City's Union Theological Seminary and was ordained as a Baptist minister in 1903, the beginning of great turmoil within American Christianity. The Protestant church in the early twentieth century was just starting to split along conservative and liberal theological fault lines. Conservative Christianity held dearly to the doctrines of biblical inerrancy and authority. Because of an inherent distrust of all things new, the conservatives often viewed the emerging modernity of the United States (mass communication, the movement of women into the workforce, industrialization, urbanization, Roman Catholic immigrants pouring into the cities, and so on) as a direct threat to their "traditional Gospel." The God preached by conservatives was a judgmental one, unerring in condemnation of human sinfulness and both distant and threatening. Liberal Christianity, for whom Fosdick would become the standard-bearer, sought to openly engage the flowering modern world and saw these new and radical social changes not as a threat but as an opportunity to reform both the teaching of the Gospel and the human soul. The God preached by liberals like Fosdick is approachable and knowable by humans in sincere prayer, where we are asked:

> . . . to desire above all else the friendship of God himself. . . . The man who misses the deep meaning of prayer has not so much refused an obligation; he has robbed himself of life's supreme privilege—friendship with God.

It was in this spirit of challenging traditional conventions about prayer and images of God that Fosdick wrote *The Meaning of Prayer*.

Taking this modernist view of prayer, Fosdick creates a spiritual arc as he invites the reader into the various methods of learning how to pray and understanding prayer, from the personal to the universal. As a typical Christian apologist, Fosdick builds argument upon argument for the need for and efficacy of prayer. In chapter 1, "The Naturalness of Prayer," Fosdick writes that prayer is a universal human need and natural act, practiced throughout history and in all faiths. Human beings pray because that impulse is built into the very fiber of our being:

> . . . the tendency to pray is native to us, that we do pray one way or another, . . . and that men have always prayed and always will pray. . . . The culture of prayer therefore is not importing an alien, but is training a native citizen of the soul.

Chapters 2, 3, and 4 continue on this intimate scale and address "Prayer as Communion with God," "God's Care for the Individual," and "Prayer and the Goodness of God." Fosdick challenges traditional childish concepts of prayer—praying to God for specific results or requests—and instead asks the believer to mature and move to an ever deeper, less self-focused form of prayer. Fosdick's God is portrayed not as a bellhop ready to deliver on demand but as an old and trusted friend and companion who seeks above all else to be in relationship with his creatures, humankind.

> . . . the practice of prayer is necessary to make God not merely an idea held in the mind but a Presence recognized in the life.

Thus confident of convincing the reader that prayer does work and that the God to whom we pray is real, Fosdick uses chapters 5, 6, 7, 8, and 9 to address what he sees as the stumbling blocks a modern believer is bound to encounter when a life of prayer is undertaken. In "Prayer and the Reign of Law," "Unanswered Prayer," "Prayer as Dominant Desire," and "Prayer as a Battlefield," Fosdick asks and answers the inevitable questions that emerge when one prays on a regular basis. Are there prayers God cannot answer because to do so would break natural law? Why do we sometimes pray and get no answer? How does one balance human desire with God's will? Because Fosdick pushes his reader to take the power of prayer seriously, he acknowledges in these chapters that the more widely prayer is applied to daily life and the life of the world, the harder it gets. Fosdick does not avoid these tough questions. He respects his readers and invites them to dig deeper and deeper into a full life of prayer. The final chapter, "Unselfish Prayer," brings the book full circle and calls the reader to move to the highest form of prayer: praying unselfishly for others.

Christian Themes

Fosdick was the first widely known modern American Liberal Christian. At a time when society was just beginning to change at a breathtaking pace, Fosdick sought in *The Meaning of Prayer* to argue for a modern, relevant faith, one that did not fear the world but instead engaged it with curiosity and a willingness to tackle the hard questions of belief in God and the reality of prayer. Fosdick's liberal take on Christianity finally declares that the act of prayer is universal, that God is an eternal power accessible to all, and that all humans are born with an intrinsic need to pray that cuts across exclusive claims of "old time religion" and scientific doubt.

Fosdick's book still resonates as true more than 90 years after its first publication because it offers prayer forms that are practical, accessible, and possible for the average person. Fosdick did not write this book for theologians or scholars, though as a text on prayer it is theological. By shaping *The Meaning of Prayer* as a prayer workbook and not merely a book about prayer, Fosdick opens prayer to those in his emerging modern world who viewed prayer with rational skepticism and those who needed to find God anew and escape the tired images of the divine they inherited from childhood and traditional orthodoxy. Fosdick takes the hand of his reader, as if to say, "Let's talk about prayer as a real possibility for your life of faith," and then gently and eloquently he accompanies them on this journey into the very life of God. As Fosdick understates in his introduction:

> This little book has been written in the hope that it may help to clarify a subject which is puzzling many minds . . . a theoretical deity saves no man from sin and disheartenment. . . . Such vital consequences require a living God who actually deals with men.

Sources for Further Study

Fosdick, Harry Emerson. *The Autobiography of Harry Emerson Fosdick: The Living of These Days.* New York: Harper & Brothers, 1956. Fosdick tells of his spiritual growth into the greatest and most famous American Protestant preacher and teacher of the first half of the twentieth century.

Fosdick, Harry Emerson, and Michael W. Perry. *The Manhood of the Master: The Character of Jesus*. Seattle: Inkling Books, 2002. For those who want to explore another book of Fosdick's daily devotions, this book takes the reader through a twelve-week introduction to the life of Jesus.

Pultz, David, ed. *A Preaching Ministry: Twenty-One Sermons Preached by Harry Emerson Fosdick at The First Presbyterian Church in the City of New York, 1918-1925*. New York: The First Presbyterian Church in the City of New York, 2000. This book contains basic biographical information about Fosdick, the birth of American Liberal Christianity and several of his most famous sermons. Of particular note is "Shall the Fundamentalists Win?"

John F. Hudson

MEETING JESUS AGAIN FOR THE FIRST TIME
The Historical Jesus and the Heart of Contemporary Faith

Author: Marcus J. Borg (1942-   )
First published: San Francisco: HarperSanFrancisco, 1994
Genre: Nonfiction
Subgenres: Biblical studies; theology
Core issues: Compassion; Gospels; Jesus Christ; scriptures; the Trinity

Borg combines scholarship and personal experience to examine the idea that people's images of the historical Jesus are inaccurate because they are filtered through the lens of Christian tradition and experience. These skewed images then distort people's images of the Christian life. Borg focuses on the original message of Jesus and asserts that the Christian life is not about believing certain things about Jesus nor about living a moral life. Rather, it is about entering into a relationship with God that involves a journey of transformation.

Overview

Meeting Jesus Again for the First Time offers an intimate and revealing reflection of Marcus J. Borg's own spiritual journey. He grew up in a Lutheran family where his earliest image of Jesus was very traditional. This image began to change in elementary school as Borg began to struggle with theological issues such as the omnipresence and transcendence of God. Throughout adolescence and college, his questions and doubts only intensified, causing enormous guilt and anxiety. His quest for answers continued as he entered seminary, and it was there that he once again focused on Jesus.

In seminary, Borg learned that the Gospels were written decades after the first Easter and that they reflect the experiences of the early Christian communities and their developing understanding of Jesus. The historical Jesus was not aware that he was the second person of the Trinity, coequal with God, or the substance of God. This distinction was a revelation to Borg, who began a lifelong quest to uncover the historical Jesus. This quest initially led to many years of becoming a "closet atheist." However, in his mid-thirties, Borg had a series of experiences with what he termed "sacred mystery," through which he began to view God as the surrounding spirit that is at the center of existence. This led to a transformation in Borg's understanding of God that profoundly changed his understanding of Jesus.

Borg uses the terms "pre-Easter Jesus" and "post-Easter Jesus" to distinguish between the historical Jesus and the Christ of faith. The majority of the book focuses on the pre-Easter Jesus or the life of Jesus before his death. The post-Easter Jesus is defined as the Jesus of Christian tradition and experience.

To begin his discussion of the pre-Easter Jesus, Borg describes his involvement with a group of scholars known as the Jesus Seminar. This group meets twice a year to vote on the historical accuracy of the sayings of Jesus. The purpose of the gatherings is to see the degree of scholarly consensus on how much of the material goes back to Jesus himself.

Borg uses four broad strokes to describe the characteristics of the pre-Easter Jesus. First, Jesus was a spirit person who had an experiential awareness of God; he was also a mediator of the spirit. Second, Jesus was a teacher of wisdom who used parables and sayings to teach alternative wisdom. Third, Jesus was a social prophet who criticized the economic, political, and religious elites of his time. Fourth, Jesus was a movement founder who challenged the social boundaries of his day.

The two keywords that describe what was most central to Jesus are "spirit" and "compassion," according to Borg. At the core of Jesus' life was a deep relationship to the spirit of God with compassion as God's central quality. This is the model by which followers of God should live. Jesus was very critical of the purity system of his day, and he spoke of purity as not a matter of external boundaries but rather a matter of the heart. Jesus shattered the social boundaries of the day and presented a model of compassion that should be applied to modern politics.

Jesus was a teacher of wisdom as well as the embodiment of divine wisdom. Borg writes that Jesus' teachings offered a transforming alternative wisdom from the conventional wisdom of the day. Conventional wisdom is the consciousness shaped and structured by culture. Jesus introduced a life of internal transformation brought by a deep centering in God. This firsthand religion leads to wisdom that is centered in compassion and grace.

In early Christianity, Jesus was known as the Son of the Father, the incarnation of Sophia ("the Wisdom Woman"), the child of Abba, and the child of Sophia. Borg says that these terms should be used metaphorically as a way to describe the significance of Jesus.

Borg states that just as people's image of Jesus shapes their image of the Christian life, so does their image of Scripture. He states that there are three stories that shape the Bible as a whole. These stories include the story of the Exodus from Egypt, the story of exile and return from Babylon, and the priestly story. Jesus subverted the priestly story by undercutting the purity system and forgiving sins apart from the institution of priest and temple. The journey stories were affirmed, and another journey story was added—the story of discipleship. Discipleship means entering a relationship with God and allowing God to transform the person into being more like Christ.

Borg ends his book with a discussion about what it means to believe in Jesus. The word "believe" comes from the Latin and Greek roots meaning "to give one's heart to." It does not mean believing doctrines about Jesus, but rather it means giving one's deepest self to the post-Easter Jesus who is the living Lord. Meeting this Jesus of the present is like meeting Jesus again for the first time.

Christian Themes

The quest for the historical Jesus is one of the major themes of this book. Borg's perspective on this topic strongly reflects the consensus of the members of the Jesus

Seminar. This controversial group of scholars and lay persons meets semiannually to evaluate the historical significance of all the documents about Jesus from antiquity (30-200 C.E.). Members of the group use color-coded beads to vote on things such as the probability that Jesus actually said or did certain things. Only about 20 percent of the sayings of Jesus received red votes, meaning Jesus undoubtedly said it or something very close to it. In this book, Borg steps out of the world of academia to offer a very personal spiritual reflection on these findings.

Another major theme of this book concerns the Christology of Jesus. Christology deals with the role or identity of Jesus, including the relationship between Jesus and God. Borg states that because of the Nicene Creed, most people see Jesus' relationship to God as Son of the Father. According to Borg, this is not the only Christology, and he proceeds to explore a variety of Christological images from the New Testament period. While father/son imagery was used, there was also a Christology that saw Jesus as the embodiment of the wisdom of God. Borg offers an indepth discussion about the personification of wisdom as a woman (Sophia). Early Christians saw Jesus as the Son of the Father, the incarnation of Sophia, the child of Abba, and the child of Sophia. None of these images should be taken literally. They are metaphors used to describe the intimate relationship between Jesus and God.

Borg states that the foundational claim of the book is that there is a connection between how people think of Jesus and how they think of the Christian life. According to Borg, Jesus did not speak or think of himself as the Son of God, and his message was not about believing in him. Rather, he was a spirit person and a movement founder who invited people to enter into a journey of transformation. This journey involves giving one's heart to the spirit of Christ and becoming a person of compassion.

Sources for Further Study

Fredriksen, Paula. "What You See Is What You Get: Context and Content in Current Research on the Historical Jesus." *Theology Today* 52, no. 1 (April, 1995): 75-97. Provides an overview of recent research on the historical Jesus.

Funk, Robert W., Roy W. Hoover, and the Jesus Seminar. *The Five Gospels: The Search for the Authentic Words of Jesus.* New York: Macmillan, 1993. This highly controversial publication is a report from the Jesus Seminar concerning what they believe Jesus actually said and did.

Keck, Leander E. "The Second Coming of the Liberal Jesus?" *Christian Century* 111, no. 24 (August 24, 1994): 784-788. This article compares Borg's book with books written by John Crossan and Geza Vermes on the life of Christ.

Wildman, Wesley. "Pinning Down the Crisis in Contemporary Christology." *Dialog* 37, no. 1 (Winter, 1998): 15-21. One of five articles in this issue discussing Jesus and the crisis in Christology. Offers extensive discussion regarding Borg's Christological beliefs.

Joy Gambill

MEMOIRS OF PONTIUS PILATE

Author: James R. Mills (1927-   )
First published: Grand Rapids, Mich.: Fleming H. Revell, 2000
Genre: Novel
Subgenres: Biblical fiction; biography
Core issues: The cross; faith; Jesus Christ

In Memoirs of Pontius Pilate, *three decades after the crucifixion of Christ, Pontius Pilate, now stripped of his high office and living in exile, attempts to convince himself that political pressures left him no choice but to assent to the death of a man he knew to be innocent. Although Pilate would prefer to classify Jesus as just another of the charismatic leaders who arose among the Jews, only to be soon forgotten, Pilate now admits the possibility that Jesus may have been exactly what he said he was.*

> *Principal characters*
> *Pontius Pilate*, the protagonist
> *Jesus Christ*, who claimed to be the Messiah
> *Claudia Procula*, Pilate's wife
> *Joseph ben Caiaphas*, a high priest of the Jews
> *Herod the Great*, king of the Jews
> *Herod Antipas*, Herod's son

Overview

As James R. Mills points out in the "Editor's Note" that precedes his novel, Pontius Pilate was not a major figure in Roman history. During the reign of Tiberius Caesar, Pilate was appointed governor of Judea, Samaria, and Idumea by the emperor's chief prefect, Lucius Aelius Sejanus. Pilate held that post for ten years. However, after the aging Tiberius turned on Sejanus, denounced him, and had him and his entire family executed, Pilate became vulnerable. Eventually he was arrested on a charge of murder by his new superior, Lucius Vitellius, and sent to Rome to be tried before Caligula, the successor of Tiberius. The outcome of that trial was not recorded, though according to tradition, Pilate was found guilty and exiled to Gaul, where he later drowned himself.

Pontius Pilate is now remembered only because of his involvement in the death of Jesus Christ. In the Gospels, Pilate is shown as an indecisive man, superstitious enough to be swayed by his wife's premonitions but too timorous to chance a political misstep. Mills chose to take a different approach to the question of Pilate's character. In his novel, he imagines how Pilate would have seen his situation and how he would have remembered the Jewish prophet he allowed to be crucified. As a historian, Mills understands the political environment in which these events took place; as a Christian, he believes that Pilate must have been at least profoundly stirred by his encounter.

Except for the brief "Editor's Note," which sums up the historical facts, *Memoirs of*

Pontius Pilate is a first-person narrative, written by Pilate in his later years. In the "Prologue," Pilate explains that during his long years of exile, he has often thought about Jesus of Nazareth, and with Nero now resolved to exterminate the Christians, it seems even more important to tell the carpenter's story. This section is followed by the "Introduction," excerpted from a history of modern Palestine that Pilate began at the suggestion of his wife but laid aside after her death. Pilate's comments on the Jews and their recent history ends with the death of Herod the Great.

In the nine chapters that follow, Pilate narrates the story of the carpenter from his birth to death. The events associated with his birth are contained in a manuscript prepared by Joseph ben Caiaphas, the high priest of the Jews, to explain why the supposed messiah who has just ridden into Jerusalem presents so serious a threat to Rome. In the next chapter, Pilate, his wife Claudia Procula, Herod Antipas, and his wife Herodia speculate as to how Jesus would have spent his childhood and youth. In "A Wayside Prophet," Pilate recalls the reports he received about Jesus' sermons and his miracles. Pilate includes a letter from Caiaphas, concluding that Jesus is an apostate. In "No One Ever Spoke Like Him," Pilate quotes Claudia, whose admiration for Jesus is evident. He assures her that as long as Jesus does not break any Roman laws, he should be all right. However, there is another letter from Caiaphas, announcing that he is convening a council to decide how to get rid of Jesus. In the following chapter, Pilate notes how brilliantly Jesus avoided the theological traps presented to him; nevertheless, in the end, Jesus is betrayed and arrested.

In the sixth chapter of the book, entitled "The Affairs of Men," Pilate attempts to justify the actions that culminated in the Crucifixion. He emphasizes his own precarious position after Sejanus's fall from power. In fact, Pilate insists, he was a better governor than those troublesome Jews deserved. It was their fault if he had to kill a good many of them to give them a dependable water supply. Moreover, wild-eyed prophets were always stirring them up, and his Roman superiors expected him to preserve law and order. When he did what he had to do, he was charged with murder. Clearly Pilate puts part of the blame for his downfall on the Jews and part of it on the machinations of his enemies.

The next three chapters, which take Jesus from the Jews to Pilate to his crucifixion, follow the biblical accounts closely, with periodic pauses for Pilate to justify his actions. He is impressed by Jesus' courage throughout his long agony, but as a rational man, he has to believe that the darkening of the sky and the earthquake that accompanied his death were merely coincidental. Nevertheless, along with the star at Jesus' birth and all the incidents fulfilling the messianic prophecies, these events persuade the common people, thus accounting for the continuing spread of Christianity.

In the final chapter, Pilate compares Jesus to Socrates, another man who was killed because he wanted to change his society. In the "Epilogue," Pilate presents two possibilities. If Nero succeeds in destroying Christianity, it will be clear that Jesus was merely a pitiable madman. However, if Christianity survives and prospers and people pray for healing in his name, then, Pilate supposes, Jesus must have been the son of a god, after all.

Christian Themes

One of the central themes in Mills's novel is faith, specifically, faith in Jesus Christ. That Christ is the subject of Pontius Pilate's memoir is significant. Even though his reminiscences include comments on Jewish history, accounts of his dealings with the Jews, and descriptions of Roman political infighting, Pilate admits that his most vivid memories of his life in Palestine involve Jesus. His attempt to put Jesus on the same level as Socrates does not convince anyone, least of all Pilate himself, that the Jew was merely a good man. Though he tries to reason away the angelic annunciation, the star that brought the astrologers to Jesus' birthplace, the fulfillment of the biblical prophecies, the many miracles, and the darkness and the earthquake at the end, Pilate cannot forget a single detail about the life and death of Jesus, nor can he erase the memory of their brief encounter.

Despite his fascination with Jesus, at the end of the novel, Pilate has still not made a commitment. For one thing, Pilate prides himself on practicality. He recalls leaving the cross because he had important matters to take care of. Pilate's snobbery is another obstacle to faith. The Roman official who proudly recalls his dinners with Herod Antipas would not be at ease with Jewish fishermen. Moreover, Pilate feels intellectually superior to the Jewish fanatics who follow Jesus. His offhand comment "What is truth?" was undoubtedly meant to show his grasp of complex thought. What it really demonstrates, however, is his inability to make a commitment, either to save an innocent man or to believe in him. Thus the memoirs end without resolution. At the end of the novel, Pilate is still waiting for proof of Jesus' divinity.

Sources for Further Study

Bond, Helen K. *Pontius Pilate in History and Interpretation.* Cambridge, England: Cambridge University Press, 1998. This revisionist study argues that Pilate was a highly competent official with a talent for compromising. Map and bibliography.

Duncan, Melanie C. Review of *Memoirs of Pontius Pilate. Library Journal* 125 (April 1, 2000): 84. Mills's book shows Pilate as a man who remained fascinated with Jesus but was determined to avoid accepting responsibility for his death.

Winner, Lauren. "Three Books Dig for Insights into the Shadowy Ruler and His Wife." *Christianity Today* 44 (December 4, 2000): 87-88. Compares Mills's book, which ends with Pilate's being drawn toward Christianity, to Ann Wroe's biography and to a novel by the poet H. D. Lawrence.

Wroe, Ann. *Pontius Pilate.* New York: Random House, 1999. After extensive research, concludes that Pilate was a nervous politician, fearful of offending those in power and thus losing his office and probably his life. Bibliography and index.

Rosemary M. Canfield Reisman

MEMORIES, DREAMS, REFLECTIONS

Author: Carl Gustav Jung (1875-1961)
First published: Erinnerungen, Träume, Gedanken, 1962 (English translation, 1963)
Edition used: Memories, Dreams, Reflections, recorded and edited by Aniela Jaffé, translated by Richard Winston and Clara Winston. New York: Vintage Books, 1989
Genre: Nonfiction
Subgenres: Autobiography; biography; didactic treatise
Core issues: Illumination; knowledge; memory; myths; psychology; self-knowledge

Viewed by many theologians as one of the primary spiritual documents of the twentieth century, Memories, Dreams, Reflections *provides remarkable access to the highly spiritual mental life of a man who made major contributions to the fields of psychology and psychiatry. Jung's preoccupation with mythology, religion, and the occult had a powerful and permanent impact on contemporary culture and theology. This text anticipates the profound changes that rippled across the spiritual landscape of the modern world years after Jung's death.*

Overview

Memories, Dreams, Reflections can be considered as either autobiography or biography. Carl Gustav Jung began writing and telling the stories that would eventually become the book in 1957. He continued to work on the manuscript until shortly before his death in 1961. It was first published shortly after his death, after editing by his assistant Aniela Jaffé and others. Jung wrote five chapters himself. The rest of the book was assembled from interviews, unpublished writings, and a now-published seminar. Jaffé, with the close involvement of Kurt Wolff, selected material, edited it, arranged it thematically, and then organized it into a series of approximately chronological chapters. Jung's attitude toward the project fluctuated. For example, after reading the early manuscript, he criticized Jaffé's handling of the text, complaining of "auntifications." Also, he seemed to dread public reaction and expressly requested that this book be omitted from his collected works. However, he also seemed to want to reveal himself, to convey his intentions and the conditions from which his work grew.

The prologue to *Memories, Dreams, Reflections* makes it clear that Jung's inner experiences form the prime material of his scientific work. Indeed, the book provides little information about Jung's life or external circumstances. For example, the book mentions Jung's wife, née Emma Rauschenbach, by name only once, in a footnote, and completely omits anything about Toni Wolff, with whom he had an intense affair. Instead, it concentrates on Jung's inner reality and crises.

The text is a story of Jung's life from the perspective of old age and mature psychological understanding. The first three chapters, on his school years, reveal a highly unusual boy who was full of contradictions. He was an extraverted and successful scholar who decided on a career in medicine (psychiatry), but at the same time a deeply reflective, isolated person, prone to fantasizing. Chapters on psychiatric activities and Sigmund Freud describe Jung's early professional work with psychiatric inpatients at the Burghölzi clinic and his ill-fated relationship with Sigmund Freud, which left psychic scars. Five chapters on confrontation with the unconscious, the work, the tower, travels, and visions describe a period of inner uncertainty and exploration, which some have labeled a psychotic episode and others a creative illness, and his eventual return to a solid footing in reality. They also touch on his multicultural interests and his confrontation with his own mortality following a heart attack. Final chapters on Jung's understanding of life after death, late thoughts, and a retrospective focus on his religious views. Appendices include letters from Freud to Jung, letters to Emma Jung from America (1909) and North Africa (1920), a description of Richard Wilhelm revolving around the *Yijing* (eighth to third centuries B.C.E.; English translation, 1876; also known as *Book of Changes*), and Seven Sermons to the Dead, which convey an impression of what Jung experienced during his creative illness.

Throughout the book are materials resulting from his theological and philosophical discussions with his father, who was a minister; his close relationship with his mother, who suffered from mental illness; his experiences with séances and the paranormal; and his experiences with the two opposing sides of his personality. In all, *Memories, Dreams, Reflections* recounts forty-two of Jung's dreams and thirteen images from people he treated, reflecting the two-step process that characterizes Jung's approach to treatment: listening to messages from one's own unconscious and relating to these messages consciously.

Jung uses the techniques of dream analysis and active imagination in his transformative journey called "individuation," in which recognizing and incorporating the shadow, the dark side of personality, was a priority. This journey involved encountering various complexes (sensitive, energy-filled clusters of emotions, such as an attitude toward one's father or father figures) and archetypes (organizing principles, imprints, and symbols of an unknown and incomprehensible content, such as a mandala) and ended in a new spiritual orientation where the center of psychological gravity shifted away from the ego (Sigmund Freud's term). The new focus Jung called the self or psyche, which is the interior, personal, universal source of all that exists. Jung viewed the psyche as a combination of spirit, soul, and idea. Through the psyche, archetypes awaken and are integrated into consciousness. Jung believed that people grow into wholeness when both conscious and unconscious parts of their mind work in harmony and that people have a natural tendency to move toward balance and self-healing. The transformed self is linked to a larger claim pronouncing that the extension of human consciousness is adding to the consciousness of God.

Memories, Dreams, Reflections reveals publicly for the first time Jung's remarkable life experiences, including many religious encounters and preoccupations and a deep trust in religious or mystical feelings. Jung's attitude toward life was one of openness, especially to ideas that were irrational and mysterious. He believed in a reality that was beyond the logic of philosophy and the instruments of scientific investigation. With humility and awe, he believed that infinity stretches beyond human understanding.

Christian Themes

A recurring theme in the work is God. From the initial chapters that recount Jung's childhood as a pastor's son, to the final chapters on life after death, Jung is preoccupied with God and God-images. Jung's view was that God is wholly intrapsychic, a projection of one's inner experience. Further, God is not entirely good or kind. Jung accepted diverse and idiosyncratic manifestations of the divine, even when these manifestations fell outside of Christian orthodoxy. Jung embraced all of creation as a potential source of illumination. Jung called on humanity to be open to God in unexpected ways. These views placed Jung outside the umbrella of traditional religion, although he called himself a Christian.

Another recurring theme is the self or psyche. The self—the inner realm of reality that balances the outer reality of material objects—comprises balancing and compensatory opposites. Part of the psyche is accessible and includes senses, intellect, emotions, and desires. Another part is inaccessible and includes elements that are forgotten or denied. Jung observed that the self spontaneously produces images with a religious content. He concluded, therefore, that the psyche is by nature religious. In addition, he believed that numerous neuroses spring from a disregard for the fundamental religiousness of the psyche, especially during the second half of life.

Another theme is myth and symbols. Jung observed that the basic motifs in myths, fantasies, dreams, and symbols are the same across vastly different cultures. Therefore, he concluded that they are universal manifestations of humanity's collective unconscious, the vast, hidden psychic resource shared by all humans. For example, some images form bridges between opposites, synthesizing two opposing attitudes or conditions in the psyche by means of third forces. Jung termed these transcendent functions because the image or symbol goes beyond, as well as mediates, the two opposites and allows a new attitude or relationship between them.

Sources for Further Study

Charet, F. X. "Understanding Jung: Recent Biographies and Scholarship." *Journal of Analytical Psychology* 45, no. 2 (2000): 195-216. Discusses how Jung's spiritual inclinations contributed to his ill-fated relationship with Freud and ultimate rejection by the Freudian establishment.

Elms, Alan. *Uncovering Lives: The Uneasy Alliance of Biography and Psychology.* New York: Oxford University Press, 1994. Argues persuasively that *Memories, Dreams, Reflections* is ambiguous, just as Jung in his own life was unable to reconcile opposing tendencies.

Franz, Marie-Louise von. *Jung: His Myth in Our Time.* London: Hodder & Stoughton, 1975. Situates Jung in contemporary culture, showing how his life and thought intersect with the most important currents of modern time from spirituality to quantum physics.

Hannah, Barbara. *Jung: His Life and Work.* New York: Putnam, 1976. Provides a chatty, gossipy insider's account of many details of the life of a highly venerated person.

Homans, Peter. *Jung in Context.* 2d ed. Chicago: University of Chicago Press, 1995. Discusses how the power of Jung's ideas and personality had a permanent impact on contemporary culture.

Winnicott, D. W. Review of *Memories, Dreams, Reflections. The International Journal of Psycho-Analysis* 5 (1953): 450-455. Provides lucid insights and a critical assessment of the doctrinaire, traditional Freudian view of Jung.

Lillian M. Range

THE MERCHANT OF VENICE

Author: William Shakespeare (1564-1616)
First produced: pr. c. 1596-1597, pb. 1600
Edition used: The Riverside Shakespeare, edited by G. Blakemore Evans with the assistance of J. J. M. Tobin. 2d ed. Boston: Houghton Mifflin, 1997
Genre: Drama
Subgenres: Comedy; problem play
Core issues: Conversion; Judaism; justice; persecution; racism

In The Merchant of Venice, *the contrast between Judaic and Christian ethics forms a principal dramatic conflict as demands for justice conflict with calls for mercy. The Old Testament Law of Talion, calling for an eye for an eye, emphasizes the preeminence of justice as an ethic of retaliation. In the New Testament's Sermon on the Mount, Jesus of Nazareth proclaims the Golden Rule, pronounces the Lord's Prayer and its petition for forgiveness, and enumerates the Beatitudes, making the case for mercy in the Christian dispensation.*

Principal characters
   Antonio, a Venetian merchant
   Bassanio, Antonio's friend
   Portia, a young woman Bassanio wants to impress
   Shylock, a Jewish moneylender
   Gratiano, companion to Bassanio
   Nerissa, Portia's lady-in-waiting
   Lorenzo, Antonio's friend
   Jessica, Shylock's daughter

Overview

As is typical of William Shakespeare's comedies, *The Merchant of Venice* contains three interrelated plots. The merchant of the play's title, Antonio, has cast his fortune into several ships laden with goods he purchased abroad and now awaits the ships' return to Venice with some apprehension. When his dear young friend Bassanio asks him for the loan of a large sum of money he can use to impress Portia, a lady of Belmont whom he wishes to court, Antonio can only refer him to Shylock, a Jewish moneylender, and offer himself as surety for the loan. Antonio and Shylock have been adversaries for some time; Antonio criticizes the Jew for charging usurious interest rates as he himself lends money without charging interest. Antonio's antipathy for Shylock extends to mocking his way of life, and heaping insults on the Jew. Nonetheless, Shylock, who likewise expresses his hatred of Christians and their ways, agrees to the loan of three thousand ducats with the curious condition that if Antonio fails to satisfy the debt when due, he shall forfeit a pound of his flesh.

Bassanio, amply provided with funds sufficient to impress Portia, travels to Belmont in grand style. There, he passes a test involving three caskets that other would-be suitors, including a prince of Morocco and a prince of Aragon, have failed, when he chooses a casket made of lead instead of gold or silver. This victory wins him the Portia's hand in marriage. His companion, Gratiano, likewise gains the hand of Portia's lady-in-waiting, Nerissa. A third couple, Antonio's friend Lorenzo and Shylock's runaway daughter, Jessica, round out the marriages that Shakespeare's comedies typically celebrate.

The problematic pairing of Lorenzo and Jessica, whose relationship forms the third thread in the multiplotted play, adds real injury to the insults heaped on Shylock and fuels his resolve to seek revenge on the Christians of Venice. The couple goes to Belmont from Venice at the same time that Salerio, another of Antonio's friends, travels there, and they all arrive on the very day of Bassanio's success. Salerio bears a letter from Antonio describing the ruin of his merchant fleet and the necessity to repay Shylock. Thus the three strands of narrative come together and propel further action.

Immediately after the hastily arranged weddings and before they can be consummated, Portia dispatches Bassanio and Gratiano to Venice, offering to pay twenty times the debt on behalf of Antonio. Meanwhile, she has already conceived a plan to disguise herself as Balthazar, a doctor of the laws, sent by her cousin from Padua, the renowned Bellario, with Nerissa disguised as her clerk, to plead Antonio's case before the Duke of Venice. This gender disguise is another hallmark of Shakespeare's comedies and serves to heighten the legal contest that Portia, as architect of the plan to save Antonio, will undertake. Even before Portia's arrival in Venice, Shylock has refused payment, even triple the debt, making it clear that he wants the pound of Antonio's flesh. In his overwhelming anger at Antonio and those who would assist him, Shylock remains adamant on this point, time and again refusing to consider Portia's plea for mercy.

When Portia finds in favor of Shylock's cause, all appears lost for Antonio. As Antonio prepares for the worst, Portia cautions that according to the letter of the bond, Shylock is not allowed to draw a single drop of blood in cutting off his pound of flesh. With the tables turned, in true comic reversal, Shylock declares he will take the triple payment, but Portia declares that the offer is rescinded and that Shylock is entitled only to his bond. Further, since Shylock, an "alien," seeks the life of a Venetian citizen, half the Jew's goods are forfeited to Antonio, the intended victim, and the other half to the state, and the offender's life may be spared only by the duke's mercy. After the duke, unasked, pardons Shylock and suggests that the half of his fortune due to the state may be reduced to a fine, Antonio mercifully asks that the fine be waived and that, in return for the use of half of Shylock's fortune while he lives, Antonio will render it unto Lorenzo and Jessica on her father's death. Antonio further stipulates the conditions that Shylock convert to Christianity and that on Shylock's death, his entire fortune will go to Lorenzo and Jessica.

As the trial is over, the disguised Portia claims to have pressing business in Padua. Before she leaves, Bassanio offers her a gift. Seeing his ring, Portia claims it, much to

Bassanio's discomfiture, so much so that he first refuses to give it to her and then sends Gratiano after her with it. Nerissa, still disguised as Balthasar's clerk, likewise manages to get the ring she gave to Gratiano who, like Bassanio, has sworn never to part with his ring. In the play's final scene at Belmont, Portia and Nerissa return the rings and reveal all, but not without first questioning their husbands about their lost rings and their broken pledges to wear them always. Portia also gives Antonio a letter revealing that three of his ships have arrived home filled with riches, thus concluding the comedy with happy endings for all but Shylock.

Christian Themes

The principal Christian theme of mercy as preferable to, or tempering, justice pervades this play. In Act IV, scene 1, Portia makes an argument for mercy against Shylock's plea for his bond.

> The quality of mercy is not strain'd
> It droppeth as the gentle rain from heaven
> Upon the place beneath; it is twice blest
> It blesseth him that gives and him that takes
> 'Tis mightiest in the mighty; it becomes
> The throned monarch better than his crown
> His sceptre shows the force of temporal power
> The attribute to awe and majesty
> Wherein dost sit the dread and fear of kings
> But mercy is above this sceptred sway
> It is enthroned in the hearts of kings
> It is an attribute to God himself
> And earthly power dost then show likest God's
> When mercy seasons justice.

This argument, one of the most well-known passages in Shakespeare's works, underscores the conflict between the vengeful Law of Talion and the more merciful Golden Rule. Indeed, a central conflict between the old dispensation of Judaism and the new covenant announced by Jesus of Nazareth rests on the Christian doctrine that salvation comes through the mercy of God (grace) rather than through justice. As the trial between Shylock and Antonio concludes, Shylock becomes the victim of his own desire for justice while the Duke of Venice and Antonio both show him some degree of mercy.

From a Christian perspective, Shylock's conversion to Christianity would allow him the possibility of salvation. That Shylock does not share this religious view seems insignificant to those in the religious majority, which in the Venice setting was Roman Catholic. In 1290 Jews had been banished from England by a decree of King Edward I, and as a result, Elizabethans knew almost nothing about Jews except perhaps some stereotypes. Those Jews present in England would have conformed outwardly to the Church of England and practiced Judaism in private. Shakespeare's original audiences would have had direct experience with forced conversions from Catholicism to the Church of England to Catholicism and back to the Church of England because several English monarchs changed the state religion in the sixteenth century. Shakespeare may indeed be using the converted Jew as a metaphor for any member of a minority religion forced to choose between faith and life itself.

Sources for Further Study

Frye, R. M. *Shakespeare and Christian Doctrine*. Princeton, N.J.: Princeton University Press, 1963. Presents biblical, patristic, medieval, and early modern Christian doctrine, especially Catholic-Anglican, as background to Shakespeare's works.

Greenblatt, Stephen. *Will in the World: How Shakespeare Became Shakespeare*. New York: W. W. Norton, 2004. Provides useful information about the Roderigo Lopez affair and the current of anti-Semitism in mid-1590's London as background to *The Merchant of Venice*.

Hall, Jonathan. *Anxious Pleasures: Shakespearean Comedy and the Nation-State*. Madison, N.J.: Fairleigh Dickinson University Press, 1995. In addition to an overview of Shakespeare's political world, this book contains valuable commentary on capitalism in *The Merchant of Venice* and on Christopher Marlowe's *The Jew of Malta* (pr. c. 1589, pb. 1633).

Shaheen, Naseb. *Biblical References in Shakespeare's Comedies*. Newark: University of Delaware Press, 1993. Examines Shakespeare's knowledge of English Bibles (Geneva and others), details his textual references, and corrects an earlier misattribution of a text in *The Merchant of Venice*.

Shapiro, James. *Shakespeare and the Jews*. New York: Columbia University Press, 1996. Shapiro examines English identity and Jewish identity in the Elizabethan age; recounts myths, histories, and historical anecdotes; and includes a chapter titled "A Pound of Flesh."

John J. Conlon

MERCY'S FACE
New and Selected Poems, 1980-2000

Author: David Craig (1951-   )
First published: Streubenville, Ohio: Franciscan University Press, 2000
Genre: Poetry
Subgenre: Lyric poetry
Core issues: Devotional life; good vs. evil; Jesus Christ; sainthood

The poetry in Mercy's Face *is subtle in its craft and uncompromising in its vision as well as explicit in its commitment to Christ and his teachings. The mingling of biblical and Catholic subjects and concerns makes it appeal to a wide variety of readers. Heart and intellect combine in this distinctive and unforgettable work.*

Overview

David Craig was born in 1951 in Berea, Ohio. His variety of experiences growing up and making his way through the world led him to a revitalization of faith and a dedication to writing as a means of expressing it. His early jobs, such as driving a taxi, gave him solid experience for his first works. He received his M.F.A. and Ph.D. degrees from Bowling Green State University and took a position teaching creative writing at the Franciscan University of Steubenville, Ohio. Along with his poetry, Craig has written essays and novels, all of which center on his Catholic faith.

This collection provides a selection of Craig's earlier work and adds a section of new poems. His introduction clearly states his theme: "What seems to hold [these poems] together is an underlying awareness of God's mercy, that and, to a lesser extent, the joy which so often accompanies Presence." These strikingly original poems provide new insights into Christian views of mercy and grace. They are simultaneously traditional and experimental; their definition of Catholicism is traditional, but their forms, images, and syntax explore the possibilities of language in new ways.

The bulk of the poems in *Mercy's Face* were selected from *The Sandaled Foot* (1980), *Psalms* (1982), *Peter Maurin, and Other Poems* (1985), *Like Taxes: Marching Through Gaul* (1989), *Only One Face* (1994), and *The Roof of Heaven* (1998). The last section of the book, "Road Work," consists of new poems. Craig's books are carefully themed; some of them reflect on saint's lives and work, and others interpret the Bible or explore childhood experience as it relates to faith. Each of the poems in *Mercy's Face* provides the feel of the book from which it came. Craig enters the lives and minds of holy people in sensitive portraits of Anna-Maria Taigi, Peter Maurin, Francis of Assisi, and Thérèse of Lisieux. His biblical explorations are moving and insightful. His poems of a rough and rowdy childhood ring with truth.

Craig's poems use traditional and open styles—sonnet form, free verse, blank verse—but most of them are in a sound-sensitive free verse. Craig tends to write in sequences based on sacred sources: the words and works of a saint or the Bible itself. He makes language perform tricks—it clicks and clanks along unaccustomed grooves to provide each poem with a visual and aural texture. Nothing is worn about Craig's work, and its glittering singularity focuses the mind on the meaning underneath. Syntax and image fuse, creating startling imagery of praise. In "Gospel Poem #1," he addresses Jesus:

> Come; take the owl from the pumpkin; march
> the skins of the old days out the necessary door.
> You are the Mother walker, candle tongue,
> bee thread. Take the lies,
> exchange them for jazz on Barnaby Street,
> flower the walls with tutors of lost languages.
> Let me shout Your blare-root
> over the beams of every mule house.

The expression of praise is universal among Christian writers, but Craig's words are packed with energy. His emphases or stresses seem to impel the lines forward— suggesting Gerard Manley Hopkins, perhaps, but a Hopkins who wrote in free verse.

The precision of observation together with the exact language sometimes results in a haiku-type effect, as in the beginning of "Apple Fools":

> Apple fools, we are,
> ripe as cups of cider and the horse's
> clodded wake.

The overall effect of Craig's language is barely contained joy. The movement and images are so original that the work appeals to readers of other faiths, who will learn much about Catholicism from the well-researched saint poems as well as the more lyrical poems. Craig's work is traditional Catholic theology and imagery touched by an individual sensibility and vision.

Christian Themes

Craig's *Mercy's Face* is poetry of adoration and of the trials and epiphanies of the individual soul. His biblical sonnet sequence is a devotion-filled, sustained work that interprets the Bible and helps apply it to modern times. The sonnets are lyrical pieces expressing adoration. Other poems detail the lives of the saints and the poet's own spiritual struggles.

Craig's themes include the phases of a soul's relationship with God, like those of the Psalms of the Bible. He portrays the soul as cut off, struggling, pleading, reunited, and adoring. The emotions of each stage in the relationship are portrayed through vibrant images that echo as they transform the biblical images.

In his sequence on the Psalms, his open, honest poems follow the Psalms and interpret them in the journey of one man's soul. Craig provides exegeses in his own Psalms that are sharply insightful, contemporary, and rich in images. He recasts the surface of the Psalms in ways that reflect our present lives. It is an enlightening experience to read the Psalms together with Craig's poems based on them. Psalm 6 in the English Standard Version of the Bible begins:

> O Lord, rebuke me not in your anger,
> nor discipline me in your wrath.
> Be gracious to me, O Lord, for I am languishing;
> heal me, O Lord, for my bones are troubled.

Craig experiences the words in this way.

> Do not punish me, do not
> stamp my soul with the seal of who I am.
> Lift me up and I will rise,
> pity me, I cannot keep
> my bones, the rack upon which I starve, knit.

His response provides an unusual but insightful definition of "punish"—to seal the soul and not to allow change, the gift of grace. The troubled syntax reflects his troubled soul.

Craig explores the nature of sainthood and holy living. The unofficial hagiographies provide glimpses into the reality of sainthood, and the poet fleshes out lines in the saints' histories. Craig depicts the saints as human beings struggling with the same temptations and worldly desires as everyone else; how the saints thought and felt becomes real in Craig's portrayals. Craig's work prompts readers to explore saints on their own, trying to find not just the facts but also the spirit of their lives and thereby redefining the nature of sainthood.

The responsibilities of the Christian are also a part of Craig's subject matter. Requirements for the right life are presented straight, with no glossing over of their difficulty. Mercy is always available, but contrition is required, and sins are sins—they cannot be defined away, but must be faced and repented. In his attitude toward the Christian life, Craig resembles C. S. Lewis.

Craig's work helps to define contemporary Catholic poetry. Its lyric beauty, narrative integrity, and ever-present luminous faith provide a reading experience that will enlighten Christian readers and enhance their understanding of faith. Its good humor and humility add to its appeal.

Many of the poems are poems of difficulty and praise. However obstacle-filled the journey is, the soul has been equipped to sense God. Grace strikes the fire of joy and light from the rock of reality. These are straightforwardly Christian and Catholic poems of theological and intellectual subtlety. They will rightly find places in both academic and devotional anthologies.

Sources for Further Study

Craig, David. *The Cheese Stands Alone*. Oak Lawn, Ill.: CMJ Marian, 2003. Clear and inspiring novel by the poet shows another view of his way of applying faith to life and provides an entry into the poems.

"David A. Craig." *Contemporary Authors Online*. Farmington Hills, Mich.: Thomson Gale, 2007. A brief description of the poet's life and works.

Impastato, David. *Upholding Mystery: An Anthology of Contemporary Christian Poetry*. New York: Oxford University Press, 1996. Craig's poetry is placed among top American religious poetry in this anthology, which also provides a good introduction to the subject.

McCann, Janet. Review of *Mercy's Face*. *St. Anthony Messenger* 19, no. 10 (March, 2002) 52-54. A review/analysis of *Mercy's Face*, especially in regard to its Christian themes.

Janet McCann

MERE CHRISTIANITY

Author: C. S. Lewis (1898-1963)
First published: 1952
Edition used: Mere Christianity. New York: Macmillan, 1960
Genre: Nonfiction
Subgenres: Didactic treatise; spiritual treatise; theology
Core issues: The divine; doubt; ethics; faith; God; reason

Mere Christianity *is a compilation of a series of talks Lewis gave over the radio between 1941 and 1944. Lewis's most famous work of nonfiction apologetics, it best encapsulates his Christian philosophy. The talks were written to a common audience and begin by discussing commonsense morality. Condensing and popularizing the work of philosophers and theologians who influenced him, Lewis works his way backward from moral law to God as the lawgiver, and then expands on his understanding of Christianity. The book has greatly influenced Christian evangelization, apologetics, and ecumenism for more than half a century.*

Overview

To understand *Mere Christianity,* one of C. S. Lewis's most well-known apologetics, one must understand his audience. The work is a compilation of talks on Christian philosophy that Lewis gave to radio listeners between 1941 and 1944. Lewis is an accomplished scholar, but he is writing for a popular audience. Therefore, he leaves out a great deal of material that scholars would look for in a systematic theology; most notably, epistemology. The book takes for granted a commonsense attitude toward morality, reason, and the Bible. Many scholars criticize the book for oversimplifying some issues, but Lewis's arguments are sound if one understands his views on literary criticism, history, and Socratic logic as expressed in his other works.

The title comes from Lewis's claim to abstract from the various denominations a kind of "pure" Christianity. Like a Puritan, Lewis believes that this "undiluted" Christianity would be as potent as merum, undiluted wine. However, like a Catholic, he relies heavily on tradition and dogmatism.

The book is divided into four main parts, titled after the separate series on which they were based, aired by the British Broadcasting Corporation (BBC).

In "Right and Wrong as a Clue to the Meaning of the Universe," Lewis discusses commonsense morality. Even young children are aware of right and wrong, and there are some acts that most people recognize as evil. People engage in acts of self-sacrifice that defy pragmatic or utilitarian ethic. Lewis argues that all human beings share a basic moral law. Using Platonic reasoning, Lewis contends that such a moral law requires the existence of a moral lawgiver.

In "What Christians Believe," Lewis works through the basic concepts of divinity, in a manner similar to what Saint Augustine does in *De civitate Dei* (413-427; *The*

City of God, 1610). A moral lawgiver must be extrinsic to the universe, eliminating pantheism as an option. Polytheism fails to meet the standard, as pagan gods are capricious and have a supreme God that rules them. Lewis discards dualism since an absolute good and an absolute evil would cancel each other out, and one must be stronger than the other for there to be a moral law. Of all major religious models, Lewis argues, only monotheism supports a definitive moral law.

Lewis then offers the Hebrew Scriptures as the best historical source of a divine lawgiver revealing himself to human beings. Similarly, the canonical Gospels are the best historical texts about the life of Jesus Christ, and these books claim that Jesus is God. Jesus is the only great moral teacher to claim to be God incarnate. Therefore, Lewis challenges the "quest for the historical Jesus" with his famous "trilemma": Jesus is a lunatic, a fraud, or God, but he is not a "good moral teacher." Some accuse Lewis of a false dilemma, arguing that the Gospels may have misrepresented Jesus. However, Lewis holds that it is intellectually dishonest to accept some parts of a text as reliable and reject others. A text must be taken as a whole.

J. R. R. Tolkein once remarked to Lewis that Christ is the only historical occurrence of a "grain god." Lewis builds on that kernel to contend that Christianity is the fulfillment not only of Judaism but also of all pagan religions.

In "Christian Behaviour," Lewis covers the basic points of Christian ethics. His ethics are mainly Aristotelian, built on the concepts that "virtue is the mean" and that virtue is achieved by building good habits.

In the last part, "Beyond Personality," Lewis delves into Trinitarian theology. Here Lewis turns more speculative than orthodox. He offers thoughts that seem to be more purely his own (or at least Pythagorean) rather than merely echoing Thomas Aquinas or Saint Augustine.

Lewis suggests that there are "dimensions" of personality. In geometry, there is a huge difference between a one-dimensional line, a two-dimensional plane, and a three-dimensional cube. He suggests that something in two dimensions would be able to understand what one dimension is. However, the two-dimensional entity cannot truly comprehend three dimensions, except by a metaphor (for example, a cube is six squares).

Lewis sees something similar in the Christian understanding of God as "three persons." He compares animals to one dimension, humans to two dimensions, and God to three dimensions. Animals understand only instinct and interact with humans as if we were similarly instinctual. They are incapable of comprehending our level of rationality. Humans, however, can understand animals, but we are incapable of really understanding the level of existence enjoyed by God. God is so beyond our level of existence that humans cannot really understand his "dimension." Christ became human to help humans understand God better. The best way for humans to comprehend God's level of existence is to speak of God as three persons, just as the square might speak of the cube as six squares.

Ultimately, Lewis contends that the goal of Christianity is for the person, with Christ's help, to expand "beyond personality," to reach toward the level of existence enjoyed by God. This is achieved by allowing the Holy Spirit to guide the person's actions and by using Christ as model and mediator.

Christian Themes

Many people think that the purpose of this book is to convince atheists to become Christians. While it has been effective in this regard and while the arguments are inspired by Lewis's own conversion, his main goal is to explain Christianity (*apologesis*, after all, means "explanation"). Lewis is fully aware that Christianity cannot be proven and involves some amount of faith, but he notes atheism also requires a great deal of faith. His main goal is to show that Christianity is reasonable. It is not a random superstition or popular myth, but a complex system of thought derived from logical processes and purported historical evidence.

Therefore, like a Pauline epistle, *Mere Christianity* is built on the core claim that God became man in Jesus Christ then died and rose from the dead to allow for humans to participate in the divine life of the blessed Trinity. In this context, moral behavior is seen as the way to better participate in that divine life.

Interestingly, while most Christian concepts of the Trinity emphasize the relationship of love, Lewis seems to emphasize a relationship of power or being. The Father shares power and wisdom with the Son through the Holy Spirit. The Christian, by the indwelling of the Holy Spirit and the mediation of Christ, can participate in the Father's power and wisdom through prayer. Morality is in that sense a means of self-discipline to handle God's power properly.

Lewis's view of salvation is derived from Plato's myth of the cave, a recurring concept in both Lewis's fiction and nonfiction. Heaven is a state of reality that exists beyond people's comprehension. The goal of a spiritual life is to prepare the soul to face the raw power of that reality when the time comes. Christianity is unique because it is the only religion that has God stooping down to the human level to lift people up.

Sources for Further Study

Beversluis, John. *C. S. Lewis and the Search for Rational Religion*. Grand Rapids, Mich.: Wm. B. Eerdmans, 1985. A rationalist critique of Lewis's thought. Focuses on issues such as the argument from desire.

Kilby, Clyde S. *The Christian World of C. S. Lewis*. Grand Rapids, Mich.: Wm. B. Eerdmans, 1964. Kilby was one of the pioneers of Lewis scholarship. Includes a chapter on each of Lewis's major fictional and apologetic works, including *Mere Christianity*.

Meilaender, Gilbert. *The Taste for the Other: The Social and Ethical Thought of C. S. Lewis*. Grand Rapids, Mich.: Wm. B. Eerdmans, 1978. Covers Lewis's social and ethical works, showing the interrelationship between his fiction and nonfiction.

Milward, Peter. *A Challenge to C. S. Lewis*. Cranbury, N.J.: Associated University Press, 1995. A Catholic priest who admires Lewis critiques the concept of "mere Christianity." Draws out several flaws in Lewis's claim to represent what "most Christians believe."

Purtill, Richard. *C. S. Lewis's Case for the Christian Faith*. Rev. ed. San Francisco: Ignatius Press, 2004. Provides an introduction to and summary of Lewis's Christian apologetics, including *Mere Christianity*.

John C. Hathaway

THE METAPHYSICAL DEMONSTRATION OF THE EXISTENCE OF GOD
Metaphysical Disputations 28-29

Author: Francisco Suárez (1548-1617)
First published: Disputationer Metaphysicae, 1597 (English translation, 2004)
Edition used: The Metaphysical Demonstration of the Existence of God: Metaphysical Disputations 28-29, translated and edited by John P. Doyle. South Bend, Ind.: St. Augustine's Press, 2004
Genre: Nonfiction
Subgenres: Essays; theology
Core issues: The Deity; the divine; God

According to Suárez, the existence of God can be proven in a metaphysical manner by proving a posteriori that there must be at least one uncreated being and then proceeding a priori to establish that it is only possible for there to be one uncreated being because it is part of the essence of an uncreated being to exist and there cannot be more than one of a type of being if existence is part of its essence.

Overview

The fifty-four disputations in Francisco Suárez's *Disputationer Metaphysicae* provide a metaphysical foundation for work in theology by thoroughly analyzing the concept of being—what characteristics all beings share in common and what distinguishes the different types of beings. This work highly influenced modern philosophers such as René Descartes and Gottfried Wilhelm Leibniz. Disputations 28 and 29, the two disputations translated in *The Metaphysical Demonstration of the Existence of God*, are generally concerned with the division of being into the infinite and finite and the question of whether it is possible to prove, without recourse to divine revelation, the existence of an infinite, uncreated being—namely, God.

Disputation 28 discusses how to divide types of beings. Suárez concludes that the most apparent division of being is between the infinite and finite because of the radical disparity between God and creatures. While this is not the division that is most easily perceived by the senses, it is the most logical division and is therefore in accordance with the order of teaching. Some other divisions of being, however, are synonymous. For instance, the division of being into that which is necessary and that which is not necessary (or is contingent). A necessary being is one that must exist and cannot cease to exist. A contingent being either cannot exist or can cease to exist. Also, being can be divided into being by essence and being by participation. Being by essence means that the being has existence because of its essence (existence is a necessary attribute of the being's essence). Finally, being can be divided into uncreated and created.

Disputation 28 also addresses the question of whether the division of being is equivocal, univocal, or analogous. This is a reformulation of the question of whether the concept of being can be posited of both God and creatures. If the concept is used equivocally, it is simply taken from what is known of creatures and imposed on God in order to understand him. Suárez notes that this argument was refuted by Thomas Aquinas and that if it were true, nothing of God could be learned from knowledge of the creatures he made. If the concept of being is univocal, then it means the same thing in relation to God as to creatures. If the concept of being is analogous, however, it is extended from its meaning in creatures to apply to God by means of a likeness or proportion. Suárez concludes that the concept of being is used analogously, and thus while it is impossible to fully know the nature of God, it is possible to have a real knowledge of that nature.

Disputation 29 is concerned with the question of whether natural reason unaided by divine revelation can prove that God exists. The first question is whether it can be proven that there is an uncreated being. The second question is whether it can be proven that there is one uncreated being.

Whether there is an uncreated being can be proven in a physical or metaphysical manner. Because Suárez rejects the physical manner, he begins with the metaphysical principle that "everything which is made, is made by another. " This is true whether a thing is created, generated, or made in some other sense. This principle is proven by the fact that a thing lacks being before it is made, but for it to be made, there must be something that already has being to make it. As a result, because causation cannot proceed to infinity, there must be an uncreated being. Left unproven, however, is whether there are one or more uncreated beings.

Suárez notes that there are two basic methods of proving that there is one uncreated being, which we call God. First, the proof proceeds a posteriori, from God's effects, and the second proof proceeds partially a posteriori and partially a priori. The demonstration completely a posteriori states that beauty, order, and the interconnection of the whole universe necessarily show both that it is governed by and draws its origin from one being. Nevertheless, this proof cannot provide sufficient certainty because it is only certain as to those things that come within the bounds of human cognition by way of natural reasoning or philosophy. As a result, it is necessary to seek a demonstration of the existence of God that proceeds a priori. The demonstration a priori begins with an attribute of God that has been demonstrated a posteriori and, from that, works to a demonstration of other attributes.

The demonstration a priori begins with the demonstration a posteriori that God is a being that is necessary and self-sufficient. Recall, Suárez is attempting to prove that there must be only one uncreated being. He begins by noting that whenever it is possible for individual or singular beings to have a common character that is multiplicable (that is, they share a common essence), it is not part of their essence to be singular. Now, such singular beings are singular, but that is because, in addition to their essence, they also exist. A necessary and self-sufficient being, however, of its essence exists and is therefore singular. In other words, the existence (and, therefore, singularity) is part of the essence of an uncreated being. As a result, because singularity is part of the essence of an uncreated being, it is not possible for there to be more than one uncreated being.

Christian Themes

Because the purpose of *The Metaphysical Demonstration of the Existence of God* is to treat solely of what can be known by reason without the aid of revelation, Suárez addresses theological issues only when necessary to further explain a particular philosophical point. Nevertheless, there are a number of issues raised by Disputations 28 and 29 that are of general interest for their influence on Christian principles and issues.

The most obvious issue of interest to modern Christians is the possibility of a philosophical proof for the existence of God. Whether such a proof is even possible is still hotly contested and has been a source of continual debate among philosophers and theologians throughout modern times. The possibility of a proof still continued to receive considerable support through the time of Descartes, but such support has waned considerably since the criticisms leveled by David Hume and Immanuel Kant. Working within the tradition of negative theology, which emphasizes the incomprehensibility of God, some contemporary theologians and philosophers have questioned whether it is even appropriate to attempt to know God on a purely philosophical level.

Of a more theological nature, however, Disputations 28 and 29 contain interesting discussions of aspects of the doctrine of the Trinity (that God is three persons, but one god), of the nature of God's free will, and of how, in accordance with principles of logic, it would appear that there must have been a first man. For instance, the question about the Trinity is how the primary division of being into infinite and finite is possible because either each person in the Trinity is finite (which is impossible for divinity) or infinite (which means that infinity is multiplied). Suárez, however, concludes that there is no difficulty because the three persons share in the same divine essence— thus, they are not finite, but neither is infinity multiplied.

Sources for Further Study

Copleston, Frederick. *Later Medieval and Renaissance Philosophy: Ockham, Francis Bacon, and the Beginning of the Modern World.* Vol. 3 in *A History of Philosophy.* New York: Image Books, 1993. Copleston's nine-volume work is rightly called the best history of philosophy in the English language. His discussion of Suárez is both thorough and concise.

Doyle, John P. "Francisco Suárez: On Preaching the Gospel to People Like the American Indians." *Fordham International Law Journal* 15 (1991): 879-951. A fascinating discussion of the legal theory of one of the founders of modern international human rights doctrine.

_____. "The Suarezian Proof for God's Existence." In *History of Philosophy in the Making: A Symposium of Essays to Honor Professor James D. Collins on His Sixty-fifth Birthday*, edited by Linus J. Thro. Washington, D.C.: University

Press of America, 1982. A thorough summary and critique of Disputation 29.
Fichter, Joseph H. *Man of Spain: Francis Suarez.* New York: Macmillan, 1940. An enjoyable biography of Suárez intended for an intelligent general audience. It emphasizes the historical events surrounding Suárez's life.
Garcia, Jorge. "Francisco Suárez: The Man of History." *The American Catholic Philosophical Quarterly* 65 (1991): 259-266. A brief overview of Suárez's life and the importance of his works both in his own time and in the history of philosophy.

Joshua A. Skinner

MIDQUEST

Author: Fred Chappell (1936-   )
First published: Baton Rouge: Louisiana State University Press, 1981
Genre: Poetry
Subgenres: Autobiography; lyric poetry; narrative poetry
Core issues: Awakening; beauty; life; love; marriage

Midquest *gathers four books of poetry into a long poem so that the poet Chappell can take the measure of his existence from its origins through midlife, tracing his development as a man and an artist. Using many different forms and several distinctive narrative voices, the poem operates as a kind of "verse novel" in which the poet recalls the essential values that formed his character.*

Overview

To employ the full range of poetic forms that he had mastered, Fred Chappell drew up an intricate plan for *Midquest*, the four-volume compilation of verse that at the midpoint of a man's life recollects and takes stock of his origins, his accumulated experiences, and his sense of how he might make use of what he has learned. Each of the four separate but interlinked books—*River* (1975), *Bloodfire* (1978), *Wind Mountain* (1979), and *Earthsleep* (1980)—focuses on one of the ancient elements of the cosmos—water, fire, air, and earth. Each book consists of eleven poems that cover twenty-four hours of the poet's life from four different perspectives, although in many cases, there are extended recollections of experiences that occurred at the given hour on previous occasions. As Chappell explains, the numbers are carefully chosen and "obviously important," because "four is the Pythagorean number representing World, and 4 x 11 = 44, the world twice, interior and exterior, Etc., etc." The firm structure was necessary because Chappell wanted to employ a wide variety of verse forms, each one representing "different states of mind."

For instance, "The River Awakening in the Sea," the first poem in the book, is an open-verse interior monologue in which the poet rapturously exclaims his love for his wife in vivid, lyric language, using image clusters that convey a sense of the body alive and crackling with energy. The second poem, "Birthday 35: Diary Entry," is a reflective meditation that sets the situation, a series of couplets following Dante's well-known initiating statement "Midway in this life I came to a darksome wood" that forms the beginning of the second couplet. The third poem, "My Grandmother Washes Her Feet," is an extended monologue with interpolations functioning as a commentary on her thoughts. The sixth poem, "Dead Soldiers," introduces Virgil Campbell, a maverick individualist and a loose analogue for Dante's presentation of the Roman poet Vergil as a guide.

The seventh poem, "My Grandfather Gets Doused," is a tight arrangement of triads with an *aba, bcb* rhyme scheme deftly maintained through thirty-one stanzas before a four-line close. Chappell's maintenance of this pattern with an occasional slant rhyme but without straining or forcing the form is characteristic of his proficiency. The ninth poem, "Science Fiction Water Letter to Guy Lillian," enables the poet to bring in some of his literary friends and also operates as a kind of tour de force of compression in which Chappell gives some indication of the sort of speculative fiction he might turn to if so inclined. The last poem, "The River Again Seeks the Sea," frames the first one, completing a unit and projecting the poet and his wife into a plausible future.

Chappell says that "With this variety of forms I hoped to suggest a kind of melting pot of American quality," and in accordance with his family's heritage in the Blue Ridge mountain country of western North Carolina, he chose "that elder American art form, the sampler" as his model. Each poem is like a distinctive stitch or patch of fabric in a quilt. Within each book, there are additional organizing principles. The first poem in each book balances the last one, "and so on inward," but the sixth poem—the middle point—in each book stands alone, independent, just as its subject Virgil Campbell does. The fifth one is an interior monologue, with the flow of consciousness becoming more formal as the poet discerns and directs a growing sense of order in his life. Each separate book is devoted primarily to members of the poet's family, *River* to his grandmother and grandfather, *Fire* to his father, *Earthwind* to an extended clan in a family reunion, and *Wind Mountain* is more generalized, as in the brief sketch with the poet, his wife, and Reynolds Price in conversation ("Hallowind," set on Halloween, 1961).

The narrative consciousness is that of "Old Fred," the poet's persona who, Chappell notes, "is no more myself than any character in any novel I might choose to write." Chappell sees him as "to some extent a demographic sample," a boy raised on a farm who moved to a city, shifted from labor on the land to work with his mind, and although "cut off from his disappearing cultural traditions," is within the poem able to search for and rediscover his real values in a return to and a revitalization of an essential self. Without telling the reader too much, the poet also adds that his "deeper talents" are "apology and even recrimination," and that for the reader "some solace may be taken" from the poem. Most significantly, "Old Fred" is rooted in his region, and for Chappell this means a constant exposure in his youth to the differing versions of the old-time religion based on the Baptist faith that his family, neighbors, teachers, and preachers followed.

Christian Themes

In his introduction to *The Fred Chappell Reader* (1987), Dabney Stuart asserts that "God and the Bible suffuse *Midquest*." He points out that there are "descents into hell ('Cleaning the Well'), rebirths ('Bloodfire,' 'Fire Now Wakening on the River'), and frequent pondering on flesh and spirit ('Firewood')." It is the poet's attitude toward these experiences that is most important, because he is both a representative of a region not that familiar to most outsiders and a keen-eyed, strong-minded commentator who is far from enamored of all of the area's social, moral, and theological mores. In "Cleaning the Well," the fourth poem in *River*, the poet as a boy is ready to accept his responsibilities, a typical hard task performed in December, the dark of winter, but is fully aware of the strange place he is descending toward. "Lord, I sank/ Like an anchor," he recalls, mingling dread with a prayer for protection. Further down, he exclaims, "Whoo! It's *God/ Damn* cold!" continuing to combat "pain, disgust, and fear," while his entreaties are answered from above with an offhand humor—"Say, Fred, how's it going down there?"—until he is hauled back to earth. At first relieved, he discovers the power of the experience, and "shut my eyes to fetch/ Back holy dark," affirming his kinship with biblical predecesors ("Jonah, Joseph, Lazarus") who returned after a dark vision. His conclusion "*I had not found death good*" is mitigated by his father's casual "'Aw, you're all right,'" which is effectively the motto for moments of fear like this one. Another vision of Hell, this one resembling Dante's circles of the damned (poem 7 in *Wind Mountain*), is a wry commentary on some of Chappell's poetic peers.

The poet's amused but respectful portrayal of the communal religious mode is reflected in two other poems from *River*. The process of baptism is seen from two directions in poem 7, "My Grandfather Gets Doused" which is a high-spirited account of a reluctant, almost offhand baptism as his grandfather "hedged his final bet" in a "Cold river and a plague/ Of cold Baptist stares," and a much more fervent recounting of his grandmother's young womanhood and marriage in poem 8, where the crossing of a river is a sign of a true spiritual commitment. Chappell has a wary skepticism toward the extravagant, dogmatic fervor of the more organized religious institutions he encounters ("too many ragshank preachers") while remaining very interested in the ways people express their faith in things.

His own faith is marked by his deep feeling for the natural world, as in "Fire Now Wakening on the River" (among many other poems), in which he describes himself as "fresh born at thirty-five," a kind of resurrection from a dormant self, following a vivid romantic moment that he likens to "a forest of fire," "green growth" and "boiled juices of poison oak." The intellectual journey that the poet pursues tends to work against any easy acceptance of doctrine, and in "Firewood," poem 5 in *Bloodfire* (the stream of conscious), he confesses, with respect to "Christmas/ on Earth" that "even as I recall the beautiful/ manifesto my faith flickers and dwindles." Against this, he sets the power of his surroundings, claiming "I'm washed in the blood/ of the sun, the ghostly holy of the deep deep log." In "Earthsleep," he finds a true Eden, a divine place, in the love he shares with his wife, Susan.

> The love that moves the sun and other stars
> The love that moves itself in light to loving
> Flames up like dew
> Here in the earliest morning of the world.

Sources for Further Study

Bizzaro, Patrick, ed. *Dream Garden: The Poetic Vision of Fred Chappell*. Baton Rouge: University of Louisiana Press, 1997. A good overview of Chappell's poetry, with several extended essays on *Midquest*.

Lang, John. *Understanding Fred Chappell*. Columbia: University of South Carolina
    Press, 2000. Discusses *Midquest* with respect to Dantean allusions and parallels
    with classical mythology.
Stuart, Dabney. Introduction to *The Fred Chappell Reader* by Fred Chappell. New
    York: Saint Martin's Press, 1987. Stuart's introduction concentrates on *Midquest*.

Leon Lewis

THE MIND OF THE MAKER

Author: Dorothy L. Sayers (1893-1957)
First published: 1941
Edition used: The Mind of the Maker. San Francisco: Harper & Row, 1987
Genre: Nonfiction
Subgenres: Critical analysis; spiritual treatise; theology
Core issues: Creation; God; Holy Spirit; Incarnation; Jesus Christ; the Trinity

Sayers's goal in The Mind of the Maker *is to be an explicator of—rather than an apologist for—the doctrine of the Trinity as articulated in the Apostles' Creed and the Nicene and Athanasian creeds. She explains the Trinity in unity by way of analogy to the writer's process of creation; she also explains the writer's process of creation by means of Trinitarian doctrine. Sayers then explores the nature of work and laments the modern tendency to desacralize labor.*

Overview

In her preface, Dorothy Sayers clearly states what *The Mind of the Maker* is not. She argues that contemporary knowledge of Christian theology is appallingly limited and that true literacy among the supposedly literate is often absent; consequently, statements of fact are frequently confused with statements of belief. *The Mind of the Maker* is neither an articulation of Sayers's beliefs nor an apology for the beliefs of others. Rather, it is an explanation of the Catholic Church's statements about the nature of God. More specifically, she intends to explicate the doctrine of the Triune God as it has been stated in the Apostles' Creed, the Nicene Creed, and the Athanasian Creed.

In dealing with the divine mystery of the Trinity, Sayers approaches mystery in a different sense than that for which she is usually known. She addresses the differences between the mysteries of detective fiction and the mysteries of life at the end of the work.

In an introductory chapter, Sayers distinguishes between fact and opinion, argues that the Christian creeds purport to be statements of fact about the world and its creator, and indicates that she intends to explain these facts, then she turns to her subject in earnest.

Genesis begins by showing God as a maker. It then says he made man and woman in his image. Therefore, Sayers argues, one part of the image in which human beings were made is creativity: We are able to make things. Our understanding of God usually comes from the analogy of God as father, which does not tax the imagination too much. We imagine an ideal human father and compare his characteristics with God's. When we want to understand God's fatherly nature, we turn to fathers. However, when we want to understand his creative nature, we must turn to creative artists. By doing so, we gain the additional benefit of understanding more about the Trinity because the writer (the kind of creative artist that Sayers understands best, though the principles apply equally to other artists) is a trinity that reflects the creator of all things.

The Athanasian Creed states that there are three persons in the godhead—Father, Son, and Holy Spirit—but only one godhead. The three persons are eternally co-equal; they are distinguishable but indivisible. No one of them can (or does) exist without the other two, yet there are not three gods but one God.

This trinity exists in the writer as well. In the ideal writer, the three persons are co-equal, but Sayers notes that the three are often out of balance (even if only slightly), and she addresses what happens when that is the case toward the end of the work. Sayers's terminology for the trinity of the writer, drawn and expanded from the ending speech of her play *The Zeal of Thy House*, is Idea (corresponding to the Father), Energy (the Son), and Power (the Holy Spirit). All three are present, each contains the whole work, and each is the whole work.

The Idea is eternally present. It can be discovered only by the writer working it out in the Energy, but it is not limited by its working out in the Energy.

The Energy (also called the Activity) comprises everything the writer does in time and space to put the work together. Thinking about the work, making notes, and writing all fall into this category. The Energy is the Word made flesh. The Power is the communication of the work to others. As Sayers goes on to argue, this is both a social and an individual phenomenon. The writer becomes the reader of the work, and the response of the reader (whoever it may be) is part of the pattern.

These three can be distinguished, but they cannot be divided. The Idea can be revealed only through the Energy; the Energy finds its being in reflecting and working out the Idea; without the Power, neither the Energy nor the Idea could be communicated; and without the Energy and the Idea, the Power would have nothing to communicate.

The rest of the book examines this thesis while also incorporating other ideas from the creeds. For example, in "The Energy Revealed in Creation," Sayers points out that the work of the creative artist can reveal how God can be both immanent and transcendent: William Shakespeare's creative output is immanent, but Shakespeare himself is transcendent. In "Pentecost," she explores the work of the Holy Spirit in its role of aiding belief. The reader, encountering a work at a given point in history, will point toward its Idea (which must be taken on faith) and its Energy (which is manifest in the book as read).

In "Free Will and Miracle," Sayers offers some insight into her specific creative process in writing *Gaudy Night* and *Murder Must Advertise*. She attempts to demonstrate that forcing the characters to serve some authorial end will falsify them and the work itself, while giving them their independence will serve the needs of truth.

In the last two sections, Sayers applies the theory. Modern life is often presented as a series of problems to be solved and not as raw material with which we may work. However, the artist reveals that you need to cooperate with your materials rather than try to become the master of them. Life is not a mathematical problem or a detective story.

The popularity of the detective story lies in the ways in which it differs from life. Sayers offers a list of four ways in which the problems presented in detective fiction differ from the materials presented by life (which should not be called problems at all). Problems in detective fiction can always.be solved; they can always be solved completely; they are solved on their own terms; and when they are solved, they are completely ended.

Life does not work in this way, Sayers says. Instead of seeking solutions, we should look for a creative synthesis of the materials brought to us. Only by creative activity can we turn the evils of the world to good.

Christian Themes

In addition to the deep meditation on the nature of the Trinity and on the role of each of its persons, the work calls Christians to think and to act on their having been created in the image of God, the creator of all things.

Sayers's exploration of the origin of evil is one place where Sayers advises us to act creatively. The creation of the character Hamlet simultaneously created the category of not-Hamlet (potential evil). With David Garrick's rewriting of *Hamlet*, anti-Hamlet (or positive evil) entered the world. By looking at Garrick as a problem to be solved, we may right an evil, but we have not redeemed it. The redemption of evil—turning it to positive good—can come about only through creativity. When we laugh at Garrick, parody him, or write him into an example of literary evil, we creatively redeem the evil he has done. This redemption must take place on the same terms as the evil, just as Christ's redemption had to take place on the same terms as the evil created—those of experience in matter.

Sayers calls Christians to recognize that the reflection of the Trinity is contained in every man and woman. The Christian approach to work must reflect this; the Christian must love creation and recognize that work is creation.

Sources for Further Study

Downing, Crystal. *Writing Performances: The Stages of Dorothy L. Sayers*. New York: Palgrave Macmillan, 2004. Chapter 4, "Minding the Performance," compares Sayers and Bakhtin on the incarnational theory of literary criticism and on their statements about the hero's autonomous nature.

Kennedy, Catherine. *The Remarkable Case of Dorothy L. Sayers*. Kent, Ohio: Kent State University Press, 1990. Contains a chapter devoted to *The Mind of the Maker*. Kennedy provides analyses of Sayers's work and of her contributions to the many fields with which she was associated.

Reynolds, Barbara. *Dorothy L. Sayers: Her Life and Soul*. New York: St. Martin's Griffin, 1993. A more authoritative and scholarly biography than earlier ones, the work provides overview, detail, and analysis of Sayers' life and work in almost equal measure.

Simmons, Laura K. *Creed Without Chaos: Exploring Theology in the Writings of Dorothy L. Sayers*. Grand Rapids, Mich.: Baker Academic, 2005. A book that, in its approach to *The Mind of the Maker*, focuses on its views of work and of the incarnational nature of creativity.

Webster, Richard T. "*The Mind of the Maker*: Logical Construction, Creative Choice, and the Trinity." In *As Her Whimsey Took Her: Critical Essays on the Work of Dorothy L. Sayers*, edited by Margaret P. Hannay. Kent, Ohio: Kent State University Press, 1979. An analysis of the philosophical strategies used in the work. Examines Sayers's approach to metaphysics. Compares the view of Sayers with that of Saint Augustine.

Keith Jones

THE MIND'S ROAD TO GOD

Author: Saint Bonaventure (Giovanni di Fidanza; 1217/1221-1274)

First transcribed: Itinerarium mentis in Deum, 1259 (*The Journey of the Soul to God*, 1937; also as *The Mind's Road to God*, 1953, and *The Journey of the Mind to God*, 1993)

Edition used: The Mind's Road to God, translated with an introduction by George Boas. New York: Liberal Arts Press, 1953

Genre: Nonfiction

Subgenres: Allegory; guidebook; instructional manual; mysticism; spiritual treatise

Core issues: Contemplation; the divine; God; illumination; soul; the Trinity; union with God

Saint Bonaventure tells the story of his ascent of Mount Alverna to meditate and seek spiritual peace in the very place where Saint Francis experienced the miraculous vision of the crucified Seraph—and of his own visions and spiritual insights.

Overview

Giovanni di Fidanza was born in central Italy near Viterbo in 1221. He studied under Alexander of Hales at the University of Paris, where he later became a professor of theology. He entered the Franciscan order in 1242, was made general of the Franciscans in 1257, and became bishop of Albano in 1273. Gregory X made him a cardinal shortly before Bonaventure's death in 1274. He was canonized by Sixtus IV in 1482 and in the sixteenth century was made a doctor of the Church by Sixtus V. Bonaventure's other notable works include *De reductione artium ad theologiam* (before 1274; *On the Recution of the Arts to Theology*, 1938) and *De triplici via* (1260; *The Enkindling of Love, Also Called the Triple Way*, 1956).

In the prologue to *The Mind's Road to God*, Saint Bonaventure tells of ascending Mount Alverna thirty-three years after the death of Saint Francis and shortly after having become minister general of the Franciscans to meditate and seek spiritual peace in the very place where Saint Francis had experienced the miraculous vision of the crucified Seraph. While in that place Bonaventure had the same vision, and he reports, "While looking upon this vision, I immediately saw that it signified the suspension of our father himself in contemplation and the way by which he came to it."

The six wings of the Seraph, he writes, are to be understood as signifying the six stages of spiritual illumination by which the soul ascends to God. The way is only by the blood of the Lamb, Bonaventure adds, for the six stages of illumination begin with God's creatures and lead up to God only "through the Crucified." (The recounting of the miraculous vision illuminates Bonaventure's subtitle, "The Mendicant's Vision in the Wilderness," and makes understandable Bonaventure's honorific designation as "The Seraphic Doctor.")

The basic image of Bonaventure's spiritual allegory is that of a six-winged angel, seen as bearing three pairs of wings, each pair symbolizing one of the three major phases in the ascent to God. The first pair of stages involves reflecting on the sensible, corporeal world; the second pair consists in the contemplation of the mind's own powers; the third is contemplation of God's essence. The ascent to God, then, calls for seeing God through and in the body, then through and in the mind, and, finally, through and in the features of pure being. Bonaventure accordingly divides his treatise into seven chapters, the first six having to do with the six stages of illumination, and the seventh with the mystical experience of the union with God by which peace comes to the spirit.

Throughout his account of the stages in the ascent to God Bonaventure emphasizes that the securing of beatitude, the "fruition of the highest good," requires divine help. None can be blessed, the saint writes, "unless he ascend above himself, not by the ascent of his body but by that of his heart," and then he adds, "But we cannot be raised above ourselves except by a higher power raising us up."

Prayer is vitally important also, Bonaventure writes. Divine help comes to those who seek it by means of prayer "from their hearts humbly and devoutly." Just as Bonaventure himself was illuminated about the stages in the ascent to God only after having humbly and devoutly prayed on Mount Alverna, so others can find through prayer the kind of knowledge needed for the ascent.

The world is a ladder for ascending to God because just as a work of art reveals much about the artist, so the world bears traces of God's hand. Accordingly, Bonaventure advises, "we ought to proceed through the traces which are corporeal and temporal and outside us; and this is to be led into the way of God." To seek God through recognizing and appreciating the signs of his creative power in the world we sense is the first mode of understanding and ascent.

The second mode of understanding is by taking our own minds as the objects of reflection, for our minds "are the eternal image of God, spiritual and internal." Having learned the *way* of God by examining the world, we proceed to awareness of the *truth* of God through and in our minds.

The third and final mode of ascent is by turning our minds to what is "eternal, most spiritual, and above us," the First Principle of being, God himself.

Bonaventure summarizes his preliminary account of the three modes of understanding and ascent by calling attention to the three aspects or, one might say, prospects of the mind. In the first mode, the mind refers to body, "whereby it is called animality or sensuality"; the mind then looks into itself, and in that aspect it is spirit; finally, the mind looks above itself, and here it is properly called "mind." Body, spirit, and mind, then, are aspects of the soul realized in the contemplative ascent to God.

These three modes are twofold, he next comments, "in so far as we happen to see God in one of the aforesaid modes as *through* a mirror and *in* a mirror." Thus, just as God made the world in six days and rested on the seventh, so the "microcosm," the soul, "by six successive stages of illumination is led in the most orderly fashion to the repose of contemplation."

Corresponding to the six stages of ascent are the six stages of the soul's powers by which that ascent is made; namely, sense, imagination, reason, intellect, intelligence, and "the illumination of conscience." These powers of the soul must be exercised through prayer, holy living, and striving for truth by way of the sixfold ascent.

The soul can become aware of God's power, wisdom, and benevolence by contemplating, believing, and reasoning: By the contemplation of created things one may come to understand the significance of their actual existence; by believing one can become aware of the significance of the habitual course of things; and by reasoning one can grasp the principles of things and their potential excellence.

Having explained in chapter 1 how the soul by the use of its powers can begin the ascent to God by reflecting on the traces of God to be found in the created, corporeal things outside us, Bonaventure proceeds in chapter 2 to explain how one can move from seeing God *through* the objects of our senses to seeing God *in* the sensible world.

Bonaventure declares: We *apprehend* the world through the five senses. We then *delight* in the natural form, power, and operations of things. Finally, we *judge* insofar as we use our intellectual powers of abstraction to appreciate the principles of things. It is the "number" in things, their rhythmical proportion, that is the primary trace of God. Through apprehension, responsive delight, and intellectual judgment, then, we realize the power, wisdom, and goodness of God.

In the third chapter Bonaventure calls upon us to enter into ourselves, to examine our own minds as the mirror through which God can be seen, for in our minds "the divine image shines."

To see the reflection of God in our minds requires use of the powers of memory, intellect, and choice. Memory enables us to retain and represent all things present, past, future, simple, and eternal. (According to Bonaventure, memory "retains the past by recalling it, the present by receiving it, the future by foreseeing it.") Memory, intelligence, and will reflect the Blessed Trinity, "Father, Word, and Love," Bonaventure concludes; memory leads to eternity, intelligence to truth, the power of choice to goodness. Thus, the soul in the "trinity of its powers" is "the image of God."

Bonaventure turns now to "The Reflection of God in His Image Reformed by the Gifts of Grace." He begins chapter 4 with the remark that "since not only by passing through ourselves but also within ourselves is it given to us to contemplate the First Principle, and this is greater than the preceding, therefore this mode of thought reaches to the fourth level of contemplation." The emphasis is on the word *in*; on the third level of contemplation the soul recognized the powers of God *through* contemplation on the mind's powers, but now one is called upon to see God *in* the mind.

No one, however, can be illuminated and find the First Principle in the finite, created mind who does not receive the gift of grace. The soul cannot intuit the divine in itself unless "the Truth, having assumed human power in Christ, should make itself into a ladder, repairing the first ladder which was broken in Adam." We are called upon, therefore, to "believe in Him, hope in Him, and love Him"; Christ will then be the Mediator by whom the soul can so enter into itself as to find and accordingly take delight in the Lord *in* itself.

The third mode of contemplation, the fifth and sixth stages of the ascent to God, may now be undertaken. Bonaventure reminds us that we may contemplate God not only *outside* ourselves through his traces and *inside* ourselves through his reflected image in the mind, but also *above* ourselves "through His light, which has signed upon our minds the light of eternal Truth." By reflection on God as *Being*, one realizes God's essential attributes (this would be the fifth stage); and then by knowing God as *Goodness*, one would know the three Persons of God (the sixth stage).

Bonaventure advises (in chapter 5, "Of the Reflection of the Divine Unity in Its Primary Name Which Is Being"), "If you wish then to contemplate the invisible traits of God in so far as they belong to the unity of His essence, fix your gaze upon Being itself." God is pure Being in that there is nothing of nonbeing in God and there is absolute actuality. Pure Being is divine.

We are accustomed to thinking of particular beings and of potentialities and possibilities, and often we are absorbed with what is not actual; hence, it is difficult to fasten our minds on being, pure being that is Being, the divine unity that is God. Bonaventure writes of the "blindness of the intellect" and of the "mind's eye, intent upon particular and universal beings" that accordingly does not contemplate Being itself. However, if one can concentrate on pure Being, Bonaventure writes, "If you see this in the pure simplicity of your mind, you will somehow be infused with the illumination of eternal light."

In chapter 6, "Of the Reflection of the Most Blessed Trinity in Its Name, Which Is Good," Bonaventure begins by developing a point introduced at the close of the previous chapter; namely, that pure Being is goodness, the Good. The Good is the foundation of the contemplation of the "divine emanations," the Trinity. Since the Good is better than nonbeing, "it cannot rightly be thought of unless conceived as both three and one." The Good must be "self-diffusive"; that is, the Good must be productive of good, pouring forth love and receiving love; it must be Word and Gift in virtue of being Good; it must be Father, Son, and Holy Ghost. Hence, as pure Being, God is unity and the Good, but since the Good is necessarily a Trinity, God is necessarily both Unity and Trinity.

Bonaventure's effort to reconcile polarities and resolve paradoxes is more a celebration of God's essence and emanations than it is a clarification. The emphasis is on the blessedness of God and the wonders of discovery at the heights of contemplation. Bonaventure's principal theme remains clear even in the midst of his most intellectual, theological efforts: By reflecting on the world outside, the soul inside, and the God above, one is brought to the elevated condition of repose in the presence of God.

In the closing chapter of his work, Bonaventure emphasizes the proposition of faith that the passage up the six steps of contemplation to the seventh stage of repose and illumination by supreme wisdom is made possible by Christ: "In this passage Christ is the way and the door, Christ is the stairway and the vehicle, like the propitiary over the ark of God and the mystery which has been hidden from eternity."

The seventh and final stage of mental and mystical elevation (of the kind granted to both Saint Francis and Bonaventure on the heights of Mount Alverna by the vision of the seraph with six wings nailed to the cross) is one in which all intellectual operations cease, "and the whole height of our affection should be transferred and transformed into God." This ultimate stage of elevation, Bonaventure adds, is "mystical and most secret, which no man knoweth but he that hath received it."

Despite his effort to describe the mind's six stages in the passage that culminates in the unifying experience of divine illumination, Bonaventure exultantly concedes that "If you should ask how these things come about, question grace, not instruction; desire, not intellect; the cry of prayer, not pursuit of study; the spouse, not the teacher; God, not man; darkness, not clarity; not light, but the wholly flaming fire which will bear you aloft to God with fullest unction and burning affection."

Christian Themes

The Mind's Road to God allegorizes the Christian spiritual path as follows: The six wings of the Seraph correspond to the six stages of illumination by which the soul ascends to God. Six stages of the soul's powers enable us to ascend by six stages to God: sense, imagination, reason, intellect, intelligence, and conscience. We may ascend to God by reflecting on his traces in the sensible world, by considering our natural powers as reflecting God, and by achieving illumination through Christ as mediator. Each of these three modes of understanding is twofold: We see God through them and in them.

The six stages, then, are these: We understand God through sensible things as bearing the traces of his creative power; we see God in sensible things as essence, potency, and presence; we enter our own minds and see God's image stamped upon our natural powers; by grace we see the First Principle in ourselves; by reflecting on pure being, we know God as unity; by reflecting on the goodness of pure being, we know God as Trinity.

Sources for Further Study

Bonaventure, Saint. *Bonaventure: "The Soul's Journey into God," "The Tree of Life," "The Life of St. Francis."* Translated with an introduction by Ewert Cousins. New York: Paulist Press, 1978. This is a useful and clear presentation of three of Saint Bonaventure's most important writings.

Bougerol, Jacques Guy. *Introduction to the Works of Bonaventure.* Translated by José de Vinck. Paterson, N.J.: St. Anthony Guild Press, 1964. A helpful guide to Bonaventure's principal works.

Cullen, Christopher M. *Bonaventure.* New York: Oxford University Press, 2006. A concise volume in the publisher's Great Medieval Thinkers series, introducing Bonaventure's thought for a student and general audience. Bibliography, index.

Gilson, Étienne. *The Philosophy of St. Bonaventure.* Translated by Dom Illtyd Trethowan and F. J. Sheed. New York: Sheed & Ward, 1938. Gilson's scholarly analysis enhances his careful presentation of the historical context of Bonaventure's life and works.

Ian P. McGreal

THE MIRACLE OF THE BELLS

Author: Russell Janney (1884-1963)
First published: New York: Prentice-Hall, 1946
Genre: Novel
Subgenres: Catholic fiction; evangelical fiction
Core issues: Awakening; charity; faith; hope; love; social action

When an unknown young movie actress dies of tuberculosis, her brokenhearted admirer, an unemployed press agent, determines to give her the burial she deserves in her Pennsylvania coal-mining hometown. His promotional efforts and those of an idealistic local priest persuade her producer to release her movie and propel the dead girl into stardom. As a result, a nationwide chain reaction of interdenominational charity and goodwill transforms the lives of thousands of previously bitter and oppressed miners.

> *Principal characters*
> *Bill Dunnigan*, a flashy press agent
> *Olga Trocki*, a young Polish American actress
> *Marcus Harris*, a movie magnate who hires and fires Bill
> *Father Paul*, an idealistic but poor Coaltown priest
> *Father Spinsky*, a selfish and calculating priest
> *Jan Rubel*, the miners' union boss
> *Grace Hanover*, the mine's owner
> *Andrev*, a nature child

Overview

The Miracle of the Bells shows how much good one man, motivated by love and altruism, can engender in the world. As the novel opens, the unemployed press agent Bill Dunnigan arrives in Coaltown, an ugly immigrant mining town, with the coffin of one of its citizens, a young actress named Olga Trocki who was the daughter of a Polish ne'er-do-well. Bill had originally discovered Olga in a dance revue and helped her to an eventual starring role in a major Hollywood motion picture. Upon finishing the movie, however, Olga died of tuberculosis. Now the angry producer, Marcus Harris, has refused to release the film.

Olga wished burial in her hometown, so Bill is honoring her request. With his last dollars, he hires an undertaker and visits a priest about having the church bells rung, another of Olga's wishes. He meets Father Paul, the young, shabby priest of St. Michael's who considers himself a failure because parishioners do not value his advice for improving life in Coaltown and forsake his parish for better-heeled churches. Father Paul will not charge for the funeral, and Bill feels grateful and generous. In turn,

Father Paul feels Bill is an answer to his prayer, to bring new hope to Coaltown. The two men become friends and determine to fight their way back up. Bill feels Olga's spirit is with him, and that God, Saint Michael, and Father Paul could do with a good press agent.

Bill gets the idea to have all five local churches ring their bells continuously for five days for Olga, and he uses all his savings as a down payment for this service. Once the bells start ringing, everyone in town tries to discover the reason and learns about Olga. A mob of the curious and the press descend on Bill's hotel. He tells the Cinderella story of the poor local girl who made good in the movies, plugs her film, and spends his last dollar on a telegram to Harris in Radio City, asking for ten thousand dollars to save Harris's million-dollar investment in the shelved movie. Harris discovers that the Olga story is in all the papers. Reading good things about himself and the movie, he changes his mind and wires Bill twenty thousand dollars to continue publicizing the film.

As interest in the bells and in Olga spreads, one hundred people show up for Father Paul's mass and donate generously. Father Spinsky, a rival priest, schemes to have the funeral moved to his own church. When Bill refuses, he demands exorbitant extra fees for continuing the bell ringing. Scrambling to borrow money, Bill prays for the first time in years. With Harris's money, Bill spreads hope all over Coaltown. He invests in a young entrepreneur, Robert, who wants to open a lunchroom. Robert in turn persuades the local police (his relatives) not to arrest Bill for public disturbance. When Bill pays Father Spinsky for five days of bell ringing, Spinsky begins to wonder if Bill is Saint Michael in disguise, repents of his stinginess, and sends boxes of candles over to St. Michael's for use by the crowds who are flocking to Mass there. He sends one of his sister's famous chocolate cakes to Bill, who likes it so much he offers to set the sister up with a radio cooking show. She too repents and decides to offer her help to St. Michael's.

Father Paul awakes the next morning to discover that his statues have miraculously turned to face Olga's coffin. This event brings even greater crowds and publicity to St. Michael's. Although Paul thinks the church's foundation has shifted as a result of subterranean mine tunnels, the visiting bishop persuades him not to crush the people's faith that a miracle has occurred. Bill gives press conferences, arranges for nationwide broadcasts from St. Michael's, and distributes placards around town publicizing Father Paul's early "miners' Mass." He meets Jan Rubel, the miners' union boss, and asks him to promote this mass in the union. The belligerent Rubel, an atheist, refuses and takes a swing at Bill. Bill knocks him out, which makes Rubel respect him, and the two become allies.

Nationwide publicity for the "miracle of the bells" brings the aristocratic and suspicious mine owner, Grace Hanover, to Coaltown, where Bill greets her and disarms her by asking her to arrange the mountains of flowers arriving from all over for the funeral. Politicians and movie stars, moved by the press stories and eager to share in the limelight, also arrange to be present as pallbearers. The funeral is a huge gathering of love and service that transcends all creeds and rituals. Bill feels Olga's presence there.

At the cemetery afterward, her old friend Andrev, a nature child who is "not quite right in the head," confirms that he sees and hears her.

The morning after the funeral, one thousand miners attend Father Paul's 5:00 A.M. mass, parading through the streets with headlamps lighted, singing "Onward, Christian Soldiers." Miss Hanover has pledged to build a new hospital in Coaltown. Lightning strikes the old mine tower, which will be replaced with new, safer machinery. The atmosphere of the town has changed from grim hopelessness to faith, optimism, and the desire to help others.

Christian Themes

The principal theme of *The Miracle of the Bells* is individual transformation. Protagonist Bill Dunnigan starts out as a cynical, worldly press agent who prides himself on his ability to manipulate public opinion. The idealistic and luminous young Olga brings him out of himself, and he becomes eager to make life better for her. This leads to a quest to improve life also for Father Paul, then the citizens of Coaltown and others as well. Father Paul, introverted and discouraged, is also transformed into a courageous young priest unafraid of his parishioners and determined to succeed in bettering their lives.

As Bill spreads his goodwill and money around Coaltown, others are also transformed from enemies into allies by the power of love and fellowship. Father Spinsky, formerly greedy and uncharitable, responds to Bill's love and becomes humble and eager to help Father Paul and others. Hard-nosed producer Marcus Harris learns to think of more than the bottom line. The police, union officials, beaten-down miners, the contemptuous mine owner, and even national political and entertainment stars catch the vision of Olga's naïve yearning to help others and find enjoyment in working together to lift Coaltown and its citizens to a better life.

Along with the contagious nature of brotherly love, another theme of the novel is the eternal nature of the soul. Olga's spirit survives after death, appearing to Bill and to her childlike former friend, Andrev, to give encouragement and inspiration. Father Spinsky is also spurred to reform by a vision of Olga's dead father, an alcoholic who was turned away from St. Leo's years before. Bill becomes convinced that Saint Michael, patron of Father Paul's church, is helping him with his quest. Readers, however, are left to form their own conclusions about the miraculous turning of the Saint Michael's statues to face Olga's casket. While the settling of foundations over mine shafts is mentioned, the question is left open as to why it occurs at this particular time, in this particular way. The primary miracle referred to in the novel's title, however, is what happens in the lives of individuals when they soften their hearts toward their fellows and learn the joy of good works.

Sources for Further Study

Bazelton, David T. Review of *The Miracle of the Bells*. In *Books in Review*. New York: Prentice-Hall, 1946. Bazelton pans the implied relationship between Hollywood and religion in the novel, as well as the oversimplification of good and evil.

Carlson, Marvin. "Janney, Russell Dixon, 1884-1963." *American National Biography* 11 (1999): 858-859. Discusses *The Miracle of the Bells* as somewhat autobiographical and details political and commercial effects of its popularity and messages.

Jacobs, Harvey C. "*The Miracle of the Bells*: Freedom Rings." *Vital Speeches of the Day* 23, no. 5 (December 15, 1956): 130-132. Relates the unselfishness and community engendered in the novel to pride in the past of American education and hope for the future.

Sally B. Palmer

MISQUOTING JESUS
The Story Behind Who Changed the Bible and Why

Author: Bart D. Ehrman (1955-   )
First published: New York: HarperSanFrancisco, 2005
Genre: Nonfiction
Subgenres: Church history; critical analysis
Core issues: The Bible; Gospels; scriptures; the Word

Given the diversity within ancient manuscripts, it is understandable that intelligent, well-meaning readers have interpreted scriptures differently. Before the printing press, manuscripts of New Testament books were copied and recopied by scribes, whose changes influenced both Bible canon and subsequent interpretations. Scholars of textual criticism have analyzed those changes, concluding that some resulted from errors and others were intended to reinforce specific doctrines or refute specific critics of Christianity.

Overview

Misquoting Jesus is both Bart D. Ehrman's spiritual autobiography and an introduction to textual criticism of the New Testament. The same quest for certainty that drew the teenaged Ehrman to "born-again Christianity" and faith in "verbal, plenary inspiration" of the Bible ultimately led him to believe that the New Testament is essentially a "human" book—written, copied, translated, and interpreted by human beings.

Ehrman initially describes the process and problems associated with formation of the early Christian canon, pointing out the role of liturgy and the need to refute early heretics and pagan critics. Demonstrating that Christianity, like Judaism, is a "textually oriented religion," Ehrman illustrates problems of textual reliability confronting the church of the first three centuries, when few members were fully literate and most copyists were not professional scribes. Some difficulties arose from the *scripto continua* Greek manuscript style (which used no punctuation, no distinction between uppercase and lowercase letters, and no spacing between words); in other instances, entire passages appear to have been added in an attempt to incorporate additional stories that were part of a parallel Christian tradition.

While praising accurate copying by some early scribes (those in Alexandria), Eherman observes that truly professional copying became the norm only after the conversion of Roman emperor Constantine. Near the end of the fourth century, the Greek manuscripts were translated into an official Latin version known as the Vulgate (Common) Bible. Until the fifteenth century, texts continued to be copied in two versions: Greek (Byzantine) in the East and Latin (Vulgate) in the West. While there soon were fifty printed editions of the Vulgate, a printed Greek version was not attempted until the early sixteenth century. In the most influential Greek text (1516),

Erasmus attempted to reconcile available Greek manuscripts but sometimes resorted to translating the Vulgate back into Greek. His five editions continued to be the standard Greek text for three hundred years.

Modern textual criticism began when Oxford scholar John Mill collated approximately one hundred early manuscripts into a Greek text with variant readings in a "critical apparatus." Mill's text exacerbated existing controversies concerning the scriptures' reliability as a doctrinal guide. Modern textual critics have cataloged more than fifty-seven hundred Greek manuscripts (four basic types) and ten thousand Vulgate manuscripts. From this evidence, scholars attempt to reconstruct the earliest versions and explain changes. Ehrman devotes a chapter to contributions of important eighteenth and nineteenth century pioneers and another to describing modern methods of textual criticism. Examining specific examples of variations, he outlines the use of external and internal evidence to determine not only the earliest version but also likely reasons for changes.

Analyzing what he considers scribes' deliberate changes, Ehrman focuses on their relationship to a second and third century theological issue: the divine and human natures of Christ. He asserts that most changes served to advance what he calls the "proto-orthodox" view of Jesus as fully human and fully divine, and he cites examples of several passages modified to refute major heresies.

Probably the book's most controversial chapter, "The Social Worlds of the Text," details the theological implications of the changes Ehrman has described, specifically as they reflect early Christian attitudes toward Jews, pagans, and women. Ehrman believes that early Christians had to portray as "recalcitrant and blind" those Jews who rejected Christianity; this antipathy continued for several centuries. Discussing Christians' interaction with pagan communities (neither Jewish nor Christian), Ehrman explains the causes and extent of religious persecution; many long-held church traditions he debunks as myths. Concerning the ongoing disagreement about women's status in the Church, he observes at least two Gospels indicating that Jesus' female disciples "alone remained faithful to him at the end, when the male disciples had fled," and he sees special significance in the fact that according to all four Gospel accounts, Mary Magdalene, alone or with other women, was the first to be told of the Resurrection. Ehrman carefully examines the role of women in the early church, concluding that several textual changes have minimized contributions of women such as Phoebe, Prisca, and Julia—in fact apparently changing the name of one "apostle" from the common female name Junia to a masculine form for which "there is no evidence in the ancient world."

In the concluding chapter, Ehrman returns to discussion of his personal quest and its resolution. After years spent analyzing, collating, and interpreting early manuscripts, Ehrman still believes in the validity of searching for the "original" New Testament text, but he has also come to believe that this is "a very human book," influenced by attitudes and limitations of the original writers as well as those of later scribes. He concludes with a position akin to reader-response literary criticism, seeing accurate interpretation as a personal interaction between reader and work.

Christian Themes

Ehrman's view of textual critics as detectives piecing together manuscript clues is obvious throughout *Misquoting Jesus*. His careful examination and collation of multiple manuscript fragments reflect his undergraduate training as an English major; adapting tools of literary analysis to study of early manuscripts, he examines these for linguistic clues and reflections of cultural attitudes. Like literary scholars, he attempts to make obscure texts accessible to interested readers.

From the outset, the central issue for Ehrman is the inerrancy of the scriptures. This book records his quest for a text that his reason will allow him to accept as divinely inspired. Beginning with a belief that the Bible is literally the product of word-by-word inspiration (verbal, plenary inspiration), Ehrman confronted the problem of textual differences, an especially thorny issue since no extant manuscript can be identified as the "original" or even a direct copy of the original.

A major function of textual critics is to examine existing manuscripts and attempt to distinguish the most authentic. The first task is to address the claims of various "gospels" and other narratives, then to determine why some were included in the canon while others were excluded. This process of evaluation and explanation requires that each be reviewed in terms of numerous heresies confronting the early church.

Even after the "orthodox" canon was generally accepted, however, manuscript versions of that canon continued to differ. Ehrman classifies these variations as copying errors or intentional changes. Although he does not enumerate many copying errors, his explanation of how they occurred seems plausible. Nevertheless, for Erdman the existence of even minor copying errors seems to cast doubt on the doctrine of verbal, plenary inspiration.

Accurately assessing Ehrman's discussion of scribes' intentional changes requires more knowledge of biblical Greek than the average reader is likely to possess. Because his intent is illustrative rather than persuasive, Ehrman cites relatively few examples of changes made to address heresies and other theological controversies. His discussions are detailed, but although these explanations seem reasonable, even cursory research suggests that some biblical scholars disagree.

A major concern for Ehrman is the implications of these variations for modern readers of the canon. Though unwilling to dismiss the idea of searching for the "original" text, he has come to regard the Scriptures as "a very human book," in which individual writers made conscious editorial decisions in much the same way scribes and modern readers have made decisions about interpretation. In effect, then, Ehrman concludes that probably the most positive effect of textual criticism is that it leads to tolerance of multiple scriptural interpretations and acceptance of Christian diversity.

Sources for Further Study

Ehrman, Bart D. *Lost Christianities: Battles for Scripture and the Faiths We Never Knew*. New York: Oxford University Press, 2003. Extended discussion of issues raised in *Misquoting Jesus*, providing detailed analysis of specific forgeries, discoveries, heresies, and orthodoxies.

Komoszewski, J., et al. *Reinventing Jesus: What "The Da Vinci Code" and Other Novel Speculations Don't Tell You.* Grand Rapids, Mich.: Kregel, 2006. More orthodox religious scholars provide an opposing interpretation, answering most of Ehrman's major textual objections.

Metzer, Bruce M. *The Canon of the New Testament: Its Origin, Develoment, and Significance.* Oxford, England: Clarendon Press, 1997. Described by Ehrman as the standard authoritative scholarly account of canonical development and extensively cited by other scholars.

Meyer, Marvin. *The Gnostic Discoveries: The Impact of the Nag Hammadi Library.* New York: HarperCollins, 2005. Overview and analysis of papyrus manuscripts discovered in Egypt in 1945, emphasizing significance for modern readers.

Pagels, Elaine. *The Gnostic Gospels.* New York: Random House, 1979. Analytical study of diversity in early Christianity, emphasizing Gnostic interaction with orthodoxy and implications for studying Christianity's origins.

Robinson, James M., ed. *The Nag Hammadi Library in English.* 3d rev. ed. New York: HarperCollins, 1988. One-volume translation of papyrus manuscripts discovered in Egypt, edited by the Institute for Antiquity and Christianity.

Charmaine Allmon Mosby

MIT BRENNENDER SORGE

Author: Pius XI (Ambrogio Damiano Achille Ratti; 1857-1939)
First published: 1937 (English translation, 1937)
Edition used: The Church in Germany, Encyclical Letter of His Holiness, Pope Pius XI, Issued March 14, 1937, translated by the Vatican Press. Washington, D.C.: National Catholic Welfare Conference, 1937
Genre: Nonfiction
Subgenres: Critical analysis; encyclical
Core issues: Alienation from God; Catholics and Catholicism; persecution; religion; social action

With the rise to power of Adolf Hitler and his paganistic and anti-Semitic Nazi Party in 1933, the climate for the Catholic Church in Germany worsened. Though supposedly protected by the Concordat of 1933, the Church suffered from persecution, and Pope Pius XI wrote against Nazi ideology and practice in 1937. Though the encyclical was bold and embarrassing for the German government, which saw its anti-Catholic and anti-Semitic actions as a purely internal political matter, it had little or no effect on German policy.

Overview

Breaking with tradition, Pope Pius XI chose to issue his encyclical *Mit brennender Sorge* in German rather than Latin. It is addressed to the German Catholic bishops but is clearly and obliquely aimed at the German government. He writes that he has heard directly from bishops and their representatives of how the faithful are standing against repression, but also how so many are being led astray—clearly a reference to the atheistic Hitler Youth program. Pius goes on to review how the 1933 Concordat, an agreement between the German government and the Vatican that was desired by the German bishops themselves, was meant to allow the peaceful and unfettered work of the Catholic Church in Germany. Now, he says, it has become clear that the German government was deceitful about its motives and that the Nazis—a name never used—"from the outset aimed only at a war of extermination," a "religious war" against Catholicism. All the Church sought was peace, Pius stresses, and to that end he adhered to the letter and spirit of every treaty and agreement. He decided to keep quiet, however, until the pattern of repression was manifest to all. Recent moves against Catholic schools, a clear concordant violation, were but the latest outrage, so he says he decided to speak out.

Pope Pius tells the German bishops that the Nazi attempts to reestablish pagan religion and to lower God to worldly status and raise themselves to the divine are acts that show their disdain for God. The bishops' flocks need to be reminded that all are subject to God's universal law and be dissuaded from submitting to godless nationalism. He urges the bishops to resist openly blasphemers and "aggressive paganism."

Christ's Gospel must be taught, and the Old Testament must also be defended from anti-Semitic attacks by those blinded by "ignorance and pride." He tacitly attacks Adolf Hitler's cult of personality by holding up Christ as the only and ultimate focus of faith. To maintain that faith "pure and unalloyed," the Church is necessary. This "divine structure, which stands on eternal foundations" has a mission with which no human organization dare interfere (though the Nazis do). At the same time, the Catholic priesthood, under the direct administration of the bishops, must remain pure and never "compromise with the world," lest they lose the power to reenergize spiritually the people under their care.

The German state's oppression calls for heroic resistance in the face of seduction to apostatize, and Pius recognizes the sacrifice many have to make for their faith. He stresses that this faith must be grounded in support for the papacy, the focus of "true and lawful authority." He frets the possibility of a schismatic "national church" controlled by the Nazis and urges the bishops not to succumb to any such overtures. German culture, he warns, is subverting the Church's own religious concepts, and Pius clearly defines "faith," "immortality," and "original sin" in their Catholic contexts, warning against secular perversions. Humility and Christ's cross are mocked by the prideful in Hitler's Germany, while Nazis promise some sort of "German type" of grace that would replace God's freely given spiritual gifts: All of this is to be resisted. Morality, Pius goes on, must be grounded in God's law and not national sentiment or the will of the state as the Nazis aver (as always, the pope writes without using their name). Subjective human ideals cannot be allowed to replace eternal divine truths. Likewise, the validity of human laws is limited by their mirroring of divine law: Utilitarianism is just only insofar as it is also (divinely) morally just. Finally, he asserts that Christians have every right to live according to conscience and to educate their children in the faith, and Pius decries recent attempts in Germany to infringe on that right.

Pius then addresses himself directly to German youth. He warns them of the seduction of phony Nazi Christianity and the draw away from Catholicism. He acknowledges that many are torn between adherence to Christ's true Church and the natural attraction to a nationalist substitute and that many have been penalized for their adherence to Christ. While he assures the reader that he is not undermining national sentiment, he is speaking against the false antagonism between faith and patriotism raised by the German state. German propaganda, secular education, and the Hitler Youth create false ethical goods that draw young people away from proper morality, even to the violation of the Sabbath, and these forces must be resisted. He also speaks words of congratulation and encouragement to German priests who are serving the Church well as pastors and examples of the true Christian life, especially those called on to sacrifice themselves and undergoing personal persecution, confinement in prisons, or relocation to concentration camps. He greets and encourages members of religious orders and laity in religious associations, especially those who have suffered for their religion. He encourages parents to continue resisting Nazi education and to raise their children in the best Catholic way. The pope closes by acknowledging the current power of the "enemies of the Church" and urges all members of the Church in Germany to remain steadfast in faith and action. Should "true peace between Church and [the German] State" not be restored, Pius pledges to defend Catholic rights and freedom in God's name.

Christian Themes

Clearly Pius is addressing the essential conflict between the Christian life and that demanded by an aggressively secular and antireligious state and society. It is an ancient theme addressed directly by Jesus in the Gospels, and Pius at least tacitly places the German Church's situation in this broader historical context. Like the emperors of old, Hitler and his followers were seeking to replace true religion with a false substitute, in this case based on race, nation, and a cult of personality, and Pius urges clergy and laity alike to resist any and all attempts to diminish the Church and its authority in favor of this false Nazi creation. Pius's concerns for both a national church, which would have been a slave to Nazi ideology, and the substitution of Christian education with secular reflect the power of German state to take the place of Catholicism—where it was dominant—and to twist its values and meanings in accord with its totalitarian perversions. Resistance meant sacrifice, again a biblical value, ranging from unpopularity to death.

Pius emphasizes the freedom of Christians and their conscience, and he marks the vileness of the German state in its growing unwillingness to allow for this. However, Christian freedom also requires its exercise in close personal adherence to God's law and in an active unwillingness to compromise in the public sphere. In a corrupted state, the Christian has a special duty to maintain a clear conscience and act in consonance with it. The pope speaks with special force to the German pastors, who directly suffered both seduction and persecution as the state tried to wrest the cure of souls from their hands. Church leaders had a special duty to remain blameless and set the proper tone for Christian existence in an openly hostile society.

Sources for Further Study

Cornwall, John. *Hitler's Pope: The Secret History of Pius XII*. New York: Penguin, 2000. Highly controversial study that criticizes Pius XII for his failure to confront or condemn the Nazi state; downplays the importance of Pius XI's earlier work.

Godman, Peter. *Hitler and the Vatican: Inside the Secret Archives That Reveal the New Story of the Nazis and the Church*. New York: Free Press, 2004. Another controversial work based on a rather narrow reading of relevant sources and underestimation of the brutality of the Nazi regime.

Lewy, Guenther. *The Catholic Church and Nazi Germany*. New York: Da Capo Press, 2000. Fairly even-handed treatment of the relationship of the Nazi regime with the Catholic hierarchy in Germany and the Vatican.

Olf, Lillian. *Their Name Is Pius: Portraits of Five Great Modern Popes*. Freeport, N.Y.: Books for Libraries, 1970. Contains a biography of Pius XI and other popes, including Pius XII, pope during World War II.

Teeling, William. *The Pope in Politics: The Life and Work of Pope Pius XI.* London: L. Dickson, 1937. A British Catholic journalist suggests that the pope opposed changes in Catholicism as it was developing in the United States. Examines the pope in relation to politics.

Joseph P. Byrne

MOMENTS OF GRACE

Author: Elizabeth Jennings (1926-2001)
First published: Manchester, England: Carcanet New Press, 1979
Genre: Poetry
Subgenres: Lyric poetry; meditation and contemplation
Core issues: Death; grace; healing; love; nature; suffering

This collection of fifty-eight poems explores the brief, illuminating moments in daily life that reveal truths about relationships, nature, and human connections with God. Utilizing the direct style, unadorned language, and contemplative insights on which she built a career, British poet Jennings indicates that redemption is possible in a dark world, order can underlie randomness, grace coexists with danger, and God abides in human affairs.

Overview

Moments of Grace was published nearly thirty years after Elizabeth Jennings gained recognition as one of the original nine members of the post-World War II British literary movement simply called the Movement, a group that valued straightforward, rational verse over the romanticism that typified the works of Dylan Thomas and the emotionally weighted imagery of earlier English poetry. The plain diction and cool treatment of poetic subjects that had earned Jennings her place in the 1950's Oxford group alongside Kingsley Amis, Thom Gunn, and Philip Larkin still imbues *Moments of Grace*; the 1979 poems remain quiet and restrained as they plumb such charged topics as loneliness, abandoned relationships, and spiritual epiphanies. The scope of *Moments of Grace*—from light musings about lowly insects to quietly reverential poems and pithy reflections on death, law, and misrule—is broader than it was in Jennings's early work.

Early in Jennings's career, critics noted that she was the only woman and the only Catholic in a movement of "angry young men" with working-class roots and political agendas. A physician's daughter with religious inclinations and classical tastes, young Jennings favored formally structured poems that observe rather than moralize; singularly among Movement members, she adhered to traditional, nonpolitical subjects such as love, nature, and the passage of time. Critic Robert Conquest amusedly likened her position in the firebrand Movement to that of a schoolmistress among drunken marines. Nevertheless, by the time Jennings wrote *Moments of Grace*, the heyday of the Movement had passed; the Oxford-based poet had weathered stints in advertising, librarianship, and book publishing; and, since earning a 1949 master's degree from St. Anne's College, she had written, edited, or translated more than twenty volumes of poetry. By 1979, Jennings was a seasoned poet at midlife, probing increasingly religious and philosophical questions as well as some controversial issues.

Moments of Grace opens with "Into the Hour," a decidedly religious poem about healing. The speaker asserts that grief, loss, and ghosts of the past have given way to sunlight and a slowly spreading Paradise. The poet does not know how to pass beyond grief or how to celebrate the passage but, in a steadfastly faithful way, understands that suffering can be fruitful: "I have come/ Into the time when grief begins to flower. . . ."

The notion that suffering can be redemptive is Christian; that poetry can confirm the healing is typical Jennings. In fact, after the publication of her first full-length book of verse (*Poems*, 1953) earned an Arts Council prize and catapulted Jennings into England's literary limelight, her next ten books included two specifically focused on healing in mental institutions. *Recoveries* (1964) and *The Mind Has Mountains* (1966) describe an obdurate doctor, dispossessed patients, needles, and psychological anguish in hospitals where Jennings landed after a suicide attempt and recurrent mental breakdowns in the 1960's. These give way to a cautious sense of promise in *Moments of Grace*. Accordingly, "Into the Hour" closes with the speaker looking ahead to new love, offering a mutedly optimistic entry into the rest of the collection.

Some moments of grace described by Jennings are truly positive, arising from a child's glance, an epic sunset, or a moment's respite from a wearying day. Some moments build bridges to ancient wonders, pastoral people, or artistic creations, as outlined in "Braque's Dream," "A Proustian Moment," and "Outside Greece." More often, however, key moments reveal danger lurking beneath the surface of earthly things. In "Goldfinch," the plucky appeal of a bird masks predatory inclinations, and in "The Sermon of Appearances," dancing motes exact a price from those drawn into their glittering momentum. "Forgiveness" uncovers a cycle of anger and apologies, "An Elusive One" exposes "counterfeits of love," and secrecy separates lovers in "Love Needs an Elegy." The darkest moments, conveys Jennings, arise with arguments, exits, and betrayals. As poetry, which Jennings held is a search for order, they become manageable.

Moments of grace that are prompted by nature—stars, the Moon, seas, gardens, woods, breezes, skies, and trees aplenty—offer a window to the elusive positive or a profoundly direct link to God. Soaring birds serve as divinely inspired examples of steadfastness in "Spirits" and "A Chorus of Creation," as do "upward-turning" Tuscan trees in "Cypresses." Dramatic sunsets bring peace. Stars form bright necklaces adorning the heavens, from which a creator watches attentively. What goes awry on earth is tempered, however briefly in these moments, with nature's steadier, closer connection with God. For Jennings, moments of grace are reminders that God is present, pivotal illuminations for the disappointed, the frail, and the flawed inhabiting her poems.

Unique in the collection, "Euthanasia" addresses a highly controversial moral issue, one pivotal to the Roman Catholic Church. The poem is told from the point of view of a patient among many who fear death by legally sanctioned caregivers.

> The law's been passed and I am lying low
> Hoping to hide from those who think they are
> Kindly, compassionate. . . .

In the poem, seemingly imprisoned patients face pain with composure, but they are terrified of death by euthanasia—even though they once purported to choose death over illness. Feigning hardiness to protect themselves, they grow weaker. Ultimately, the poem pits the changeable will of patients against the law permitting euthanasia, and also against "murdering ministers" with the surreptitious power to take life.

Christian Themes

"My Roman Catholic religion and my poems are the most important things in my life," said Jennings, whose craft and faith intertwine via biblical places, religious figures, and Christian metaphors and themes in a lifetime of poems. In *Moments of Grace*, references to Gethsemane, Jerusalem, Paradise, and Eden crop up in the final few lines of poems whose titles and treatment are otherwise secular, as does the sun as metaphor for a Communion wafer. To profess love's willingness to overcome adversity, another poem draws on biblical phrasing—"seven times seven"—used in scripture to signal God's works. Some poems, including "A Beseeching," move beyond reference and metaphor to formal prayer: They acknowledge the reign of the Lord or the Virgin and then request divine help.

Christian themes are most explicit in "Christmas Suite in Five Movements," the closing work that recounts Christ's birth. Vacillating between images of a crying, needy babe and an adult Christ bearing crucifixion scars, Jennings's version of Christmas emphasizes vulnerability. It also expresses a mutual need of humans for Christ and Christ for humans.

> . . . This God fears the night,
> A child so terrified he asks for us.
> God is the cry we thought came from our own
> Perpetual sense of loss.
> Can God be frightened to be so alone?
> Does that child dream the cross?

As portrayed by Jennings, the Christ child is not the pacific infant of traditional holiday fare; he is very noisy, very fearful, and very human. Similarly, when the story jumps in time from the newborn to the mature Christ, it highlights emotional and physical discomforts—a disturbing dream, exhaustion, blindness from the sun, as well as a great deal of dust, heat, poverty, and cold. Why? The raw humanity underscores what Jennings calls the "terrible truth" of Christ's suffering. Graphically portrayed, Christ's suffering makes redemption real for people bearing their own burdens, including the burdens of unfulfilled love, misspoken words, and ebbing powers depicted in *Moments of Grace*.

Jennings's Christmas suite closes without fanfare, focusing on the "tiny flesh/ And flickering spirit" of the Christ child. In a mixture of the Lord's Prayer, the sacrament of Communion, and a sense of Christianity enduring, the closing lines of the collection offer quiet but potent hope: "Give us this daily Bread, this little Host."

Sources for Further Study

Foisner, Sabine. "Elizabeth Jennings: Against the Dark." In *English Language and Literature: Positions and Dispositions*, edited by James Hogg. Salzburg, Austria: University of Salzburg Press, 1990. Shows how Jennings renders imagination sacred, facilitates communion with God, affirms order over earthly chaos, and garners salvation from suffering.

Gramang, Gerlinde. *Elizabeth Jennings: An Appraisal of Her Life as a Poet, Her Approach to Her Work, and a Selection of the Major Themes of her Poetry.* Lewiston, N.Y.: Edwin Mellen Press, 1995. Despite awkward phrasing and text wedded to the obvious, includes a comprehensive bibliography and an interview with Jennings.

Riggs, Thomas, ed. *Contemporary Poets.* 7th ed. Detroit: St. James Press, 2001. Examines contemplation, projection, saints (including Saint Catherine and Saint Augustine), and mystical revelation in Jennings's work.

Shelton, Pamela, ed. *Contemporary Women Poets.* Detroit: St. James Press, 1998. Traces Jennings's entries into the experiences of artists, religious figures, the desperate, and the aged.

Wheeler, Michael. "Elizabeth Jennings and Gerard Manley Hopkins." In *Hopkins Among the Poets: Studies in Modern Responses to Gerard Manley Hopkins*, edited by Richard F. Giles. Hamilton, Ont.: International Hopkins Association, 1985. Compares similar poetic treatments of innocence, suffering, and childhood. Notes parallels in tone and alliteration.

Wendy Alison Lamb

MORTE D'URBAN

Author: J. F. Powers (1917-1999)
First published: 1962
Edition used: Morte d'Urban, with an introduction by Elizabeth Hardwick. New York: New York Review Books, 2000
Genre: Novel
Subgenres: Literary fiction; satire
Core issues: Catholics and Catholicism; clerical life; pastoral role; preaching; priesthood; works and deeds

A mission preacher in the Clementine order, Father Urban Roche is transferred from his preaching circuit, centered in Chicago, to the foundation of a retreat house in a remote area of Minnesota. Affable and energetic, he serves also as a parish priest and builds a coterie of sponsors around him. He also establishes a circle of clergy jealous of his prominence. His success is based on secular values of sociability rather than spirituality. Talk about golf and baseball and activities filled with drinking, smoking, and cursing are the substance of his daily life, reflecting a desiccated religious one.

Principal characters
: *Father Urban Roche*, a mission preacher in the Chicago province of the Clementine order
: *Billy Cosgrove*, a somewhat shady Chicago patron of Father Urban
: *Paul*, a chauffeur, Billy's right-hand man
: *Father Boniface*, head of the Chicago province
: *Father Wilfrid "Wilf" Bestudik*, rector of the retreat house
: *Father John "Jack" Kelleher*, a colleague of Father Urban
: *Brother Harold Peters*, a general aid at the retreat house
: *Sam Bean*, a Minnesota businessman
: *Sylvia Bean*, Sam's wife
: *Father Phil Smith*, the pastor at St. Monica's Church
: *Monsignor "Red" Renton*, a consultor in the Great Plains Diocese
: *Father Udovic*, a chancellor of the diocese
: *Mrs. Thwaites*, a wealthy, widowed patron of the Clementines
: *Dickie Thwaites*, Mrs. Thwaites's son
: *Katie*, Mrs. Thwaites's servant
: *Sally Hopgood Thwaites*, Mrs. Thwaites's daughter
: *Bishop James Conor*, head of the diocese

Overview

Morte d'Urban (literally meaning "death of Urban") describes the rise and fall of Father Urban Roche, a priest in the Chicago province of the Order of Saint Clement, an order dedicated to preaching and teaching. Urban became a Clementine after being inspired as a boy by one of their dynamic, outgoing preachers, Father Placidus. One of the Clementines' leading preachers, he travels by train throughout the Midwest giving parish missions. Father Urban, however, considers the Clementines a mediocre group. They compete with the Dalmatian and Dolomite orders. The province head, Father Boniface, transfers him to a newly established retreat house in Duesterhaus, Minnesota, removing him from the mission circuit. Urban is accompanied by Jack Kelleher, a burned-out preacher who clings to tiresome Clementine devotional publications. Father Urban's patron, Billy Cosgrove, is a wealthy yet shady character.

Arriving at the retreat house, Father Urban finds it a rambling complex, renovated in a happenstance manner. The rector is the parsimonious Father Wilfrid "Wilf" Bestudik, assisted by Brother Harold Peters, a jack of all trades. Father Urban retires to his sparse bedroom, underheated to reduce costs. In their first chapter meeting, they haggle over mundane matters such as the naming of their location (eventually St. Clement's Hill), the design of a tedious brochure to attract retreatants, and squirrels and rats on the premises. A rivalry exists between Wilf and Urban. The former is a narrow-minded pinchpenny and the latter, indulgent and garrulous. The rector expects Urban to submit to drab routines, repressing his "star" power. Nonetheless, their petty arguments over how to set up a Nativity crib or expenses for using a phone or electric heater are usually won by Urban. Passive-aggressive resistance makes the rector submit.

Father Urban goes as a visiting parish priest to St. Monica's in Great Plains, seat of the diocese. The rectory is large and comfortable; the parish church, cramped and dilapidated. Father Phil Smith, the ailing pastor, is taken south by Monsignor "Red" Renton for a vacation. Father Urban takes charge of the parish, conducting a census, inaugurating new programs, and enlivening rectory spirits. Sam Bean, a well-to-do businessman, and his wife, Sylvia, become friends with Father Urban after one of his talks. Sylvia comes to admire the priest, often loaning him her sports car. Father Urban replaces Father Smith in taking weekly Communion to Mrs. Thwaites, a patron of the Clementines, who comes to relish his advice and companionship.

Father Smith dies while playing golf in the Bahamas. Father Urban, absorbed in the social dynamics of the parish, tries to persuade the bishop to let him replace the former pastor. Unsuccessful, he nevertheless wins support among the Clementines for two projects. Funded by Billy, the Clementines purchase farmland adjacent to their retreat house for a golf course, hoping to attract retreatants of a higher social class. Moreover, the Milestone Press, operated by the order, receives a subsidy from Mrs. Thwaites to publish a series of unmarketable books edited by her son, Dickie Thwaites. One of these is a Catholic edition for children of the stories of King Arthur and the Knights of the Round Table. A particularly challenging passage to edit is the nature of the relationship between Sir Lancelot and Queen Guinevere.

Supervising the building of the golf course, Father Urban effectively becomes manager of the "Hill." Monsignor Renton informs Father Urban that Bishop James Conor is intent on taking it over for a seminary. A poor golfer, the bishop plays in a game at the Hill in which one of his balls hits Father Urban, leaving him unconscious and hospitalized. This event initiates a downward spiral for Father Urban: The bishop indicates that he is no longer planning the seminary, and Father Urban is left with recurring headaches. Recuperating at the home of Mrs. Thwaites, Father Urban learns that she is cheating her Irish servant, Katie, of her wages in games of dominoes. He mildly admonishes the order's patron about Katie's straitened conditions. Father Urban's patron Billy and his sidekick, Paul, accompany Urban on a fishing trip. Urban comes to see more clearly Billy's boorish, violent nature. When he prevents Billy from drowning a deer, Billy falls into an infantile rage. Mrs. Thwaites's daughter, Sally, tries to seduce Father Urban. He resists but, having had a drink with her, falls into a reverie of what his life would have been had he not become a priest.

Elections for a new provincial result in the appointment of Father Urban. However, the reforms his supporters had expected of him never occur. A broken man, he comes to administer as lamely as had his predecessor. Demoralized by personal losses and suffering chronically from ever more severe headaches, he is fading away, ironically echoing the decline of King Arthur and Sir Launcelot.

Christian Themes

The book of Hebrews (5:1) states that a priest is a man taken from among men to do for them those things that pertain to God. *Morte d'Urban* describes the fragility of the priest's human condition in relation to his divine duties. Until the middle of the twentieth century, the American Catholic Church comprised working-class European immigrants or their recent descendants. The parish priest was a figure of totem sanctity and authority. The book evokes another title, the story of the legendary King Arthur by Sir Thomas Malory, *Le Morte d'Arthur* (1485), reminding readers of the esteem in which the parish priest was held by his parishioners. However, in the atmosphere of rising prosperity and increasing higher education following World War II, some in the Catholic laity increasingly perceived their priests' "feet of clay." It was to this audience that the novels of J. F. Powers appealed, particularly *Morte d'Urban*, which describes clerical foibles and failures.

The dilemma of the irreligious life of people in religion is a perennial theme in Christian literature. One finds it in Dante's *La divina commedia* (c. 1320; *The Divine Comedy*, 1802), Geoffrey Chaucer's *The Canterbury Tales* (1387-1400), and Graham Greene's novel *The Power and the Glory* (1940). In *Morte d'Urban*, Powers sets this dilemma within the context of a parochial, materialistic, mid-twentieth century America, applying the satirical style of Sinclair Lewis from works such as *Main Street* (1920), *Babbitt* (1922), and *Elmer Gantry* (1927).

Father Urban is not as much a religious person as a clerical version of an affable salesman or promoter, somewhat more given to moral rhetoric. However, even this posture arises not from theological principles so much as from his efforts to maintain an agreeable social environment. Spirituality and liturgy are only tangential to his life. His occasional religious thoughts focus mainly on aspects of church history or homely admonitions that he can present more effectively in his preaching. The book's title ironically recalls that of Sir Thomas Malory's *Le Morte d'Arthur*, which retold the tales of the heroic King Arthur and his knights of the Round Table. However, the *morte* (death) of the title refers not to the death of a hero such as King Arthur but to the desiccated spirituality of an ordinary man.

Sources for Further Study

Evans, Fallon, and Thomas Merton. *J. F. Powers*. St. Louis, Mo.: Herder, 1968. A collection of articles including four on *Morte d'Urban*, one by the famous Trappist writer Thomas Merton.

Hagopian, John V. *J. F. Powers*. Twayne's United States Authors 130. New York: Twayne, 1968. This concise examination of Powers's life and work (to the mid-1960's) emphasizes the acuteness and subtlety of his observations of Catholic clerical life, especially as presented in *Morte d'Urban*.

Settimo, Scott R. "What Fellowship Has Light with Darkness? A Carmelite Reading of J. F. Powers." Master's thesis. St. Benedict, Oreg.: Mount Angel Seminary, 2005. Analyzes works of J. F. Powers in relation to their treatment of progress, or the lack of such, in spritual growth.

Tartt, Donna. "The Glory of J. F. Powers: A Writer's Work Is Resurrected." *Harper's* 301, no. 1802 (July, 2000): 69-74. A positive reassessment of Powers's work two decades after he had achieved the pinnacle of his production and critical acclaim.

Edward A. Riedinger

MUSIC TO DIE FOR

Author: Radine Trees Nehring (1935-   )
First published: Wichita, Kans.: St. Kitts Press, 2003
Genre: Novel
Subgenre: Mystery and detective fiction
Core issues: Faith; friendship; responsibility; trust in God

Carrie McCrite, manager of an Arkansas highway tourist center, is attending a travel convention on a working vacation. When the evening's lead entertainers, Chase Mason and Tracy Teal, do not appear for dinner, she volunteers to check on their whereabouts. Carrie finds Chase huddled over a body in a Folk Center shop, terrified and crying. It turns out the murdered man, who knew Tracy, had kidnapped her little daughter Dulcey. Now the little girl has vanished. Carrie and her friend Henry King untangle a web involving arson, hillbilly pot growers, and secret parentage before the murder is solved and Dulcey found.

> *Principal characters*
> *Carrie McCrite*, a widow, tourist station manager, and sometime amateur sleuth
> *Henry King*, a retired Kansas City police detective and Carrie's friend
> *Tracy Teal*, a famous young country music star
> *Chase Mason*, Tracy's husband, an equally famous country musician and guitarist
> *Dulcey Mason*, Tracy and Chase's four-year-old daughter
> *"Mad Margaret" Culpeper*, the ancient matriarch of an Ozark hill family
> *Micah*,
> *Zephaniah*,
> *Habakkuk*, and
> *Nahum*, Margaret's sons
> *Beth*, Carrie's friend
> *Ben Yokum*, a backstage hand at Ozark Folk Center
> *Bobby Lee Logan*, a blacksmith, musician, and childhood friend of Tracy
> *Farel Teal*, a murder victim, Tracy's cousin

Overview

At the beginning of *Music to Die For*, upon settling in for her vacation at the Ozark Folk Center, Carrie McCrite goes walking in the woods. Besides birds and spring wildflowers, she notices a faint, haunting melody. A few moments later, an eccentric old woman walks past, muttering, "The gowerow has taken the child." Carrie puzzles over this but then shrugs and goes in to dinner. There, her friend Beth asks for her help in finding the star performers, country musicians Tracy Teal and her husband, Chase Mason, who have not yet appeared. Carrie goes out to look. Behind a door, she overhears the two stars talking with Chase's mother, Brigid, about Tracy and Chase's daughter Dulcey's having been kidnapped. She introduces herself and takes them back to the banquet, where they perform. However, they leave immediately afterward.

Carrie follows, walking out into the craft shop area. There, she hears muffled gasps coming from the dressmaker's shop. She opens the door and comes across Tracy, crying in the dark. When Carrie lights a candle, she sees the body of Farel Teal, Tracy's cousin, on the floor. He has been stabbed in the chest, and a note is in his hand, mentioning a blue birdhouse and Dulcey.

Tracy and Chase do not want to call the police yet, for fear of prompting harm to their daughter. It strikes Carrie that both are acting a bit strangely, however, and she leaves to call the sheriff's office about the body. Carrie wishes that Henry King, a retired Kansas City police detective, were there to offer help and advice. Since he is not, it falls to her to help the obviously shaken couple. She rides with them to Farel's cabin. No one is there. As they leave, a figure dashes into the house. A moment later, the place goes up in flames. Tracy collapses, and Carrie tries to comfort her on the drive back to the park.

The next morning, Carrie pokes around the Folk Center grounds, soliciting background information on the Masons' career and the local scene. At noon, much to her relief, Henry arrives. Carrie briefs him on the situation. Ruefully, they decide that sleuthing must take precedence over their original plan to attend workshops on Ozark folk crafts. Henry concurs with Carrie's plan to find and query Margaret Culpeper, the old woman whom Carrie heard muttering on the day of her arrival. They leave to visit her; perhaps her strange words are more than coincidental.

Carrie and Henry find Margaret in a clearing as picturesque and junky as any Ozark travel photo. Warming to Carrie's own (if exaggerated) Culpeper connections, Margaret invites them into one of the surrounding weathered shacks. As long as her shotgun-toting son Micah is present, Margaret chatters inconsequential family gossip. Once Micah disappears, she answers Carrie's question about the gowerow—a folk monster—with a surprise revelation. Her boys are holding Dulcey. She assures Carrie and Henry that they will not hurt the child; they just want the ransom. When she learns who Dulcey is—and recognizes her as her granddaughter—she offers more help. She dare not counter her "boys" openly, she says, but that evening she will be babysitting Dulcey. She can then take the child down the mountain to her son Nahum's house. He will keep her secret, and Carrie and Henry can pick her up there.

Carrie and Henry leave, amazed to have solved the kidnapping so easily. Unfortunately, the plan to recover Dulcey encounters some hitches. When Carrie approaches the house, she is grabbed and bound, then dumped on the floor next to a similarly trussed Tracy, who had also come looking for her daughter. Two of Margaret's sons,

Habakkuk and Zephaniah (Hab and Zeph), have decided that Tracy will make another ransomable hostage. Carrie, however, fears that she may be disposable. She tries to comfort herself by reciting Psalms. Eventually she and Tracy are moved. Tracy wakes and tells Carrie about her marriage problems, which led indirectly to this crisis. Carrie tells her not to worry about Dulcey; her daughter is safe. Carrie assumes that Henry went up the path and took Dulcey from Margaret, since Nahum was not at home.

Margaret appears. With the excuse of helping the captives to the bathroom, she confirms Carrie's news about Dulcey, then unties both women and urges them to flee. Before they can, Hab bursts in with his gun. A shot rings out and Hab falls to the floor, injured. Ben Yokum, a stagehand at Ozark Folk Center, climbs in the window. Henry and the sheriff follow, coming down the hall. It turns out that the sheriff has long suspected Hab and Zeph of growing marijuana.

In the aftermath, all the puzzles are solved. Farel Teal did originally kidnap Dulcey, albeit with Tracy's cooperation, in revenge for a song that Chase stole from him and Tracy. Ben Yokum stabbed Farel; he saw Tracy fighting with him and concluded she was in danger. Bobby Lee Logan (a blacksmith, musician, and childhood friend of Tracy) set the fire at Farel's house to cover up Farel's involvement with the Culpepers' drug business. Chase and Tracy, whose marriage had always been shaky, are reconciled.

Christian Themes

Music to Die For is representative of mystery and detective genre fiction that has been written specifically for a Christian audience. Some features typical of Christian (sometimes more broadly identified as inspirational) genre fiction are that it avoids depiction of certain behaviors on the part of the main characters (such as drinking, cursing, and nonmarital sex) and that it presents a "faith journey" on the part of a protagonist. Both of these criteria are met by *Music to Die For*. The novel is the second of a series that features Carrie McCrite and Henry King as amateur sleuths, and its author, Radine Trees Nehring, won the 1998 Christian Writer of the Year Award, presented by the American Christian Writers.

Specific Christian themes are subtle but definitely present. While the plot contains no overtly "churchy" elements—in fact, all readers can enjoy it simply as a mystery without considering its spiritual themes—Carrie McCrite nevertheless is a woman of indelible faith. Her faith in God allows her to enter dangerous situations without disabling fear. When facing the unknown, she automatically says a silent prayer. Carrie knows her Bible and, when someone needs comforting, often recalls an appropriate Psalm or other passage to share with them.

Accompanying her faith is Carrie's strong sense of responsibility. When finding herself in a dangerous situation, she has no doubt that her responsibility is to do whatever it takes to untangle the trouble and resolve the situation fairly. She is willing, even eager, to learn and try new activities, from herbal cultivation to the details of good detective practice, despite her grandmotherly demeanor and her past life as a dependent wife. Part of her openness to new experiences and knowledge stems from her sheer curiosity and the lure of a challenge, but she also wants to be prepared to face the responsibilities that descend upon her regularly.

Like almost all mystery novels, *Music to Die For* is concerned with restoring moral order and bringing wrongdoers to justice. However, there is another dimension of theme also, the importance of human connections. Friendships are important in Carrie's world. Without her network of friends, living in an isolated clearing in the Ozarks as she does would be very lonely, even frightening. Family is important too, and even if the Culpeper family is eccentric, there is no doubt of Margaret's joy when she discovers her lost granddaughter. Nor is there a doubt of Tracy's happiness upon discovering that her long-lost biological father is Ben Yokum. Likewise, Tracy is willing to give her marriage another try, even after she realizes that Chase originally married her only to lay claim to her trademark song. As for Chase, the sobering experience of almost losing Tracy and Dulcey has begun to temper his arrogance and impatience by the story's end. Concern for these human connections is not uniquely Christian, but the author's, and the characters', Christian faith strengthens their importance here.

Sources for Further Study

Nehring, Radine Trees. Radine's Books. http://www.radinesbooks.com. The author's Web site lists her other books and writings.

_____. *A Valley to Die For.* Wichita, Kans.: St. Kitts Press, 2002. First of Nehring's series of ". . . to Die For" mysteries, in which Carrie moves to Arkansas, meets Henry, and solves the murder of a friend.

"Radine Trees Nehring." *Tulsa World*, May 26, 2002, p. 5. Nehring tells the story of her road to becoming a mystery writer.

Emily Alward

MY GOD AND I
A Spiritual Memoir

Author: Lewis B. Smedes (1921-2002)
First published: Grand Rapids, Mich.: Wm. B. Eerdmans, 2003, with introductions
   by Rod Jellema and Jon Pott and a coda by Cathy Smedes
Genre: Nonfiction
Subgenres: Autobiography; meditation and contemplation; spiritual treatise
Core issues: Calvinism; ethics; forgiveness; friendship; hope

In a combination of memoir and theology, Smedes chronicles the major events of his
life and describes how God was present in his life at each juncture. Throughout most
of his early years he was convinced he was unworthy of God's love, but in college he
was introduced to a Calvinist way of thinking that allowed him to appreciate God's
grace. As a seminary professor and author, he grew in his relationship with God to the
point of being "almost friends." As an old man, he finds his feelings about God "ta-
pered down" to gratitude and hope.

Overview

The maternal grandparents of Lewis Smedes were from Friesland, the northern-most province of the Netherlands. Their daughter Renske (her name was later short-ened to Rena), after marrying Melle Smedes, sailed to America and settled in Mus-kegon, Michigan. When Lewis was two months old, his father died, and the family struggled to make ends meet. As an adolescent, he became convinced that he was one of the reprobates, chosen by God for damnation before he had been born. He de-scribes himself in high school as a lonely loser, someone to be pitied. If God was pres-ent during this time in his life, he did not make himself known.

Upon graduation from high school, Smedes moved to Detroit to work at Smedes Steel, his Uncle Nick's company. After one year he left to enroll at Moody Bible Insti-tute in Chicago in the hope of coming to terms with God. Although this hope was not realized at Moody, his coming to terms with God took place in the chance discovery of a theology book in a used bookstore near Moody. The book taught him for the first time in his life that what he needed to do was to stop considering his own acceptability or unacceptability and allow God to accept him.

Next he enrolled at Calvin College in Grand Rapids, Michigan. He describes it as a serious liberal arts school operated by Dutch Calvinists who wanted their children to get the intellectual equipment they needed to serve God and bring a patch of his king-dom into his broken world. Smedes converted to this brand of Calvinism, and it was the faith that sustained him for the rest of his life. At the same time he joined the Christian Reformed Church because it had a great vision of God as the Creator and Redeemer of the whole world and because of its orderliness, sobriety, and respect for education. He liked the practice of baptizing babies into the family of God, not treating them as lost sinners who still had to walk down the sawdust trail to be saved.

After earning his bachelor's degree, Smedes spent one year at Westminster Theological Seminary in Philadelphia and subsequently returned to Grand Rapids to study at Calvin Theological Seminary. He married Doris Dekker during this period, and after seminary graduation they set off for Amsterdam, where he pursued his doctorate at the Free University. Having successfully defended his doctoral dissertation, Smedes served a small congregation in Paterson, New Jersey, located in a rundown section of town. After a few years of serving this multicultural community, he was invited by the Calvin College Board of Trustees to become a teacher of religion and theology at the college. He immediately developed a fondness for Calvin students. Calvin students were not like the students at Ivy League universities, but what they lacked in academic achievement they made up for in Calvinistic seriousness.

A few years after they arrived at Calvin College, Doris Smedes gave birth to a premature baby who lived for only a few hours. This shaped Lewis's beliefs about God. John Calvin had taught that all things happen when and how and where they happen precisely as God decreed them to happen. Smedes could not believe that God had arranged for the tiny child to die before he had barely begun to live. He learned that he could not accept such hard-boiled theology. The Smedeses adopted three children.

In 1968 Smedes received an invitation to spend a year teaching at Fuller Theological Seminary in Pasadena, California. Halfway through the year after arriving, he joined the faculty as a tenured member. There he spent the rest of his working days.

For several years, Smedes suffered from severe bouts of depression. While undergoing a course of intensive psychotherapy, he lived in a secluded cabin for a couple of weeks. During this isolation, he seemed to hear the voices of his family and closest friends saying "I cannot help you." Then God came to him and said, "I will never let you fall. I will always hold you up." After that day, his depression was never again severe.

When Smedes retired from Fuller Theological Seminary, people asked him what he planned to do in retirement. Sometimes he replied that he was going to develop a closer relationship with God. They usually chuckled in view of his already close relationship with God, but he was serious. Abraham was God's friend, and Smedes wondered why he could not be close friends with God. Part of the problem was that he found it hard to think that God could like him and admire him. In old age, he finally began to believe that he was someone God could admire. Toward the end of his life, he was finally on the way to really believing that God wanted to be his friend—not instead of, but besides, being his Maker and Redeemer.

In his old age, Smede had two primary feelings about God: gratitude and hope. When he was young, he hoped that Christ would never come, that Christ would stay in heaven and leave him alone. In old age, he yearned for Christ's presence. Soon after he wrote *My God and I*, that hope was realized.

Christian Themes

Lewis Smedes's approach to Christian ethics is based on the doctrine that God is a triune God. First, God the Father shows his creatures what is right and what is good.

Second, God the Son has shown these creatures a new ethic, a more excellent way of following the old one, which involves an unselfish love. Third, the Spirit of God opens our eyes and ears to see and hear the voices of the human situation, which requires a moral decision.

Smedes discusses the relation between believers and unbelievers by developing a bridge metaphor. Some Christians hold that the differences between believers and unbelievers are so great that no bridge can be built to allow these two groups of people to conduct meaningful conversations with each other. Smedes finds this view faulty, and he holds that believers and unbelievers have enough in common to cross over and learn from one another.

Smedes subscribes to the Calvinists' worldview, which he describes as follows. First, God made the world good. Second, human beings brought evil into the world near the beginning of their arrival. Third, in the end God will come to make the world good again. Fourth, in the meantime, his creatures are to create some imperfect models of the good world that will one day come about. In addition, we are to live with hope. Hope is a blend of three psychological ingredients: a dream, a desire, and faith.

Sources for Further Study

Smedes, Lewis. *Forgive and Forget: Healing the Hurts We Don't Deserve*. San Francisco: Harper & Row, 1984. This volume explores the phenomenon of human beings forgiving one another.

_____. *How Can It Be All Right When Everything Is All Wrong?* San Francisco: Harper & Row, 1982. When human beings experience great evils in their lives, it is difficult to understand how God allows them to occur. This book is an original and insightful treatment of this difficult problem.

_____. *Mere Morality: What God Expects from Ordinary People*. Grand Rapids, Mich.: Wm. B. Eerdmans, 1983. Smedes's views on ethics made accessible to a popular audience.

_____. *Sex for Christians: The Limits and Liberties of Sexual Living*. Grand Rapids, Mich.: Wm. B. Eerdmans, 1976. God's expectations for Christians involving sexual practice and conduct.

Stob, Henry. *Ethical Reflections*. Grand Rapids, Mich.: Wm. B. Eerdmans, 1978. Stob was an influential teacher of Smedes and had much to do with shaping his ethical views.

Gregory Mellema

THE MYSTICAL ELEMENT OF RELIGION
As Studied in Saint Catherine of Genoa and Her Friends

Author: Baron Friedrich von Hügel (1852-1925)
First published: London: J. M. Dent, 1908, 2 vols.
Genre: Nonfiction
Subgenres: Biography; critical analysis; mysticism
Core issues: Asceticism; charity; devotional life; mysticism; problem of evil

Hügel wrote this biography of Saint Catherine of Genoa partly because he admired her intelligence and her ability to examine her mystical experiences in the light of both Scripture and Renaissance Platonism. In addition to details on her life, he provides his views on the nature of religion and brings opinions from science and philosophy to bear on religion and mysticism.

Overview

The son of an Austrian diplomat and a Scottish gentlewoman, Friedrich von Hügel spent his childhood and youth mainly on the Continent. His marriage to Lady Mary Herbert, a recent convert, drew him into English Catholic circles, among whom he established himself as a moderating influence.

A prolific writer, von Hügel became interested in Catherine Fiesca Adorna (1447-1510), known to history as Saint Catherine of Genoa, in 1884 when he picked up a copy of her life and teachings at the British Museum. However, fourteen years elapsed before he published a small book on questions suggested by her life, and another ten years before the present two-volume *The Mystical Element of Religion* appeared. Why, one might ask, was this relatively minor saint chosen as the subject of such a monumental work? Among the reasons that the author puts forward are that she represents not the Middle Ages nor the Counter-Reformation from which the more notable mystics have come, but the high tide of the Italian Renaissance; she was never a member of a religious order and owed almost nothing to spiritual directors; and she was highly intelligent and able to interpret her own experience in the light not merely of Scripture but also of Renaissance Platonism. As has been said, she was the perfect heroine for a Victorian novel and Hügel was the complete Victorian.

The book is divided into three parts. Part 1, "Introduction," sets forth the three elements that the author believes are essential in a religion that is to meet our needs. The first or historical element corresponds to the needs of childhood, which demand that religion be founded on fact and embodied in a social institution. The second or intellectual element corresponds to the needs of youth, when the argumentative and reflective capacities come into play and eventuate in a system of doctrine and a view of the world. The third or experimental element corresponds to the needs of maturity, when belief and reason ripen into volition and action, and when religion is felt rather than seen and argued about. The author returns to these elements in his conclusion.

In part 2, "Biography," Hügel takes up the life and teachings of the saint and the beginnings of her official cultus. As a beautiful girl of sixteen, Catherine was married by her aristocratic family to Giuliano Adorno, the wealthy but irresponsible scion of a rival clan. The marriage was unhappy. However, ten years of loneliness and of frantic activity went by before, in a moment of transport, "she was drawn away from the miseries of the world; and, as it were beside herself, she kept crying out within herself: 'No more world; no more sins!'" For four years she lived as a penitent, giving herself to menial tasks among the poor, wearing a hair shirt, and moving with downcast eyes, seemingly dead to all around her. Meanwhile, Giuliano had suffered financial ruin and had become a convert, and they moved from their palace to a humble house near the great hospital of the Pammatone where they ministered to the sick and the poor. Later they moved into the hospital, living without pay and at their own expense. Catherine served as matron for a number of years, including the plague year 1493, during which she caught the fever as a result of kissing the lips of a dying woman. In 1497 Giuliano died, and Catherine, although still living within the hospital, was gradually forced by illness to give up her work. During these last years of her life, she had a small following of disciples; these, when she died, arranged for her to be buried, not beside her husband as she had desired, but in the pilgrimage church of San Nicolo.

It is to two of these disciples that we owe the *Life and Doctrine*, published in Genoa in 1551, but based on material gathered by Ettore Vernazzo (1470?-1524), a notary who helped Catherine during the plague and who devoted the remainder of his life to charitable work, and Don Cattaneo Marabotto (1450?-1528), a secular priest who was Catherine's confessor for the last ten years of her life. Vernazzo's daughter Battista (1497-1587), an able and saintly woman, seems to have taken the work in hand and given it final shape. According to Hügel, only a small part of the book is narrative, the rest being discourses by the saint; and although it contains brief passages that must have been recorded when they were spoken, most of the book is secondary so that the whole is "largely insipid and monotonous." The two "works" usually attributed to Saint Catherine are from the same hands: The *Treatise on Purgatory* is a seventeen-page excerpt from the *Life and Doctrine*, and the *Spiritual Dialogue* is a composition of Battista Vernazza designed to systematize the teachings found in the *Life and Doctrine*.

Apart from the desire to record her teaching, Catherine's biographers were guided by two main interests. One was to put divine favors on record. These were not many. On one occasion, when asked by Vernazzo to narrate graces shown to her, she replied that it was impossible to describe her interior experiences and that "as to exterior things, few or none had taken place in her case." Still, it was reported that she would lie on the ground for hours in a state of trance, that during her fasts (forty days twice a year) her stomach rejected food, that she could tell unconsecrated from consecrated wine, and that the hand with which Don Cattaneo blessed the elements had for her a sweet odor. The other main concern was to put in a favorable light certain of Catherine's departures from conventional piety: that she took Communion daily, that she went for years without confessing to a priest, that she did not take advantage of indulgences, and that she would not pray to saints. Both of these concerns were important in the eyes of the cult that grew up soon after Catherine's death, notably after her body was found not to have undergone decay.

Hügel goes into every detail. Of Catherine's absorption in prayer he notes that from the time of her conversion until her health failed (some twenty-six years of active life) these absorptions (she did not like the word "ecstasy"), which occurred almost daily and lasted up to six hours, were controlled by herself although they came and went so quickly as to seem involuntary. Often they were occasioned by her reception of the Eucharist, together with which they constituted her chief source of spiritual growth. In Hügel's judgment she seems to have experienced only one form of absorption, that which is known as the Prayer of Quiet. These, he says,

> are treated substantially as times when the conscious region of her soul, a region always relatively shallow, sinks down into the ever-present deep regions of subconsciousness; and hence as experiences which can only be described indirectly,—in their effects, as traced by and in the conscious soul, after its rising up again . . . to its more ordinary condition.

Hügel denies that Catherine's teachings are "pneumatic," in the sense that they were given to her during these absorptions. Rather, he suggests, the soul itself was fed on these occasions, and its capacities for intellectual expression were increased when she returned to ordinary consciousness. He further notes that in Catherine's later years, when she was no longer able to work and when the rhythm of her life was broken, her protracted absorptions diminished and, toward the end, were interspersed with a different kind of trance, outwardly indistinguishable from her healthy absorptions, but which she recognized as alien and complained that they did her harm. It was, however, in the last year of her life that Catherine was granted what was perhaps the most stirring of all her experiences.

> There came upon her an insupportable fire of infinite love; and she declared that there had been shown to her one single spark (scintilla) of Pure Love, and that this had been but for a short moment; and that, had it lasted longer, she would have expired because of its great force.

According to Hügel this "scintilla-experience," the richest in her life, must be kept in mind if we are to understand her most profound teachings. Yet essentially it was no different in kind from her earlier experiences, being "a gift of herself by herself to God; and yet her very power and determination to give herself were rendered possible and became actual through the accompanying gift of God."

Catherine was never a teacher in the formal sense. What her followers called her doctrine is simply a compilation of detached sayings without context. To aid in deciding which are authentic, Hügel used the tests of rhythm, simplicity, and originality. (We are told that she often "made rhymed sayings in her joy.") The sayings, while touching many matters and giving vent to many moods, are all true to Catherine's central experience of God's unifying love and can easily be grouped under the great theological heads of God and Creation, sin and redemption, and last things.

For Catherine, God is a "living fountain of goodness." All creatures participate in this goodness even when they are in mortal sin; otherwise they would perish. God, she says, seems to have "nothing else to do than to unite Himself to us." As for man, "lift sin off from his shoulders and then allow the good of God to act." True self-love is love of God, and all other love is self-hatred. It is nonsensical to say that God is offended by our acts; say rather that we damage ourselves. God is the true center of each rational creature. "My *Me* is God, . . . not by simple participation but by a true transformation of my Being."

How there can be evil in the presence of an all-loving God is not easy to understand, especially for those who are consumed with the thirst for unity that Catherine shares with all the Neoplatonist school, for reality constitutes a graduated series with the sensible world at the bottom and with God at the top. "Listen," she says, "to what Fra Jacopone says in one of his *Lauds*: 'True elevation is in heaven; earthly lowness leads to the soul's destruction.'" On this view, everything is good in its place; evil is merely displacement. However, this solution to the problem does not represent Catherine's better thinking, for she recognized in self-determining creatures not only the varying degrees of goodness but also the capacity for self-making and self-marring. Indeed, nothing is more characteristic of her own experience than the continuous awareness of her own bad side, which must be fought with and subdued again and again. With the aid of God's grace one makes progress but never attains perfection. Time and again she had thought her love was complete, but when she saw more clearly she was aware of great imperfections. "God-Love was determined to achieve the whole only little by little, for the sake of preserving my physical life, and so as to keep my behavior tolerable for those with whom I lived."

Catherine's doctrine of last things is closely connected with her teachings concerning sin and redemption. There is no break between our present life and our life after the body's death. While still in the flesh, the penitent soul experiences God's love as refining fire, even as souls in purgatory are cleansed of such stains as remain after death. Voluntary acceptance of the suffering necessarily attaching to the pleasure seeking of the false self renders suffering wholesome. Impenitent souls are those who have so far unmade themselves as to be no longer capable of recognizing God's love. To these nothing remains but to endure the pain, although even in these there must remain a residue of moral goodness that cannot but mitigate what they have to bear. This is hell; and it is the same whether it be experienced here or hereafter.

Part 3, "Critical," is a wide-ranging survey of scientific and philosophical opinions as they bear on religion in general and on mysticism in particular. There are interesting comparisons between Saint Catherine (canonized in 1737) and other mystics, most notably Saint Teresa of Ávila; learned discussions of Pseudo-Dionysius and other Neoplatonists; and a sympathetic presentation of quietism (Madame Guyon) and the doctrine of pure love (Fénelon). Catherine's doctrines are discussed at length and compared not merely with received doctrines of the Church but also with the teachings of many of Hügel's contemporaries. Hügel saw no difficulty in reconciling mysticism and science, insisting that, as over against various schools of Idealism, it is a leading characteristic of Catholic teaching to insist on the full reality of the "determinist Thing" alongside the freedom of Spirit—a principle he finds illustrated in Catherine's karmalike doctrine of purgation.

Hügel holds that there are three main elements of religion corresponding to three main forces of the soul. In his final summary he returns to these, arguing that although each of them is necessary to a true religion, any one of them divorced from the other two is destructive of itself and of religion. For example, institutionalism led to the Spanish Inquisition, rationalism to the Goddess of Reason being installed at Notre Dame of Paris, and emotionalism to the apocalyptic orgies of the Münster Anabaptists. Even where the imbalance does not reach these proportions, it leaves the church weak and divided, as in the parties of the Church of England: High, Broad, and Low Church.

Mysticism, which is one manifestation of the third or experimental element of religion, is as susceptible as the other elements of exaggeration and abuse. This is apparent when, as sometimes happens among followers of Pseudo-Dionysius, love of God is thought of as competing with love of God's creatures, and the inference is drawn that God is not loved until he is loved alone. However, in contrast to exclusive mysticism of this kind there is an inclusive mysticism that places God not alongside his creatures but behind them "as the light which shines through a crystal and lends it whatever lustre it may have." Among inclusive mystics, says Hügel, in spite of the uncertainty on many points of her life and of defects in her natural character and limited opportunity, Saint Catherine of Genoa "shines forth . . . with a penetrating attractiveness, rarely matched, hardly surpassed, by Saints and Heroes of . . . more massive gifts and actions."

Christian Themes

Hügel's selection of Saint Catherine of Genoa as the subject of his biography is made clear when he reveals the importance with which he regards mysticism. Mysticism is an essential element of a developed religion, he says, and the properties of mysticism are best studied in the lives of individual mystics. The traditional lives of mystics are commonly overlaid with legends, and must be subjected to historical criticism. Hügel carefully and critically analyzes the works of earlier writers on the saint as he examines every detail of her life, especially those relating to mystical experiences. He notes that because those who have enjoyed a full mystical experience frequently suffer from mental and nervous illness, care must be taken to distinguish symptoms of illness from spiritual insights.

Hügel especially praises inclusive mysticism, which recognizes the necessity of diverse types of souls and finds in the Kingdom of God the "means of an ever more distinct articulation, within an ever more fruitful interaction, of the various gifts, vocations, and types of souls which constitute its society." Among inclusive mystics, he notes one of the most prominent to be Saint Catherine of Genoa, which makes her a fitting subject for his study.

Sources for Further Study

De la Bedoyère, Michael. *The Life of Baron von Hügel*. New York: Scribner, 1951. A full-length biography including a full account of his role in the Modernist controversy as a friend and correspondent of Alfred Loisy and of George Tyrell.

Johns, David L. *Mysticism and Ethics in Friedrich von Hügel*. Lewiston, N.Y.: E. Mellen Press, 2004. Includes a bibliography and index.

Leonard, Ellen M. *Creative Tension: The Spiritual Legacy of Friedrich von Hügel*. Scranton, Pa.: University of Scranton Press, 1997. This biography focuses on Friedrich von Hügel's writings and spiritual activities. The author covers his life, philosophy, and spiritual vision. Includes a selective bibliography and index.

Whelan, Joseph P. *The Spirituality of Friedrich von Hügel*. Foreword by B. C. Butler. New York: Newman Press, 1971. Von Hügel's teachings concerning Christ, God, and the Church as they help to illuminate the problem of sanctity in the modern world. Includes a bibliography.

Jean H. Faurot

MYSTICAL THEOLOGY

Author: Pseudo-Dionysius the Areopagite (fl. c. 500 C.E.)
First transcribed: Peri mustikes theologias, c. 500 C.E. (English translation, 1897)
Edition used: "The Divine Names" and "Mystical Theology," translated with an introductory study by John D. Jones. Milwaukee, Wis.: Marquette University Press, 1980
Genre: Nonfiction
Subgenres: Mysticism; spiritual treatise; theology
Core issues: Cause universal; God; mysticism; reason; silence; the Trinity

This very short treatise of five chapters is, as Pseudo-Dionysius himself shows, the pinnacle of his teaching, a strongly Neoplatonic treatise on mystical theology.

Overview

Little in fact is known of the author now called Pseudo-Dionysius the Areopagite apart from what can be adduced from his writings. This alleged disciple of Saint Paul and first bishop of Athens is commonly identified today as a late fifth or early sixth century Syrian monk. He had immense influence on Christian spirituality through the commentaries written on his works by Maximus the Confessor in the seventh century. In the ninth century he was translated into Latin by Johannes Scotus Erigena. Thomas Aquinas often cited him as an authority.

Mystical Theology, which begins with a prayer to the Trinity, is addressed to Timothy—perhaps Saint Paul's disciple by that name. In regard to his own teaching, Dionysius claims the authority of Saint Bartholomew the Apostle. The chapters are geared toward motivating the reader to seek union with God in mystical contemplation rather than being content with some rational understanding of him. For this purpose the author insists that we not only purify ourselves morally but even leave behind rational thought and sense experience. Like many writers of this genre, he issues a warning against sharing this treatise with the uninitiated. The work falls very clearly on the side of the theology of negation or apophaticism.

We truly get to know God not by apprehending him with our understanding. The reasoning powers must enter into a passive stillness, allowing the highest faculty in the human person to possess God with a knowledge that exceeds understanding. This knowledge is a darkness that is beyond light. At this level we praise God by a transcendent hymnody; namely, by letting go of all thoughts and images and simply giving our naked self to God to be united with him.

The affirmative way begins with what is most like the Deity and then surpasses it. The negative way begins by denying what is most different from the Deity and arises to the negation of all categories of thought. Dionysius illustrates this assertion by tracing his own path through his previous writings. In *Symbolic Divinity* (no longer extant), the search for the Deity began with metaphorical titles drawn from the world of sense and applied to the nature of God, such as his functions, instruments of activity, places, passions, and emotions. In *Peri theion onomaton* (c. 500; *Divine Names*, 1897) the author begins from the titles of God formed by the intellect. Finally, in the *Outlines of Divinity* (no longer extant), it is the revelations that come through the sacred Scriptures that are his source. Dionysius notes that the higher one ascends, the greater is the brevity of speech. This, his highest treatise, is the briefest of all.

He sums up his teaching in his last sentence: "The Deity transcends all affirmation by being the perfect and unique Cause of all things, and transcends all negation by the preeminence of Its simple and absolute nature—free from every limitation and beyond them all"—in a word, incomprehensible.

An earlier age of faith more in tune with mystical experience held Dionysius in higher regard than does our present age, which is more rationalistic in its theological approach. Orthodox Christian theologians are a bit uncomfortable with him because of what they see as an excessive emphasis on the Godhead and unity, to the detriment of the substantiality of the Trinity of Persons. There is some fear that the Neoplatonic philosopher eclipses the theologian. Dionysius's writings do suffer from an obscurity of style that makes translation uncertain. This obscurity does not arise from a lack of skill on the part of the author but out of a desire to conceal the lofty truths he is dealing with from the ridicule of the profane. He is very concise (especially in this last treatise), uses Platonic expressions, and invents new words and striking new expressions. Some see him as having an important role in Christian dialogue with Eastern religions.

Christian Themes

A summary of Pseudo-Dionysius the Areopagite's primary theological assertions in *Mystical Theology* would include the following points:

- The Deity possesses all the positive attributes of the universe, yet more strictly it does not, for it transcends them all.
- The Deity is beyond all distinctions of good and evil.
- By rejecting all knowledge, we can possess a knowledge that exceeds understanding, the darkness of unknowing.
- This negative method must be wholly distinguished from the use of positive statements.
- The higher we ascend, the more we are reduced to silence.
- The universal Cause, transcending all, is neither impersonal nor lifeless nor irrational nor without understanding, but is beyond all qualities, faculties, and categories of rational thought.
- The Deity is not Spirit, Sonship, or Fatherhood.

Sources for Further Study

Maximus Confessor. "The Ascetic Life" and "The Four Centuries on Charity." Translated and annotated by Polycarp Sherwood. Westminster, Md.: Newman Press, 1955. The writings of Maximus helped to restore the balance between Neoplatonism and Christian orthodoxy; his commentaries on Dionysius enabled the work of Dionysius to have a profound effect on Christian spirituality.

"Mystical Theology": The Glosses by Thomas Gallus and the Commentary of Robert Grosseteste on "De mystica theologia." Translated with an introduction by James McEvoy. Dudley, Mass.: Peeters, 2003. Serious students of Bonaventure will be especially interested in the historic glosses. Bibliography, index.

Pseudo-Dionysius the Areopagite. *The Divine Names.* Translated by the Editors of the Shrine of Wisdom. Brook, Surrey, England: Shrine of Wisdom, 1957. God is first considered in his undifferentiated aspect; then his differentiated aspect is examined in terms of his attributes represented by the divine names.

Sparrow-Simpson, W. J. "The Influence of Dionysius in Religious History." In *The Divine Names and the Mystical Theology*, translated by C. E. Rolt. London: Society for Promoting Christian Knowledge, 1940. Remains perhaps the best study available in English concerning Dionysius's overall place in the Christian tradition.

M. Basil Pennington

MYSTICISM
A Study in the Nature and Development
of Man's Spiritual Consciousness

Author: Evelyn Underhill (1875-1941)
First published: 1911
Edition used: Mysticism: A Study in the Nature and Development of Man's Spiritual Consciousness. New York: Dutton, 1961
Genre: Nonfiction
Subgenres: History; mysticism; spiritual treatise
Core issues: Awakening; contemplation; conversion; illumination; mysticism; purgation; recollection; self-abandonment; silence; simplicity; soul; union with God

Born into a middle-class family in which there was no particular emphasis on religion, Underhill was converted to Christianity after a visit to a convent in 1907 and, although at first inclined to join the Roman Catholic Church, remained with the Church of England and became fully committed in 1921. In her work she emphasized the importance of worship, the course and spirit of Western mysticism, pacifism, the ministry of spiritual direction, and spiritual retreats. The heart of Mysticism *is her extensive analysis of the highest examples of the spiritual life, primarily the great mystics of the Middle Ages. Her description of the mystical way has become normative.*

Overview

Evelyn Underhill begins *Mysticism* with the awakening of the self to a consciousness of Divine Reality. This experience, usually abrupt and well recognized, is accompanied by feelings of intense joy. She suggests that it is an intense form of "conversion" or "sanctification." It is usually a crisis experience. She cites the example of Saint Francis of Assisi, who went into the church of San Damiano to pray and, "having been smitten by unwonted visitations, found himself another man than he who had gone in." Some people like George Fox, founder of the Quakers, however, have a more gradual experience. In awakening, the person surrenders totally to God, and a passionate love for God, for the Absolute, is born.

As Underhill says, "the business and method of Mysticism is Love." According to "An Epistle of Discretion" (probably by the same anonymous author as *The Cloud of Unknowing*, first transcribed in the late fourteenth century), God "may not be known by reason, [God] may not be gotten by thought, nor concluded by understanding; but [God] may be loved and chosen with the true lovely will of thine heart." As John of Ruysbroeck put it, "where intelligence must rest without, love and desire can enter in."

The process of purification, purgation, begins. The soul, meeting God, realizes its sinfulness, its willfulness. Catherine of Genoa's first response to her vision of God's unmeasured love was "No more world! no more sin!" The first steps are contrition and repentance. According to Richard of Saint Victor, though, the "essence of purgation is self-simplification." The perpetual process of purification has both negative and positive sides. The first is detachment, the stripping away or purging of all that is superfluous, illusionary, or distracting. It is the essence of the "evangelical counsels": poverty, chastity, and obedience. Many, though not all, of the great mystics have been members of religious orders or have adopted monastic practices, at least during this period of their lives. Underhill defines poverty as "a breaking down of [humanity's] inveterate habit of trying to rest in, or take seriously, things which are 'less than God': i.e., which do not possess the character of reality."

The more positive or active side is mortification, the changing of one's character, the forming of new habits. It is a dying and finding new life. According to fourteenth century mystic John Tauler, "this dying has many degrees, and so has this life. A man might die a thousand deaths in one day and find at once a joyful life corresponding to each of them." Asceticism for the mystics is a means to an end, not an end in itself. Another fourteenth century mystic, Henry Suso, practiced extreme mortification for sixteen years, and then "on a certain Whitsun Day a heavenly messenger appeared to him, and ordered him in God's name to continue no more." He ceased at once "and threw all the instruments of his sufferings . . . into a river." Catherine of Genoa went through a penitential period of four years, constantly haunted by a sense of sin, and then in an instant it seemed as though her sins were cast into the sea and she was free. In modern terms, their attitude toward spiritual disciplines was simply "No pain, no gain." Their goal was freedom from the world, freedom from self-will.

Interspersed with purgation is illumination, God's revelations of the divine. Some called it *Ludus Amoris*, the game of love that God plays with the seeking soul. The mystic is consoled by glimpses of the Divine Reality. Though a sense of self remains, and thus a distance from God, the soul is treated to moments of transcendence, rapture, ecstasy. Some experience a total oneness with nature. Others hear voices or celestial music, see visions, feel heat or stabbing joy, write automatically. This is not the unitive state, because the self remains separate and intact and the moments of illumination are measured.

This state is not to be sought for its ecstasies or clutched as though it could be selfishly preserved. Underhill is careful to note that true mystics seek God alone, not spiritual thrills. She criticizes the early eighteenth century French mystic Madame Guyon (whose doctrines of Quietism were considered heretical by the Roman Catholic Church) as "basking like a pious tabby cat in the beams of the Uncreated Light." The purpose of illumination is to call the soul onward in its quest. Quoting John of Ruysbroeck: "Here there begins an eternal hunger, which shall never more be satisfied. It is the inward craving and hankering of the affective power and created spirit after an Uncreated Good."

The pious soul is now tuned to recollection, quiet, and contemplation, topics to which Underhill devotes several chapters. This is the mystic's education of the faculty of concentration, the power of spiritual attention. This is where the mystic ascends the ladder toward heaven, practices "degrees of prayer." This is not petition but the yearning of the soul for God. Recollection begins in meditation and develops into interior silence or simplicity. This melts into true Quiet. This deepens into ordinary contemplation and then into the contemplation proper, which is passive union with God. The "personality is not lost: only its hard edge is gone," says Underhill.

However, as the mystic travels toward union, he or she must cross the desert, that period of blankness and stagnation known as the dark night of the soul, so named by John of the Cross. All consolations are withdrawn. Often the person is assailed by slanders and trials without, doubts and temptations within. It is the final purgation of selfhood, "self-naughting." The aspiring soul must struggle on, usually on the basis of naked faith and sheer will. All sense of God's presence is gone. A sense of one's hopeless and helpless imperfection weighs heavily, and there is complete emotional exhaustion, spiritual aridity. Sometimes death seems preferable to struggle. The goal is total surrender and utter humility. Those who persevere may obtain union with God, the unitive life. Underhill underscores the "may" because it is a gift from God's grace, not the result of a person's work or willing. The mystics teach that the lessons of the way are just as valuable as the attainment; thus the soul who strives and does not attain union is also blessed.

Union is often described under the metaphor of spiritual marriage between the soul and God. Richard of Saint Victor described the result: "When the soul is plunged in the fire of divine love, like iron, it first loses its blackness, and then growing to white heat, it becomes like unto the fires itself. And lastly, it grows liquid, and losing its nature is transmuted into an utterly different quality of being." The result is not passive exaltation but energetic action. Joan of Arc led the armies of France. Catherine of Genoa administered hospitals; Catherine of Siena became a peacemaker between warring states; Teresa of Ávila reformed her order. Francis of Assisi became God's troubadour. Many mystics wrote of their insights and counseled those in need of spiritual nurture. They led productive lives of balanced wholeness.

One of the most attractive features of the book is an appendix that gives the history of mysticism in outline form, citing all the great mystics, their dates, relationships to one another, and their principal ideas. The high points of mysticism were in the eleventh and fourteenth centuries. A bibliography follows with a listing of the major works by each mystic of note. Another feature of this book that appeals to the student is the outline at the beginning of each chapter. These allow the reader to follow the continuity of Underhill's argument and then to read more deeply in the sections with special appeal or to find parts one has previously read. Since this is a rather massive book, the help is welcome.

Christian Themes

Underhill's *Mysticism* identifies five distinct stages through which the mystical life develops as the soul finds its way to union with God: awakening, in which one makes a commitment to seek God with all of the heart; purgation, in which one, realizing one's own finitude and imperfections, seeks to become detached from all sensible things through discipline and mortification; illumination, in which God gives the soul various "consolations" as encouragement—voices, visions, trances; the dark night of the soul, in which all sense of God's presence vanishes and the mystic must struggle on toward the goal of faith; and finally union, in which the soul is united with God.

Underhill's interest in *Mysticism* is in the philosophical basis for mysticism, an understanding of the universe as constituted on two levels: that of the physical senses and that of the spiritual realm. She does not analyze or critique at any length, however, the Neoplatonism on which most understandings of mysticism have been based. Her interest is more psychological than philosophical or theological. In looking at the psychological aspects of the mystical life, Underhill notes with the anonymous author of *The Cloud of Unknowing* that "By love [God] may be gotten and holden, but by thought . . . never." Throughout she stresses the psychological maturity and balance that has characterized the great Christian mystics.

Sources for Further Study

Cropper, Margaret. *Life of Evelyn Underhill: An Intimate Portrait of the Groundbreaking Author of "Mysticism."* 1958. With a new foreword by Dana Greene and an introduction by Emilie Griffin. Woodstock, Vt.: SkyLight Paths, 2003. A reissue of an absorbing spiritual biography by an early biographer and friend of Underhill. This detailed account of Underhill's life remains an excellent introduction to her work.

Greene, Dana. *Evelyn Underhill: Artist of the Infinite Life.* 1990. Notre Dame, Ind.: University of Notre Dame Press, 1998. Greene is well read in Underhill's works, has done extensive research and interviews, and knew Underhill personally. Thus, this thorough biography goes beyond life facts to include Underhill's mentors, environment, milieu, and passions. Includes a bibliography and index.

Griffin, Emilie. Introduction to *Evelyn Underhill: Essential Writings.* Maryknoll, N.Y.: Orbis Books, 2003. A very well-written, authoritative, and concise summary of Underhill's life and achievements. An excellent introduction.

Underhill, Evelyn. *The Letters of Evelyn Underhill.* Edited with an introduction by Charles Williams. Westminster, Md.: Christian Classics, 1989. Underhill's letters reveal the pervasiveness of her spiritual preoccupations.

Nancy A. Hardesty

THE NAME OF THE ROSE

Author: Umberto Eco (1932-   )

First published: Il nome della rosa, 1980 (English translation, 1983)

Edition used: The Name of the Rose, translated by William Weaver. New York: Harcourt Brace Jovanovich, 1983

Genre: Novel

Subgenres: Historical fiction (fourteenth century); mystery and detective fiction; thriller/suspense

Core issues: Clerical life; justice; knowledge; reason

By reading the signs in the world around them the way they might read the letters and words in the books on theology or philosophy in the abbey library, two monks unravel a murder mystery at a medieval monastery. Both the clues they discover and the phrases of scripture at the heart of ongoing religious debate are open to numerous interpretations. Truth, whether about events in the world or about the divine, cannot be revealed through intellectual pursuits alone.

> *Principal characters*
> *William of Baskerville*, a Franciscan monk who solves mysteries through the use of reason
> *Adso of Melk*, the first-person narrator, a novice monk traveling as William's scribe
> *Abo*, the abbot
> *Jorge of Burgos*, an elderly monk
> *Malachi of Hildesheim*, the librarian
> *Berengar of Arundel*, the assistant librarian
> *Adelmo of Otranto*, a monk attracted to Berengar
> *Salvatore*, a former heretic
> *Bernard Gui*, a representative of the pope
> *Michael of Cesena*, an advocate of poverty for clerics
> *Benno of Uppsala*, a monk who is chosen as the new assistant librarian upon Berengar's death

Overview

Through the use of a preface, Umberto Eco presents *The Name of the Rose* as a book he came upon by chance. That book was a translation of a manuscript written by Adso of Melk, a monk in the fourteenth century. The fictional framing of the novel and distancing of the narrator from the story alert the reader to the theme of the way knowledge and understanding are gained and the novel's questioning of the accuracy and relevance of what is learned.

Adso of Melk, a young novice monk, relates the story of how he accompanies the Franciscan monk William of Baskerville to an abbey in northern Italy, where a meeting between opposing factions in the Church will soon take place. The pope, who is very rich, wants to keep factions of monks who advocate poverty for the clergy from gaining power. The abbey is in a state of anxiety because a monk has recently died; the monks believe he was murdered and that supernatural, evil forces are loose in the abbey. As more deaths follow, William uses logic to discover how the monks died. William advocates observing carefully to understand the signs that will reveal truth. In contrast, others, such as the inquisitor Bernard Gui, rely on superstition and assumptions. William believes for a time that the murders follow a pattern laid out in the Apocalypse (Book of Revelation), and the elderly monk Jorge of Burgos encourages this line of thinking to distract William from the truth. There was not, in fact, a single murderer, although poison, which Jorge smeared on the pages of a book, did kill several monks. William realizes that the first death was a suicide.

The deaths in the novel result from the monks' passions, both physical and mental. Adelmo of Otranto commits suicide after regretting his relationship with Berengar of Arundel; physical attraction between the monks is a common theme in the book, and Adso's youthful attractiveness is several times the subject of comment. Adso spends much of the novel pining after a young woman whom he encounters and with whom he has had sexual relations; he grieves deeply when Bernard Gui accuses her of witchcraft and takes her away to be burned. The monks' passion for books and knowledge compels them to risk the demons said to be hiding in the forbidden library, the labyrinthine floor plan of which makes seeking books a risky proposition. For several, the desire to read the forbidden book of Aristotle on laughter leads to death as they lick their fingers trying to turn the pages and consume the poison Jorge has left there.

At the novel's end, William solves the mystery, but it is too late to do any good. The abbey is destroyed in the fire that begins when William and Adso struggle with Jorge over the forbidden book. Adso returns to Melk. There, late in his life, he records the events of his youth.

Christian Themes

On one level, *The Name of the Rose* is a murder mystery solved by a clever detective. However, like the clues that William and Adso find, there are many layers of meaning. Before publishing the novel, Umberto Eco earned the distinction of being a leading literary theorist, best known for his work in semiotics. Semiotics, the study of signs, is a way of understanding how meaning is created or understood, whether in a work of literature or in life. A sign can be any unit of information that conveys meaning—a word, an article of clothing, a drop of blood at a murder scene. Eco theorized both that signs have multiple meanings and that a methodical approach is the best way of comprehending a series of signs. Many aspects of Eco's semiotic theory are evident in the novel. Eco theorized that meaning is created in literature in part through reference to other works of literature. In the novel, William's and Adso's method of solving the crimes owes an obvious debt to Sherlock Holmes and his friend Dr. Watson.

The church history and theological debates of the Middle Ages are important factors of the novel's setting in a medieval abbey. The monks are caught in a political conflict between the pope and the king of France and engaged in power struggles between groups of clergy. They also face the issue of how or whether to remain celibate, and, if they do not, must choose between women, seen as sources of evil and temptation, and fellow monks. However, the monks, who spend their days working on copying and preserving manuscripts, are most interested in intellectual issues. In fact, the murders occur largely because those who die are seeking knowledge that has been declared inappropriate for them.

This theme of seeking forbidden knowledge extends throughout the novel. Although the abbey houses one of the finest libraries in the world, monks who live and work there cannot enter and must request books from the librarian. The abbot himself must approve some requests, and no one is allowed to see certain books. Even the library's floor plan is designed to discourage access to materials. Knowledge is potentially dangerous and threatening to religious belief. Jorge, by poisoning the pages, makes the work of Aristotle literally deadly. The cause of most of the deaths, he is in some respects most guilty of intellectual pride. The Bible refers to Jesus as the Word made flesh. In the sacrament of the Eucharist, the body of Christ is consumed in the form of bread. Jorge and other monks kills themselves by eating the pages of the forbidden book that he has smeared with poison; the narrator contrasts this act of eating printed words with consuming the body of Christ in the Eucharist.

At the end of the novel, William and Adso are left with the question of whether events occur in a knowable order or at random, with an order that is imposed by the observer. Every clue they study has more than one meaning. This uncertainty in determining truth applies not only to the novel's murder mystery but also to the religious truths the monks attempt to decipher. God's ways are not easily revealed to man; Eco thus reinforces the theme that intellectual pride is a sin, inadequate to reveal God's mystery.

Sources for Further Study

Bondanella, Peter. *Umberto Eco and the Open Text: Semiotics, Fiction, Popular Culture*. Cambridge, England: Cambridge University Press, 1997. Analyzes Eco's fiction in the context of his literary theory, showing how his semiotics, or theory of signs, is applicable to the detective work in *The Name of the Rose*.

Caesar, Michael. *Umberto Eco: Philosophy, Semiotics, and the Work of Fiction*. Cambridge, England: Polity Press, 1999. Comprehensive overview of Eco's theories, with explanations of how they influence and appear in his fiction.

Inge, Thomas M., ed. *Naming the Rose: Essays on Eco's "The Name of the Rose."* Jackson: University of Mississippi Press, 1988. Anthologizes some of the best essays on the novel to the time of publication. Contains a checklist of articles on and reviews of the novel.

Ross, Charlotte, and Rochelle Sibley, eds. *Illuminating Eco: On the Boundaries of Interpretation*. Burlington, Vt.: Ashgate, 2004. A collection of essays chosen to show the variety of approaches British scholars have taken to Eco's novels and theoretical works. Includes contributions by Eco.

Joan Hope

THE NATURE AND DESTINY OF MAN
A Christian Interpretation

Author: Reinhold Niebuhr (1892-1971)
First published: Vol. 1, *Human Nature*, 1941; vol. 2, *Human Destiny*, 1943
Edition used: The Nature and Destiny of Man: A Christian Interpretation. Louisville,
   Ky.: Westminster John Knox Press, 1964
Genre: Nonfiction
Subgenres: Church history; theology
Core issues: Faith; Protestants and Protestantism; reason; religion; scriptures

*According to Niebuhr, human beings are part of the natural world but their spirit
gives them transcendent power over it. They are capable of self-consciousness and
are free to act. This freedom, however, is limited by personal and historical circumstances. Because human beings cannot know their destiny or fully understand the ultimate meaning of life, they are anxious about their future. History demonstrates the futility of believing that human reason alone can find meaning or bring salvation on
earth. Christian faith, through the grace of God's forgiveness of sin and redemption,
provides a way out of this dilemma.*

Overview

In *Human Nature*, the first volume of *The Nature and Destiny of Man*, Reinhold
Niebuhr surveys human history from Plato to modern times, focusing on political, religious, and philosophical movements and theories, highlighting human beings' efforts to understand themselves and to craft their own destiny. From ancient civilizations through the Renaissance and Romanticism up to modern culture, the intellectual
leaders in each era defined human nature with a historical bias and sought to remedy
social evils with limited insight. The ancient Greeks, principally Plato, held that each
human consisted of a soul, body, and spirit. Human beings' ability to reason, it was argued, distinguishes them from all other animals on earth. Humans are the only self-
conscious animal, able to stand outside themselves or see themselves as objects in nature. They also can manipulate history, within certain limits, because they are able to
choose how to act. As creatures who live in and are bound by time, people's lives are a
linear, measurable flow. Their spirits also give them a kind of perpendicular existence.

Through transcendence, humans can know God, whose image resides naturally in
human nature, giving humans some idea as to the nature of God. A view of God's relation to humans is contained in the ideas of religious and secular thinkers up to modern
times and turns on the notion that humans have the power to transcend their finiteness
either with their reason or with their faith in and relation to God. Religious and philosophical thought from the ancient Greeks to the modern theorists is concerned primarily with the relation of reason, spirit, and nature. The naturalistic view sees humans as

creatures bound to nature, and therefore having vitalistic impulses, and bound to God through their spirits. Each of the major intellectual movements, classical, Renaissance, Romantic, and modern, emphasized one or the other of these conceptions of humankind or conceived a blend of both. Renaissance thinkers celebrated humankind's mastery over nature through the powers of the human mind and emphasized the importance of science in humankind's intellectual development.

Modern conceptions of humankind combine the Romantic idea of humanity's relation to nature with the Renaissance faith in reason and individuality, freedom of the human spirit as opposed to the Christian notion of humankind's predestination. Modern people, Niebuhr concludes, cannot decide whether they control their destiny through their reason or are controlled by nature through their affinity with it. The power of the individual seems boundless, given technology and science, but the autonomy of the individual is lost in the very forces that culture has developed.

Niebuhr points out that the behavior of humans, even their destiny, is inescapably contingent on historical circumstances, and to think otherwise, to think that humans do not need divine guidance because they have the power of reason, is to commit the sin of pride. Too much faith in human reason leads to idolatry; too little faith in God leads to cynicism. Without Christian faith, humans are left with the feeling that life is meaningless. Niebuhr agrees with philosopher Søren Kierkegaard's thesis that humans suffer from inherent and inescapable anxiety caused by the dread of individual annihilation. Human history reveals a struggle for survival that pits humans against humans and disrupts the harmony of nature. Freedom allows humans to make choices, but these choices are tainted by self-interest, which leads to inequality, injustice, conflict, and sin.

In *Human Destiny*, the second volume of *The Nature and Destiny of Man*, Niebuhr explains that his interpretation of history is based on the belief that Christ's coming represented a divine purpose, which shall be fulfilled in the Second Coming. Christ symbolizes God's presence in humankind's destiny, which is realized by adherence to God's law. Humans must overcome conflicts between self-love and brotherly love, *agape* and *eros*, and egoism and Christian altruism. The resurrection promised by Christ awaits those who are guided by sacrificial love, not self-love. The paradox of Christian ethics stems from the idea that one gains freedom by submitting to God's law of love and that one finds oneself by losing oneself in Christ. The ideal life is to live in harmony with nature, guided by mutual love, and to bring the soul in harmony with God through self-sacrificing love.

The coming of Christ symbolized a twofold grace, that of forgiveness of humankind's sins and that of empowering human beings to redeem themselves through love. Without God's grace, humans lack the spiritual and moral strength to overcome sin. Christ's coming gave humans hope of final redemption through the spirit. History is growth, not simply progress through time. Humans are continually challenged to use their reasoning to address events as they arise, but the ultimate escape from finitude and egoism lies beyond human history. Christian faith leads one to accept what human reason and human experience cannot prove, that eternity is not a physical consummation of historical growth; rather, it is the elevation of the spirit into the timeless realm of God's grace. To break the cycle of sin and despair, Niebuhr argues, one must accept the paradox of faith, that freedom comes from knowing that one is not free and that one escapes sin by freeing the spirit of egoistic demands. In doing so, one achieves spiritual wisdom that comes from faith.

Christian Themes

Niebuhr argues that human nature is uniquely dual. Humans are finite creatures, whose brief lives on earth are subject to the demands of nature and to their personal struggle to satisfy their individual needs. Through the power of reason, humans can choose how they live and think; they therefore have some control over their lives, but because they cannot escape their egoism and self-interest, conflict inevitably arises between individuals, social groups, and nations, even between humans and nature. In Christian terms, humans live in a state of sin as long as their actions are guided by self-interest and the belief that one can find happiness and fulfillment by the use of reason alone. Christian faith is necessary because it shows the way out of sin and the way to spiritual fulfillment. The tension between the freedom to direct the course of history and the inability to overcome finite human nature can be relieved only by surrendering to a complete faith in God's wisdom, as it revealed in the New Testament and embodied in the figure of Christ.

A life lived by Christian faith balances the needs of the individual and the needs of others; it creates a harmony with nature, with the self, and with others. The sin of inequality and the taint of conscience are also eliminated. One gains eternal life by accepting God's twofold grace, that of redemption from sin and that of resurrection through spiritual elevation. A belief in the redemptive power of God's love frees one from the anxiety caused by knowing that one will die and the feeling that life has no purpose or meaning beyond the present. Christian faith frees one from the guilt of sinfulness because of Christ's redeeming act of self-sacrifice, and Christian faith offers eternal life.

Sources for Further Study

Brown, Charles C. *Niebuhr and His Age: Reinhold Niebuhr's Prophetic Role in the Twentieth Century*. Philadelphia: Trinity Press International, 1992. Relates Niebuhr's thoughts to political and social history in the second half of the twentieth century; reviews and evaluates *The Nature and Destiny of Man*.

Clark, Henry B. *Serenity, Courage, and Wisdom: The Enduring Legacy of Reinhold Niebuhr*. Cleveland, Ohio: Pilgrim Press, 1994. Surveys the whole of Niebuhr's thinking, showing its political relevance and its place in theological and ethical debate; includes a survey of criticism of Neibuhr's ideas.

Fox, Richard Wightman. *Reinhold Niebuhr: A Biography*. New York: Pantheon Books, 1985. Reviews the structure and purpose of *The Nature and Destiny of Man* and its political impact; a substantial bibliography is included.

Lovin, Robin W. Introduction to *Nature and Destiny of Man: A Christian Interpreta-

tion by Reinhold Niebuhr. Louisville, Ky.: Westminster John Knox Press, 1964. Analyzes the major ideas and structure of *The Nature and Destiny of Man*.

Novak, Michael. "Father of Neoconservatives: Nowadays, the Truest Disciples of the Liberal Theologian Reinhold Niebuhr Are Conservatives." *National Review* 44, no. 9 (May 11, 1992): 39-42. Shows the extent to which Niebuhr's religious ideas have political and economic relevance and the power to stir debate between the Right and Left.

Bernard E. Morris

A NEW KIND OF CHRISTIAN
A Tale of Two Friends on a Spiritual Journey

Author: Brian D. McLaren (1956-   )
First published: San Francisco: Jossey-Bass, 2001
Genre: Novella
Subgenres: Essays; journal or diary
Core issues: Church; discipleship; evangelization; friendship; Protestants and Protestantism

An evangelical pastor tells of how an older layman helped him think through his disillusionment with late twentieth century American Protestantism. With his friend's help, the pastor comes to recognize the difficulties as systemic but not irresolvable. The typical failures of both conservative and liberal Protestants are often traceable to the time-conditioned Christianity that emerged through confrontation with "modernity," not the nature of the Gospel itself. The disruptions involved in engaging an increasingly postmodern culture thus offer great hope for renewal and for a shift in mindset that may allow the churches to transcend stultifying patterns of thought and action.

Principal characters
Dan Poole, the narrator
Dr. N. E. "Neo" Oliver, Dan's friend

Overview

A New Kind of Christian begins when Dan Poole, pastor of Potomac Community Church in suburban Maryland, meets his daughter's science teacher, Dr. N. E. Oliver ("Neo" to his friends), on a day when he is considering abandoning the pastorate. Dan can no longer live in harmony with a church culture that he now sees as stagnant and self-satisfied, and he is suffering in his faith because the kind of Christian he feels unable to serve is the only kind of Christian he knows how to be. Neo takes a generous interest in Dan's plight, and Dan quickly discovers a thoughtful Christian in the erudite, personable, Jamaican-born science teacher; he is struck by Neo's ability to abandon evangelical myopia without at the same time falling into liberalism or vacuousness, and he decides to cultivate the friendship.

From their first, extended conversation over coffee and bagels, it becomes apparent that Neo, a former pastor, has long pondered the kinds of Church problems that are on Dan's mind and has developed a theory to illuminate them. To Neo, Dan's apprehensions are symptoms of a larger cultural paradigm shift. Though culture is always evolving, Western society is currently experiencing its deepest mental reconfiguration since medieval culture began to give way to "modernity" in the 1500's under the combined pressures of modern science and Protestant Christianity. In Neo's estimation, the modern culture that thus arose fixed its sights on values such as objectivity, proof, argument, mechanization, institutionalization, secularization, individualism, and consumerism. While this cultural focus yielded various great achievements (many important technologies, for example), it also was based on a view of the human person that now appears incomplete, resulting in a single-minded pursuit of progress and control that marginalizes the aesthetic, spiritual, and interpersonal needs of human life. The cultural shift to postmodern thinking thus involves a general recognition that the modernistic mentality must be transformed into something more open, comprehensive, and humane. In Neo's view, Dan is experiencing cognitive dissonance as a result of the ways Western Christianity has assimilated itself into its modernistic cultural environment; modern Christianity is embattled because modernity in general, not necessarily Christianity as such, is being radically challenged by an increasingly postmodern culture.

Dan finds Neo's ideas to be a source of insight, hope, and challenge. Over several months, the two continue to converse about the problems and opportunities that emerge when modern-style Protestant Christians are confronted with postmodernity. Neo typically attempts to transcend the customary options in many modern Christian quandaries, holding that "people are often *against* something worth being *against* but in the process find themselves *for* some things that aren't worth being *for*." Together, he and Dan discuss contemporary attitudes about heaven and hell and who goes where; the role and interpretation of the Bible in the Church; faith and finances; the trivializations caused by law-centered and individual-centered morality; inadequate conceptions of Christian truth; patterns of theological smugness and vitriol; the pervasiveness of hollow or self-absorbed spirituality and of "numbers-oriented" evangelism.

Neo is suddenly called upon to move to Seattle to bury his father and care for his ailing mother. In the few months before Neo's mother dies, he and Dan continue their friendship, exchanging insights and support via e-mail and telephone. With the passing of his mother and the sale of his parents' house, Neo receives a large inheritance and is inspired to spend a year of self-renewal traveling the globe. He tells Dan that he has also resolved to reenter the pastorate after his return, devoting his remaining years to facilitating the emergence of a postmodern Christianity.

During Neo's travels, Dan, himself recommitted to the pastorate, gets in touch with one of Neo's friends from church, who shares with Dan a group of e-mails from Neo containing some positive conjectures about postmodern ministry. Seminaries will need to embrace a more holistic view of Christian leadership, becoming less like theology schools and more like the Catholic religious orders. Churches must refuse to be nostalgic ghettos or marketers of a commodity and instead must claim the freedom needed to empower Christians to live God's love for the real world. Because the problem is with the modern worldview itself, incrementally added "techniques" miss the point; a comprehensive paradigm shift is necessary. As Dan concludes his memoir of their friendship thus far, he is still awaiting news of Neo's return.

Christian Themes

In his introduction, Brian McLaren explains that *A New Kind of Christian* began as a work of nonfiction, born of his own crises and conversations as pastor of an evangelical church attempting the leap into postmodernity. His lively insights and genial style struck a nerve at the beginning at the twenty-first century, and *A New Kind of Christian* generated two sequels, *The Story We Find Ourselves In* (2003) and *The Last Word and the Word After That* (2005), establishing McLaren as the figurehead of an adventurous movement calling itself Postmodern Christianity, or the Emergent Church.

McLaren's musings fit well into the venerable tradition of Christian reform, calling the faithful back to the centrality of Christ's charity and denouncing false accretions that have pushed it to the margins of Christian life. He is preceded in his critique of unreflectively modernized Christianity by a number of major theological thinkers, including Blaise Pascal, John Henry Newman, Søren Kierkegaard, Fyodor Dostoevski, and Romano Guardini. The "postmodern Christian" critique is fully new, however, insofar as it adds particular concern for current tendencies in secular philosophy and popular culture. It also gains a very distinctive flavor from its immediate context, a local conversation probing the thought patterns of American free-church Protestants as well as, less directly, liberal mainline Protestantism.

Its concreteness is one of the book's chief characteristics. Though the book is highly idea-driven, the incarnation of those ideas in dialogue and narrative is no coincidence. The context of talk among Christian friends encourages a sympathetic reading and, more important, suits the book's concern with exploring worldviews, not abstract systems. This holistic approach to faith and thought also contributes to the appreciation of vital traditions, rather than mere "correct ideas," as a locus of insight in premodern, Catholic, and Eastern Christianity, and as a core priority for the postmodern church. Even the adventurous and iconoclastic urgency of Neo's views about the need to free American churches to move beyond their successes in modern terms—mighty accomplishments such as pristine systematic theologies and robust church attendance—is ultimately subordinated to a holistic approach, insofar as it expresses the desire to restore to its proper centrality the model of Christian life as a pilgrimage of faith.

In complement to the enthusiasm McLaren's book has expressed and garnered, there has been no shortage of theological counter-critiques. Nevertheless, because of the book's approach, perhaps the most direct concerns regard not the book's orthodoxy but the wisdom of its general outlook. For example, if Postmodern Christianity is fundamentally suspicious of real intellectual and churchly authority, what will guide its freedom to rise above the level of whimsy and fragmentation? More compelling still is the question of whether such a movement's Christian spirituality will be profound enough to keep it from degenerating into just another activist modern ideology? The sheer diversity of the values that Dan and Neo espouse (values such as spirituality, activism, anti-individualism, and anti-institutionalism) makes such questions a principal undertone of the book for many Christian readers.

Sources for Further Study

Benedict XVI. *God Is Love; Deus Caritas Est*. Washington, D.C.: United States Conference of Catholic Bishops, 2006. Seminal papal letter pondering Christianity's heart and the fountainhead of all Christian renewal. Classical vision complements and contrasts with postmodern critique.

Brueggeman, Walter. *Texts Under Negotiation: The Bible and Postmodern Imagination*. Minneapolis, Minn.: Fortress Press, 1993. A biblical scholar presents ways that postmodern perspective can enable more fruitful reading of the Bible's story.

Groeschel, Benedict, et al. *A Drama of Reform*. San Francisco: Ignatius Press, 2005. A Catholic perspective on street-level church renewal; the story of a Franciscan reform coming out of the South Bronx. Beautifully photographed.

Guder, Darrell, et al. *Missional Church: A Vision for the Sending of the Church in North America*. Grand Rapids, Mich.: Wm. B. Eerdmans, 1998. A postmodernstyle ecclesiology, envisioning the whole Church as God's agent commissioned for bringing about his reign in the world.

Joseph Van House, O.Cist.

A NEW SONG

Author: Jan Karon (1937-   )
First published: 1999
Edition used: A New Song. New York: Penguin Putnam, 2005
Genre: Novel
Subgenres: Evangelical fiction; romance
Core issues: African Americans; alienation from God; awakening; connectedness; faith; pastoral role; responsibility

Father Timothy Kavanagh has retired as rector of his Mitford, North Carolina, mountain church and is called to an interim appointment on Whitecap Island, off the coast of North Carolina. While his old parishioners have become friends and still rely on him for help, problems, both spiritual and physical, beset his new congregation, even before a severe storm sweeps over the island. With God's help, he finds the strength to solve these new problems without abandoning his old responsibilities.

> *Principal characters*
> *Father Timothy Kavanagh,* the protagonist, an Episcopal priest
> *Cynthia Coppersmith Kavanagh,* Timothy's wife
> *Dooley Barlowe,* a neglected sixteen-year-old boy given a home by Kavanagh
> *Morris Love,* a disabled Whitecap neighbor, a gifted organist
> *Jeffrey Tolson,* a former Whitecap choir director
> *Janette Tolson,* Jeffrey's abandoned wife
> *Otis Bragg,* a wealthy businessman
> *Marlene Bragg,* Otis's wife
> *Hélène Pringle,* the Kavanaghs' tenant

Overview

Father Timothy Kavanagh, protagonist of four earlier Mitford novels (*At Home in Mitford,* 1994; *A Light in the Window,* 1995; *These High Green Hills,* 1996; and *Out to Cannan,* 1997), has been retired for six months from his Episcopalian ministry in Lord's Chapel in the mountain town of Mitford. Approaching his sixty-sixth birthday, he wonders how next to serve God, but he has already accepted an interim appointment at the church of St. John's in the Grove on Whitecap Island, about six hundred miles from Mitford. He and his wife, Cynthia Coppersmith Kavanagh, a prominent children's book writer and illustrator, prepare to leave Mitford but cannot leave their responsibilities behind.

Dooley Barlowe is a particular responsibility. Taken in by Kavanagh when eleven, Dooley is now sixteen, wants a car, and wants to remain in Mitford. While denying him a car, Kavanagh believes he has made satisfactory arrangements for Dooley to remain in Mitford under close supervision. They plan to continue the search for his lost siblings, abandoned by their alcoholic mother. That mother, now recovering, is engaged to a stable man; the couple wants Kavanagh to return to Mitford to marry them. The Kavanaghs also must rent out the rectory that Kavanagh bought when he retired. Their tenant is a Frenchwoman, Hélène Pringle, who apparently wants to teach piano in Mitford. They take her at her word. Reluctantly, they leave for the island, arriving in a storm.

The storm foreshadows challenges to come. Whitecap Island, linked to the North Carolina mainland by a ferry and a frequently broken bridge, is a community like Mitford, but the Episcopalian pastor has departed, leaving broken bridges among his parishioners and neighbors. The principal problem is that Jeffrey Tolson, the former choir director, has run off with the church organist, abandoning his wife, and children and failing to provide financial support for them. He is not welcomed by church members, especially wealthy businessman Otis Bragg and his wife, Marlene, who believe that their money should control church affairs. Although Father Kavanagh abandons his usual noncombative style to confront Tolson in great anger, what he wants is Tolson's repentance and acceptance of responsibility, not his expulsion. Tolson, however, believes his acceptance in the church is obligatory because his family has been important in the church. Tolson's arrogance is overwhelming. He cannot find work on the island, but he refuses to work on the mainland because the commuting would be inconvenient. He has no work, so he believes he has no financial obligation to his wife and children. The woman with whom he has eloped has left him. Busy condemning Jeffrey, church members have ignored the plight of the abandoned and penniless wife, Janette, who has lapsed into suicidal depression. Father Kavanagh faces down Bragg to obtain money for her hospitalization and, because relatives cannot take care of all of the children, takes the youngest, Jonathan Tolson, into his home, although the aging priest and his wife find it difficult to deal with a child of three. Janette has given up hope and any sense of connectedness. Kavanagh visits her and gently persists until he gets her to respond to him. Church members finally acknowledge their responsibility and how to address it: Since Janette is an accomplished seamstress, they place orders with her and offer her hope for an income.

Father Kavanagh also takes on the challenge of Morris Love, a Whitecap neighbor. Plagued with a series of physical disabilities including Tourette's syndrome, mocked when he tried to attend school, and abandoned by most of his family, he has, under his late grandfather's care, become a brilliant organist and composer. Nonetheless, he has closed himself in his house and refuses any human contact except that of a highly educated African American woman whose mother took care of Love until her death. The physically disabled and the victims of segregation—Whitecap's Episcopal Church has not welcomed African Americans—have a common bond. Love rejects Kavanagh's many overtures, but Kavanagh again persists. Kavanagh is away on a trip when a serious storm ravages the island. He returns to find that his family, the young Tolson, and the family pets have been given sanctuary in Love's home. Afterward, Love rudely rejects any further contacts. Kavanagh can do nothing but pray.

He must also pray about problems in Mitford. Prevented from returning to Mitford, first by an unsympathetic bishop and later by the storm, Kavanagh finds pain awaiting him there. A pilot friend flies food to Whitecap Island, and friends make it possible for Dooley's mother and his future stepfather to be married on the island, but Dooley himself has innocently been implicated in a crime and arrested. Kavanagh's tenant, Hélène Pringle, has been caught stealing from the rectory and has filed a lawsuit against him. He finally learns that the source of her bitterness is in the money that has been used to underwrite Hope House, a Mitford sanctuary for the aged with which Kavanagh is involved; she believes she deserves part of the money. If Love has been embittered by bad parenting and physical disabilities, Pringle has been deliberately taught to hate her American relatives.

That Kavanagh is able to reconcile these people, change their lives, and return them to membership in their communities is the product of his continual prayer, his faith in God, his acknowledgment of his own helplessness and need for God's help, and his strong sense of perseverance. His Whitecap Island triumph is a homecoming celebration, when the church has been restored after the storm and most of the characters (except for Jeffrey Tolson) have been reconciled with the Christian community. Eventually, the Mitford problems are resolved. The book ends as Father Kavanagh again meets Tolson.

Christian Themes

Storm-ravaged Whitecap Island, with its fragile links to the mainland, is a metaphor for the souls of those who attempt to cope with serious problems while alienated both from God and from the Christian community. Father Kavanagh suffers a sense of his own vulnerability, but he aids those in need through his fervent faith in God and in Christ as a personal savior, through the example he presents of a Christian life, and through his unceasing prayers. Kavanagh believes that the God of love helps humans endure troubles, not escape them. While the Episcopalian faith is frequently associated with ritual and liturgy, Father Kavanagh uses the liturgy only to forge links between humans and God, with each other, and with the congregations of the past, not for the liturgy's own sake. He departs from liturgy when inspired to do so. He calls on the Bible, but he calls on appropriate secular verse to heal when it is appropriate.

Father Kavanagh's faith, however, is not simply directed toward emotional support. He also demands personal accountability, confronting both the successful businessman Otis Bragg and the man who has abandoned his family, Jeffrey Tolson. Kavanagh and his wife, despite the personal pain the situation causes them, have his Mitford tenant, Hélène Pringle, arrested for theft, although later they are willing to drop charges. They model personal responsibility for their parishioners, both by the care they take of others in Mitford and on the island and by their willingness to sacrifice themselves to the needs of others. In Mitford, they look after Dooley Barlowe and continue a search for the boy's lost siblings. On the island, they take in a three-year-old whose mother is hospitalized, despite the pain the situation causes Cynthia Kavanagh, unable to bear a child, when she must return the boy to his mother.

Sources for Further Study

Jones, Malcolm, Patricia King, Sherry Keene-Osborn, and Mike Hendricks. "Touched by the Angels." *Newsweek* 133 (May 3, 1999): 71-72. Focuses on Jan Karon, Iyanla Vanzant, and Anne Lamott as three best-selling mainstream religious authors.

Stanton, Luke A. "Karon, Jan." In *Current Biography Yearbook 2003*. New York: H. W. Wilson, 2003. Comprehensive short biography of Karon accompanied by a description of her writings.

Whitcomb, Claire. "Introducing Jan Karon: The View from Main Street." *Victoria* 12, no. 1 (January, 1998): 26-29, 104. Describes the genesis of the Mitford novels in the real town of Blowing Rock, North Carolina, and the development of the novels themselves.

Winner, Lauren F. "New Song, Familiar Tune." *Christianity Today* 43, no. 8 (July 12, 1999): 62, 64-65. Briefly describes the Christian journey of Timothy and Cynthia Kavanagh from Mitford to Whitecap Island.

Betty Richardson

NEW TESTAMENT LETTERS

Author: Saint Paul (c. 10-c. 65 C.E.)

First published: Pauli Epistolas, c. 50-c. 65 C.E. (English translation, 1380)

Edition used: The New Oxford Annotated Bible with the Apocryphal/Deuterocanonical Books, edited by Bruce M. Metzger and Roland E. Murphy. New York: Oxford University Press, 1991

Genre: Nonfiction

Subgenres: Letters; theology

Core issues: The cross; ethics; faith; freedom and free will; grace; Jesus Christ; salvation

A person is justified by faith, not by the works of the law. Thus Paul describes the saving significance of the death of Jesus, which incorporates all people into the family of God. Whether Jew or Gentile, all were incapable of reconciliation with God through their own efforts but were reunited through grace. While not intending to break with Judaism, Paul implemented this principle and thereby established Christianity as a separate religion that became predominantly Gentile.

Overview

Several years following the death of Jesus of Nazareth (30 C.E.), a young Jewish scholar, from the town of Tarsus in what is now Turkey, experienced a dramatic transformation on the road to Damascus. A persecutor of the fledgling Christian movement, Paul had a vision in which Jesus appeared to him and called him to become his apostle to the Gentiles. As part of his missionary journeys across the northern Mediterranean region, Paul was a prolific letter writer, offering direction, support, encouragement, and correction to his network of congregations.

There are several ways to approach the letters. The most common way is to speak in terms of canon. By the late second century, Paul's letters were accepted into the New Testament and given authoritative status for the life and faith of the Church. Thirteen letters are ascribed with the name of Paul. Many are named for residents of cities where congregations were located: Romans, 1-2 Corinthians, 1-2 Thessalonians, Philippians, Ephesians, and Colossians. One is the name of a region: Galatians. Several are names of individuals: Philemon, 1-2 Timothy, and Titus.

In the canon, the organizing principle is not chronological. Rather, the letters are arranged according to length. Paul's importance led composers of the King James Bible to attribute to Paul also the anonymous letter to the Hebrews, a conclusion rarely accepted today. The canonical approach also recognized the possibility that Paul wrote other letters including two other letters to the Corinthians (1 Corinthians 5:9, 2 Corinthians 2:4) and one to Laodicea (Colossians 4:15). These letters, and possibly others, were assumed to have been lost. Other letters attributed to Paul, such as 3 Corinthians and the correspondence between Paul and the Roman philosopher Seneca, were considered to be later imitations of Paul's writing.

A second approach to Paul's letters has been to focus on the historical context. The Acts of the Apostles, which describes three missionary journeys of Paul and a final journey to imprisonment in Rome, has often been used to establish a framework for the letters. Accordingly, 1 Thessalonians is the first of Paul's letters written from Corinth in the spring of 50 C.E. Over the next six or seven years, other letters would have followed while Paul was traveling in the Aegean Sea area, in the following general order: 2 Thessalonians, Galatians, 1-2 Corinthians, and Romans. The remaining "prison" letters are designated to Rome prior to Paul's martyrdom under Nero around 65 C.E.

Many scholars have now opted to take a more critical historical approach, noting that Acts fails to mention any of the letters of Paul, that the author was likely not eyewitness for most of these events, and that there are significant disagreements between Acts and Paul's letters. Rather, it is preferable to begin a historical construction based on Paul's letters. The material from Acts is thus weighed against what Paul himself says in his letters. Other imprisonment locations, such as Ephesus, are considered for Paul's prison letters.

The historical-critical approach also raises the question of authorship. Seven letters are universally considered authentic: Romans, 1-2 Corinthians, Galatians, Philippians, 1 Thessalonians, and Philemon. 1-2 Timothy and Titus are frequently disputed because the theology and hierarchical church structure suggest a second century context. Others question the authenticity of Ephesians, Colossians, and 2 Thessalonians based on vocabulary usage and sentence structure.

At the same time, careful analysis of several authentic letters of Paul suggests that they are compilations of shorter letters. Philippians is likely made up of two separate letters, while 2 Corinthians is a compilation of four or five shorter letters including those previously identified as "lost." Even 1 Corinthians may have changed, with the famous "Let a woman be silent" passage added by later scribes.

A very real, human Paul comes across in his letters. He sometimes turns angry and sarcastic, as in Galatians, when attacked by opponents. At other times, as in Philippians, he is very personable and appreciative. In Philemon he comes across as manipulative, and in 2 Corinthians he seems depressed. In his greetings, he notes his dependence upon the grace of God. From a theological standpoint, many prefer Romans, a letter written near the end of his missionary travels in 57 C.E. as an introduction to a congregation he wishes to visit.

Christian Themes

It is surprising that Paul mentions little about the life and teachings of the historical Jesus. Yet Paul himself notes that he never met him face to face. There is nothing about Jesus' childhood or parents, no descriptions of a Galilee ministry, no Lord's Prayer or Sermon on the Mount, no parables or miracles. Other than a short reference to the Last Supper, Paul's focus is on the death and resurrection of Jesus.

As a Pharisee, Paul had already accepted the concept of the final resurrection. However, the Damascus road experience convinced Paul that the resurrection had already occurred in history in the person of Jesus, evidence that Jesus was the long-awaited Jewish Messiah. Thus he places himself as last in the list of those who witnessed appearances of the risen Jesus (1 Corinthians 15). This witness became the driving force for Paul's missionary travels, his energy, passion, and urgency. In his first letter (1 Thessalonians), Paul expresses the belief that Jesus will return within his lifetime to complete the resurrection of the dead. Later he qualifies that view, accepting the inevitability of his own death (1 Corinthians 15, 2 Corinthians 5, and Philippians 1:21) and the continuation of the Church living in hope.

It is the death of Jesus that provides meaning. He tells the Corinthians that he decided to know nothing but Christ crucified, a concept that he identified as foolishness to the Greeks and a scandal to the Jews. Paul thus discovered the value of suffering so that he could speak of his own self as dying with Christ and as bearing the marks of Christ's death in his own body. Christ's death, for Paul, was carried out "for others." It took place "for our sins."

A student of the prophets, Paul saw this sacrificial death as the extension of God's grace beyond Judaism to the gentile word. Admission of Gentiles into the Church was accepted in a gathering of Christian leaders in Jerusalem in 49 C.E., but it was in his letter to the Galatians (and more fully in Romans) that Paul argued that Gentiles are justified by faith, not by works of the law. The critical test for this view was his rejection for Gentiles of circumcision as the initiation ritual, but it also became evident in the abandonment of kosher food laws, Sabbath observance, and a law orientation in general. Paul is thus responsible more than any other for Christianity having developed as a religion separate from Judaism. However, it is important to note that in Romans 9-11, he stresses the continued validity of God's covenant with the Jews.

Paul's letters are best known for their theology, yet there is also a significant amount of ethical advice. This is a result of his focus on Christian freedom. Ethics is not determined by law but by the guidance of the Spirit, who breathes life into the individual. It is not what is lawful that matters but what builds up the community, to which Paul refers as the "Body of Christ" (1 Corinthians 12). An ethic of love (1 Corinthians 13) and service characterizes the Christian life.

Sources for Further Study

Dunn, James. *Theology of Paul the Apostle*. Grand Rapids, Mich.: Wm. B. Eerdmans, 2006. Basing his work primarily on Paul's letter to the Romans, Dunn constructs a theology around topics such as God, humankind, sin, Christology, salvation, the Church, and the Christian life.

Murphy-O'Connor, Jerome. *Paul: A Critical Life*. New York: Oxford University Press, 1996. An account of Paul's letters based primarily on information gathered from the letters themselves rather than from the Acts of the Apostles. Includes contextual information from numerous first century sources.

Roetzel, Calvin J. *The Letters of Paul: Conversations in Context*. Louisville: Westminster John Knox Press, 1998. Treats each letter in terms of possible dating, situation, and literary structure. Includes arguments for dividing later letters from authentic letters of Paul.

Stendahl, Krister. *Paul Among Jews and Gentiles, and Other Essays*. Philadelphia, Pa.: Fortress Press, 1976. A series of essays, based on careful word study, that show that Paul's primary goal was to incorporate Gentiles into the family of God.

Wright, N. T. *Paul in Fresh Perspective*. Minneapolis, Minn.: Fortress Press, 2006. Part 1 focuses on themes of Creation and covenant, Messiah and apocalyptic, Gospel and empire. Part 2 deals with structures such as rethinking God, reworking God's people, and reimagining God's future.

Fred Strickert

NEWPOINTE 911

Author: Terri Blackstock (1957-   )
First published: Private Justice, 1998; *Shadow of Doubt*, 1998; *Word of Honor*, 1999;
    Trial by Fire, 2000; *Line of Duty*, 2003. Grand Rapids, Mich.: Zondervan Press
Genre: Novels
Subgenres: Mystery and detective fiction; thriller/suspense
Core issues: Doubt; good vs. evil; justice; marriage; problem of evil; trust in God

The Newpointe 911 series portrays Christians in the modern world as they face conflicts, crises, and challenges to their faith. Each book in the series is not only a mystery but also a lesson for Christians that reveals that they can survive only by holding onto their faith and accepting the plan that God has for them.

Principal characters
    Mark Branning, a firefighter
    Allie Branning, Mark's wife
    Craig Barnes, a fire chief
    Stan Shepherd, a detective in the Newpointe police force
    Celia Shepherd, Stan's wife, accused of poisoning him
    Dan Nichols, a firefighter who becomes paralyzed
    Jill Nichols, Dan's wife and a lawyer
    Ray Ford, a fire chief
    Nick Foster, a firefighter and pastor of local church
    Issie Foster, Nick's wife
    Ashley Morris, a rebellious teen

Overview

Newpointe 911 is a series of five mysteries based on the trials and tribulation of a group of firefighters and their families, friends, and neighbors in Newpointe, Louisiana. The books have the main characters solve mysterious deaths and other crimes while maintaining a Christian perspective on the evils of humankind and keeping in mind God's plan for every person. The series has its share of crime and violence, ranging from a serial killer in Newpointe who is stalking the wives of firefighters to a massive series of explosions in a thirty-story tower in New Orleans that produces a chain-reaction collapse of the tower that is reminiscent of what happened to the towers at the World Trade Center. These manmade disasters and crises may test but never seem to shake the characters' faith in God or their belief that death frees one from the difficulties of their physical being. The first and last books of the series provide insight into the themes of the series and the problems experienced by its characters.

The first book in the series, *Private Justice*, sets the tone for the series, as characters face life-changing events that cause them to question their faith. The wives of firefighters in the town are being murdered. The survivors are frightened and seeking answers on how good people could be struck down by an unknown evil. Among them are Mark and Allie Branning, whose marriage is disintegrating even as danger closes in on them. As Mark struggles to protect his wife, who believes he has cheated on her, he begins to question whether God has forsaken him or if he has forsaken God. Mark seeks his answers in Scripture, realizing that memories of his alcoholic father and a fear of following that path had pulled him away from the Church. As the pair seek to escape a killer who stalks them, Allie sees her husband in a new light, as a man who will sacrifice his own life to save her. Her earlier anger and suspicion melt away, and the pair renew their faith in God and each other in order to reconcile their marriage.

As with all the novels in the series, the characters struggle with the difficult reality that God allows bad things to happen to good people. The deaths of three women, all married to firefighters, including one with two small children, causes the main characters to question whether God is looking out for them. Suspicion of friends and neighbors threatens to tear apart the community, and the discovery that the killer is one of the firefighters further causes the people of Newpointe to wonder whether they have been forsaken by God.

Yet death and mayhem are not the only challenges faced by Newpointe residents. Everyday life provides its own difficulties, including the pressures of marriage as husbands face danger in their everyday work. The characters experience dramatic changes in their lives as the series continues. In the first book, romance blooms between firefighter Dan Nichols and Jill, a successful attorney. The two are later married. The same occurs for the town's pastor, Nick Foster, who romances, then marries Issie, the woman responsible for coming between the Brannings in the first book of the series. As pastor of the church to which the Nichols and Brannings belong, Nick must juggle the demands of his congregation while working as a firefighter to make ends meet. His financial difficulties are only a sample of the economic struggles of the poor Newpointe community.

There are additional pressures of family, the desire to have a family, and past failings. Dan Nichols is haunted by memories of his absentee parents, including a mother who did not attend his wedding and whom he has not seen for a decade. Lacking the experience of having good parents, he suffers doubts about his own ability to raise children even as he and his wife struggle to create a family. The Brannings, Mark and Allie, must juggle life as parents while both work outside the home.

The development of the characters continues through the remaining four books. The series was originally to last only four books, but the events of the World Trade Center in September, 2001, caused Terri Blackstone to add a book that uses the disaster as a backdrop for more lessons about Christian faith.

The second book in the series, *Shadow of Doubt*, centers on the poisoning of a Newpointe detective, Stan Shephard, who falls into a coma. His wife, Celia, is accused. The death of her first husband through poisoning places her in the role of a would-be serial killer, and her faith in God and the faith of her husband in their marriage and God is strained as the evidence builds against her.

In *Word of Honor*, a bomber strikes at the post office, and the death of three people and the serious injury of a child tests the residents of Newpointe. A hostage taking adds to the suspense along with a rush to judgment that places a prime member of the community and many of her friends in danger.

In *Trial by Fire*, the burning of the town church forces part-time firefighter and part-time pastor Nick Foster to question God's wisdom and grace and his own dedication to his chosen fields.

The five-book series includes many lessons on Christianity and a belief in God's plan. However, the final book best presents many of these challenges and lessons on how Christians should use prayer to guide them to accept God's plan while realizing that their earthly life is not as important as life after death. In *Line of Duty*, the final book, the Newpointe firefighters are on call when a series of bombs explode in a New Orleans high rise. Based on the struggles faced by firefighters and their families during the World Trade Center collapse, the book relates how the community of Newpointe must handle the deaths and injuries of several of its firefighters. The collapse of the building produces its own lessons as the trapped firefighters are helpless, uncertain about survival of some of their loved ones and wondering if they will die themselves. Their only avenue is prayer. Facing death, the trapped firefighters must come to terms with never seeing their families again or accepting the possibility that their colleagues may die. Only through prayer and an acceptance that their lives are part of God's greater plan are they able to get through nearly impossible times.

Not all the lessons of life are played out among the central characters. In *Line of Duty*, Ashley Morris is a rebellious teen who has deserted her mother and is living with a group of teens, who spend their days in a drunken or drug-induced haze. Ashley's mother is caught in the building explosion and killed. Suddenly orphaned, Ashley spends much of the book reconsidering her life and the direction she has taken. She finds that she no longer fits in with her rebellious friends, but her attitude and appearance prevent her from fitting in with the people of Newpointe. Ashley considers suicide then revenge against the man who has killed her mother. The book's climactic scene has the girl confronting her mother's killer with the means of killing him but choosing against revenge, instead managing some form of forgiveness for his act.

At the same time the firefighter Dan Nichols must face the loss of his ability to move his legs. As he moves from a life built on physical strength to one plagued by physical weakness, he concludes that God has a new plan for him, a different life that must be accepted. His decision is based on Scripture, including the story of Job and God's decision to allow Satan to harm a just believer as a test of his faith. Only by strengthening that faith and surrendering to God's will can he survive the test and continue to live his life, Dan realizes. The book and series end with Dan a paraplegic but more accepting of his fate and more at ease with his condition. Dan's illness also affects his mother, a woman who had neglected him during his childhood while pursuing a life of wealth and comfort. Suddenly faced with the death of her son, she seeks to redeem herself by helping care for him during his illness.

Christian Themes

The Newpointe 911 series presents the Christian perspective in a suspense and mystery format appealing to modern readers. The continuing cast of characters must face personal and community catastrophes while maintaining their Christian beliefs and faith and learn to accept that God's plan may force them to put their own plans aside. The five books in the series portray the many difficulties faced by Christians in maintaining their faith while struggling to understand how a loving God could allow horrible things to happen to good people. In showing how the faithful are tested, the series highlights one of the oldest precepts of Christianity, dating back to Job, that the righteous will suffer hardships and that they must maintain their faith.

The series also presents a stark battle between good and evil and shows how that battle sometimes consumes the lives of good people. The most graphic example is the final book in the series, *Line of Duty*, in which a mass murder was committed by a man who was driven to evil acts by corruption and the evil of others. Through most of the series, the crimes take second place to the everyday crises faced by Newpointe residents. Marriages are shaken by suspected infidelity, past troubles explode in the present, and friendships are strained. The characters must rely on divine guidance throughout their lives while asking questions of faith on why God allows suffering to continue.

Sources for Further Study

Butler, Tamara. Review of *Line of Duty* by Terri Blackstock. *Library Journal* 128, no. 18 (November 1, 2003): 66. A brief review of the last in the Newpointe 911 series by this Christian mystery writer.

Byle, Ann. "Author Quits Romance Writing for Christian Books: Terri Blackstock Caught Upswing in Christian Fiction Market." *The Grand Rapids Press*, December 4, 2004, p. D9. Blackstock talks about her switch from writing romances to Christian fiction in 1995.

Hanna, John, ed. *Faces of Faith*. Gainesville, Fla.: Bridge-Logos, 2006. Highlights a group of people, mostly women, who accepted God. The book includes a biography of Terri Blackstock, the story of her conversion, and a brief discussion of her various book series.

Nappa, Mike. *True Stories of Answered Prayers*. Wheaton, Ill.: Tyndale House, 1999. Includes brief stories about famous people who faced difficult times and found prayer and God to be the answer. The book includes a discussion of Terri Blackstock and her conversion from secular writer to religious author.

Douglas Clouatre

NO GREATER LOVE

Author: Mother Teresa (1910-1997)
First published: Novato, Calif.: New World Library, 1997, edited by Becky Benenate and Joseph Durepos
Genre: Nonfiction
Subgenres: Handbook for living; meditation and contemplation
Core issues: Catholics and Catholicism; church; clerical life; connectedness; love; poverty

Widely regarded as a "living saint" during her lifetime, Mother Teresa is now officially recognized as "Blessed" by the Catholic Church. Written near the end of her life, this book shares her insights into living a life in Christ, including prayer, work and service, family and children, poverty, suffering, and holiness. The book also contains an interview with José Luis González-Balado and a biographical sketch.

Overview

Mother Teresa spent the bulk of her life ministering to the poorest of the poor on the streets of Calcutta. She begins *No Greater Love* by discussing the importance of prayer in her life. Prayer is her lifeblood. She is utterly dependent on God, and prayer connects her to God. She encourages all to pray, not only with words but also through silence. In silence, we can open our hearts to the presence of God, place ourselves humbly before him, and listen for him. In our prayer, we should give God all of ourselves, offering love and praise and seeking union with God. Only then can we go out and minister to the world.

Mother Teresa's ministry was centered on love. She cared for the poor's physical needs, but her main focus was on loving them. In her chapter on love, she emphasizes that this was the central focus of Jesus' message. Jesus came to reveal God's love to humankind and to command us to love one another. Mother Teresa's life exemplified the meaning of love and of giving. She encouraged all people to give—not only tangible gifts such as money, food, and clothing but also the intangible gifts of ourselves, such as a smile or a caring ear. She encouraged people to give not just from their abundance but to the point of feeling the sacrifice of giving. It is also important, Mother Teresa maintains, to teach children how to give.

All are called to holiness. God created us to be holy. Mother Teresa tells us that we are called to turn our lives over to God through humility and prayer. It is only through stripping away the ego and offering our lives to God that we can love others the way God loves us. In learning to love as God loves, we learn to be holy.

We also serve God through our work, whether that work takes place in the world or within our families. God calls each to a different role, but whatever help we offer to another person, whatever service we perform for another, we also perform for Jesus. We must use our God-given talents to glorify God. By the same token, Mother Teresa says that the love we show to our family members reflects the love of God. It is within the family that children learn to love and to share that love with others. Our work within the family is some of the most important work we can do. Mother Teresa holds the family in the highest esteem. She laments that people today seem to be afraid of having children and that all too often today's children are not loved. She also holds the vocation of parenting in high regard. She urges families to slow down and make time for one another. She tells families to pray together and, most important, love one another.

Mother Teresa served the poor, but in *No Greater Love* she emphasizes that it is not the lack of material goods that causes the most harm but rather the loss of human dignity. That sort of poverty is not limited to those who are materially poor. In fact, Mother Teresa states that the spiritually poor are much worse off. She can feed the hungry and provide a bed for the homeless, but healing anger and loneliness takes much longer. Loving someone is often the greatest service we can provide. There is much we can learn from the poor. Despite their extreme hunger and physical pain, the poor in Mother Teresa's experience are not bitter, and they are willing to share what little that they have.

Part of providing love is offering forgiveness. In order to be able to forgive, we need to realize that we ourselves are in need of forgiveness. Mother Teresa stresses the importance of the sacrament of Confession. In the confessional, Christians turn their sinfulness over to God, begging for God's forgiveness and through penance healing the divide that has come between us and others, and us and God. Mother Teresa relates her own habit of going to confession once a week. Like a young child going to her father to say she is sorry after doing something wrong, she goes to request forgiveness from her father in heaven, offering her failures to God and humbly receiving his mercy. Familiar with suffering, Mother Teresa encourages her readers to accept suffering as part of life and to offer it up to Jesus. In suffering, she advises readers to remember Christ's suffering and his resurrection; there is always hope, even in suffering. The same holds true of death, which is merely a means of returning to God.

Mother Teresa also speaks about the meaning of vocation. Vocation is God's call to us. Mother Teresa describes how she received her original call to religious life, and her second call to begin ministering to the poor. Vocation requires us to surrender our lives to God. To do so, we must have a loving trust in God.

No Greater Love concludes with an interview Mother Teresa gave to José Luis González-Balado, as well as a short biographical sketch.

Christian Themes

Jesus preached a message of love and radical poverty. He told those who wanted to follow him to love God, love their neighbor, and give all that they had to the poor. Mother Teresa dedicated her life to following those edicts, as do her fellow Missionaries of Charity. They minister to those whom the world has forgotten, seeing Jesus in each person for whom they care. In *No Greater Love*, Mother Teresa provided a window on her life and that ministry.

The book is essentially a handbook for living the Christian life. While all are not called to make a radical choice of poverty as Mother Teresa did, everyone is called to minister to those nearest at hand. We are called to love, beginning with those in our own families and then reaching out to the greater community. We are called to be generous and to give what we have to the poor. We do not need to make grand gestures; it is often in the smallest acts that love can be found.

Mother Teresa provides a wonderful example of how to live the Christian life. She lived Jesus' message of love and, in this volume, invited others to do the same. She knew that the road to the Christian life is not easy; it often involves suffering and pain, loneliness and hunger that are both spiritual and physical. She invited her readers, however, to turn that pain over to Jesus, seeing Jesus in one another and loving as Jesus loved.

Sources for Further Study

Schaefer, Linda. *Come and See: A Photojournalist's Journey into the World of Mother Teresa.* Sanford, Fla.: DC Press, 2003. Schaefer volunteered with Mother Teresa and ultimately received permission to photograph the experience. This book illustrates that amid pain and suffering there was also much joy to be experienced in this life of service.

Teresa, Mother, with José Luis González-Balado. *Mother Teresa: In My Own Words.* New York: Gramercy Books, 1996. González-Balado, a Spanish journalist and editor, knew Mother Teresa from 1969 until her death. This is a collection of her stories and prayers that illustrates her spirituality and presents her advice for following in the footsteps of Jesus.

Teresa, Mother, and Anthony Stern. *Everything Starts from Prayer: Mother Teresa's Meditations on Spiritual Life for People.* Ashland, Oreg.: White Cloud Press, 1998. Contains Mother Teresa's insights on prayer, which are appropriate for members of all faiths seeking a deeper connection with God.

Patrice Fagnant-MacArthur

NORTH OF HOPE

Author: Jon Hassler (1933-　　)
First published: 1990
Edition used: North of Hope, with an introduction by Amy Welborn. Chicago: Loyola
　Press, 2006
Genre: Novel
Subgenre: Catholic fiction
Core issues: Hope; love; prayer; priesthood

*A priest facing a midlife crisis must decide between two loves, one for a woman from
his past and one for his God. In the process, he must reconcile the apparent incongru-
ities of divine and human love, faith and doubt, the monastic and the communal life in
order to connect the temporal world with the eternal. In tending to his parishioners, he
realizes that they have likewise ministered to him.*

    Principal characters
        Father Frank Healy, the protagonist, a priest
        Father Adrian Lawrence, Frank's mentor
        Eunice Pfeiffer, a retired rectory housekeeper
        Father Zell, a nineteenth century missionary
        Libby Girard Pearsall, a nurse
        Tom Pearsall, a physician
        Verna Jessen, Libby's daughter
        Judge Bigelow, a bar owner
        Roger Upward, Verna's dead Ojibway lover

Overview

An expansive four-part novel, *North of Hope* chronicles Father Frank Healy's efforts to revive his languishing vocation as a Catholic priest. As he admits in therapy,
"I've sprung a very big leak, and my spirit is draining away."

Part 1 recounts Frank's adolescence in the northern Minnesota town of Linden
Falls, including his dying mother's seminal wish that her son join the priesthood. This
message is relayed through Eunice Pfeiffer, who kept a deathbed vigil while Frank
served as altar boy at Christmas Mass. Adrian Lawrence, the parish priest, befriends
Frank and quietly supports his desire to serve God. Frank's choice is also manipulated
by Eunice's pious mothering. Unable to gain the affections of the widower, she devotes herself to making a priest of the widower's son. Another influence on Frank's
decision is his hero, Father Zell, a nineteenth century missionary who served the
Ojibway Indians and died from exposure while carrying Communion wafers across
frozen Lake Sovereign.

In 1949 during his senior year, Frank's first and only crush is on Libby Girard. A newcomer to Linden Falls, she catches Frank's eye at the cinema. A voice in Frank's head intuits that "she's the one," and Libby finds in the gentle teenager a refuge from her volatile home life. Though the confidants share walks to school, Frank watches from the sidelines as Libby wins her share of admirers. When she entreats Frank to take her to his house for a few hours' respite, he panics and abandons her. Libby aims to marry early and cannot fathom Frank's contemplation of the priesthood. Frank experiences his first dance and kiss with Libby, pleasures followed by heartbreak as, in quick succession, she gets pregnant, withdraws from school, marries the father of her child, moves to a farm, and gives birth. Frank heads to Aquinas Seminary to begin theological studies. To mortify his soul and to erase memories of Libby, he denies himself sufficient sustenance and warmth. When a recently divorced Libby gatecrashes the male enclave, Frank is both embarrassed and tempted by her disclosure of love. Ultimately he rejects her proposal for a life together.

Part 2 continues Father Frank Healy's story decades later, during the winter of 1977-1978. The college where Frank served as headmaster has closed because of declining enrollments, and his displacement creates a midlife crisis of faith. He returns to his hometown parish to assist his aging mentor, Father Lawrence. Nicknamed "Loving Kindness" by younger priests who mock his sermons, the elderly Adrian welcomes Frank to St. Ann's. Frank also travels to the Basswood Indian Reservation to say weekly Mass at Our Lady's, another facility threatened with closure. To his astonishment, Libby lives across from the mission in a building that houses both a clinic and accommodations for its doctor. It is not by choice that Libby and her third husband, Tom Pearsall, are in residence. Tom must complete community service for a drug sentence in Minneapolis, and Libby, a nurse, has accompanied him. She hopes this barren outback will keep her husband within the law and allow her daughter, Verna, a chance to heal from her sexual and drug addictions. Neither hope seems promising. Verna acquires replacement lovers and Tom, flouting his Hippocratic Oath, supplies illegal drugs for Judge Bigelow to peddle from his bar, the Homestead. The suspicious death of Verna's Ojibway lover, Roger Upward, complicates matters when federal investigators enter the scene. As Frank comforts this distraught family, his feelings for Libby, never entirely extinguished, are renewed.

Part 3 focuses on human suffering, both the physical ailments of age and addiction and the emotional trauma of abuse and grief. After his mentor suffers a heart attack and is hospitalized, Frank replaces Adrian as pastor of St. Ann's. A suicidal Verna is consigned to a mental health facility, the aptly named Hope. Frank escorts Libby on her visits to the ward and learns that her second husband sexually abused Verna. Amid these crises, Libby and Frank replenish their friendship and begin a ritual of midnight telephone calls. The priest admits his love for Libby but remains true to his vow of chastity, despite temptation and opportunity. Frank's realization that pastoral work is another form of his beloved teaching allows him finally to settle in at St. Ann's.

Part 4 of the novel, like the human lives it depicts, is not tidy but offers resolution. Verna bares her soul to Frank: She has engaged in sexual relations with her stepfather,

Tom. The incest Libby knew occurred in her second marriage is revealed to have carried over into her third. It is news Libby struggles to process, and she leaves Tom. Despair and loneliness, added to her awareness of Frank's renewed commitment to the priesthood, drive Libby to attempt suicide. Frank, apparently divinely guided, senses her desperation and intervenes. Hoping to avoid prosecution for statutory rape, Tom endeavors to fake his death but is double-crossed by Judge Bigelow. In an ironic reversal of Father Zell's noble sacrifice, the doctor drives through the icy surface of Lake Sovereign and drowns. Eunice Pfeiffer's conscience compels her confession to Frank that she took liberties with his mother's final words. She explains it was merely Mrs. Healy's hope, and not her edict, that he become a priest. Frank, however, has made peace with his vocation and his God. In the process of ministering to others, he has been healed through communion with them.

Christian Themes

Jon Hassler writes with insight about the Church in contemporary America, where much in its culture starves, rather than feeds, the spiritual hunger of clergy and laity. *North of Hope*'s depiction of a priest in crisis compares favorably to Graham Greene's *The Power and the Glory* and J. F. Powers's *Morte d'Urban*. In addition to challenges facing priests in a secular society, the novel explores hope amid despair, prayer in daily life, and the healing properties of love.

As indicated by its title, the novel's dominant theme is hope, a rare commodity, as Hassler's characters find themselves north of hope both geographically and emotionally. Variously they desire restored faith in God and humanity, renewed health, recovery from addiction, dignity in old age, economic opportunity, and true love. However, hope seems alien to this isolated region. As Libby laments, "It's like hope doesn't reach this far north." Even a fragile faith offers solace to the desperate, as Frank and his parishioners learn. When Libby and Verna take steps to mend their shattered family, it is their mutual hope for a better relationship that allows them to acknowledge each other's pain and look past their own.

Whether spoken intentionally or uttered unaware, prayer is practiced by both the doubtful and the faithful in *North of Hope*. There are formal prayers, such as Father Lawrence's liturgical recitation during his terrifying heart attack and his ever-expanding prayer list for the deceased. Frank's conversational prayers range from his request that God keep Libby at a safe distance to his commentary on loneliness: "Dear God, the barriers between us. The walls." Libby, an agnostic, envies Frank's faith, but her thoughts as she plans her suicide become a form of prayer. Though Frank has imagined God to be a loner like himself, only the intercession of an involved God can adequately explain how her words reach Frank, miles away.

Ultimately, *North of Hope* is a love story. If prayer dismantles the walls humans have erected between themselves and their God, love bridges the distances that separate people. Though Frank and Libby do not consummate their love, each comes to recognize the value of their intellectual and emotional connection and the intimacy that close friendship engenders. The loving-kindness preached by Father Lawrence proves to be the balm, after all, for lonely individuals and wounded families afflicted by the diseases of modern life.

Sources for Further Study

Block, Ed. "A Conversation with Jon Hassler." *Image: A Journal of the Arts and Religion* 19 (Spring, 1998): 41-58. In this interview, Hassler reviews his career as a writer and examines the many connections between his faith and his fiction.

Brown, W. Dale. "Jon Hassler: Happy Man." In *Of Fiction and Faith: Twelve American Writers Talk About Their Vision and Work*. Grand Rapids, Mich.: Wm. B. Eerdmans, 1997. Traces characters' values and behaviors to the author's Catholicism.

Hassler, Jon. "Conversation with Jon Hassler: *North of Hope*." Interview by Joseph Plut. *Renascence: Essays on Values in Literature* 55, no. 2 (Winter, 2003): 145-164. Hassler shares the origins of certain characters, settings, and events in *North of Hope*, including biographical links.

Low, Anthony. "Jon Hassler: Catholic Realist." *Renascence: Essays on Values in Literature* 47, no. 1 (Fall, 1994): 59-70. Examines Hassler's oeuvre in the light of its religiosity and realism.

Narveson, Robert D. "Catholic-Lutheran Interaction in Keillor's *Lake Wobegon Days* and Hassler's *Grand Opening*." In *Exploring the Midwestern Imagination*, edited by Marcia Noe. Troy, N.Y.: Whitston, 1993. Compares Hassler's interdenominational presentation of Christian life in rural Minnesota with that of Garrison Keillor.

Dorothy Dodge Robbins

THE NUN'S STORY

Author: Kathryn C. Hulme (1900-1981)
First published: 1956
Edition used: The Nun's Story, edited by Roger Sharrock. New York: Pocket Books, 1958
Genre: Novel
Subgenres: Biography; Catholic fiction
Core issues: Attachment and detachment; clerical life; discipline; humility; monasticism; obedience and disobedience

This fictionalized life of a Roman Catholic nursing nun begins with her initial decision to join a convent and ends with her reemergence from religious life. It illustrates the life of service of a woman of faith, ranging from caring for the mentally ill to missionary work in the Belgian Congo and, ultimately, her decision to join the anti-Nazi resistance movement in Europe during World War II.

> *Principal characters*
> *Gabrielle Van der Mal*, later Sister Luke, a nursing sister of the Order of the Sisters of Charity of Jesus and Mary
> *Dr. Van der Mal*, Gabrielle's father
> *Dr. Fortunati*, a surgeon at the mission hospital in the Congo
> *Sister William*, a nursing nun who inspires Sister Luke to join the order
> *The Reverend Mother Emmanuel*, head of the order

Overview

The mention of the word "nun" evokes in many people's minds an image of a black-clad figure, walking silently, eyes cast down. That a woman would choose to be cloistered in communion only with God and unaware of and unknown to her fellow human beings is a fascinating concept. Published originally in 1956, *The Nun's Story* is based on the life of a real woman, a trained nurse, Marie Louis Habets, with whom Kathryn Hulme worked in the years following World War II, when both women were aid workers for the United Nations Relief and Rehabilitation Administration (UNRRA). The two women were trained together and became friends and roommates at Wildflecken, a camp from which more than twenty thousand displaced persons would be repatriated to their homelands, primarily Poland.

The Nun's Story opens in the 1920's in Belgium, where Gabrielle Van der Mal, the daughter of a noted surgeon, enters the convent of the Sisters of Charity of Jesus and Mary. As a nursing student, Gabrielle first feels a calling to the religious life after she accompanies a group of sick pilgrims to Lourdes. Gabrielle is impressed with the care and gentleness of the nuns who work with the patients. Moreover, the piety of the pilgrims is evident, even when they are not cured of their physical illnesses. When the group returns home, Gabrielle begins to feel developing within her a vocation to the religious life.

Nuns vow to live a life of poverty (lacking personal possessions), chastity (keeping oneself sexually pure), and obedience (submitting oneself to the authority of one's superiors). The education of a novice nun is designed to create a sense of unity and camaraderie with the other members of the order. Like military recruits, nuns learn that the unit is more important than the individual, and each individual is trained to act without a moment's hesitation on an order given by a superior.

During her first year and a half in the convent, Gabrielle has many obligations and must learn all the minutiae of a life lived in community—the pattern of life called "the Rule" by its adherents. She learns that what the order demands more than anything else is a detachment from earthly relationships and material possessions. "Detachment" means having no possessions; even the clothing one wears belongs to the community. It requires instant obedience to orders from one's superiors and absolute adherence to the schedule established by the convent. Detachment also means withdrawal from parents and family and even the public admission of one's personal failures. Despite the hardships of her first year, Gabrielle remains committed to her goal. After taking her first temporary vows, Gabrielle, now renamed Sister Luke, is sent to study at the School of Tropical Medicine with the goal of her becoming a nursing nun in the Belgian Congo. Because of her years of medical study and education, she proves to be an exceptional student and graduates fourth in a class of eighty students.

Now ready for medical service in the Congo, Sister Luke prepares to make the lifelong commitment to Christ by taking her final, permanent vows and becoming a newly professed nun. She thinks she is ready for the big step and plans to live a life of service to the Church in the missions. She is not assigned to the missions, however, but to a mental sanatorium run by the order. When Sister Luke arrives at the asylum, she discovers that the patients are not medicated into obedience but are treated with care and respect. Her experiences at the sanatorium are capped when one patient, under the illusion that she is the Archangel Gabriel, tries to strangle Sister Luke and stabs another one of the nuns to death. Through her horror and sorrow, Sister Luke begins to understand the thinking behind the Rule: It helps her to carry on and to keep herself under control even during such horrific experiences.

In the months that follow the tragedy, Sister Luke, through her discipline and devotion to duty, earns the respect of the Mother Superior and is finally permitted to serve in the missions in the Congo. She becomes a surgical assistant to Dr. Fortunati, a brilliant if somewhat disrespectful doctor. He comes to respect Sister Luke's ability, but he sees better than she does how her natural instincts for patient care make her a less than perfect nun, and he bluntly tells her so. Her desire to help injured workmen at an accident scene forces the young nun to admit that the doctor is right; when she is harshly punished for leaving the hospital without permission from her superiors, she realizes that she will never be able to be the kind of nun the Rule calls her to be.

Eventually Sister Luke applies to be relieved of her vows and begins the lengthy process of emergence. Her last days as a nun are painful, partly because of the impersonal nature of her dismissal. Seventeen years of service are forgotten in the bitterness of her departure, even though she is filled with new purpose and new goals. The novel ends as Sister Luke, now once more Gabrielle, prepares to find members of the underground and, if possible, work for the freedom of her native Belgium from its German oppressors during World War II.

Christian Themes

One of the dominant themes in *The Nun's Story* is the idea of submission of the self to a community. From the very beginning, Gabrielle learns that the one thing a nun must never do is to "singularize" herself—that is, to stand out from the group with which she associates herself. For example, the head of Gabrielle's order, the Mother Superior, is a very important and educated person: She has served as a missionary in India, a teacher in Poland, and a supervisor of many nursing nuns across the whole of Europe. She has degrees in philosophy, the humanities, and medicine. Still, when the Mother Superior visits the convents under her supervision, she makes a point of knowing every sister by name and speaks patiently and gently to the youngest beginners in the order. She even chooses, when taking part in the mandatory sewing circles run by the convent, to repair the stockings of the lowest workers—the gardeners and laundry nuns. Her humility is considered the essence of submission—she neglects to remind others of her own significant position because she seeks to promote the idea of service.

Another dominant theme is the idea of attachment and detachment. The ideal nun, or "living rule," is a woman who can observe even the intense suffering of one of her fellow sisters or supplicants without becoming emotionally connected. While idealized detachment is perceived by outsiders as emotional coldness, within the order detachment is promoted as a recognition of one's rejection of worldly issues and emotions in favor of an all-consuming devotion to God and God's works. Furthermore, detachment allows each sister to perform her work effectively, without being distracted by what suffering of others.

Ultimately, however, *The Nun's Story* is about being true to oneself—and the idea of calling, or God's plan for one's life: Gabrielle learns through her experiences as a nun that her personality is unsuited to that calling, and she finally finds herself more suited for work in the resistance against Nazi aggression.

Sources for Further Study

Hulme, Kathryn C. *Undiscovered Country: A Spiritual Adventure*. Boston/Toronto: Little, Brown, 1966. Hulme's autobiography, with a much-expanded description of her life with Marie-Louis Habets as well as her earlier life, including her years in Paris.

_____. *The Wild Place*. New York: Little, Brown, 1953. An account of Hulme's years at Wildflecken working for the UNRRA. Winner of the Atlantic Monthly Nonfiction Award.

Patterson, William Patrick. *Ladies of the Rope: Gurdjieff's Special Left Bank Woman's Group*. Princeton, N.J.: Arete, 1998. A memoir of Hulme's years in Paris as a pupil and later a disciple of G. I. Gurdjieff, philosopher and mystic. Tells of her becoming a member of the the Rope, a group of women dedicated to spiritual development.

Schleich, Kathryn. *Hollywood and Catholic Women: Virgins, Whores, Mothers, and Other Images*. New York: iUniverse, 2003. The author discusses the attitude of the Church throughout history and how Hollywood has adopted its point of view in films such as *The Song of Bernadette* (1943), *The Bells of St. Mary's* (1945), *A Nun's Story* (1959), *Agnes of God* (1985), and even the comedy *Sister Act* (1992).

Julia M. Meyers

OCTOGESIMA ADVENIENS

Author: Paul VI (Giovanni Battista Montini; 1897-1978)
First published: 1971 (English translation, 1971)
Edition used: Catholic Social Thought: The Documentary Heritage, edited by David
    J. O'Brien and Thomas A. Shannon. Maryknoll, N.Y.: Orbis Books, 2002
Genre: Nonfiction
Subgenres: Encyclical; theology
Core issues: Capitalism; justice; morality; social action

This work reiterates the importance of earlier writings on Catholic social teachings. In the first half, it extends the scope of these teachings to a variety of issues, including the problems of large urban areas, discrimination, inequities that result from social and economic change, and the protection of the environment. The second half examines broader political concerns such as the legal protection of human rights, the illegitimacy of Marxism, and problems with economic liberalism. The conclusion argues that Catholic social teachings can adapt to new circumstances and that the faithful should act to improve the world.

Overview

Pope Paul VI's *Octogesima Adveniens* takes its title, as do all major papal writings, from the first few words of the Latin version of the document. In this case, the words mean "the eightieth anniversary" and refer to the eightieth anniversary of Leo XIII's *Rerum Novarum* (1891), the first papal social encyclical. Paul VI is following the tradition of Pius XI, whose 1931 social encyclical was entitled *Quadragesimo Anno* (forty years) and also paid homage to *Rerum Novarum*. Later, in 1991, John Paul II would again refer to *Rerum Novarum* with his *Centesimus Annus*.

Octogesima Adveniens reads like an encyclical, but it is properly classified as an apostolic letter, a typic of document that is usually addressed to a Vatican official or a group of bishops. *Octogesima Adveniens* is addressed to Cardinal Maurice Roy, president of the Pontifical Commission on Justice and Peace, which was established by Paul VI. It is likely that *Octogesima Adveniens* was intended to give prominence to that body. The work consists of fifty-two sections without any chapter divisions.

Paul VI begins by speaking of the universal appeal of the Church's message about human beings and social life, and makes reference to the people whom he has met during his pontificate. This is significant as Paul VI was the first modern pope to travel extensively. The Church, Paul VI asserts, does not require the same structures in all places, but the same moral concerns should be expressed to all people.

Sections 8 through 21 address specific social concerns. The topic receiving the most attention in these sections is the impact of urbanization. Paul VI decries large urban areas with vast numbers of poor living in substandard conditions. He expresses a vision whereby Christians can bring "a message of hope" to the city and states that "this can be done by brotherhood which is lived and by concrete justice."

Paul VI then raises several other concerns about social life. He briefly refers to the youth of the world and is concerned whether the world will provide a proper environment for them. He has a brief section on women in which he expresses concern regarding sex discrimination and hopes for equality of rights. There follows a section on workers in which he reaffirms a right to work and speaks of the important role of labor unions, although he expresses concern that labor unions are not always able to perform their role, which he sees as collaboration in society. There follows a brief section on compassion for those who experience social and political changes and are thereby placed on the fringes of society. Paul VI offers some brief thoughts on discrimination based on race, origin, color, culture, sex, or religion and says that all must be eradicated.

There are two sections that relate to seeking employment. One section affirms a new idea in the social encyclicals—the right to emigrate for economic reasons—and calls on Christians to assist those migrating for economic well-being. The other section related to employment indicates that the state has a positive role in encouraging the creation of new jobs.

After a brief section on social communication, there is a section addressing moral concerns related to the environment. Paul VI says that "man is suddenly becoming aware that by an ill-considered exploitation of nature he risks destroying it and becoming in his turn the victim of this degradation."

Section 22 through 41 consider more theoretical concerns about public life. Paul VI addresses the need for legal rules that protect rights, but he also acknowledges that legal rules alone will not be enough for the recognition of rights. There must be a culture that respects the rights of human beings. Paul VI affirms the importance of equality and participation within political society, both of which point to democratic life.

Paul VI then addresses the Catholic Church's social views regarding relations to others. He asserts that the Church's social teachings are not an ideology and are therefore neither Marxist nor liberal. He acknowledges that many Christians are drawn to forms of socialism because it expresses a concern for justice, solidarity, and equality. He adds that those same people "refuse to recognize the limitations of the historical socialist movements." By this Paul VI indicates that he feels that socialist regimes have not lived up to their ideals. He is particularly critical of Marxism, which sees as leading to a "totalitarian and violent society." Here he seems to be responding to what at the time was a newly emerging movement within Catholic theology that adopted elements of Marxism and was known as liberation theology.

Paul VI quickly adds that liberalism is not the answer and that Christians should not expects utopias in this world. He is particularly concerned about the use of natural science to create an earthly utopia.

The final portion, sections 42 through 51, addresses the role of Christians in the world today. Christians and other people of goodwill must work to change attitudes and structures in the world. There is no one single action for all people as there are a variety of circumstances and many ways of working for justice in the world.

Christian Themes

Morality and, in particular, justice within the social sphere are important themes. Paul VI argues that the Catholic Church is concerned with moral social structures and actions by individuals in the world. Paul VI wants urban areas in which people are treated with justice, and he decries the injustices he has seen in his travels to urban areas around the globe. He argues that youth, women, workers, and emigrants should not be discriminated against and should be treated with dignity. People must treat the environment in a just and moral way because if they do not, the damaged environment will harm human beings in the future.

Paul VI rejects Marxism and socialism because they do not bring justice to the world. At the same time, individualistic liberalism is also not just. Paul VI wants justice in the world but warns against any arrangement to attempt to bring about perfect justice in the world.

Social action is also an important theme in this work. The beginning of the document calls for social action and engagement throughout the world. Individuals are called to engage in social action in a variety of ways—ranging from activities at their own workplace to work involving migrants.

The final portion of the document focuses on social action. It says that "there is a need to establish a greater justice in the sharing of goods." This social action must not use force but must encourage cooperation and solidarity among human beings. This social action must lead to changed attitudes in individuals and changed social structures because those too can be unjust. Christians can and should work within the political sphere. Politics should be used to rectify the situations in which many people live. While there is a place for social action within politics, there are many means of correct social action. In the end, the document offers "to all Christians . . . a fresh and insistent call to action."

Sources for Further Study

Cochran, Clarke E., and David Carroll Cochran. *Catholics, Politics, and Public Policy: Beyond Left and Right*. Maryknoll, N.Y.: Orbis Books, 2003. This work discusses themes in the documents of Catholic social teachings and makes several references to *Octogesima Adveniens*.

Pontifical Council for Justice and Peace. *Compendium of the Social Doctrine of the Church*. Washington, D.C.: United States Conference of Catholic Bishops, 2005. This work attempts to systematize and synthesize the many documents, including *Octogesima Adveniens*, that are part of Catholic social teachings.

Weigel, George, and Robert Royal, eds. *Building the Free Society: Democracy, Capitalism, and Catholic Social Teaching*. Grand Rapids, Mich.: Wm. B. Eerdmans, 1993. This work includes eleven essays, each examining a different important document, including one on *Octogesima Adveniens*, in the tradition of Catholic social teachings.

Michael L. Coulter

"ODE: INTIMATIONS OF IMMORTALITY"

Author: William Wordsworth (1770-1850)
First published: 1807
Edition used: Selected Poems and Prefaces by William Wordsworth, edited with an introduction by Jack Stillinger. Boston: Houghton Mifflin, 1965
Genre: Poetry
Subgenre: Lyric poetry
Core issues: Beauty; children; memory; nature; psychology; soul

In this meditative ode, Wordsworth finds consolation for and ultimately acceptance of his own mortality and lost sense of the glories of nature by evoking memories of his own childhood experience. For the poet, the ultimate ground of faith is the child's innate awareness of its own immortality and heavenly origin.

Overview

William Wordsworth's "Ode: Intimations of Immortality from Recollections of Early Childhood" was written over a two-year period from 1802 to 1804 and published in 1807. According to his sister Dororthy's journals, Wordsworth began the poem sometime before the end of March, 1802. The first four stanzas of the ode were completed by April 4, 1802, which is the date assigned by Samuel Taylor Coleridge to his "Dejection: An Ode," which was written in response to Wordsworth's poem. In 1802 William and Dorothy were living at Grasmere cottage, within walking distance of Coleridge's house in the same neighborhood. The proximity of the two poets fueled a magical collaboration, of which the two odes are a prime example. After hearing Wordsworth read the first few stanzas of his ode, Coleridge was inspired to answer some of the questions and problems it raised.

A period of two years intervened between Wordsworth's writing of the first part and the poem's completion. The poem was originally published under the abbreviated title "Ode." As he did with many of his poems, Wordsworth continued to revise the ode throughout his lifetime, adding the famous epigraph, "The Child is father of the Man," in an 1815 edition. In a note on the poem dictated to Isabella Fenwick in 1843, Wordsworth identifies the poem's principal theme as the "Immortality of the Soul." According to Wordsworth, the poem emerges from two recollected feelings of childhood: the lost vividness of sense objects, which appear different to the adult poet from how they appeared to him as a child; and the child's inability to accept his own mortality and to reconcile the fact of his own death with the world around him.

The poem begins with Wordsworth's fond memories of his childhood and his early experiences of nature. In this past time, the natural world appeared to the speaker as though "appareled in celestial light" (line 4). Now, in the present, this former, dreamlike appearance of the external world has changed. The poet laments hauntingly that "The things which I have seen I now can see no more" (9). Wordsworth elaborates on this change in stanzas 2-3. The speaker recognizes that the inherent beauty of nature has not changed, but even in the midst of the natural beauty of the world around him, the speaker is saddened: "To me alone there came a thought of grief" (22). Throughout this first part of the poem, Wordsworth continues to contrast the individual beauties of nature that surround him with his own inward sense of isolation and loss. At the end of the fourth stanza (56-57), the poet signals the depth of this intensely personal crisis with the question:

> Whither is fled the visionary gleam?
> Where is it now, the glory and the dream?

In the second part of the poem, stanzas 5-8, Wordsworth announces his poetic doctrine of the preexistence of the soul and asserts that the infant's soul is not entirely forgetful of its origins but still sees heaven as lying about itself. However, according to the poet, we experience a progressive change as we grow older, a darkening of this vision of our heavenly home, as "Shades of the prison-house begin to close" (68). Mortal life has its own pleasures, which contribute to our forgetfulness of our heavenly origins. In stanza 7, Wordsworth presents his account of the psychology of child development through an analysis of play. For the poet, the whole life of the child is gradually transformed into an "endless imitation" (107). In the eighth stanza, he addresses the child directly and asks why the child is in such a hurry to take up the yoke of adulthood, to lose its wisdom and freedom, to forget its true nature and heavenly origin, and to give up its vision of the natural world, the loss of which the poet so deeply regrets.

In the third and final section of the poem, stanzas 9-11, the poem evidences a major shift as Wordsworth discovers a way out of his crisis. The poet is convinced that something lies buried deep in human nature that remembers our divine origin and essence. For Wordsworth, the recollection of childhood feeling and experience holds nothing less than the ground of faith itself and a lasting source of joy. Wordsworth now celebrates those very things that precipitated his crisis and that gave rise to the occasion of the poem in the first place. The forgetfulness and confusion that so profoundly disturbed the poet give rise to a realization that the earth is not our proper home. The child's memory of the soul's origins is a source of light to our adult life. Through our memories of childhood, this knowledge is always accessible. Thus the poet is able to reject his grief and sense of loss and embrace the deep contentment of what he calls the "philosophic mind," which is a product of age and the passing of time (186). For Wordsworth, this new awareness, which comes from insight into one's own immortality, yields a love of nature equal to that experienced in childhood.

Christian Themes

Over the years as well as in Wordsworth's own lifetime, a number of people have objected to Wordsworth's apparent adherence in this poem to the idea of "metempsychosis," or the transmigration of the soul, a notion of the soul's immortality that seems much more Eastern in its orientation than the traditional Christian formulation. This criticism of the poet's conception of immortality extends beyond an orthodox Christian audience. According to Richard McKusick, Henry David Thoreau in his journals further complains of "Wordsworth's assimilation of the Platonic doctrine of the soul's preexistence to the traditional Christian belief in heaven." In Thoreau's mind, Wordsworth seems to be claiming that the soul's existence before incarnation is not only separate but also superior to earthly life. In line 80, Wordsworth seems to be contrasting "the glories he hath known," the soul's experience and remembrance of its heavenly origins, to its mundane existence in this dimmer earthly plane. Elsewhere, in line 86, the poet characterizes the heavenly realm of the soul's origins as an "imperial palace," a place far removed and much lamented by the soul now imprisoned in human form. In response to both Wordsworth's Christian critics and more secular readers like Thoreau, one can reasonably ask if the poem reveals a Christianizing tendency in its treatment of the soul's origins and immortality—or, conversely, can the ode be viewed in any way as Christian at all?

Wordsworth himself was apparently made aware in his own lifetime of this problem. In response to his contemporary critics, he asserted that he used the notion of the soul's preexistence in the ode as a poetic idea, not as a statement of belief. Wordsworth wrote that the idea of the soul's previous existence as portrayed in the poem is "too shadowy a notion to be recommended to faith," that it is only one "element in our instincts of immortality." However, the poet goes on to say that although the concept of the soul's existence prior to earthly life is not given by revelation as received in Scripture, it is not contradicted either. According to Wordsworth, the story of the Fall itself provides an analogy to his use of the idea of the soul's preexistence. As Wordsworth continued to revise and expand on his earlier poetry over the course of a long lifetime, it becomes obvious that his ideas began to tend more toward the conservative orthodoxy of the Victorian period. The so-called Sage of Rydal Mount, admired and revered by the British public of the mid-nineteenth century, came to supplant the radical Romantic poet who wrote his earliest and best-known work in comparative youth amid the heady passions of the French Revolution. Thus, Wordsworth himself may have come to regard his earlier poems through glasses of a more conservative and orthodox tint in his later years.

Sources for Further Study

Brooks, Cleanth. *The Well-Wrought Urn: Studies in the Structure of Poetry*. San Diego: Harcourt Brace, 1947. See Brooks's chapter "Wordsworth and the Paradox of the Imagination" for one of the most influential modern readings of Wordsworth's "Ode: Intimations of Immortality."

Hall, Spencer, and Jonathan Ramsey. *Approaches to Teaching Wordsworth's Poetry*. New York: Modern Language Association, 1986. See especially Mahoney's essay on the connections between Wordsworth's ode and Coleridge's answer in "Dejection: A Ode."

McKusick, Richard. *Green Writing: Romanticism and Ecology*. New York: St. Martin's Press, 2000. McKusick reads Wordsworth, Coleridge, and a number of other English and American Romantics in relation to modern ecological ideas about humans' relationship with the natural world.

Ulmer, William A. *The Christian Wordsworth, 1798-1805*. Albany: State University of New York Press, 2003. Ulmer argues that a Christian influence is apparent in Wordsworth's poetry from the start of his career.

Tony Rafalowski

OF LEARNED IGNORANCE

Author: Nicholas of Cusa (Nicholas Kryfts; 1401-1464)
First published: De docta ignorantia, 1440 (English translation, 1954)
Edition used: Of Learned Ignorance, in *Selected Spiritual Writings,* translated by H. Lawrence Bond with an introduction by Maurice Watanabe. New York: Paulist Press, 1997
Genre: Nonfiction
Subgenres: Meditation and contemplation; spiritual treatise
Core issues: Knowledge; mysticism; wisdom

Human beings have an innate desire to learn, and the wisest of them discover that they will always be ignorant of certain things. They can never fully know themselves, yet God knows them. God is the maximum of what can be known and also, in the creation of the world and the Incarnation of Jesus Christ, the minimum. The paradox of a God and a knowledge that is both maximal and minimal, like the paradox of "learned ignorance," is basic to a proper understanding of human nature.

Overview

Addressing his treatise to Giuliano Cesarini, a friend and mentor from his days as a law student at the University of Padua, Nicholas of Cusa in *Of Learned Ignorance* (also known in English translation as *On Learned Ignorance*) apologizes for its unusual title, *De docta ignorantia* (translated into English in 1650 as *The Idiot*). He explains that he is concerned with theological reasoning and cites many philosophers and theologians in the first of the three books that make up this work. Perhaps the most important is the fifth century church father who wrote as Dionysius the Areopagite (known also as Pseudo-Dionysius or Pseudo-Areopagite). Because no one can know God, Dionysius said in *De mystica theologia* (c. 500; English translation, 1910), one can know only what God is not. However, one can learn something about God by this *via negativa,* or "negative way."

The first book develops the thesis that there is a maximum and a minimum of everything, including knowledge: an absolute extension and contraction. These are transcendent terms, Nicholas explains, so far beyond the human capacity for understanding that they seem paradoxically to coincide. The only satisfactory term for them is God. Because nothing falls outside divine providence, God is the absolute maximum; and because this maximum is somehow contained in creation, God is also the absolute minimum. Humans can comprehend only the finite consequences in between these opposites.

In book 1, Nicholas draws from geometry. He reasons, for example, that a triangle becomes a single line when its apex is extended infinitely. In the process, he finds an interesting analogy of the Trinity which is also unity. Then, in book 2, he turns to astronomy and discusses the movement of heavenly bodies. He challenges the once common view that the universe is a perfect sphere and that heavenly bodies circle the

Earth in perfect symmetry. He is not trying to create a Copernican revolution, as some historians suggest, so much as he is saying that all astronomic measurements are relative and only the Creator has an absolute grasp of things. (In this respect, he is actually closer to Albert Einstein and the special theory of relativity.) Finally, in book 3, Nicholas turns to Christian doctrine, meditating on the mission of Jesus Christ from his vantage as a longtime monastic and newly ordained priest. By understanding how God became man, he suggests, one can begin to understand the medial role of human nature, in between nature and divinity.

Like many works of his day, Nicholas's has a series of short chapters, each with a descriptive heading. He often says he is working by analogy, using geometrical and astronomical figures as "metaphors." He thus tries to draw his friend, and any subsequent readers, into the sort of thinking that can appreciate what it means to be truly ignorant. As was common at the time, he cites numerous authorities to strengthen his argument. Book 1 takes most of its examples from pagan philosophers in Latin editions. Book 2 continues to draw from pagan writers as it develops the theme of an orderly cosmos, but it ends with a series of biblical paraphrases. Book 3 relies almost entirely on biblical texts, though it may echo some sermons of Nicholas's fellow countryman Meister Eckhart (Johannes Heinrich Eckhart von Hochheim, 1260-1328).

The term "learned ignorance" has a double meaning. It refers to the ignorance of ostensibly learned men, the pseudoknowledge paraded about by those who know less than they think. (Nicholas knew them well, having served at several German universities.) It also refers to the ignorance that is learned, with pains and often at a cost, by those who care to understand the world. Such people learn their own ignorance, especially in matters of divinity. However, this knowledge prepares them to receive God's revelation through Jesus Christ.

Another key term throughout the three books is "coincidence" (from *co* + *incidentio* "falling together"), specifically the "coincidence of opposites." The maximal coincides with the minimal, the opposing forces within the Creation coincide in God, and God makes use of coincidences to educate human beings. English has lost the old sense of "coincidence" as "agreement," most often among people, so the word "concurrence" might better convey the multiple senses of Nicholas's *conicidentio*. This concept allows Nicholas to reconcile the scholars who seek knowing and the mystics who seek not-knowing. It allows him to suggest that all paths of life, active and completive; all theologies, positive and negative; and all forms of discourse, lay and scholarly, are ultimately consistent in the mind of God. Coincidence is thus an enabling device, created by God and given to Nicholas, he says, as a gift.

In his epilogue to his friend and first reader, Nicholas says that God has enabled him to comprehend the incomprehensible and therefore has given him a principle for approaching even the most difficult passages in the Bible.

Christian Themes

Christianity has always taken a somewhat skeptical approach to "the wisdom of men" as compared with "the power of God" (1 Corinthians 2:5). Indeed, Jesus occasionally showed the same distrust of professional teachers when confronted by Pharisees as Socrates did when faced with Sophists. Writing at a time when university classes in divinity had become sophisticated at least, and occasionally sophistic, Nicholas found it appropriate to mention Socrates at the outset. "Socrates believed he knew nothing except that he did not know," he wrote, quoting Plato's *Apologia Sōkratous* (399-390 B.C.E.; *Apology*, 1675). Christian scholars can do no better than to learn their own ignorance and its consequence: their absolute reliance on God.

Nicholas realizes that the world looks different when viewed *sub species aeternitatis* (from the vantage of eternity). No one on earth would think that a triangle could become a line or that the Earth could move around the Sun, but Christianity allows one to think anagogically and to try to find the spiritual sense in God's word. The same sort of thinking can lead to a new vision of the Creation and an enhanced appreciation of the Creator.

Nicholas's doctrine of the coincidence of opposites seemed sophistical to some contemporaries. It may remind a modern reader of Parmenides on the lack of difference between being and nonbeing. However, it was meant as a means to resolve contradictions. As he ends the discussion of the heavens in book 2, Nicholas quotes Colossians 1:16: ". . . all things were created by him [God], and for him." He might have extended the quotation to note that Christ served "to reconcile all things unto himself" (1:20). When the world is viewed in the context of its creation and salvation, some petty disagreements disappear.

During his lifetime, Nicholas worked hard to achieve church unity, both north-south across the Alps and east-west across the Mediterranean. Born during the Great Schism in the Western or Roman Church, he wrote an important tract, *De concordantia catholica* (1433; *The Catholic Concordance*, 1991). He knew that the usual tendency is to dichotomize, sending the best to heaven and the others elsewhere. He wanted the sort of eccumenicity that later officials of his church would foster. After being made a cardinal in 1448, he wrote a final work calling for peace among the world religions: *De pace fidei* (1453; *On Interreligious Harmony: Text, Concordance, and Translation of "De pace fidei,"* 1990). One key to mutual understanding, he suggested, was awareness of one's own ignorance.

Sources for Further Study

Bellitto, Christopher M., Thomas M. Izbicki, and Gerald Christianson, eds. *Introducing Nicholas of Cusa: A Guide to a Renaissance Man.* Mahwah, N.J.: Paulist Press, 2004. Fifteen interconnected essays on Nicholas and his thought. Includes H. Lawrence Bond's glossary of Nicholas's terminology and a guide to English-language research on Nicholas.

Casarella, Peter J., ed. *Cusanus: The Legacy of Learned Ignorance.* Washington, D.C.: Catholic University of America Press, 2006. Thirteen essays on philosophical, theological, and scientific themes in Nicholas's work. One explores his mathematical metaphors, while another discusses ideas about planetary motion.

Hopkins, Jasper. *A Concise Introduction to the Philosophy of Nicholas of Cusa.* 2d ed.

Minneapolis: University of Minnesota Press, 1980. An introductory essay on key concepts of Nicholas's thought, supplemented by a chronology of major works and a bibliography of primary and secondary texts.

Jaspers, Karl. *Anselm and Nicholas of Cusa*. Translated by Ralph Manheim. New York: Harcourt, 1966. A highly readable selection from *The Great Philosophers* (1957; English translation 1962). Considers Nicholas's personality in relation to his world system.

Nicholas of Cusa. *Selected Spiritual Writings*. Classics of Western Spirituality 89. Translated by H. Lawrence Bond with an introduction by Maurice Watanabe. New York: Paulist Press, 1997. The preface offers a good introduction to the man, his theology, and its importance. The translations are carefully annotated to identify Nicholas's sources.

Yamaki, Kazuhiko, ed. *Nicholas of Cusa: A Medieval Thinker for the Modern Age*. Richmond, Surrey, England: Curzon Press, 2002. Twenty-five essays on Nicholas, eight of them in English. Of particular interest are studies of his epistemology and multiculturalism, written in English by Japanese scholars.

Thomas Willard

ON BEING A CHRISTIAN

Author: Hans Küng (1928-   )
First published: Christ sein, 1974 (English translation, 1976)
Edition used: On Being a Christian, translated by Edward Quinn. New York: Pocket
    Books, 1978
Genre: Nonfiction
Subgenres: Church history; critical analysis; theology
Core issues: Daily living; faith; Jesus Christ; truth

Küng's thesis is directed at the reader in his first sentence: "Why should one be a Christian?" As a display of apologetics, Küng chooses to work "from the bottom up," that is, from his understanding of everyday human reality, to create a case for the validity of the Christian faith. Although Küng does not ignore the overriding issues of transcendence and salvation, he keeps them firmly rooted in a description of modern life. Küng's insistence that "truth is not merely facticity" attempts to reply to both literalist and modernist claims about the possibility of faith statements.

Overview

Hans Küng, born in Switzerland, is a Catholic priest and a prolific author. The appearance of *On Being a Christian* in English in 1976 brought a primarily academic theologian to wide public attention. At the time, Küng was a professor of theology at Tubingen, Germany. The book's perspective, which can now be appreciated as expressing a moderate theological liberalism, added to the official Vatican concern about Küng's 1970 book, *Unfehlbar? Eine Anfrage (Infallible? An Inquiry,* 1971). In 1979, he lost his license to teach as a Roman Catholic theologian but continued teaching at Tubingen until his retirement in 1996. In his retirement he has explored the concept of a "global ethic," drawing on insights from all religious traditions.

In *On Being a Christian,* Küng's first response is to turn to the world situation as he sees it, to a secular world apparently in the throes of great change, and to its social and political claims on human beings. He wonders if the Catholic Church, in the midst of all this, has lost its relevance, or more possibly, its soul. He begins with the claim that "to save man's humanity . . . there must be genuine transcending, a genuinely qualitative ascent to a real alternative (to) one-dimensional thinking, talking and acting."

Küng next moves to the question of the world religions. "Not only Christianity, but also the world religions are aware of man's alienation, enslavement, and need of redemption," he writes, and he sees in this shared knowledge a confirmation of the need for transcendence. However, he does not accept a universalizing "religion" in general: Similarities exist but serious differences must be acknowledged. The telling distinction is to be found in the person of Jesus of Nazareth. He identifies the distinctions among the world religions and the various secular humanisms as follows: "Christianity only exists where the memory of Jesus Christ is activated in theory and practice."

Küng then turns to the relationship between Christianity and Judaism. Christianity and the memory of Jesus Christ must be firmly rooted in the understanding that Jesus was a Jew. Küng sensitively describes the "Judaisms" of Jesus' historical period and the ways in which Jesus diverged from them. What then, he asks, was the center of Jesus' proclamation and his actions? Küng understands that center to be the proclamation of the Kingdom of God, which he calls "the designation of God's cause." Küng sees the Jesus of the Gospels not proclaiming himself but rather an "oddly radical identification of God's cause with man's."

This examination of Jesus leads to a discussion of the debate about the nature and being of God, especially in the problematic designation of "Father" used in the Christian creeds. Again, Küng sees a radical revision. "Father" is not used in the Greek sense of physical progenitor (Zeus), nor in the patriarchal sense of the exerciser of sovereign rights. This is instead the "Father" of the parable of the prodigal son, "who meets men as a God of redeeming love." Jesus, it follows, is God's "personal ambassador, trustee, confidant, friend of God . . . when he proclaims God as Father . . . he rises above the religious fears and prejudices of his time [and] identifies himself with the people who are ignorant of religion." Here Küng finds the alternative to one-dimensional life, "a real alternative with different values, norms and ideals." However, this alternative is not without cost.

Küng turns to the death of Jesus. The opening question must be why he had to die. By asserting that "Jesus' violent end was the logical conclusion of his proclamation and behavior," Küng carefully lays out the political and religious provocations of Jesus' ministry, and what interest each group had in seeking his death. In this discussion, Küng moves from historically accepted material to issues of faith. He notes the difficulties in the narratives of the Resurrection. Once again, he speaks of radicalization; "The resurrection faith is not an appendage to faith in God, but a radicalizing of faith in God." The Resurrection, then, is another manifestation of "God's cause."

Küng's concluding section is entitled, "Being Christian as Being Radically Human." Küng returns to the secular sphere, where he is cautiously critical of "political theology." Writing at a time when Latin American liberation theology was ascendant in many places, Küng calls for "no uncritical identifications." Just as he views Jesus as unallied with any of the political movements of his time, Küng urges Christians not to join uncritically with contemporary political movements whether of the left or the right. Politics must be subject to the scrutiny of the Gospel. Küng concludes, repeating his question: "Why should one be a Christian?" His final answer is that "By following Jesus Christ, man in the world of today can truly humanly live, act, suffer and die; in happiness and unhappiness, in life and death, sustained by God and helpful to men."

Christian Themes

In *On Being a Christian*, Küng's first concern is to address the question of the distinctiveness of Christianity. He locates this distinctiveness in the person of Jesus Christ. From this, Küng turns to Christology, an analysis of what may be known about

Jesus Christ, how it may be known, and what to do with this knowledge once one has it. This involves a discussion of the historical-critical method of biblical study, which attempts, among other things, to place the biblical narratives in their historical contexts and to realign the reader's perception of the narratives with how a person of the period might have understood them.

Küng examines the ethical teachings of Jesus Christ within their historical contexts as well as vis-à-vis the actual content of the narratives. Suffering is one of the themes that emerges in the context of the Crucifixion. The miraculous, not only Jesus' miracles in the Gospel narratives, but also the even more pressing questions of the Resurrection and the virgin birth, also receive careful examination. The practice of being the Church is his next theme. Küng posits that being the Church is a distinct way of being, and he works through what that means by drawing not only on the teachings of Jesus and Paul but also on the practices of the early Church. His final discussion of evangelism considers how the understanding of the Gospel that he has so far portrayed may be presented in a diverse and increasingly secularized world.

Sources for Further Study

Küng, Hans. *Christianity: Essence, History, and Future.* New York: Continuum, 1995. Examines Christian history through several periods from the eschatologically minded early Christian period to the contemporary ecumenical period. Diagrams, maps, and sidebars make skimming easy, but the full 936 pages are for the determined reader.

_____. *My Struggle for Freedom: Memoirs.* Grand Rapids, Mich.: Wm. B. Eerdmans, 2003. Küng's account of his early life, vocational call, education, and faith development, written entirely in present tense. Concludes at the close of Vatican II. Illustrated.

_____. *Theology for the Third Millennium: An Ecumenical View.* New York: Doubleday, 1988. An effort to create a pan-Christian theology to carry churches toward unity in the twenty-first century. Helpful but perhaps too hopeful.

Nowell, Robert. *A Passion for Truth: Hans Küng, A Biography.* New York: Crossroad, 1981. Written in response to the revocation of Küng's license to teach Catholic theology, this work presents a defense of his life and work.

Bonnie L. A. Shullenberger

ON CHRISTIAN THEOLOGY

Author: Rowan Williams (1950-   )
First published: Malden, Mass.: Blackwell, 2000, edited by Gareth Jones and Lewis
   Ayres
Genre: Nonfiction
Subgenres: Hermeneutics; theology
Core issues: Church; Eucharist; God; Incarnation; prayer; social action

*Christianity is a community of individuals who share a common hope and a common
vocation to holiness. By praying, reading the Scriptures, and participating in the Sacraments, especially the Eucharist, Christians gain the strength to fulfill the primary
mission of the Church: to take their faith into the world by engaging in conversations
with those who differ with them. Christian theology, then, is not a set of doctrinal
statements to be learned by rote but instead a means by which people can evaluate
their beliefs and their practices.*

Overview

   On Christian Theology is one of many works by Rowan Williams, whose erudition,
superb style, and profound vision earned him a reputation as one of the finest theologians of his era. Born in Wales, Williams earned two degrees at Christ's College,
Cambridge, and a D. Phil. from Christ Church and Wadham College, Oxford. After
being ordained a priest of the Church of England, he remained in the academic world
for the next decade and a half, becoming a recognized poet and a prominent theologian as well as a social activist. In 1991, Williams was elected bishop of Monmouth,
Newport, Wales. Nine years later, he became archbishop of Wales, and in 2003, he
was enthroned as archbishop of Canterbury. However, his administrative duties did
not prevent Williams from continuing to pursue his scholarly interests and to publish
works on a wide variety of subjects.

   On Christian Theology is a collection of eighteen essays and lectures that were produced by Williams in the 1980's and 1990's. Although the subjects of these pieces
vary, the collection is unified by Williams's vision of what Christianity is meant to be.
It is also given coherence by the fact that the purpose of the essays is as much to define
theology and to explain its purpose as it is to illustrate its applications.

   In his prologue, Williams defines the twofold task of the theologian: on one hand,
to observe the ongoing life of the Christian community, and on the other, to remind
the members of the community of their historical roots. Theological thought, he argues, is divided into three styles. The "celebratory" style uses the full range of sound,
imagery, and symbolism to create a transcendent vision. Examples of this style would
be hymns, psalms, and religious poetry.

   The "communicative" style is experimental, tentative, and courageous, for it involves taking the Gospel into alien environments. Williams cites as one example the

inclusion of Stoic and Platonic ideas in patristic works. More recently, there have been attempts to read Marxist theories as applications of the Gospel. Feminist works, too, have been read as reflections of the Gospel in practice. Williams admits that the results of such attempts may vary. At the very least, they can succeed in opening lines of communication between Christians and people who had previously assumed that the Gospel was irrelevant. Even if the outsiders remain unconvinced, this endeavor may enable Christians to see that the Gospel has broader applications than they had realized and that it has depths of meaning they had not previously perceived.

The third style, the "critical," is insistently rational and systematic. It is important, for it provides continuity with the historical church. By insisting on fundamentals, it also guards against the emotional responses that can be provoked by the "celebratory" style and the indulgent tolerance that can result from the "communicative" style. However, Williams points out that the critical style, which depends on scholarly skepticism, can proceed to doubt or even unbelief. At its best, however, it will end with a return to faith and a celebratory acknowledgment of the mysterious nature of a very real God. Though Williams admits that some of his essays could be classified as closer to one style or another, he insists that all three styles are all essential to the development of Christian theology.

Williams has provided further coherence to his collection by organizing the essays by subject matter. In part 1, "Defining the Enterprise," Williams discusses such matters as theological integrity, the difference between tolerance of the beliefs of others and acceptance of the idea of religious pluralism, and the importance of Scripture. Part 2, "The Act of God," begins by pointing out the importance of seeing God as the creator and viewing all human beings as his creatures. Williams then discusses the implications of the Incarnation, the Crucifixion, and the presence of the Holy Spirit. In part 3, "The Grammar of God," Williams applies his ideas about the Trinity to three complex issues: revelation, ontology, and pluralism. Part 4, "Making Signs," which begins with "Between the Cherubim: The Empty Tomb and the Empty Throne," moves logically to an exploration of the meaning of the Sacraments. In the final section, "Living the Mystery," Williams moves to practical applications of his theology, emphasizing the importance of community and then outlining New Testament ethics, which he sees as mandating opposition to war and to any form of racism.

In his "Preface," Williams expresses his gratitude to friends and former students, as well as his wife, who over the years have challenged his ideas, often disagreeing with him, thus enabling him to refine his thoughts. Throughout *On Christian Theology*, Williams frequently mentions other theologians, past and present, courteously refuting what he perceives as errors but pointing out ideas he finds valuable. Thus Williams illustrates his belief that even critical theology is a search for the truth by means of civil discourse.

Christian Themes

Although he has been labeled a theological conservative and a social liberal, in *On Christian Theology* Williams emphasizes his belief that Christian faith and practice must always be open to discussion and even to modification. Despite his own commitment to Anglicanism, he does not define the Church denominationally. Instead, he sees it as a community of people with the same hope, a closer relationship with God, and the same vocation, to reflect that relationship in their dealings with other human beings.

The Christian community is also united by their belief in the identity of Jesus Christ, revealed in the Gospels as the Incarnate Son of God. They see the three major events in the Gospels as the Incarnation, the Crucifixion, and the Resurrection. The sacraments of baptism and the Eucharist are both essential in the life of a Christian. Baptism represents an individual commitment to Christ; the Eucharist is a reliving of the events of the Gospel, a deliverance from sin, and a reminder that by making a commitment to Christ, one has become a member of the Christian family.

Like Christ, Christians are expected to surrender to God in prayer and in action. Like Christ, they must remain open to others, thus witnessing to the fact that every human being is one of God's creatures. This is the basis of Williams's pacifism. Williams also applies the biblical strictures against judging others not only to racial injustices and the mistreatment of women in the past but also to present-day judgments about the appropriate place in society and in the Church of women and of homosexuals. Again, Williams would have the Christian community be inclusive rather than exclusive. He would have Christians direct their efforts toward developing their own holiness, so that they can reflect the love of a perfect God in an imperfect world.

Sources for Further Study

Breyfogle, Todd. "Time and Transformation: A Conversation with Rowan Williams." *Cross Currents* 45 (1995): 293-312. Williams comments on music, literature, and theology; the ordination of women in the Anglican Church; and theological differences within the Church.

Higton, Mike. *Difficult Gospel: The Theology of Rowan Williams.* London: SCM-Canterbury Press, 2004. Argues that Williams sees theology as necessarily tentative because the body of Christ consists of billions of people, each with a different response to God. A useful guide.

Hobson, Theo. "Rowan Williams as Anglican Hegelian." *Reviews in Religion and Theology* 12 (2005): 290-297. Explains how Williams utilizes Hegel's insights to show that Anglicanism offers the best basis for the ideal Christian society.

Kelsey, David H. Review of *On Christian Theology. Modern Theology* 16 (2000): 562-564. Points out that despite being written at different times, the essays in this volume are consistent stylistically, intellectually, and theologically.

Shortt, Rupert. *Rowan Williams: An Introduction.* London: Darton, Longman, and Todd, 2003. A lengthy biographical chapter is followed by sections on Williams's philosophy and theology, spirituality, and politics. Bibliography and index.

Rosemary M. Canfield Reisman

ON DIVINE LOVE

Author: John Duns Scotus (1266-1308)

First published: As part of *Commentaria Oxoniensia ad IV libros magistri Sent-entiarum*, after 1300 (*Proof for the Unicity of God*, 1950; better known as *Ordinatio: Philosophical Writings*, 1962)

Edition used: Duns Scotus on Divine Love: Texts and Commentary on Goodness and Freedom, God and Humans, edited by A. Vos, et al. Burlington, Vt.: Ashgate, 2003

Genre: Nonfiction

Subgenre: Theology

Core issues: Acceptance; *agape*; the Eternal Now; grace; love; salvation

Duns Scotus expounded his views on divine love as part of an ongoing medieval theological and philosophical debate on the nature of salvation within a wider context of the nature and being of God and how he relates to humans. Duns Scotus held that the primary concepts within this doctrine of salvation were love, merit, and the will, both human and divine. His views were in contrast to those of contemporary theologians such as Thomas Aquinas, who upheld the primacy of reason, the intellect, knowledge, and faith. Duns Scotus also redefined the nature of the Trinity to show that the Holy Spirit is the divine love.

Overview

John Duns Scotus was probably born in the small town of Duns, in the Borders region of Scotland. In 1279 he entered the Franciscan convent in nearby Dumfries, then the next year went to Oxford University. For eight years he studied the basic liberal arts courses, then arranged into the quadrivium of four subjects and the trivium of three. Having completed these courses, he became a student of theology in 1288. On March 17, 1291, he was ordained. In 1297, he received the baccalaureus, which enabled him to lecture, with the view to his becoming a doctor of philosophy and a university professor.

The main way to do this was to give a lecture course of a year's length based on the *Sententiarum libri IV* (1148-1151; *Four Books of Sentences*, 2000) of the medieval theologian Peter Lombard, after spending a year preparing these lectures. This is when Duns Scotus wrote his *Lectura*. Basically they were lecture notes on the sentences, set out in the formal scholastic manner: proposition to be defended, questions on it, possible answers, possible objections, and refutation of objections. For some reason, he did not receive his doctorate immediately after having distinguished himself in these lectures. He attracted, it seems, some thousands of students, and was given the nickname of "Doctor Subtilis," the subtle doctor. He also had the tag "Scotus" (the Scotsman) added to his name.

In 1301 Duns Scotus was sent to the University of Paris, which had been the center of fierce theological strife, to teach the course again, plus teach a philosophy course and enter into debate about the immaculate conception of the Virgin Mary. So well did he defend this doctrine that it became adopted by the university, though it did not become official Catholic dogma till 1854. In 1303 he was expelled from the university in the conflict between the pope and the French king. He possibly went to Cambridge University at this time but was back in Paris the next year. It was only then he received his doctor of theology degree, or *magister theologiae*. He started working with his assistants on his major work of scholarship, the *Ordinatio*, which was to become the official commentary on the sentences.

This was interrupted by more controversy in Paris, and in 1307, the Franciscan order sent Duns Scotus to Cologne, Germany, to teach at the theological college there. He suddenly died on November 8, 1308, the *Ordinatio* still unfinished and now known as the *Opus Oxoniense* (the Oxford work). His students put together what else they remembered from his lectures, this being the *Reportatio parisiensis* (1302-1305). Not until the 1920's were the *Lectura* discovered, and not till the 1950's was a critical edition of Dun Scotus's complete works produced. There is yet to be a complete English translation of the Latin.

Duns Scotus did not write any single text entitled "On Divine Love." That title came from a commentary put together by Research Group John Duns Scotus working out of Utrecht University in the Netherlands. They collected together a number of his writings on the topic, putting Scotus's Latin text on one side, an English translation on the other side, and then adding a commentary at the end of each section. This is the text this article will address. The sections are taken from volumes 6, 16, and 17 of the 1950's edition, some of which is drawn from the *Lectura* and some from the *Ordinatio*.

The book is divided into six chapters. The first deals with necessity and contingency, the second applies these concepts to theological ethics, and the third discusses "the act of love" and eternal life. The subject of election and merit constitutes the fourth chapter, followed by a chapter on God's will and its goodness. The last chapter is "An Infinite Act of Love." The concepts of necessity and contingency may not seem to have much to do with love, but Duns Scotus makes these foundational to his notions of freedom, merit, and grace. Logically, something contingent did not have to be; something necessary did. Do we necessarily love God, or can it be otherwise, out of choice?

Christian Themes

A number of core themes emerge. First, in the Franciscan tradition, love and the will are the two fundamental concepts that link God and humans. The concepts come together in election and by an understanding of the nature of the Trinity. One of the medieval debates was whether God's will was irresistible. If it was, would that not make humans automatons and therefore incapable of love or being loved? Duns Scotus held that humans were free, which made it possible for humans to will to love God and authenticate that freedom by an act of love.

Like most medieval theologians, Duns Scotus was concerned with finding some merit in humans by which God might accept them, even though God had chosen (elected) individuals to receive his salvation and gain eternal life. Scotus saw that humans, of themselves, in their fallen state, needed to have put in them a "disposition" (*habitus*) to love. There is an ethical necessity to love the perfect good (God), but an inability to do so. This implanting of a disposition is an act of grace, following on from people's election. However, the will of each person can still choose whether to act on that disposition and actually choose to love God. This is the one possible act of merit and what make each person "loveable" to God.

The inevitable question that attaches itself to all discussions of election is whether once elected, one is always elected, whatever one does. Although Scotus holds that all past acts are necessary (you cannot change history), he argues that God lives in eternity, so past, present, and future are collapsed into the Eternal Now. Therefore, even though God elected one contingently, it could have been otherwise. If one sins and rejects God's love, then it becomes that otherwise with God: One has not been elected, that is, one is reprobate.

Having returned God's love through an implanted disposition, one then has to love oneself and one's neighbor. Which comes first? Duns Scotus holds that a right love for oneself must precede love for one's neighbor, which he sees as mirroring our love for ourselves.

This concept is taken by Duns Scotus into understanding the Trinity. God must love the divine essence, since it is perfectly good. The object of his love is Christ, the Son. So we have God the lover and God the beloved. The divine love that goes from one to the other is the Holy Spirit, the third person of the Trinity. The divine love is none other than the Holy Spirit.

Sources for Further Study

Cross, Richard. *Duns Scotus*. New York: Oxford University Press, 1999. One of the Great Medieval Thinkers series and probably the easiest overall introduction to his work, from a leading Duns Scotus scholar.

Ingham, Mary Beth. *Scotus for Dunces: An Introduction to the Subtle Doctor*. St. Bonaventure, N.Y.: Franciscan Institute Publications, 2003. Ingham is a leading scholar on Duns Scotus. She considers "rational love" in her section "Reading Scotus Today."

Ingham, Mary Beth, and Mechthild Dreyer. *The Philosophical Vision of John Duns Scotus*. Washington, D.C.: Catholic University of America Press, 2004. This is much more of an academic textbook than the above. It shows Duns Scotus as philosopher and moralist as well as theologian. Chapter 6, "The Rational Will and Freedom," is the most relevant.

Vos, Antonie. *The Philosophy of John Duns Scotus*. Edinburgh, Scotland: Edinburgh University Press, 2006. A summary of Duns Scotus's life as well as an overall view of his writings from this leading Dutch Reformed scholar.

Williams, Thomas, ed. *The Cambridge Companion to Duns Scotus*. Cambridge, England: Cambridge University Press, 2003. A series of essays covering various aspects of Duns Scotus.

Wolter, Allan B. *Scotus and Ockham: Selected Essays.* St. Bonaventure, N.Y.: Franciscan Institute Publications, 2003. This is more of a philosophy text, but it does discuss Duns Scotus in a wider context. Wolter takes Duns Scotus to be more Aristotelian and less Augustinian than some other scholars.

David Barratt

ON FIRST PRINCIPLES

Author: Origen (c. 185-c. 254 C.E.)
First published: Peri archōn, 220-230 C.E. (English translation, 1936)
Edition used: Origen de Principiis, vol. 4 in *The Ante-Nicene Fathers*, edited by Alexander Roberts and James Donaldson. Grand Rapids, Mich.: Wm. B. Eerdmans, 1979
Genre: Nonfiction
Subgenre: Theology
Core issues: The Bible; Creation; the Deity; freedom and free will; God; Holy Spirit; Incarnation; Jesus Christ; reason; salvation; soul; the Trinity; wisdom; the Word

Beginning with what is clear from the teaching of the Church, Origen speculates about the unanswered questions regarding the Trinity, human salvation, free will, and the way to interpret Scripture.

Overview

Origen was the first Christian to write systematic theology, to explain how all the things the Bible teaches can be true, and to show how those truths relate to one another. In *On First Principles*, Origen begins the first book with a preface that states what is clear from the teaching of the Apostles. First, there is only one God the creator, who gave the Law and sent Jesus Christ. Second, God the Son was born of the Father, was the servant of God in the creation of all things, became a man, was born of a virgin, died, and rose from the dead. Third, the Holy Spirit inspired the prophets and apostles. Fourth, souls exist with free will and rationality, and they are rewarded or punished after death. Fifth, a devil and bad angels exist. Sixth, the world began and will end. Seventh, the Scriptures were written by the Holy Spirit and have both an obvious and a hidden meaning. Eighth, good angels help in human salvation. Origen says that anyone who wants to make a "connected series and body of truths" must begin from this foundation.

The first book of *On First Principles* begins by disproving the idea that God exists materially. While various Scriptures give this impression, Origen shows that they are metaphors. God is also incomprehensible, far better than any human understanding can fathom. Of God the Son, Origen says that he is also the wisdom and Word of God. Because God has always been the Father and has always possessed wisdom and his Word, God the Son must be coeternal with the Father. He is also the life by which all things live and the truth by which all things truly exist. While some might have reasoned that God exists and communicates through a divine Word, no one would think of the existence of the Holy Spirit without the revelation in Scripture. Nothing in the Bible even implies that the Holy Spirit was created, so it must be uncreated and coeternal with God the Father. This Holy Spirit works exclusively with believers. God the Father gives all beings existence, God the Son gives some beings rationality, and God the Spirit gives the rational beings who obey God holiness. Those to whom the Spirit gives holiness must continue to long for more, lest they become satiated and fall away through neglect.

Thinking of falling away through neglect makes Origen wonder whether the good angels and the bad demons were created that way or became what they are through their own choice. Ezekiel 28 and Isaiah 14 convince him that all the spiritual powers were created good. Those who are now angels continued to obey God, but those who are demons fell away. However, Origen speculates, since every rational being has free will, it is possible that some demons may repent and be restored to their former positions.

Next, Origen wonders about the sun, moon, and stars, concluding that they are rational creatures whom God has ordained to serve humanity. Likewise, the angels discharge various functions assigned to them by God in accordance with their behavior before the earth was created. Origen concludes this first book by asserting that there can be movement by rational souls between the three ranks of angels, demons, and people. He has already asserted that angels can become demons, and demons by repenting can become angels, but in this final section he says that people can become angels. He even says that these souls may become forever one spirit with the Lord until no one can distinguish between these souls and God.

In the second book, Origen raises the question of whether or not the world was created. He finds it impossible to believe that such a well-ordered world could exist by chance and argues that the world needs an architect. He says that free will negates the Stoic notion that the events of the world repeat themselves endlessly, and he projects three possible ends for the world. One is that matter will be annihilated, a second is that bodies and spirits will become ethereal, and a third is that soul will leave the realm of change and move into an unchanging heaven.

Origen next refutes those who say the God of the Old Testament is not the Father of Jesus Christ. He then shows that goodness and justice require each other, against those who say that the Old Testament God is just and the New Testament God is good. About the Incarnation, Origen speculates that God chose the most obedient human soul to unite with himself, and that as Christ's human soul always freely chose to do the good, its nature was changed so it became immune to sin. About the Holy Spirit, Origen says it explains the hidden meaning of the Scripture to the believer and even communicates unutterable consolation.

Turning to the nature of the soul, Origen defines the soul as the living part of a being and says that saving the soul of a person restores all its rational powers. Next Origen considers the objection that a just God did not create the world because people are born into such different situations, some into privilege and some into privation. He answers this charge by arguing that in a prebirth existence every soul either moves toward God or away from him. Those who choose God are rewarded in their birth circumstances, and those who reject him are punished. In the final judgment after death, people's souls and bodies will be reunited, God will consider all the circumstances of earthly existence, and he will reward or punish people accordingly. Finally Origen disagrees with those who think eternal life to be one of fleshly indulgence, saying that the keenest desire of the soul is for understanding and that this is the need that will be satisfied in the heavenly world.

The third book deals with free will, which Origen defines as the rational part of a person that chooses which of the external promptings and internal desires it will follow. He cites many portions of Scripture that assume people can do what they choose, but then he addresses the passages in Scripture that seem to assert the contrary. Beginning with God's hardening of Pharaoh's heart, Origen explains that the same sun melts the wax and hardens the clay. Thus, while many Egyptians turned to God during the plagues, Pharaoh freely choose to defy God. Explaining Romans 9:16—"It is not of him that wills, . . . but of God that shows mercy"—Origen argues that this is just another example of a situation in which humans do things but the Scripture attributes the overall result to God. The most difficult verses to explain away are Romans 9:18-21, which assert that God has mercy on whom he will have mercy and hardens those whom he hardens. Origen cannot easily explain away these verses, so he cites several other verses wherein Paul teaches free will and says that we must not think the Apostle contradicted himself. Because Paul clearly believes in free will, this passage cannot teach otherwise, despite what it apparently affirms. In the rest of this book, Origen argues that the way the devil tempts people shows that they have free will.

The fourth book deals with the interpretation of the Bible. Using many examples, Origen teaches that the Scripture must be interpreted on three levels corresponding to the flesh, soul, and spirit in the human being. The flesh is the obvious meaning, the soul is the meaning that edifies, and the spiritual is God's hidden wisdom for the perfect individual. In order to make the necessity of this threefold interpretation obvious, God put various absurdities into the Bible. For example, the law forbids the eating of vultures. Since no one, even in a famine, would think of eating a vulture, this prohibition must have a soulish or spiritual meaning. Origen finishes his work with a recapitulation of his teachings about the Trinity, defending them as being taught by the spiritual sense of the Scripture.

Christian Themes

Origen explains the how the Father, Son, and Holy Spirit can be different and yet be coeternal and all fully God. He defends free will and explains the threefold meaning of Scripture. Althought the Church valued Origen as the first theologian and intiailly accepted his theology, it later rejected his speculations about the prebirth activities of souls; reincarnation; the interchangeability of demoniac, human, and angelic souls; and the final absorption of all into God.

Sources for Further Study

Crouzel, Henri. *Origen*. Translated by A. S. Worrall. San Francisco: Harper & Row, 1989. An overview of Origen's life and theology.

Ferguson, Everett, ed. *Encyclopedia of Early Christianity*. 2d ed. New York: Garland, 1997. Provides an extensive article on Origen.

Kannengiesser, Charles, and William Petersen, eds. *Origen of Alexandria: His World and His Legacy.* Notre Dame, Ind.: University of Notre Dame Press, 1988. Scholarly papers on various aspects of Origen's life, thought, and impact.

McGrath, Allister. *Historical Theology: An Introduction to the History of Christian Thought.* Malden, Mass.: Blackwell, 1998. Provides the background for Origen's theology.

Charles White

ON LISTENING TO ANOTHER

Author: Douglas V. Steere (1901-1995)
First published: 1955
Edition used: "On Beginning from Within" and "On Listening to Another." New York: Harper & Row, 1964
Genre: Nonfiction
Subgenre: Devotions
Core issues: God; listening; prayer; Quakers; silence

Beginning in the 1930's, Steere, one of the eminent spiritual guides and writers of the twentieth century, led an ecumenical vanguard in constructing bridges between Protestantism and Catholicism and between Christians and non-Christians. In what was delivered in part as the Swarthmore Lecture at the London Yearly Meeting in 1955, Douglas Steere used the common experience of listening and being listened to as a fresh way of laying before his hearers the genius of Quaker worship and vocal ministry.

Overview

Listening, as Douglas V. Steere understood it, involves far more than hearing. It is nothing less than a disclosure of the inner person, "where words come from," as the Indian chief Papunehang exclaimed of John Woolman's prayer delivered in a language he could not understand. All of us have experienced both listening and not listening, being listened to and not being listened to, in this sense. Steere contends that true listening requires discernment not merely of the external sounds but of what the speaker is trying to communicate that is beyond words, what lies beneath the layer of words at the level of the heart. Every conversation involves more than a speaker and a hearer. It has to do also with what each person meant to say, with what each understood the other to say, and with many other levels of listening. More important still, it involves a spectator listener within each speaker who listens as that person speaks and grasps what is going on at all levels.

Yet deep and genuine listening is rare, Steere claims, for the kind of love that is required for it seldom is present. All listeners experience lapses as a consequence of bored inattention, adverse judgments on what is being revealed or on the person revealing it, and the imposition of one's own subconscious interpretations because of unfaced fears, evaded decisions, repressed longings, or hidden aspirations. Here the inward spectator must never let up on vigilance toward the outward listener.

A good listener will be characterized by vulnerability, acceptance, expectancy, and constancy. The critical factor, Steere insists, is openness in the listener, which can create a climate for self-disclosure "where the deepest longings in the heart of the speaker feel safe to reveal themselves, . . . where nothing needs any longer to be concealed." This degree of openness will make a listener vulnerable, for the speaker will know that person has been through some testing, too. Father Damien on the Hawaiian island of Molokai, for instance, put a new note of reality into his ministry to lepers there when, after years of service, he began his sermon one Sunday, "We lepers."

The good listener will also accept the other person just as that person is, Steere suggests. Acceptance does not mean "toleration born of indifference" but "an interest so alive that judgment is withheld." By expectancy the good listener "reaches through" to partially concealed capacities in the speaker "by something that is almost akin to divination." Good listening depends too on a fourth quality, Steere writes, namely, constancy, "an infinite patience grounded in faith in what the person may become." All other qualities, however, circle back to the first: caring enough to risk being involved.

Listening so as to lead another into a condition of disclosure and discovery goes beyond human listening. Over the shoulder of the human listener, as it were, Steere writes, is "the silent presence of the Eternal Listener, the Living God." Steere asks, in penetrating to the depths of another, "do we not disclose the thinness of the filament that separates [persons] listening openly to one another, and that of God intently listening to each soul?" As Søren Kierkegaard points out in *Purity of Heart Is to Will One Thing* (1847), the listener stands alone on the stage with God as the audience while the deliverer of the message prompts from offstage in the wings. Psalm 139 reminds us that we can conceal nothing from the Eternal Listener, and it is the presence of this Listener that clarifies and discloses. Such is the point Fyodor Dostoevski makes in the Grand Inquisitor scene of *Bratya Karamazovy* (1879-1880; *The Brothers Karamazov*, 1912) as Jesus stands silent before the accusations of the Inquisitor until his listening "penetrates to the core of the Cardinal and reduces him to silence."

The Eternal Listener has exemplified the qualities of vulnerability, acceptance, expectancy, and constancy. He entered flesh and blood and went to the cross to demonstrate how much he cared. As Abbé Huvelin once told Friedrich von Hügel, no Sermon on the Mount could ever have secured our redemption; God had to arrange this by dying so as to convince us he cared supremely. Jesus modeled acceptance, expectancy, and constancy. Steere asks, Can one find any starker demonstration of unqualified *acceptance* than Jesus' association with tax collectors, prostitutes, and outcasts of Jewish society? Or of *expectancy* in what his acceptance did to the impetuous, vacillating Peter, Mary Magdalene, or Zacchaeus? Or of *constancy* as he rallied the dismayed, fearful, scattered, fleeing band of followers to send them out as witnesses?

What really matters, Steere comments, is not what the listener is but what the listener *is* in what he or she *does*. In encounter with a human listener, a speaker is never unaware of the judgment upon his or her life by the listener, nor can the listener resist judging the speaker. However, it is encounter with the Eternal Listener that really matters, Steere claims, for this Listener's very existence, if not ignored, "rebukes and clamps down the evil and calls out and underlines the good, drawing from the visible participants, things they did not know they possessed." On the Emmaus Road, for instance, Jesus set the hearts of his two companions to glowing. As Bernard of Clairvaux expresses it, the Living Listener "seems able to take fearlessly the speakers' own diseased irradiations, lethal though they may be, to absorb them, and to transform them." The more conscious the human listener is of the effect of the Living Listener, the more certain that person becomes "that only the cleansing radiations of an utterly loving and charitable one will do." The Living Listener's presence totally alters the situation.

This is especially true of prayer, Steere contends. Prayer may begin as a soliloquy, for human beings must begin where they are. What veterans in prayer counsel is that we persist until we stop talking and start listening. The situation in corporate worship is similar. Worshipers gather with a heavy load, their minds far from worshiping. Worship, after all, is for the weary and heavily laden. What matters is that the Divine Listener changes these cares, reorders them, drops them into the background, and reduces them to silence as worshipers become still enough to hear God. The test of worship or vocal ministry rests in its ability to draw worshipers to an attentive awareness of the Living Listener until they themselves become listeners.

The Quaker (Friends') form of corporate renewal may appear strange to many but, Steere writes, "the living Listener's magnetic transforming caring is present and able to meet [the worshipers'] needs and to draw the worshippers into his service." Quaker worship has its own set of problems, but it does not experience some of those experienced in either Free Protestant or liturgical churches. In laying aside traditional patterns, Quakers place immense responsibility upon the shoulders of each listener to praise, give thanks, confess sins and receive forgiveness, offer petitions or make intercessions, and yield to what God requires. The danger is that this freedom may lead to an abandonment of discipline or cause lapses into artificial reliance on cold psychological devices.

Quaker corporate worship requires both voluntary and involuntary attention to the subject of worship. The more one knows of the subject, the better the concentration, Steere remarks. Concentration upon the Divine Listener is the small part the worshiper can and must perform if the service is to be fruitful. Quakers do not speak much about their voluntary acts of attention because they recognize "the drastic variations in temperament and personal needs in so intimate a matter as coming into the presence of God." Readying oneself in silence, however, is as natural in preparing to enter the presence of God as it is to prepare oneself to meet a distinguished person. Sitting quietly in the midst of other silent worshipers helps restore attention as inner and outer distractions tug away at the mind. Most Friends know it is futile to fight against distractions or be despondent about them, for all persons, no matter how saintly, experience them. By accepting, acknowledging, and quietly ignoring them, they fade into the background. Some enfold them into a prayer. Others reflect on what the distractions might communicate. Most ignore them and return to the Center.

Thankfulness to God for himself, his love, his constancy, and his caring passes naturally into adoration. Regular contact with the Bible and Jesus' life, ministry, death, and resurrection may supply ample reasons for such thankfulness. Such an experience, however, leads to "no snug coziness." Adoration, rather, stirs a desire to penetrate further the abyss of being that is the living God.

Quakers enter the service not just as private worshipers but in a company of worshipers. They know something of the needs of their fellow worshipers and of the world and are thus brought into intercession for them. Steere contends that if we do not bring others before God, then the leading of the spirit "has neither sincerity nor deep intent behind it." In intercession we often realize how little we care and how much God cares and how long he has cared. Thence we offer what we are and what we have to God. "To leave a meeting without this offering is to leave too soon."

What begins as a voluntary act of guided attention may be lifted up, Steere says, and "drawn irresistibly by the living power of the all tender One whom we confront in worship." Here the query becomes "Did you finally find the Listener taking over?"

Quaker worship often concludes without a vocal ministry and has demonstrated again and again that a company of worshipers can receive a message without words from the Word, Steere writes. Protestant services suffer from wordiness and a forensic character. Friends have always preferred deeds above words. Nevertheless, words do carry power and authority when they "come up fresh and breathless, come up still moist and glistening from the sea of existence." What is spoken must come from the source itself. Quakers have wrestled from the beginning with the problem of the relation of words to the Word. Sometimes they have lapsed into conversational-type homilies or ethical counsels, only to rediscover that a prophetic ministry is a listening ministry. The eighteenth century Quaker Quietists such as Job Scott protested the ministry of words not "freshly tempered, hammered out, and reshaped in the powerful forge of the silent listening meeting." The fire for vocal ministry is laid by reading the Bible and other great literature, prayer, writing, and using the power of reason. Ultimately it is a matter of the worshipers' own personal commitment to the Inward Guide and the welfare of those for whom they cared. What turns the worshiper into a minister is the disclosure before the Living Listener. Inward caring for others and inward disclosure of their conditions and needs are the most important preparation for speaking. Here one learns to trim away nonessentials. Quaker worship has not fulfilled its purpose until worshipers put themselves at the disposal of the Listener and one's fellow human beings for whom God cares. It is here that Friends discover "concerns," "a costly inner leading to some act that in the course of its fulfillment may take the very life of the one it engages." Friends know the meaning of Meister Eckhart's remark that "a person can only spend in good works what he/she earns in contemplation." All depends on openness to the Divine Listener.

Christian Themes

On Listening to Another defines and elevates listening to a fundamental Christian act. Listening is the ground of all true conversation, prayer, worship, vocal ministry, and what Friends call "concerns." Listening takes place at various levels, but genuine listening exacts a price. Qualities of a good listener are vulnerability, acceptance, expectancy, and constancy. Within every conversation the Eternal Listener is also present to clarify and to confront in an inner encounter; the more conscious a listener is of this Presence, the more disclosure can occur. Listening is a key to private prayer and corporate worship where all gather around the Eternal Listener. Finally, silence enhances the listening process.

Sources for Further Study

Steere, Douglas V. *Doors into Life from Five Devotional Classics*. New York: Harper & Bros., 1948. Introductions to *The Imitation of Christ*, Francis de Sales's *Introduction to the Devout Life*, John Woolman's *Journal*, Søren Kierkegaard's *Purity of Heart*, and Friedrich von Hügel's *Selected Letters*.

_____. *On Beginning from Within*. New York: Harper & Row, 1943. An essay on the need for saints in modern society to effect spiritual renewal.

_____. *Prayer and Worship*. New York: Association Press, 1938. An essay on the relationship between private and public prayer.

_____. *Together in Solitude*. New York: Crossroad, 1982. A collection of essays, including the remarkably insightful "On Being Present Where You Are."

E. Glenn Hinson

ON LOVING GOD

Author: Saint Bernard of Clairvaux (1090-1153)
First transcribed: De amore Dei, c. 1126-1141 (English translation, 1909)
Edition used: On Loving God. In *Treatises II*, vol. 5 in *The Works of Bernard of Clairvaux.* Washington, D.C.: Cistercian, 1974
Genre: Nonfiction
Subgenres: Meditation and contemplation; spiritual treatise
Core issues: Agape; God; love

This spiritual treatise on the essence of Christian living, written in response to some questions addressed to Bernard by Haimeric, cardinal deacon and chancellor of the See of Rome, sets forth Bernard's basic principles of his whole treatment of love: The reason for loving God is God himself.

Overview

Bernard was born of a noble family, one of seven sons and a daughter. He was prepared more for the clerical life than for the martial arts, and when he decided to enter the cloister he spent a year in preparation and recruited some thirty relatives and friends. He entered Citeaux in 1112 and three years later was sent to start the abbey of Clairvaux, where he served as abbot until his death. He founded some sixty monasteries and assisted in the founding of more than three hundred others. Though his desire was for a secluded life, his great abilities involved him in the politics of church and state. He ruined his health with excessive asceticism when young, but found a freedom to live a life of complete love for God and for his fellows. He left many rich writings, including a commentary on the Song of Songs.

On Loving God was written in response to some questions addressed to Bernard by Haimeric, cardinal deacon and chancellor of the See of Rome. It incorporates a letter earlier addressed to the monks of the Grande Chartreuse, epistle 11 in Bernard's corpus.

Immediately Bernard sets forth his basic response and the basic principles of his whole treatment of love: The reason for loving God is God himself. The measure for such love is to love without measure. These principles contain everything, yet they are not enough; it is necessary to know what they contain.

What Bernard says is very simple. He starts with three elementary chapters about the reasons for loving God, which he sets forth in a very logical yet very suggestive way. (Books of meditation as such did not come into being among the Cistercians until the thirteenth century, but this book is in fact a method of meditation. In other words, it is not broken up into points of meditation, but if we follow the steps of Bernard we will see a clear, logical order.)

We should love God because of his gifts to us: first of all himself, then all the gifts of nature, and finally the gift of ourselves.

God gave himself to us in a wholly gratuitous love. To quote Saint John, "He first loved us." Almost in the style of a newspaper report, Bernard asks: Who, to whom, how much? Who loves? He who has not need of his creatures loves with the love of majesty that does not seek its own. The whole of the spiritual life is a response to this gratuitous love. Whom does he love? His extreme opposite, the nefarious sinner, who has disobeyed him. How has he loved? To the fullest extent possible: He has given his very Son to be crucified for us.

When Bernard comes to speak about the gifts of God in nature in general, he is eloquent, but this section lacks the strength and insight of the preceding and following. Bernard has a rich existential understanding of humanity.

God deserves to be loved even by infidels who do not know God but know themselves. Bernard's view of human nature is very optimistic, to the glory of God the creator. If we know ourselves, we are already on the way to God, because God created us in his own image. He has endowed us with supreme dignity of freedom and the ability to know our own dignity.

Our dignity lies in our freedom to love God, Bernard writes. If we are aware we can love God, then what keeps us from loving him? We do not use our freedom precisely because we are not aware of it. Our understanding has been obscured by sin and passion. We cannot see on our own; we need the grace of Christ, which has been given to us. So we are twice the beneficiaries: in creation and in re-creation. We need to look at the mysteries of Christ, the author of life, who submitted himself to death on the cross. The whole of creation comes back to life in the resurrection of Christ. Surrounded now by the fruits of the tree of the cross we can be nourished. We pick them and eat them by meditating on the mysteries of faith that make Christ present in our hearts. This develops into contemplation. His love prepares our love and then rewards it.

No one can seek God unless that person has first been found by God, Benedict states, and the seeker is led to find God in order that he or she might seek God more.

Love is natural and it is good. It is one of the four basic instincts in us: love, joy, fear, and sorrow (Bernard is following Boethius here), the roots of all our activities. Love is central. These instincts are given to us by God so that we can serve him with the help of his grace.

The most basic form of love is carnal and social love. Carnal love is that natural love we have to care for our own bodies, keeping them within the limits willed by God, which gives glory to him. We cannot just care for ourselves, however. We have to restrain our love of self in order to love others so that we can find our place among them and share all that God has given to us in common. To see and do this we need both self-denial and God's grace. The first degree of love, the love of self, has to be understood in this fuller sense—loving self as a social person, disciplining oneself to be socially integrated.

Bernard sets forth four degrees of love. His division is not so much psychological as philosophical or theological, coming from the nature of the human person. Still, Bernard constantly brings in our experience of these and this is psychological. Bernard's four degrees of love can be stated as follows: We love ourselves for our own sake. We love God for our own sake. We love God for his sake. We love ourselves for God's sake.

This clear ordering of things is typical of Bernard, the order of his mind perceiving the order in things. What is most interesting is the way in which Bernard moves from one to the other in developing these degrees of love. What is basic throughout is an obedience to the will or plan of God.

That God wants us to love ourselves is expressed in the needs of our nature. Fundamental to all spiritual life is this: that we start with what is. We ourselves are a gift of God. However, we ourselves share a common human nature with our neighbor; therefore our neighbor is our other self, equally to be cared for. If there is a conflict between our needs and those of our neighbor, nature calls upon us to provide first for our fellow creature. This is Bernard's high sense of human nature. His argument is cogent—we all expect a parent to sacrifice for a child; we honor one who lays down life for another.

Bernard moves on. When we sacrifice ourselves for our brother or sister, reaching out to the other, God will reach out to us, and we will move to the second degree of love. We will know God's help and care and love him for it. As we experience God's help we are able to help others more with his help. In this experience we come to know God's loving care for all. God himself is perceived as good and we love him for his goodness, for himself. As we come to love God in himself, we love because we love. Our love grows constantly. We are now free from any why. Our love, like God's, becomes wholly gratuitous, and in this we begin to love ourselves as God does. Bernard declares that this degree of love is not possible on earth. We still have to care for ourselves. However, if we do this for God's sake, we are approximating the divine love.

In the included letter to the Carthusians, Bernard makes an important contribution to one of the theological controversies of the time. Some argued that charity in us is but the indwelling of the Holy Spirit. Bernard comes out for what became the commonly accepted doctrine. Charity is God; it is the divine substance, but it is also the gift of God. Where charity signifies the Giver, it is of the substance; where it is gift, it is a quality.

Christian Themes

Bernard's message in *On Loving God* can be summarized briefly as follows:
- The reason for loving God is God himself.
- The measure for such love is to love without measure.
- We should love God because of his gifts to us: first of all himself, then all the gifts of nature, and finally the gift of ourselves.
- The whole of the spiritual life is a response to God's gratuitous love.
- If we know ourselves, we are already on the way to God, because God created us in his own image.
- No one can seek God unless one has first been found by God and is led to find God in order that one might seek him more.
- We love ourselves for our own sake; we love God for our own sake; we love God for his sake; we love ourselves for God's sake.

Sources for Further Study

Butler, Cuthbert. *Western Mysticism.* London: Constable, 1922. Reprint. New York: Harper & Row, 1966. This classic excellently places Bernard of Clairvaux and his contribution in its historical context in the development of spiritual theology.

Evans, G. R. *Bernard of Clairvaux.* New York: Oxford University Press, 2000. Includes chapters on Bernard's life, monastic theology, academic theology, exegesis and theology, positive theology, negative theology, moral theology, and political theology. Bibliography, index.

Gilson, Étienne. *The Mystical Theology of Saint Bernard.* Translated by A. H. C. Downers. New York: Sheed & Ward, 1939. The most insightful study of Bernard of Clairvaux available in English, written by an eminent medieval scholar. Gilson also includes a masterful study of Bernard's sources.

Leclercq, Jean. *Bernard of Clairvaux and the Cistercian Spirit.* Translated by Claire Lavoie. Cistercian Studies 16. Kalamazoo, Mich.: Cistercian, 1976. Leclercq, who did the critical edition of Bernard's writings and one of the more important biographical studies, here offers an updated and somewhat popularized presentation of the monk and his milieu.

Pennington, M. Basil. "Two Treatises on Love." In *The Last of the Fathers.* Still River, Mass.: St. Bede's, 1983. A comparative study of Bernard's *On Loving God* and the study on love of his friend, William of Saint Thierry, who was both disciple and mentor.

Sommerfeldt, John R. *Bernard of Clairvaux on the Spirituality of Relationship.* New York: Newman Press, 2004. Includes chapters headed "Bernard, Society, and the Church," "The Monastic Order of Daniel," "The Clerical Order of Noah," "Noah's Many Virtues," "The Lay Order of Job," "Job's Ministry of Governance," "The Dissidents," and "Daniel, Noah, and Job: A Hierarchy?" Bibliography, index.

M. Basil Pennington

ON PROVIDENCE

Author: Ulrich Zwingli (1484-1531)
First published: Ad illustrissimum Cattorum principem Philippum, sermonis de providentia Dei anamnema, 1530 (English translation, 1922)
Edition used: On Providence, and Other Essays, edited by William John Hinke. Durham, N.C.: Labyrinth Press, 1983
Genre: Nonfiction
Subgenres: Didactic treatise; exegesis; theology
Core issues: Baptism; Eucharist; faith; freedom and free will; predestination; Protestants and Protestantism; salvation

On Providence *is one of the foundational works of the Swiss Reformation. The treatise combines philosophical and theological arguments to explain not only the nature of divine providence but also the principal articles of Zwingli's faith. Providence is defined as God's enduring and unchangeable governance over all things. Neither good works nor prayer can influence what cannot be changed. Sacraments, such as the Eucharist and baptism, are mere symbols and do not impart grace. Salvation comes only through God's grace freely given.*

Overview

Ulrich Zwingli wrote his Latin treatise *On Providence* at the behest of Landgrave Philip of Hesse and saw it published in Zurich on August 20, 1530. The text is based on his recollection of a sermon he delivered at the landgrave's castle in Marburg the preceding year, just prior to the formal commencement of the Marburg Colloquy (October 1-4, 1529). Zwingli's treatise comprises a dedicatory epistle addressed to Philip of Hesse, seven chapters, and an epilogue in which he recapitulates his insights into the nature of divine providence. Its pages also reflect some of the contentious theological issues he debated with Martin Luther, Philipp Melanchthon, and other Protestant leaders present at the Marburg Colloquy.

Proceeding by definition and syllogism, Zwingli reasons that divine providence in fact exists, because God's nature is such that he cares for and regulates all things. Any thought that the Supreme Deity might lack the willingness or the ability to foresee and regulate the universe for the better is, in his view, inconceivable and would contradict that Deity's necessary attributes: goodness, absolute wisdom, unrestricted power, and immutability. Theologians and philosophers who argue in favor of human free will ultimately diminish or abolish providence when they falsely presume that something can occur without God's prescient knowledge.

Zwingli expresses formal acceptance of panentheism in the third chapter when he discusses God's relationship to creation and the secret concordance of pagan and Christian doctrines. Because God is infinite, he writes, nothing can exist outside of him; all of his works and creatures exist in him and through him, and are a part of him.

Zwingli finds evidence of this not only in Holy Scripture but also in the wisdom of the ancients. He voices approval of the Pythagorean doctrine of rebirth, or palingenesis; he applauds Gaius Pliny's understanding of nature; he welcomes Plato's and Seneca's contributions to natural theology.

Chapters 4 and 5 deal with humankind's place in the universe, the nature of sin, and God's reasons for predestining humanity's fall. According to Zwingli, humans were created in God's image. Humans are the only being endowed with both mind and body, and for this reason, they are superior to all other animals. Humans are also the only terrestrial creature capable of receiving God's law, which, once given, exposes them to sin. When wolves, eagles, and stallions act according to their nature, they transgress against no law, because none was given them. Humans, on the other hand, are constantly torn between the wickedness of the flesh and the integrity of the spirit, because they have received knowledge of God's law. The law, Zwingli contends, is not given to instill fear or damn as some individuals teach, but to expose humans' deformity.

Why did God impose the law, if he foresaw its consequences? So that humans could recognize God's righteousness. Without evil, Zwingli reasons, there can be no knowledge of good. Humans had to experience wickedness themselves before they could comprehend the magnitude of God's righteousness. In foreseeing humanity's fall, God also provided for humanity's redemption. Redemption was not an afterthought of God's creation, but rather a sure sign of his foresight and mercy.

In chapter 6, the longest of the treatise, Zwingli explains his views on predestination, election, faith, and the Sacraments. Faulting Saint John Chrysostom's position on predestination, he maintains that God is the author, mover, and instigator of all creation. When a robber slays an innocent person, he is merely a tool in God's hands. Those who see the robber as the primary agent, according to Zwingli, fail to distinguish properly between cause and instrument. If the robber's action initiates in God, is God then guilty of this crime? No, he is not. God breaks no law, because he is subject to none. Is the robber then guilty? Yes, he is. Granted, the robber is forced to act, but the champions of free will and enemies of providence, as Zwingli calls them, are wrong to exonerate him, for he has broken the law.

Lashing out against both papists and "sacramentarians," Zwingli rejects the doctrine of justification through faith and works. Human deeds, either good or evil, cannot affect God's will, which is one, eternal and immutable. Prayer cannot influence what is ordained, nor can the use of sacraments. When Jesus Christ held out a loaf of bread and said "This is my body," he did not mean that the bread was his material body, says Zwingli, but rather a symbol of his presence. The Eucharist is thus little more than a pledge and a symbolic reminder of cleansing and atonement.

Faith, according to Zwingli, is bestowed only on the elect. Its possession offers a clear sign of election, but those who lack it are not necessarily damned. Non-Christians of singular virtue, such as Socrates or Seneca, show greater promise of election, in his opinion, than the Roman pontiff or his Dominican and Franciscan minions. What of infants who die before they receive baptism? They too can expect salvation, especially if they are children of the faithful. Like prayer, the rite of baptism has no effect on God's preordained will.

In the book's final chapter and epilogue, Zwingli reiterates the central thrust of his argument, namely that nothing happens by accident. To think otherwise is, in his view, inconsistent with religion.

Christian Themes

Philosophers and theologians have debated the existence and nature of divine providence since antiquity. Zwingli's treatment of this complex issue from a Protestant Christian perspective required discussion of many related theological notions, such as God's nature, the authority of Scripture, salvation, grace, baptism, the disputed doctrine of free will, and the disputed efficacy of faith and works. Considering the profundity and the scope of its issues, Zwingli's treatise *On Providence* rightly ranks as one of the foundational works of Reformation theology.

In addition to the importance of Holy Scripture, the influence of classical scholarship and pagan philosophy is particularly apparent in this work. The Swiss reformer disagreed with Erasmus of Rotterdam and other Christian humanists on some fundamental issues, but he shared with them the same basic tools of exegesis: a solid foundation in biblical languages and a desire to reconcile classical wisdom and Christian society. Much of what Pythagoras, Socrates, Plato, Aristotle, Pliny, and Seneca discovered through nature and reason was, in Zwingli's opinion, perfectly consistent with Holy Scripture. Like Erasmus, moreover, he embraced the purity of classical Latin and shunned the eccentricities of scholastic jargon.

At the Marburg Colloquy, Zwingli and Luther reached agreement on most key points of doctrine, such as salvation by grace and the overriding authority of Scripture. They also succeeded in avoiding confrontation over the role of faith in salvation. The principal point of contention between them lay in their opposing interpretations of the Eucharist. For Luther, the expression "This is my body" was literally true; for Zwingli, it was a figurative statement. Although Zwingli did not name any of his Marburg adversaries in the treatise *On Providence*, it is clear that Luther was prominent among those he condemned as sacramentarians for their belief in the power of the Eucharist. According to Zwingli, it was wrong to attribute divine powers to anyone, or anything, but God.

Sources for Further Study

Gordon, Bruce. *The Swiss Reformation*. Manchester, England: Manchester University Press, 2002. A survey of events and ideas of the Swiss Reformation, with emphasis on Heinrich Bullinger and Zwingli.

Locher, Gottfried W. *Zwingli's Thought: New Perspectives*. Leiden, the Netherlands: E. J. Brill, 1981. A comprehensive study of Zwingli's thought, with a chapter on his doctrine of predestination and comparisons of Zwingli to Luther, John Calvin, and Erasmus.

McEnhill, Peter, and George Newlands. *Fifty Key Christian Thinkers*. New York:

Routledge, 2004. Includes an entry summarizing Zwingli's life and the fundamental principles of his faith.

Snavely, Iren. "The Evidence of Things Unseen: Zwingli's Sermon *On Providence* and the Colloquy of Marburg." *The Westminster Theological Journal* 56 (1994): 399-407. Examines the events surrounding the Marburg Colloquy and their reflection in Zwingli's treatise.

Stephens, W. Peter. *Zwingli: An Introduction to His Thought*. Oxford, England: Clarendon Press, 1992. Discusses Zwingli's stance on central issues, including baptism, the Eucharist, salvation, works, and the respective roles of church and state.

Jan Pendergrass

ON THE FREEDOM OF THE WILL

Author: Desiderius Erasmus (1466?-1536)
First published: De Libero Arbitrio, 1524 (English translation, 1961)
Edition used: A Discussion of Free Will in *Collected Works of Erasmus*, edited by
Charles Trinkhaus. Toronto: University of Toronto Press, 1999
Genre: Nonfiction
Subgenres: Didactic treatise; exegesis; theology
Core issues: Faith; freedom and free will; grace; Lutherans and Lutheranism; obedi-
ence and disobedience; salvation; scriptures

*Erasmus seeks to refute Martin Luther's assertion that free will exists in name only.
According to Erasmus, not only does free will exist but it can also contribute to the attainment of eternal salvation. Luther and his followers frequently twist the meaning of
Holy Scripture with abusive exegetical techniques. They fail to consider the context of
passages they cite; they ignore common figures of speech; and they make hasty gener-
alizations. He urges Luther to show more moderation in his views.*

Overview

During the early days of the Reformation, many observers considered Desiderius
Erasmus a natural ally of Martin Luther. The two men shared a common interest in
evangelical humanism, and they voiced similar concerns regarding institutional
abuses within the Catholic Church. Erasmus, however, disagreed with Luther on fundamental theological questions and wanted no part in the German reformer's rebellion against authority. Following the advice of friends and influential patrons, he
wrote *On the Freedom of the Will* to refute article 36 of Luther's incendiary *Assertio
omnium articulorum Martini Lutheri per bullam Leonis X novissimam damnatorum*
(1520; article 36 has been translated as *An Assertion of All the Articles of Martin Luther Which Were Quite Recently Condemned by a Bull of Leo X, Article 36*, 1999). By
limiting his critique mainly to that one article, Erasmus hoped to avoid a harsh confrontation with Luther and, at the same time, to demonstrate his own allegiance to
Rome. In article 36, Luther characterized free will as "a fiction among real things"
and "a name with no reality."

Erasmus describes the issue of free will as one of the most impenetrable labyrinths
to be found in Holy Scripture. In recent years, he adds, it has become a subject of mild
debate between Andreas Bodenstein of Karlstadt and Johann Maier of Eck, and now
Luther, invoking the authority of John Wyclif, has stirred it up again with greater ve-
hemence. While some things in Holy Scripture are perfectly clear, others such as the
precise nature of the Trinity or the finer points of the Immaculate Conception are not.
In such instances, excessive subtlety can serve only as a prelude to pointless theoretical quarrels. Erasmus believes, in contrast to Luther, that "a certain power of free will
does exist." The question of free will is also closely linked to salvation:

> By "free will" here we understand a power of the human will by which man may be able to direct himself toward, or turn away from, what leads to eternal salvation.

Luther, says Erasmus, cast aside the authority of numerous biblical scholars who endorse the doctrine of free will. Not counting Lorenzo Valla, whom theologians discredit, only two writers, Mani of Babylonia and Wyclif, agree with Luther. However, the debate, as Erasmus sees it, is more appropriately one of interpretation than of numbers. There are many passages in Scripture that support the existence of free will and some that seem to oppose it altogether. Because Holy Scripture cannot contradict itself, one must examine the context and the purpose of each passage to grasp its true meaning and resolve any apparent conflict.

Erasmus feels that Luther and his followers frequently distort the meaning of Holy Scripture to make it conform to their own religious persuasions. When dealing with similes and parables, they fail to consider the context and the drift of the passages they cite. When it suits their purpose, they neglect common figures of speech and cling to literal interpretation, or they take a particular case and pass it off as a general principle.

Erasmus concedes that God's grace is necessary for salvation, but he rejects the view that humans are free only to sin, or worse, that free will is only an empty name. Holy Scripture, he argues, is full of passages that offer a choice between two paths of conduct. Some promise rewards to individuals who perform good works, while others threaten individuals who disobey God's commandments. In the end, such passages become meaningless if everything is subject to absolute necessity.

Does not God's foreknowledge abolish free will? Erasmus believes it does not. As Lorenzo Valla once argued, events do not happen because God foresees them; he foresees them because they are going to happen. Foreknowledge does not negate free will. What then of God's will and the doctrine of predestination? Do they not speak against human freedom? Not entirely, says Erasmus. There is a fine distinction between God's absolute will and his ordained will. No one can oppose God's absolute will, but many do resist his ordained will.

Pointing to the work of "certain orthodox Fathers" (such as Saint Bernard of Clairvaux), Erasmus identifies three stages in every good deed that humans perform. They are knowing what is good, willing it, and performing it. The first and last stages rely entirely on God's grace and leave no room for free will. However, the second stage requires a collaboration of human will and grace, whereby grace serves as the principal cause. Whatever good may be derived from human actions should be attributed, for the greatest part, to God's grace; but the human will must also contribute its share. Although people may receive healthy eyesight and ample light for vision, they can still close their eyes and refuse to see.

According to Erasmus, Luther overstates his case. Christians should prefer a more "moderate view" on the question of human freedom, one that not only preserves free will but also recognizes the preeminence of God's grace.

Christian Themes

On the Freedom of the Will raises a crucial theological question: To what extent, if any, does human merit contribute to salvation? By ascribing a greater role to divine grace and a lesser one to free will and human effort, Erasmus hoped to produce a compromise that would be equally acceptable to both Lutherans and orthodox Catholics. Although he clearly disagreed with Luther in substantial ways, he did not deny that Luther had some valid arguments. In particular, he praised the German reformer's fundamental belief that Christians must place their entire trust in God and not rely on their own merit for salvation; but he also felt that Luther was wrong to deny completely the soteriological importance of free will.

What disturbed Erasmus most, however, was the virulent, uncompromising nature of Luther's campaign against the tradition and authority of the Catholic Church. As he stated in his introductory remarks to *On the Freedom of the Will*, some cures are simply more harmful than the afflictions they seek to remedy. Like Luther, he felt that moral corruption had seriously compromised the integrity of the Catholic Church at all levels, yet he did not believe that open confrontation would contribute to meaningful reform. If there was going to be a debate, he felt it should be conducted with moderation and evangelical mildness.

The debate opposing Erasmus and Luther on free will did not end there, nor did it remain a polite exchange of ideas as Erasmus clearly had hoped. Confident that truth was on their side, the Lutherans and other Protestant groups persisted in their defiance of Catholic authority. In December of 1525, Luther replied to the Dutch humanist's criticism by publishing his *De servo arbitrio* (*Martin Luther on the Bondage of the Will*, 1823). The work was a stark rebuttal of Erasmus's views on free will, salvation, foreknowledge, the origin of evil, and the authority of the Catholic Church. This prompted Erasmus to reaffirm his critique of Luther doctrine, this time with rancorous venom, in a two-part treatise titled *Hyperaspistes* (1526-1527; English translation, 1999 and 2000). By that point in time, all hope of reconciliation had vanished.

Sources for Further Study

Augustijn, Cornelis. *Erasmus: His Life, Works, and Influence.* Toronto: University of Toronto Press, 1991. A comprehensive biography and analysis of the major works; includes detailed discussion of Erasmus's debate on the freedom of the will.

Forde, Gerhard O. *The Captivation of the Will: Luther Versus Erasmus on Freedom and Bondage.* Grand Rapids, Mich.: Wm. B. Eerdmans, 2005. Reviews the major points of contention between Luther and Erasmus.

Rummel, Erika. *Erasmus.* New York: Continuum, 2004. A general study of Erasmus's views on pedagogy, society, religion; his role as a biblical scholar; and his opposition to Luther.

Schoeck, R. J. *Erasmus of Europe.* 2 vols. Edinburgh, Scotland: Edinburgh University Press, 1990 and 1993. Follows Erasmus through every stage of his life; the second volume includes a detailed chapter on the free will debate.

Wengert, Timothy J. *Human Freedom, Christian Righteousness: Philip Melanchthon's Exegetical Dispute with Erasmus of Rotterdam.* New York: Oxford University Press, 1998. Compares Erasmus's and Philip Melanchthon's opposing views on the question of human freedom.

Jan Pendergrass

ON THE INCARNATION OF THE WORD OF GOD

Author: Saint Athanasius of Alexandria (c. 293-373 C.E.)
First transcribed: De incarnatione Verbi Dei, before 325 C.E. (English translation, 1880)
Edition used: Saint Athanasius on the Incarnation: The Treatise "De Incarnatione Verbi Dei." Rev. ed. Translated and edited by a Religious of Community of Saint Mary the Virgin. Crestwood, N.Y.: St. Vladimir's Orthodox Theological Seminary, 1993
Genre: Nonfiction
Subgenres: Didactic treatise; exegesis; theology
Core issues: Atonement; Incarnation; Jesus Christ; redemption; sacrifice; union with God

Responding to doubts from believers and objections from nonbelievers, Saint Athanasius explains why the Son of God entered the world as the human Jesus Christ. Because of humanity's disobedience to God, humanity could not recover from the corruption that had entered the world except through the Word's loving act of being born, living a sinless life, dying, and being raised again. Events in history and the witness of the Bible confirm that Christ is God incarnate, but understanding the truth of the Scriptures requires a pure mind and a pure life.

Overview

Saint Athanasius of Alexandria writes that the Redeemer is also the Creator. God became incarnate to redeem fallen humankind and renew all creation. In addition, Christ, the Son of God—the incarnate, redeeming Word—is also the creating Word, who made the universe in the beginning. For the universe is not self-generated nor preexistent as many philosophers think, but was made by God through his Word. It was the fall of humanity, through the exercise of free will, that occasioned God's response of love in sending his redeeming Word. This response could be thought of as inevitable because of God's goodness. It was impossible for God to leave humankind declining on a path toward inevitable extinction. Human repentance does not suffice as a means of self-restoration to divine favor. Repentance might stop future sin, but it will not repair the corruption of the race that has already been brought about by previous sins, and the sinner is inclined to return to sin again. For this reason, the Word entered the world.

The Word, who received his humanity from a pure virgin, did not just become embodied but was born and did not just appear but lived, so that by becoming subject to human life and death, he might break the hold that death had over the entire human race, according to Saint Athanasius. Like a king who did not neglect his fair city after it had been attacked by robbers but rather saved and restored it, so has the Word restored the plundered nature of humankind.

The second reason for the Incarnation is that although humans were made in the image of God, through neglect they failed to know their maker and turned instead to worshiping false gods. Humans proved to be still incapable of knowing God by the means God had subsequently sent, the law of Moses, the prophets, and holy men. Therefore it became necessary for the very image of the Father to come and effect the re-creation of humankind.

This coming in the flesh did nothing to change Christ's nature as God, as the sun is not changed by the contact of its rays with the earth, Saint Athanasius explains. When Christ died in what for the human mind is a paradoxical death, the sun hid its face and the mountains quaked, showing by those miracles that Christ was God. In answer to the question of why, if the one who gave life to all had to die to pay the debt owed by all, he did not choose some private means of dying instead of subjecting himself to a public execution; Saint Athanasius says that no death by sickness, age, or hunger would have sufficed for the one who came to conquer death. Christ accepted the harshest form of death, on the terms of his enemies, to defeat death in all its forms by rising on the third day after his execution. His victory over death is confirmed by his disciples, who are willing to die as martyrs for their faith at the hands of those who hate them, and who scorn death as something no longer to be feared.

Saint Athanasius found further testimony to Christ's resurrection in his unprecedented influence on the lives of men and women throughout the world, Jew and Gentile alike. If Christ had not been resurrected, how could the pagan gods have been routed from the minds of so many? He noted that the Savior works powerfully in the world and wondered how the Giver of Life could remain dead.

After discussing Christ's incarnation and victory over death in the Resurrection, Saint Athanasius proceeds to a refutation of nonbelievers. To Jews, Christ is a stumbling block, but their very Scriptures prophesy abundantly about his miraculous birth from a virgin, his death on the cross, and his resurrection. All their prophecy points to Christ and ends with Christ. To Gentiles, Christ is foolishness. They mock Christians but fail to see the folly of their gods and idols. They say that Christians hold to a belief unfitting of a God, namely, that a God would debase himself to enter creation. However, Saint Athanasius writes, if Gentiles listen to their philosophers, who hold that the universe is animated by the divine Logos, they would understand that these philosophers also allow for the presence of God in a material body. Plato himself writes of God having come to rescue the tottering universe. The pagan gods, moreover, are refuted by Christ's own works and those of his disciples, and the pagan gods, being false gods, are powerless to stop the defection of their former worshipers. Saint Athanasius says if you study the Scriptures yourself, you will learn these things, but know that to understand the Scriptures, a good life and a pure soul are required. You cannot understand without these.

Christian Themes

Saint Athanasius's *On the Incarnation of the Word of God* follows his *Contra gentes* (c. 318, *Against the Heathen*, 1892). The two works may be regarded as form-

ing a single project, a systematic treatise following an apologetic. Athanasius's predecessor Origen of Alexandria did the same on a larger scale in *Kata Kelsou* (248, also
known as *Contra Celsum*; *Origen Against Celsus*, 1660) and *Peri archōn* (220-230,
also known as *De principiis*; *On First Principles*, 1936).

Saint Athanasius maintains the Christological position that eventually defeated
Arianism, which considered the divine Logos as a creature of God, begotten as a
product of the Father's will as a medium between the supreme God and creation. Athanasius, maintaining that begetting is an aspect of nature and not will, teaches that the
Son possesses the same divine nature as the Father and is equal to the Father. He argues that the incarnation of the Word was absolutely essential for human salvation.
There was no other remedy for fallen humankind, which had succumbed to corruption
and would eventually have extinguished itself. The redemption of humankind required the Word's incarnation and death because humans could not escape the corruption, the penalty for sin, on their own. The Word Incarnate restored God's creation,
which had become disoriented by sin, because the indwelling of God the Word in the
human body freed it from its natural liability, and the entire human race was freed by
Christ's union with it. Athanasius not only responds to believers' doubts about the
identity of the Redeemer with the Creator-Word but also refutes objections from Jewish and pagan critics of the doctrine of the Incarnation.

Saint Athanasius accounts for the universality of life, death, and Resurrection of Jesus Christ, a very particular and concrete historical series of events, by saying that
"the common savior of all has died on our behalf." Christ's resurrection is the first
fruit of the resurrection to come of those who believe in him. Athanasius shows how
the birth, life, and death of the Savior Christ is foretold in the Hebrew scriptures. He
also incorporates Greek philosophy, not to explore divine nature but to confirm Christian doctrine. The Greeks, he says, especially the Platonists, fail to understand that the
invisible and infinite God has indeed entered history and yet remains eternally with
his Father, has died but is the Giver of life, and is not only human but also is God the
Word. The concluding chapters take up a basic principle of his theology, that understanding these truths requires purity of mind and heart.

Sources for Further Study

Anatolios, Khaled. *Athanasius: The Coherence of His Thought*. New York: Routledge, 1998. This introduction to Athanasius's life, writings, and theology emphasizes the importance of reading Athanasius on his own terms and not those of later
controversies.

Brakke, David. "Athanasius." In *The Early Christian World*, edited by Philip F. Esler.
New York: Routledge, 2000. Discusses the contribution of Athanasius to the development of the Nicene trinitarian formula. Provides an overview of contemporary scholarly debate on Athanasius.

Pettersen, Alvyn. *Athanasius*. Harrisburg, Pa.: Morehouse, 1995. Focuses on Athanasius's key role in the success of the Nicene formula and the defeat of Arianism.

Thomson, Robert W. *Athanasius "Contra Gentes" and "De Incarnatione."* Oxford,

England: Clarendon Press, 1971. Provides a new translation of these works together with the Greek text.

Young, Frances M. *From Nicaea to Chalcedon: A Guide to the Literature and Its Background*. Philadelphia: Fortress Press, 1983. A useful overview of the entire period of the trinitarian and Christological controversies, including the influential role played by Athanasius.

Daniel J. Nodes

ON THE TRUTH OF HOLY SCRIPTURE

Author: John Wyclif (c. 1328-1384)
First published: De veritate sacrae scripturae, wr. 1377-1378, pb. 1904-1905, re-
vised 1905-1907 (English translation, 2001)
Edition used: On the Truth of Holy Scripture, translated with an introduction and
notes by Ian Christopher Levy. Kalamazoo, Mich.: Medieval Institute, 2001
Genre: Nonfiction
Subgenres: Didactic treatise; hermeneutics; theology
Core issues: Church; faith; pastoral role; scriptures; truth

*Holy Scripture is most properly defined as spiritual truth, according to Wyclif. A
manuscript version of the Bible is scripture only in a derivative, material sense, inasmuch as it signifies the transcendent reality of God's wisdom. Holy Scripture embraces every Catholic truth and should serve as a standard for all human affairs. It
obeys its own divine logic, and none of its parts may be deemed false or contradictory.
Faith is required before the literal and figurative truth of Scripture becomes apparent.*

Overview

On the Truth of Holy Scripture is one of twelve treatises contained in John Wyclif's
Summa theologiae (wr. 1375-1381; a summary of theology). Internal evidence suggests that the treatise was composed over the course of about one year, from the fall or
winter of 1377 until late 1378. Its thirty-two chapters reflect not only the author's mature thought on the nature and authority of Holy Scripture but also his growing estrangement from the Roman curia at the onset of the Great Western Schism (a split
within the Catholic Church).

The first nine chapters of *On the Truth of Holy Scripture* deal with a variety of
hermeneutical issues, ranging from discussion of the various levels of Holy Scripture
to the concept of divine logic. According to Wyclif, the highest and most authoritative
level of Holy Scripture is the "book of life," or spiritual truth. The fifth and lowest
level of Scripture is represented by individual manuscripts, the spoken word, or other
physical reminders of God's will and ordination; these, however, do not actually contain the truth in any ontological sense but can lead to it when properly interpreted.

Because God cannot lie or contradict himself—otherwise he would not be God—it
follows that his word can contain neither deceit nor contradiction. Scripture, Wyclif
insists, is never self-contradictory, but rather it is "equivocal" (*aequivoca*), meaning
that it can signify different things on different levels at different times. When sophists
armed with human logic assert that the Bible contains contradictory statements, they
indulge in blasphemy. Blinded by sin, they cannot or will not learn the divine logic of
Holy Scripture. They fail to distinguish between literal and figurative manners of
speech, or they reason out of context without consideration for the whole.

Christians, Wyclif contends, should humbly submit to the eloquence of Scripture, because it is inherently superior to the grammar and logic of human reason. Faith and constant exposure to God's word are required before one can ascend to the first level of Scripture and fully grasp God's "intended meaning" (*virtus sermonis*).

In chapters 10 to 15, Wyclif examines the relationship between scriptural authority and ecclesiastical law. No doubt, he argues, both the Old and New Testaments are authentic parts of Scripture. Although faith moves Christians to accept the authority of these texts a priori, reasons may be adduced a posteriori to justify and fortify that faith. In response to those who call into question the authority of Holy Scripture by pointing to minor verbal discrepancies between Old and New Testament passages, Wyclif counters that the fifth and lowest category of Scripture is merely a physical representation of divine truth. Because Holy Scripture mirrors God's will, it becomes for Wyclif the ultimate source of truth and the standard by which all authority, including that of papal bulls and canon law, may be judged.

According to Wyclif, the vicars of Christ deviated from the law of Scripture during the period following Constantine the Great's alleged donation to the Church in the fourth century C.E. Since that time, "the Church has proven herself deceptive, mistaken, and ignorant," and the papacy has issued "a procession of contradictory bulls." Wyclif does not deny the authority of bishops and popes to issue statutes in the interest of governing the Church, yet he firmly insists that their proclamations must not contradict prior statutes or Holy Scripture.

In chapters 14 to 19, Wyclif considers various manners in which lecture-hall sophists falsify Scripture. In his view, all errors of interpretation are in some way rooted in sin. While some forms of sin are venial, others are deliberate and pernicious. Individuals who maintain that Scripture contains contradictions or lies—even "pious lies"—are guilty of falsifying God's intended meaning, but not all such individuals are malevolent. As Saint Jerome teaches, only those who arrogantly and obstinately defend erroneous opinions may be considered heretics.

In the book's final thirteen chapters, Wyclif turns his attention to the discussion of practical and doctrinal issues relating to Church governance, including the nature of evangelical law, the organization of the Church, the fulfillment of pastoral duties, the significance of Mosaic Law in the age of grace, and criteria for the judgment of heresy.

Wyclif admits that laws are necessary to assure peace and stability, yet laments that a lust for "worldly dominion" has corrupted the medieval Church. To seek holy office "chiefly for reasons of pride or profit" is a mortal sin. Every Christian, he writes, should be familiar with Holy Scripture, but this holds especially true for priests. Church law requires bishops and archbishops to know the entirety of Holy Scripture, and their primary duty should be to preach the word of God. "If a bishop does not preach," Wyclif boldly asserts, then "he is not a bishop."

Clerics who neglect their duties should be censured and, when appropriate, removed from office. Excommunication, however, should be used for the purpose of saving souls, or for removing "poisonous sinners" from the Church, but not as a means for "exacting money for the clergy." Only qualified theologians should judge heresy, and they should proceed with moderation. If the Church cannot enforce its laws in accordance with Holy Scripture, says Wyclif, then the laity must intervene. Hence, under certain circumstances, it may be lawful for civil authorities to pursue the vices of delinquent priests or to confiscate Church property.

Christian Themes

Wyclif's purpose in writing *On the Truth of Holy Scripture* was primarily academic and faith-bound. He sought to preserve the authority and integrity of Holy Scripture against the perceived impiety of those who would quibble over the literal meaning of biblical passages in the late medieval lecture halls at Oxford University. In his view, theologians ought to accept the authority of Scripture through faith, rather than impose the standards of human logic on it for the vainglorious purpose of extracting contradictions, lies, or falsehoods from God's written word.

By insisting that Holy Scripture resides not on parchment but rather in Christ, Wyclif deemphasized the sacred importance of the physical, scribal records of Christianity. Such records, he noted, could be miscopied, falsified, defiled, or even destroyed. Instead, he identified Holy Scripture in its most proper form as a transcendental "book of life"—an incorruptible and infallible archetype of truth present in God's mind, embodied in Christ, and inscribed in the hearts of faithful Christians.

In Wyclif's approach to hermeneutics, recourse to formal methods of interpretation became less important (but not irrelevant) for a proper understanding of biblical truths. Proper interpretation became more a matter of attitude and less one of method. In his view, those who understand Holy Scripture will live in accordance with Christ's law and will already possess the "intended meaning" of the written word, no matter how paradoxical it might appear to human logic. Knowing in the heart what Christ means, means knowing what Christ meant.

It would be difficult not to notice the circularity of Wyclif's hermeneutical approach. In all likelihood, its glaring "irrationality" must be seen as a deliberate and mature reflection of the Englishman's humble submission to the logic of Holy Scripture.

Sources for Further Study

Evans, G. R. *John Wyclif: Myth and Reality*. Downers Grove, Ill.: InterVarsity Press Academic, 2005. A biography portraying the Englishman not as a religious firebrand but as an "able academic" whose links to Lollardy and the Reformation have been overstated.

Ghosh, Kantik. *Wycliffite Heresy: Authority and Interpretation of Texts*. New York: Cambridge University Press, 2002. According to Ghosh, Wyclif's "textual idealism" paradoxically ignores essential hermeneutical problems by relegating them to "the irrelevant category of scripture *quinto modo*."

Levy, Ian Christopher. *John Wyclif: Scriptural Logic, Real Presence, and the Parameters of Orthodoxy*. Milwaukee, Wis.: Marquette University Press, 2003. Examines the fundamental concepts of authorship, intended meaning, and scriptural logic within the framework of Wyclif's theological realism.

Tresko, Michael. "John Wyclif's Metaphysics of Scriptural Integrity in the *De veritate sacrae scripturae.*" *Dionysius* 12 (1989): 153-196. Discusses Wyclif's opposition to the threat of biblical literalism in fourteenth century nominalist thought; recommended reading.

Jan Pendergrass

ONE TUESDAY MORNING

Author: Karen Kingsbury (1964-   )
First published: Grand Rapids, Mich.: Zondervan, 2003
Genre: Novel
Subgenres: Evangelical fiction; historical fiction (twenty-first century)
Core issues: Agape; awakening; compassion; death; faith; healing; love; memory

In a Christian reading of the worst terrorist attack in the history of the United States, Kingsbury's novel portrays how faith sustains believers in God and saved former non-believers after the destruction of the World Trade Center in 2001. She puts September 11 in the context of God's plan for humankind and for individual characters, showing how this grand trial provides an opportunity for people's Christian faith to transform themselves and each other.

> *Principal characters*
> *Jake Bryan*, a New York firefighter who believes in God
> *Jamie Bryan*, Jake's wife, a nonbeliever
> *Sierra Bryan*, Jake and Jamie's young daughter
> *Eric Michaels*, an investment broker in California, a nonbeliever
> *Laura Michaels*, Eric's wife, a believer
> *Josh Michaels*, Eric and Laura's young son
> *Clay Michaels*, Eric's brother, a police officer and believer

Overview

Winner of the 2004 Silver Medallion book award (now called the Christian Book Award), given by the Evangelical Christian Publishers Association, *One Tuesday Morning* presents the parallel and interrelated stories of two fictional families, one from the East Coast and one from the West Coast. Author Karen Kingsbury shows how the September 11 terrorist attacks on New York City's World Trade Center affect the spiritual journeys of these families, couples, and individuals. The novel begins with a funeral of a New York firefighter who died young from a heart attack. Firefighter Jake Bryan and his wife, Jamie, childhood sweethearts, share a deep love for each other and their young daughter, Sierra. Jamie is terrified that her husband will die fighting a fire. However, Jake has faith in God's plan for himself and his family and wants his wife to return to loving God as she did before the deaths of her parents in an auto accident when she was a teenager. He writes comments in his Bible and in a daily journal to encourage and record Jamie's progress toward God, so that she can read it as a guide to recover her faith when she is ready.

In Southern California, the marriage of Eric and Laura Michaels is faltering. Formerly close to his wife, Eric has closed his heart to God and his wife after their daughter was stillborn. He turns his focus to work as an investment broker, neglecting Laura and their young son, Josh. Eric's brother Clay, a police officer, spends time with Laura and Josh; they become especially close when Eric disappears on a business trip to the World Trade Center office during the September 11 collapse.

As Jake ascends the stairs of the World Trade Center's south tower to save people on the Tuesday morning of September 11, 2001, he passes Eric Michaels, on a business trip from California, who is descending the stairs to safety. When Eric falls, Jake helps him, dropping his helmet, which Eric hands to him; inside is a picture of Jake's young daughter with her printed name, Sierra. Eric is struck by how much Jake looks like him. Jake and his best friend, Larry Henning, die together in the collapse of the south tower, sacrificing their lives to save other people. Eric is found under a fire truck from Jake's station, suffering from amnesia; he remembers the name Sierra and he is thought to be Jake.

In order to help the man she thinks is her husband recover his memories, Jamie Bryan reads her husband's journal and Bible and gives them to Eric. Impressed by Jamie's goodness, Eric is also touched by the goodness of Jake Bryan and his love for his family as well as his desire for his wife to go to God. Within three months, both are healed and transformed into believers. Jamie discovers Eric's real identity and helps him reunite with his wife. Eric vows to invest his love and time with his wife and son, both of whom he had ignored in his devotion to work. Jamie, strengthened by her faith in God, becomes strong enough to raise her daughter without Jake. Kingsbury ends the novel with a vision that Jake and Jamie's daughter, Sierra, has of her father smiling down on her from heaven.

Christian Themes

One Tuesday Morning is Bible-based, rooted in the words of the Bible as a source of strength and comfort to the characters, who attempt to live by the words of God. Jake's Bible centers the narrative. He contemplates it and writes his thoughts about passages in it every day. In the Puritan tradition, he also writes his thoughts in his journal every day, but he contemplates his wife's spiritual journey more than his own. Significantly, he writes in private, so that his wife does not feel pressured to accept Jesus as her savior before she is really ready. Hoping that someday his beloved wife will be open to reading his words and accepting God in her life, he feels that her lack of faith is the only element lacking in their relationship. Jake's concern for his wife's salvation despicts for the reader the depth and joy of love and faith.

The many layers of words in Jake's Bible and journal provide the opportunity for salvation for both Jamie and Eric. The dead Jake's living words serve as a model of God-centered life for the tabula rasa of the amnesiac Eric. The investment broker who has neglected his wife, son, and God learns how to love God. Inspired by God's love, Eric vows to invest his love in his wife and son. He returns to California transformed. Filtered through the words of Jake Bryan, the Bible saves two nonbelievers. Following the biblical model, Kingsbury uses the words of her novel to tell stories that instruct and inspire. She uses analogies to teach and enliven Christian themes. She foreshadows death with images like sand castles and a melting ice cream cake. She suggests changes and connections in the Staten Island Ferry to and from Manhattan and plane trips from coast to coast.

Kingsbury stresses the Christian belief in family, emphasizing and juxtaposing relationships of brothers, sisters, fathers, mothers, wives, and husbands. Jake is a good father, Eric an absent father. Eric's brother Clay helps his sister-in-law and niece until their real husband and father return. Jake's fictional fire station is a community of brothers, most of whom die on September 11, leaving a sisterhood of widows who sustain one another through faith in God. Jake's words in his journal, inspired by God, and his words on God's Word in the Bible help his spiritual brother Eric to seek his heavenly father. Although the 9/11 tragedy broke up families through death, the faith tested in this horrific trial helps to heal them. The example of the resurrection of Christ, which teaches the birth of hope from despair, guides earthly families. The geographical scope of the novel, which brings together two families from each coast, suggests that the United States is a family, closer and renewed after its greatest tragedy.

The novel attests to the power of transformation through faith. Framed with the deaths of firefighters, it both highlights Jamie Bryan's fear that her husband will die fighting a fire and transforms it into a love that is depicted in the image of a smiling Jake Bryan, smiling down on his young daughter, gladdening and strengthening her.

Sources for Further Study

Block, Eleanor S. "The Press Reacts to September 11, 2001: A Review of Recent Literature." *Communication Booknotes Quarterly* 35, no. 1 (Winter, 2004): 7-23. Reviews *One Tuesday Morning* in the context of other post-9/11 literature.

Hamilton, Lee H., and Thomas H. Kean. *The 911 Report: The National Commission on Terrorist Attacks Upon the United States.* New York: St. Martin's Press, 2004. Offers background for the September 11 attacks, describes what happened on that day, explains the lessons learned, and suggests global strategies to prevent a recurrence.

Kingsbury, Karen. *Beyond Tuesday Morning.* In *One Tuesday Morning/Beyond Tuesday Morning.* Grand Rapids, Mich.: Zondervan, 2006. This sequel to *One Tuesday Morning* tells the story of how widow Jamie Bryan, after a long period of grieving and guided by her dead husband's written words, chooses life and love in a strange plot twist.

Williams, Wilda. Review of *One Tuesday Morning. Library Journal* 128, no. 6 (April 1, 2003): 84. Williams concludes that Kingsbury's fans will "definitely want this."

Joanna Yin

THE ORTHODOX CHURCH

Author: Timothy Ware (Kallistos Ware; 1934-   )
First published: 1963
Edition used: The Orthodox Church. 2d ed. New York: Penguin Books, 1997
Genre: Nonfiction
Subgenres: Church history; theology
Core issues: Bishops; cause universal; church; devotional life; faith; religion

The Orthodox Church is the living, continuous body of the faithful in Jesus Christ, reaching back through its succession of bishops to the Apostles. Through its Sacraments, the gift of God's Holy Spirit won by Christ's incarnation, life, death, and resurrection is offered for the redemption of humankind. The Eastern Orthodox Church has a special historical affinity with the eastern Roman and Byzantine eras of antiquity. It is intent on preserving its Tradition as the Church of Christ, his Apostles and successor bishops, the martyrs, church fathers, and the great councils of the first eight centuries. Organized and governed locally and regionally, it is a worldwide community united in faith and love.

Overview

From the first Pentecost the Gospel was preached to Jews in Palestine and then to Gentiles throughout the world. For three centuries under constant threat of persecution, the Church's status in the world changed in the first quarter of the fourth century from persecuted to tolerated to preferred. During Constantine's reign, the Church marked the beginning of its coming of age. Although already living in its Tradition, the Church used its freedom from persecution to organize its governing structures and articulate its beliefs. By the Seventh Ecumenical Council (787), the Church had established its principal lines of doctrine, worship, and organization. By the eleventh century, the gradual estrangement between Christians in the eastern and western regions of the Roman Empire resulted in a formal schism, or splitting, of the Church into Roman Catholic and Eastern Orthodox. The loss of a common language, theological disputes, and different conceptions of the visible organization of the Church, with Rome's alignment with the Frankish Empire, contributed to this splitting. The separation was exacerbated after the Eastern Empire fell to the Ottomans in the mid-fifteenth century. As a result of Constantinople's fall (1453), Moscow became the new Christian capital in the East, the "Third Rome." The Church in Russia had survived the Mongol occupation but was to suffer persecution under Communist governments. In modern times the Eastern Orthodox Church exists in five situations: a minority community in the eastern Mediterranean corresponding to the four ancient patriarchates; the churches of Greece and Cyprus; the churches in Eastern Europe; the Orthodox living in the West; and the Orthodox living in Africa, the Far East, and elsewhere.

Orthodoxy is characterized by a commitment to preserving the faith and practice "which Jesus imparted to the Apostles" and which since that time has been handed down from ancestors to posterity, forming a living continuity with the Church of ancient times. The main outward signs of Orthodox Tradition are the Bible, which is the living "verbal icon" of Christ, the Creed, the decrees of the Seven Ecumenical Councils, the teachings of the church fathers, Orthodox doctrinal statements since 787, the Liturgy and Sacraments, Canon Law, and the Holy Icons. These signs express in various ways the timeless true mysteries of the Orthodox faith: one God in three persons, the Son eternally begotten of the Father, the Holy Spirit proceeding from the Father, and the human person made body and soul in the image and likeness of Father, Son, and Holy Spirit. "Image" includes those powers of reason and virtue that each person has as a child of God; "likeness" is the goal that requires effort to be attained.

The sin of disobedience of the first humans affected their descendants with mortality and corruption and an environment that inclines them to sin; however, the fact of their sin and guilt is the result of each individual. Sin sets up a barrier between humankind and God that humans cannot overcome on their own. Thus, as an act of love, God sent his Son into the world as the man Jesus Christ, whose life, death, and resurrection resulted in God's sending of his Holy Spirit to humankind. Humanity's goal is nothing less than achieving the divine likeness human beings were meant to possess. This is achieved by living, through the grace of God, a life of humility, repentance, and charity in fulfillment of the great commandments to love God and to love one's neighbor.

The Church and the Sacraments are the means whereby Christians receive the necessary gift of God's Holy Spirit to receive deification. To preserve that heritage without succumbing to an indiscriminate antiquarianism requires a "creative fidelity." The Orthodox Church humbly believes that it is "the one, holy, Catholic, and Apostolic Church." It reflects the Triune divine nature by its unity in diversity. It is Christological both in its members and in the Eucharist; as the body of Christ, the Church is also the dwelling place of the Holy Spirit. While giving worship only to God in Trinity, the Church honors its saints.

While special honor is bestowed on Mary as *Theotokos*, Mother of God, and as *Panagia*, All-Holy, the Church is the communion of all saints and those called to be saints, to whom God has granted salvation. Through its Sacraments, liturgy, and cycle of worship, the Church already begins to bestow God's blessings on the living. It is legitimate to hope and pray that all will be saved, but hell exists because free will exists, "for hell is nothing else than the rejection of God." As the visible Church, it does not deny the possibility that others are part of the whole Church whose membership God alone knows. The reunification of all Christians, based on the necessary foundation of unity in the faith, is what the Orthodox pray for and expect.

Christian Themes

The Orthodox Church traces the line of continuity from Jesus Christ and the Apostles to the Eastern Orthodox Church today. Adherence to the ancient Christian Tradition is what both distinguishes and joins Orthodoxy to other Christian communities. As a hierarchical and sacramental Church, it is in closest agreement on critical points of dogma with the Roman Catholic Church: the Trinitarian God, Jesus Christ as true God and true man, and the Eucharist as the true body and blood of Christ. The Tradition also, however, points up departures that have arisen.

The Orthodox Church has kept its creed intact. It has not experienced a scholastic revolution and it has not undergone a Reformation and Counter-Reformation. It has not added the Filioque and doctrines of the Immaculate Conception and Purgatory to the Apostolic teaching. Its organization is based not on a doctrine of papal supremacy but on a collegial assembly of bishops. The Orthodox accord the pope a primacy, but one that would act always in cooperation with the other bishops.

The Orthodox Church and Christians in the West are only recently rediscovering each other. At first Christianity in the West may have seemed to the Orthodox too rationalistic and monarchical; to the West, Orthodoxy has seemed too mystical, too amorphous, expressing its doctrine more in the context of worship than systematically and academically, as the West has done. Both communities of Christians are learning from each other. The Orthodox Church has preserved the patristic and monastic heritage that many Christians seek to rediscover. Similarly, the beauty of its liturgies and the doctrinal fidelity of its icons have become sources of renewed inspiration in the West. Christians in the West have made great application of scholarship, particularly in the cooperative efforts of philosophy and science and the interaction with an increasingly secularized society. From these developments Orthodoxy can learn. Timothy Ware considers the Orthodox Church as the elder brother preserving the family's legacy but grateful to its younger brothers for helping it understand that legacy. To a "divided and bewildered Christendom" it offers a faith preserved intact and also living.

Sources for Further Study

Behr, John, et al. *Abba: The Tradition of Orthodoxy in the West.* Crestwood, N.Y.: St. Vladimir's Orthodox Theological Seminary, 2003. A festschrift in honor of Ware's retirement. Contains twenty essays on various aspects of Orthodoxy in the world today.

Florovsky, Georges. *Bible, Church, Tradition: An Eastern Orthodox View.* Belmont, Mass.: Nordland, 1972. A collection of essays by a principal Orthodox theologian of the twentieth century. Offers insight into the patristic interpretation of the Bible and the patristic mind.

L'Huillier, Peter. *The Church of the Ancient Councils.* Crestwood, N.Y.: St. Vladimir's Orthodox Theological Seminary, 1996. A detailed examination of the canons of the first four ecumenical councils of the Church, pointing to their importance for today's Christians.

Patrinacos, Nicon D. *A Dictionary of Greek Orthodoxy.* New York: Greek Orthodox Archdiocese of North and South America, 1984. Alphabetically arranged articles on topics of Orthodox faith, doctrine, and history.

Spidlík, Tomás. *Spirituality of the Christian East: A Systematic Handbook.* Vol. 2. Kalamazoo, Mich.: Cistercian, 2005. Written by a Catholic priest, this volume joins the first volume (published in 1986) as a scholarly but accessible introduction to elements of Eastern Christian spirituality and religion.

Ware, Timothy. *The Orthodox Way.* Crestwood, N.Y.: St. Vladimir's Orthodox Theological Seminary, 1979. A collection of sayings from the fathers of the Church, the liturgy, and prayers to illustrate the doctrines of the Orthodox Church and its spirituality.

Daniel J. Nodes

ORTHODOXY

Author: G. K. Chesterton (1874-1936)
First published: 1908
Edition used: Orthodoxy. New York: Dodd, Mead, 1943
Genre: Nonfiction
Subgenres: Autobiography; essays; humor; meditation and contemplation
Core issues: Capitalism; doubt; ethics; faith; reason; sin and sinners

In this volume of clever apologetics and sparkling humor, with a dash of spiritual autobiography, Chesterton analyzes the intellectual and emotional appeal of Christian ideas. His vigorous endorsement of Christian philosophy not only inspired the so-called Catholic literary revival but also provided subsequent conservative Christian authors with a model of persuasive rhetoric for popular spiritual writing, influencing Dorothy Sayers, C. S. Lewis, and many others.

Overview

Though sometimes vaguely regarded as a minor British literary figure, G. K. Chesterton is considered by many informed readers to be one of the great writers of the English language in the twentieth century. A prolific author of astonishing creativity, he published dozens of books (including novels, biographies, and social, literary, and religious criticism), hundreds of short stories and poems, and thousands of essays. Though nowadays perhaps most often remembered as the author of the well-known Father Brown detective stories, he was a public intellectual in the media of his time. His enduring cultural significance is found in his sometimes prescient, sometimes naïve critiques of modernist ideas, and in his vigorous, witty defense of the intellectual respectability of traditional Christian doctrines. *Orthodoxy*, one of his most important books, presents his effervescent *apologia pro vita sua.*

The title of chapter 6, "The Paradoxes of Christianity," articulates what in a real sense is the subject of the whole volume. Though Chesterton condemns the use of "mere paradox," his characteristic humor is pervasively couched in paradoxical terms: *Orthodoxy* reads like Saint Paul's epistles as written by Oscar Wilde. With glittering wit, Chesterton endorses Christian doctrine as the logical upshot of a humble and democratic common sense. To some readers his unrelenting inversion of truisms may grow predictable and tedious; to others, the verbal pyrotechnics are redeemed by an abundance of unfashionable truths memorably expressed.

Chesterton explains how he came to Christianity but provides neither conventional autobiography nor ordinary apologetics. Offering "mental pictures" rather than deductions, he tries to show how his instinctive view of life—a view in sharp contrast to the drift of modern thought—was ultimately recognized by him as consonant with historic Christian faith. (A decade and a half later, in 1922, he embraced Roman Catholicism.) His "ultimate attitudes towards life" include the idea that the meaningfulness of the world requires a personal agency behind it, an agency to whom people owe the good of their lives and to whom deference is due.

Chesterton encapsulates the main problem for philosophers in this question: "How can we contrive to be at once astonished at the world and yet at home in it?" He describes the important influence fairy tales had upon his outlook. "These tales say that apples were golden only to refresh the forgotten moment when we found that they were green." This "mixture of the familiar and the unfamiliar" he calls "romance," and he presents Christian faith as uniquely equipped to provide a place for such romance in the world. In effect, he presents Christian doctrines and symbols as the most satisfying expressions of life's mystery.

Chesterton critiques the sensibility of his times, which he sees as involving both a lack of balance among the various attitudes human life requires and a loss of belief in the reality of truth. Modernist views seem to him materialistic and therefore skeptical and self-defeating. They undermine human reason, will, and energy, so they ultimately result in what he calls (it is the title of chapter 3) "the suicide of thought." The German philosopher Friedrich Nietzsche is a frequent target, and some of Chesterton's cogent observations point to philosophical weaknesses arguably still found decades later in so-called postmodernist philosophers.

Only in his final chapter ("Authority and the Adventurer") does Chesterton at last address the important question of why thinkers should fully accept Christianity rather than merely extract from it whatever worldly truths it may have discerned. He responds to agnostic or atheistic objections, arguing that the skeptic's case invariably derives from a mistake about the facts. It is skeptics who reject concrete evidence such as human testimony because of their commitment to an abstract dogma about what is possible, he says. "It is we Christians who accept all actual evidence."

Chesterton may intend to suggest that Christian belief has been shown to be better, or at least no less acceptable, than materialist belief. To reach this conclusion, however, he must rely upon his view that complexity in the world implies (divine) personal agency, and in the end he concedes that this conviction is "undiscussable . . . a *primary* intellectual conviction." If this conviction may seem more in question today than it did a century ago, the issue remains central to the ongoing debate over Darwinian evolution and so-called Intelligent Design. Chesterton's brief discussion of evolution presents the subject, depending on how it is understood, either as perfectly innocuous or as yet another example of the suicide of thought.

Chesterton could insist that his concern is only to explain his beliefs rather than to compel the belief of others, for the argument he discusses is not, he says, his real reason for accepting Christianity. He is persuaded not because Christianity has told him this or that particular truth but because it "has again and again said the thing that does not seem to be true, but is true." Critics will note that if the romance of orthodoxy depends on the individual believer's way of telling the story or involves the relativity of incommensurable primary intellectual convictions, then heterodoxy may yet have a word to be said for it.

Christian Themes

Because Chesterton's topic is the way in which Christian ideas have often received unexpected vindication in the human effort to make sense of life, his discussion touches on various Christian themes. Some of these include the Trinity; such virtues as courage, modesty, and charity; the certain wrongness of suicide, in connection with which Chesterton first recognized the concurrence of his thoughts with Christianity; and the possible rightness of celibacy, which he claims not fully to understand.

The discussion of capitalism and wealth in the latter part of the book continues the traditional Christian debate about the theological significance of poverty and riches. Chesterton argues (in chapter 7, "The Eternal Revolution") that only the Christian doctrine of Original Sin provides a logical basis for the defense of democracy against the rule of a wealthy elite. The ideas of Original Sin and the Fall play a central role throughout his reflections on modern intellectual life.

In chapter 8, "The Romance of Orthodoxy," Chesterton presents the Christian view as the natural foundation for metaphysical, moral, and political freedom, contrasting it with materialism as well as with such religions as Buddhism and Islam. Again and again, he portrays the right thinking of orthodoxy as a thrilling romance, one that renders the profound mystery of life its due, remains in tune with common sense yet is the opposite of received opinion, and retains the power to remind us of the forgotten magic of everyday truth.

Sources for Further Study

Ahlquist, Dale. *G. K. Chesterton: The Apostle of Common Sense.* San Francisco: Ignatius Press, 2003. The companion volume to a popular television series hosted by Ahlquist, who is both president of the American Chesterton Society and associate editor of the Ignatius Press edition of Chesterton's collected works.

Chesterton, G. K. *"Heretics," "Orthodoxy," "The Blatchford Controversies."* Vol. 1 in *Collected Works.* San Francisco: Ignatius Press, 1986. Provides a broad context for understanding *Orthodoxy* by including Chesterton's earlier critique of the religious ideas of his contemporaries, *Heretics* (1905), as well as still earlier material relating to the his participation in the controversies promoted by Robert Blatchford (editor of the socialist weekly *The Clarion*).

Kenner, Hugh. *Paradox in Chesterton.* New York: Sheed & Ward, 1947. The Canadian literary critic Hugh Kenner, one of the architects of the canon of modernism, devoted his first book to a study of Chesterton's use of paradox.

Kibler, Craig M., ed. *Orthodoxy: The Annotated Edition.* Lenoir, N.C.: Reformation Press, 2002. Extensive commentary on Chesterton's text by a Christian journalist who has also published an annotated edition of *Heretics* (2005).

Lauer, Quentin. *G. K. Chesterton: Philosopher Without a Portfolio.* New York: Fordham University Press, 1988. An academic expert on the philosophy of G. W. F. Hegel and on the phenomenology of Edmund Husserl defends the philosophical significance of Chesterton's thought.

Wills, Garry. *Chesterton*. Rev. ed. New York: Doubleday, 2001. Wills, a prolific public intellectual, both a Catholic critic and a critic of Catholicism, reexamines
Chesterton's faith and works four decades after his first book on Chesterton.

Edward Johnson

OUT OF MY LIFE AND THOUGHT
An Autobiography

Author: Albert Schweitzer (1875-1965)
First published: Aus meinem Leben und Denken, 1931 (English translation, 1933)
Edition used: Out of My Life and Thought: An Autobiography, translated by C. T.
  Campion. New York: Henry Holt, 1933
Genre: Nonfiction
Subgenres: Autobiography; meditation and contemplation
Core issues: Conscience; devotional life; ethics; life; love; morality; mysticism; reli-
  gion; service; truth

*After serving as curate at Saint Nicholas in Strassburg and having subsequently been
appointed principal of the theological seminary there, Schweitzer decided on his thirtieth birthday to become a medical doctor and to devote his life to the service of natives in equatorial Africa. In 1912 he established his hospital at Lambaréné, Gabon,
and he spent the rest of his life working there, periodically traveling to Europe and the
United States to lecture or present organ recitals. He played a major role in influencing sentiment against the testing and proliferation of nuclear weapons and won the
Nobel Peace Prize in 1952.*

Overview

Albert Schweitzer's *Out of My Life and Thought* is a spiritual autobiography in that
it is both an account of spiritual progress and an expression of it. His book could very
well have been entitled "Out of My Thought, My Life," for the thinking he calls "elemental" concerns itself with the fundamental conditions and opportunities of life and
is itself an expression of the will-to-live. It is Schweitzer's thesis, exemplified in the
course of his creative life of service, that elemental thought, in aiming at truth, effects
a transition from the will-to-life to the will-to-love. His autobiography is an account
spiritualized by just such a process—a course of fundamental thinking leading to the
will-to-love and, accordingly, to a religion of love that proves itself in life-affirming
service to others.

A gifted organist, philosopher, theologian, pastor, and writer, Schweitzer decided,
at the age of thirty, to become a medical doctor and to devote his life to the service of
natives of equatorial Africa. He had conceived the idea during his days as a student,
and he reports that "It struck me as incomprehensible that I should be allowed to lead
such a happy life, while I saw so many people around me wrestling with care and
suffering." At Gunsbach in 1896, while on holiday away from the university at
Strassburg, Schweitzer decided that he would be justified in living until he was thirty
for science and art, and then should devote the remainder of his life to the "direct service of humanity." His decision to become a doctor and to serve in Africa was
prompted in the autumn of 1904 by his reading an article on the needs of the Congo

mission, published in a magazine of the Paris Missionary Society. A few months later, on his thirtieth birthday, January 14, 1905, he decided on equatorial Africa as his place of service and, despite the opposition of his friends and relatives, began planning to enter medical college. He persevered despite being told that he was throwing away his many talents in order to bury himself in the jungle. He writes that "it moved me strangely to see them [people who passed for Christians] so far from perceiving that the effort to serve the love preached by Jesus may sweep a man into a new course of life."

Schweitzer's account of his life experience (to 1931, when he still had thirty-four years to live) alternates reports of significant events in his life with reviews of his thoughts and commitments. It becomes apparent as one reads that the events of his life stimulated thought, thought gave rise to commitment, and commitment showed itself in action. The thesis he argues is proved in the life he led.

While at Strassburg studying philosophy and theology, Schweitzer undertook an inquiry that later assumed the title *Eine Geschichte der Leben-Jesus Forschung* (1906; *The Quest of the Historical Jesus*, 1910). Schweitzer's studies led him to the conclusion that Jesus accepted the late-Jewish Messianic worldview involving the imminent end of the world and the establishment of the kingdom of God. The idea that Jesus held views later shown to be false is repugnant to many Christians, Schweitzer points out, but he argues that the religion of love that Jesus taught need not be dependent upon the worldview in which it first appeared. Although we cannot accept the dogma involved in the late-Jewish Messianic expectation, Schweitzer writes, "the spirituality which lies in this religion of love must gradually, like a refiner's fire, seize upon all ideas which come into communication with it," and hence, he concludes, "it is the destiny of Christianity to develop through a constant process of spiritualization." The religion of love persists whatever the prevailing *Weltanschauung* of any particular period; the spiritual and ethical truth continues to be influential whatever temporal view may clothe it.

Schweitzer and his wife arrived in Lambaréné in the spring of 1913, and the construction of the jungle hospital began. The intensive medical work was interrupted the following year with the beginning of the war in Europe. The Schweitzers were interned at the Lambaréné mission-station, and on the second day of their internment Schweitzer began work on a problem that had occupied his mind for a number of years—the problem of civilization. The product of his labors was to be published under the title *Kulturphilosophie* (*The Philosophy of Civilization*, 1946), but not until its completion in 1923, when the first two volumes were published.

Having called into question the common opinion that humankind naturally develops in the direction of progress, Schweitzer sought to resolve the problem of restoring civilization. Having realized that "the catastrophe of civilization started from a catastrophe of world-view," he explored the idea of civilization itself. His conclusion was that "the essential element in civilization is the ethical perfecting of the individual and of society as well," that the "will to civilization is . . . the universal will to progress which is conscious of the ethical as the highest value of all." The worldview that is required, then, is one that consists in an ethical affirmation of the world and life. What is needed is "an act of the spirit" whereby progress is understood to be internal, not external; spiritual, not material; life- and world-affirming, not negating.

What Schweitzer sought in order to complete his basic idea of the conditions of true civilization was a fundamental truth, an "elementary and universal conception of the ethical," that would enable the connection between a spiritual worldview and civilization to be realized. For months he grappled with the problem, but it was not until he was traveling upstream on the Ogowe River to visit the ailing wife of a missionary that he suddenly conceived the answer: "Late on the third day, at the very moment when, at sunset, we were making our way through a herd of hippopotamuses, there flashed upon my mind, unforeseen and unsought, the phrase 'Reverence for Life.'"

What is Reverence for Life? Schweitzer asks, and in response he suggests that we look away from the manifold, the product of thought and knowledge, and turn attention to the immediate fact of consciousness, the assertion, "I am life which wills to live, in the midst of life which wills to live." Life-affirmation, Schweitzer writes, is a "spiritual act" by which a person becomes devoted to life with reverence "in order to raise it to its true value."

A "thinking" being, Schweitzer insists, is one who gives to every life the same reverence given one's own. Thus, such a being "accepts as being good: to preserve life, to promote life, to raise to its highest value life which is capable of development; and as being evil: to destroy life, to injure life, to repress life which is capable of development." This principle, stemming from the will-to-live, is the fundamental principle of morality. "The Reverence for Life, therefore," Schweitzer concludes, ". . . contains world- and life-affirmation and the ethical fused together." The spiritual and ethical perfection of humanity becomes the highest ideal.

Schweitzer concludes that the solidarity with all life cannot completely be brought about, for each human being "is subject to the puzzling and horrible law of being obliged to live at the cost of other life, and to incur again and again the guilt of destroying and injuring life." The thinking, ethical being, Schweitzer adds, "strives to escape whenever possible from this necessity."

The discovery of and commitment to the reverence for life enabled Schweitzer to complete the first two volumes of his *Philosophy of Civilization: Verfall und Wiederaufbau der Kultur* (1923; *The Decay and Restoration of Civilization*, 1946) and *Kultur und Ethik* (1923; *Civilization and Ethics*, 1946). Schweitzer bemoaned the modern renunciation of thinking. Elemental thinking shows that the will to truth must involve the will to sincerity, and the will to sincerity and truth leads to the reverence for life, which contains within itself resignation (one sees the world as it is, with all its suffering), world- and life-affirmation (one thinks through to a solidarity with other wills-to-live), and the ethical (the call for action issued by love).

Schweitzer describes the worldview that involves reverence for life as an "ethical mysticism." He contends that rational thinking, "if it goes deep, ends of necessity in the non-rational of mysticism." The essential element in Christianity, then, as preached by Jesus, is that "it is only through love that we can attain to communion with God. All living knowledge of God rests upon this foundation: that we experience Him in our lives as Will-to-Love."

Christian Themes

Schweitzer believed that religion of love Jesus taught makes it clear that ethics is the essence of religion. It is the destiny of Christianity to develop through a process of spiritualization made evident in the religion of love. Christians must bring themselves into spiritual relation with the world and become one with it through active service out of a reverence for life. Elemental thought that penetrates to the nature of things leads to a world- and life-affirmation that stems from an ethics based on the will-to-live and, accordingly, on a reverence for all life. We experience God in our lives as the will-to-love.

Sources for Further Study

Cousins, Norman. *Albert Schweitzer's Mission: Healing and Peace.* New York: Norton, 1985. Part 1 is an adaptation of Cousins's *Dr. Schweitzer of Lambaréné* (1960) and provides a sensitive and sympathetic portrait based on a visit Cousins made to the jungle hospital; part 2 contains previously unpublished correspondence involving Schweitzer, Jawaharlal Nehru, Dwight Eisenhower, Nikita Krushchev, John F. Kennedy, and Cousins, centering on Schweitzer's effort to awaken world consciousness to the catastrophic dangers of nuclear war.

Joy, Charles R., ed. *Albert Schweitzer: An Anthology.* 1947. Enlarged ed. Boston: Beacon Press, 1956. Joy has edited an excellent and moving anthology drawn from Schweitzer's most effective writings. It includes a chronological summary of Schweitzer's life (to 1956) and a bibliography.

Schweitzer, Albert. *Civilization and Ethics.* Part 2 of *The Philosophy of Civilization.* Translated by C. T. Campion. New York: Macmillan, 1929. The central spiritual and ethical philosophy is here developed at length.

_____. *On the Edge of the Primeval Forest.* Published with *The Forest Hospital at Lambaréné.* Translated by C. T. Campion. New York: Macmillan, 1948. Schweitzer's African reminiscences, dealing in part with the problems of colonization among primitive peoples.

_____. *The Quest of the Historical Jesus: A Critical Study of Its Progress from Reimarus to Wrede.* Translated by W. Montgomery. New York: Macmillan, 1945. Insisting on Jesus' messianic worldview, Schweitzer calls attention to his religion of love.

Ian P. McGreal

OUT OF THE RED SHADOW

Author: Anne de Graaf
First published: Minneapolis, Minn.: Bethany House, 1999
Genre: Novel
Subgenre: Historical fiction (twentieth century)
Core issues: Children; communism; guilt; healing; nature; social action

For many years, Jacek has believed his daughter Amy dead. Now she appears like a ghost from the past, married, a mother, and searching for her father. Because of his long history as a Central Intelligence Agency (CIA) agent operating in Cold War Poland, Jacek cannot reveal his identity, but he does vow to protect Amy and her family and to destroy her former lover, Piotr Piekarz, a rising leader in the Solidarność movement sweeping over the country. Even as Jacek strives to keep his distance, he cannot help becoming more involved with Amy's family, to the extent that he ultimately must save her son, Tomasz, from life on the streets of Berlin and help to preserve her family in the face of the growing Communist threat to the Polish people's quest for self-governance.

Principal characters

> *Jacek Skrzypek*, also known as *Jacek Duch*, a CIA agent who has for some time been operating in the Służba Bezpieczeństwa (Secret Police or SB) of Poland
> *Roman*, Jacek's contact in the SB
> *Amy Piekarz*, Jacek's daughter
> *Jan Piekarz*, Amy's husband
> *Tomasz "Tomek" or "Tomku" Piekarz*, Jan and Amy's son
> *Elżbieta "Żanetka" or "Żanetko" Piekarz*, Jan and Amy's oldest daughter
> *Małgorzata "Gonia" Piekarz*, Jan and Amy's youngest daughter
> *Piotr Piekarz*, Amy's former lover, Jan's brother, a leader in the Solidarność movement
> *Halina Piekarz*, Piotr's wife
> *Hanna Piekarz*, Piotr and Jan's mother
> *Tadeusz Piekarz*, Piotr and Jan's father, a Protestant minister
> *Ewa* and *Bogdan*, friends of Amy, Jan, and Piotr, also involved in the resistance movement
> *Gabi* and *Jurek*, two CIA agents assigned to protect Jacek

Overview

Out of the Red Shadow, winner of the Christy Award 2000 for international historical fiction, is the third and concluding novel of Anne de Graaf's *The Hidden Harvest*.

Set in Cold War Poland, the political turmoil of the country is echoed in the emotional upheaval in the lives of Jacek Duch and his daughter's family and illustrated through a perspective that shifts from Jacek to Tomek (later Tomasz) Piekarz, his sister Żanetka, and Piotr Piekarz, their uncle.

Jacek's perspective provides the frame for the narrative, starting from his unexpected meeting with the daughter he has for years believed dead. Long an undercover agent for the Central Intelligence Agency (CIA), Jacek feels his position in the Służba Bezpieczeństwa (SB) has become imperiled. In an effort to deflect attention from himself, he has initiated a surveillance campaign spying on the minority Protestant population to jeopardize the growing Solidarność movement. Amy is now an adult and married to Jan Piekarz, son of Tadeusz Piekarz, a Protestant minister who discovered Jacek's identity during World War II but kept it secret all these years. Because of their religious affiliation, the family has been caught in the SB's surveillance, and Jacek must destroy the tapes of their conversations that reveal his own identity in a conversation with the "outlaw" Jacek discovers is Piotr Piekarz, Amy's brother-in-law and former lover. As part of his plan to protect Amy and her family, Jacek decides Piotr, a Solidarność leader and the only person who knows of Jacek's relationship to Amy once his father, Tadeusz, dies, must be eliminated. As a result of Jacek's tip to the SB, Piotr is arrested.

After Jacek is nearly arrested by the Americans for an attempted assassination on the life of President Jimmy Carter, he goes into hiding from both the SB and the CIA. He sets himself up in an apartment near Amy and her family in Gdańsk, so he can begin getting to know them, if only from a distance. A chance encounter with her son, Tomek, cements his need to feel close to them.

Tomek and Żanetka reveal the internal life of a family in which the children must grow up too quickly. The story of their uncle Piotr's wedding and arrest are related through Tomek's perspective and supplemented by Piotr's own letters, written to Amy and Jan from prison, in which he reflects on his loveless marriage to Halina and his commitment to the Solidarność cause. As Tomek grows up, his relationship with his parents becomes increasingly strained; he rejects his father, suggesting that Piotr should have been his father instead of Jan.

Żanetka struggles to fit in at school as she grow up, learning from the troubles within her family. Uncle Piotr has been imprisoned for some time; his whereabouts were unknown until one day when Jan discovers where he is being held. Amy sets off to see him, taking Gonia with her. Through Żanetka we learn of four-year-old Gonia's death from falling down a staircase at the prison during a brief moment when Amy and Piotr are alone and momentarily distracted by a whisper of their former romance. The grief in the family is terrible and shortly compounded by Tomasz's decision to run away. After an especially brutal argument with his father, Tomasz leaves Gdańsk, hitchhiking to the West and making his way to Berlin, where very quickly he descends to a life of uncertainty, crime, drugs, and desperation on the streets.

Back in Gdańsk, Tomasz's frantic family begins searching for him. Having formed an unlikely and tenuous friendship with Jacek, Piotr begs him to find Tomasz. As

Jacek begins his quest, the Solidarność movement is gaining momentum under the charismatic leadership of Lech Wałęsa. Jacek heads to Berlin, using his CIA credentials to access government records and betraying his existence to an old enemy, Gabi, formerly one of two CIA agents detailed to protect him.

Piotr is released from prison. Jacek finds Tomasz and takes him away from Berlin to begin the painful and horrific process of addiction withdrawal, which they accomplish in an isolated rural cabin. When Tomasz is finally ready, Jacek sends him back to his family.

Jacek gets to Gdańsk first, chased by Gabi, who is intent on killing him for betraying Jurek, another CIA officer, to the SB. Nevertheless, he completes his personal mission to tell Amy who he is. Tomasz follows on the train, discovering the mass *milicja* waiting to descend on a Solidarność rally. With a new recognition of the significance of freedom and the efforts of the underground, he races to warn his uncle. Piotr initially does not believe him, but the tanks roll in and the *milicja* begin shooting.

Gabi shoots Jacek. Piotr and Tomasz help him to shelter, but she follows them, threatening all of the family who run in to escape from the snipers. To protect Jacek, Tomasz jumps between him and Gabi. In the chaos that follows, she runs away. Jacek has final words with his family, asking for forgiveness and recognizing in Amy's friend Ewa the face of his true love, Monika, destroyed by the Soviets during the Cold War.

Christian Themes

Overarching the story of *Out of the Red Shadow* is the introductory epigram of James 1:17, assuring the people of the beneficent and unchanging nature of God. The book is divided into six parts, each introduced by a biblical epigram that re-creates the rite of the Eucharist as practiced in Reformed Protestantism and that underscores the intertwined nature of the Polish resistance movement and the country's relationship with religion.

Psalm 80:4-5 introduces part 1 and Jacek's story. Because of his obligations as a CIA operative working for the SB, he has had to make many regrettable choices and witnessed many horrific things that now, as an old man, he must face. Amy's sudden appearance prompts him to reflect on all the mistakes and missed opportunities of his life, his own "bread of tears," that not only affected him but in many cases inflicted tragedy on others during the years of the Cold War in Poland. Retreating to a mountain lodge and isolating himself gives Jacek the opportunity to seek solace and find strength to return to the world. During this time, the Solidarność movement is beginning to emerge, as well, fomented in the people's protest against postwar Communist oppression.

The taking of the Eucharist is outlined in parts 2 through 4, through Matthew 6:11, 1 Corinthians 10:16, Matthew 4:4, and John 6:51, respectively. In part 2 one reads the prayer for daily sustenance, the daily life and needs of the diverse Piekarz family, and the growing demands of the Solidarność movement. Part 3 concerns the devastating loss of Gonia and the seeming insufficiency of prayer to ameliorate the family's response to her death. In part 4, Tomasz leaves to seek the materialism of the West, forgetting that "bread alone" is inadequate for life. In part 5, Tomasz's recovery will admit the "living bread" of Christ that Tomasz and Jacek also find manifested in their encounters with nature.

Closing with Jacek's framing narrative enables de Graaf to reiterate the constancy of God asserted in the opening epigram. She draws on Psalm 78:2, recalling that even when people act irresponsibly or unfaithfully, God does not desert them. This is effectively underlined when Żanetka's dying grandmother, the voice of Scripture in the novel, tells her granddaughter that she has an "intercessory heart," a reminder of the Eucharist as the celebration of Christ's role as intercessor for the people of the earth.

Source for Further Study

De Graaf, Anne. http://www.annedegraaf.com. The author's Web site contains biographical information, a list of publications, excerpts, reviews, and a blog.

Jennie MacDonald

OXYGEN
A Mission Gone Desperately Wrong—
and No Way Out Short of Blind Faith

Authors: Randall Scott Ingermanson (1958-   ) and John B. Olson
First published: Minneapolis, Minn.: Bethany House, 2001
Genre: Novel
Subgenres: Science fiction; thriller/suspense
Core issues: Doubt; ethics; faith; love; sacrifice

En route to Mars, four astronauts face mechanical malfunctions and an explosion aboard ship that threaten to end their lives. Paranoia grips the crew as each member fears that another member may be a saboteur. Unable to trust her fellow astronauts, the lone avowed Christian on the journey places her trust in God, but it is a faith tempered by doubt. Acts of Christian self-sacrifice, combined with human ingenuity, effect the resolution of this science-fiction thriller.

Principal characters
> *Valkerie Jansen*, a microbial ecologist and a Christian
> *Bob Kaganovski*, the chief engineer of Ares 10
> *Kennedy Hampton*, mission commander and pilot
> *Lex Ohta*, an astronaut and geochemist
> *Steven Perez*, NASA Administrator
> *Nate Harrington*, mission director
> *Josh Bennet*, capsule communicator (capcom)
> *Senator Axton*, a U.S. congressman
> *Sidney Nichols*, Jansen's former boyfriend, a fundamentalist
> terrorist
> *Sarah Laval*, former fiancé of Bob Kaganovski, a born-again
> Christian

Overview

In *Oxygen*, biochemist John B. Olson and physicist Randall Scott Ingermanson produce a work of science fiction that poses an intriguing question. If a catastrophe should strike midway between Earth and Mars, what should an astronaut trust: God or technology? The protagonist, Valkerie Jansen—astronaut, scientist, doctor, and Christian—responds in a way that honors both her faith-based heritage and her empirical training.

In this account of a mission gone awry, events begin on Tuesday, August 14, 2012, in Alaska and end on Friday, July 4, 2014, on Mars. During the short two-year span, Jansen is selected to the astronaut corps, trains for a flight, and begins the mission to

Mars. The pressure of time is a significant catalyst: NASA must launch Ares 10 as scheduled or the program will be scrapped; Jansen has months, not years, to complete her training; and, following a series of mishaps, the astronauts have limited time to find a solution to their depleting oxygen supply. Furthermore, if NASA is to profit from televised coverage and gain public support for future flights, it must meet expectations for a Fourth of July landing. This haste is conveyed effectively in the novel's format. Comprising four long sections that house forty short chapters, the novel is fast-paced.

Part 1, "Human Factors," opens with Jansen camped in Alaska, collecting biological samples from an active volcano as part of her postdoctoral work. Poisonous gases leak from the earth's crust and she instinctively seeks higher ground. When the gases reach into the treetops she climbs, she returns to camp, punctures her Jeep's tires, and inhales the stale oxygen they provide. Her survival instinct and vast scientific knowledge are a combination sought by NASA. In a coincidence that is at odds with an otherwise believably scripted work, two NASA officials arrive by helicopter during this episode to interview their applicant. Instead of conducting an interview, they find themselves rescuing the oxygen-deprived Jansen, airlifting her to safety. The episode tells them what they hoped to discover in their interview, and they offer her a dream job.

Throughout much of the novel, the relationship between crew members is a tenuous one. Even prior to the flight disasters, tension exists. Others are suspicious of Jansen's Christian beliefs, which she downplays in their presence. Fundamentalist protesters mob NASA's gates, angered at the agency's search for evidence of life on Mars. Their presence embarrasses Jansen and inflames fellow astronauts. In particular, Chief Engineer Bob Kaganovski worries that Jansen might thwart the discovery of life on Mars to avoid a potential conflict with Creationism. Jansen's fellow astronauts are aggrieved she has replaced the more affable Josh Bennet, the former leader of their mission, who remains behind to assume responsibilities as capcom.

The rough launch in part 2, "The Point of No Return," creates mechanical and physical problems for the crew even before they leave Earth orbit. Commander Kennedy Hampton suffers a detached retina that leaves him blind in one eye, though a greater blindness is his lack of faith in his crew and in God. His paranoia infects the morale of his crew, and they begin to question loyalties. Desperate to continue the mission, he withholds information from NASA about damage to onboard systems, endangering the lives of his comrades.

In part 3, "The Belly of the Beast," Kaganovski and Hampton take an unplanned spacewalk to assess vehicle damage and attempt repairs. When Kaganovski touches an exposed wire, he causes an explosion of such intensity that a metal seam ruptures. Jansen must aid injured astronaut Lex Ohta, repair the breach to prevent further loss of oxygen, and rescue the bewildered spacewalkers. As the origins of the explosion remain unknown, the consensus among crew and NASA is sabotage: Someone attached a bomb to the ship prior to launch. Tight security precludes all but one of six individuals as the culprit: the four crew members and two ground commanders. With a dwindling supply of oxygen, Jansen induces a state of coma in her fellow crew members (consequently reducing their oxygen intake) and monitors their conditions over several months. Alone she ponders existential questions: her role in the mission, God's role (if any) in their rescue, the nature of her being, the nature of God. Attempting to douse her faith with cold logic, she finds she cannot; it is too ingrained.

After siphoning oxygen from another ship, the crew reaches Mars. Their final journey in part 4, "Independence Day," is an arduous trek for two to the Mars Habitation Module (Hab). Unbeknownst to Kaganovski and Hampton, the female crew adds their ration of oxygen to the men's tanks, fearing that without it their colleagues will not survive. Returning to the Ares 10, the men discover the lifeless women, realize their sacrifice, and transport their bodies for later burial. A despondent Kaganovski realizes his love for Jansen and his renewed faith in God. Later a noise outside the Hab disturbs Kaganovski. He enters the rover, and in a scene reminiscent of Mary Magdalene discovering Christ's empty tomb, fails to find Jansen's body. She steps into view and speaks his name. Jansen's resurrection, and subsequently Ohta's, is not a miraculous return to life but a reawakening from an induced coma. The mystery of the explosion is revealed as well. Bennet, the replaced astronaut, confesses to having attached a canister of arctic bacteria to the ship with which he hoped to seed life on Mars, thereby furthering space exploration. Its premature explosion was unintended. The novel concludes with an image of Kaganovski on bended knee proposing to Jansen with the Martian landscape behind them. Not only has their mission succeeded; so, too, has their love.

Christian Themes

The counterpart of faith is doubt, and their contradiction is explored fully in *Oxygen*. Science is a field that relies on experimentation and logic to ascertain truths about the universe. God becomes an improvable element through normal scientific channels, but when faced with the loneliness of space, these voyagers consider his presence with greater frequency the further they travel from Earth. After inducing comas in her comrades, Valkerie Jansen is left alone with her thoughts, which become prayer in outer space. Hurtling toward Mars, she contemplates her relationship with God and its impersonal nature. She asks for a sign; she hears the rumblings of a damaged spacecraft. Clear proof is evasive, yet when she tries to dismantle her faith through empirical examination, it refuses to abandon her.

Her shipmate Bob Kaganovski, an avowed skeptic despite twelve years of Catholic education, demands proof of God's existence. His former fiancé, the born-again Christian Sarah Laval, was persuaded by friends not to marry "outside the yoke" (to a nonbeliever). Confronted with his own mortality, Kaganovski realizes what he must do before death: forgive Sarah and relinquish the bitterness he carried with him into space. With that burden lifted, he recovers his spiritual identity. His developing love for another believer, Jansen, and her Christian witness—expressed not in words but through selfless actions—lead him to repentance and acceptance.

Ethics is central to the novel's focus on science and religion, strange bedfellows when events begin but wedded partners by the narrative's end. Neither is perfect; both fields are revealed to suffer serious ethical lapses. NASA, spurred by fears of government cuts, hastens preparations for the Mars mission and launches in unfavorable conditions, a decision that spawns calamity. By valuing public relations and funding over safety, NASA cheapens life. Likewise, protesters who fear what space might reveal about life's origins value ignorance over knowledge, impeding research that might extend the human race. As one of the astronauts notes in a broadcast from space, Mars might be where humans reside when Earth can no longer sustain them. In a subplot, Jansen's college boyfriend is revealed to have died in an explosion at a Yale laboratory. Ironically, in his protest against stem cell research, he destroyed human life. Jansen has distanced herself from such violent Christians.

In Jansen, science and faith blend. She lives the Christian ethos by applying her scientific knowledge to the service of others. As doctor, scientist, and Christian, Jansen does everything within her power to sustain human life, even relinquishing precious oxygen so that others might live.

Sources for Further Study

Duncan, Melanie. Review of *Oxygen*. *Library Journal*, September 1, 2001, 156. Examines the novel's genre-blending elements and concludes that science fiction melds with mystery in a satisfying marriage.

Mort, John. Review of *Oxygen*. *Booklist*, June 1, 2001, 1844. An appraisal of the novel's technical savvy, compelling story line, and spiritual elements.

Tomasso, Phillip. Review of *Oxygen*. *Curled up with a Good Book*. http://curledup .com. Focuses on novel's stylistic features that contribute to its readability; also notes its relevance to contemporary issues.

Dorothy Dodge Robbins

PACEM IN TERRIS

Author: John XXIII (Angelo Giuseppe Roncalli; 1881-1963)
First published: 1963 (English translation, 1963)
Edition used: Pacem in Terris, translated by the National Catholic Welfare Conference. Boston: St. Paul Editions, 1963
Genre: Nonfiction
Subgenres: Didactic treatise; encyclical; spiritual treatise
Core issues: Catholics and Catholicism; cause universal; ethics; justice; pastoral role; peace; social action

This encyclical of Pope John XXIII, addressed to not only the worldwide Catholic community but also all humanity, proclaims the necessity for immediate world peace and outlines a program of action to be taken by all nations and peoples to successfully achieve worldwide peace. The encyclical establishes a growing progression of social and political rights, starting with the rights of the individual among individuals, between the individual and the nation, the nation among nations, and between nations and the global community. It reflects the political situation of the Cold War and the growing arms race, and calls for disarmament and the subsequent banning of nuclear weapons. The encyclical ends with the identification of the pastoral role in realizing this program for peace on earth.

Overview

The early 1960's saw the world facing the grim reality of the Cold War and the nuclear arms race, with the threat of a nuclear holocaust. The Berlin Wall, constructed in 1961, had become a chilling symbol of the polarization of relations between the Soviet Union and the Western capitalist nations. The Cuban missile crisis in 1962 had brought the world to the very brink of war, and Pope John XXIII had been personally involved as a correspondent between President John F. Kennedy and Soviet leader Nikita Khrushchev. This alarming event, however, precipitated an eloquent response from the Vatican in the form of the encyclical *Pacem in Terris*. Issued on April 11, 1963, at the start of the Easter weekend, the encyclical was addressed to not only the Catholic community, or even just the Christian community, but also "all men of good will." It acknowledged peace as a goal and necessity that transcended all denominational and national boundaries, and it appealed to all on the level of common humanity.

The entire encyclical was an affirmation of human rights and duties, appealing to its audience on the grounds of a common humanity within a global community. While it echoes and develops certain ideas put forth in Pope John's 1961 encyclical *Mater et Magistra* (English translation, 1961), it is the first Vatican document to address issues essentially on an international order. In the introduction, Pope John states that the only way to establish peace on earth is to follow God's order. This divine order is outlined in the first four of five parts of the encyclical.

Part 1 is primarily a discussion of the rights of the human being, such as a "worthy standard of living"; religious, economic and political freedoms; and the right to immigrate and emigrate. This statement of human rights also reflects the political and social times of the mid-twentieth century, when civil rights were a major issue, especially concerning racial segregation and inequality in the southern part of the United States (incidentally, Martin Luther King, Jr.'s "Letter from the Birmingham Jail," in which King argues that active nonviolent resistance is the only true Christian response to injustice, was published in the same week as Pope John's encyclical). The human rights outlined in part 1 also bear resemblance to the United Nations' 1948 "Universal Declaration of Human Rights," and by aligning Catholic teachings with the goals of a worldwide government, the Vatican showed that its interest lay in not only the Catholic community but also the entire world.

Part 2 addresses the responsibility of figures of public authority. Public authority should be representative of the divine order, and therefore all laws should be made to uphold the moral order and to protect and promote the rights of humans outlined in part 1. These individual rights must be upheld and respected by public officials as it is the primary duty of public authority and government is to serve the greater good.

Part 3 is concerned with the relations between sovereign nations. Individual nations, like individual people, have rights and dignity, and no other nation should infringe on or violate the rights of another nation. The same values of liberty and justice that should govern the single nation should also govern the relations between nations on the global level, and therefore no nation should threaten the liberty or freedom of another nation. Pope John identifies the most significant threat to all liberty and freedom to be nuclear warfare, and a powerful section of part 3 calls for immediate and total disarmament. The global fear inspired by the magnitude of these weapons violates human security and makes global peace impossible.

Part 4 asserts that the "universal common good" takes precedence over the interests of individual nations and calls for a "worldwide public authority" similar to the United Nations, only stronger, to sufficiently protect the individual or nation being threatened by a nation that has violated the divine moral order.

Part 5, "Pastoral Exhortations," is a call for members of the Church community to take a more active part in the promotion of rights outlined in the first four parts. It acknowledges the recent scientific and technical advances made and entreats that advances in the teaching of ethics and religion be made so as to ensure that all further scientific and technical progression adheres to the ethics of the moral order. Pope John calls for cooperation between those involved in science, politics, and religion to actively achieve global peace. He also urges all members of the Catholic community, including the laity, to incorporate these peaceful values into their lives, to actively work toward the peaceful world order proscribed in the encyclical, and to assist the non-Catholic and non-Christian members of the global community in political and social orders so that they effectively move toward the goal of realizing world peace.

The encyclical was part of Pope John's efforts to revitalize the church and its teaching in the mid-twentieth century by calling the Second Vatican Council in 1962.

However, stricken with stomach cancer, Pope John died two months after issuing *Pacem in Terris*, before the completion of the Council.

Christian Themes

Pacem in Terris is an encyclical, and its argument for world peace invokes several Christian themes of nonviolence and pacifism. Proponents of pacifism find scriptural basis for nonviolence in Jesus' message of forgiveness, compassion, and in his unwillingness to resort to physical violence, even in instances of defense.

The section on disarmament, in which Pope John argues for the necessity of ceasing all warfare in the nuclear age, is an argument built on the concept of just-war teachings. Just-war teachings delineate the criteria in which war may be morally justified or necessary. The seven criteria are as follows: just cause, competent authority, last resort, comparative justice, proportionality, right intention, and probability of success. However, warfare as destructive and undiscriminating as nuclear warfare, which would kill thousands of civilians and leave monumental devastation in its wake and possibly precipitate an even more catastrophic nuclear response, cannot be justified under the seven tenets of just-war theory.

The Catholic Church also has a rich history of actively promoting and teaching social justice, and *Pacem in Terris* takes part in this history in its fervent advocacy of the special dignity and rights of the individual human being as a child of God. The ecumenical nature of the encyclical demonstrates that Jesus' message of peace, compassion, and love transcends national, political, religious, and social boundaries and exhorts unity and equality among all people. Pope John, throughout *Pacem in Terris*, builds on the teachings of both biblical Scripture and previous popes, particularly those of his immediate predecessor, Pius XII, establishing *Pacem in Terris* as firmly rooted in Catholic theology.

Sources for Further Study

Catholic Church, National Conference of Catholic Bishops. *The Challenge of Peace: God's Promise and Our Response*. Washington, D.C.: Office of Publishing Services, United States Catholic Conference, 1983. This pastoral letter from U.S. Catholic bishops declares that nuclear war can never be justified by just-war teachings. Echoing *Pacem in Terris*, it calls for immediate disarmament and cessation of nuclear war.

Curran, Charles E. *Catholic Social Teaching 1891-Present: A Historical, Theological, and Ethical Analysis*. Washington, D.C.: Georgetown University Press, 2002. Follows the development of methodological approaches to modern Catholic social teachings and ethics as rooted in theology.

Massaro, Thomas J. *Catholic Perspectives on War and Peace*. Lanham, Md.: Rowman and Littlefield, 2004. Provides an insightful overview of Catholic teachings on war and peace, including just-war theory and pacifism. It traces the developments of particular teachings and examines recent Christian approaches to peacemaking.

Roncalli, Angelo. *Journal of a Soul.* Translated by Dorothy M. White. New York: McGraw-Hill, 1964. Autobiography of Pope John XXIII, compiled from diaries he began at age fourteen. Offers insight into how doctrines of peace affected and shaped Pope John's spirituality.

Jessica H. Gray

PARADISE LOST

Author: John Milton (1608-1674)

First published: 1667 (ten books), 1674 (twelve books)

Edition used: Paradise Lost, in *Complete Poems and Major Prose,* edited by Merritt Y. Hughes. New York: Odyssey Press, 1957

Genre: Poetry

Subgenres: Epic; narrative poetry; theology

Core issues: The Fall; good vs. evil; obedience and disobedience; Puritans and Puritanism; salvation; sin and sinners; spiritual warfare

Milton's epic poem in twelve books depicts "man's first disobedience" in the larger Christian scheme of religious history, from Satan's rebellion to the Second Coming. It describes Satan's antagonism toward God after his defeat, God's decree of redemption, Adam and Eve's life prior to their fall, the War in Heaven, the creation of the universe, Satan's corruption of Adam and Eve, the regeneration of Adam and Eve, their expulsion from Eden, and the working out of God's plan of salvation.

> Principal characters
> God the Father
> God the Son
> *Satan*, the fallen angel Lucifer
> *Adam and Eve*, the first humans
> *Raphael*, an archangel
> *Michael*, an archangel

Overview

Considered the greatest epic poem in English literature, John Milton's monumental *Paradise Lost*, a twelve-book narrative poem written in iambic pentameter, tells the story

> Of Man's first disobedience and the fruit
> Of that forbidden tree whose mortal taste
> Brought death into the World, and all our woe,
> With loss of Eden. . . .

Like classical epics of Greco-Roman antiquity, *Paradise Lost* opens in the midst of things (in medias res), at a central point of the action. In books 1 and 2, Satan and his peers have been defeated in the War in Heaven and, now in Hell, turn their vengeful thoughts toward another world, Earth, about to be created for some "new Race called *Man*." As infernal deliverer of fallen angels, Satan, "author of evil," promises to lead them out of Hell, thereby solidifying his hold on the throne of Hell. "Better to reign in

Hell, than serve in Heaven," Satan asserts, and he hopes to make God repent his act of creation. In escaping from Hell, Satan allies himself with his offspring, both Sin, the gatekeeper of Hell, and Death, in opposition to God. After voyaging through Chaos, the "unbottom's infinite Abyss," he deceives the archangel Uriel in order to discover the location of Paradise and then practices deception in tempting Eve.

Meanwhile, in book 3, in Heaven, where all measures of time—past, present, and future—coexist, God the Father, knowing that Satan will deceive Man, announces that Man, despite continual ingratitude and faithlessness, will find salvation. The Father ordains the Son's incarnation and commands that he shall reign as universal king, "both God and Man."

In book 4, Satan invades the "blissful solitude" of Adam and Eve in Eden, a paradoxical realm of "Eternal Spring" without decay. Satan learns from Adam and Eve that of all Eden offers, they are "not to taste that only Tree/ Of Knowledge," and it is "death to taste that Tree." Satan decides to "excite thir minds/ With more desire to know," thinking "they taste and die: what likelier can ensue?" He wants to convince them that the Tree is not a symbol of obedience to God's will. He never imagines that his action will bring forth God's goodness by providing a means of redemption.

In book 5, God the Father sends Raphael to warn Adam and Eve of the danger and to impart the knowledge they need to resist Satan. Raphael explains the threat resulting from the War in Heaven, recounted in book 6. Moved by jealousy of the Son's elevation, Satan incites a third of the angels in Heaven to rebel against God, who, on the third day of the war, sends the Son to end the rebellion. Satan and his evil angels, now "to disobedience fall'n" and envying the "state" of Adam and Eve, plot to seduce them and all their progeny that they, too, may share in "Eternal misery." Raphael also explains the workings of physical nature in book 5 and, in book 7, the creation of the universe, stressing natural theology as the expression of God's mind through his works. Raphael imparts knowledge as a defense against evil. In book 8, Adam reveals the effect that Eve has upon him; Raphael tells him to love Eve but love God first by obedience.

In book 9, Satan, incarnated as a serpent, argues that he can improve on perfection. He convinces Eve, now separated from Adam, that God maliciously denies them fruit of the Tree of Knowledge to keep them "low and ignorant." Eve, in trusting appearances rather than the divine command not to eat of the Tree, reaches for the fruit: "she pluck'd, she eat" and "Earth felt the wound." Common belief at the time generally accepted nature's involvement in the Fall. Adam, "against his better knowledge," also eats "of that fair enticing Fruit." Earth again shudders at this completion of "the mortal Sin/ Original."

In book 10, God the Son, "mild Judge and Intercessor," pronounces the Genesis "curse" upon Adam and Eve as well as the serpent, the curse upon the serpent involving a hint of its eventual defeat: "Her seed shall bruise thy head, thou bruise his heel." God explains that change and decay will now occur in everything, in all possible forms with all possible consequences. Eve, moved by God's grace, initiates Adam's as well as her own regeneration. She accepts responsibility for their sin and prompts

Adam to remember the hint of victory to come.

God the Father, in book 11, directs Michael to banish Adam and Eve from Paradise, now subject to death, "a long day's dying," and to give them hope in "what shall come in future days." In books 11 and 12, Michael outlines the history of salvation up to and including Redemption and return of the Savior, his account grimly realistic. Adam and Eve, "the World . . . all before them," take their "solitary way" out of Eden, with an obtainable "paradise within thee, happier far."

Christian Themes

In *Paradise Lost*, Milton's Puritanism and his broad Christian humanism transform all aspects of the epic poem. His blindness (since at least 1651) presented no impediment to his achievement. The style, technique, and features of the epic were derived from Homer's *Iliad* (c. 750 B.C.E.; English translation, 1611), Homer's *Odyssey* (c. 725 B.C.E.; English translation, 1614), and Vergil's *Aeneid* (c. 29-19 B.C.E.; English translation, 1553). Milton, however, asserts the uniqueness and superiority of his epic because of its Christian truth rather than pagan myth. In books 1, 3, 7, and 9, the blind Milton indicates that, if he receives the inspiration he seeks and if he can attain an "answerable style," he will surpass the ancient epics in importance of subject and in majesty of language. He invokes God's spirit that he may glorify him by showing his power and asks for aid in the task to "assert Eternal Providence/ And justify the ways of God to men." He combines his inspiration with vast sacred and secular learning. *Paradise Lost* reconciles the justice of God's providential design with human freedom and responsibility, defending it with respect to the existence of evil, a form of literature known as theodic.

Milton's defense of God's ways, as far as they fall within the scope of human comprehension, is centered in book 3, where God the Father explains why the Fall occurs and how it shapes all human history. He announces that justice must be exacted for sin; that though deceived by Satan, man has free will, the power not to sin; and that man shall find mercy. God the Son offers himself as payment for sin, that God's authority and mercy be upheld; otherwise evil would go unpunished and justice be betrayed. The dialogue between the Father and the Son presents salvation as a gift of God, eternal life through the Son, who fulfills God's law "by obedience and by love." The dialogue closely follows Paul's Epistles to the Romans and the Hebrews; Pauline theology was central to Milton's Puritanism. Milton rejects the Calvinistic view that God created each individual for salvation or damnation. He stresses man's freedom to choose and that whatever evil does, God will make good of it.

In addition, Milton's presentation of the Son redefines the epic hero as one who overcomes evil with good, patiently suffering in the hope that God's larger plan is fulfilled. In Milton's seventeenth century epic, Christian values of love, faith, obedience, and humility superseded the heroic codes of the ancient Greek and Roman epics. In book 12, Adam and Eve and their children must follow in the "Redeemer" to secure salvation. They will thus subvert "worldly strong, and worldly wise" by "things deem weak" and by "small" accomplish "great things." Also, after the death of the Apostles, the Holy Spirit, directly received, will guide and support believers in the wisdom and truth of salvation, since the teachings of the Gospel become corrupted. In book 1, Milton writes that the Spirit prefers "before all Temples th' upright heart and pure." Milton's Puritanism remained strongly anti-institutional, as expressed in *De doctrina Christiana libri duo Posthumi* (wr. c. 1658-1660, pb. 1825; a treatise on Christian doctrine).

Sources for Further Study

Danielson, Dennis, ed. *The Cambridge Companion to Milton.* 1989. 2d ed. Cambridge, England: Cambridge University Press, 1999. Essays by scholars and critics, with a useful bibliography.

Kelley, Maurice. *This Great Argument: A Study of Milton's "De Doctrina Christiana" as a Gloss upon "Paradise Lost."* Princeton, N.J.: Princeton University Press, 1941. According to reviewer A. S. P. Woodhouse, "For the student of the history of thought the volume is a clear and useful compendium of Milton's opinions on a large range of theological topics. . . . Kelley demonstrates in detail . . . that many of [*Christian Doctrine*'s] doctrines are reflected in *Paradise Lost.*"

Lewalski, Barbara. *The Life of John Milton: A Critical Biography.* Rev. ed. Oxford, England: Blackwell, 2002. Focuses on Milton's religious, political, and literary development.

Miller, Timothy C. *The Critical Response to John Milton's Paradise Lost.* Westport, Conn.: Greenwood, 1997. A documentary history of reviews and articles, with an introductory account.

Timothy C. Miller

PARADISE REGAINED

Author: John Milton (1608-1674)
First published: 1671
Edition used: Paradise Regained, in *Complete Poems and Selected Prose,* edited by
   Merritt Y. Hughes. New York: Macmillan, 1985
Genre: Poetry
Subgenres: Biblical fiction; epic; narrative poetry
Core issues: Good vs. evil; Gospels; Jesus Christ; salvation; self-control; self-
   knowledge; spiritual warfare

Milton's epic sequel to Paradise Lost *presents Satan tempting Jesus in the wilderness.
Jesus, the second Adam, overcomes Original Sin, to which Adam fell prey in the previous epic, to redeem humankind and regain paradise. Jesus' resistance to temptation
allows him to defeat Satan and reveals to readers Jesus' role as the Son of God. Milton, who was both a Puritan and a Christian humanist, shifts the epic's generic concerns from martial heroism to a Messianic heroism, thus elevating constancy and
Christian faith in the face of temptation as the greatest of heroic acts.*

> *Principal characters*
> *God the Father*
> *Jesus Christ,* Son of God, the protagonist
> *Satan,* the fallen angel Lucifer, the antagonist
> *Mary,* Jesus' mother
> *John the Baptist,* Jesus' cousin
> *Belial,* Satan's adviser
> *Simon* and
> *Andrew,* Jesus' followers

Overview

Paradise Regained is poet John Milton's sequel to his great epic poem *Paradise
Lost* (1667, 1674), in which he began his history of sin and redemption by telling the
story of the fallen angel Lucifer (Satan) and the loss of innocence through Adam and
Eve's original sin and their expulsion from the Garden of Eden. Whereas *Paradise
Lost* consisted of ten books (twelve in its 1674 revised version) of blank verse, *Para-
dise Regained* consists of only four. In the poem's induction, Milton announces that
he will complete the history of sin and redemption begun with *Paradise Lost.* Thus,
Paradise Regained retells Luke's account of Jesus' temptation in the desert by Satan.

   Milton begins his story with Jesus' baptism by John the Baptist. At this event, a
voice from Heaven announces that Jesus is the Son of God, a term whose meaning is
crucial to the story as Jesus grows in knowledge of himself and his role as the Messiah. Jesus, returning to his mother Mary's house, hears from Mary the story of his mi-

raculous birth, announced by the angel Gabriel. Jesus then wanders in the desert for forty days and nights as he ponders how to begin his mission.

Meanwhile, Satan has observed Christ's baptism and heard the announcement that Jesus is the Son of God, though he is unsure of what the term "Son of God" means. Calling a council of devils, Satan resolves to corrupt Jesus as he did Adam. God the Father views all these characters from Heaven and tells the angel Gabriel that Jesus' time in the desert will be his trial period, which he will pass just as Job did. In the wilderness, Satan, disguised as an old man, confronts Jesus. Posing as Jesus' friend and adviser, Satan tempts Jesus (who now feels the pangs of hunger after his forty days in the wilderness) by telling him to turn the stones into food. Jesus, however, sees through Satan's disguise and says that man lives by God's Word, not by bread. During Jesus' absence, Andrew and Simon, Jesus' followers, search for him and meditate on his significance, while Mary keeps her faith in God's promise.

Satan calls another devils' council to debate how to destroy Jesus. The fallen angel Belial advocates tempting Jesus with women, but Satan disdainfully cites the examples of great men who resisted lust. After his council, Satan returns to Jesus and spreads before him a proper offering to the Son of God, a banquet in the wilderness—all the world's fine foods with beautiful women for attendants. Jesus sees through Satan, realizing that the real temptation here is to take food as a gift from Satan; he rejects Satan's offer, saying that he could command a greater feast if he wanted. Next, Satan offers Jesus wealth, without which (Satan indicates) the Son of God can never rule a great kingdom. Jesus counters that true heroism, like that of Socrates and Job, lies in self-control, not in controlling others.

Next Satan takes Jesus to a mountaintop to view the world's empires. Satan reminds the Savior that he is the heir to King David's throne and offers to help him regain that throne. First Satan shows Jesus the Parthian Empire, Rome's great eastern rival, brave and warlike. Satan promises to deliver Parthia to Jesus, but Jesus rejects warfare. Then Satan shows Jesus the city of Rome, with its glories and its corruption, implying that Jesus, as David's heir, can overthrow the degenerate Tiberius, who has already abandoned Rome for the island of Capri, and free both the Romans and the Jews from Tiberius's oppression. Jesus rejects Satan's arguments: Parthian valor and Roman glory are based on killing and slavery. The Messiah seeks instead the glory that comes from living a life of virtue. He also unsettles Satan by reminding him that the oppression of Rome's or Parthia's subjects was, after all, Satan's handiwork.

Satan, realizing Jesus' disdain for political power, directs his attention to Athens and the prospect of intellectual glory, as represented by Greek poetry, philosophy, law, and oratory. Once again Jesus remains firm, seeing no value in learning and eloquence purchased at the cost of faith. Showing an awareness of classical culture that Satan had not expected, the Savior distinguishes between the cleverness of the Greeks and true wisdom, which combines knowledge with judgment and moral commitment. Whatever is good in Greek learning, Jesus asserts, is already found in the scriptures; moreover, the Greeks are intellectually limited because, as pagans, they do not know the one true God.

A desperate Satan, still believing that the title "Son of God" has no special meaning, makes his final temptation. After trying unsuccessfully to weaken Jesus with a night of storms and nightmares, Satan flies Jesus to the pinnacle of the temple at Jerusalem and dares him to stand or fall, saying that angels will lift him up. Jesus replies, "Tempt not the Lord thy God." With this, Jesus reveals his true nature as the Son of God. Satan falls into defeat. Angels then fly Jesus to a valley, where they put forth a feast for him. In a conclusion capturing both Jesus' humility and his grandeur, the angels sing hymns of praise to Jesus, after which he quietly returns to his mother's house.

Christian Themes

The seventeenth century English poet John Milton wrote two great epic poems: *Paradise Lost*, in which he depicted Adam's fall into Original Sin, and its sequel, *Paradise Regained*, which celebrates humankind's redemption through Jesus, often called the second Adam. Milton was both a Puritan, whose stern Christianity demanded a radical break with worldly values, and a Christian humanist, eager to place ancient Greek and Roman culture in the service of Christianity. While these two positions could be in tension, Milton reconciled them by retelling the Gospel narrative as a classical epic on a par with Homer's *Iliad* (c. 750 B.C.E.; English translation, 1611) and Vergil's *Aeneid* (c. 29-19 B.C.E.; English translation, 1553). However, where classical epics portrayed great heroes defeating enemies in physical combat, Milton makes Jesus a hero like Job in the Old Testament: one who suffers but maintains his faith in God. Through the analogy between the heroes of classical, pagan epics and the Jesus of his Christian epic, Milton created a new epic hero: one whose domain was elevated, as it deserved to be, over all epic heroes of all time.

Jesus' example as an epic hero thus counterpoints and trumps those of his mythic predecessors. At the same time, his tribulations humanize him and his response to Satan's temptations exemplify the potential in all human beings to choose a Christ-like way of behaving in a world full of temptation. Milton brilliantly interweaves his theme of conflict and struggle with that of identity. Thus *Paradise Regained* reveals Jesus as the Son of God through the means of rejected temptations. For example, Jesus forgoes physical combat in favor of spiritual warfare, eloquence in favor of self-knowledge, and control of others in favor of self-control. Each of Satan's temptations tries to lure Jesus into choosing to become a false Messiah.

Milton's unorthodox attitude toward the Trinity influenced his portrayal of Christ in both *Paradise Lost* and *Paradise Regained*: Milton believed that the Son of God was not coeternal with God the Father. Instead, he believed that both Jesus as the Son of God and the Holy Spirit were parts of God but not the essence of God. Nevertheless, just as light and its source cannot be separated, so God and the Son of God were, in that sense, inseparable. This belief allowed Milton to present a more simply human Jesus, one who had to arrive at self-knowledge through the trials depicted in the poem.

Milton reveals Satan's characteristic mixture of cunning and moral limitation through his inability to see the Messiah in terms other than wealth, power, or fame. Jesus, however, experiences an evolution in his self-understanding: When Jesus overcomes his first temptation, he sees himself as a man who lives by God's word; by the last temptation, he identifies himself with God. The temptations serve to show readers the nature of the true Messiah by revealing what he is not, as Jesus rejects the false concepts of the Messiah to which Satan appeals. Ironically Satan achieves only what God intended; by trying to destroy the Savior, Satan simply facilitates Jesus' process of manifesting his role as the Son of God.

Sources for Further Study

Lewalski, Barbara K. *The Life of John Milton: A Critical Biography*. Oxford, England: Blackwell, 2000. A full and detailed biography of Milton by a scholar who has written on *Paradise Regained*.

_____. *Milton's Brief Epic*. Providence, R.I.: Brown University Press, 1966. A magisterial treatment of the religious background of *Paradise Regained*, with particular attention to the Book of Job and its historical interpretation.

Mayer, Joseph G. *Between Two Pillars: The Hero's Plight in "Samson Agonistes" and "Paradise Regained."* Lanham, Md.: University Press of America, 2004. A study of *Paradise Regained* and *Samson Agonistes* (1671) as poems about temptation and the development of the heroes.

Pope, Elizabeth Anne. *Paradise Regained: The Tradition and the Poem*. New York: Russell and Russell, 1962. A helpful examination of the poem through the religious commentaries, legends, and sermons familiar to Milton and his original readers.

Stein, Arnold. *Heroic Knowledge: An Interpretation of "Paradise Regained" and "Samson Agonistes."* Minneapolis: University of Minnesota Press, 1957. An intelligent, free-ranging series of essays on Milton's major late works as dramatic poems and the problems they present.

Wittreich, Joseph Anthony. *Calm of Mind*. Cleveland, Ohio: Case Western Reserve University Press, 1971. A collection of valuable critical studies on *Paradise Regained* and *Samson Agonistes*, including issues in their interpretation.

Anthony Bernardo

PASSING BY SAMARIA

Author: Sharon Ewell Foster (1956-   )
First published: Sisters, Oreg.: Alabaster Books, 2000
Genre: Novel
Subgenres: Evangelical fiction; romance
Core issues: African Americans; alienation from God; connectedness; forgiveness; innocence; prayer; racism

Hatred, violence, and murder can poison the lives they touch in multiple ways. Shaken by the lynching of her childhood friend, cheerful Alena lets her pain and outrage turn into sullen hatred. Sent to her aunt's mission in Chicago for her own safety, she lashes out at everyone she meets in her new life there, pushing away James, who is unmistakably fond of her. After her bitter words nearly goad another good man to his death, prayer and an imminent race riot open her heart to the need to forgive even those who do evil.

Principal characters
  Alena Waterbridge, a naïve young woman
  Amos, Alena's father, a farmer
  Evelyn, Alena's mother and Amos's wife
  Patrice, Alena's aunt, who runs a mission house in Chicago
  James Pittman, a former Army major, editor and owner of a
    Chicago newspaper
  Jonathan, James's assistant
  Dinah, Jonathan's sister
  Pearl, a porter and man-about-town
  Deac, Pearl's older colleague
  Eric Bates, a Mississippi sheriff
  Miranda Bates, the sheriff's wife

Overview

Even though they are poor black farmers in the Mississippi Delta, Alena Waterbridge's parents have managed to give her a happy, sheltered upbringing. Surrounded by love and nature's bounty, at eighteen she had never suspected that her life might have to change. When she finds her childhood friend J. C.'s body in the woods near her home, the victim of a brutal lynching, her trauma is unbearable. Ignorant of the ugly realities of racism of the era, she cannot understand why the grown-ups around her fail to protest. At J. C.'s funeral, she starts an angry tirade. Realizing how dangerous this is and unable to keep her quiet, her parents decide to send her far away, to Chicago, where her Aunt Patrice lives.

Driving twenty hours in a horse-drawn cart to reach the station, Amos and Evelyn take her to catch a Chicago-bound train. Alena, furious at having her life plans interrupted this way, distances herself from them emotionally before they part. During the long ride north, her emotions harden further. She determines not to let herself care about anyone else. Pearl, a porter, always on the lookout for young innocents to seduce, invites her into the porters' car for a meal. ("Colored" passengers cannot eat in the dining car.) Deac, watching Pearl's machinations, cautions him against toying with Alena. Pearl shrugs off the warnings and tells Alena that he will meet her again later, in Chicago.

Aunt Patrice is a bubbly but practical woman who sees through Alena's petulance from the beginning but believes that time and love will heal her. She chatters enthusiastically about people and projects waiting for Alena in the neighborhood, ignoring the girl's lack of response. Chicago's crowds and sights do impress Alena, and deep inside, she realizes that she is not equipped to handle the world on her own terms. She helps with mission projects, but reluctantly, keeping up her facade of icy disdain.

The south State Street neighborhood where she and Aunt Patrice live bustles with black-owned stores and services and people trying to build a better life. James Pittman, just back from service in the Army, is working to turn his news sheet into a crusading newspaper for the black community. Dinah, a volunteer at the mission, teams with Alena to deliver food baskets to the many poor families surrounding them. Even while she works with them, Alena resents James's assistant Jonathan and Jonathan's sister Dinah for being white. On the other hand, James, to whom she feels subconsciously attracted, is too good as a possible boyfriend. She refuses the opportunity to write for his paper and persuades herself that he is pining for her.

Meanwhile, Pearl finds Alena and invites her to run away with him to a more exciting life. The next day, Alena taunts Jonathan so cruelly that he insists that he and James start right away on their hazardous research into housing discrimination. James and Jonathan are swept into a riot, and Jonathan is dragged into the lake. Aunt Patrice, having heard Alena scream at Jonathan, finally loses her patience. She tells Alena that everyone has indulged her in her misery long enough and that she is killing people with her mouth no less than the brutal white sheriff back in Mississippi, Eric Bates, kills them with his hands. Alena, stricken, still clinging to her plan to meet Pearl, hides in a storeroom and goes through a dark night of the soul. She tries to pray, but her prayers do not help. Finally, she picks up her suitcases and stands, waiting for Pearl, in the street outside the mission. To her surprise, fire is raging in the neighborhood. Crowds of panicked people run past. Alena looks up to see James, grimy and desperate, trying to save his press from the flames. Almost involuntarily, she steps toward him, and he comes the rest of the way to her. She drops her suitcases.

In the aftermath, calm returns to Chicago as National Guard troops, aided by James and other veterans, are called in to help. Pearl never reaches Alena. Almost trampled by rioters, he is found injured by Deac, who had foreseen a bad end to Pearl's plans. Jonathan, believed to be dead, reappears, and the South Side neighborhood begins to rebuild. James and Alena, their relationship redeemed by Alena's change of heart, start planning their wedding. Alena, now eager to build a life in Chicago, plans a trip home to Mississippi to reconcile with her parents.

The visit goes well until it is time for Alena to leave. The racist Sheriff Bates—who has read about, and been infuriated by, the Illinois authorities' evenhanded response to the race riots—decides he cannot allow any such influences in "his" county. Knowing Alena has come home, he sets out to ambush her in her own yard. Chance or divine mercy intervenes: Just as he lunges toward Alena in the dark, Alena's dog Cottonball trips him, so that he falls and is impaled on his own weapon. Alena, horrified to realize her narrow escape, nevertheless goes to his funeral to extend sympathy and forgiveness to Bates's widow Miranda.

Christian Themes

Alena's story is an exploration of the power of forgiveness. Because Alena holds onto her anger for so long, building it into "a high place in her heart," what happens when she lets it go is extraordinary. Few people can forgive their would-be murderer, let alone offer condolences to his widow or inspire a whole church congregation to a mission of reconciliation at his funeral. It takes faith and courage to confront oppressors gently, but most of all it takes a conviction of God's love.

Despite her dramatic reversal of attitude, such forgiveness does not descend on Alena immediately. First she must give her hatred and resentment up to God. It is notable that when she first tries to do so, huddled in the storeroom, she is not sure if she has reached God. However, having unloaded her confusion into God's hands, she is subtly changed, so that when the moment comes when her life's direction hangs in the balance, she makes the right decision. Once she no longer "has to hate," she can connect with those near her in genuine friendship and love. She can help build bonds of community in her Chicago neighborhood. Finally, she can reach across the boundaries to the "Samaria" of the book's title—those strangers who may even seem to hate her. Hence the ideal of connectedness complements the primary theme of forgiveness. Without the latter, fragile and precious relationships with others cannot endure.

Also notable is the book's focus on prayer. Not only is prayer the path by which Alena connects with God; it is a resource and discipline by which one can deal with problems that otherwise appear hopeless. Deac prays for Pearl, in the hope that the younger man be saved from his downward spiral of bad behavior. Miranda Bates and her pastor pray all night, after she fails to dissuade her husband from his plan to murder Alena. As in life, prayers are not always answered in the way the requestor expects. In *Passing by Samaria*, at least, there is no doubt that prayer contributes to God's working his will in mysterious ways.

Sources for Further Study

Enright, Robert, and Joanna North. *Exploring Forgiveness*. Madison: University of Wisconsin Press, 1998. Twelve essays examine personal and social aspects of forgiveness from a wide range of faith perspectives. Foreword by Desmond Tutu; extensive bibliography.

Foster, Sharon Ewell. *Ain't No River*. Sisters, Oreg.: Multnomah, 2001. Foster's second book takes a contemporary D.C. woman home to North Carolina, where reconciliation with God helps her put her life together again.

Grossman, James R. "African-American Migration to Chicago." In *Ethnic Chicago: A Multicultural Portrait*, edited by Melvin G. Holli and Peter d'A. Jones. Grand Rapids, Mich.: Wm. B. Eerdmans, 1995. Survey of the continuing migration from the South and its creative results, providing useful context for *Passing by Samaria*.

Hunt, Sharita. "God's Reading Rainbow." *Black Issues Book Review* 3, no. 3 (May/June, 2001): 50-51. Reviews several Christian books for African Americans, including *Passing by Samaria*.

Stanley, Kathryn V. "The Ministry of Fiction." *Black Issues Book Review* 7, no. 1 (January/February, 2005): 52-53. A profile of Foster that includes a mention of *Passing by Samaria* as well as other work.

Emily Alward

PAUL
A Novel

Author: Walter Wangerin, Jr. (1944-   )
First published: Grand Rapids, Mich.: Zondervan, 2000
Genre: Novel
Subgenres: Biblical fiction; historical fiction (first century)
Core issues: The cross; faith; freedom and free will; grace; Jesus Christ; salvation

Ever since Luke wrote the Acts of the Apostles, authors have tried to amplify his account of Christianity's greatest figure, second only to Jesus. Wangerin portrays Paul as the missionary to the Gentiles, driven by an appearance of Jesus on the Damascus road, traveling the northern Mediterranean, preaching, establishing congregations, writing letters, and troubleshooting against law-oriented and glory-oriented opponents who sought to undercut his grace-centered message of inclusion.

Principal characters
  Paul, a first century missionary
  Barnabas, an early missionary partner
  James, leader of the Jerusalem church and an opponent of Paul's
    theology
  Timothy, a young protégé and assistant
  Titus, the first gentile convert
  Aquila, a tent maker from Corinth
  Prisca, Aquila's wife
  Seneca, a contemporary Roman philosopher

Overview

The task of writing an account of Paul carries with it a number of challenges. The primary biblical sources, Paul's own letters and Luke's Acts of the Apostles, do not always agree on important details. Even with Paul's own letters, scholars debate which are authentic and which were written by subsequent generations. Likewise, there is the question of what information to include from second and third century "apocryphal" works. Then there is always the question of what liberties to take with the gaps in Paul's life and which details to add from what modern historians, archaeologists, and social scientists have learned about the first century Greco-Roman world.

Walter Wangerin, Jr., addresses some of these issues by writing a fictional account of Paul's life with multiple storytellers. The main perspectives come from Timothy and Prisca, who give their impressions in thirty-two of the book's ninety-nine chapters. Others, such as James and Barnabas with nine chapters each and Titus with four chapters, play a less prominent role because they are limited to certain periods in

Paul's life. Rhoda gives voice to only one short chapter as a character borrowed from Peter's story to depict Paul's impact on Jerusalem's younger generation. The character Jude appears in only six early chapters to fill out the scanty details about Paul's Damascus road experience. Among these imaginary reflections by biblical characters, Wangerin intersperses twelve chapters by Luke, simply recounting, word for word, the story of Acts. Similarly, five chapters convey the very words of Paul's letters to the Thessalonians, Galatians, and Corinthians (with the latter divided into shorter fragments according current scholarly views).

Taking a cue from second century apocryphal letters, Wangerin includes eight carefully positioned chapters that describe key movements in the life of the contemporary Stoic philosopher and playwright Lucius Annaeus Seneca (Seneca the Younger). While never mentioned in the biblical text, Seneca provides an appropriate comparison and contrast to the character and career of Paul; both were martyred under Roman emperor Nero in the mid-60's.

Generally, the novel follows the outline of the Book of Acts, with chapters organized in five geographical sections: Damascus (chapters 2-16), Antioch (chapters 17-33), Corinth (chapters 34-58), Ephesus (chapters 59-78), and Jerusalem (chapters 79-95). With the prologue (chapter 1) set in Corinth, it is clear that Wangerin's focus is on the missionary Paul. In the epilogue, four chapters sum up Paul's later years in Rome.

As in Acts, the story begins in Jerusalem with Paul's involvement in the trial and death of Stephen. "I did like Stephen." With those words James, the leader of the Jerusalem church, is introduced as Paul's eventual antagonist, leading the confrontation of a law-oriented Christianity with the freedom-thinking Hellenists. Paul journeys to Damascus, where God changes his life forever. It is through the eyes of the aged Jude, however, that this event is viewed. Jude provides a physical description of Paul similar to the apocryphal Acts of Paul: bald with one continuous eyebrow, small in stature, energetic, a fast walker with bowed legs, and an equally fast talker. The question is, What did God's intervention mean? For Paul's companions, and also for Jude, it is God's judgment. For Paul, however, it is God's call to become apostle to the Gentiles.

The story skips quickly to Antioch, where Paul works in a church, presented at its idyllic best. The lovable Barnabas cannot get enough of delicious pork; Titus, moved by the spirit, sings and dances; and the Christians gather weekly to hear Simeon of Cyrene recount the story of the cross. A prophetic message by Simeon's wife sends Barnabas and Paul out as missionaries. Paul's effectiveness is evidenced by his preaching and healing at Lystra. So is the danger, as he is stoned and left by the roadside for dead. Paul, however, is a determined fellow. A young widow offers a special request: that Paul teach her son Hebrew and his Jewish heritage. Thus Timothy follows, and Paul's traveling seminary begins. Paul is then summoned to Jerusalem to discuss the gentile mission. The noncompromising side of Paul leads to fractured relationships, both in Jerusalem and in Antioch, but Paul's position prevails. The Gentiles are saved by faith; circumcision will not be required.

Though feeling defeated in the East, Paul is met in Corinth with a spiritually uplifting moment on Acro-Corinth. Prisca, wife of the Corinthian tent maker Aquila, is drawn to Paul's spoken message, and she and Aquila host the now aging and scarred preacher in their workshop-home. The church grows and thrives; even Erastus, the manager of public markets, joins the throng. Still, growth also brings divisions and countermessages oriented to glory or to law. In Corinth, Phoebe's intervention rescues Paul in court. Later, in Ephesus, Prisca risks her life to free Paul from prison. Paul's long correspondence with the Corinthians works to restore unity.

Paul returns to Jerusalem, where he presents the personally gathered collection to assist a group of Nazarites to keep their vow. This leads to misunderstanding, arrest, and imprisonment while Paul awaits his eventual transfer to Rome. Just as in Luke's story, Paul's arrival and preaching in Rome offer a fitting climax.

Christian Themes

For Wangerin, Paul is the embodiment of the living voice of the Gospel. So it is that the first word out of Prisca's mouth in the prologue is "There was a Voice in the morning. There came a Voice through the wet air, like a long flag lifted on the wind. . . ." Just as most Christians' encounter with Paul is through an oral reading of his letters each Sunday, so they are linked with Prisca, who hears for the first time the voice of Paul preaching in Corinth's busy market. The words are the same: "I would not have you worry about those fallen asleep," copied carefully by Timothy for the letter to Thessalonica while Paul preached on that spring day in 50 C.E.

Wangerin is particularly concerned with how the voice of Paul connects with human need. Prisca is a hurting individual, newly arrived in Corinth after having been driven away from her family and her Roman home, alienated from religious conflict under Claudius, and just learning of her mother's sudden death. Paul's message speaks directly to her heart, giving her hope and purpose. Certainly others of Prisca's world were in a similar predicament. The aged Jude of Damascus, for example, who is haunted by loneliness after the death of his wife and threatened by anything new, retreated to his security of tradition. Likewise Seneca, facing illness in Egypt, the death of an uncle, shipwreck, and exile, turns to Stoicism and eventual suicide.

Something about Paul's message resonates with Prisca. Christ's message "Behold I make all things new!" comes to life through Paul's voice, providing the excitement of life in the spirit as well as the risk of carrying the wounds of Christ in one's body. Wangerin's Paul always proclaims anew the message of life in the risen Jesus, articulates faith in relationship to the crucified Christ, and announces the freeing power of the spirit and the unifying principle of love that formulated the Christianity of Prisca's day and continues to speak today.

Sources for Further Study

Bornkamm, Günther. *Paul*. Minneapolis, Minn.: Fortress, 1995. The previous generation's best-known fictional biography of Paul, originally written in German.
Dunn, James. *Theology of Paul the Apostle*. Grand Rapids, Mich.: Wm. B. Eerdmans, 2006. Based primarily on Paul's letter to the Romans, Dunn reconstructs his theol-

ogy and thoughts on God, humankind, sin, Christology, salvation, the Church, and the Christian life.

Murphy-O'Connor, Jerome. *Paul: A Critical Life*. New York: Oxford University Press, 1996. An account of Paul's life based primarily on information gathered from the letters themselves rather than from the Acts of the Apostles. Includes contextual information from numerous first century sources.

Roetzel, Calvin J. *The Letters of Paul: Conversations in Context*. Louisville, Ky.: Westminster John Knox Press, 1998. Treats each letter's possible dating, situation, and literary structure. Includes arguments for dividing later letters from authentic letters of Paul.

Stendahl, Krister. *Paul Among Jews and Gentiles*. Minneapolis, Minn.: Fortress, 1977. A series of essays based on careful word study that shows Paul's primary goal, to incorporate Gentiles into the family of God.

Wright, N. T. *Paul in Fresh Perspective*. Minneapolis, Minn.: Fortress, 2006. Part 1 focuses on themes of creation and covenant, Messiah and apocalyptic, Gospel and empire. Part 2 deals with structures such as rethinking God, reworking God's people, and reimagining God's future.

Fred Strickert

PEARL

Author: Mary Gordon (1949-   )
First published: New York: Pantheon Books, 2005
Genre: Novel
Subgenre: Literary fiction
Core issues: Fasting; forgiveness; guilt; love; purity; sacrifice

American activist Maria Meyers, who has spent most of her adult life rebelling against Catholicism and authority, learns that her daughter Pearl, a university student in Dublin, is publicly starving herself in atonement for the death of a friend. Gordon's study of an attempted suicide explores the troubled relationship between love and possession, guilt and sacrifice, acceptance and forgiveness, exacerbated by the volatile political situation in Northern Ireland.

> *Principal characters*
> *Maria Meyers*, a former political activist and a single mother
> *Pearl Meyers*, Maria's twenty-year-old daughter
> *Joseph Kasperman*, Maria's lifelong friend and Pearl's surrogate father
> *Mick Winthrop*, an American performance artist
> *Stevie Donegan*, Mick's illegitimate son
> *Breeda Donegan*, Stevie's Irish mother

Overview

In a 2005 interview, Mary Gordon called herself "a practicing Catholic. . . . The church is in my blood and my bones." Nevertheless, she refuses to be identified as a "Catholic writer," a term she considers marginalizing; she prefers to work with ideas rather than doctrine. Her sixth novel, *Pearl*, begins in New York City on Christmas, 1998, when childhood friends Joseph Kasperman and Maria Meyers have reached their fifties.

Joseph, a quiet, responsible man who hesitates to say what he really thinks, is Maria's financial guardian and a surrogate father to her daughter Pearl. Maria, who was an activist and protester during the Vietnam War years, inevitably rebelled against her conservative father and his Catholic faith, abandoning both. Later she had a brief affair with a Cambodian doctor who had managed to flee the brutal Pol Pot regime for the United States. After he returned to Cambodia with critically needed medical supplies, he vanished, unaware that she was pregnant with Pearl. Having chafed under her father's strict surveillance, Maria refused to bring up her beloved daughter in any religion. She has always protected Pearl from life and the Catholic Church.

On Christmas, Maria waits impatiently for Pearl's holiday phone call. Instead she receives an emergency message from the State Department informing her that her daughter, a linguistics student in Dublin, has just chained herself to a flagpole at the American embassy. For six weeks Pearl has been fasting and now refuses water as well. Horrified, Maria quickly boards a plane for Ireland.

Religion and politics lie at the heart of a centuries-old conflict that culminates at this time between the six counties of Northern Ireland, mostly Protestant and loyal to Britain, and the fiercely Catholic Irish of the south. The year before, when Pearl arrived in Dublin, she learned of the rebel Bobby Sands, the Irish Republican Army martyr who had starved to death protesting the British rule of Northern Ireland. His story fascinated her, particularly "his faith in the power of suffering." Pearl informally joined a splinter group of revolutionaries calling themselves the Real IRA. Among them was an older American, Mick Winthrop, who still spent most of his time with his wife and children in the United States. Some years ago, Mick had admired Breeda Donegan, the sister of another jailed rebel, and had donated money to the revolutionary cause in exchange for her buying his membership in his idol's family and fathering an illegitimate son, Stevie Donegan. Pearl befriended Stevie, teaching the dyslexic youth how to read and to fold the origami birds that still hang in his flat.

On Good Friday, 1998, Irish voters accepted a proposed peace treaty between the Catholic IRA and the Protestant Unionists. Breeda, an innocent just beginning to think for herself, quietly supported the agreement, as did Pearl. However, the Real IRA did not, cruelly bombing the marketplace of Omagh in protest; nearly thirty were killed and hundreds wounded. Gentle Pearl was appalled. After Mick and the others decided to play a crude joke to shift blame to the police, Stevie was unluckily involved, caught, and humiliated. Because Pearl lost her temper and insulted Stevie, she blamed herself when he subsequently died in an accident, and Breeda, his mother, cursed her bitterly.

At present, chained to the flagpole in front of the American embassy, Pearl is neither anorectic nor suicidal, but like Bobby Sands, by self-starvation she is publicly witnessing Stevie's death and protesting the violence. She recognizes that she too is tainted with "the human will to harm." She wants to die; she has gained a purpose. Believing her death will be more meaningful than her life, she has planned it for Christmas to create maximum effect. Even as an ambulance crew attempts to hydrate her, she is convinced that she is dying.

Pearl is calm, sure, and euphoric from fasting—all of which disappears once she is freed from the flagpole and fed intravenously. The book then follows the struggle to keep her alive. Even as she manages to pull out her feeding tube in the hospital, she experiences fear, shame, and finally hunger as she begins to heal.

Meanwhile, Maria is temporarily barred from seeing her daughter. In frustration she recalls her father, with whom she refused all contact even in his final illness, and begins to comprehend the nature of his love. No longer sure of herself, Maria is forced to recognize that she has no control over this situation. Always she has tried to protect her daughter with love, but it has not been enough. Joseph, who has joined them, adores Pearl and desperately wants to save her but does not know how. He attempts to take control in order to protect her, but Pearl is really the one who gains control; she must be the one to decide whether she will live.

Christian Themes

Religion underlies nearly all of Gordon's writing, creating a moral and ethical structure against which her characters react. *Pearl* is laden with obvious biblical allusions to the Holy Family, many of them used ironically. Maria is the flawed single mother of a divine victim—a sacrificial Child so pure she seems almost to glow, suggesting Saint Matthew's "pearl of great price" (13:46). Pearl herself has an absent father, a "ghost" who vanished almost immediately after her conception, and a loving foster father who cares for her welfare. (Joseph also identifies himself with Judas.) This family model is distorted further by Mick (the absent father), Breeda, and the boy Stevie (who perhaps evokes Saint Stephen, the first Christian martyr). The will to harm that Pearl identifies in herself may likewise correspond to the stain of Original Sin.

Gordon likes to deal with concepts; she has said, "I seem always to be writing about a sense of failure in achieving an ideal." One such ideal is purity, which can be easily perverted, a powerful double-edged sword that may protect or maim. Maria's concept of purity is simplistic—sexual purity or childlike innocence, the Church's definition and also her father's. Pearl, who never makes demands for herself, seems the pale embodiment of purity, especially in the hospital when her hand appears translucent from her fast. In Joseph's eyes she has always been pure; his disastrous offer of marriage is a misguided attempt to shelter her spiritual purity from the world. A negative manifestation of this ideal appears in the actions of Cambodian leader Pol Pot, for whom purity means revolution, the purging of outside contamination through the slaughter of doctors, intellectuals, and dissidents.

Gordon has noted her mistrust of "the religious impulse unmediated by reason," and it is this error that Joseph, Pearl, the Real IRA, and even Breeda make—choosing moral but extreme positions amid powerful emotions but without the aid of reason. The two women experience intense guilt as a result of Stevie's accident; Joseph and Maria (who is more rational than spiritual) likewise suffer guilt for the mistakes they have made.

After Pearl begs Maria to contact Stevie's mother, Breeda assures Maria that she has forgiven Pearl and that it is only "an accident of time" that prevented Pearl and Stevie from reconciling before his death. Maria then becomes aware that a similar situation exists between her and her dead father. She thought him overprotective before she herself experienced the anguish of a distraught parent, and she realizes that forgiveness is a choice. Surrendering her anger, she prays: "Father, forgive me. Keep her safe. There is nothing I understand; there is nothing I can do." At this point, when Maria has finally reached this state of humility, she is truly able to comfort her daughter.

Sources for Further Study

Bennett, Alma. *Mary Gordon*. New York: Twayne, 1996. The first full-length study of Gordon's work examines her thematic treatment of sacrifice and the religious impulse.

Bush, Trudy. "Hunger Strike." *The Christian Century* 122, no. 8 (April 19, 2005): 24. A perceptive analysis of Maria's conflict between her loss of faith and her need for the structure and patterns of religion.

_____. "Notions of Purity: An Interview with Mary Gordon." *The Christian Century* 122, no. 8 (April 19, 2005): 23. Gordon discusses positive and negative concepts of purity in *Pearl*, ultimately defining it as "giving one's utmost . . . doing whatever we do for the thing itself."

Reich, Tova. "A Comfortable Martyrdom." *The New Leader* 87, no. 6 (November/December, 2004): 33. Extensive exploration of the religious symbolism in *Pearl*, including Pearl's biological father Ya-Katey, whose name suggests "the YK of the divine ineffable name" in Jewish tradition.

Zinsser, William, ed. *Spiritual Quests: The Art and Craft of Religious Writing*. Boston: Houghton Mifflin, 1988. Includes the text of Gordon's speech "Getting Here from There: A Writer's Reflections on a Religious Past" and a list of religious writings that have influenced her.

Joanne McCarthy

PEARL

Author: Pearl-Poet (fl. late fourteenth century)
First transcribed: Late fourteenth century
Edition used: The Poems of the Pearl Manuscript: Pearl, Cleanness, Patience, Sir Gawain and the Green Knight, edited by Malcolm Andrew and Ronald Waldron. Berkeley: University of California Press, 1978
Genre: Poetry
Subgenre: Meditation and contemplation; narrative poetry
Core issues: Children; death; revelation; salvation

Distraught after the death of his daughter, the narrator falls asleep on her grave. He speaks to her in a dream-vision, and she instructs him about Heaven, her position in it, and how to obtain salvation. The Dreamer receives a glimpse of the Heavenly Jerusalem and the Lamb of God within it. The poem ends with his awakening, and his resolution to submit to God's will.

Overview

Pearl survives in only one manuscript, which contains two of the greatest poems in Middle English, *Pearl* and *Sir Gawain and the Green Knight*, as well as two other poems, *Cleanness* and *Patience. Sir Gawain and the Green Knight* is an Arthurian romance infused with Christian concerns, while *Pearl* and the other two poems deal with explicitly Christian matters. The poems may be the work of the same, unknown author, referred to as the Pearl-Poet or the Gawain-Poet. The poems are written in a northern dialect; therefore, although the poems are contemporary with Chaucer, they are much more challenging to read in their original language.

However, their being written in the provincial dialect does not mean that these poems are inferior literature. Rather, they are the work of a skillful and well-educated poet who is familiar with the new fashions in poetic construction as seen in Chaucer, but who chooses to write primarily in older forms. *Sir Gawain and the Green Knight* is the preeminent example of long-line alliterative poetry of the so-called alliterative revival (William Langland's *Piers Plowman*, c. 1362, c. 1377, c. 1393, is the other major example).

Pearl is a tour de force of poetic construction. First, the poet blends the newer fashion of rhyming poetry with the older alliterative forms. Each stanza has a rhyme scheme and usually divides into units of meaning along the fissures (*abab, abab, bcbc*). Alliteration is also used consistently, underscoring core concepts. Both poetic strategies can be seen from the first lines of the work: "Perle plesaunte, to princes paye/ To clanly clos in golde so clere:/ Oute of orient, I hardyly saye,/ Ne proued I neuer her precios pere." The line-end rhymes and mid-line alliteration coexist, creating poetry rich in both beauty and meaning.

Pearl's sophisticated structure extends beyond the integration of rhyme and alliteration. The poem is divided into twenty sections, each a group of stanzas connected thematically. The linking concept is seen in the concatenating word that appears in the first and last lines of each stanza. These concatenating words underscore the core concerns of the poem itself. For instance, in the first stanza group, the linking word is "spot." The narrator speaks of his grief for his child, whom he thinks of as having been a "precious pearl without spot," raising the question of why God allows the death of innocents. The unblemished "pearl" is contrasted with the dirt in which it is now buried. The "spot" where the narrator lies is envisioned as a garden, but the presentation is ambivalent. Soil is life giving, but the dead are buried within it. New plants grow, but only if a seed dies. Using the various meanings ("place," "blemish") of the concatenating word "spot," the poem begins its multifaceted consideration of death, mourning, and one's relationship to God.

A final arc of structural complexity can be seen in the poem's linking of its first and last lines. The opening line of the poem ("Perle plesaunte, to princes paye") is echoed in its final line ("Ande precious perlez vnto His pay"). Structurally, the poem becomes, like its predominant image, the pearl, round and perfect. Here, as with the rhyme, alliteration, and concatenating words, the form and content of the poem complement one another.

However, this strategy of echoing the first line of the poem in its last, creating a circular structure, does not imply that essentially nothing happens in the poem. In fact, the echoing underscores precisely what has changed. At the beginning, the narrator envisions his lost daughter as a pearl, so precious as to have been desirable to a prince. He is thinking in solely earthly terms—an earthly prince and earthly worth. By the end of the poem, the narrator's understanding has matured. The prince of the final stanza, for whom we are to become like "precious pearls," is Christ.

Indeed, the relationship of the earthly and the heavenly is a central concern in the poem. As the Pearl-maiden makes clear to the narrator, it is necessary that we develop our understanding beyond the merely earthly; we need to begin seeing things through a heavenly perspective, even though we can never fully do so. Moreover, the majesty of Heaven is ultimately incomprehensible to the merely human. In the second stanza group, for instance, the narrator asserts that what he has seen is more beautiful than he can possibly describe. However, the earthly is what we know, and the poem shows how the earthly can be used to help us reach toward and better understand the heavenly.

The poem is constructed as a dream-vision, a common medieval genre. Dante's *La divina commedia* (c. 1320; *The Divine Comedy*, 1802), William Langland's *Piers Plowman*, Geoffrey Chaucer's *Book of the Duchess* (c. 1370), and the anonymous Old English poem "The Dream of the Rood" (written before c. 700) are other well-known medieval dream-visions.

Christian Themes

The poem's central Christian symbol is the pearl itself, and the poem begins by developing a multifaceted presentation of what the pearl could mean. The narrator says he had a pearl so beautiful that princes would have loved it, but he lost it. At first the pearl seems to be merely an object (albeit valuable), but the pronouns used (both "it" and "her") reveal that more is going on. The poem soon implies that the pearl is someone whom the narrator loved and who has died, and at line 483, it reveals that she was his infant daughter.

As the poem continues, the pearl-symbol acquires increasing significance. In the first section of the poem, the pearl is both precious gem and lost child. In the second, as the narrator's dream-vision begins, the symbol of the pearl plays a core role in the poem's depiction of Heaven. The marvelous landscape that the dreamer sees is both beautiful and so abundant that things that are precious on earth are common here; the "gravel" on the ground is "precious pearls."

When the dreamer sees the Pearl-maiden, the meaning of the central symbol deepens further. The Pearl-maiden's garment is adorned with pearls, symbolizing her purity. She wears a crown covered with pearls, the symbol of what is promised to the faithful as their reward in Heaven. The large pearl on the Pearl-maiden's chest connects with the parable of the pearl of great price. Indeed, the Pearl-maiden is described as pearl-like, in words (line 190) previously used to describe the narrator's lost pearl (line 6), making the connection between his loss and the girl he sees. By the end of the poem, the narrator has learned that he must submit to God, despite his grief, and strive to live according to his will, which will polish his soul like a spotless pearl, to be treasured and cherished by the prince.

The pearl is the central Christian and most developed image in the poem, but additional, related motifs can readily be located. The use of precious stones to symbolize the abundance and beauty of Heaven occurs later in the poem, in the description of the Heavenly Jerusalem. In addition, the concatenating words of each section draw attention to important Christian concepts of the poem.

Sources for Further Study

Brewer, Derek, and Jonathan Gibson, eds. *A Companion to the Gawain-Poet*. Rochester, N.Y.: D. S. Brewer, 1997. Provides an introduction to scholarship about the author and historical information about the time of composition. See particularly pages 143-155.

Finch, Casey. *The Complete Works of the Pearl Poet*. Berkeley: University of California Press, 1993. Accessible, newer, but not always literal translation that places the original on left-hand pages, and the modern English translation on right-hand pages. With introduction, explanatory notes, and glossary. Volume also contains *Sir Gawain and the Green Knight, Cleanness, Patience*, and *Saint Erkenwald*.

Hillmann, Sister Mary Vincent. *The Pearl: A New Translation and Interpretation*. Notre Dame, Ind.: University of Notre Dame Press, 1967. Older but reliable literal translation that places the original on left-hand pages, and the modern English translation on right-hand pages. With explanatory notes and glossary.

Putter, Ad. *An Introduction to the Gawain-Poet*. New York: Longman, 1996. See specifically chapter 4, "Pearl." Putter is informed by and references prior scholarship on the poem but does not exclusively summarize. Designed for a student audience, so it is accessible for a general reader.

Rhodes, Jim. *Poetry Does Theology: Chaucer, Grosseteste, and the Pearl-Poet.* Notre Dame, Ind.: University of Notre Dame Press, 2001. See particularly chapter 3, part 3. Scholarly, but difficult in places for the casual reader unfamiliar with some terminology.

Spearing, A. C. *The Gawain-Poet: A Critical Study.* Cambridge, England: Cambridge University Press, 1970. Older but classic study by a foremost scholar. See particularly chapter 4. Spearing's audience is other scholars but his work is nevertheless accessible for a wider audience.

Michelle M. Butler

THE PENITENT MAGDALENE

Author: David Brendan Hopes (1953-   )
First published: Steubenville, Ohio: Franciscan University Press, 1992, edited by
   David Craig
Genre: Poetry
Subgenre: Lyric poetry
Core issues: Contemplation; the Eternal Now; grace; resignation

Thirteen key moments of epiphany in Christian history—including Mary Magda-
lene's repentance, the Annunciation, Veronica wiping the blood from Christ's face,
the reunion of Saints Anthony and Paul, and the deeds of the earliest Franciscans,
Bernard of Quintavalle and Brother Leo, are captured in lyrical bursts of various
lengths, many inspired by other art forms, such as Renaissance and Baroque paint-
ings or even a simple small-town passion play.

Overview

Thirteen poems exploring various aspects of Christian experience make up this
chapbook by David Brendan Hopes; most, like the title poem, focus on specific Christian images or events, though a few, such as "The Soul May Be Compared to a Figure
Walking" and "From the Infinite Names of the Center," explore universal spiritual
experiences not limited to the Christian tradition.

The first three poems in *The Penitent Magdalene* present contemplative responses
to specific works of Christian art. The second poem, *"The Annunciation*/Jan van
Eyck," offers enough descriptive detail for the reader to imagine the painting—an
early fifteenth century painting of the Annunciation—though the description is also
commentary and interpretation. These interpretations both penetrate van Eyck's fourteenth century vision and present it to the modern audience. For example, the descent
of the Holy Ghost is described as a "circus dancer on a golden wire," an apt description of van Eyck's stylized ray from the window to Mary's head. Yet when the next
line notes that the dove is out of proportion to the figures of Mary and the Angel,
Hopes affirms a late-medieval principle of religious art, that it presents spiritual essence rather than material reality. In the words of the poem, "the miracle/ survives the
carnival of externals," both echoing the previous reference to the "circus dancer" and
the original meaning of "carnival" as "farewell to the flesh," the feasting that precedes
a religious fast.

The third poem, *"The Meeting of St. Anthony and St. Paul*/Sassetta," responds to a
painting of the same era as the van Eyck painting and also housed in the National Gal-
lery of Art in Washington, D.C. Just as the previous poem contained a playful description of the "golden wire," this one describes the stylized golden haloes surrounding
the heads of the saints as "rings of light." Again, the fifteenth century perspective of
the painter clashes with the vision of the modern reader, and the poem mediates. The

description offers two explanations of the weird geometry of the painting's composition: the tenth line calls the figures of the two saints "crooked," but then line eleven adds "or aligned with some unsuspected center." That is the aesthetic geometry of Sassetta's religious art: The space of the painting is an extension not of the physical space of the viewer but of the spiritual space of the religious subjects.

The title poem, the twelfth and penultimate selection, invokes a baroque canvas painted two centuries after van Eyck's and Sassetta's works. "Georges de la Tour: *The Penitent Magdalene* Circa 1640" does not describe the painting until 60 lines into the poem. Yet the poem does not rest in description, bringing the reader ("you") actively into the painting and therefore the poem. Because de la Tour positions a mirror in the painting pointing directly toward the viewer, the poem reveals that if Mary Magdalene looked in the mirror, she would see "you," the viewer, looking at her. The last movement of the 101-line poem (the second longest in the collection) imagines the reader/viewer crying out to Mary Magdalene, causing her to look at her observer, as they join in a flame of passion (suggested by the candle flame and its reflection, the focal point of the painting).

The poem captures the ambiguity of the painting—a temporal ambiguity, not a moral one. The Magdalene of de la Tour is caught not in the moment of repentance but on the verge. On the floor are her cast-off jewels ("orphaned" is the verb Hopes uses), but she is still wearing the red dress of a prostitute. As in his treatment of Sassetta's painting, Hopes uses the geometry of the composition to illuminate its religious import. Noting that the candle flame, which is the visual center of the group, parallel's the Magdalene's breast, Hopes reminds the reader of the dual significance of fire imagery in Christian tradition: both the burning of sensual passion (Magdalene before repentance) and the soul's yearning for God (the penitent Magdalene).

Other poems in the collection that do not deal with religious paintings nevertheless share the confrontation of the modern mind with older religious traditions. Three "Saint Francis Poems" present the ability of the medieval imagination to personify abstractions: the first convert to the saint's order, Bernard of Quintavalle embracing Lady Poverty; Brother Leo adoring Lady Chastity; and Clara Scifi giving herself to Lord Obedience. However, even when the poems do not present the intrusion of an earlier religious tradition into the modern world (as in "A Passion Play" in which modern working-class Ohioans continue a medieval tradition by performing an Easter drama), a more profound intrusion—that of the eternal into our temporal world—infuses them all.

Christian Themes

Both the Annunciation poem and the title poem deal with the spiritual theme of resignation but not necessarily in the traditional way. The highest form of human resignation, Mary's affirmative reply to God that made the Incarnation of Christ possible, is the core of the Annunciation story for Christians and presumably for van Eyck's painting. Yet Hopes emphasizes the physicality of the spiritual elements in the painting: the angel whose weight bends the floor and the ray of divine light that looks more like a gold wire. In the same way, the religious tradition of Mary Magdalene's story leads the reader to suspect a rejection of sensuality immediately after the moment depicted in de la Tour's painting. However, the poem imagines instead a passionate union of the viewer and the Magdalene in the moment after she looks in the mirror.

By capturing Mary Magdalene at a peak moment, both the painting and the poem express the Christian paradox of the Eternal Now, in which eternity penetrates time. The moment Mary conceived Christ, the subject of the Annunciation poem, is of course the premier example for Christians of the eternal moment. Yet the Magdalene poem, as well as the one on Sassetta's *Meeting of St. Anthony and St. Paul*, deals with the breaking of eternity into time. Sessetta depicts several events, widely separate in time, in the same space, and Hopes uses the cockeyed geometry of the canvas to describe the disorientation.

Grace, the unexpected gifts from God, shines through each of the poems in this collection. In modern Christian poetry, it tends to take the form of the unexpected. The speaker of "A Passion Play" clearly does not expect to see anything profound at a rural outdoor amateur theater.

Sources for Further Study

Abbot, Anthony S. Review of *Upholding Mystery: An Anthology of Contemporary Christian Poetry*, edited by David Impastato. *Theology Today*, July, 1997. A review of an anthology that includes some of Hopes's poems, categorizing him as a writer of "the natural world."

Hopes, David Brendan. "The Boy Stood on the Burning Deck: Knowing the Mediocre and Teaching the Good." *English Journal* 75 (1986): 42-45. Elucidates Hopes's criteria for what he considers good poetry, helping readers understand his own poetry. Mediocre poetry for Hopes is that which tells readers nothing new.

_____. *A Childhood in the Milky Way: Becoming a Poet in Ohio*. Akron, Ohio: Akron University Press, 1999. This prose autobiography connects Hopes's childhood in Akron with his poetry about God and nature.

Maksel, Rebecca. Review of *Bird Songs of the Mesozoic: A Day Hiker's Guide to the Nearby Wild*, by David Brendan Hopes. *Booklist* 101 (2005): 926. A brief review of a book of nature essays by Hopes, citing his ability to "find the magical in the quotidian," the same ability that makes his religious poetry effective.

John R. Holmes

PENSÉES

Author: Blaise Pascal (1623-1662)
First published: 1670 (English translation, 1688)
Edition used: Pensées, translated by W. F. Trotter with an introduction by T. S. Eliot.
   New York: E. P. Dutton, 1958
Genre: Nonfiction
Subgenres: Meditation and contemplation; philosophy; theology
Core issues: Conversion; faith; God; reason

Human beings seek happiness but cannot find it fully apart from a faithful relation to God. God's existence cannot be proved by human thought. It is reasonable, however, to wager that God does exist. The God who redeems human beings is not the God of "the philosophers and scholars" but the biblical God of Abraham, Isaac, Jacob, and Jesus.

Overview

During the night of November 23, 1654, the French philosopher and mathematician Blaise Pascal experienced a profound religious conversion. Thereafter he always carried with him a description of the event:

> From about 10:30 at night, until about 12:30. FIRE. God of Abraham, God of Isaac, God of Jacob, not of the philosophers and of the learned. Certitude, certitude, feeling, joy, peace. God of Jesus Christ . . . Jesus Christ. . . . Let me never be separated from Him.

Pascal went on to write his *Pensées* and thereby became one of the most passionate defenders of the Christian faith.

Pascal's best-known contribution to religious philosophy is called "Pascal's Wager." In the section of his *Pensées* devoted to it, he speaks about the search for God. For Pascal, that search *is* the quest for meaning in life, not least of all because God provides the hope that we can be redeemed from misery and death. The question of one's immortality is of particularly great consequence. If only death awaits even the noblest lives, we will possess no lasting satisfaction. To have only doubt is a great burden where such questions are concerned, but even worse is a failure to try moving beyond that condition. As Pascal's conversion experience suggests, he thought that religious experience could convey a kind of certitude, at least in the moment of its happening. He recognized, too, that life goes on and is never completely immune to doubt and uncertainty. Where the meaning of life is at stake, Pascal understood, we are dealing with faith, which means that the risk of making and sustaining a commitment is always present.

Pascal argues that we ought to bet religiously that life does make sense. That wager, he underscored, is about God's existence and purposes. For if God does not exist, life's meaning will at best be tragic and at worst simply annihilated. We ought to wager that God exists, asserts Pascal, and live accordingly. To do so, he contends, is not irrational but exactly the opposite. In our human situation it is not given to us to demonstrate that God exists, and yet an analysis of our predicament suggests that faith in God is sensible.

The importance of the latter claim is clarified when Pascal writes that ". . . man is but a reed, the most feeble thing in nature; but he is a thinking reed. . . . Thought constitutes the greatness of man." Pascal believes that reason is limited, but it must not be disparaged, for "all our dignity consists . . . in thought." For Pascal, religious faith is a further expression of human dignity. The thoughtful person, Pascal believes, will see that the wager makes sense:

> Let us weigh the gain and the loss in wagering that God is. Let us estimate these two chances. If you gain, you gain all; if you lose, you lose nothing. Wager, then, without hesitation that He is.

The clincher in this argument, Pascal believes, is that this wager is forced. Not to choose is also a choice, for a decision is made by refusing to try, to enter in, to venture. Lack of belief excludes one from the benefits of faith. This situation has an either/or quality. We have to choose.

Christian Themes

Having distinguished between the God of philosophers and scholars and the God of Abraham, Isaac, Jacob, and Jesus, Pascal elaborates his convictions about God and God's relation to humankind. As a Christian, Pascal affirms that his religion teaches two essential truths: There is a God we can know; there is also a corruption in human nature that renders us unworthy. God, however, is "a God of love," adds Pascal, and God will "fill the soul and heart of those whom He possesses." Such claims, however, are not rationally demonstrable. On the contrary, religion often places us in a precarious position, saying that people are in "darkness and estranged from God." Religion pushes reason to its limits, but, Pascal asserts in one of his most famous lines, "the heart has its reasons, which reason does not know." He goes on to argue that primarily the heart, not reason, experiences God. Indeed faith is characterized by heartfelt experience of God.

As Pascal saw it, one's decision as to whether life makes sense does not depend ultimately on reason alone but at least as much on one's willingness to act when confronted by a forced wager. This is Pascal's fundamental spiritual point. He argues that this situation need not offend reason. Indeed, defining life as meaningful is no greater affront to reason than the opposite decision. One has everything to gain and nothing to lose, at least in the long run, by believing. An eternity of happiness is at stake.

In fact, when forced to gamble, the paradox is that the *reasonable* action is to let choice transcend reason in order to allow oneself to be possessed by God. According to Pascal, those who demand certainty prior to commitment fail to understand the human situation. If one objects that religion is too uncertain and God too difficult, while sufficient meaning can be found without entanglement in the vagaries of either, Pascal thinks the issue of life beyond death is crucial where life's significance is concerned. He finds it hard to conceive that death is not the end for us unless a loving God exists.

"To deny, to believe, and to doubt well," Pascal thought, "are to a man what the race is to a horse." Pascal likens life to a game, but one that should be played out earnestly. To do so takes one beyond reason, for "the last proceeding of reason is to recognize that there is an infinity of things beyond it." Played well, the game of life teaches reason to trust the heart. Yet that result can occur only when we give reason its due as well. Each has its own order. In searching for meaning in life, Pascal recommends that we must be careful not to confuse the two or try to reduce one to the other. Life might be simpler if we could do the latter, but Pascal insists that this is impossible. There are two levels, two ways of proceeding. They can supplement each other, but they do not always blend. We must learn to live with both and discount neither. It is this complexity that forces us to wager where the meaning of life is concerned.

When we ask, "Does life make sense?" Pascal's first reply is: "Not of itself and not on its own." Life does not come with built-in answers for our questions, in spite of hopes that it will. But for Pascal this outcome does not mean that life has no meaning in itself. Nor does it follow, as some philosophers assert, that all meaning is dependent on us and varies with each person. Pascal thinks life has meaning in itself, but our awareness of and participation in it are not assured unless we gamble. We must make the wager. Then the purpose of life may become clear.

Sources for Further Study

Hammond, Nicholas, ed. *The Cambridge Companion to Pascal.* New York: Cambridge University Press, 2003. This volume contains interpretive and critical essays by leading scholars who assess Pascal's philosophical and religious views.

Kolakowski, Lezek. *God Owes Us Nothing: A Brief Remark on Pascal's Religion and on the Spirit of Jansenism.* Chicago: University of Chicago Press, 1995. An important philosopher of religion reflects on the main points of Pascal's views about faith and the relationship between God and humankind.

Melzer, Sara E. *Discourses of the Fall: A Study of Pascal's "Pensées."* Berkeley: University of California Press, 1986. Critical discussion of the major dilemma in *Pensées,* that is, a strong claim for belief in a transcendent God (although limited by human language and understanding) set against an element of uncertainty.

Morris, Thomas V. *Making Sense of It All: Pascal and the Meaning of Life.* Grand Rapids, Mich.: Wm. B. Eerdmans, 1992. Provides a lucid introduction to the key themes and issues in Pascal's thought.

Natoli, Charles M. *Fire in the Dark: Essays on Pascal's Pensées and Provinciales.* Rochester, N.Y.: University of Rochester Press, 2005. This book probes Pascal's reflections on salvation and the mystery and revelation of God.

O'Connell, Marvin R. *Blaise Pascal: Reasons of the Heart.* Grand Rapids, Mich.:

Wm. B. Eerdmans, 1997. An important biography that situates Pascal's life and thought in the religious and political context of his time and place.

Pascal, Blaise. *The Provincial Letters.* 1656-1657. Reprint. Translated by A. J. Krailsheimer. New York: Penguin Books, 1967. Widely read and controversial when they appeared in 1656-1657, Pascal's letters satirize Jesuit theology and defend the Jansenists against heresy charges. The book was placed on the Index of Prohibited Works in 1657.

Wetsel, David. *Pascal and Disbelief: Catechesis and Conversion in the "Pensees."* Washington, D.C.: Catholic University of America Press, 1994. A helpful discussion of Pascal's approach to an affirmative religious faith, which Pascal develops and defends in a context of skepticism.

John K. Roth

PHANTASTES
A Faerie Romance for Men and Women

Author: George MacDonald (1824-1905)
First published: 1858
Edition used: Phantastes: A Faerie Romance for Men and Women, with an introduction by Lin Carter. New York: Ballantine, 1970
Genre: Novel
Subgenre: Romance
Core issues: Attachment and detachment; death; hope; nature; pilgrimage; self-knowledge

MacDonald's "faerie romance" suggests that both the external world of nature and the internal world of human imagination point us to God. In the natural world and in the workings of our own minds, wonder and awe lead us to seek and explore. Besides beauty and the desire for love and union, we sense the ominous presence of the darker self, temptation, threat, and death. The yearning to understand the laws that govern the workings within and outside us can draw us to God, and finally we exclaim, with Anodos, "A great good is coming."

Principal characters
Anodos, the protagonist
The white lady, object of his quest
Sir Percival, a knight
The Shadow, the antagonist, an alter ego of Anodos
The wise woman, a being of comfort and advice

Overview

The tale begins as youthful Anodos, searching his father's old desk, encounters a little creature who identifies herself as his fairy grandmother and informs him that he will visit Fairy-land. Anodos goes to sleep and, when he awakens, finds himself in an enchanted forest. He wanders east through various realms of Fairy-land in search of adventure, knowledge, and identity, yet he remains in a dream. Wandering in this dream state becomes the novel's structural pattern: Anodos constantly wonders at his surroundings yet reports his experiences realistically. It has been noted that the protagonist's name may come from a Greek word meaning "pathless." Beyond the fragmented plot, however, lies the unifying factor of Anodos's subtle moral development.

This entrance into Fairy-land and its various realms introduces the theme of entering new worlds. The new worlds symbolize mental states. The theme of yearning so pervasive in the book stems from a consciousness of other worlds. At one point a beech maiden protects, soothes, and instructs Anodos. She is a tree who longs to be a woman, and Anodos notes that, as he had longed for Fairy-land, she now yearns for the world of men. The longing to be something new stems from a consciousness of a lack and a reality beyond. As Anodos enters new worlds, in typical quest romance fashion, he encounters unexpected trials, temptations, and helps. His early encounter with the knight Percival, who saves him from a deadly foe, provides him with an ideal of manly action. Anodos's meeting an enchanted woman provides him with an ideal of beauty and a longing that motivates all his travels. His desire for love and beauty drives him ever onward.

The dreamlike, imaginative world of Fairy-land plays against the idea of the waking world. Anodos observes that the fairy world sometimes invades the world of men, and men are astonished at its variant causality. Late in the tale, Anodos muses about whether he can transform the experiences of his journey in Fairy-land into his common life. This hope to translate and bridge is as much of a quest as any he encounters, though subtler. At one point Anodos addresses his audience and notes that Fairyland's abundant and incredibly outlandish oddities must be treated by the wanderer as if they were real, though the wanderer may feel foolish for doing so.

At the heart of Anodos's restrained progression is his growing desire that another self arise within him. This yearning for a new self to surface from the remains of the crushed self of the past lies at the heart of his journeys. Anodos observes that the self must die over and over, be buried, and rise to new life from the old abyss. In his hope to renew, Anodos encounters various helps, the chief of which is the archetypal wise woman in the cottage, a leitmotif in the book. She is, in her different manifestations, a being of comfort and advice. As in other tales by George MacDonald, the wise woman of the cottage is a supernatural, godlike figure who provides knowledge and encouragement.

The plot is driven by seemingly random, if wonderfully rich, imagination; the ordering of episodes seems in most cases nonlinear, dreamlike. In this spirit the moral character development of Anodos through the novel seems minimal. At one point in the novel Anodos awakens, sees a forest stream, and follows it, confessing that his principle of movement since he entered Fairy-land has been to follow whatever has been in motion. In the course of his random wanderings, however, he confesses his yearning for the ability to act decisively. His talents are for song and sight, but not for moral deeds. Time after time he knows an action to be perilous and contrary to good sense but chooses it anyway. Anodos's gifts are gifts of mind, but not gifts of action. Nevertheless, near the end of the tale Anodos acts heroically.

As squire to Percival, Anodos finds himself with the knight on a track in the forest leading to a place of worship. Many pilgrims clad in white robes move toward a temple. Percival feels that they are going to hear the words of a prophet, but Anodos has misgivings, qualms that are confirmed when he sees with his superior sight the subtle sacrifice of two unwilling victims. Anodos resolves upon decisive action, trades his battle-ax for a white robe, makes his way to the temple, ascends, and topples the idol there. A large, wolflike creature, the pagan heart of this worship, emerges and attacks. Anodos strangles and kills it before the worshipers in turn take his life. Finally, Anodos has acted decisively.

Though it appears that in dying Anodos has merely entered another new world, the world of death is characterized by a more fervent hope than previously seen. At the end of the story Anodos says that he has thought of the woman of the cottage often and her knowledge of something too good to be told. At the end of the book Anodos hears a tree whispering to him, "A great good is coming—is coming—is coming—to thee, Anodos," and the protagonist states his conviction that the good is ever on its way. This book is finally about hope.

Christian Themes

A central Christian theme in *Phantastes* derives from the biblical idea of being strangers and pilgrims in the earth. MacDonald explores what it means to be a stranger as Anodos fluctuates in his pilgrimage between awe and dread throughout Fairy-land, the peculiar land that constitutes the setting of *Phantastes*. MacDonald conveys Anodos's ambivalence by the complexity of his response to Fairy-land. Anodos does not seem intimidated either by the strangeness of the place or by his own sometimes blundering efforts to navigate through it. Though some of the forest trees seek his destruction, though the white lady is ever elusive, and though he is trailed by his ominous Shadow self, Anodos continues his pilgrimage in faith and hope.

MacDonald conveys the Christian idea of displacement by showing Anodos's constant yearning to understand the laws that govern Fairy-land. Though the protagonist is ever the foreigner, often breaking the rules of common sense and even conscience, his quest is unified by his dogged searching, primarily for moral strength within himself. Though he wanders interminably through episode and topography, Anodos's pursuit is unified by the quest for a better self. Being lost in Fairy-land becomes a metaphor for his being at odds with himself. His quest then for the integrated self is essentially a longing for moral improvement through noble suffering and service.

Phantastes thus illustrates the Christian longing for an integrated self in a state of communion with the deity. Although Anodos struggles throughout against the natural aversion to pain and death, when he finally encounters death it turns out to be a realm of blessed hope. Perhaps because he gives his life fighting for right, he is rewarded with continuing hope. At the end of the novel, as Anodos reflects on his Fairy-land experiences, his recollections of his anguish there are attractive, and Fairy-land's past delights, remembered inconclusively and in terms of present sadness, are divine. Redemption is thus a central impulse of the novel. Anodos does not finally arrive at unity with God in a beatific sense, but he is no longer a stranger to himself. He concludes that he has found the deeper Fairy-land of the soul and is convinced that a great good awaits him yet.

Sources for Further Study

Gaarden, Bonnie. "Cosmic and Psychological Redemption in George MacDonald's *Lilith*." *Studies in the Novel* 37, no. 1 (Spring, 2005): 20-36. Gaarden applies Jungian psychology to *Phantastes*' sister volume, *Lilith* (1895), examining Christian redemption in that novel.

Gray, William N. "George MacDonald, Julia Kristeva, and the Black Sun." *Studies in English Literature, 1500-1900* 36, no. 4 (Autumn, 1996): 877. Gray reads *Phantastes* through the lens of critic Julia Kristeva, focusing on the opening of the novel and Anodos's journey into Fairy-land.

MacDonald, Greville. *George MacDonald and His Wife*. 1924. Reprint. Whitehorn, Calif.: Johannesen, 1998. The essential biography by MacDonald's son. Besides giving invaluable historical background, it traces the development and relationship of both MacDonald's faith and his fiction.

Scott Samuelson

PHILOKALIA
New and Selected Poems

Author: Scott Cairns (1954-   )
First published: Lincoln, Nebr.: Zoo Press, 2002
Genre: Poetry
Subgenres: Devotions; lyric poetry; meditation and contemplation
Core issues: Acceptance; attachment and detachment; Incarnation

Cairns is one of several Christian poets who emerged in the 1990's with an ambitious intellectual agenda and a broad definition of the reverberation of religious faith.

Overview

Scott Cairns, who taught at Old Dominion University in Virginia before moving to the University of Missouri, is a profoundly Christian poet, but he applies Christianity to a particularly broad range of experience, and his incarnational emphasis sometimes leads him to address physical and sexual subjects that many Christian poets have eschewed. Cairns takes the title of this collection from the *Philokalia*, a collection of sacred texts ranging from late antiquity to the late medieval period, cherished in the Eastern Orthodox tradition. Literally, *philokalia* as a word in Greek means "love of the beautiful," although Cairns clearly means to refer to the collection, not merely to the word as such. Cairns is an Eastern Orthodox believer who came to this tradition as an adult, and refractions of the qualities found in the original *Philokalia*—a stress on devotion, on daily acts of piety, on the religious significance of the natural world, and on religion as an ongoing, dedicated process, not an isolated gesture of zeal—are to be found throughout Cairns's collection.

Philokalia is composed of a selection from each of Cairns's poetry books of the 1980's and 1990's–*The Theology of Doubt* (1985), *The Translation of Babel* (1990), *Figures for the Ghost* (1994), and *Recovered Body* (1998)—followed by a generous selection of then uncollected poems, including Cairns's important "Adventures in New Testament Greek" series. The title poem of Cairns's first volume, "The Theology of Doubt" accepts moments of unbelief as the price for equally spontaneous moments of belief. "The Theology of Delight," similarly, celebrates a random joy in the world through which divine luminosity can manifest itself. "Approaching Judea" is a whimsical poem featuring a pilgrim who comes to the Holy Land in pursuit of the unlikely quarry of moose, but which carries with it deeper meanings about the nature of the spiritual search.

The Translation of Babel was Cairns's breakthrough book, and, as the title indicates, aspires to find a poetic language that can testify to the potential reparation of the fallen nature of humankind. A series called "Acts" is not based directly on the biblical book but concerns how the continuum of ordinary human feeling can acquire an aura of the sacred. Cairns also includes "The Translation of Raimundo Luz," a sequence centering on a fictive version of the Brazilian city of Florianópolis, as a complement to the spiritual themes that became characteristic of Cairns's poetry and on which this selection concentrates.

Figures for the Ghost refers to the Holy Ghost, the third person of the Trinity. "The Holy Ghost" uses rowing as a metaphor for a sense of mission in life, a reaching out to others motivated by the persuasive force of the Spirit. "Prospect of the Interior" continues the rowing metaphor but takes up a riskier and more agonizing journey.

The poems that first appeared in *Philokalia* itself take up the balance of the volume. "The Spiteful Jesus" castigates retributive conceptions of Jesus fashioned by authoritarian faith communities in order to discipline their members, opting instead for a radical and unexpected forgiveness. "Three Descents" contrasts the pagan figures of Aeneas and Orpheus to Jesus. Aeneas and Orpheus plumb the full dimensions of individual political and personal dramas, but only Jesus can serve as the pivot around which the total drama of existence turns. "The Modern Poets" reveals that there can be a sense of spiritual indwelling even amid the deracinated sites of modern cities, and in the modern poets who write about them.

The most important poems in this section are "Adventures in New Testament Greek." The *metanoia* poem, for instance, concentrates on the themes of repentance and a contrite heart that the Greek word indicates. Refreshingly, though Cairns does not treat *metanoia* simply as the Greek equivalent of "repentance" but illustrates how it exemplifies a joyous turn, not just a dutiful swerve away from sin but a delighted embrace of the path of righteousness. Similarly, in the *mysterion* poem Cairns goes beyond a normative sense of "mystery" to canvass how mystery in the Christian sense is both here and there, both immanent and transcendent. Perhaps the most compelling of the "Adventures in New Testament Greek" series is the *hairesis* poem. *Hairesis* means "choice" in Greek, and it is the source of the word "heretic"; heretics "choose" to split off from the main body of doctrinal belief. While not encouraging heresy as such, Cairns, however, makes his audience see that every act of belief is some kind of choice, and he encourages a sense of choice, of mental self-determination, as a prerequisite to a meaningful confession of faith.

In all the New Testament Greek poems, Cairns is not intent on explicating individual words so much as on talking about how the biblical language has an aura of its own that, despite the huge success of the Bible in translation, is only partially translatable into the lexicon of other languages. Similarly, in "Sacred Time" Cairns points out that this familiar phrase is as much spatial as temporal and that we domesticate it when we make sacred time just an intensified version of the model of temporal extension to which we are already accustomed. This tension between nuance and understanding, plenitude of definition and popular accessibility, ranges throughout Cairns's oeuvre.

Christian Themes

Cairns is Eastern Orthodox, but he was not raised in that faith tradition, coming to it as an adult through his reading in ancient sacred texts. Cairns is comparable to contemporary Eastern Orthodox converts like the theological writer Frank Schaeffer, who combine a devotion to Orthodox liturgy and tradition with a Protestant piety and fervor—although Cairns is much more liberal politically. Cairns's poetry can suggest a difference between American poetic converts to Eastern Orthodoxy from Protestantism and those formerly Protestant poets who have converted to Roman Catholicism. Whereas the Catholic convert Robert Lowell, in the work he published in the late 1940's and 1950's, assumed a deliberately ornate style, Cairns's plainspoken style is reminiscent of contemporary Protestant poets such as Walt McDonald or Julia Kasdorf. He does not often use rhyme or traditional verse forms, and, despite the complexity of some of his vocabulary and allusions, does not wish to make reading the poem a difficult experience. Cairns combines an Orthodox sense of liturgical blessing and internalized pilgrimage with a Protestant stress on the accessibility of the Word in the biblical sense—and the word in a poetic sense—to every professing congregant. Cairns is not seeking after conventionally devotional subjects; if he is a poet of divine redemption, he is also a poet of the human sin and despair that in Christian terms necessitates such redemption.

Cairns refers to theological concepts such as *apocatastasis* (the doctrine that all that has been lost will be found someday and that good and evil will ultimately be reconciled), which, although generally Christian concepts, receive special emphasis in Orthodox Christianity with its emphasis on resurrective life and participation in the spirit of God. He tries to take these abstract concepts and endow them with the sinew of poetic language.

Sources for Further Study

Cairns, Scott. *Compass of Affection*. Orleans, Mass.: Paraclete Press, 2006. *Philokalia*, an omnibus collection of new and selected poems, was published in 2002 by the Nebraska-based Zoo Press. Zoo Press experienced financial difficulties shortly thereafter, and many of its books, including *Philokalia*, were pulled from publication and, as of 2006, were are not available for purchase in bookstores. This volume is substantially similar, though not identical, to *Philokalia* in content; it includes a number of new poems Cairns wrote after 2002. It is likelier to be available through bookstores and libraries.

Cantwell, Kevin. Review of *Philokalia*. *Prairie Schooner* 77, no. 4 (Winter, 2003): 192-196. A positive review that stresses the ambition and reach of Cairns's religious vision.

Holden, Jonathan. "'Both Good and Beautiful': A Review of Poetry by Scott Cairns." *New Letters* 70, no. 2 (Spring, 2004): 207-209. One of Cairns's influences and the subject of the dedication of his poem "Salvation" gives a sophisticated account of Cairns's poems as unconventional religious verse that can appeal to both the believing and nonbelieving reader.

Wolfe, Gregory. Review of *Philokalia*. *Image* 42 (January, 2004): 3-4. Even though Cairns's liberal politics and convictions are very different from Wolfe's conservative views, the editor of *Image* takes a very positive stance toward Cairns's work, appreciating his nimble shifts in emphasis and perspective and the generous sense of the celebratory possibilities of Christian verse that his poetry offers.

Wright, David. "Poetry, Prayer, and Parable: The Playful Provocations of Scott Cairns." *Christianity Today* 47, no. 10 (October, 2003): 17-19. Traces the development of Cairns's career and gives particular attention to biblical themes in the volume.

Nicholas Birns

PHILOSOPHY OF EXISTENCE

Author: Karl Jaspers (1883-1969)
First published: Existenzphilosophie, 1938 (English translation, 1971)
Edition used: Philosophy of Existence. Translated with an introduction by Richard F.
  Grabau. Philadelphia: University of Pennsylvania Press, 1971
Genre: Nonfiction
Subgenres: Essays; philosophy; theology
Core issues: Contemplation; faith; freedom and free will; knowledge; reason; religion; truth

Existential philosophy is for Jaspers a matter of seeking reality at its source and within oneself. No philosopher, however, can offer a standing dogma for all times; he or she is always in ongoing dialogue. Jaspers's book consists of three lectures in which he asks first about being, which he sees as all-encompassing totality as world and as consciousness; next, about the meaning of truth, which he sees as pragmatic truth, intellectual truth, and existential truth in touch with transcendence; and last, about reality, which he sees as transcendence.

Overview

Karl Jaspers saw being as polarity: It is the all-embracing out of which all comes to exist, but it is also the vast consciousness within. Where being appears, is world; where being is immanent, is consciousness. Jaspers's thinking about being is like meditation about a web that embraces, sustains, and brings forth all, including oneself. All-embracing totality melts away when one approaches it as an object of research. For example, a living human being's true nature disappears when one attempts to understand human beings in terms of anthropology. To understand humanness, one must be human—just as it is necessary to experience art in order to know art.

Next, Jaspers focuses on the nature of truth. Where variant truths clash, one can discern three basic variants. First is the truth of "being-there" (living), which is a function of staying alive and expanding life. This truth validates itself through practical usefulness. This truth has neither general validity nor compelling certainty. This truth supports living; its untruth is what damages, limits, and paralyzes life. As life changes, so does its truth change; hence, this truth remains a relative concept. Self-interested life speaks on condition of promoting its own existence. It speaks as in combat with other interests or as identity with other interests. Every life already contains its demise; being-there contains no lasting happiness.

The second truth is the truth-of-intellect, which is part of a locked whole. My true self never becomes my property; it develops. I experience myself as moving and changing through time. Truth-of-consciousness takes its compelling nature from empirical evidence; truth-of-intellect is conviction. Truth-of-intellect validates itself when the thought fits into the totality of ideas and, by fitting into it, also corroborates the totality of ideas. As intellect, an atmosphere of a concrete and unified entirety speaks. The speaker and the one who comprehends what is spoken are parts of this atmosphere.

Finally, the third truth, truth-of-existence, is simple immediacy that does not need to know itself. Existence experiences truth in faith as having broken through "being-in-the-world" to transcendence, to which true self returns. Truth-of-existence yields actualized consciousness of reality. Communication occurs in loving combat—not a combat for power and dominance but a combat for obviousness and clarity.

All truth is in the polarity of "exception" and "authority." Exception challenges common truth; authority gags especially that truth which seeks absolute independence. While exception must yield to what is common, its battle with common thought is necessary, since it serves to test common thought. Paradoxically, every attempt at comprehending truth emerges from the receptivity to exception. Thus, exception influences the next authority. Authority compels and forces from outside, but in such a way as to speak from within. Authority rests in transcendence, out of which the one commanding it also is its obedient subject. The individual's education comes from the authority in which he or she believes. The authority in which my self has matured is part of my transcendental foundation. When freedom challenges authority, self and identity develop, keeping authority inside the individual as transcendence. Freedom urges toward confirmation by authority, or it urges to oppose authority. Authority offers supportive strength to newly evolving freedom, or authority offers shape and solidity by its resistance to freedom. For the sake of this process, even the most independent person must wish for authority in the world.

One can understand authority objectively by way of seeing its decline. Authority loses truth when it seems to become forcible power in one's life without a foundation of living sources of truth. Then, it commands thoughtless obedience instead of surrender to transcendent authority. Being commanded to obey a religious behavior, for example, is different from feeling the inner urge to obey a religious behavior. The former is a sign of authority in decline as it becomes force; the latter is transcendent authority. In sum, exception and authority are polarities: (1) They are both rooted in transcendence. (2) Both are unfinished. (3) Both are historical. (4) Both contain truth that, as object, forever escapes one.

The path that goes beyond the polarity of authority and exception is rationality. Taking that path is the task of philosophy. Rationality goes beyond scientific thinking toward an all-embracing connectivity that seeks to highlight what ultimately embraces all. Rationality is willingness to communicate; it wants to let all become concept. Rationality seeks unity by way of full and complete openness—in contrast to truth fanaticism. Rationality is where open eyes see reality itself with all its possibilities and possible interpretations; however, this open eye may not wax judgmental or dogmatic. Rationality is "mysticism of the understanding."

Reality—becoming aware of the space of the all-embracing within one—is like changing dark walls into clear glass. I can see the expanse and all that is and can be present to me. This question about reality is the ultimate question of philosophizing. In its own way, all is reality and yet persists as mere perspective. The sum of all researchable parts is never a total reality. Researched nature appears to be reliable, but human technology ultimately is no different from the magical incantations in primitive cultures.

One cannot measure reality. When one tries to determine a factual circumstance, one must construct it first. Thus, all facticity is already theory and not deep reality. The reality of our own being does not exist outside ourselves; we are gifts to ourselves. Thus, our reality of existence is not *the* reality. Actual reality is being that cannot be thought of as potentiality; however, I can think only of such as can be thought of as potentiality. For that reason, reality resists all thinking about it, receding from the understanding until it finds a point of rest in transcendence. While hidden, transcendence is present philosophically as reality. Transcendence is the power through which I am myself. The most decisive language of transcendence is the language of freedom itself. Philosophical faith requires us to remain in the world and to find nothing more important than to apply all our strength to what appears to make sense while, at the same time, not forgetting the diminution of all in the face of transcendence. All that is manifested in being-there is what it is only as a secret codification of transcendence.

Christian Themes

Philosophically, one attempts to show the path to approach reality by way of truth. One seeks to grasp being, which is everywhere, but which is nowhere really apparent. Reality, which supports all, is experienced in religion as certainty, as authoritatively warranted, as something believed that is fundamentally different from all philosophizing. In religion, reality is spoken of as myth and as revelation. Myth, fairy tale, tragedy, and sublime poetry can be of greatest depth and meaning where they do not explain and where they are logically at the most nonsensical. The general truth is that where only story is narrated, there is reality. The language of fantasy meets reality, which recedes from any exploration otherwise. When we hear being in the secret code of story, then we hear reality. The language of mysterious codes in philosophy is the language of transcendent reality; in religion, that language is myth and revelation. Reality can be accessed only by believing recognition and by believing experience. As the reality of the world offers itself through the senses, so transcendence is accessible through philosophical or through religious faith.

Religious symbols cannot preserve the exclusivity of their specific sanctity for the philosophical mind. They remain symbols only as long as they are not part of dogma or purposive activity. Religious faith in revelation has placed transcendence in a historical singularity, which is to be objectively and exclusively valid for all and which is the condition for salvation. From the perspective of philosophy, religion here is attempting to force all other historicity into one historicity that is to be regarded as exclusively valid. Such an absolute world history, however, denies all other historicity, which should participate in dialogue. That denial includes the historicity of the individual, who has roots in transcendence and must thus not be subsumed under a single world historicity. One gives up rationality by changing freedom and openness into an absolute system that denies variances.

Religion is different from philosophy. Philosophy cannot offer certainties. Philosophizing, I experience the reality of transcendence in immediacy through myself as that which is not me in myself. Philosophical faith speaks and lives in communication with the realm of dialogue of various thinkers, all of whom participate in and none of whom owns philosophy. Philosophical faith has no creed because it has no dogma, although it touches reality.

Juxtaposing philosophy and religion, one must consider both to be at the same level; one may not consider one to be superior to or protected from the other. Though philosophy is in alienation from religion, it must fight religion as an untruth. The philosopher is part of the tension of religious reality, but philosophy is not a foundation for religion; instead, it is in polarity with religion, a polarity without which religion appears to sink away. Philosophy assumes that thought which seems to endanger religion is actually no danger at all for a *true* religion. Whatever cannot last in thinking, cannot really be authentic. The same is true for a religion that defensively refuses to listen or to be questioned; such defensive religion therefore should quite properly come seriously under attack.

One might think that philosophy must therefore be rejected as ruinous and dissolving religious thinking. However, the process of knowing includes philosophizing, which opens us to the expansion of the all-embracing, to risk loving battle through an exploration of every sense of truth, to keep rationality alert before even the most strange and the most failed, and to find one's way back home to reality.

Sources for Further Study

Ehrlich, Leonard. *Karl Jaspers: Philosophy as Faith*. Amherst: University of Massachusetts Press, 1975. An analysis of Jaspers's understanding of philosophical thought as the expression of faith, in the underlying unity of the subject and the objective, examining such key themes as the role of freedom and transcendence.

Horn, Hermann. "Karl Jaspers, 1883-1969." *Quarterly Review of Comparative Education* 23, nos. 3/4 (1993): 721-739. Several parts of this review of Jaspers's ideas on education elucidate concepts from *Philosophy of Existence*.

Jaspers, Karl. "On My Philosophy." In *Existentialism from Dostoyevsky to Sartre*, translated by Walter Kaufmann. 1941. New York: Penguin Books, 1975. Simple and straightforward in tone, style, and content, this essay echoes several themes from *Philosophy of Existence*.

Kirkbright, Suzanne. *Karl Jaspers: A Biography*. New Haven, Conn.: Yale University Press, 2004. Kirkbright draws on Jaspers's lifelong diaries and correspondence to portray the philosopher whose work on truth, integrity, and interpersonal communication was so starkly contrasted by the Germany of his times.

Thornhill, Chris. *Karl Jaspers: Politics and Metaphysics*. New York: Routledge, 2002. Examines the epistemological, metaphysical, and political work of Jaspers, who, according to Thornhill, deserves more attention in the context of hermeneutics, anthropological reflections on religion, idealism, and metaphysics.

Reinhold Schlieper

THE PHILOSOPHY OF EXISTENTIALISM

Author: Gabriel Marcel (1889-1973)
First published: 1956
Edition used: The Philosophy of Existentialism, translated by Manya Harari. New
    York: Citadel Press, 1966
Genre: Nonfiction
Subgenres: Autobiography; critical analysis; essays; philosophy
Core issues: Ethics; freedom and free will; knowledge; life; reason; religion

*This volume brings together four essays previously published separately in French by
the French Catholic existentialist Marcel. English-language readers familiar with
the non-Christian existentialism of Jean-Paul Sartre since the late 1940's generally
associated the term "existentialism" with the antireligious views of Sartre and his associates. In this book, Marcel connects existentialism to Christian perspectives, and
he offers a criticism of Sartre's views on human freedom.*

Overview

In his introduction to *The Philosophy of Existentialism,* Gabriel Marcel describes
the first three essays, which make up most of the book. The first, "On the Ontological
Mystery," gives the main outlines of Marcel's own thinking. The second, "Existence
and Human Freedom," offers a critical discussion of the work of Jean-Paul Sartre.
The third, "Testimony and Existentialism," gives Marcel's own perspective on existentialism. These three essays also appear in chronological order, since Marcel wrote
them in 1933, January of 1946, and February of 1946, respectively. A fourth, short autobiographical piece, "An Essay in Autobiography," published in 1947 in a collection
of writings devoted to Marcel's work, appears at the end. Thus, the four essays can be
taken as representing the development of Gabriel Marcel's thought and as his response to existentialist philosophy in its heyday in the late 1940's.

"On the Ontological Mystery" poses a distinction between problems and mysteries. Problems are questions that are, at least in theory, resolvable. However, the ontological, which Marcel defines as the sense of being, is not a problem, but a mystery.
Connected to the mystery of the sense of being is the sense of presence, the sense of
one's own presence and the sense of the presence of things and of something beyond
oneself. Modern life, with its absorption in problems and in the technical means to
solve problems, tends to overlook being and presence. The fascination with technology, in particular, tends to involve human beings in a pride in their own control of the
world and to render them incapable of controlling their own control. Marcel suggests
an association between the ontological mystery and Christianity, particularly Catholicism. The sense of presence, for example, can be understood as the religious experience of the Eucharist. However, Marcel maintains that openness to the irreducible
fullness of existence may entail Christianity for those who live within the historical

tradition of Christianity, but that no particular religious perspective is logically necessary for the recognition of the ontological mystery.

The second essay, "Existence and Human Freedom," takes up the ideas developed in the first and directs these ideas toward the most famous (or notorious) spokesperson of existentialism, Jean-Paul Sartre. In this essay, Marcel concentrates on Sartre's first book, the novel *La Nausée* (1938; *Nausea*, 1949), but he also touches on several of Sartre's other works. Those who read Marcel's description of Sartre's novel with the first essay of this book in mind will be struck by the difference between the two writers' subjective approaches to existence. For Marcel, being is a mysterious fullness. For Sartre, as seen through the ideas of his protagonist Roquentin, being is something that produces feelings of formlessness, stickiness, emptiness, and disgust. Marcel raises the question of why the existence of things apart from oneself should necessarily give rise to such negative reactions. An analysis of Sartre's ideas of human freedom is central to Marcel's criticism of the Sartrean system of values. Sartre argues that freedom consists of making choices and that it is through making choices that one becomes free. It is also the case, though, that all choices are absurd. Since all choices are made in absolute freedom, there is no reason to choose one thing rather than another. The philosophy of the freedom of emptiness is based on Sartre's materialism and his atheism. There is nothing inside of things or behind them, and this is what gives existence its quality of provoking vertigo and nausea. Marcel points out, though, that if we simply exercise our freedom through making choices, we have no basis for judging the choices that people make. The French who chose to collaborate with the German occupiers during World War II (which had ended only a decade before Marcel published his book) acted in ways that were no better and no worse than those who took part in the resistance. Sartre's materialism and relativism led Marcel to ask whether Sartre, at odds with the French communists in 1946, would move closer to Marxism in the future. Over the following two decades, as Sartre allied himself with the extreme left in French politics, Marcel's question proved to be prophetic.

"Testimony and Existence," the third essay, continues to criticize Sartre, but in this piece Sartre becomes more of a foil to illustrate Marcel's own variety of existentialism. For Marcel, being means bearing witness. This is bearing witness before a transcendent other, presumably God, but also bearing witness before other people. Therefore, giving testimony about being is a social act. Sartre takes a negative view of other people and of acts for other people. For Sartre, a gift is a strategy to possess and ultimately destroy others. Marcel responds, though, that gifts are testimonies of relations with other people.

The final essay in the volume, "An Essay in Autobiography," is a reflection on Marcel's own life and on the readings, thoughts, and experiences that led him to his philosophy. He describes the "desert universe" of abstract learning in the schools and the influence of French philosopher Henri Bergson. At the end, he reaches the conclusion that the deepening of metaphysical knowledge involves delving into experience, rather than the development of technical solutions to problems.

Christian Themes

The Christian themes in Marcel's work are subtle, and often implicit rather than explicit. One of the most fundamental themes is that of the fullness of being. Existence for Marcel is not a void into which we find ourselves thrown, as it seems to be in the writings of many others described as existentialists. It is replete with other people and with an Other that permeates all. This is not an exclusively Christian theme, as Marcel recognizes in his first essay. Nevertheless, it creates an opening to Christianity.

The theme of presence is connected to that of the fullness of being. Presence involves both the subject in the world and the experiences of that subject. It is both being present and receiving the presence of other people and the presence of God through other people and through the world.

Marcel's writing may seem a bit perplexing to many first-time readers because he does not seem to expound a doctrine or set of ideas in any systematic way. Instead, his writings have the quality of looking around and exploring his thoughts. This can be thought of as a theme in his writing, and a theme that draws on a long tradition in Christian literature. This is the theme of the journey of illumination, in which a writer moves toward understanding through reflection.

Running through all of Marcel's work is the theme of the mystery, a word with long-standing Christian connotations. The mystery of being is the source of its fullness, and it is the ultimate presence in the world. The distinction between the mystery and the problem parallels the Christian distinction between faith and works. Problems, as issues that have technical and intellectual solutions, involve the works of people. The mystery, though, is something that can be realized only through deepening experience.

Sources for Further Study

Cooney, William, ed. *Contributions of Gabriel Marcel to Philosophy: A Collection of Essays*. Lewiston, N.Y.: Edwin Mellen Press, 1989. The essays are divided into four parts that look at Marcel's thought in the context of his life, Marcel's work in the theater, his thoughts on the nature of being, and the way Marcel and other existentialists approached the issues of death, hope, and God.

Moran, Denis P. *Gabriel Marcel: Existentialist Philosopher, Dramatist, and Educator*. Lanham, Md.: University Press of America, 1992. Provides an intellectual biography of Marcel and examines the relationship of Marcel's drama to his philosophy. The author then uses the concepts in Marcel's work to discuss contemporary philosophies of education.

Schilpp, Paul Arthur, and Lewis Edwin Hahn. *The Philosophy of Gabriel Marcel*. La Salle, Ill.: Open Court Press, 1984. From the Library of Living Philosophers series, this volume offers twenty-two essays on Marcel's philosophy written by major twentieth century thinkers. Each essay is followed by a response from Marcel himself. Also contains a bibliography of the writings of Gabriel Marcel. The book was composed during the last years of Marcel's life.

Traub, Donald F. *Toward a Fraternal Society: A Study of Gabriel Marcel's Complete*

Approach to Being, Technology, and Intersubjectivity. New York: P. Lang, 1988. Examines what the author sees as Marcel's experiential thinking as a means of achieving understanding among people and of creating a fraternal order in society.

Van Ewijk, Thomas J. M. *Gabriel Marcel: An Introduction.* Glen Rock, N.J.: Paulist Press, 1965. An introductory work intended to acquaint the general reader with the philosophical work of Marcel. Includes a biographical chapter. Other chapters are devoted to some of the main themes and concepts in Marcel's work.

Carl L. Bankston III

PIERS PLOWMAN

Author: William Langland (c. 1332-c. 1400)
First transcribed: c. 1362, c. 1377, c. 1393
Edition used: Piers Plowman: A Parallel-text Edition of the A, B, C, and Z Versions,
   edited by A. V. C. Schmidt. London: Longman, 1995
Genre: Poetry
Subgenres: Allegory; lyric poetry; narrative poetry
Core issues: Pilgrimage; redemption; repentance

In a series of eight allegorical visions, Langland considers what is necessary to achieve a just society and spiritual salvation. The first two visions examine the active life and satirize abuses of power. With the third vision, Langland turns to the spiritual realm to explore whether one is saved through one's own efforts or whether salvation depends on grace.

> *Principal characters*
> *Will*, the narrator
> *Holy Church*, the ideal Catholic church
> *Lady Mede*, reward; rival of Holy Church
> *False*, betrothed to Mede
> *Conscience*, inner knowledge of the good
> *Clergie*, learning, often corrupt
> *Ymaginatif*, one of Will's guides, imagination
> *Piers*, a plowman; ideal humanity; Peter; Christ
> *Work-in-Time*, Piers's wife
> *Haukin*, the active man, a waferer (seller of wafers) and minstrel
> *Kynde*, nature
> *Dowel*, honest layperson; learning
> *Dobet*, righteous religious figure; teaching; generosity
> *Dobest*, love; active caring
> *Patience*, a poor pilgrim

Overview

Piers Plowman exists in at least three versions. The A text, dating from about 1362, contains a prologue and eleven passi, or cantos. The Latin word "passus" means step or stage of a journey and is both singular and plural. About a decade later William Langland expanded the work from 2,400 lines to 7,277, arranged in a prologue and twenty passi. This expanded B text, dating from about 1377, is regarded as the most authoritative. Sometime in the 1380's Langland began another revision to create the C text (1393), which contains 7,338 lines, divided into a prologue and twenty-two passus. Because the revision of the C text was left unfinished at Langland's death, scholars are reluctant to regard it as definitive. In addition to the A, B, and C texts, there is a Z text, even shorter than A, which survives in a single manuscript at the Bodleian Library, Oxford University.

The allegorical poem *Piers Plowman*, an outstanding example of the later fourteenth century alliterative revival, combines various popular medieval literary forms. It presents a quest or pilgrimage, as the narrator Will seeks Truth, Dowel, Dobet(ter), and Dobest. This quest occurs within the context of dream visions that satirize secular and religious figures corrupted by greed. The poem includes debates, and many scenes recall the mystery and morality plays of the period.

As the prologue begins, Will falls asleep and dreams of a landscape flanked on one side by a tower belonging to Truth (God), that is, Heaven, and a valley with a large castle or dungeon representing Hell. In between is "A fair feeld ful of folk" that is this world with its living inhabitants. In passus 1, Holy Church expounds Will's dream as he sleeps and urges Will to seek Truth. The main action of this first vision involves the conflict between Holy Church and Theology over the nature of Lady Mede. The former regards her as corrupt, whereas the latter argues for her legitimacy because rewards may be justly earned. Throughout, the poem distrusts learning and the clergy, who have been tainted by avarice. Theology may thus represent the misuse of learning, and in this vision, Mede is indeed banished. The medieval mind, however, was unitary. It did not so much see the world as either/or but rather as both, as Christ is both God and man. So here Theology is not necessarily wrong, even though the poem sides with Holy Church. (Revisions in the C text explicitly attempt to reconcile various opposing views.)

In the second vision, Conscience preaches to the same people Will had seen in his first dream. The sermon is so effective that even the Seven Deadly Sins consider repenting. Langland here presents an entertaining procession of these offenses, beginning fittingly with pride and ending, equally appropriately, with slow-moving sloth. The penitents who set off on the quest for Truth get lost. Langland introduces Piers the plowman, who offers to guide the pilgrims if they will first help him finish plowing his half-acre of land. In fact, physical labor becomes a substitute for pilgrimage and produces a properly ordered society. Knights guard laborers and those who teach and pray. Truth is so impressed with Piers's achievement that in passus 7 he sends Piers a pardon for himself and his heirs. The text, consisting of two lines from the Athanasian Creed, promises salvation to all who act well and damnation to those who do not.

A priest who examines the document denies that it is a pardon at all. The disagreement between Piers, an ideal character in the poem, and the priest may suggest that the priest is corrupt. The priest wants a plenary pardon from sin regardless of how one behaves. Yet the poem may challenge the view seemingly embraced in these first two visions that good deeds are sufficient for salvation, because the pardon says nothing about God's grace. Piers tears up the pardon, perhaps because it contains nothing that the Bible had not promised already and perhaps because he recognizes that the priest is right. Regardless of his motive, he resolves to devote less time to work and more to spiritual matters.

In the succeeding dreams, Will seeks Dowel, Dobet, and Dobest. Different characters offer him diverse definitions of these allegorical figures. All the glosses may contain a measure of truth, even though Will rejects some and favors others. The dreams provide Langland the opportunity to instruct his audience about biblical and church history from creation to the present and to debate theological points in lay terms without always arriving at resolutions. The poem ends inconclusively, with Conscience embarking on a pilgrimage to seek Grace and Piers plowman. Such an ending indicates that as long as one lives, one cannot abandon the search for salvation.

Christian Themes

Two central questions of Christian theology concern defining the just society in this world and finding salvation in the next. *Piers Plowman* addresses both of these issues. The first two visions focus mainly on the first question. Though Langland is sometimes presented as a revolutionary, his ideal commonwealth is hierarchical. When in the prologue the rats want to bell the cat (perhaps an allusion to Parliament's attempt in 1376 to limit the king's power), a mouse says that everyone is better off with an unfettered ruler. If the king ruled with the advice of Reason and Conscience, and if all who could do so labored in their vocation, everyone would live comfortably. Holy Church, as early as the first passus, says that Will already knows Truth, which is that love is the key to the just society.

It is also the source of salvation. A key question that the poem explores, however, is whose love? Is it enough for one to love others, including one's enemies, to give charity, to shun the Seven Deadly Sins? Passus 11 presents the Roman emperor Trajan, who was saved through his love of others and his good life, even though he was not baptized. In passus 12 Ymaginatif argues that Aristotle and Solomon also achieved salvation because of their actions. Langland constantly stresses the importance of good deeds. One of his repeated targets of satire is the granting of pardons that eliminate the need for action. Such indulgences troubled many Catholics and would help spark the Protestant Reformation.

Yet human action alone is also inadequate, as Langland indicates in his parable of the Tree of Charity that Piers shows Will in passus 16. The tree represents three ways of living properly: in matrimony, widowhood, and virginity. As the vision proceeds, Will sees the devil shake this tree and steal the fruit (its souls) away to hell. Only Christ can retrieve what the devil has taken. Similarly, in passus 17 Langland redefines the parable of the Good Samaritan. Traditionally, it is read as Christ's message to help others, to give love and charity. To that meaning Langland adds another, for in the poem the Samaritan is Christ, the wounded man assailed by sin, whom only God's love can retrieve from eternal death. Works and grace thus emerge as the twin pillars on which salvation rests.

Sources for Further Study

Godden, Malcolm. *The Making of "Piers Plowman."* London: Longman, 1990. Examines the differences among the three texts of the poem and sets the work in its historical and literary context.

Scott, Anna M. *"Piers Plowman" and the Poor*. Dublin: Four Courts Press, 2001. Focuses on the way Langland portrays poverty and the poor in fourteenth century England and how the work exemplifies its cultural milieu.

Witting, Joseph S. *William Langland Revisited*. New York: Twayne, 1997. A close reading of the B text. A good, accessible introduction to the poem.

Joseph Rosenblum

THE PILGRIM'S PROGRESS
From This World to That Which Is to Come

Author: John Bunyan (1628-1688)
First published: Part 1, 1678; part 2, 1684
Edition used: The Pilgrim's Progress from This World to That Which Is to Come, edited with an introduction by Roger Sharrock. London: Oxford University Press, 1966
Genre: Novel
Subgenre: Allegory
Core issues: Faith; grace; pilgrimage; Puritans and Puritanism; redemption; salvation; sin and sinners

In his "relation of the merciful working of God upon my soul," Bunyan's concern is to tell how "great sins do draw out great grace." Although Bunyan, like other Puritans, had imbibed deeply of Calvinist or reformed theology, he revealed a profound dependence on the more experiential thinking of Martin Luther, whose Commentary on Galatians *etched itself deeply on his mind and heart precisely because it accorded so well with his own battle with doubt and guilt.*

> *Principal characters*
> *Christian*, the protagonist, a pilgrim seeking the Celestial City
> *Evangelist*, who warns Christian to flee
> *Mr. Worldly-Wiseman*, who counsels against Evangelist's advice
> *Good Will*, who is prompted by Christian's repentance to open the way to the Celestial City
> *Interpreter*, who enlightens Christian from Scripture
> *Simple*,
> *Sloth*,
> *Formalist*,
> *Hypocrisie*,
> *Timorous*, and
> *Mistrust*, who tempt Christian to detour from his goal
> *Watchful*,
> *Piety*,
> *Prudence*, and
> *Charity*, who encourage Christian
> *Apollyon*, the Destroyer whom Christian vanquishes
> *Faithful*, Christian's companion during the middle of his journey
> *Talkative*, who is faithless despite his pretenses
> *Judge Hate-Good* and
> *Vanity*, who attempt to destroy Faithful

Hopeful, Christian's companion on the last leg of his journey
Despair and his wife Diffidence, giants who try to destroy
    Christian with doubt
Knowledge,
Experience,
Watchful, and
Sincere, shepherds who offer sustenance
Ignorance, a thief who tries to enter the Celestial City
Christiana, another pilgrim who makes the journey (part 2)
Great-Heart, who guides and protects Christiana

Overview

In *The Pilgrim's Progress from This World to That Which Is to Come*, John Bunyan strove to dramatize through allegory the pilgrimage that a Christian must undertake to get safely "from this world to that which is to come." Bunyan's protagonist, Christian—warned by the allegorical figure Evangelist to flee the "wrath to come"—forsakes a wife and four children (the same number Bunyan left behind when he went to prison in 1660) when they refuse to accompany him, despite the chidings and ridicule of neighbors. Although two neighbors, Obstinate and Pliable, try to drag him back by force, he manages to make it through the Slough of Despond and past Mr. Worldly-Wiseman, who counsels him against Evangelist's preaching, to the Strait Gate through which one must pass to go to the Celestial City. Good Will opens the Gate for him when he discovers Christian's brokenhearted repentance for sin.

Entering the Gate, Christian makes his way to Interpreter's House (suggested perhaps by the church at Bedford), where Interpreter enlightens him from Scriptures about the difficulties of the journey and explains how he can overcome them. Rested and illumined, Christian heads directly to the cross, where the heavy burden of sin and guilt he has borne fall immediately from his back. He proceeds with greater confidence without this burden, but he faces difficulty all along the way, constantly tempted to leave the path by such figures as Simple, Sloth, Formalist, Hypocrisie, Timorous, and Mistrust. Resting after an arduous climb up the hill Difficulty, he reads from his Roll (the Scriptures) for encouragement, then places it under his head and goes to sleep. When he awakens, he leaves without the Roll and has to return "with sorrow" to find it, for he cannot reach the Celestial City without it.

At the Porter's Lodge, Watchful, Piety, Prudence, and Charity supply much-needed encouragement and, still fearful for the rest of the journey, arm him with Sword, Shield, Helmet, Breastplate, All-Prayer, and Shoes that will not wear out. They also show him a vision of the Delectable Mountains of Immanuel's Land within sight of the Celestial City. Thus outfitted, Christian overcomes Apollyon (the Destroyer) in hand-to-hand combat. All-Prayer enables him to pass unharmed through the Valley of the Shadow of Death that winds just above Hell itself. There Christian overtakes Faithful, who shares with him the cost of discipleship. Along the way, they encounter Talkative, whose faith "hath no place in his heart, or house, or conversation," but rather "all he hath lieth in his *tongue*, and his Religion is to make a noise *therewith*." Extended conversation with Talkative gives Christian and Faithful a chance to explain what true religion consists of: an experimental confession of faith in Christ; a life answerable to that confession (a life of holiness); and, above all, the practice of faith.

Upset with the peevishness of the pilgrims, Talkative bids them farewell. Once again, Evangelist appears and encourages them just in time, for they now reach Vanity Fair, which has claimed the lives of many faithful pilgrims. The Fair offers for sale all sorts of worldly merchandise. Not unexpectedly, fairgoers take offense at the clothing, speech, and disdain of the pilgrims and consequently beat Christian and Faithful, smearing them with dirt, locking them in a cage, and ridiculing them. When the brash pair preach and win some converts, Judge Hate-Good and a jury composed of no-goods of Vanity try and condemn Faithful to death. Christian, however, though remanded to prison for a time, manages to escape.

No sooner has Christian lost Faithful than he is joined by Hopeful for the last leg of his journey. Deceptive company and dangerous temptations still lurk along the way, trying to lure them astray. They nearly perish at Doubting-Castle, owned by the giant Despair and his wife Diffidence, but Hopeful helps Christian overcome his depression by recalling previous victories. Just when the giant is ready to destroy them, Christian finds a key in his bosom, called Promise, that will open any lock in Doubting-Castle. They come quickly to the Delectable Mountains and are within sight of the Celestial City.

Shepherds—Knowledge, Experience, Watchful, and Sincere—feed them and direct them to the right path, warning them to beware of flatterers and not to sleep on the Enchanted Ground. Ignorance joins them, thinking he can enter the Celestial City even though he has not passed through the Strait Gate, and keeps them company the rest of the way. Little-Faith, a good man from the town of Sincere, joins them in time to get a lecture about Esau's selling of his birthright and about the courage of Christian. Flatterer nearly diverts them from the way, but Christian and Hopeful pass through the Enchanted Ground without going to sleep and enter safely into Beulah Land, where angels meet them.

One danger still stands between them and the Celestial City: the River of Death. Their hope in Jesus Christ, however, gives them courage to pass through to the other side. Ignorance reaches the very gates of the heavenly Jerusalem but is thrown into outer darkness because he has entered as a thief and robber. Only the pilgrims who have come by the way of the Wicket Gate were welcomed.

The story of Christiana, which Bunyan added in 1694, repeats his theme of the Christian pilgrimage, and most of the personae are the same. Great-Heart, however—who plays a nominal role in Christian's saga—becomes the hero and guide in Christiana's, lending the male power that her feminine sensibilities are thought to require and fighting her battles on her behalf. Christiana's journey lacks the terror and sheer drama of Christian's. By this time, Bunyan seemed ready to open heaven's gates more readily for those who would claim some morsel of sincerity. None of the pilgrims has to pay the price Faithful did; the age of persecution has passed.

Christian Themes

The Pilgrim's Progress can be properly understood only within the framework of Puritan theology. In the Puritan view, the most urgent human concern is salvation—to go to heaven. Although salvation is a free gift of God, it requires a complete detachment from all earthly ties and single-minded preoccupation with heavenly concerns during this life. The way is difficult and few make it through from the City of Destruction to the Heavenly Jerusalem.

Saturated with scriptural language, metaphors, and ideas in the style characteristic of "mechanick preachers" of the seventeenth century, Bunyan's allegory expounds a typically Puritan message in an un-Puritan manner. Indeed, as Bunyan confessed in his "Apology," he hesitated for a while to publish lest he offend Puritan sensitivities about using allegory, but he received enough encouragement to go ahead anyway.

The narrative conveys and confirms the primary Puritan beliefs: that God's grace is sufficient to enable the Christian to remain faithful during the arduous pilgrimage from life to death; that the goal of Christian life is the heavenly city, and life here and now is only a preparation to which the faithful must commit themselves unreservedly; that the Bible is the main guide for the journey, but other agents (the Church) also offer vital encouragement and assistance; and that true religion consists in deed rather than in word.

Sources for Further Study

Bunyan, John. *Grace Abounding to the Chief of Sinners*. Edited by Roger Sharrock. London: Oxford University Press, 1966. This earlier autobiography (1666) lays the foundation for Bunyan's allegory.

Collmer, Robert G. *Bunyan in Our Time*. Kent, Ohio: Kent State University Press, 1989. A collection of distinguished literary criticism and appraisals of Bunyan. Includes essays on his use of language, satire and its biblical sources, and *The Pilgrim's Progress* as allegory. Of particular interest are the essays on Marxist perspectives on Bunyan and a comparison between Bunyan's quest and C. S. Lewis's quest in *The Pilgrim's Regress* (1933).

Furlong, Monica. *Puritan's Progress*. New York: Coward, McCann & Geoghegan, 1975. Although dated, this is an excellent starting point for research. A good summarized discussion of both parts 1 and 2 of *The Pilgrim's Progress*. Includes a solid introduction to John Bunyan and the life of the Puritans. Excellent but dated bibliography.

Horner, Barry E. *John's Bunyan's Pilgrim's Progress: Themes and Issues*. Vestavia Hills, Ala.: Solid Ground Christian Books, 2003. A study guide, including bibliographical references, index.

Johnson, Barbara A. *Reading "Piers Plowman" and "The Pilgrim's Progress": Reception and the Protestant Reader*. Carbondale: Southern Illinois University Press, 1992. Approaches the works through the history of their readership and critical reception, including both Protestant and Puritan readings. Bibliographical references, index.

Newey, Vincent. *"The Pilgrim's Progress": Critical and Historical Views*. Liverpool, England: Liverpool University Press, 1980. Brings together critical essays on *The Pilgrim's Progress* to provide fresh, detailed, and varied approaches to this work. Discusses the tension between allegory and naturalism and Bunyan's handling of the language and values of the people. Indispensable to the serious scholar of this work.

Wakefield, Gordon S. *Bunyan the Christian*. London: HarperCollinsReligious, 1992. Perhaps the best commentary on the work, addressing stylistic, historical, social, and especially evangelical issues. Bibliographical references, index.

E. Glenn Hinson

A PLACE CALLED WIREGRASS

Author: Michael Morris (1966-   )
First published: Tulsa, Okla.: RiverOak, 2002
Genre: Novel
Subgenre: Romance
Core issues: African Americans; awakening; despair; freedom and free will; friend-
  ship; healing; Methodists and Methodism; service

Faith strengthens Erma Lee Jacobs and Miss Claudia, who open their hearts to the
possibilities of God's forgiveness for their weaknesses and guidance to face chal-
lenges. Religion provides shelter for those women who need to retreat and heal while
offering them spiritual rebirth as they escape the emotional residue of their unhappy
pasts. Nurturing friends and family members establish an inspirational community,
strengthening the protagonists' resolve to establish a safe home for other wounded
people to restore and replenish their spirits so they can seek truth, develop trust, give
love, and embrace hope.

Principal characters
  Erma Lee Collins Jacobs, the protagonist
  Bozell Jacobs, her violent husband
  Cher Jacobs, Erma Lee's granddaughter
  Suzette, Erma Lee's daughter and Cher's mother, in prison
  Gerald Peterson, Erma Lee's boyfriend
  Miss Claudia Ranker Tyler, Erma Lee's employer
  Patricia Tyler Murray, Miss Claudia's daughter
  Missoura, Miss Claudia's friend
  Lee Avery, a preacher
  LaRue Rouche, Cher's father

Overview

Victimized by an abusive father who battered his mother, Michael Morris trusted
his religious faith during his childhood to help him survive spiritually. For his first
novel, he appropriated those experiences to create his protagonist, Erma Lee, and depict her awakening and transformation from a person who sees herself as an unworthy, abused wife to one who values her family, friends, and community. Erma Lee initiates her spiritual transformation by escaping from her unfaithful, violent husband,
Bozell Jacobs, and her emotionally cold Mama. Abandoning her tedious factory job
in Cross City, Louisiana, Erma Lee drives with her granddaughter Cher, of whom she
has custody, to Wiregrass, Alabama, the hometown of their cousin Lucille, who once
bragged at a family reunion that plentiful, well-paying jobs were available in that
town.

When Erma Lee and Cher arrive in Wiregrass, they discover that their cousin distorted the truth but are nevertheless determined to stay. Erma Lee enrolls Cher in school and rents a furnished mobile home at the Westgate Trailer Park, owned by the nosy Miss Trellis. A high school dropout, Erma Lee secures a job in the Barton Elementary School cafeteria, stretching her small paychecks to buy groceries and pay expenses. Erma Lee worries about how she will be able to support Cher throughout the upcoming summer. The school's principal, Patricia Murray, asks Erma Lee to tend to her sickly mother, Miss Claudia Tyler, during the Easter vacation.

When she sees Miss Claudia's elaborate house, Erma Lee, feeling ashamed of her background, pessimistically assumes that the wealthy Miss Claudia, the widow of a local store owner, will reject her. Instead, she is surprised when Miss Claudia embraces her, urging Erma Lee to read her Bible and discuss religious issues. Meeting finely dressed churchwomen who visit the ailing Miss Claudia, self-conscious Erma Lee feels insecure and flawed, comparing herself to them and fretting that she will be fired. Evasive about her past, Erma Lee hides her secrets, lying that her daughter Suzette is hospitalized for a mental condition instead of admitting the truth, that she is incarcerated in prison for dealing drugs and abandoning Cher.

Erma Lee and Cher attend Easter services with Miss Claudia at her friend Missoura's Bethel AME Church, a black congregation that unconditionally accepts the white women's presence, praising and blessing them. Miss Claudia's minister, the Reverend Winters, and many of the First Methodist Church's members seem preoccupied with material rather than spiritual wealth, considering attending services a duty rather than a spiritual opportunity. An elderly man chastises the Reverend Winters and the congregation for ignoring him and others in need.

After Erma Lee's car breaks down, she meets mechanic Gerald Peterson, a widower, who encourages her to attend his church and participate in community events. She accompanies Gerald to Wiregrass Community Church, a nondenominational group, where the minister, Lee Avery, preaches about his flaws and how he befriended God, who forgave him. Church, Avery notes, is not for perfect people but a place to fix problems. Inspired by Avery's words, Erma seeks the peace he describes, asking God for help. She feels compelled to be baptized again, recalling how when she was a child her Aunt Stella took her to vacation Bible school at the Antioch Missionary Church, where Erma Lee memorized Bible verses and was saved, receiving a Bible stamped with her name. She stopped worshiping because she heard the minister and a church member pity her for being poor. Later, Gerald welcomes Erma Lee to a secluded, Edenic area of his farm, a spot he considers his emotional sanctuary, referring to it as paradise. Erma Lee realizes she can trust and perhaps love Gerald.

As her friendship with Miss Claudia deepens, Erma Lee experiences unconditional acceptance and love. A former seamstress, Miss Claudia makes exquisite clothes for Erma Lee and Cher to wear on special occasions. Her friendship gives Erma Lee courage to divorce her husband. Erma Lee begins to respect herself and feels like she belongs in Wiregrass. Miss Claudia's generosity extends beyond material items; she gives Erma Lee her trust, revealing that she also was a battered wife and telling Erma

Lee about how Missoura and her husband aided Miss Claudia's escape from her abusive first husband.

Although Cher does well in school, especially in mathematics, she longs to be reunited with her father, LaRue Rouche, whom she cannot remember because he left when she was a toddler. Cher keeps a photograph of her parents underneath her pillow and furtively calls her father. Erma Lee discourages Cher from seeking a relationship with LaRue, refraining from telling Cher the truth about her parents. Defying her grandmother's wishes, Cher runs away with her father. Financially aided by Miss Claudia, Gerald accompanies Erma Lee to rescue Cher, whom LaRue has exploited to acquire money for heroin.

The theme of rescue continues in Miss Claudia's efforts to establish a shelter for battered women in Wiregrass. Privately battling leukemia, Miss Claudia confronts public opposition and denial of that social problem from members of her church, who she had expected would support her efforts. Erma Lee protects Miss Claudia's health secret and nurses her as she declines. After Miss Claudia's death, Erma Lee and Missoura start a shelter in an empty grocery store, vowing to continue Miss Claudia's legacy of generously giving love to people in need.

Christian Themes

Although he grew up in the Baptist church, Morris does not identify himself with any specific denomination as an adult, stating he is a Christian who worships at a variety of churches. His characters' faith is more important than their religious affiliations. He did not create Erma Lee and her story with the intention of writing Christian fiction; rather, he simply envisioned this work as a depiction of how faith can heal wounded spirits.

Through his characters, Morris emphasizes his belief that seeking a direct connection with God can comfort people who are facing problems and conflicts in their lives. Miss Claudia often tells Erma Lee that God exists within her and that she is never solitary, because God is always present. She reminds Erma Lee that God gives her strength and will watch over her and guide her. Miss Claudia emphasizes that God has a plan for every person. She urges Erma Lee to pray, sharing her burdens with God. Both women consider reading the Bible soothing, and Miss Claudia arranges for Erma Lee to receive her Bible after she dies. She discusses themes of sacrifice, suffering, and resurrection while explaining how dogwood blossoms symbolize the cross on which Jesus died.

Morris depicts his personal frustrations with people who attend church but fail to act in a Christian manner to all people, including those of different ethnicities and social classes. Erma Lee detects such behavior in the Methodist women who flock to Miss Claudia's house when she is ill but dismiss Erma Lee as someone beneath them. Despite their church affiliation, they fail to act charitably to people in need. Erma Lee and Miss Claudia, by contrast—two women of different social classes but united in their Christian belief and behavior—epitomize how people should live their faith, not just talk about it, and transform negative situations into positive actions. Their kindness, generosity, sense of duty, and charity to each other reinforce the Christian concept that family is not simply defined by blood. Erma Lee ultimately learns to recognize her own spiritual richness and love herself as she sees through hypocrites and antagonistic people and situations. Her experiences deepen and enrich her faith.

Sources for Further Study

Dixon, Joyce. "A Q&A with Michael Morris." In *A Place Called Wiregrass*. San Francisco, Calif.: HarperCollins, 2004. Transcription of interview, originally posted on the Southern Scribe Web site, that relates Morris's experiences with religion and how he expresses faith through his fiction.

Hilliard, Juli Cragg. "Michael Morris: Writing at Last." *Publishers Weekly* 250, no. 37 (September 15, 2003): S10. This profile discusses new Christian books written by four authors, noting how Morris's religious views influenced his writing.

McGregory, Jerrilyn. *Wiregrass Country*. With material by Jerry DeVine, Delma E. Presley, and Henry Willett. Jackson: University Press of Mississippi, 1997. This volume in the Folklore in the South series explores cultural aspects of the Wiregrass region, including music, community activities, and storytelling; provides insights into the characters and situations in Morris's book.

Summer, Bob. "*Wiregrass* Springs up Fast." *Publishers Weekly* 249, no. 23 (June 10, 2002): 19. Discusses why Morris's novel was marketed as Christian fiction despite his assertion that he did not write it specifically for a Christian audience.

Elizabeth D. Schafer

THE PLACE OF THE LION

Author: Charles Williams (1886-1945)
First published: 1931
Edition used: The Place of the Lion. Grand Rapids, Mich.: Wm. B. Eerdmans, 1965
Genre: Novel
Subgenres: Fantasy; mystery and detective fiction
Core issues: The divine; friendship; good vs. evil; Incarnation; selfishness

*Williams's novel concerns itself with the idea of the Incarnation—not merely in the
Christian understanding but also in the sense of the coming of spiritual realities into
the material world. In a small English village, Platonic ideals are taking physical
form, first as animals and then as geological and meteorological occurrences.
Friends and lovers, parents and children must sort out their responses to one another
and to these occurrences as destruction looms. One man seeks the reasons for the bi-
zarre events, not only to save his best friend and his intended lover but also to assure
himself of the principles on which he has staked his existence.*

Principal characters
    Anthony Durrant, the editor of a review of cultural criticism
    Quentin Sabot, Anthony's friend and colleague
    Damaris Tighe, a doctoral student, with whom Anthony is in love
    Mr. Tighe, Damaris's father, an entomologist
    Mr. Berringer, the leader of a mystical group, in a coma

Overview

    Charles Williams was born in 1886 to a genteel but impoverished, devout Anglican
family. He was able to spend two years at University College, London, before circumstances forced him to withdraw to find employment. From 1908 until his death in
1945, Williams was an editor at Oxford University Press. When Oxford University
Press moved from London to Oxford in 1939, Williams moved as well, becoming part
of a literary circle that included C. S. Lewis and J. R. R. Tolkien. Among his editorial
projects for Oxford University Press was the oversight of the first English-langauge
editions of the work of Søren Kierkegaard. As a writer, Williams produced novels,
poetry, drama, theology, biography, and literary studies. Williams's novels were once
described as "metaphysical thrillers," playing out, to a certain degree, the principal
themes of his theology: Incarnation, coinherence, and substitution. By Incarnation, he
meant not only Christ's incarnation but also the cloaking and revealing of divine realities in material forms. By coinherence, he meant the shared life of the Creation,
human and nonhuman and supernatural, which is experienced and exchanged in a
mystical dance. The exchange of one of those beings with another is substitution, supremely exemplified by Christ but expressed in daily life by sacrifices both great and

small. Williams's vision of the divine never lifts its gaze from the ordinary.

All of these themes are present in *The Place of the Lion*. In a quiet English village named Smetham, two friends, Anthony Durrant and Quentin Sabot, are rambling in the countryside when they encounter a group of villagers searching for a lioness said to have escaped from a traveling circus. Later in their ramble they see, or think they see, a lion bent over the inert form of a man. The man turns out to be a Mr. Berringer, the leader of a local, mystically inclined group. Berringer is unconscious, and the friends carry him into his house.

Damaris Tighe, whom Anthony loves, is approached by a member of the mystical group to give a paper for their meeting. Damaris, who writes about Plato and Aristotle and their influences in the Middle Ages, attends the group but finds her paper disrupted by a hysterical outburst by one of the members, who thinks she sees a snake. Meanwhile, Anthony is visiting Damaris's father, who is an avid butterfly collector. Mr. Tighe has had a vision of a vortex of butterflies disappearing into one giant butterfly. Later, in a conversation with a bookstore clerk named Richardson, Anthony learns more about some members of the mystical group and the fact that they seek knowledge for self-advancement. Richardson tells Anthony about a book on angelic powers and principalities that Berringer has given to him. The book concerns, among other things, the apparitions of the Divine Universals. Anthony and Richardson assume that what is happening in the village may be related.

Quentin, who has become increasingly fearful, has disappeared into the hedgerows surrounding the village. The house where Berringer lies unconscious is enveloped by flames that cannot be quenched, much to the consternation of the local firemen. Ghastly unseasonal heat lays over the region; houses collapse for no reason. A unicorn appears in the center of the village, and the townspeople hide in their houses.

Damaris, who has taken no notice of these events except to the extent that they interfere with her studies, has her own confrontation with one of the Divine Universals, which appears in the form of a pterodactyl. She is rescued when Anthony calls her name, and she recognizes him and her own true self at last. She goes out to seek Quentin, while Anthony and Richardson each head out to confront the divine beings in their own ways.

Christian Themes

While it might be argued that in *The Place of the Lion* Williams is pursuing some kind of Neoplatonic worldview, with the notion of the Divine Universals (or perhaps one could say the Platonic Ideals) of the animals that spring into being, it is also accurate to say that Williams is making reference to the Christian conception of Creation, wherein all that is springs from one single source. Mr. Tighe's vision of a vortex of butterflies seeking to form a single, giant butterfly is a mystical insight into the way that all creation seeks to return to its single source, the power of which leaves Mr. Tighe able to utter only a single word, "Glory!" Berringer, on the other hand, in his single-minded meditations on strength and power, calls to himself the lioness which has wandered from the traveling circus; in his meditation she is transformed into the archetypal Lion. In the contrast of these two occurrences is the underlying Christian theme of how one approaches things. Mr. Tighe's vision is of beauty and "glory" because his love of butterflies is innocent and selfless; he sees beyond the material form to the source from which all form emerges: "glory," a word Williams used to express the ecstasy that comes with whole and unselfish love. Berringer's call to the Lion has nothing of love or selflessness in it: He and his group seek power through their mystical exercises. Berringer finds his source of power, or rather it finds him, but it leaves him unconscious and eventually consumes him.

Williams has a constant theme, namely, that Heaven and Hell are a choice, and that the choice is made in the minutiae of daily life. Damaris's irritable and single-minded pursuit of her studies leads her to use other people to advance herself, notably Anthony, who loves her. When the pterodactyl, emblematic of her own selfishness, appears outside her window, it comes with a foul stench that sickens her. It is the voice of Anthony calling her, giving her her name in a voice of love, that rescues her. Williams called this ability to speak to and connect to other people in the work of love "coinherence." In the end it is by naming that Anthony restores the world to its proper functioning. It is through this naming, or baptism—the most primal Christian sacramental act—that the Glory reveals itself as the source of unselfishness and the fount of love.

Sources for Further Study

Howard, Thomas. *The Novels of Charles Williams*. Reprint. San Francisco: Ignatius Press, 1991. Provides thorough readings of all seven of William's novels with an afterword arguing for Williams's place in literary studies.

Huttar, Charles A., and Peter J. Schakel, eds. *The Rhetoric of Vision: Essays on Charles Williams*. Lewisburg, Pa.: Bucknell University Press, 1996. A collection of essays on every aspect of Williams's work, including his unique theology, which informs *The Place of the Lion*.

Shullenberger, Bonnie. "Love, That Grows from One to All." *The Anglican* 30, no. 1 (January, 2001). A brief but comprehensive introduction to the novels and theology of Charles Williams.

Williams, Charles. *Descent of the Dove: A Short History of the Holy Spirit in the Church*. Reprint. Grand Rapids, Mich.: Wm. B. Eerdmans, 1980. Williams's eclectic history of the Church, which W. H. Auden was said to have regularly read every year.

_____. *He Came Down from Heaven*. Grand Rapids, Mich.: Wm. B. Eerdmans, 1984. Williams's doctrine of the Incarnation, including a chapter on his "theology of romantic love."

Bonnie L. A. Shullenberger

A PLAIN ACCOUNT OF CHRISTIAN PERFECTION

Author: John Wesley (1703-1791)
First published: 1766
Edition used: A Plain Account of Christian Perfection. London: Epworth Press, 1952
Genre: Nonfiction
Subgenres: Sermons; spiritual treatise
Core issues: Awakening; conversion; evangelization; Holy Spirit; Methodists and
Methodism; mysticism; perfection; Protestants and Protestantism; sanctification;
sin and sinners

A supplement to Wesley's journals, this volume documents his adherence to the perfectionist Christian ideal.

Overview

The circuit rider in American history was usually a Methodist; but it would be a mistake to superimpose our image of the frontier evangelist on the founder of Methodism, who, for all his traveling and out-of-doors preaching, was an Oxford don who had taken Anglican orders. During their university days, John Wesley and his brother Charles (the hymn writer) were leaders in a group known as the Holy Club, devoted to charitable works and to holy living. Nothing in the regimen of this pious band gives any hint of the great popular revival movement with which the names of the Wesleys and of George Whitefield (another member of the Holy Club) are so closely connected. The exception might be a certain mystical and ascetic ideal of Christian living that, in John Wesley's view, was an essential part of the Anglican tradition and that he fought to retain in the societies that he founded, often in opposition to other evangelical leaders, including Whitefield.

Wesley is remembered chiefly as a man of action. Of his writings, only the *Journal* has excited general interest, and that less for its literary qualities than for the story it narrates. Excerpts from the *Journal* were published serially as part of his attempt to allay prejudice and to promote understanding. *A Plain Account of Christian Perfection* may be thought of as a supplement to the published *Journal*. In the 1760's some people were saying that Wesley had shifted his ground on the matter of Christian perfection. This provided him an occasion to publish the cumulative record. The main statements from which he quotes are his first published sermon, "Circumcision of the Heart"; a tract, "The Character of a Methodist"; another published sermon, "Christian Perfection"; and two booklets, *Thoughts on Christian Perfection* (1759), and *Further Thoughts on Christian Perfection* (1763). Excerpts and summaries from these are pieced together chronologically and are interspersed with hymns, personal recollections, and reports of conferences and conversations. Because the purpose of the book is to show that his stand on perfectionism remained the same throughout his ministry, one is prepared for a good deal of repetition. On the other hand, Wesley's teaching does not seem to have been quite as uniform as he claimed. It has been said of Wesley that, although he was an insatiable reader (he read as he traveled on horseback), he was never a close reader, and one gets the impression that he was not a close reader of what he himself had written.

A Plain Account of Christian Perfection begins with Wesley's youthful resolves. He was twenty-two when, reading Jeremy Taylor's *Holy Living and Dying* (1831; originally as *The Rule and Exercises of Holy Living*, 1650, and *The Rule and Exercises of Holy Dying*, 1651), he was persuaded of the importance of purity of intention and of the need to dedicate every part of his life to God. This resolve was strengthened when he went on to read Thomas à Kempis and William Law. Studying the Bible in this light, he saw the "indispensable necessity of having the mind which was in Christ" and of "an entire inward and outward conformity to our Master." His sermon "Circumcision of the Heart" (1733) belongs to this first period. In it he defines holiness as a habitual state of the soul, so renewed as to be "perfect as the Father in heaven is perfect." The first and great commandment is said to contain all the virtues. The one thing that God desires of us is the living sacrifice of the heart that he has chosen. No creature is to share our love for God, for he is a jealous God. "Desire not to live but to praise his name; let all your thoughts, words, and works tend to his glory."

When we turn to Wesley's next publication, "The Character of a Methodist" (1739), we are on different ground. These are not the vaporings of an Oxford fellow but the manifesto of an evangelist answerable for his vocation. As a Methodist, Wesley does not sigh after perfection; he vaunts it—a Methodist prays without ceasing. In retirement or in company, his heart is ever with the Lord. He loves his neighbor as himself, including his enemies. His heart is purified from envy, malice, and every unkind temper. He keeps all the commandments with all his might.

Other leaders in the evangelical revival were not long in voicing their opposition to these claims. In response, Wesley published the sermon "Christian Perfection" (1740). Drawing heavily from the Bible, Wesley allowed that Christians are not perfect in the sense of committing no mistakes, but he argued that intention is all that counts. Sins have to be intentional. Even newborn Christians are perfect in that they do not commit sins, while more adult Christians are perfect in the higher sense of being freed from evil desires. "It remains, then, that Christians are saved in this world from all sin, from all unrighteousness; that they are now in such a sense perfect, as not to commit sin, and to be freed from evil thoughts and tempers." Much in the same tenor is the preface that Wesley wrote for a book of hymns (1741). Christians are freed from pride; they feel it is not they that speak or act but God in them. They no longer desire anything for themselves, neither possessions nor relief from pain. It is impossible for them to entertain evil thoughts. Their minds do not wander when they pray. They are free from all fear and doubt. Temptations fly about them, but their souls are unmovable.

Then, as if making a new start, Wesley allows that the change does not come all at once: God's work is partly instantaneous, partly gradual—at one moment the believer received a clear sense of forgiveness, at another the abiding witness of the Holy Spirit, at another a clean heart. There are times of lamentation mixed with times of rejoicing.

On occasion God lets them see all the abominations of pride and self-will that are hidden in their hearts; but "in the midst of this fiery trial . . . they feel after a full renewal," and God, observing their desire, visits them anew with his Son and with the Holy Spirit. Wesley appends a footnote (1765) calling attention to what he had said in 1741 about the hidden corruption of the heart, to prove to his critics that he had even then been mindful of the believer's possible deficiency of self-knowledge.

In 1744, at the first annual Methodist conference, an early session was given to considering "the doctrine of sanctification or perfection." Owing to the presence in early Methodism of Calvinist and Arminian parties, the statements agreed to are little more than scriptural texts that speak of God saving Israel from all uncleanness and of Christ giving himself that his Church might be without spot and wrinkle. Wesley mentions successive conferences where the issue hung fire. That of 1758 was memorable as subscribing to the distinction between intentional and unintentional transgressions of the law and in acknowledging that unintentional transgressions require atonement as much as intentional ones do.

This is the starting point for Wesley's *Thoughts on Christian Perfection*. The work is conciliatory. Wesley goes so far as to say that "sinless perfection" is a phrase he avoids using because some people use the word *sin* carelessly to include involuntary as well as voluntary transgressions. The rest of the book is devoted to problems that perfectionism poses for the pastoral ministry. Methodist preachers, usually self-taught laymen, are advised not only of their duty to preach the necessity for holiness but also of their responsibility for counseling those who believe that they have received this blessing. Some of the questions dealt with seem trivial, such as whether one who has reached perfection will prefer pleasing food to unpleasing, and whether the children of perfect parents will be born without sin. More serious is the question of how one can tell whether a person is perfect. Wesley's answer is not very different from that of other spiritual advisers: I know that this person is not a liar, and if he says that he feels no sin but all love and that he has the witness of the Holy Spirit, then I ought in all reason to believe him.

A letter from one of Wesley's London converts serves well to illustrate the experiences of one passing from justifying faith to what came to be known as the second blessing. Jane Cooper wrote Wesley on May 2, 1761, relating her prayers and distresses. Moved by his sermon on the text, "We wait for the hope of righteousness," she began to wait and pray for the blessing. With the music of George Frideric Handel's *Messiah* running through her head, she appropriated to herself the prophecy, "The Lord whom ye seek shall suddenly come to his temple" and sit there "as a refining fire." She felt as if she were nothing and enjoyed great quiet, but she was not sure whether God had destroyed her sin. She conversed with friends, opened the Bible at random, and read, "The unbeliever shall be cast into a lake of fire" and again, "Be not affrighted: ye seek Jesus. He goeth before you into Galilee." One of her friends reminded her that God is no respecter of persons, and in a moment she found full salvation. "I saw Jesus altogether lovely; and knew he was mine in all his offices." Some six months later Jane Cooper died, but Wesley is able to append a letter from one who was witness of her last days. In spite of strong convulsions and extreme pain, she was reasonable to the end. Her last words were, "My Jesus is all in all to me: glory be to Him through time and eternity."

Further Thoughts on Christian Perfection was Wesley's response to the extravagances of a revival that had visited London the previous year. Earlier he had issued a tract called "Cautions and Directions Given to the Greatest Professors in the Methodist Societies," warning preachers against pride, enthusiasm, antinomianism, and other dangers that he saw in store. *Further Thoughts on Christian Perfection* incorporates this tract, while addressing itself also to substantive issues. Questions that had earlier been debated by preachers at the annual conferences were now being argued by everyone. The book is heavy on the side of doctrine. Classical Protestantism had distinguished between justification (pardon of sins through faith in Christ's atoning death) and sanctification (the inner working of the Holy Spirit), holding that the former is instantaneous and the latter gradual. Wesley, like the German Pietists from the time of Johann Arndt, complained that the clergy neglected to preach sanctification, thereby making Christianity seem too easy. This was no doubt a legitimate complaint; nevertheless, in refusing to deal publicly with questions concerning the work of the Holy Spirit in each person's soul, the established churches steered clear of much futile controversy. Wesley held that in most cases sanctification proceeds gradually and that the believer attains complete holiness only in the instant preceding his death, but he insisted, both on the basis of Scripture and on the evidence of his own pastoral experience, that some are entirely sanctified soon after their conversion. It was inevitable that many would ask, How can I know? In answer, Wesley could refer only to the inner testimony of the Holy Spirit. There were endless questions, however: for example, whether one could be mistaken about the witness; whether the witness could be lost even though a person remained in a state of grace; and, indeed, whether one can fall out of a state of grace. All of these questions Wesley answered in the affirmative. "Have any a testimony from the Spirit that they shall never sin? We know not what God may vouchsafe to some particular persons; but we do not find any general state described in Scripture, from which a man cannot draw back to sin." This explains the emphasis that Wesley placed on deathbed behavior and last words.

Further Thoughts on Christian Perfection concludes with a series of "reflections," which Wesley recommends to his readers for "deep and frequent consideration, next to the Holy Scriptures." These are interesting mainly because they echo a long mystical tradition and can be represented by the following:

- The best helps to growth in grace are the ill usage, the affronts, and the losses which befall us.
- True resignation consists in a thorough conformity to the whole will of God. . . . In order to do this, we have only to embrace all events, good and bad, as His will.
- To abandon all, to strip one's self of all, in order to seek and to follow Jesus Christ naked to Bethlehem . . . to Calvary, where He died on the cross, is so great a mercy, that neither the thing, nor the knowledge of it, is given to any, but through faith in the Son of God.

- True humility is a kind of self-annihilation; and this is the center of all virtues.
- Prayer continues in the desire of the heart, though the understanding be employed on outward things.
- God does not love men that are inconstant, nor good works that are intermitted. Nothing is pleasing to Him but what has a semblance of His own immutability.

As a popular evangelist, Wesley spoke ill of mysticism, even in so honored a person as the English devotional writer William Law. In his early years, however, Wesley had visited Law, and on Law's recommendation he had read widely in mystical theology, both ancient and modern. Thus, it is not surprising that we find here passages reminiscent of mystical writers. All that is surprising is that they are appended to a work written long after he had cut himself off from this tradition—unless, as seems likely, these are reflections penned by Wesley in his Holy Club days. If this is the case, and if some of the reflections are lifted, in whole or in part, from mystical authors, we understand somewhat better how Wesley can place them next to the Scriptures. In any case, their appearance at the end of his last published work on perfection provides unintentional evidence of the underlying unity of Wesley's convictions through the years.

Christian Themes

Wesley's perfectionism, therefore, held that to be a Christian is to have the mind of Christ and to live in entire conformity to his example. Holiness is a habitual state of the soul so renewed as to be "perfect even as the Father in Heaven is perfect." The sincere convert to Christianity is perfect from the beginning, in the sense that he cannot commit sin; the more advanced convert is perfect in the sense that he has no evil thoughts or desires. Finally, the higher perfection is directly attested to a person by the abiding presence of the Holy Spirit within him.

Sources for Further Study

Abraham, William J. *Wesley for Armchair Theologians*. Louisville, Ky.: Westminster John Knox Press, 2005. Part of the publisher's Armchair Theologians series, designed to introduce the most important Christian thinkers to a lay audience. Lively and engaging. Illustrations, bibliography, index.

Flew, R. Newton. *The Idea of Perfection in Christian Theology: An Historical Study of the Christian Ideal for the Present Life*. 1934. Oxford, England: Clarendon Press, 1968. Holds that despite appearances to the contrary, Quakerism, Pietism, and Methodism were a return to a more Catholic view of Christianity obscured by the Protestant Reformation. Chapter 19, "Methodism," while deeply sympathetic with Wesley's teaching, makes most of criticisms that occur to the reader of *A Plain Account of Christian Perfection*.

Hattersley, Roy. *The Life of John Wesley: A Brand from the Burning*. New York: Doubleday, 2003. Shows the human, social, and spiritual sides of Wesley. Includes a fifteen-page bibliography and index.

Knox, R. A. *Enthusiasm: A Chapter in the History of Religion with Special Reference to the Seventeenth and Eighteenth Centuries.* 1950. New York: Oxford University Press, 2000. Chapters 18 through 21 are on Wesley and Methodism. Critical but respectful treatment of Wesley by an English monsignor.

Rack, Henry D. *Reasonable Enthusiast: John Wesley and the Rise of Methodism.* 3d ed. London: Epworth Press, 2002. A tome at 662 pages, covers Wesley and his theology from his youth through the consolidation of Methodism and the 1780's. Bibliography, index.

Turner, John Munsey. *John Wesley: The Evangelical Revival and the Rise of Methodism in England.* London: Epworth Press, 2002. Places Methodism in the context of the worldwide revival of the early eighteenth century, along with Wesley's political and social influence. Bibliography, index.

Wesley, John. *The Journal of John Wesley: A Selection.* Edited with an introduction by Elisabeth Jay. New York: Oxford University Press, 1987. Based on the "standard" *Journal*, deciphered in 1909. Provides a nice snapshot, in 290 pages, of Wesley's journals.

_____. *The Works of John Wesley.* Edited by Albert C. Outler. Nashville, Tenn.: Abingdon Press, 1984. Representative sermons, letters, theological statements, and polemical writings, with helpful introductory material by the editor. Contains the sermon "Christian Perfection" and "Thoughts on Christian Perfection."

Jean H. Faurot

THE POISONWOOD BIBLE

Author: Barbara Kingsolver (1955-   )
First published: New York: HarperFlamingo, 1998
Genre: Novel
Subgenre: Literary fiction
Core issues: Faith; marriage; pastoral role; preaching; social action

Kingsolver's novel tells of the travels and work of the Prices, a missionary family from the southern United States, in the prerevolutionary Belgian Congo.

> *Principal characters*
> *Orleanna Price*, the wife of Nathan Price, who accompanies him and their four daughters to the Congo
> *Nathan Price*, a character known through the narrations of his wife and four daughters
> *Leah Price*, one of the adolescent twins, bookish and introspective
> *Adah Price*, the other twin, who is hemiplegic and speaks in palindromes
> *Rachel Price*, the oldest daughter
> *Ruth May Price*, the youngest daughter
> *Eeben Axelroot*, a bush pilot
> *Mama Bekwa Tataba*, a native woman who does housework for the Prices
> *Brother Fyntan Fowles*, a Catholic missionary
> *Celine Fowles*, Fyntan's wife
> *Anatole Ngemba*, a village teacher, translator, political activist, and Leah's husband
> *Pascal,*
> *Patrice,*
> *Martin,* and
> *Nataniel*, the Ngembas' children
> *Tata Ndu*, the village chief
> *Nelson*, a young man who replaces Mama Tataba
> *Aunt Elisabet*, Anatole's mother's sister
> *Mama Mwanza*, a Congolese woman

Overview

The Poisonwood Bible is the story of the Price family's arrival in the Belgian Congo in 1959, their establishment of a household and mission in the village of Kilanga, and the ultimate leavetaking of all but Nathan and Leah Price from the newly independent Congo. Arriving as independent missionaries loosely affiliated with American Baptists, the Price family sets up headquarters in a house recently vacated by another missionary. The novel is told in five distinct voices: Orleanna's, Leah's, Ruth's, Rachel's, and Adah's. Nathan Price has no voice in the novel, despite his position as head of the family. Through their narrations of life in the Congo, he emerges as a stubborn, compassionless man, a family despot—feared and unresponsive to pleas and needs expressed by the women in his care.

What the reader learns is filtered through the eyes of distinctly different sisters and their mother. All, however, convey clearly that Nathan Price arrogantly refuses native customs and ways of being in favor of his own righteous practices and beliefs. His high-mindedness causes suffering and loss from the beginning. For example, he ignores Mama Tataba's advice about planting his garden in protected, raised hillocks, as the natives do, so in the first hard rain all the plants are washed out. He persists in regarding the natives as lost and backward, insulting the village chief and insisting on baptizing children in the river even though the village people know that crocodiles pose a threat to anyone in the river. He pays no attention to the realities of the language or culture around him, and, ironically, his mispronunciation of *bangala*, which he shouts out at the close of his sermon every Sunday, announces that Jesus is "poisonwood," which will make them itch like the poisonwood tree, instead of what he wishes to say, "that Jesus is precious."

Language and miscommunication are central to the novel. Each daughter represents a response to life and to the African experience through language. Rachel, the eldest, perpetually misuses words, signaling a basic confusion about English, an inability to which she clings as she fails to comprehend the value of native Congolese culture and social structure. For her, Africa remains a land that needs rescuing by any Western power with the time and patience to accomplish the task. Ultimately, Rachel relocates and keeps a hotel in South Africa, serving the white minority culture. She survives three husbands, remains nonintrospective, and lacks the desire or mental acuity to be critical of American or European involvement in Africa.

Adah, the silent twin, observes everything. She speaks only in palindromes to herself and no one else. Her internal monologues focus on the inconsistencies in Nathan Price's approach to religion, her relationship to her sisters, and the ideas and customs they experience as outsiders in the Congo. Returning to America with her mother after Ruth's death, Adah regains her voice, becomes a doctor, and devotes her life to discovering the "life histories of viruses." Through her, the reader shares Orleanna's life in America after she leaves Nathan in Africa.

The dedication of the other twin, Leah, to learning French and Kikongo and her willingness to learn political and national truths from the village teacher, Anatole Ngemba, mirror her openness to Congolese culture. She remains in the struggling world of the Congo as Anatole's wife after her family returns to America, coping and building a life in the same way she labored to learn the grammar of new languages and the political realities of colonialism.

Ruth, the youngest, plays with the village children and teaches them games and some English. She learns from them, illustrating her child's ability to accept the surface of life and fit in somehow. Her naïve descriptions of family situations and events eloquently illustrate the tensions in her family. Orleanna plays the role of suffering helpmate for Nathan in the Congo. Unprepared for the poverty and grinding work of simply surviving, she does her best, holding on to a semblance of manners and decorum in a jungle-bordered clearing. She takes verbal and physical abuse until Nathan refuses to leave the Congo after the nation has declared independence and Ruth dies. Then she begins to speak her mind and finally leaves, walking with Leah and Adah to any city where she can find transportation back to the United States. In Georgia, she lives a solitary life, compromised in health by her Congo years and continually looking for forgiveness. She has no chance to talk to anyone but Adah about her surreal life in the Congo.

Nathan, deserted by his wife and daughters after Ruth's death, stays on to preach. He attempts to win converts but becomes suspect as a spirit man who can turn himself into a crocodile. Following an accident during which children drown in a river after their boat is overturned by a crocodile, villagers chase and corner Nathan in an old coffee field watchtower and burn the tower with him in it. A tyrant, he has failed as a husband, father, and missionary, utterly unable to communicate because he is incapable of listening. By contrast, Brother Fowles, a Catholic missionary, takes a Congolese wife. With their children they reside in the Congo with respect for the culture and functioning as part of a humanitarian network that eases lives all over the country.

Eeben Axelroot, a South African-born white bush pilot, represents the worst of the race bred in Africa, accustomed to a position of legally enforced racial superiority. His knowledge of the country allows him to conduct lucrative smuggling and interfere with local governments by aiding Westerners in finding thugs to carry out their schemes and violence. A womanizer and profiteering presence, he exploits Rachel sexually and simply uses her as he uses Africa, for his personal gratification.

Nelson, an orphaned Congolese boy who works for the Prices; Aunt Elisabet and Mama Mwanza, women who have survived the rigors and dangers of Congolese life; and Tata Ndu, the village chief, play roles in the novel that show how Congolese people interact with Westerners and survive foreign intervention in their lives. Their interactions with members of the Price family reveal the wisdom of Congolese religion, ways of governance based on respect for the elders and consensus building, family support, and the Congolese principle of communal sharing of food and goods to ward off illness and death. Hearing their stories, readers develop a sense of the divide between Western and Congolese cultures. The clash of ideas and values seems unavoidable.

The rift in the Price family's lives, the devastation of the Congo by the Belgian colonials, and America's complicity in the destruction of independent Congo's first prime minister, Patrice Lumumba, create a complex pattern of miscommunication, exploitation, and power. Anatole Ngemba narrates the point of view of nationalistic Congolese persons working for independence and peaceful ways to move from Belgian rule to self-rule. His rational, intelligent voice puts him at odds with the brutal,

American-backed Mobutu Sese Seko and results in his imprisonment at different times. He, Leah, their four sons, and his Aunt Elisabet emigrate to Angola looking for a better life in an African country run by Africans. Their future seems difficult at best.

Christian Themes

Barbara Kingsolver calls *The Poisonwood Bible* a political allegory. Her choice of the missionary Prices as a lens for life in the Belgian Congo creates a frame to consider Western exploitation of Africa. The attitudes of the Price women, from disgust to acceptance, and their observations along with Nathan's complete lack of respect for the Congo's human or social conventions present a spectrum of Western culture's attitudes about Africa. The morality of imposing Christian religious values on people one does not know or respect becomes an issue as the family interacts with villagers.

Insensitive responses to need and village custom undercut Nathan's spiritual authority, while his daughters Leah, Adah, and Ruth accept both friendship and help from neighbors. Rachel remains self-centered throughout, resentful toward her father and Africans alike. Her insensitivity is not personal; it is based on a feeling of entitlement and her assumption that whatever she wants is right. She comes close to being amoral, since her desires form the core of her values. Orleanna becomes complicit in Nathan's excesses by failing to object to his private or public cruelty. Her mother-love is undercut by a weak defense of herself and her daughters. In contrast, the African neighbors of the Prices treat them humanely, saving their lives on several occasions and thereby raising the question of which society is more morally grounded. In their lives in Kilanga, religion becomes personal and each Price family member exhibits varying degrees of sensitivity and compassion.

Nathan Price's self-righteous preaching and insistence on his authority to change life in Kilanga stand for the West's power relationship to Africa. Ignoring centuries of custom and survival in the tropical jungle, he overlooks the reality that daily struggles focus on survival, not redemption. He has no interest in acquiring information, learning the language, or facing real human problems of existence. His answer for everything is ideology in the guise of religious beliefs. Later in the novel, political ideology motivates meddling in the name of anticommunism, but it is hard to separate American political interference from Nathan's methods. They stem from the same self-righteous motivation. Africa and Africans in the novel suffer colonial exploitation of their resources, religious meddling with their belief systems, political disregard for centuries-old methods of rule and social structure, and international collusion to take natural resources from independent countries by interfering in local political contests.

The question of forgiveness surfaces throughout the book. Whether it has to do with resentments between the Price sisters, Nathan's brutality toward Orleanna while he preaches God's love, the villagers' suspicion that the Prices have brought bad luck to them, the political intolerance of one Congolese regime for another after Belgium has left the country, the Belgian colonial exploitation of the Congo, Eeben Axelroot's seduction of Rachel, or Orleanna's failure to keep Ruth May alive, *The Poisonwood Bible* offers myriad chances for readers to consider who deserves and who bestows forgiveness. The precepts of Nathan Price's religious forgiveness pale in the crowd of personal and devastating circumstances in the novel. The source of forgiveness in the world emerges as a main concern.

Sources for Further Study

Jacobson, Kristin J. "The Neodomestic American Novel: The Politics of Home in Barbara Kingsolver's *The Poisonwood Bible.*" *Tulsa Studies in Women's Literature* 24, no. 1 (Spring, 2005): 105-127. Compares and contrasts *The Poisonwood Bible* with Louisa May Alcott's *Little Women*, with particular attention to the genre of the (neo)domestic novel.

Kakutani, Michiko. "No Ice Cream Cones in a Heart of Darkness." *The New York Times*, October 16, 1998. Review of the book that takes up the symbolic significance of several main characters in line with political allegory.

Kerr, Sarah. "The Novel as Indictment." *The New York Times*, October 11, 1998, p. SM53. An examination of *The Poisonwood Bible* and Kingsolver's ideas about writing and influencing the world.

Ognibene, Elaine R. "The Missionary Position: Barbara Kingsolver's *The Poisonwood Bible.*" *College Literature* 20, no. 3 (Summer, 2003): 19-36. This lengthy analysis concludes that "words, Kingsolver warns, have multiple meanings, especially in the Congo. To decode those meanings, readers must 'look at what happens from every side. . . .' Kingsolver dares us to do so and to discover the moments of truth in the telling."

Riswold, Caryn D. "Four Fictions and Their Theological Truths." An assistant professor of religion surveys four novels, including *The Poisonwood Bible*, concluding that "Kingsolver describes justification by grace and the difficulty of living liberated from guilt."

Karen L. Arnold

THE POLITICS OF JESUS
Vicit Agnus Noster

Author: John H. Yoder (1927-1997)
First published: 1972
Edition used: The Politics of Jesus: Vicit Agnus Noster. 2d ed. Grand Rapids, Mich.:
Wm. B. Eerdmans, 1994
Genre: Nonfiction
Subgenres: Biblical studies; exegesis
Core issues: Ethics; nonviolent resistance

The life and teachings of Jesus are not to be understood simply in a personal, intro-
spective manner; they are also political, having social implications. Yoder's book
demonstrates the profound humanity of Jesus, whose suffering provides for Chris-
tians the critical basis for social ethics, including the usually overlooked issues of
passivism and jubilee. The New Testament affirms that the Christian community ex-
ists to reject violence of any kind.

Overview

John H. Yoder's major work is an exegetical defense of passivism and a call to social involvement by Christians. He argues that Christians too often read the scriptures
only in terms of personal salvation as relief of personal anxiety, when in fact the scriptures demand that Christian disciples understand the collective, social implications of
faith in Jesus Christ. Many erroneously conclude that the message of Jesus was irrelevant or that he was disinterested in political situations. Yoder argues to the contrary,
that Jesus was specifically political, and that his death by crucifixion demonstrates his
renunciation of a dehumanizing political system operative in his day:

> [T]he cross is beginning to loom not as a ritually prescribed instrument of propitiation
> but as the political alternative to both insurrection and quietism.

Yoder's claims stand in opposition to other political and religious viewpoints, such
as liberation theology, Marxist ideology, subjective irrelevance, and Jewish zealotry,
all of which have been prominent at various points in history. Yoder argues that nonviolent, social involvement, modeled by Jesus in the New Testament, is the appropriate model for Christians. He initially argues this based on a close reading of the Gospel of Luke, then follows with an examination of Pauline writings. Yoder points out
that the most significant temptations of Jesus, as recorded in the New Testament, concern an appeal for him to use violence in response to injustice.

The Christian community is to be a new kind of community. Justification is to be
understood in more than personal guilt before God, who grants amnesty on the basis
of one's faith. Rather, justification has to do with breaking down walls that separate

segments of a larger society. It has to do with making peace with those who might otherwise be enemies. Yoder reads that to be in Christ is to be part of a community wherein creation is new. He goes beyond an individual reading of one's existential status before Christ to focus on the collective community ethic that is literally a new creation. Community members practice nonviolence, not as a retreat from the political concerns about them but in a proactive manner and, if need be, in the face of violent opposition. The community is also to recognize that suffering and death have redemptive value for society; real power is realized in the face of evil that is an affront to the stability of society, not merely to individual happiness.

Closely related to the nonviolence advocated and practiced by Jesus, Yoder understands, other ethical concerns naturally follow. The concept of jubilee, an Old Testament event, was preached by Jesus and should be practiced by contemporary Christian communities. Jubilee includes letting the land lie fallow for a year, releasing debt, liberating slaves, and redistributing capital. This is not a utopian vision, he argues, but would in fact have prevented "many bloody revolutions" if the "Christian church had shown herself more respectful than Israel was of the jubilee dispositions contained in the law of Moses." Essential elements of the message of Jesus—for example, the Lord's Prayer and the Sermon on the Mount—should be understood as examples of a community called to practice jubilee.

Yoder provides exegesis and examples from the Old Testament to demonstrate that Jews have had a history of nonviolent responses to injustice. This history was understood by Jesus and the community of believers, and it is foundational for recognizing that Jesus was not disinterested in the political and social concerns of his day. To the contrary, his recorded death is evidence of his social and political involvement. His teachings challenged the status quo of his society. Moreover, his nonviolent response to personal threat establishes the primary method for his disciples when they engage injustice within society and when they encounter similar accusations or retribution. Yoder also quotes significant passages from the Old Testament and from nonscriptural Jewish history in which random nonviolent responses to injustice occurred. These examples underscore his point that such methods of resistance were not uncommon in the cultural memory of the contemporaries of Jesus. Jesus expected this type of response from believers based on their a priori understanding. Since the time of Jesus, however, the Christian church has too often ignored this foundational position.

Rather than resisting political regimes by force, Christians are to be subject to the governmental powers on earth. Yoder argues that personal responses, even by passivists, miss the point of this biblical injunction. He claims that the biblical passages in Romans 13 and Matthew 5-7 are not in contradiction; both passages "instruct Christians to be nonresistant in all their relationships, including the social." Both passages call Christians to renounce vengeance and

> to respect and be subject to the historical process in which the sword continues to be wielded and to bring about a kind of order under fire, but not to perceive in the wielding of the sword their own reconciling ministry.

Christian Themes

Yoder addresses Christian themes common in both Protestant and Catholic theology as expressed in varying degrees throughout history. Perhaps the key distinction of Yoder's work, however, is his corporate, rather than a personal, reading of those themes. Instead of focusing on the Jesus story's implications for individuals, for Yoder, all of the New Testament ideas coalesce into a messsage of social responsibility that is to be implemented, rather than ignored. He reads the traditional biblical concepts of justification, the Kingdom of God, discipleship, grace, and faith in light of the active, collective social and political involvement exemplified in the life of Jesus. Principally, this life is a life of nonviolent resistance. It is a call to the cross, by which Yoder seems to mean that Christians must be prepared literally to suffer at the hands of those who would inflict injustice. A collective, nonviolent response to injustice, however, not only demonstrates the methodology of Jesus; practically, it should also have an efficacious result. If collectively practiced by Christians, rather than ignored or misinterpreted, such nonviolent responses could render defenseless the motives of the oppressor. In the meantime, such a response bears witness to the action to which Christians are truly called.

Yoder's exegesis takes seriously the problem of social unrest, and his writing underscores the fact that Christianity is not an easy religion. The fact of punishment, even death, as a result of resisting unjust powers within a given society, however, is not reason to ignore the biblical teachings and human example of Christ.

Sources for Further Study

Carter, Craig A. *The Politics of the Cross: The Theology and Social Ethics of John Howard Yoder*. Grand Rapids, Mich.: Brazos Press, 2001. According to one reviewer, "first systematic survey of Yoder's work" and the first place to turn for elucidation of Yoder's *The Politics of Jesus*.

Hauerwas, Stanley, ed. *The Wisdom of the Cross: Essays in Honor of John Howard Yoder*. Grand Rapids, Mich.: Wm. B. Eerdmans, 1999. The essays address questions surrounding nonviolence, biblical interpretation, method or antimethod, ecclesiology, and other aspects of Yoder's thought, attesting the diversity of his theological concerns. Bibliographical references.

Hughes, Richard T., ed. *The Primitive Church in the Modern World*. Urbana: Illinois University Press, 1995. A collection of essays originally presented at Pepperdine University in 1991. Includes an essay by Yoder. Contains an index and bibliographical references.

Niebuhr, Richard H. *Christ and Culture*. New York: Harper & Row, 1951. A classic study that offers five positions that Christian communities have historically held in relation to faith and society.

Rouner, Leroy S., ed. *Foundations of Ethics*. Notre Dame, Ind.: Notre Dame University Press, 1983. Part of the Boston University series on the study of philosophy and religion, this collection contains an essay by Yoder. Index, bibliographic references.

Whitmore, Todd, ed. *Ethics in the Nuclear Age: Strategy, Religious Studies, and the Churches*. Dallas, Tex.: Southern Methodist University Press, 1989. A collection of essays from the Colloquium on Religion and World Affairs, held at the University of Chicago. The volume includes an essay by Yoder.

Kenneth Hada

PONTIUS PILATE

Author: Roger Caillois (1913-1978)
First published: Ponce Pilate, 1961 (English translation, 1963)
Edition used: Pontius Pilate, translated by Charles Lam Markmann, with an introduction by Ivan Strenski. Charlottesville: University of Virginia Press, 2006
Genre: Novel
Subgenres: Biblical fiction; historical fiction (first century); literary fiction
Core issues: Jesus Christ; justice; sacrifice; stoicism

Caillois's fictional depiction of the arrest, trial, and judgment of Jesus makes a strong case for the necessity of the sacrifice of the Son of God for the redemption of humankind. Pilate's freeing of Jesus deprives the world of Christianity and changes the course of history. Without the Divine Sacrifice, there is no Christian faith and no doctrine of salvation. Caillois's investigation into Pilate's thought and the arguments proposed by the various characters in the novel lead the reader on a fascinating journey into the mysteries of Divine Sacrifice.

Principal characters
Pontius Pilate, the protagonist, procurator of Judea under Roman emperor Tiberius
Procula, his wife
Mardouk, his closest friend
Annas and
Caiaphas, Jewish priests
Menenius, a politician, adviser to Pilate
Judas, disciple and betrayer of Jesus
Jesus, the Son of God, King of the Jews, the Messiah
Barabbas, a prisoner

Overview

Roger Caillois's novel *Pontius Pilate* is a compeling look at the dilemma that Pontius Pilate, procurator of Judea, may have faced in making the decision to execute Jesus. Caillois examines Pilate's thought processes as he listens to those who would condemn Jesus and consults with individuals whose judgment he trusts. The novel is composed of seven chapters and an epilogue. In five of the seven chapters, Caillois presents a conversation between Pilate and one of the individuals or groups who might have been influential in his decision about Jesus. The last two chapters reveal Pilate's final turmoil and moments of irresolution before he arrives at his final decision.

In the first chapter, Pilate is informed of the arrest of Jesus and told that Annas and Caiaphas, the Jewish high priests, wish an audience with him immediately. The Sanhedrin (the supreme Jewish council with authority in all judicial, religious, and administrative matters regarding the Jewish community in Jerusalem) has sat in judgment of Jesus and condemned him to death; the priests request Jesus' crucifixion within the day. This chapter provides the reader with an understanding of Pilate's situation in Judea and of his difficulties in dealing with what he views as the religious fanaticism of the Jews. Pilate, as a subordinate Roman official, is in a precarious position; he must consider his course of action in the light of how his superiors will react to it. Thus, in an attempt to transfer the problem to another official, he sends Jesus to Herod, tetrarch of Galilee, but to no avail. The Sanhedrin quickly informs Pilate that Jesus, by calling himself King of the Jews, has attacked the sovereignty of Rome. The matter is no longer merely religious; it is now political as well. Herod sends Jesus back to Pilate, who realizes that he is trapped and will have to decide the matter. Pilate's inclination is to free Jesus, whom he finds guiltless and preferable to the fanatics who are clamoring for his death, but he fears repercussions that could lead to his dismissal as procurator and to the end of his career. Pilate's reflection on his dilemma is interrupted by a centurion who comes to tell him an angry mob is demanding the death of Jesus and by a slave sent by his wife Procula. The first chapter ends with an account of a dream about Jesus that has frightened her. Pilate promises to consult his Chaldean friend Mardouk about the dream.

In chapter 2, Pilate seeks the advice of the prefect Menenius, his senior administrative officer who is an adept politician with many years of experience in outlying parts of the Roman Empire. Pilate explains to him that the priests have fulminated street riots as a means of pressuring him to execute an innocent man and to capitulate to their demands, thus letting them control the power of Rome. The astute Menenius immediately sees the errors to be avoided. Pilate must neither accept responsibility for Jesus' death nor give him the protection of the Roman army. Menenius suggests that Pilate, following tradition, offer to free a prisoner, either Jesus or Barabbas. The mob will choose Barabbas, and Pilate, evidencing his disapproval, will thus absolve himself and Rome of responsibility for Jesus' death. Menenius then stresses the importance of Pilate's performing the ritual gesture of hand washing to show that he is blameless. Menenius himself will provide the pitcher, basin, and bowl. Pilate is perplexed, then ashamed that Menenius considers him capable of executing an innocent man to avoid consequences that might be detrimental to his career. Imbued with Stoic philosophy, Pilate is repulsed by the injustice of Menenius's plan yet lacks courage to incur the displeasure of the propraetor, his administrative superior in the province. Then, Pilate conveniently remembers Judas, the madman waiting to speak with him.

In chapter 3, Judas explains the necessity of the condemnation and crucifixion of Jesus and tells Pilate that he and Pilate must fulfill their roles as divine instruments for the salvation of the world. Judas says he is telling this to Pilate because he fears that Pilate might summon up enough courage to stand against the Sanhedrin and free Jesus. Judas then falls into a fit, and Pilate, completely confused, decides to consult his friend Mardouk, a Chaldean well versed in matters of religion and interpretation of dreams.

Chapter 4 recounts the meeting of Pilate and Jesus, who, after stating that he has come for an express purpose, refuses to answer Pilate's questions. Caillois's depiction of the interrogation follows that of the biblical account except that, instead of ordering Jesus to be scourged, Pilate merely turns him over to the soldiers to do what they will with him. Pilate states that he believes Jesus to be innocent. The crowd, however, demands his crucifixion, and Caiaphas reminds Pilate that Jesus claims he is King of the Jews. With this statement, Caiaphas challenges Pilate's loyalty to Rome. Pilate assures the crowd that Jesus will be punished and offers them the choice of freedom for Barabbas or Jesus. They choose Barabbas. It is at this point that Pilate hands Jesus over to the soldiers. Jesus is flogged and a crown of thorns is placed on his head. Pilate then presents Jesus to the crowd, which screams for immediate crucifixion. Pilate refuses and says he will pass sentence the next day at the tribunal of Gabbatha.

That evening, Pilate visits Mardouk and finds some respite from his turmoil. He shares Procula's dream amd the ravings of Judas with Mardouk, who tells him of the Essenes and of their belief in the coming of a Redeemer. He then foretells the future after the crucifixion. Pilate returns home, reevaluates the problem, dreams feverishly, mixing a number of metaphysics in his mind, and finally becomes fascinated by the freedom of choice available to the human species. The next day at Gabbatha, Pilate frees Jesus, who continues preaching and lives to a venerable age. The world, however, never knows Christianity, and none of the events foretold by Mardouk occur, except Pilate's exile and suicide.

Christian Themes

The major Christian theme of the work is first expressed by Menenius when he repeats the argument of Caiaphas for the crucifixion of Jesus: that the sacrifice of one man for the salvation of an entire people is an admirable thing. Neither Caiaphas nor Menenius understands the true meaning of the statement. Caiaphas wishes to maintain the established Jewish religion and his own power. Menenius is simply advocating that the end—to forestall rebellion against Rome and the ensuing killings of many Jews—justifies the means. In chapter 3, Judas bluntly states that Jesus must be crucified for the world to be saved from eternal damnation and that he and Pilate are the instruments that God is using to bring this about. Caillois builds intensity in his novel as Pilate's visit to Mardouk reveals all that will happen as a result of the crucifixion of Jesus. The reader realizes the effect of the divine sacrifice on human history, on the history that he shares with all of humankind. Pilate's decision to spare Jesus and the resulting obliteration of all that the reader knows as human existence is overwhelming. Caillois's fictional account and reverse outcome of the trial of Jesus challenges the reader's complacency.

Sources for Further Study

Bond, Helen K. *Caiaphas: Friend of Rome and Judge of Jesus?* Louisville, Ky.: Westminster John Knox Press, 2004. Addresses the religious and political roles of Jewish priesthood and motives behind Caiaphas's involvement in trial of Jesus, us-

ing historical and archaeological sources; considers Caiaphas as a literary character in the four Gospels.

_____. *Pontius Pilate in History and Interpretation*. 1998, Reprint. Cam-
bridge, England: Cambridge University Press, 2004. Examines the presentation of
Pilate in the Gospel of Mark and the works of Philo and Josephus. Examines Pilate's role in Judea.

Carter, Warren. *Pontius Pilate: Portrait of a Roman Governor*. Collegeville, Minn.:
Liturgical Press, 2003. A portrait of Pilate that sharply contrasts with that of
Caillois. Carefully documented, with biblical references.

Crozier, W. P., ed. *Letters of Pontius Pilate: Written During His Governorship of
Judea to His Friend Seneca in Rome*. Amsterdam, Netherlands: Fredonia Books,
2002. Pilate discusses problems governing Judea, his policies, his impressions of
Jesus, and who he believed Jesus to be.

Strenski, Ivan. Introduction to *Pontius Pilate*. Charlottesville: University of Virginia
Press, 2006. Offers an excellent comparison of biblical version and Caillois's version of the Crucifixion story, addressing Caillois's philosophical position and the
connection between the novel and Algerian War.

Shawncey Webb

POPULORUM PROGRESSIO

Author: Paul VI (Giovanni Battista Montini; 1897-1978)
First published: 1967 (English translation, 1967)
Edition used: Encyclical Letter of His Holiness Paul VI, by Divine Providence, Pope, to the Bishops, Priests, Religious, the Faithful of the Whole Catholic Word, and to All Men of Good Will, on Fostering the Development of Peoples. London: Catholic Truth Society, 1967
Genre: Nonfiction
Subgenre: Encyclical
Core issues: Capitalism; charity; connectedness; peace; poverty; social action

In this encyclical, composed shortly after Vatican Council II, Pope Paul VI addresses the problem of world poverty. He proposes that the issue is widespread and severe and therefore in need of international attention. He emphasizes the universal destination of goods, which he argues places limitations on the rights to private ownership and free trade. Paul calls for attentiveness to the needs of the poor and he encourages the virtue of solidarity. While he focuses on economic development, Paul insists that true development cultivates the growth of what is fully human, including knowledge, virtue, and spiritual concern.

Overview

Pope Paul VI begins *Populorum Progressio* by explaining that he has turned his attention to the progress of the peoples of the world because of the widespread hunger, poverty, endemic disease, and ignorance present in underdeveloped nations. He explains that he has seen the social evils firsthand and states that the problems are urgent.

Paul breaks *Populorum Progressio* into two main sections: humankind's complete development and the common development of humankind. In the first section, Paul repeatedly acknowledges that progress is a "two-edged sword." He explains that colonialism has led to technological advances but has often entailed self-seeking activities, missionary work has spread the Gospel through charitable activity but has also engaged in cultural imposition, and industrialization has led to economic growth but has encouraged the evils of unbridled liberalism as well as the neglect of moral and spiritual goods.

To avoid the negative effects of progress, Paul proposes that social activity should seek to address the whole person. With this holistic view in mind, Paul provides a list of conditions important for human development. He describes these conditions on three levels: first, material necessities, social peace, education, and refinement and culture; second, awareness of human dignity, spirit of poverty, interest in the common good, and desire for peace; and third, sharing in God's life. Paul writes that every person has certain aptitudes and tasks to contribute to society and the building of God's kingdom.

Paul encourages the wealthy to stand in solidarity with those who are impoverished. Solidarity entails acknowledging the sufferings of our brothers and sisters and doing what we can to eliminate their difficulties. In particular, Paul emphasizes the universal destination of goods, which implies that wealthy individuals should share their fruits with those who lack material necessities. Paul states that the universal destination of goods is primary to the rights to private property and free trade. If property is abused while others endure severe hardship, Paul proposes that the government should have limited power to intervene to foster a just distribution of goods.

Paul extends the call for both solidarity and brotherly love to a national and international level. He explains that nations must have effective economic structures to address the needs of the impoverished. He critiques unbridled liberalism, stating that while competition among equals encourages economic growth, competition among those with different resources places the power of competition in the hands of the wealthy and often leads to economic tyranny. Despite his emphasis on the need for effective economic structures, Paul encourages the pursuit of reform rather than revolution. He proposes that the latter often leads to greater evils and therefore is contrary to progress. That being said, Paul calls for significant and urgent reform, and he states that such development ought to occur on a large-scale level. He states that large organizations must have clear goals, plans, methods, and authority; their activities should seek to serve human nature; and, if possible, they should have a religious orientation. Paul also writes that education is essential for economic reform.

In the second part of *Populorum Progressio*, Paul expands many of his earlier observations to the international level. He focuses on the duties of wealthy nations, which he summarizes in three virtues: solidarity, social justice, and universal charity. Concerning solidarity, Paul writes that wealthier nations should share the fruit of their land with those less fortunate. He encourages the development of a world fund, which would receive contributions from wealthier nations and would be distributed to those nations in need. To promote solidarity and the effective distribution of goods, Paul stresses the importance of communication concerning the needs of the impoverished nations and the most efficient means for wealthy nations to share their resources.

In his discussion of social justice, Paul focuses on trade relations. He explains that impoverished nations lack marketable goods and that international trading often leads only to greater debts and the obligation of paying interest. Paul writes that competition has important limits, and he proposes that these limitations should be acknowledged on an international level. He argues that steps must be made to equalize trade relations so that all countries can benefit from their mutual interactions. Further, Paul encourages the development of international organizations and warns against the evils of nationalism and racism.

Paul also addresses developing nations. He explains that the reception of aid from wealthy nations is only a short-term solution. Citizens of impoverished lands must take a central role in the progress of their nations. They must actively discern the forms of aid that they would like to receive to avoid unnecessary dependence on undependable assistance. Paul also states that developing nations need access to education, which fosters technological advances and long-term production of resources. Paul encourages developing nations to attain peaceful relations with neighboring countries so that the nations may seek economic reform by pooling their resources.

While Paul focuses on economic reform, he continually states that developing nations are in need of moral and spiritual resources as well. Paul states that the foundation of economic poverty and likewise economic development is the absence or presence of brotherly and sisterly charity.

Christian Themes

In *Populorum Progressio*, Paul VI offers focused reflection on the Christian themes of solidarity, options for the poor, and Christian anthropology. He explains that all people have the same supernatural destiny and are called to contribute to the building up of the human community. This shared destiny brings people in unity with their brothers and sisters. A fruit of this unity is the virtue of solidarity, which entails being aware of the sufferings of others and assisting those in need.

Central to solidarity is the need to be attentive to the situation of the impoverished. Paul acknowledges that the voices of the impoverished tend to go unheard because they lack the wealth and power to gain the attention of others. Therefore, all people must make efforts to acknowledge the needs of others so that the poor will also have the opportunity to contribute to society. In particular, Paul states that private property should be expropriated when owners abuse their land while others go without necessities. Further, Paul encourages the development of a world fund and calls for reflection on how international trade relations can be equalized.

Paul also makes frequent mention of the need to develop a genuine understanding of humans. Paul states that economic development alone is not sufficient. He argues that for people to be fully human, they must have a peaceful family and political community, education, moral formation, and spiritual orientation toward their origin and end. Paul argues that Christian social teaching is more than a set of principles and rules because this teaching promotes the fulfillment of human life. Promoting Christian social teaching, then, is not an imposition on others but an act of charity expressed for the benefit of others.

Sources for Further Study

Himes, Kenneth R., ed. *Modern Catholic Social Teaching: Commentaries and Interpretations*. Washington, D.C.: Georgetown University Press, 2005. This scholarly collection includes four foundational essays and fourteen commentaries on influential church documents. Each essay includes thorough bibliographical information. Brief index.

Pontifical Council for Justice and Peace. *Compendium of the Social Doctrine of the Church*. Translated by Vatican Press. Washington, D.C.: United States Conference of Catholic Bishops, 2005. This reference work provides a comprehensive synthesis of central concepts in Catholic social ethics. Includes thorough reference and analytical indexes.

_____. *The Social Agenda: A Collection of Magisterial Texts*. Città del Vaticano: Libreria Editrice Vaticano, 2000. This work is a concise compilation of official church statements thematically organized to discuss eleven issues central to Christian social ethics.

Royal, Robert. "Reforming International Development: *Populorum Progressio*. In *Building the Free Society: Democracy, Capitalism, and Catholic Social Teaching*, edited by George Weigel and Robert Royal. Grand Rapids, Mich.: Wm. B. Eerdmans, 1993. Royal is critical of Paul VI's call for national and international organization as a way to address poverty.

Kevin Schemenauer

THE POWER AND THE GLORY

Author: Graham Greene (1904-1991)
First published: 1940
Edition used: The Power and the Glory. New York: Viking Press, 1958
Genre: Novel
Subgenres: Catholic fiction; literary fiction
Core issues: Alienation from God; Catholics and Catholicism; fear; guilt; Latin Americans; persecution; sacrifice

In a novel inspired by real events, Greene's nameless priest is hunted by an atheistic police lieutenant during the Mexican government's persecution of the Catholic Church in the late 1930's. Although the priest struggles to escape over the mountains to safety, he is repeatedly lured back into danger by a treacherous peasant, the needs of his people, and his own guilt.

> *Principal characters*
> *The whiskey priest,* a Catholic fugitive
> *The police lieutenant,* a revolutionary idealist
> *The mestizo,* a scheming peasant
> *Padre José,* a cowardly priest
> *Brigida,* the whiskey priest's difficult child
> *James Calver,* an escaped American criminal

Overview

Graham Greene, baptized an Anglican, became an atheist at Oxford University and converted to Catholicism at the age of twenty-one. He preferred to say he was not a Catholic novelist but rather a novelist who happened to be Catholic; nevertheless, his faith informed his work. As a journalist, he traveled to Mexico to write *The Lawless Roads: A Mexican Journal* (1939), a nonfiction account of religious persecution in the states of Tabasco and Chiapas. Antireligious laws were most severe in Tabasco, where all Catholic churches were destroyed and the celebration of Mass, confession, and rites for the dying were forbidden. The governor decreed that all priests must leave the state, marry, or be shot. There, Greene encountered stories of the hunted, alcoholic priest who became his protagonist in *The Power and the Glory*.

Greene's "whiskey priest" is a questionable hero. He has evaded the authorities for ten years, yet he still feels a pastoral duty: Without him, the people cannot receive God through the sacrament of Communion. Fear dominates his life. A small man, he dreads pain; only brandy can give him courage when necessary. He has sinned, for in a moment of loneliness he has fathered a child. He knows he is unworthy of the priesthood but cannot abandon those who need him, even though he wants to—unlike Padre José, a disgraced old priest who chose to marry his housekeeper rather than die and who faces continual humiliation.

The whiskey priest's pursuer is an ascetic police lieutenant, a priest of the new order, whose real life began with the socialist revolution a few years before. He wholeheartedly believes that religion has had a corrupting influence on the lives of his people. Although he has destroyed lives and property for his ideals, he views the world as rational, and his faith lies in the power of a godless state. Ironically, he also seeks another wanted man—a murderer named James Calver.

The priest flees to a banana plantation, then to the poor village where his little daughter Brigida already seems wise beyond her years and on the brink of corruption. He desperately wants to save her but feels helpless when he cannot reach her. She does not, however, betray him to the lieutenant. During his flight the priest acquires an unwelcome companion, a miserable peasant of mixed Spanish and native blood. The mestizo follows him, whining, urging him to rest, offering advice he neither needs nor wants. A disreputable figure with two yellow fangs protruding over his lower lip, the mestizo intends to surrender him for a reward of seven hundred pesos. The two men strive to outwit one another; even so, the priest refuses to confront him and ultimately pities him, realizing that he too is made in the image of God.

A crucial scene occurs when the unrecognized priest, attempting to buy wine necessary to celebrate Mass, is jailed for violating the temperance law. He finds himself in a dark and filthy cell, a sort of underworld, packed in with others whose faces he cannot see. In the blackness he confesses his identity and his sins to fellow prisoners, who sympathize and refuse to expose him to the authorities. When he is released in the morning, the lieutenant, learning he has no money, impulsively gives him a coin for food.

Once the priest is safely across the mountains, he again encounters his Judas. The ragged mestizo appears with a note from the wounded killer Calver, begging the priest to return to hear his confession. This note is part of a trap set by the police, and the priest fully understands he will be going to meet his death. After the lieutenant finally captures him, the two men have a lengthy debate on the philosophical merits of church and state. The lieutenant tells him, "You're a danger. That's why we kill you. I have nothing against you. . . . It's your ideas."

At police headquarters, the priest asks to make his confession to Padre José. Against all his principles, the lieutenant approaches Padre José with the request—for him, an act both of charity and of treason against the government—but the old man, suspecting a trick, refuses. The lieutenant informs the whiskey priest, slipping him a small flask of illegal brandy to steady him before his impending execution. For the lieutenant, a world without the priest seems suddenly empty.

Christian Themes

Greene is not a didactic author. With insight and grace he describes the human condition and human anguish. His whiskey priest, a typical protagonist, is an imperfect soul who accepts and loves God but somehow fails to comprehend his great mercy. Haunted by the sins he has committed, he regards himself as beyond redemption, but in spite of his weaknesses he is essentially a good man, as is the lieutenant. Can there be salvation for such men? Although the question is left hanging, Greene suggests that the answer is yes.

Greene's fallen world is one that Saint Augustine would recognize. Augustine's doctrine of humanity, which strongly influenced the early Christian church, is that, through Adam's sin of disobedience, his descendants are stained by Original Sin and can escape it only by the grace of God. The means of grace are the Sacraments of the Church, regardless of the unworthiness of whoever performs them. In his long dialogue with the lieutenant, the whiskey priest acknowledges the power of the Sacraments as well as the Catholic belief in transubstantiation, whereby the bread and wine of Communion become—in essence, not in appearance—the body and blood of Christ. As an appointed conduit of God's grace, the priest believes he truly "can put God into a man's mouth," no matter what he himself may have done.

The priest blames himself and his own inadequacies for his failures. As soon as he offers his shirt to the shivering mestizo, he regards the act as a sin of pride. He has violated his vow of chastity; he lies; he is an alcoholic; he is tempted into deceit. He recognizes his own fallen nature in his daughter, but he is unable to repent of her conception: "What was the good of confession when you loved the result of your crime?" He cannot regret that she exists, whom he loves most intensely but fears he cannot save.

The priest feels alienated from God and knows he deserves damnation. He cannot even make a good act of contrition, because he has forgotten the words of the prayer, perhaps from terror. He is willing, however, to sacrifice himself for others, praying that God will save his daughter in exchange for his own death. He becomes Christlike when he returns to absolve the dying criminal Calver, in effect giving up his own life for another man's chance at eternal life. The lieutenant calls him a martyr, but the priest rejects the title because he thinks martyrs have no fear.

Greene, however, seems to endorse the idea that God allows evil to exist in the world to give fallen human beings an opportunity to rise above it. Although the whiskey priest lives in a state of mortal sin and dies unshriven, one sees his imprint on those he leaves behind. He inspires others to emulate him in his kindness and courage—for he is brave, in spite of himself. His deeds of compassion and charity appear to outweigh his human weakness and to suggest that a loving God will forgive and understand.

Sources for Further Study

Allott, Kenneth, and Miriam Farris. *The Art of Graham Greene*. New York: Russell and Russell, 1963. Envisions *The Power and the Glory* as a spiritual way of the cross, as the priest separates himself from his known life.

Baldridge, Cates. *Graham Greene's Fictions: The Virtues of Extremity*. Columbia: University of Missouri Press, 2000. This first evaluation of Greene's work since his death in 1991 examines his conception of God as revealed through his fiction.

Bosco, Mark, S.J. *Graham Greene's Catholic Imagination*. New York: Oxford University Press, 2005. Explores Greene's theological vision and his achievement as a master of the Catholic novel prior to Vatican Council II.

De Vitis, A. A. *Graham Greene*. New York: Twayne, 1964. Sees the novel as a study of good and evil in the fallen world and an extended allegory of Everyman.

Kurismmootil, K. C. Joseph, S.J. *Heaven and Hell on Earth: An Appreciation of Five Novels of Graham Greene*. Chicago: Loyola University Press, 1982. Contrasts the priest as a picaresque saint with the lieutenant as socialist ascetic.

Miller, R. H. *Understanding Graham Greene*. Columbia: University of South Carolina Press, 1990. Analyzes the priest's physical and spiritual journey, his ministry, and his pursuit by God.

Joanne McCarthy

THE POWER OF POSITIVE THINKING

Author: Norman Vincent Peale (1898-1993)
First published: New York: Prentice-Hall, 1952
Genre: Nonfiction
Subgenres: Guidebook; handbook for living
Core issues: Daily living; doubt; fear; guidance; psychology; self-knowledge

In 1952, Peale, the pastor at Marble Collegiate Church in New York City, published a book destined to sell more than twenty million copies over the next half century. That volume was the model for thousands of self-help books that followed, including several by Dr. Peale himself. The book is unparalleled in having restored the faltering faith of millions and providing a combination of inspiration and self-directed psychology.

Overview

Norman Vincent Peale was ordained in the Methodist Episcopal Church in 1922 and held several pastorates until changing his affiliation to the Dutch Reformed Church so that he could become the pastor in 1932 of Marble Collegiate Church, a Dutch Reformed Church founded in 1628. He remained as that church's pastor of Marble Collegiate for fifty-two years. He and his wife, Ruth, founded *Guideposts* magazine in 1945; by the 1950's, it had the largest circulation of any religious magazine in America. Peale's life was the subject of a 1964 movie entitled *One Man's Way*.

The theme of *The Power of Positive Thinking* is that one's faith in oneself will allow good things to happen. The book is a guide to enhancing self-esteem and thereby achieving success. Thus, despite the fact that its author is a religious man, the volume is not strictly a religious book. Peale took his inspiration from his own life. He acknowledged having had an inferiority complex as a younger man and believed that his feeling of inferiority held him back. As a result, he had long preached a message that merged theology and psychology: that maintaining a positive attitude will lead to success and happiness. He was subsequently called the father of the self-esteem gospel, a mixture of modern psychology and the Bible. Peale was not one to use the Bible like a baseball bat, to swat the unknowing reader heavy-handedly. Rather, he was tolerant of his readers', and parishioners', weaknesses. His book recognizes that prayer is the greatest energy in the universe and a link between people's thoughts, feelings, and actions. One reviewer stated that the book should be called "The Power of Prayer."

Peale preaches that perseverance is the key to success in any activity and that faith releases enormous power in the believer. Thus, the key to success in any endeavor is to think positively. In fact, the first sentence in the book reads, "Believe in yourself," and that is a good summary of the book. Peale offers dozens of examples of real-life experiences during which people used the principles presented in his book to change their lives or otherwise develop their faith. Peale advises readers to apply positive thinking in every aspect of their lives; he encourages them, for example, to try to like people that they do not particularly like. Although he does not specifically advise readers to be phony, Peale supports contrived emotions when he says that individuals should practice liking other people until they genuinely do. Peale observes that getting involved in other people's problems can take one's mind off one's own difficulties.

Another of the book's motivational approaches is based on goal setting. Peale argues that many people do not accomplish anything because they do not know what it is that they really want to accomplish. This aspect of Peale's thought is only a minor part of the book, but it would lead to hundreds of similarly focused books by other writers.

Despite the book's popularity, there were criticisms. Simply making religion compatible with success was objectionable to some critics. Some thought the material "too positive." One reviewer argued that Peale was implying that the primary purpose of God was to dispense divine vitamins to those who wanted improved health and wealth. Some fundamentalist groups believed Peale's message to be blasphemous because of his absence of fear-based theology. It was argued by some that positive thinking was not really religious and was applicable only to the salvation that concerned modern man—namely that which occurs in this world, not the next. The book was criticized for neglecting the commandments of humility and self-sacrifice and for teaching that Christianity was a practical discipline. Some Christians looked askance at Peale's evident philosophy that worldly success could indicate a blessedness to come.

Peale was one of America's most influential clergymen during the 1950's and throughout the remainder of his life. For more than half a century, he was heard on his daily radio show, and in later years his sermons were broadcast on television. He was constantly in demand as a motivational speaker. His rhetoric only made his books more popular. He wrote more than forty books, and *The Power of Positive Thinking* was published in forty-one languages. He was a major influence on religion and the field of personal motivation.

Christian Themes

The heart of *The Power of Positive Thinking* deals with how to eliminate the handicap of self-doubt and how to reduce worry, stress, and resentment. Included are prayerful exercises that readers can use daily to reinforce the habit of eliminating negative thoughts. The book is spiritual in that it advocates a fuller life in Christ. The dominant theme is that negative thoughts prevent people from achieving happiness and success, but the power of positive thinking will result in a positive change in an individual's life. There is no fear-based theology in the book. Peale does, however, invoke positive biblical passages throughout, such as "If God be for us, who can be against us?" (Romans 8:31) and "I can do all things through Christ who gives me strength" (Philippians 4:13). In fact, Peale often told people to recite the passage from Philippians to enhance their belief in themselves.

One of Peale's biographers, Carol George, called his theology "eclectic, synthetic, obviously uncreedal, and unsystematic." She went on to say that his theological blend of "evangelical Protestantism, metaphysical spirituality, and the American dream" was perfectly suited to the cultural currents of the 1950's. Based on the book's continuing sales, that blend is also apparently well suited to the cultural currents and modern sensibilities of decades since. Essentially, Peale's message combines hope, faith, and Christian symbols with an individualized program in self-help and healing. The book has remained a classic for more than half a century because it speaks of simple faith as the most powerful thing in the universe. Peale framed his religious experiences within the world of which he was a part. Just as Christ spoke and taught in a simple manner with parables, so does Norman Vincent Peale. Peale's book enabled him to comfort and offer personal direction to the lives of millions.

Peale wrote several sequels to *The Power of Positive Thinking*, which share the original's theme and continue to promote sales of the original volume. Peale's work was also the inspiration for books by Dr. Robert H. Schuller, who preaches a concept known as "possibility thinking."

Sources for Further Study

George, Carol V. R. *God's Salesman: Norman Vincent Peale and the Power of Positive Thinking*. New York: Oxford University Press, 1993. Partly biographical and partly analytical, George's book is widely available in libraries.

Gordon, Arthur. *One Man's Way: The Story and Message of Norman Vincent Peale, a Biography*. New York: Prentice-Hall, 1972. Excellent biography of Peale to the time of publication; does not cover the last thirty years of his life.

Peale, Norman Vincent. *The Power of Positive Living*. New York: Doubleday, 1990. A sequel to the classic volume, with the principles being extrapolated for the 1990's generation of readers.

_____. *This Incredible Century*. Pauling, N.Y.: Peale Center for Christian Living, 1991. Essentially a biography of the twentieth century, written from Peale's perspective of positive thinking.

_____. *The True Joy of Positive Living*. New York: Morrow, 1998. An autobiography and memoir in which Peale explains how positive thinking influenced his life.

Peale, Norman Vincent, and Smiley Blanton. *The Art of Real Happiness*. London: Vermilion, 2000. Shows readers how to cope with depression and anxiety, and how to find peace of mind and contentment.

Dale L. Flesher

A PRAYER FOR OWEN MEANY

Author: John Irving (1942-   )
First published: New York: Morrow, 1989
Genre: Novel
Subgenre: Literary fiction
Core issues: Conversion; friendship; martyrdom; redemption

Owen Meany, Irving's diminutive protagonist, considers himself to be an instrument of God. Indeed, he acts upon and influences the lives of most of the people whom he touches, none more than the book's narrator, John Wheelwright. John considers Owen to have been the instrument of his conversion to Christianity. The questions raised by the book regarding predestination are intriguing, as is the Christ figure that Owen is clearly intended to be.

Principal characters
    Owen Meany, the protagonist
    John Wheelwright, Owen's closest friend and the narrator
    Tabitha Wheelwright, John's mother and Owen's benefactor
    Dan Needham, John's stepfather
    Harriet Wheelwright, John's grandmother
    Hester Eastman, John's cousin and Owen's lover
    The Reverend Lewis Merrill, pastor of the Congregational Church
    Mr. and Mrs. Meany, Owen's parents
    Randy White, headmaster of Gravesend Academy

Overview

In the first sentence of *A Prayer for Owen Meany*, the adult John Wheelwright, the narrator, tells the reader three things: that Owen Meany was the smallest person he ever knew; that he was the instrument of John's mother's death; and that Owen is the reason John believes in God:

> I am doomed to remember a boy with a wrecked voice—not because of his voice or because he was the smallest person I ever knew or even because he was the instrument of my mother's death, but because he is the reason I believe in God; I am a Christian because of Owen Meany.

This sentence lays out some of the complex issues of the novel in simple terms. The novel then proceeds to tell the story of John and Owen, the boy with the "wrecked voice," from their childhood to their adulthood.

As children, John and Owen live in Gravesend, New Hampshire, where John is the grandson of Harriet Wheelwright and a descendant of John Adams; Owen, by contrast, is the son of an owner of a granite business. They go to church together (where a favorite Sunday School game was picking Owen up and passing him around over the heads of the other children), they play Little League baseball together, and they attend school together. John Irving renders the "wrecked voice" to which the opening sentence refers in full capital letters; in fact, that Irving intends Owen to be associated in the reader's mind with Christ is made partially clear by this use of capital letters for Owen's words, a device that parallels the printing of the words of Christ in red in some versions of the Bible. The capital letters also represent Owen's otherworldly voice, described by the narrator as a "voice from another planet" and "a voice not entirely of this world." However, one of the strongest connections with Christ is made when Owen's father tells John that Owen was born to a virgin mother, that there was no sexual congress to account for his conception.

John is the illegitimate son of Tabitha Wheelwright, who sometimes refers to him as her "little fling." Tabitha holds the secret of his parentage closely; no one knows who John's father is, and Owen seems rather more curious about the father than is John. Tabitha had regularly attended singing lessons in Boston, to which she took the train and stayed overnight for her early lesson. On one of these trips, she became pregnant with John, but no one has an inkling as to who her lover might have been. When John is ten, Tabitha marries Dan Needham, a teacher at Gravesend Academy, who adopts John. Though he is a poor student, he is assured of enrollment in the prestigious private school because his stepfather is a faculty member. Owen has no such assurances, though Tabitha insists that he attend the academy as well.

The event around which all others in the novel revolve occurs when John and Owen are eleven. Owen hits a foul ball in a Little League game. It strikes Tabitha in the head and kills her. Tabitha's death is as devastating to Owen as it is to John. Indeed, it is this accident that convinces Owen that he is "God's instrument" and that his hands are the instruments that took her. (Throughout the novel, the use of hands as symbols is repeated, prefiguring Owen's own death.) Owen gives John his most treasured possession: his collection of baseball cards. As Dan helps John understand, Owen's gift is both a sacrifice and an offering of himself.

Reinforcement of Owen's role as a Christ figure is literally underscored when he serves as the Christ child in the manger for the annual Christmas pageant at the Episcopal Church. (Even though Owen is more than eleven years old, he is small enough to fit into the manger and is therefore cast as the Christ child.) During this same period, Dan, the director of the local theater group, uses Owen as the Ghost of Christmas Yet to Come in his annual portrayal of Charles Dickens's *A Christmas Carol*. During his performance, Owen sees his name and the date of his death on Scrooge's gravestone. Owen believes he has been given a vision of the day and circumstances of his own death.

Owen and John enter Gravesend Academy in the fall of 1958, and Owen becomes a power in the school as The Voice, writer of editorials for the school newspaper, *The Grave*. As a columnist, Owen exerts considerable power in the school; as a tutor, he essentially gets John through. While they are at Gravesend, Owen and John also perfect "the shot," a basketball maneuver performed when Owen jumps into John's arms and dunks the ball into the basket. They time themselves on their performance and eventually perform the shot in less than four seconds.

When Randy White is made headmaster of the school, Owen's days there are numbered. Owen's criticisms of White and of the school make him something of a marked man. After a series of incidents, White manages to find enough evidence of misbehavior to have Owen expelled: As John puts it, "they crucified him." Having lost his offers of scholarships to Harvard and Yale, Owen goes to the University of New Hampshire and joins the Reserve Officers' Training Corps.

Owen joins the army and applies for duty in Vietnam, firm in his belief that he is supposed to die in the performance of a heroic deed, rescuing nuns and Vietnamese children. Ultimately, that is exactly what happens, except that it happens in Phoenix, Arizona. Owen and John are attempting to help some Vietnamese orphans, accompanied by nuns, to reach a bathroom. A deranged brother of a man killed in Vietnam tosses a grenade into the bathroom to kill the children. Owen and John—by use of "the shot"—save the children, but Owen covers the grenade with his arms, and they are blown off. He dies on the lap of one of the nuns.

Christian Themes

As James M. Wall notes in his review of the novel for *The Christian Century*:

> When evil befalls the innocent, the response is either to curse God or to embrace an ultimate reality which alone can give meaning to a broken world. Owen decides to embrace God; and all who know him are forced either to accept God or to reject God's instrument and suffer the consequences.

Owen—the "wrecked voice," The Voice, instrument of God—brooks no fools and states truth plainly, clearly, and (as the capital letters imply) loudly. He has strong views of what constitutes Christians and Christianity. "If you don't believe in Easter . . . [d]on't call yourself a Christian," he says. Later, in a Bible class, he calls the disciples "stupid" because, he says, they never understood what Jesus was telling them. He nevertheless takes all of the scripture and religion classes offered at the academy. When he reaches his senior year, there are no more classes available, so he undertakes independent study with the Reverend Lewis Merrill, basing a term paper on Isaiah 5:20, "Woe unto them that call evil good and good evil." This particular theme has considerable meaning when Randy White, the pompous, self-deluded headmaster at Gravesend Academy sets out to destroy Owen. White does manage to damage Owen, but his malice carries the seeds of his own destruction. Owen overcomes White's evil; White himself does not.

Owen as the instrument of God's will is perhaps at once the most amusing and most baffling feature of the novel: His role as a Christ figure, clearly intended, is nevertheless mysterious and counterintuitive. There is little of the pious or saintly about Owen Meany. He is a heavy smoker, and for a time he lives with Hester Eastman ("Hester the Molester"), John's cousin. He has pronounced notions about religion and expresses some fairly biased opinions about Catholics in general and about nuns in particular. He calls them "penguins" and considers them "unnatural," although given his earlier vision of his own death, his sentiments might make his aversion understandable. His role as the instrument of the beloved Tabitha's death provokes the greatest dissonance with the Christ symbolism that engulfs him: He embraces his having caused Tabitha's death as a sign that he is God's instrument rather than the instrument of evil—despite the hurt he has caused. Instead, he accepts, or does not question, events and appears to exude a love and wisdom that allow Tabitha to live on. A surprising instrument of God, Owen gives of himself unstintingly and allows the divine to work through him. John, looking back, realizes that he has become a Christian because of him, recalling that until his mother died and Owen gave him his collection of baseball cards,

> . . . the notion that anything had a designated, much less a special purpose would have been cuckoo to me. I was not what was commonly called a believer then, and I am a believer now; I believe in God, and I believe in the "special purpose" of certain events or specific things.

Sources for Further Study

Campbell, Josie P. *John Irving: A Critical Companion.* Westport, Conn.: Greenwood Press, 1998. Campbell looks at all of Irving's novels written prior to 1998 and examines their themes and the critical response to the books.

Davis, Todd F., and Kenneth Womak. *The Critical Response to John Irving.* Westport, Conn.: Praeger, 2004. A scholarly treatment of Irving's work, including book reviews, essays on the novels, and the critical response.

Reilly, Edward C. *Understanding John Irving.* Colombia: University of South Carolina Press, 1991. Examines the life and works of John Irving, including themes, symbols, and motifs used in his novels.

Shostak, Debra. "Plot as Repetition: John Irving's Narrative Experiments." *Critique: Studies in Contemporary Fiction* 37, no. 1 (Fall, 1995): 51-70. Shostak compares *The World According to Garp* and *A Prayer for Owen Meany,* paying particular attention to the way Irving plots these novels as well as his use of symbols and images. She focuses as well on the novel's Christian themes.

Wall, James M. "Owen Meany and the Presence of God." *The Christian Century* 106, no. 10 (March 22, 1989): 299-300. Sees the novel as focused on the problem of evil and Owen as "the vehicle of Irving's vision that promises . . . 'Woe unto them that call evil good and good evil.'"

June Harris

PRAYING GOD'S WORD
Breaking Free from Spiritual Strongholds

Author: Beth Moore (1957-   )
First published: Nashville, Tenn.: Broadman & Holman, 2000
Genre: Nonfiction
Subgenres: Guidebook; handbook for living
Core issues: Daily living; guidance; prayer; self-control; spiritual warfare; trust in
   God; the Word

Even committed Christians suffer from addiction, disobedience, and despair. Moore
states that as contemporary culture seems to drift farther away from the will of God, it
is easy to be deceived or entrapped through Satan's power. In Praying God's Word,
she shows believers how God has armed them with divine weapons that can "demol-
ish strongholds" and bring them closer to his presence. The weapons—Scripture and
prayer—are formidable when used together and can foster more intimate communion
with God.

Overview

Popular Bible teacher, conference speaker, and author Beth Moore writes about
powerful "strongholds" that can ensnare individual believers and consume "so
much . . . emotional and mental energy that abundant life is strangled." Early in the
book, she assures readers that she herself has been released from bondage and stands
as living proof of the power of "praying Scripture to overcome strongholds." Most often, Moore argues, battles are waged not in the physical world but in the minds of believers. She sees pride, insecurity, depression, and sexual addiction as emotional responses to the lies Satan tells Christians.

Moore first explicates what will become the central Scriptural passage of her work,
2 Corinthians 10:3-5, which begins

> For though we live in the world, we do not wage war as the world does. The weapons we
> fight with are not the weapons of the world. On the contrary, they have the power to de-
> molish strongholds.

The "weapons we fight with," Moore tells readers, are Scripture and prayer, and together, they are strong enough to set captives free.

Each of the book's main chapters is organized around a lesson that describes how
to overcome a particular stronghold. Moore lists fourteen: idolatry, unbelief, pride,
deception, insecurity, rejection, addiction, food-related strongholds, guilt, despair resulting from loss, unforgiveness, depression, sexual strongholds, and finally, the enemy, Satan himself. While these are distinct problems, they are related; thus, some
themes recur throughout the book. For example, it might be the stronghold of pride

that prevents someone from granting forgiveness. Deception leads to addiction. Insecurity can come from guilt and rejection.

In each lesson, Moore describes the problem and gives examples of ways in which it can diminish the joy of life in the body of Christ. For example, in a chapter titled "Overcoming Deception," she offers a list of common lies that creep into the thoughts of those whose defenses are weakened: "I'm worthless," "I'll know when to stop," and "There's nothing wrong with this relationship."

After examining the nature of a particular problem, Moore outlines key passages of Scripture that address it. Some reassuring words follow, and she often relates the message of the chapter to her own life or to testimonials of her students or friends.

The final section of each chapter contains a series of "scripture-prayers," intimate prayers that readers might use to ask for God's aid as they seek release and comfort. Because the invitation to "pray God's Word" is the central part of Moore's message, the scripture-prayers represent the largest portion of each chapter and thus the book as a whole. Moore invites readers to say the words aloud and to study the Bible verses that are referenced parenthetically after each prayer. The words of prayer are meant to combat negative messages and to prepare hearts and minds for direct communication with God.

Praying God's Word is structured so that readers can begin with any chapter, focusing only on those that interest them or reading them all in order. The mixture of scriptural exegesis, personal anecdotes, and practical advice makes it a popular title for Bible-study groups and seminars. It was a recurring title on the Christian Booksellers Association's best-sellers list from its publication in 2000 until late 2002.

Christian Themes

Like many evangelicals—Christians who accept a literal interpretation of the Bible and who believe one must be "born again" in Christ in order to enter heaven—Moore sees events in world politics and trends in social culture as evidence of increased evil activities and thus of the imminent return of Christ prophesied in the biblical book of Revelation. For this reason, she believes that contemporary Christians will be challenged to a greater degree than ever before. Whereas previous generations of believers might have been able simply to pray for release from the bondage of addiction or other strongholds, leading up to the last days, Satan's activity will increase and so must the arsenal of the Christians.

Moore's teachings are informed by the presumption of a coming apocalyptic struggle between the forces of good and evil. "Just in case anyone is still clinging to a few doubts," she writes in the chapter on "Overcoming the Enemy," "let me assure you, *the devil is real.*" For Moore, the devil is an active, deceptive, and crafty force who preys on mental and emotional weaknesses and wants to keep Christians in bondage. One of the themes at work in *Praying God's Word* is the idea of slavery versus freedom. It is quite possible, Moore reminds readers, to be a born-again Christian and still be overcome by powerful forces that prevent true spirit-filled living.

Another significant message not made fully clear until the end of the book is

Moore's belief in the redemptive power of God's love. Though the early chapters and the scripture-prayers show evidence of a mature and tested faith, the last chapter connects the prescriptive teachings back to the struggles Moore alludes to early in the work. In this section, she shares obviously painful stories about her own apparent history of abuse. Though she does not give specific details of the events, she *does* provide examples of the ways in which the memories of those events damaged her self-esteem, her views about relationships, her moods, and even her spiritual development. In retrospect, she sees that Satan was working especially hard on her during those years because those were also the years during which she was building what would become a large, interdenominational Bible ministry. As she waged almost daily internal battles and felt like giving up (and even, she admits, killing herself), she did not realize then what was at stake. Her prayer for readers is that they learn from her lessons and find the courage to live the life that God has planned for them.

Sources for Further Study

Cowman, Mrs. Charles E. [Lettie Burd]. *Streams in the Desert*. Los Angeles: Oriental Missionary Society, 1925. Rev. ed. Grand Rapids, Mich.: Zondervan, 1999. Mrs. Cowman's popular devotional journal (and its revised editions) has been a best-selling title for nearly a century and is an early model of books like Moore's.

Moore, Beth. *Breaking Free: Making Liberty in Christ a Reality in Life*. Nashville, Tenn.: Broadman & Holman, 2000. Published the same year as *Praying God's Word*, this more extensive work describes the journey of transformation believers undergo as they seek union with God.

Vara, Richard. "A Victorious Life: Local Bible Teacher Builds National Women's Ministry." *Houston Chronicle*, January 8, 2000, 1. Article looks at how Moore came to be a Bible teacher and how she founded the Living Proof Ministries.

Jennifer Heller

THE PRESENCE OF THE WORD
Some Prolegomena for Cultural and Religious History

Author: Walter J. Ong (1912-2003)
First published: New Haven, Conn.: Yale University Press, 1967
Genre: Nonfiction
Subgenres: Essays; history; theology
Core issues: Listening; memory; psychology; silence; time; the Word

The Presence of the Word *develops Ong's ideas about the effects of scientific development and technology on people and how they think. It also addresses religious implications of the conflict between the word as sound (oral communication) and the word as sign or letter (written communication).*

Overview

When Walter J. Ong, Jesuit priest and theologian, delivered the Terry lectures on religion in the light of science and philosophy at Yale University in 1964 (published three years later as *The Presence of the Word: Some Prolegomena for Cultural and Religious History*), he had already published several volumes exploring the religious importance of evolution and scientific development, the interpenetration of religious and secular cultural history, and the influence of technology on human patterns of thought. Ong was widely known as the author of *Ramus, Method, and the Decay of Dialogue: From the Art of Discourse to the Art of Reason* (1958), considered a profound contribution to the history of sixteenth century education. The research for his 1955 doctoral dissertation at Harvard University had been the basis not only for that volume but also for an associated bibliographical study, *Ramus and Talon Inventory* (1958), which Ong dedicated to his mentor, Marshall McLuhan, "who started all this."

McLuhan, who had directed Ong's 1941 master's thesis on the poetry of Gerard Manley Hopkins at St. Louis University and stimulated his interest in French humanist Petrus Ramus, was soon popularizing, in *The Gutenberg Galaxy* (1962) and *Understanding Media* (1964), the idea that shifts in communications media such as the development of writing and literacy or the invention of the printing press had played transformative, perhaps determinative, roles in the development of human thought. The medium, McLuhan insisted in one of his catchy exaggerations, is the message. Though his ideas sometimes overlap McLuhan's, Ong's approach tends to be more detailed and nuanced, and is explicitly relational (rather than reductionist). Ong was influenced by many other scholars in his reflections on the contrast between "orality" and "literacy," including Albert Lord and Eric Havelock, who redefined the relations of oral poets such as Homer and literary philosophers such as Plato to oral and literate cultures.

Though McLuhan converted to Catholicism and his "global village" is related to the "noosphere" of the French theologian and scientist Pierre Teilhard de Chardin,

Ong has the more abiding interest in the religious implications of media-driven changes in human thought. Very roughly speaking, the first three chapters of *The Presence of the Word* ("The Word and the Sensorium," "Transformations of the Word," and "Word as Sound") lay out the theory, and the next three chapters ("The Word as History: Sacred and Profane," "The Word and the Quest for Peace," "Man's Word and God's Presence") focus on the religious implications.

For Ong, the word as sound comes naturally to human beings, while the word as visual sign or letter begins a complex process of enculturation that grows even more consequential when cultures of writing become cultures of printing. With the advent of electronic communications media, certain aspects of oral societies reassert themselves, albeit in transformed ways. Societies organized around different media support a different organization of the senses (the "sensorium"), different habits of thought, and even different personality structures.

In primary oral (nonliterate) cultures, persons have a presence to one another as voices. In a "visualist" written culture (script or chirographic, initially, and later print or typographic), persons give way to viewpoints and perspectives, and eventually to quantifiable bodies in measurable space. Before printing, script culture was still influenced by the oral legacy of the past, but that influence fades as print takes hold on consciousness. In secondary oral cultures, such as the American, there is a mixture, as oral patterns reassert themselves (with a difference) in new electronic guises.

Ong insists that "sight registers surfaces," while "sound manifests interiors." The word as sound has "a permanent inwardness," but the written word is associated with (causes and is caused by) a way of thinking that focuses on externalities. In this world of objects, persons are "an embarrassing kind of objects. . . . Persons and the consciousness they exhibit are unaccountable intrusions. . . ." In the end, Ong's work is as much the insinuation of a kind of "personalist"—or even "existentialist"—understanding of human situatedness as it is the assertion of definite historical theses.

Christian Themes

Ong's account of the sensory shifts in human media must be viewed against the background of his Christian evolutionary optimism. Influenced in part by the cosmological speculations of Teilhard de Chardin, Ong insisted (in *American Catholic Crossroads: Religious-Secular Encounters in the Modern World*, 1959) that "once the fact of evolution (of the cosmos, of life, and of our knowledge) is known, the Christian must recognize as God's work this upward movement in the universe, from brute matter to inorganic matter to man, and in human society from disjointed, less self-aware forms of social consciousness to a global awareness." In his collection *In the Human Grain: Further Explorations of Contemporary Culture* (1967), published just before *The Presence of the Word*, Ong asserted

> In the past it was easy to identify God with what man did not know of the universe. . . . Such a concept of God . . . makes God only a substitute for physical science, with the result that, as our knowledge grows, God becomes less and less necessary. . . . The God

of Judeo-Christian revelation manifests himself in what men *know* of the universe, not in what they do *not* know. . . . Early man's ignorance deformed his religious sensibility and . . . predisposed his religion to superstition. . . . The Christian dispensation is closely tied to the evolution of the material world, and to its very materiality. For the Christian, matter, changing in time, is a positive good, and the future is colored with hope.

This positive view of matter imports an enthusiasm for science and for secular knowledge generally. Ong is concerned with what is lost, as well as what is gained, in cultural change, with modes of deference and self-assertion, impulses of conflict and forms of cooperation. Ong's account of the sensory dynamics of human communication also has implications for the mystery of incarnation and the understanding of divine communication. Just as the word is both interior and exterior, so Jesus is both divine incarnation and human transcendence.

According to Ong, the word as sound is living presence, existing only in its own perishing. The voice expresses the innerness of the self and speaks to the innerness of the other. The shift from sound and person to sight and object—from "I" and "Thou" to "It," in the terms popularized by philospher Martin Buber—has involved a silencing of the human life-world, and that in turn has led to "a certain silence of God" in the modern world. (At one point, Ong reluctantly acknowledges a connection between his views and those of the philospher Martin Heidegger.) The "visualist" tendencies Ong critiques, he believes, have encouraged us to try to understand others, and ultimately ourselves, as externalities, as "surfaces." However, that is a doomed project, as our presence to ourselves, and to each other, involves interiors, which cannot be reduced to surfaces; interiors can be sounded, but not seen. Invisible, God speaks—or would, if we but knew how to listen.

Sources for Further Study

Farrell, Thomas J. *Walter Ong's Contributions to Cultural Studies: The Phenomenology of the Word and I-Thou Communication.* Cresskill, N.J.: Hampton Press, 2000. A valuable study of Ong's work by a scholar who has taken on the project of bringing Ong to a wider audience.

Farrell, Thomas J., and Paul A. Soukup, eds. *An Ong Reader: Challenges for Further Inquiry.* Cresskill, N.J.: Hampton Press, 2002. A convenient, up-to-date anthology of Ong's writing.

Gronbeck, Bruce E., Thomas J. Farrell, and Paul A. Soukup, eds. *Media, Consciousness, and Culture: Explorations of Walter Ong's Thought.* Newbury Park, Calif.: Sage Publications, 1991. Fifteen essays linking Ong's work to a variety of subjects—Kant, Francis Bacon, feminism, Iran, the unconscious, and computer science.

Olson, David R. *The World on Paper: The Conceptual and Cognitive Implications of Writing and Reading.* Cambridge, England: Cambridge University Press, 1994. Critiques Ong and others in the context of a reassessment of the priority of speech to writing.

Ong, Walter J. *Faith and Contexts*. Atlanta, Ga.: Scholars Press, 1992-1999. Four volumes of Ong's essays on religious themes, edited by Thomas J. Farrell and Paul A. Soukup.

Weeks, Dennis L., and Jane Hoogestraat, eds. *Time, Memory, and the Verbal Arts: Essays on the Thought of Walter Ong*. Selinsgrove, Pa.: Susquehanna University Press, 1998. An anthology of essays by various scholars examining Ong's impact on literary theory and analysis.

Edward Johnson

PRISON MEDITATIONS OF FATHER ALFRED DELP

Author: Alfred Delp (1907-1945)

First published: Im Angesicht des Todes, 1956 (English translation, 1962, as *Facing Death*)

Edition used: Prison Meditations of Father Alfred Delp, with an introduction by Thomas Merton. New York: Herder & Herder, 1963

Genre: Nonfiction

Subgenres: Journal or diary; letters; meditation and contemplation

Core issues: Catholics and Catholicism; death; God; good vs. evil; persecution; religion; sin and sinners; social action; suffering; surrender

Father Delp's meditations on Christianity, the pervasiveness of sin, and death are most rewarding if read in their entirety. Thomas Merton's introduction, written in 1962, is a thoughtful and challenging statement, an affirmation of faith that is at the same time a word of warning to those who fail to realize the dangers of division in the nuclear age.

Overview

Alfred Delp was born in Mannheim, Germany. He joined the Jesuits when he was nineteen, after having become a convert to Catholicism. He was editor of *Stimmen der Zeit* (voices of the time) from 1939 until 1942, when the Nazis suppressed the publication. In 1943, at the height of World War II, he joined in the work of the Kreisau Circle, an anti-Nazi group devoted to planning a new social order built on the principles of Christianity. Delp joined the circle at the invitation of Count Helmuth von Moltke, and with Moltke he stood trial for treason and was sentenced to be executed. The execution took place in Plotzensee prison on February 2, 1945.

The principles of Christian spirituality revealed in *The Prison Meditations of Father Alfred Delp* are wrapped in the personal experiences of a man sentenced to die by the Nazis. Delp and a group of his friends were arrested by the Gestapo in 1944. He had joined a secret group called the Kreisau Circle who expected German chancellor Adolf Hitler's defeat and were planning a new social order to be built on Christian lines after World War II. These "rechristianising intentions" were considered heresy. Charges that he was part of a plot to assassinate Hitler were dropped; the trial was plainly a religious one. Delp maintained that he was condemned because he "happened to be, and chose to remain, a Jesuit." After a mock trial and a perfunctory sentencing he was executed in Plotzensee prison on February 2, 1945.

The insights that he gained during his last months of life have universal validity for contemporary Christian spirituality. They are bare and unsentimental; he had no time for extraneous matters. As he awaited the executioner's certain but unscheduled arrival, he wrote:

On this ultimate peak of existence at which I have arrived many ordinary words seem to have lost the meaning they used to have for me and I have now come to see them in quite a different sense. Some I don't even care to use at all any more; they belong to the past which already is far away. Here I am, on the edge of my cliff, waiting for the thrust that will send me over. In this solitude time has grown wings—angels' wings; I can almost sense the soft current as they cleave the air, keeping their distance because of the immense height. And the noises from below are softened and quietened—I hear them rather as the distant murmur of a stream tossing and tumbling in a narrow gorge.

What he could see from the cliff's edge is recorded for us in excerpts from his diary; meditations on Advent, Christmas, and Epiphany; some short essays; reflections on the Lord's Prayer and a pentecostal liturgy; and his parting words after the death sentence. These writings, written in the face of Nazi terror, peer deep into the dark heart of modern evil and point unfailingly to the saving reality of faith in God.

Father Delp's description of his time is disturbingly realistic for our own. From "the very shadow of the scaffold" Father Delp saw that his world had entered a new era that had as its recurring theme a humanity that is profoundly godless, no longer even capable of knowing God. Drowned by the noises of everyday life, forbidden by restrictions, lost in the hurry of "progress," stifled by authority, misled by fear, the ordinary person's "spiritual mechanism has rusted and become practically useless." He portrayed Western humanity as "spiritually homeless, naked and exposed." The modern world seems "incapable of being God-conscious." Ground down by the totalitarian machinery of a ruthless nation-state, Father Delp had no illusions about the strength of human evil in the modern age.

The Church was not spared by the critique coming from the shackled priest in solitary confinement. He wrote:

> But recently the man turning to the Church for enlightenment has all too often found only a tired man to receive him—a man who then had the dishonesty to hide his fatigue under pious words and fervent gestures. At some future date the honest historian will have some bitter things to say about the contribution made by the churches to the creation of the mass-mind, of collectivism, dictatorships and so on.

Admitting that the Church was no longer one of the controlling powers in human affairs, Delp urged believers to leave the familiar territory of religious habit and a privileged clergy. He found himself surrounded by "mechanical 'believers' who 'believe' in everything, in every ceremony, every ritual—but know nothing whatever about the living God."

Father Delp's meditations are not just the cynical analyses of a doomed man; they are a message of hope despite the harsh realities portrayed. Indeed the very shock that arises when one knows what one is capable of, as well as the "failings of humanity as a whole," are essential elements in the journey to renewed contact with God. Two things must be accepted unreservedly according to Delp: first, "that life is both powerless and futile in so far as by itself it has neither purpose nor fulfillment"; and second, "it must be recognised that it is God's alliance with man, his being on our side, ranging himself with us that corrects this state of meaningless futility." The recognition of our separation from God is Delp's most important message, for it helps us to realize that only by the direct intervention of God, "who breaks the fetters, absolves the guilt and bestows the inevitable blessing," can humankind recognize its true identity. "The essential requirement is that man must wake up to the truth about himself." In the unfolding of history, even the dark history of the 1940's, this word of truth is carried into effect.

Once that recognition of the true state of affairs occurs, persons are free to turn away from "passionate preoccupation with self" and turn toward God. Delp's suffering led him to see that thinking only in terms of self destroys self. The "happy" alternative is that one "needs the eternal, the infinite." The hunger and thirst and awareness of lack turn life into "a continuous Advent" that is hope itself. As humankind turns toward God, consciously trying to make contact with him, we find we are no longer on our own. Freedom is restored for real contact with the living God. This surrender of self Delp calls "God-conscious humanism."

The conversion of a soul is an act of God and requires an inner turning, but it does not take place in a vacuum. For the reestablishment of contact with God to occur, a new social order is demanded. "As long as human beings have to exist in inhuman and unworthy conditions the majority will succumb to them and nothing will make them either pray or think." The spiritual insights that Delp found in his isolation are to be applied to all of life, to the whole human race. Only then are they valid for the prisoner of God-forsakenness.

Delp believed that every human being required space in which to grow. This space includes an "existence minimum" of living space, stable government, and adequate nourishment; an ethical minimum of honesty in society, dedication to the search for truth, and a sense of service; and a "minimum of transcendence"—an ultimate goal to live toward. Delp sums these up "in the words respect, awe, devotion, love, freedom, law." Individually they are expressed in character; collectively in family, community, economy.

In themselves these insights are valuable and good, but the force of Delp's writing is the personal incarnation of this spirituality. The principles expressed by one who was forced to test their validity in the face of death carry the force of truth. His struggles and doubt are there in black and white. Near the end, he wrote, "So is it madness to hope—or conceit, or cowardice, or grace?" but he also added, "One thing is gradually becoming clear—I must surrender myself completely." This process of surrender to God worked out before our eyes in his writings is a treasure for all Christians who seek God in a seemingly godless age. He concluded his wrestling with these words:

> I will honestly and patiently await God's will. I will trust him till they come to fetch me. I will do my best to ensure that this blessing, too, shall not find me broken and in despair.

Christian Themes

Delp's meditation, produced at the height of World War II and under the greatest pressures a human being can face—imprisonment, persecution, and knowledge of certain, imminent death—is a testament to his Christian faith. In the worst days of Nazi oppression, he produced an honest appraisal of modern Western humankind, concluding that humanity is profoundly godless and seemingly incapable of knowing God. The task, as he saw it, was to help create the fundamental conditions that would reestablish living contact with God, who alone can give meaning and purpose to life. This regeneration must come from God, is to be received by the believer, and is inextricably bound to a renewal of the entire social order.

Sources for Further Study

Coady, Mary Frances. "Hitler and the Jesuits." *Commonweal* 121, no. 18 (October 22, 2004): 20-21. Coady addresses the anti-Nazi work of the Jesuits during World War II, in particular the priests Lothar König, Augustin Rösch, and Alfred Delp.

_____. *With Bound Hands: A Jesuit in Nazi Germany—The Life and Selected Prison Letters of Alfred Delp*. Chicago: Jesuit Way, 2003. The first full-length English-language biography of Delp.

William Loyd Allen

PRISON MEDITATIONS ON PSALMS 51 AND 31

Author: Girolamo Savonarola (1452-1498)
First published: Infelix ego and *Tristitia obsedit me*, 1498 (English translation, 1534)
Edition used: Prison Meditations on Psalms 51 and 31, edited and translated by John
   Patrick Donnelly, S.J. Milwaukee, Wis.: Marquette University Press, 1994
Genre: Nonfiction
Subgenres: Devotions; meditation and contemplation; spiritual treatise
Core issues: Despair; fear; hope; repentance; trust in God

*Savonarola wrote these two Psalm meditations after he was tortured and before he
was burned at the stake, expressing his anguish at being weak and signing a confession recanting his beliefs and prophecies. In the first meditation, he makes a plea to
God for mercy; in the companion meditation, he laments his sadness and places his
hope in God.*

Overview

Written during Girolamo Savonarola's final weeks in his Florentine prison, a term
that would end with his fiery execution, these Psalm meditations, originally written in
Latin, are his most-read works. He wrote these works after being tortured and signing
a confession that recanted his faith, then regretting his weak will in the face of torture.
His meditation on Psalm 51 is complete and offered in the form of a highly personal
prayer to God who alone can provide hope as Savonarola faces his many enemies. His
incomplete meditation on Psalm 31 presents only the first two verses and develops as
a spiritual conversation between the writer and Sadness and Hope personified. Immediately popular, within two years Psalm 51 went through eight Latin editions and
seventy-eight in Latin and vernaculars by 1600; Psalm 31 has seen more than eighty
editions.

Each verse of Psalm 51 prompts a meditation. Sinful, Savonarola is abandoned by
all but God, his only hope. Yet God is all, "the supreme reality . . . indescribable majesty," how can he presume to approach God? However, God is also supreme mercy,
and Savonarola asks that God take away his misery. By the blood of Christ his salvation is made possible, and so he asks that God turn him toward himself, forgive his
sins, and "justify [him] through your grace." As God's mercy aided Peter, Mary Magdalene, and the penitent thief, so may God deign to aid Savonarola: "blot out my iniquity . . . wipe clean my heart." The author has benefited from God's mercy before, but
his fear and love of self and the world assure him that he is still "imperfectly clean"
and in need of further cleansing with tears, the Scriptures, and divine graces. His sin
was against God and therefore against himself, and it sits before him always. His sin
was love of a creature (unspecified, perhaps himself) that interfered with his love of
God, and fear of humans (under torture?) before fear of God. His tormentors claim
that God has withdrawn all help, and Savonarola begs that God prove them wrong. He

admits that Original Sin has twisted him and therefore made him prone to iniquity and sin and in need of God's mercy and kindness.

God is also complete and full of love, and Savonarola prays that by virtue of God's boundless love for his creation, he will save him. God's promise is contained in the stories of David and the prodigal son, and the promise is truth, and God loves truth. Savonarola is the prodigal son and relies only on the grace of Christ. The worldly philosophers do not understand the power of God's promise as does Savonarola, to whom it has been revealed, and Savonarola begs that his hope will be fulfilled. God's promise is the cleansing that will result in joy and peace. However, Savonarola's "bones remain broken," and God continues to count his sins. He prays that God see the divine image in him and not his sinfulness. Betrayed by his heart, the author prays that God will re-create it and renew it through grace "so that it may burn [him] with a heavenly love." For whom has God denied or cast away? The Canaanite woman, despite her status, had faith and hope that were fulfilled (Matt 15). The fact that Savonarola calls out to Jesus, who is Lord, shows that the Spirit is in him, and he prays that the Spirit may not be taken away. He asks that "the joy of salvation" be returned with hope founded on God's scriptural promises to answer the prayers of the faithful. He prays for a strengthening of his own spirit that he may do God's will and work. He will "teach transgressors" God's ways if his spirit is strengthened, so that just as Saul was converted while a great transgressor, so other miracles might be performed to God's glory.

Still, his sins weigh him down, and he needs freeing as did Jonah, Lot, and Peter. He prays that God might open his lips that God be praised, as by the apostles, prophets, and saints, and in childlike humility and purity. God requires praise, not sacrifice, unless that be a broken spirit and contrite heart. Like Mary Magdalene, Savonarola offers tears and contrition as an acceptable sacrifice. Finally, he asks that God treat his Church with kindness, weak and shrunken as it has become. This will prompt a new spirit of justice to prevail, and sacrifice of justice will replace the "abomination" of the empty ceremonies offered in its place.

Savonarola's meditation on Psalm 31 opens with his lament for his own Sadness, woe, and despair. He calls on Hope, who will bring joy and consolation and scatter his enemies. His hope is in God, and he reviews God's goodness and power and love: "Throw yourself upon him and he will catch you and save you." His hope is above all that God will forgive him his sins and make possible his salvation. Only Christ's merits and divine grace make this possible, a fact that the "philosophers" ignore, and so they misunderstand true justice. He is consoled. However, Sadness returns with an army, mocking his lack of hope, challenging his faith. Divine aid is a myth, she mocks, rely on human help. Hope then appears and consoles him, reminding him to practice patience and to look for invisible rather than visible aid. Turning to divine help once again, Savonarola asks for forgiveness and spiritual strength. Sadness again mocks him, for he is still in physical fetters. Sadness reminds him pitilessly that God is just as well as merciful, and Savonarola cannot stand before divine justice. Hope then returns from Heaven and tells him that God's justice is for the wicked, not the penitent and faithful. Savonarola is faithful and penitent and a one-time recipient of mercy, so why should he despair? He is heartened and soon prays for divine refuge from the hand of humankind. Sadness appears again with her mob and reminds the friar of his many acts of rebellion and ingratitude to God, which certainly must be punished. At this, Hope reappears and sets his mind at ease: God's mercy is infinite. All people sin, but faith provides a guarantee of mercy and salvation, at least in the next world. The text ends with the words of verse 3.

Christian Themes

Savonarola's meditations explore the relationship of humans and God, sin and divine mercy, and maintenance of faith and hope in the face of calamity and despair. Bolstered by Scripture in the first study and Hope personified in the second, Savonarola lays himself verbally before the omnipotent God without whose salvation he is nothing. In an Augustinian fashion, in the first meditation Savonarola explores God's promises in Scripture and is reminded time and again that grace and forgiveness flow from Christ's side and will wash him clean. Yet he remains dogged by uncertainty that his own penitence and faith are powerful enough, and he echoes the fear of the early Martin Luther that what God has provided him thus far is not enough. This lack of certitude also permeates the second meditation, as he allows himself to have his faith in God's promises undermined by his own personified Sadness. Doubts continually assault him, and Hope has continually to reassure him of the falsity of his qualms. Like the philosopher Boethius's Lady Philosophy, Hope provides a foundation of consolation whose full contours are clear even if the work was stopped abruptly.

Sources for Further Study

Erlanger, Rachel. *The Unarmed Prophet: Savonarola in Florence.* New York: McGraw-Hill, 1987. An energetically written biography of Savonarola that emphasizes the intersection of moral and political reform in his writings and public activities.

Martines, Lauro. *Fire in the City: Savonarola and the Struggle for the Soul of Renaissance Florence.* New York: Oxford University Press, 2006. Sympathetic discussion of the man and his influence as a religious reformer in Florence. Martines wraps his venerable expertise and sound judgments in vivid prose.

Savonarola, Girolamo. *Selected Writings of Girolamo Savonarola: Religion and Politics, 1490-1498.* Translated and edited by Anne Borelli and Maria Pastore Passaro. New Haven, Conn.: Yale University Press, 2006. This is a significant collection of many of Savonarola's major and minor works, most of which have not been published in English before, including sermons, biblical commentaries, and other moral guides essays.

Joseph P. Byrne

THE PROBLEM OF CHRISTIANITY

Author: Josiah Royce (1855-1916)
First published: 1913
Edition used: The Problem of Christianity, with an introduction by John E. Smith and
with a new foreword and a revised and expanded index by Frank M. Oppenheim.
Washington, D.C.: The Catholic University of America Press, 2001
Genre: Nonfiction
Subgenres: Church history; critical analysis; essays
Core issues: Church; constancy; ethics; forgiveness; morality; problem of evil; re-
demption

Royce published The Problem of Christianity *late in life after significant changes in
his philosophy. He explores the Christian ideas of community, sin, atonement, and
saving grace, and he conceives of a Universal Community made up of truth seekers
whose collective process of interpretation leads to shared knowledge. This is a community of grace, and disloyalty to it is a grave sin. A voluntary act by an intermediary
can bring about atonement and reinstate the grace of the community.*

Overview

The Problem of Christianity is based on a series of lectures that Josiah Royce delivered at Oxford University toward the end of his life. During these lectures he stated
"the problem" in various ways, but his basic question was, "In what sense, if any, can
the modern man consistently be, in creed, a Christian?" This question implies a potential contradiction between being a Christian and being a "modern" human. However,
Royce, who recognized the desire for salvation as a fundamental human drive, had
long since decided that Christianity was the human race's "most effective expression
of religious longing."

In the book, Royce wishes to investigate what it means to belong to a Christian
community—or, for that matter, any community. He rejects the notion that belonging
means abandonment of the quest for living truth, unthinking adherence to static doctrine, or surrender of the will to a dominant individual. As essentially social beings, he
says, people come together in a church to express their individual longing for salvation, and collectively they seek the truth that leads to salvation.

Royce amplifies on the Christian ideas of community, sin, atonement, and saving
grace. That a community comes together to pursue shared individual goals implies
that its members are loyal to one another for the sake of those goals. Further, a community of people exercising free choice is preferable to one made up of "puppets."
Therefore, inevitably, community members run the risk of betrayal. In a Christian setting, to act against shared goals is to commit treason against the community and, implicitly, against one's own best interests.

Royce turns to the questions of forgiveness and atonement. Historically, most societies, including Christian communities, have required transgressors to accept responsibility and express remorse for misdeeds. According to Royce, however, this is not enough to repair the injury to the community or to the transgressor's self. Of course, one who has "sinned" against the community may be forgiven, in the sense that the community will not exact any penalty, but the sin itself remains a permanent historical fact. Forgiveness alone cannot repair the injury, and unless that injury is repaired, the transgressing individual lives in what Royce calls "the hell of the irrevocable." As for the injured community, the fact remains "that we are helplessly dependent on human fidelity for some of our highest goods, and so may be betrayed. . . ."

The community must perform the act that will heal its own spirit by restoring trust. That is, atonement is required to reverse the consequences of the betrayal and effect a true reconciliation. Atonement has a special meaning for Royce. It is performed by a third party acting on behalf of the community in a way that makes the community stronger for having experienced both the betrayal and the reconciliation. Royce has in mind Christ's willing sacrifice of his life to atone for the sins of humanity. It is humanity's acceptance of this sacrifice that made Royce decide Christianity was the "most effective expression of religious longing." He adds that Christianity expressed this truth as "a report concerning the supernatural work of Christ."

Christian Themes

It would be easy, but it would be a mistake, to perceive Royce as putting philosophy ahead of religion—conceiving an ideal community and then singling out a faith, which just happened to be Christian, as the best example of that ideal. A faithful Christian, Royce wanted to understand what made his religion unique and supremely worthy of adherence, and he did so through the medium of philosophy. He also employed philosophical investigation to help him and his students comprehend all the phenomena of life: the nature of human society, religious experience, ethical action, suffering, and the problem of evil.

Earlier in life, he had been convinced that all truth, including the apparent contradictions of ordinary life, was to be found in what is called absolute idealism. Royce was one of a few American philosophers who believed in this concept, developed by the German philosopher Georg Wilhelm Friedrich Hegel. However, by the time Royce came to write *The Problem of Christianity*, he had changed his idea about the nature of this consciousness. Initially, for him, it had resided in a single, absolute mind, or all-encompassing consciousness. Later, he saw it as residing in a community of truth-seeking individuals who constituted a kind of second-order self while retaining their individual identities. This was a community of hope and grace, best exemplified, in Royce's estimation, by the churches to which Saint Paul had ministered. On the other hand, Royce was disappointed in some doctrine-bound churches that seemed to have lost sight of the truth-seeking spirit that ought to guide them.

In large part, Royce revised his concept of absolute idealism to meet earlier criticisms by his contemporaries. In particular, his good friend the philosopher William James had complained that absolute mind, by resolving all the suffering and apparent evils of life, seemed to relieve individuals of moral responsibility. Royce himself was wary that inflexible church doctrine could have the same effect. Though a devout Christian, he rejected the idea that belonging to an organized religion requires one to adhere to static beliefs.

In *The Problem of Christianity*, Royce replaces absolute mind with Universal Community. He identifies a process in which a truth-seeking spiritual force guides individuals toward the salvation for which everyone longs. Royce acknowledges that doctrine is not static but can evolve continually. He maintains that, far from claiming a permanent lock on the truth, Christian communities, however imperfect, should be bound together by loyalty to one another and to the quest for spiritual reality. In that sense, he declares, "the Church, rather than the person of the founder, ought to be viewed as the central idea of Christianity."

As to the problem of evil, it was not simply apparent in Royce's life, but a part of direct personal experience. In 1907 Royce and his wife committed their eldest son to a state mental institution, without any expectation of his recovery from severe depression and delusion. Three years later, their son died of typhoid fever. Historically, all Christians have struggled with the question of why God would permit this type of suffering. As an idealist, Royce might be expected to conclude that it was "all for the best." However, he was unwilling to explain it away in this fashion.

In his view, evil is an inevitable fact of an imperfect, changing world. What concerns him is the response of fragile human beings to evil. His answer involves a sort of counterpressure to evil: We should remain loyal steadfastly to moral goodness and spiritual truth, which are also forces in the real world and are the opposite of evil. Evil can never be finally defeated in the everyday world. However, in this world, the will to confront and overcome evil is one source of meaning and value for the Christian community.

Sources for Further Study

Clendenning, John. *The Life and Thought of Josiah Royce, Revised and Expanded Edition*. Nashville, Tenn.: Vanderbilt University Press, 1999. A biography of Royce, revised and expanded since its original publication, after the discovery of previously unpublished correspondence by the subject.

James, William. *The Varieties of Religious Experience*. In *The Works of William James*, edited by Frederick Burkhardt. Cambridge, Mass.: Harvard University Press, 1985. Originally published in 1902. In a sense, this book by Royce's good friend was a foil to Royce's philosophy. James was concerned with the religious experience of exceptional individuals, while Royce focused on that of ordinary people.

Oppenheim, Frank M. *Royce's Mature Philosophy of Religion*. Notre Dame, Ind.: University of Notre Dame Press, 1987. Tracing the evolution of Royce's ideas from early life, this Jesuit scholar emphasizes the continuing relevance of Royce nearly a century after the philosopher's death.

Peirce, Charles S. *Reasoning and the Logic of Things: The Cambridge Conferences*

Lectures of 1898. Edited by Kenneth Laine Ketner. Cambridge, Mass.: Harvard University Press, 1992. The American philosopher Charles Peirce presents his philosophy of semiotics, an important influence on Royce's concept of the community of interpretation.

Smith, John E. *Royce's Social Infinite: The Community of Interpretation*. Hamden, Conn.: Archon Books, 1969. Discusses important influences, especially that of Charles Peirce, on the major element in Royce's thought.

Thomas Rankin

THE PRODIGAL GIRL

Author: Grace Livingston Hill (1865-1947)
First published: 1929
Edition used: The Prodigal Girl. Chappaqua, N.Y.: Family Bookshelf, 1989
Genre: Novel
Subgenre: Romance
Core issues: Coming of age or teen life; discipline; prayer; sin and sinners

In The Prodigal Girl, *Chester Thornton and his wife want what is best for their five children, and they equate their indulgence of their children's desires with parental love. However, when their firstborn son incurs gambling debts and their eldest daughter engages in risqué behaviors, Chester alters course. The Thorntons relocate to a secluded cabin to raise their children in a Christian environment, but teenage Betty rebels against chores and home schooling by running away with a disreputable boyfriend. When searching proves futile, the family prays for her well-being. Despite a harrowing accident and illness, the prodigal and repentant daughter returns.*

> *Principal characters*
> *Chester Thornton*, father
> *Eleanor Thornton*, Chester's wife
> *Chris Thornton*, Chester and Eleanor's eldest son
> *Betty Thornton*, Chester and Eleanor's daughter, the prodigal girl
> *Jane Thornton*, Chester and Eleanor's middle child
> *Doris and John Thornton*, Chester and Eleanor's younger twins
> *Dudley Weston*, Betty's boyfriend
> *Minister Dunham*, the Thornton children's tutor
> *David Dunham*, minister's son

Overview

When Grace Livingston Hill died at eighty-two, she had penned more than one hundred Christian romance novels. Chief among them is *The Prodigal Girl*, a chronicle of two parents' efforts to transform sinful children into obedient daughters and sons of Christ. The plot of this novel deviates from Hill's standard fare. Many works contain a rags-to-riches motif (indigent Christian girl meets wealthy Christian man who rescues her from dire circumstances through marriage). Instead *The Prodigal Girl* features the Thorntons, a middle-class family whose fortunes have improved, but whose standard of living is reduced by the father's choice. Teenaged Betty, lured by the temptations of fast boys, fast cars, fast dances, and sloe gin, impulsively elopes with the unprincipled, but flashy Dudley Weston on a winter's night in 1929.

As the novel opens, businessperson Chester Thornton contemplates celebrating a successful venture by rewarding his children with luxuries. Christmas approaches, and he imagines surprising Betty with a sports car now that she is old enough to drive. These thoughts entertain him until when riding the train home, he overhears a ruffian who boasts about his lustful exploits and mentions Betty's name. Blinders off, Chester arrives home and is further disillusioned. He sees his children for what they are: his son, a drunken gambler; his daughter Jane, an exhibitionist; and his prized Betty, a slut. During dinner his youngest offspring, the twins, share their lesson from school that day: evolution! Chester has seen and heard enough; he forbids his children to leave the house, but the teenagers sneak out with his wife's knowledge. A convert to modern child psychology and permissive parenting, his wife sticks to her ways until her husband physically collapses later that night and she joins his crusade.

When Chester locates Betty in a car parked outside a bar, he pulls her from the arms of her boyfriend. The father criticizes his daughter's loose behavior, and she laughs. Reminiscent of the family's dinnertime discussion (when the children proved more knowledgeable than their parents about evolutionary science and adamant about its veracity), his advice on sexual mores is evidence, in Betty's eyes, of her father's outdated Victorian values. When he explains the wages of sin, she retorts, "What right would God have to make laws for us? If He put us here on the earth and made us live whether we wanted to or not, it's up to us to have as good a time as we can, isn't it? If there is a God." Her narcissism, skepticism, and disrespect reveal to her father the depth of their generational and spiritual divide.

When Chester realizes his children are not the angels he had envisioned, he measures their upbringing against his own and identifies the missing elements. He too was raised in a large household, but one that was disciplined, removed from the vices of the city, and centered on daily prayer and Bible study. As a countermeasure to his children's lax morals, he re-creates his childhood environment by transporting them to that very cabin in a secluded forest where he grew up. As money appears the root of many of their evils (Tom's gambling, Betty and Jane's immodest attire, and the teens' purchase of alcohol), he prefers that his family not know about his recent monetary gains and allows them to think their fortunes have declined. Reduced means act as an antidote to overindulgence, and the children learn to relish pleasures like hikes through the woods and ice skating (but only after they have cleared the snowy paths and the pond by virtue of their own labors).

Because the Thornton children are withdrawn from school, a devout local man is hired as their home tutor. Minister Dunham's curriculum is based entirely on the Bible; from this single volume he instructs them in literature, history, mathematics, and most crucially, Christian fundamentals. Initially reluctant, the children, with the exception of Betty, are persuaded by his knowledge and his sincerity. Daily family prayer is instituted in the evenings. While her brothers and sisters engage in spiritual activities with their parents, the sight of her father on his knees praying aloud to God repulses Betty, who steals upstairs and locks her door. Deprived of the fun she once enjoyed and feeling imprisoned, Betty plans her escape. A letter to Dudley and some lies told to her family enable her to sneak out one night and hike through the snow to the village train terminal.

The prodigal daughter's anticipated elopement is disastrous. Dudley arrives drunken and late to their rendezvous. He drives recklessly into New York City, causing an accident that lands both of them in the hospital, Dudley with severe injuries. Betty finds her way to an aunt's city apartment, but the maid bars the girl's entrance because of her tattered appearance. After selling her watch to purchase a ticket, a hungry and penniless Betty journeys homeward by train and by foot. Suffering from hypothermia, she is rescued (by chance or perhaps divine intervention) when the minister's son, David, finds her asleep in a snowdrift. Delirious, she calls him "God's child," and he delivers her to worried parents who celebrate her return. Back home she recovers physically and spiritually, accepting Jesus Christ as her savior and David as her fiancé.

Christian Themes

While certain material in Hill's novel may strike readers as dated, the core issues are still relevant. Problems continue to exist between parents and children. Academic curriculums and the social environment of public schools cause some parents to choose home schooling. While rebellious teenage behavior may change with the times (Betty's kissing and backtalk notwithstanding, she remains a virgin after eloping with Dudley), most parents are troubled by their children's experimentation with alcohol, drugs, and sex, and by their disrespect for authority.

In *The Prodigal Girl*, Hill presents the temptations and the penalties of sin for both the children and the parents. After his awakening, Chester admits his indulgent parenting and his sin of neglect. To lead his family spiritually, he must guide by example and mete out discipline when needed. However, Chester is neither without mercy nor does he abandon his children in times of trouble. When Chris's gambling debts mount, Chester hires a lawyer and helps him repay the money, keeping his son from jail. During Betty's absence, Chester spends a long night entreating God's assistance and begging mercy for his own sins. Likewise, Eleanor acknowledges her role in the children's misbehaving. Feeling duped by permissive attitudes, she vows to consult biblical teachings and not popular texts when seeking counsel on mothering.

However, parents cannot raise children in the way of the cross alone; they need the assistance of institutions that affirm the values of the Christian household. The Thorntons rely on home schooling and seclusion for a period of time to reform their children, but they realize they must rejoin the world at large. To live in isolation is not a solution. In the final chapter, plans are made to return to the city and open a Christian school under the direction of Minister Dunham and his son, David, who is completing theological studies to join his father's ministry. Hill's *The Prodigal Girl* emphasizes that discipline, instruction, and prayer are fundamental to the reform of the sinner and to sustain a Christian lifestyle, and it is for this purpose the school is to be established.

Sources for Further Study

"Grace Livingston Hill." In *Twentieth Century Romance and Historical Writers*, edited by Lesley Henderson. Chicago: St. James Press, 1990. Features information on Hill and her popular Christian romance novels.

Karr, Jean. *Grace Livingston Hill: Her Story and Her Writing.* Mattituck, N.Y.: Amereon House: 1982. Republication of the 1948 biography that includes an analysis of major works in chronological order. Traces the author's career from her first publication at age twenty-two to the novel she was composing when she died at eighty-two.

Munce, Robert L. *Grace Livingston Hill.* Wheaton, Ill.: Tyndale House, 1986. Written by her grandson, this biography recounts Hill's two marriages; the first ending with her husband's death, the second in a separation. Discusses Hill's family, many of whom were writers, and assesses Grace's reputation and legacy as a writer of Christian fiction.

Paulsen, Joanna. *Grace Livingston Hill: A Checklist.* Mattituck, N.Y.: Amereon House, 1981. Comprehensive bibliography listing all of Hill's novels.

Dorothy Dodge Robbins

PROPHESY DELIVERANCE!
An Afro-American Revolutionary Christianity

Author: Cornel West (1953-   )
First published: Philadelphia: Westminster Press, 1982
Genre: Nonfiction
Subgenre: Didactic treatise
Core issues: African Americans; capitalism; ethics; good vs. evil; justice; racism

The major focus of West's prophetic Christianity is liberation and social justice in this world, although he also expresses a vague hope for otherworldly salvation. Profoundly disaffected with modern capitalism, he advocates an alliance between African American religious thought and a democratic version of Marxism, which he considers the best approach for ending poverty, racial inequalities, and oppression. Calling for equal respect for persons of all races, nationalities, and sexual orientations, he focuses primarily on the invidious discrimination against Africans and African Americans.

Overview

A variety of writers and political activists influenced the thinking of Cornel West. Growing up in Oklahoma during the Civil Rights movement, he admired the work of liberal leaders like Martin Luther King, Jr., while he was also impressed by the militancy of Malcolm X and the Black Panther Party. As a student at Harvard University, he was particularly influenced by Professor Richard Rorty's pragmatic philosophy. As a leftist with a strong commitment to African American Christianity, West naturally was attracted to the emerging currents of liberation theology, particularly James Cone's Afrocentric perspective. His doctoral dissertation, later revised for a book, was an analysis of the ethical aspects of Marxism. During his early career at Union Theological Seminary, he published *Prophesy Deliverance!* at the age of twenty-nine.

Emphasizing morality and secular liberation, West writes that the most basic message of prophetic Christianity is "that every individual regardless of class, country, caste, race, or sex should have the opportunity to fulfill his or her potentialities." He makes a distinction between "penultimate liberation" and "ultimate salvation." The first category involves the "betterment of humankind," including an expansion of human freedom and democracy. West makes only a few passing statements about the nature of ultimate salvation, describing it as the "transcendence of history," which presumably involves an end to human evil and suffering. Criticizing the traditional emphasis on "the salvation of individual souls in heaven," he declares that prophetic Christians must "insist upon both this-worldly liberation and otherworldly salvation as the proper loci of Christianity."

West devotes a large percentage of *Prophesy Deliverance!* to summarizing the history of philosophical and theological ideas. He presents admirable summaries of the enlightenment of the eighteenth century, the romantic movement of the next century, and the various strands of Marxism, postmodernism, and pragmatism. When analyzing the African American intellectual tradition, he critiques four traditions: the "exceptional" tradition, the "assimilationist" tradition, the "marginalist" tradition, and the "humanistic" tradition. He firmly defends the latter, which he defines as including the struggle for self-determination, individual rights, and a self-identity for African Americans.

West's views on prophetic Christianity are rooted in the historical experiences of the African American churches, which have usually been less concerned about doctrine and more concerned about improving social conditions than churches with predominantly white congregations. He presents an interesting summary of how pre-Civil War churches provided oppressed slaves with comfort as well as opportunities for organized protest, and he emphasizes that preachers were among the most outspoken and influential of the abolitionists. Likewise, he argues that the Civil Rights movement would have been inconceivable without the crusading leadership and support of the churches.

While always respectful of Martin Luther King, Jr., and other civil rights leaders, West criticizes their "ineluctable shortsightedness" insofar as they were unable to "transcend political liberalism." Unable to recognize the inherent inequalities of modern capitalism, they presumably failed to understand that political liberalism was incapable of delivering the African American the freedom that it promised. In contrast to his critique of King's Southern Christian Leadership Conference, West praises Malcolm X for his "wholesale rejection of liberalism," as well as his vision of black liberation within the context of "the anticolonial struggles occurring around the world." Likewise he praises the ideology of the Black Panther Party and the League of Revolutionary Black Workers as well as the "revolutionary Christian perspective" of the National Committee of Black Churchmen.

Although quite critical of the practices of modern Communist regimes, West asserts that the fundamental objective of Marxism is "self-fulfillment, self-development, and self-realization of harmonious personalities." In advocating Marxist analysis, West distinguishes among different streams of Marxist ideology. Highly critical of Soviet versions that derive from the thought of Vladimir Ilich Lenin, he endorses the "progressive" perspective of Eduard Bernstein's *Die Voraussetzungen des Sozialismus und die Aufgaben der Sozialdemokratie* (1899, *Evolutionary Socialism*, 1907), which looked to the achievement of socialism through democratic, nonviolent means. While admitting that the Marxist tradition has been dominated by the Leninist stream, West argues that the best hope for liberation lies in a synthesis of Bersteinian Marxism and a revolutionary Christian perspective.

According to West, black theologians share much in common with Marxist theorists, as both use a dialectical method to "unmask falsehoods." This method consists of a three-step approach of negating white interpretations of the Gospel, preserving the traditional African American perceptions of the Bible, and transforming these historical understandings into new ones relevant to contemporary concerns. In this way, black theologians seek to understand the plight of black people from the perspective of a benevolent deity and "to preserve the biblical truth that God sides with the oppressed and acts on their behalf."

At the time he was writing *Prophesy Deliverance!*, West was enough of a realist to acknowledge that the United States was highly unlikely to adopt a socialist system anytime in the near future. Presumably he wanted to encourage more intellectuals to support a revolutionary ideology, with the hope of establishing a foundation for future liberation. In subsequent years, however, West concluded that a synthesis between Marxism and prophetic Christianity was impractical, and he began to describe himself as a "non-Marxist socialist," while campaigning for progressive reformers like Ralph Nader and the Reverend Al Sharpton.

Christian Themes

West's use of the word "prophesy" does not refer to any predictions about the future, but rather to the moral condemnation of evil, combined with active efforts to bring about greater justice, equality, and benevolence toward the poor and oppressed. For models, West points to the prophetic works of Jesus of Nazareth, later Old Testament prophets, opponents of slavery, civil-rights leaders, and African American liberation theologians. In this vein, he quotes Luke 4:18, a passage in which Jesus proclaimed that he was anointed to preach the good news to the poor, to heal the afflicted, and to liberate those who were oppressed.

While frequently classifying himself as a Christian thinker, West shuns the role of theologian and writes that he has no interest in attempting to systematize the doctrines and dogmas of the Christian tradition, even expressing skepticism that they can be "rendered coherent and consistent." Thus, he has little to say about Christian doctrines such as the Trinity, biblical miracles, or the uniqueness of Christian revelation. Profoundly influenced by the quasi-Marxist school of liberation theology, he views himself as primarily a cultural critic with philosophic training who works out of the Christian tradition.

West combines his pragmatic philosophy with a rather mystical interpretation of the Christian message. He writes: "Jesus Christ is the Truth, a reality that can only be existentially appropriated (not intellectually grasped) by fallen human beings." He views the suffering of Jesus as a metaphor of the human condition, demonstrating that God is on the side of the oppressed. The "existential appropriation of Jesus Christ" requires the "putting of oneself on the line" in the struggle in behalf of social justice, racial equality, and social amelioration. The Christian religion, moreover, "is first and foremost a theodicy, a triumphant account of good over evil."

While West articulates great respect for chosen biblical texts, his biblical references almost always relate to secular concerns, and he unequivocally declares that "God's will" is to promote "the precious values of individuality and democracy." Applauding Malcolm X for evolving a "revolutionary Islamic perspective" similar to his own viewpoint, he finds that the doctrinal differences between Islam and Christianity are of little significance. Although West is highly critical of fundamentalism and conservative versions of Christianity that concentrate on otherworldly salvation, he has no quarrel with conservative Christian beliefs as long as they are combined with progressive social teachings. He has nothing but praise for the example of the House of the Lord Pentecostal Church of Brooklyn, led by the Reverend Herbert Daughtry, a minister who combined a conservative and charismatic religious message with organized efforts to combat poverty and racial injustice.

Sources for Further Study

Cowan, Rosemary. *Cornel West and the Politics of Redemption.* Cambridge, England: Polity Press, 2002. A critical but sympathetic analysis, suggesting that liberation theology is the key to understanding West's writings and political activities.

Johnson, Clarence. *Cornel West and Philosophy.* New York: Routledge, 2002. A comprehensive examination of West's philosophical writings, including his views of pragmatism, existentialism, Marxism, religion, ethics, and social justice.

Morrison, John. *Cornel West.* Philadelphia: Chelsea House, 2004. An admiring, relatively short account, written primarily for young readers.

West, Cornel. *The Cornel West Reader.* New York: Basic Civitas Books, 2000. An anthology of West's writings. Contains an autobiographical sketch and several revealing interviews.

Wood, Mark David. *Cornel West and the Politics of Prophetic Pragmatism.* Urbana: University of Illinois Press, 2000. A left-wing critique of West's shift in position from an earlier commitment to revolutionary socialism to one of progressive reformism.

Yancy, George, ed. *Cornel West: A Critical Reader.* Malden, Mass.: Blackwell, 2001. An interesting collection of scholarly essays about all aspects of West's life and thought.

Thomas Tandy Lewis

THE PROTESTANT ETHIC AND THE
SPIRIT OF CAPITALISM

Author: Max Weber (1864-1920)
First published: Die protestantische Ethik und der Geist des Kapitalismus, 1904-1905 (English translation, 1930)
Edition used: The Protestant Ethic and the Spirit of Capitalism, translated by Talcott Parsons. Mineola, N.Y.: Dover, 2003
Genre: Nonfiction
Subgenres: Church history; critical analysis; history
Core issues: Calvinism; capitalism; Catholics and Catholicism; Protestants and Protestantism; psychology; Puritans and Puritanism

According to Weber, modern capitalism is the result of the Protestant Reformation, particularly John Calvin's concept of predestination. The omnipotent and omniscient God has chosen a select few to enter heaven; the rest are destined for hell. God has also called humans to add to his glory by fulfilling his calling in this world. Given the psychological pressure to believe that they are among the select few, people work diligently and rationally with the result that wealth accumulates and capitalism results.

Overview

Max Weber's *The Protestant Ethic and the Spirit of Capitalism* was one of the seminal works of the twentieth century. An analytic sociologist as well as an economist, Weber's scholarly interests and accomplishments transcended any individual academic discipline, and his book includes not only sociology and economy but also history, political science, theology, and psychology.

What Weber attempts to discover in this work is the connection between the economic system of capitalism and theological ideas of the sixteenth century Protestant reformer John Calvin and his Calvinist followers. He begins with the long-held observation that in Weber's Germany, Protestants rather than Catholics were to be found as business leaders, skilled laborers, and heads of its capitalist enterprises, and he theorizes that the reason was to be found in their religious beliefs.

Weber discusses what he calls "the spirit of capitalism," using several aphorisms of Benjamin Franklin, such as "Time is money" and "Money is of the prolific, generating nature." This, the author argues, is not mere avarice, but rather the belief that it is the ultimate duty of individuals to increase their wealth, which he calls the ethos of capitalism. He admits that capitalism has manifested itself in most civilizations, including Europe in the Middle Ages, but those civilizations lacked the ethos or spirit that Weber finds is at the core of modern capitalism.

This root of the ethos of capitalism is what Weber famously refers to as a "calling," a new concept that emerges from the Protestant Reformation. It is religious in origin—an individual is called by God—and applies both to owners and managers as well as workers and laborers. Just as an individual is called to work in a particular occupation or profession, a person is called to make money. This, Weber argues, is connected to a commitment to asceticism, not the asceticism of medieval monks but an ascetic life in the world rather than the monastery. Measured economically, the acquisition of money does not manifest itself in living a more luxurious or comfortable life in a material sense but rather in believing psychologically that one has fulfilled one's calling, a calling ordained by God.

Weber states that Martin Luther employed the idea of a calling, but Luther was a traditionalist, so his use of the concept was more conservative than revolutionary, in that individuals were to accept their lot as it was given by God rather than change their circumstance. The author also discusses Protestant pietism, John Wesley's Methodist movement in England, several Baptist sects, and the Quakers, but finds his Protestant-induced spirit of capitalism best revealed in the consequences of the ideas of Calvin, notably the concept of predestination. Because of his omniscience and omnipotence, God knows all, and he has elected some for salvation, with the remainder, probably the majority for Calvin, damned to hell. The church and its sacraments cannot save one, because an individual's final destination has already been determined since the beginning of time, given the nature of God's foreknowledge. According to Calvin, human beings are in the world only to increase the glory of God, and they do this through the fulfillment of what God has called them to do.

Given the stakes—heaven or hell for all eternity—the question of whether one was among the elect was of a burning concern with a deep psychological dimension, but hints or clues of one's election might be evidenced by the successful application to one's calling, or occupation, in this world. Conversely, Weber claims that Luther's conception of the religious life was more medieval in its quest to seek God through a mystical faith rather than a rational method for transforming one's life through fulfilling one's calling. For the Calvinists, including the Puritans in England and England's North American colonies, successful work did not result in salvation, but it could well be a sign of salvation. As Weber notes, in practice this led to the belief that God helps those who help themselves. As Saint Paul said, "He who will not work shall not eat." Luxury for its own sake is a "sin," as is wasting time. In England, the Puritans closed the theaters and attempted to restrict Sunday sports, and for Calvinists/Puritans, sexual relations were acceptable only for the conception of children, not for enjoyment in their own right.

Modern capitalism is also a product of the rational use of capital in economic enterprises as well as the rational organization of labor, neither of which Weber claims existed before the sixteenth and seventeenth centuries. Calvinism demanded not just the occasional good works within a religious institutional framework but rather a rational program, a unified system, a life of good works. Paradoxically, although the seeds of the Protestant ethic were planted in the religion of Calvinism, where the central imperative was the afterlife and whether it would be heaven or hell, in time the connective root to religion was severed, but the reward of fulfilling one's calling became an ethical end in itself, based more on habit and cultural tradition than conscious reflection.

Weber's thesis remains relevant as well as controversial a century after its publication. However, it has been widely noted by critics writing in an age when the social sciences have become more "science" than "social" that *The Protestant Ethic and the Spirit of Capitalism* is overly impressionistic, lacking the hard quantitative data that could validate its claims.

Christian Themes

Weber's focus in *The Protestant Ethic and the Spirit of Capitalism* is on the economic development of capitalism rather than on the Christian religion. However, inasmuch as he argues that modern Western capitalism was a consequence of the Protestant Reformation, particularly Calvinism, he discusses other Christian concepts and practices only when those themes had a relationship to the root or seed that resulted in the forest, or jungle, of modern capitalism. For him, the key figure is Calvin and the key concept is predestination, which logically flows from the definition of God as all powerful and all knowing, a description that encompasses the God of all of Western monotheism, including Judaism and Islam as well as Christianity. Saint Augustine and other early church fathers included predestination in their theological analyses, but it became the central pillar for Calvin, who did not shy away from its stark consequences, which logically led to the denial of human beings having free will.

If Calvin and Calvinism is the major theme in *The Protestant Ethic and the Spirit of Capitalism*, Weber also discusses, in part for purposes of comparison, the nature of medieval Catholicism, particularly the religious practices of the monastic orders who chose to retreat from the world in a quest for God rather than engage the world as, Weber argues, the Calvinists did. He also discusses the beliefs of Martin Luther and his salvation by faith, although unlike many historians of Luther, he finds Luther closer to Catholicism than Protestant Calvinism.

Finally, some economists and historians, notably R. H. Tawney, suggest that Weber got the connection between Calvinism and capitalism backward, and that it was the economic changes of the late Middle Ages and the Renaissance that required a new religious response to the traditional corporatism of Catholic civilization.

Sources for Further Study

Delacroix, Jacques, and Francois Nielsen. "The Beloved Myth: Protestantism and the Rise of Industrial Capitalism in the Nineteenth Century." *Social Forces* 80 (December, 2001). The authors criticize Weber for his failure to offer sufficient empirical evidence for his thesis.

Novak, Michael. "Max Weber Goes Global." *First Things: A Monthly Journal of Religion and Public Life* 152 (April, 2005). Novak argues that the Catholic tradition also contributed to the rise of modern capitalism.

Swatos, William H., and Lutz Kaelbar, eds. *The Protestant Ethic Turns One Hundred.*

Boulder, Colo.: Paradigm, 2005. A valuable series of essays assessing the Weber thesis at the time of its centenary.

Tawney, R. H. *Religion and the Rise of Capitalism*. New York: Harcourt, Brace, 1926. Tawney turns Weber's thesis on its head, arguing that Protestant Calvinism was a consequence of the emergence of modern capitalism rather than its cause.

Eugene Larson

PSALMS

Authors: Traditionally ascribed to David (c. 1030-c. 962 B.C.E.) and others

First transcribed: Tehillim (Hebrew), *Psalmoi* (Greek), dates unknown (English translation, 1384)

Edition used: The Holy Bible Containing the Old and New Testaments: New Revised Standard Version. Nashville, Tenn.: Thomas Nelson, 1990

Genres: Holy writings; poetry

Subgenres: Devotions; lyric poetry; theology

Core issues: The Bible; devotional life; faith; prayer; trust in God

Psalms is an Old Testament book of one hundred fifty religious songs, written by a variety of Hebrew authors over the span of several hundred years. The Psalms include several types of songs that vary considerably in style, content, and form. They are cited often in the New Testament, where many of them are associated with the life of Jesus the Messiah. The importance of the Psalms is illustrated further by their continued use throughout history both in public liturgy and in private devotions.

Overview

The English title Psalms derives from the Greek word *Psalmoi*, the book's title in the Septuagint version, which dates from the second century B.C.E. In its original Hebrew language, the title of Psalms is *Tehillim*, meaning "praises." The Psalms, however, are not uniformly praises; they also include other genres such as lament, wisdom, and historical recital songs.

In the Hebrew Bible, Psalms is the first book in the Writings, the third part of the Hebrew canon, and in the English Bible, Psalms is the first of the poetical books. The 150 Psalms are organized into five divisions (called "books"), each ending in a doxology: book 1, Psalms 1-41; book 2, Psalms 42-72; book 3, Psalms 73-89; book 4, Psalms 90-106; and book 5, Psalms 107-150. It has been suggested that the five books may represent stages in the collection process; they may be thematic groupings that move from lament to praise; or they may be an attempt to parallel the five books of Moses (Genesis to Deuteronomy).

David is credited with the authorship of seventy-three Psalms. The remaining seventy-seven are attributed to a variety of authors, including Moses (Psalm 90), Solomon (Psalms 72 and 127), Heman (Psalm 88), and Ethan (Psalm 89). A number of Psalms are attributed to musical guilds known as the Sons of Korah and the Sons of Asaph, while still other Psalms are of anonymous origin.

Of the 150 Psalms, 116 have headings (often called "superscriptions") containing one or more of the following: the author's name, the traditional setting of the Psalm, typological designation, musical accompaniment, and other musical instructions. For example, the heading of the Third Psalm reads, "A Psalm of David, when he fled from Absalom his son." Although the scholarly consensus maintains that these headings are not a part of the original composition, the presence of the headings in both the Septuagint and in the Qumran scrolls suggests that they are at least very ancient. Furthermore, the fact that headings are found on the imbedded Psalms that begin at 2 Samuel 23:1 and Habakkuk 3:1 may show that the practice of attaching a heading was a normal part of composition.

The Psalms are lyric poetry and exhibit the universal features of poetry. Although poetry may take many forms, it can be distinguished from prose by its concentration on figurative language and word play, its combination of word sounds, its utilization of meter, and its terseness within a verse structure. The poetry of Psalms takes full advantage of metaphor, simile, personification, hyperbole, and other figures of speech. The most famous metaphor in the Bible is "The Lord is my shepherd" (Ps. 23:1).

The verse structure of Hebrew poetry is based on parallelism of lines. A verse may consist of one, two, or three lines, but most often it will be two lines, with the second line related in some fashion to the first line. The second line may restate the thought of the first line (synonymous parallelism); it may state the antithesis of the first line (antithetical parallelism); or it may complete the thought of the first line (synthetic parallelism). Note the following examples: Psalm 19:1-2 "The heavens declare the glory of God; the skies proclaim the work of his hands" (synonymous); Psalm 1:6 "The Lord knows the way of the righteous, but the way of the ungodly shall perish" (antithetical); and Psalm 119:9 "How can a young man keep his way pure? By guarding it according to thy word" (synthetic).

Although parallelism of lines is the most distinctive mark of Hebrew poetry, another technique used in the Psalter is the acrostic poem (Pss. 25, 34, 111, 112, 119, and 145), in which each verse begins with successive letters of the alphabet. Psalm 119 is unique in that it consists of twenty-two sections, one for each letter of the Hebrew alphabet, and every verse within a section begins with the same letter.

As with all poetry, a significant attraction of Psalms is its ability to draw the reader into the poetic world through visual imagery, imaginative symbols, and appeals to the readers' emotions. This affective dimension of the Psalms speaks to the heart and to the passions with a fervent freshness and honesty that does not neglect the exasperating complexities of human existence. The Psalms give witness to both the greatest joys of life and to its greatest agonies. The emotions of the psalmist range from despair ("My heart is in anguish within me, the terrors of death have fallen upon me" Ps. 55:4) to elation ("Bless the Lord, O my soul: and all that is within me, bless his holy name" Ps. 103:1) and every feeling between those extremes.

By employing a variety of psalm types, the Hebrew psalmists were able to frame appropriate responses to the diversities of the life of faith. In his groundbreaking work Hermann Gunkel identified five basic genres of psalms: the individual lament, the communal lament, the communal hymn, the individual thanksgiving psalm, and the royal psalm. These genres do not exhibit strict, ironclad structures, nor do they explain the nature of every song in the entire collection, but they are helpful guides to the basic forms of biblical psalmic expression.

The most common genre in the book of Psalms is the lament, which is the worshiper's cry to God for deliverance from distress. The sufferer's trouble may take the form of sickness (Psalm 6), personal or corporate sin (Psalm 51), oppression (Psalm 10), or an accusation (Psalm 17). The lament usually begins with an address to God ("Save me, O God" Ps. 54:1), followed by the specific complaint ("strangers have risen up against me" Ps. 54:3). The worshiper may then confess his/her trust in God ("God is my helper" Ps. 54:4) and offer up a petition to God ("heal me" Ps. 6:2). The lament may include a declaration of assurance that God has heard the prayer ("he has delivered me" Ps. 54:7) and conclude with a promise to praise God with a thanksgiving offering ("I will freely sacrifice unto you" Ps. 54:6).

The thanksgiving psalm is based on the final element of the lament. After the petitioner's prayer has been answered, the petitioner will offer the promised sacrifice and celebrate publicly with a psalm of thanksgiving as a testimonial to all who are present. This type of psalm normally includes three basic parts: the reason for praising God ("I will extol you, O God, for you have lifted me up" Ps. 30:1), the narration of the specific deliverance being celebrated ("I cried unto you and you healed me" Ps. 30:2-5), and a renewed vow to praise God ("I will give thanks to you forever" Ps. 30:12).

Unlike the thanksgiving psalm, which is based on a specific event in the life of the worshiper, the hymn is a psalm of descriptive praise that is uttered in praise of God's more comprehensive virtues ("Praise him for his mighty acts" Ps. 150:2). The hymns hold in tension the dialectic between God's transcendence and his immanence by emphasizing his power in creation and his care in providence, his majesty in kingship, and his nearness in the salvation of the Exodus (Psalms 113, 135).

Other types of psalms are less prominent, such as the royal psalms (Psalm 72), the historical psalms (Psalm 78), the songs of Zion (Psalm 122), and the wisdom psalms. Psalm 1 is a wisdom psalm, and includes several of the key themes that may be found in the genre. These characteristic themes are the family, God's law, justice, life's choices, life's inconsistencies, and the trust or fear of God.

Christian Themes

Although the book of Psalms is Hebrew literature from the Old Testament and is sometimes called the songbook of Israel's second temple, Christians have consistently witnessed to the power of the Psalms to give voice to their prayers and their expressions of worship. The Psalms have this power because, unlike other parts of Scripture, they are not God's words directed toward Israel; they are instead Israel's words directed to God in worshipful and prayerful response to his presence and actions among them. As long as Christians continue to acknowledge God's presence and activity in the Church, the Psalms will serve as a meaningful expression of the Christian response to God in worship and prayer.

Psalms suggests to the Christian that worship is deep, intense, and passionate, and that prayer is honest and fervent. In fact, the Psalms' honesty and fervency may offend modern Christian sensibilities at times, especially on those occasions when the psalmist prayed for the violent destruction of enemies and their children (for example, Ps. 3:7). These imprecatory psalms are difficult to reconcile with Christ's command to love our enemies. It should be remembered, however, that these psalms are cries for help, emerging from situations of deep suffering and oppression, and that the New Testament allows for God's intervention as vindicator of his people (Rom. 12:19; 1 Thess. 1:8; 2 Tim. 4:14; Heb. 10:30-31; Jude 14-15; Rev. 6:10).

Claus Westermann and Walter Brueggemann have shown that the diversity of psalmic types testifies to a dynamic life of faith. The lament and the hymn are opposite poles of Christian experience, but most of human existence falls somewhere between these extremes. Brueggemann argues that the lament speaks to the times of pain, the hymn rejoices in times of great joy, and the other types of psalms relate to periods of settled, average existence. Furthermore, the life of faith is not static; rather, people are often in movement from one stage to another. The Psalms address this dynamic element of Christian life.

In addition to the experiential themes that emerge from the Psalms, numerous theological topics stand out as well. The psalmists' cries for help assume that God is savior and deliverer, an assumption that is given specific witness in the thanksgiving psalms, and is expanded in the hymns by mention of the Exodus. God's saving work includes his providential care, his forgiveness of sin, his healing of sickness, and his giving of his Spirit (Ps. 51:10-11). Additionally, God is portrayed prominently as creator and sovereign of the universe. As king, God is enthroned in heaven, active on earth, and coming to reign over the world (Psalm 96).

Sources for Further Study

Brueggemann, Walter. *The Message of the Psalms: A Theological Commentary*. Minneapolis, Minn.: Augsburg, 1984. A postcritical approach to the Psalms in which the precritical devotional approach and the historical critical approaches balance and correct each other.

Eaton, J. H. *The Psalms: A Historical and Spiritual Commentary with an Introduction and New Translation*. London: T & T Clark, 2003. Includes a helpful summary of the theology of the Psalms and the interpretation of Psalms through history. Applies each Psalm to Christian spirituality.

McCann, J. Clinton. *A Theological Introduction to the Book of Psalms: The Psalms as Torah*. Nashville, Tenn.: Abingdon, 1993. Exegetical and theological commentary from a Christian context, including a chapter on Jesus Christ and an appendix on the singing of the Psalms.

Mays, James. *Psalms*. Louisville, Ky.: John Knox, 1994. Perceptive theological commentary that appreciates the canonical context of the Psalms and their use by New Testament writers and later Christian interpreters.

Terrien, Samuel. *The Psalms: Strophic Structure and Theological Commentary*. Grand Rapids, Mich.: Wm. B. Eerdmans, 2003. Critical and theological commentary rich in Ancient Near Eastern references and useful bibliographic sources. A scholarly yet passionately expressive volume.

Lee Roy Martin

PURITY OF HEART IS TO WILL ONE THING
Spiritual Preparation for the Feast of Confession

Author: Søren Kierkegaard (1813-1855)
First published: 1847
Edition used: Purity of Heart Is to Will One Thing: Spiritual Preparation for the Feast of Confession, translated with an introductory essay by Douglas V. Steere. New York: Harper & Bros., 1938
Genre: Nonfiction
Subgenres: Didactic treatise; meditation and contemplation; sermons
Core issues: Confession; doubt; God; good vs. evil; perfection; suffering; truth

This volume of meditations in preparation for the office of Confession, although an amplified sermon, is not meant to be preached but to be read; still, it is a sermon, with a text, appropriate divisions, long, somnolent stretches, and a conclusion exhorting the reader to change his or her ways. "Purity of heart," Kierkegaard's name for holiness, is conceived as right willing, or what God wills.

Overview

The seventh son of a wealthy wool merchant, Søren Kierkegaard resided all his life in the large family dwelling in central Copenhagen, where he was prominent as a literary figure. An unhappy love affair, quarrels with other writers, and, in his last years, disputes with the Church—all documented in lengthy journals—make up the story of his life. Graduated in theology, he put off taking orders (Lutheran); still, an overriding sense of what the Gospel can mean to those who embrace it with faith and love led him to sandwich between his various poetical and philosophical writings a number of "Edifying Discourses," of which the present book is a memorable example.

Purity of Heart Is to Will One Thing is a penitential sermon intended to accompany the office of Confession. To be sure, it is an amplified sermon, not meant to be preached but to be read; still, it is a sermon, with a text, appropriate divisions, long, somnolent stretches, and a conclusion exhorting the reader to change his or her ways. The sermon, which enjoins holiness, deserves a place in the literature of Christian perfection. "Purity of heart," Søren Kierkegaard's name for holiness, is conceived as right willing, that is, willing the Good, or what God wills—"the one thing needful." The text comes from James 4:8: "Draw nigh to God and He will draw nigh to you. Cleanse your hands, ye sinners; and purify your hearts ye double-minded." "Double-minded" (Greek *dipsychos,* a term peculiar to Jewish-Christian wisdom literature) means doubting, wavering, uncertain, and especially division of interest between the world and God. Appropriately in a preconfessional sermon, the preacher's main concern is to expose double-mindedness (or, as we might say, bad faith, not in the sense of deceiving others but in the deeper sense of deceiving oneself). In any case, the opposite of double-mindedness, that is, willing one thing, does not lend itself to any elaboration. For Kierkegaard, it is equivalent to obeying the secret voice of conscience.

The divisions of the sermon (obscured by extraneous section headings in the American version) are conveniently stated by the author in more places than one. The argument falls into two main parts: a shorter part in which it is maintained that to will one thing one must lift one's eyes to the heavens, for there is nothing on earth that can be willed with an undivided will; and a much longer part in which typical duplicities that creep into the creaturely will when it tries to conform itself to the will of the Creator are systematically exposed. In this second part, the author further distinguishes between willing and doing. The problem when one tries to will what heaven wills is that self-interest keeps creeping in.

The first, relatively short, part of the sermon, called "Willing the Good," is of interest mainly in view of the claim of secular humanists that doubters can give meaning and weight to their lives by willing one thing without any reference to the Good. Select a cause, give it your all, and save your soul in so doing. Whether it is the best cause will always be debatable, but all that you need ask is whether it is a cause with which you have enough affinity to be authentic in the role you will be undertaking to play. A life is too precious to waste in drifting with the tide. Be somebody! Maybe you will find out that you are strong enough not even to need a cause to lean on. Choose your goal and follow it ruthlessly to the end!

How far does willing one thing—any one thing—equal purity of heart? Suppose the extreme case, Kierkegaard proposes. Can the unmitigated seeker after pleasure or wealth or power win a halo merely in virtue of the consistency with which the goal is pursued? No doubt such a person can—in the eyes of the double-minded. If halos were for average persons to bestow, quite possibly they would immortalize great sinners who have done what the bestower would sneakingly have liked to do. Questions arise, however. When one devotes oneself to pleasure or power or wealth or fame, is that person in fact willing one thing? First, may that person not be mistaken about the world? How can anyone will one thing in a world where everything changes, often into its opposite? "Carried to its extreme limit," says Kierkegaard, "what is pleasure other than disgust? What is earthly honor at its dizzy pinnacle other than contempt for existence? What are riches, the highest superabundance of riches, other than poverty?" Second, is not such a person's conception of self mistaken? One may imagine, perhaps, that one is self-made, the only one strong enough to overcome the indolence and mediocrity that enslave the human spirit. In thinking so, however, one is surely deluded. Moreover, Kierkegaard remarks, "if you should meet him in what he himself would call a weak moment, but which, alas, you would have to call a better moment," you might find him envying "that man of single purpose who even in all his frailty still wills the Good."

The second, much longer, part of the sermon is called "Willing the Good in Truth." It is addressed to upright souls, to conventional Christians, to those who, like the Pharisee in the parable, are in the habit of addressing God with a certain complacency, and who are not like other people—extortioners, unjust, adulterers, or even like yon publican. Its purpose is to show that good people ought not to get into the habit of approaching God too familiarly, not because of minor lapses but because of what might appear to one standing on the other side as treachery or double-dealing.

In division A of this second part, the sermon appeals to the hearers to get themselves together: "If it be possible for a man to will the Good in truth, then he must be at one with himself in willing to renounce all double-mindedness." In developing this point, the preacher suggests that we ask ourselves whether we serve the Good with a single eye or with an eye out for rewards and punishments. Only briefly does Kierkegaard touch the question traditional to mystical theology as to whether perfect love of God requires that a person set aside all thought of eternal beatitude. Mainly, under rewards and punishments, Kierkegaard is thinking of the here-and-now question of whether serving the Good can or ought to be independent of one's business and social interests. The double-mindedness here involved is fairly gross, although not always easy to root out. Kierkegaard compares it to the predicament of the man who loves a beautiful heiress: Would he love her as much if she were poor and ugly? More subtle than the outright question of rewards and punishments (or gains and losses) is the case in which an ambitious person, with an eye out for the main chance, is transfixed with a vision of the Good, and henceforth makes the service of the Good a career. He or she may become a great person, a universal benefactor. The question remains, however, with what will does that person serve the Good: Is the Good never subservient to personal ambition? With persons less capable of holding to a single course in life, double-mindedness is more likely to take the form of compromise. There is the person who is sometimes called a Sunday Christian. Such a person has, says the preacher, "a living feeling for the Good." If one speaks to such a person of God's love and providence, especially if one does so in a poetic fashion, the person is deeply moved. However, when an occasion presents itself in which that person might serve as an instrument of God's love and providence, it will probably find him or her engrossed in private affairs.

In division B of this second part, the sermon appeals for total commitment. "If a man shall will the Good in truth, then he must be willing to do all for the Good or be willing to suffer all for the Good." The "or" is important. Admittedly, doers of the good will have to suffer, but their suffering has some point to it. The word "or" reminds us that, besides persons who are fitted for an active life and who can serve the Good outwardly, there are many who are not fitted for an active life and who can serve the Good only inwardly. What doers and sufferers have in common is indicated by the word "all." Whichever their lot, they must do or suffer all for the Good.

In treating of the active life, Kierkegaard minimizes the difference between various callings. For some, doing all means giving up a place in the world, leaving possessions, not even turning back to bury a father. However, for others, it may mean assuming wealth and power and managing these faithfully. As regards the Good, there is no difference between these callings, nor is the difficulty or magnitude of the task worthy of any note. Quarreling and comparisons involve double-mindedness. This is a minor point, however. Kierkegaard's main concern in this section is the danger that arises whenever one tries to realize the Good in the temporal order. He calls it cleverness. "In its given reality the temporal order is in conflict with the Eternal." Cleverness, however, makes its appearance. Remember Jesus' temptations. By altering the Good here and there the clever one can win the world's goodwill. Many will join together under the conviction that the Good, instead of being something that human beings need, is something that stands in need of humankind. So, the clever one is able to accomplish something in the world. However, asks the preacher, does memory never visit the popular idol? "Can you remember the deceptive turn you gave the thing, by which you won the blind masses? . . . Very well. Let it rest. No one shall get to know. . . . But eternally, eternally it will continue to be remembered."

Now, what has the sermon to say to the sufferer—to "the person whom nature, from the very outset, as we humans are tempted to say, wronged, one who from birth was singled out by useless suffering: a burden to others; almost a burden to himself; and yes, what is worse, to be a born objection to the goodness of Providence"? Kierkegaard is thinking, no doubt, of the physically afflicted; but in his opinion the physical distress is less a problem than the mental anguish of being forever cut off from a happy life on earth. We laud the joys of childhood, of youth, of domestic life, says the preacher; but for the sufferer there is no happy childhood: If he is asked, "Why do you not play with the others?" he turns away. At the time of love, nobody loves him; and when anyone is friendly he knows that it is from compassion. So, he withdraws from life. Even at death, the handful of mourners say to each other that it is a blessing. He did, indeed, take part in life, says the preacher, in that he lived; but one thing he never knew, and that was "to be able to give and to receive like for like." What has the sermon to say to the true sufferer? It will not mock him by saying, "You too can accomplish something—for others." It will say, in truth, "You can still do—the highest thing of all. You can will to suffer all and thereby be committed to the Good. Oh, blessed justice, that the true sufferer can unconditionally do the highest quite as well as fortune's favorite child!" Indeed, says Kierkegaard, it is from the sufferer and not from the outward achiever that we learn most profoundly and most reliably what the highest is.

Such, in skeletal form, is the sermon. Kierkegaard has introduced the sermon with a long meditation on the time for confession, and has followed it by what is almost another discourse reminding the reader of the necessity for decision. In these two additional parts, which one may bring together under the expression, "the eleventh hour," Kierkegaard touches on the central theme of his philosophy, namely, human beings' consciousness of eternity, together with the dread that it causes in their hearts and the decision which it holds continually before them. King Solomon said, "For everything there is a season" (Ecclesiastes 3:1); so, it is natural for us to suppose that there is a season for remorse and repentance just as there is a season for rejoicing and for sorrow. However, the eleventh hour is not a season but an understanding of life that should accompany us in every season. "It is a silent, daily anxiety," says Kierkegaard. Every hour is appropriate for confession, and confession is always the eleventh hour. That it is an hour of decision is Kierkegaard's concluding word. God "has set eternity in the heart" is another of Solomon's sayings (Ecclesiastes 3:11). God has installed in each of us the voice of conscience with "its eternal right to be the exclusive voice." The preacher is no more than a prompter. He has nothing to tell his hearers beyond reminding them of their own inner voice, which the voices of the crowd make it difficult to hear. Eternity, says Kierkegaard, scatters the crowd, giving to the individual infinite weight. Viewed in another manner, conscience is the presence in the temporal order that is prepared to change a nullity into an individual through decision. The talk does not ask you to withdraw from life, from a useful calling, from agreeable society. It does demand that you be eternally concerned, that you bring not merely your life goal under the aegis of the Good but also the means by which you hope to achieve this goal. Once again, to you who suffer: Solomon says, "Sorrow is better than laughter; for by the sadness of the countenance, the heart is made better" (Ecclesiastes 7:3). Hence, the talk asks you, How has your condition changed? This is not a question about the state of your health: The talk will not be diverted into that channel. It asks rather "whether you now live in such a way that you truthfully will only one thing." "Not a change in suffering (for even if it is changed, it can only be a finite change), but in you, an infinite change in you from good to better." You may be denied sympathy: People may be afraid to mention your suffering. Do not feel bitter about this. Ask only whether at your grave those standing by, instead of mumbling prayers of thanks that the sufferer is dead, will say, "The content of his life was suffering, yet his life has put many to shame."

Christian Themes

Kierkegaard's sermon reminds us that, if one is to draw near to God, one must do so by sincerely willing to be holy even as God is holy. He makes the following main points: Only persons who will the Good can be said to will one thing. If one is to be sincere in willing the Good, one's will must be stripped of the entanglements of self-interest. A person who wills the Good in sincerity must be willing to do all or to suffer all for the Good. Finally, one wills the Good by obeying the voice of conscience, which speaks in time with the authority of eternity.

Sources for Further Study

Evans, C. Stephen, ed. *Kierkegaard on Faith and the Self*. Waco, Tex.: Baylor University Press, 2006. A collection of essays on Kierkegaard as a Christian philosopher. Bibliography, index.

Giles, James, ed. *Kierkegaard and Freedom*. New York: Palgrave, 2000. Essays on aspects of Kierkegaard's concept of freedom, including Peter Rogers's "Self-Deception and Freedom in Kierkegaard's *Purity of Heart*." Bibliography, index.

Kierkegaard, Søren. *The Living Thoughts of Kierkegaard*. Presented by W. H. Auden. Bloomington: Indiana University Press, 1952. Selections arranged under such headings as "The Present Age," "Aesthetics, Ethics, Religion," "The Subjective Thinker," "Sin and Dread," and "Christ the Offense." Includes an appreciative introduction.

Rohde, Peter. *Søren Kierkegaard: An Introduction to His Life and Philosophy.* Translated with a foreword by Alan M. Williams. London: George Allen & Unwin, 1963. Sound insights presented for the general reader.

Stendahl, Brita K. *Søren Kierkegaard.* Boston: Twayne, 1976. A convenient review of the writings that offers a substantial general introduction to Kierkegaard's thought. Bibliography.

Thomte, Reidar. *Kierkegaard's Philosophy of Religion.* Princeton, N.J.: Princeton University Press, 1948. Surveys the development of Kierkegaard's religious thought.

Jean H. Faurot

THE PURPOSE DRIVEN LIFE
What on Earth Am I Here For?

Author: Rick Warren (1954-   )
First published: Grand Rapids, Mich.: Zondervan, 2002
Genre: Nonfiction
Subgenres: Devotions; handbook for living; instructional manual
Core issues: Church; daily living; discipleship; holiness; salvation; trust in God

Created out of a desire to reach those who do not attend church and foster healthy churches, The Purpose Driven Life *leads readers through a forty-day devotional series focused on helping individuals understand their purpose in life. In contrast to self-help books promoting personal ambition, this book declares that the meaning of one's life comes from a proper relationship to God through Jesus Christ, not from focusing on the self. Warren identifies five purposes for life: people are planned for God's pleasure, formed for God's family, created to become like Christ, shaped for serving God, and made for a mission.*

Overview

Based on a biblical model of taking forty days to develop new patterns for ministry, Rick Warren's *The Purpose Driven Life* is divided into forty chapters, one for each day of a spiritual pilgrimage toward better understanding God's purpose in the reader's life. The first seven days are devoted to examining the purpose and meaning of life. To signal how this volume contrasts with many works that are focused on making people feel good and be successful, Warren begins with a clear statement that the purpose of life is much larger than personal fulfillment, peace of mind, or happiness. The meaning and purpose of life come not from focusing on the self but from knowing and working with the author of life, namely God. This seven-day segment of the book emphasizes the providence of God in creating people to enjoy God's fellowship forever through faith in Jesus Christ. Life on earth is intended by God as a preparation for eternity, and this process is part of God's purpose for each human being.

The second seven-day segment of the book treats the first purpose of life that Warren has identified: People are planned for God's pleasure. People please God first of all through worship—through singing, praising, praying, giving, and honoring God with trust and adoration. Such worship involves surrendering to God as one learns to walk in friendship with God. God also takes pleasure in helping people discover their gifts or abilities and use them for God's glory.

The third segment treats the second purpose: People are formed for God's family, or the church. Warren argues that because God is love, God values relationships. Even the nature of the Trinity reveals this relational quality in God as Father, Son, and Holy Spirit. Those who accept the Son, Jesus Christ, become adopted members of the family of God. Learning to be a loving member of this community on earth is central to life and a vital preparation for eternity with God in the community of heaven.

The fourth segment presents the third purpose: People are created to become like Christ. Warren explains that people are made in the image or likeness of God, meaning that they are spiritual beings designed to live for eternity; furthermore, they are intellectual, relational, and have a moral conscience. Because people are also fallen or sinful, people need the redemptive work of Christ to change their warped image into a holy one that reflects God's righteous character. In this process people do not become gods but do become adopted children of God who are patterned after the perfectly obedient Son of God, Jesus Christ. The focus here is on developing character that is godly. In this process of becoming a true disciple of Jesus Christ, the individual is to be transformed by the truth of Scripture, the trials of life, and the challenges of overcoming temptations. Such spiritual growth requires obedience and time.

The next seven-day segment discusses the fourth purpose: People are shaped for serving God. Warren says people are made to be more than consumers. Each person is created to serve God and such service is not optional. The happiness and joy of each person is realized in fulfilling God's purpose. This service is different for each person because how people are to serve God is determined by each one's SHAPE, an acronym for *s*piritual gifts, *h*eart or godly desires, *a*bilities, *p*ersonality, and *e*xperience. Serving God involves serving people, focusing on other people's needs, and moving beyond one's own selfish ambitions. Through redemptive work in Jesus Christ, God especially uses the hurts and disappointments of life to help individuals grow and mature. Service to God must be accomplished through God's purposes and strength.

The sixth and final segment evaluates the fifth purpose: People are made for a mission. According to Warren, God is at work in the world and calls people to join in this work. Christians are called to share what God is doing in their lives so that others can come to know and understand God's purposes for each person's life. The great commission of Matthew 28:18-20 and Acts 1:8 is the commission of each disciple of Jesus Christ to give witness to God's work in believers. The mission is to move beyond thinking about the self to reach a world that does not yet know God or God's ways.

The five purposes discussed in this book are rooted in the great commandment (Matthew 22:37-39) and the great commission of Jesus Christ. These can be summarized in five phrases from Jesus' teachings: "Love God with all your heart," "Love your neighbor as yourself," "Go and make disciples," "baptize them into [God's family]," and "teach them to do all things" through discipleship. Warren argues that when people keep these five purposes in balance, they can experience a meaningful and fruitful life, one that honors God by accepting and promoting God's holy purposes.

Christian Themes

Warren deals with the major biblical themes of sin, salvation, sanctification, and the choice people make for eternal life by accepting Jesus Christ or for eternal separation by rejecting Christ. He translates these Christian doctrines into language accessible to those not acquainted with church jargon and makes them enlightening to those already familiar with such terminology. Warren's stance against sin, New Age beliefs, and self-centered, self-help philosophies is strong.

The focus of this book is on positive steps people can take to discover God's design for their life. This work is strongly informed by a biblically rooted conviction that the providence of God determines the course of life, yet this volume also affirms the opportunity for each person to respond to God and be saved. Warren is also careful to note that people are saved to serve, to make a positive contribution to the life of the church and the world.

The Purpose Driven Life emphasizes that God wastes nothing in human experience. It states that life is not an accident. Each event and experience has the potential for helping people grow closer to God and learn to trust God more. In this process, God is far more concerned about character than comfort. By God's grace, one's greatest ministry comes from one's deepest hurts and greatest weaknesses. Only when God is one's strength, can God work best for God's glory. This book also emphasizes the centrality of the Bible in helping one discover the purpose and meaning of life. Scriptures provide a foundation for understanding God's purpose for life and protect believers from being swept along by the relativism of the postmodern era.

In keeping with traditional Christian teaching, Warren declares that God is the one who gives life meaning. Only by keeping God at the center of one's life can one realize the purpose and meaning of life. As Warren concludes, a purpose driven life is a God-directed life.

Sources for Further Study

Abanes, Richard. *Rick Warren and the Purpose That Drives Him: An Insider Looks at the Phenomenal Bestseller*. Eugene, Oreg.: Harvest House, 2005. An informed review of the life and work of Warren. Abanes offers answers to criticisms of Warren's books and ministry.

Byasse, Jason. "Re-Purposed: What Is a Church For?" *Christian Century* (March 9, 2004): 28-29, 31-32. A thoughtful evaluation of *The Purpose Driven Life*. Byasse finds it a biblically and theologically responsible rethinking of church practice but questions its use for liturgical context.

Gunther, Marc, and Christopher Tkaczyk. "Will Success Spoil Rick Warren?" *Fortune* 15, no. 9 (October 31, 2005): 108-110, 112, 114, 116, 118, 120. This secular management article evaluates the nature and legacy of Warren's leadership in writing and ministry. Concludes that Warren is the major religious entrepreneur of his generation.

Stafford, Tim. Review of *The Purpose Driven Life: What on Earth Am I Here For? Christianity Today* (March, 2004): 29. Evaluates Warren's book as redefining the nature of a balanced Christian life in an ordinary church, whether Pentecostal, Episcopal, or Baptist.

Warren, Rick. *The Purpose Driven Church: Growth Without Compromising Your Message and Mission*. Grand Rapids, Mich.: Zondervan, 1995. Warren describes how to develop healthy Christians and biblical church leadership, the measure for obedience to the purpose of God for a given church.

Daven M. Kari

QUADRAGESIMO ANNO

Author: Pius XI (Ambrogio Damiano Achille Ratti; 1857-1939)
First published: 1931 (English translation, 1931)
Edition used: On Reconstructing the Social Order (Quadragesimo Anno). Chicago: Outline Press, 1947
Genre: Nonfiction
Subgenre: Encyclical
Core issues: Capitalism; church; communism; justice; poverty; social action

In thanksgiving for the insights and benefits of Leo XIII's Rerum Novarum, *Pius XI presents* Quadragesimo Anno *on the anniversary of the latter's promulgation. Pius updates and clarifies principles central to Leo's work, such as private property, just wages, and worker associations.* Quadragesimo Anno *is influential for Pius's expression of the principle of subsidiarity and his critique of both unrestricted liberal economies and socialism.*

Overview

Pius XI begins *Quadragesimo Anno* by honoring and summarizing Leo XIII's *Rerum Novarum* (1891). He recalls that Leo faced the Industrial Revolution, which contributed to inordinate wealth for a few and wretched working conditions for the majority. Leo critiqued both economic liberalism and socialism as found in the late nineteenth century, and he advised away from class struggle and toward recognition of mutual complementariness. Many applauded Leo's reflections, but some remained critical. Before defending Leo from his critics, Pius first highlights the benefits that had flowed from Leo's foundational encyclical.

Pius writes that *Rerum Novarum* had encouraged many Christian leaders to reflect on social issues within a Christian framework. He states that Leo's encyclical had also won acceptance outside of the Catholic Church as evidenced by nations that instituted new labor laws. Further, Pius explains that although many were leery of worker associations prior to *Rerum Novarum*, many clergy and laypersons have since sacrificed much to provide organized support for underprivileged workers.

After summarizing *Rerum Novarum*, Pius clarifies and updates four issues that Leo had addressed: church authority, private property, just wages, and worker associations. First, Pius discusses the responsibility of the church to address social issues. Whereas Leo sought to defend the right of church leaders to speak on social issues, Pius's writing style indicates that the church's authority to speak on such issues is assumed rather then debated. Pius explains that while church leaders do not have authority to speak on matters of scientific technique, they do have authority to offer guidance on matters related to the moral law. Because economic issues overlap with the moral law, Pius writes that he has the responsibility to address the relevant issues.

Pius then discusses private property. Benefiting from the forty years of discussion that had followed *Rerum Novarum*, Pius writes that private property has a twofold character: individual and collective. Workers should have a right to attain private property, but the fruits of the land ought to be distributed for the benefit of the common good. The state should maintain the right to private property and should have limited authority to moderate the distribution of wealth to curb radical abuses. Pius maintains that the wealthy should be encouraged to distribute their wealth for the common good. Accordingly, Pius promotes investments aimed at producing jobs.

Pius's discussion of the just distribution of wealth provides a transition to his discussion of just wages. He indicates that many factors ought to be considered in determining the appropriate wage for employees. He gives four considerations particular attention: the needs of the worker and his family, the condition of the business, the public economic good, and the relation of wages to those of other workers as well as the goods being sold. Next, Pius explains that without intermediary organizations like worker associations, the state is left to deal directly with individuals. As a result, the voice of impoverished individuals often remains unheard and the responsibilities of the state become overburdening. Pius promotes the subsidiary function, a principle that states that larger organizations should allow smaller associations to accomplish those tasks they are competent to complete. Pius argues that with intermediate associations, the gap between social classes will be reduced, the needs of individuals will be more easily addressed, and state leaders will be freed from performing small and distracting tasks. In particular, Pius encourages the formation of associations among those who work in the same or similar occupations.

Pius then provides an updated look at the manifestations of economic liberalism and socialism as found in 1931. He explains that while economic liberalism should not be condemned in itself, he argues that this economic structure leads to devastating consequences when business leaders are given unlimited license. Such a license contributes to three conflicts: the struggle among business leaders for economic supremacy; fight to gain control of the state; and conflict between states. To avoid these conflicts, Pius encourages limited government intervention and the promotion of the virtues of justice and charity.

Pius explains that socialism had divided into two forms. The form known as communism promoted unrelenting class warfare and the elimination of private property. The more moderate form of socialism rejected violence and somewhat modified both class struggle and the denial of private property. In the end, however, Pius concludes that any social structure that can be appropriately named socialism is incompatible with the teachings of the Catholic Church. He defends this claim by explaining that socialism is materialistic and employs force to the point of violating human freedom.

Finally, Pius calls for Christian reform. He proposes that the foundations of social evils are the disordered passions that result from sin. He decries the selfishness of greedy business leaders and the dangerous and compromising working situations that are offered to women and children. Further, he raises concerns about those employees whose working situations separate them from their families and do not allow them to spend their Sundays in dedication to God. In the final paragraphs, Pius highlights a claim he repeats throughout his work, the need for the virtues of charity and justice. He also encourages the virtues of moderation and perseverance, and he praises those who have selflessly developed worker associations. Moreover, he asks priests to train workers so that they may be sources of Christian light in the workplace. Lastly, Pius reminds all Christians of their need for God's grace and the importance of following God's plan.

Christian Themes

A major Christian theme that Pius XI highlights in *Quadragesimo Anno* is the importance of tradition. Pius recognizes that his insights have largely benefited from *Rerum Novarum* and the forty years of discussion that have resulted from Leo's foundational work. Rather than writing as if he were the sole source of his reflections, Pius, through his format, acknowledges his debt to the tradition that has preceded him. The first quarter of the work is a summary of Leo's work, and the remainder of Pius's encyclical provides clarifications and updates of issues discussed by Leo.

By using *Rerum Novarum* as a foundation, Pius solidifies certain principles in the tradition of Christian social ethics. He explains that church leaders have the responsibility to speak on moral issues. He clearly explains that private property has both an individual and communal character. He gives fuller consideration to matters central to the determination of a just wage. He also maintains the importance of intermediary associations and formulates the principle of subsidiary function, which later becomes a central principle of the tradition.

In addition, Pius engages in the church's ongoing dialogue with economic liberalism and socialism. He critiques unbridled liberal economies. He also proposes that socialism, as he defines it, is in itself contrary to the Christian faith. Finally, Pius recalls the ultimate destiny of humankind and the priority of remaining in God's grace over the accumulation of material wealth. His reflections engage the social structures of his time and encourage further clarification of Christian social principles. Pius's decision to explicitly acknowledge the social tradition that precedes him is repeated by many who follow him as the bishop of Rome.

Sources for Further Study

Himes, Kenneth R., O. F. M., ed. *Modern Catholic Social Teaching: Commentaries and Interpretations.* Washington, D.C.: Georgetown University Press, 2005. This scholarly collection includes four foundational essays and fourteen commentaries on influential church documents. Each essay includes thorough bibliographical information. Brief index.

Nell-Breuning, Oswald von, S.J. *Reorganization of Social Economy: The Social Encyclical Developed and Explained.* Translated by Bernard W. Dempsey, S.J. New York: Bruce, 1936. Extensive commentary on *Quadragesimo Anno* from an author who himself was central in the formation of the encyclical. Brief index.

Pontifical Council for Justice and Peace. *Compendium of the Social Doctrine of the Church.* Translated by Vatican Press. Washington, D.C.: United States Conference of Catholic Bishops, 2005. This reference work provides a comprehensive synthesis of central concepts in Catholic social ethics. Includes thorough reference and analytical indexes.

Pontifical Council for Justice and Peace. *The Social Agenda: A Collection of Magisterial Texts*. Città del Vaticano: Libreria Editrice Vaticano, 2000. This work is a concise compilation of official church statements thematically organized to discuss eleven issues central to Christian social ethics.

Kevin Schemenauer

QUESTIONS FOR ECCLESIASTES

Author: Mark Jarman (1952-   )
First published: Brownsville, Oreg.: Story Line Press, 1997
Genre: Poetry
Subgenres: Lyric poetry; narrative poetry
Core issues: Expectancy; faith; illumination; knowledge; silence; works and deeds

Jarman uses the medium of poetry to address questions of faith and his relationship with God. He tests the merit of a worldview dominated by Christian thought and asserts that questioning doctrinal tenets rather than believing without question is essential to spiritual growth.

Overview

The son and grandson of ministers in the Disciples of Christ Christian Church, Mark Jarman employs his skills as a writer to address essential aspects of the Christian faith. The poet was initially impressed by his maternal grandmother, Nora Pemberton, who was an unpublished poet and short-fiction writer, and his father, Donald Ray Jarman, who as a preacher had a masterful command of language. He was further inspired by British poet Donald Davie, whom he admired for his willingness to openly express his Christian faith in his poetry. Of him Jarman has written, "Davie's religious life was intimately involved with this poetry. This realization . . . led me to engage my own religious beliefs directly in my writing." *Questions for Ecclesiastes* continues a conversation about God, expressions of faith, and why faith matters in daily life begun in Jarman's first book of verse, *North Sea* (1978), in which he initiated the theme of questioning the real-life applicability of Christian teaching and the example of Jesus.

Jarman is unique as a poet of Christian-themed verse because he challenges intellectual complacency. For him it is insufficient to mouth doctrine or espouse Jesus as a role model. For example, in the title poem, "Questions for Ecclesiastes," Jarman narrates an autobiographically inspired incident in which a minister (his father) is called to the home of a young female suicide to offer the family comfort and religious perspective. The aim of the poem is to question God's will in the death of the girl and also the usefulness of the preacher as an emissary of divine will. Divided into nine paragraph-style stanzas, the poem begins in the past tense and ends in the present tense, allowing the speaker to retell the story and then analyze its outcome. Six of the stanzas start with "What if." Eight of the nine present essential questions about blind faith, and the ninth ponders why God keeps the incomprehensible "a secret" from both those willing to believe and the already devout Christian. Throughout the poem, the preacher's words and gestures at consolation are made to seem useless because he cannot explain why the girl killed herself, and his talking is contrasted to God's silence on the matter. The tension creates what Jarman calls the "urgency" that "gives religious poetry its power." Jarman stated that he adopted the rhythm of this poem from that of the book of Ecclesiastes in the Old Testament of the King James version of the Bible. One of the accomplishments of the poem is its responsiveness to biblical language on a contemporary theme.

Jarman's personae embrace the potency of faith and organized religious worship as formative in ordinary life. In testing the merit of a worldview shaped by Christian doctrine, Jarman's poems assert a positive place for faith and doubt in the mind and heart of the Christian. "Transfiguration," with its poignant final stanza opening "I want to believe," captures the struggle for the Christian to believe in such logic-defying aspects of Jesus' life as his resurrection and transfiguration. This poem, divided into seven stanzas, opens with Jesus, as described in the Gospel of Mark, flanked by Old Testament figures Moses and Elijah, who accompany him on his ascent into heaven. The first stanza sets the scene, allowing the focus to shift to the metaphoric aspects of "transfiguration" as the kinds of change in the body of the sick person and in the human person of Jesus. The poem develops by elaborating on the promise of eternal life and the quest of the faithful who "want to believe" that the transfiguration happened, that the sick can be cured, and that the changes one under-goes in life are really part of a larger plan designed by God. The persona of this poem, like others in the collection, is that of the unsettled Christian who has more questions than answers about theological matters.

Questions for Ecclesiastes, a National Book Critics Circle Award finalist and win-ner of the Lenore Marshall Poetry Prize, is important because it previews the first of the "unholy sonnets" that grew into Jarman's 2000 book-length collection of the same name. These sonnets were inspired by British poets John Donne and Gerard Manley Hopkins, known for their contribution to the sonnet form and to English-language po-etry dealing with the Christian struggle. Although most of Jarman's sonnets are seri-ous in tone and topic, a few, such as sonnet 12, illustrate Jarman's humor and dry wit. In this poem, a "pious man" who is a bit too verbal in his love of God, loses everything to a flood and asks God why this had to happen to him. He is disarmed by God's can-did and irreverent reply, "I can't say/ Just something about you pisses me off." Using the child's hand game of making a church with the fingers, Jarman suggests that wor-shipers are trapped by "Holy Terror" (sonnet 2). In sonnets 10 and 11, he contem-plates the role of the poet as the divine singer, in the tradition of King David.

Not all the poems in *Questions for Ecclesiastes* are on religious themes. Jarman also writes eloquently of his love for his wife and daughters and shows his keen eye for detail in describing scenes in nature.

Christian Themes

Having established the range of God's interactions in everyday life and people's at-traction to or need for the idea of God, Jarman spotlights his thesis that because no one can live up to the ideal faith described in Scripture, the quest to believe is as important and somehow more real than believing without questioning. In the poem "The Last Supper," the speaker considers the many imitations in life and art of the Last Supper to be found in suburban houses and suggests that the Last Supper is the story of a family trying to reconcile its competing interests, just as the Christian is called to reconcile or balance faith and reason. Belying the apparently happy gathering of the family is the "loneliness of God," whose will is not fully known or embraced. In the final poem of the book, "The Worry Bird," the speaker remembers how his parents told him to give all his cares to the worry bird, a garage-sale bird statue that sat in his bedroom. The bird takes on the traits of the Holy Spirit in the mind of the mature poet, who has been acculturated to pass his cares on to God.

In Jarman's poetry, little in the world makes sense. Things are constantly changing—his children grow up, his parents age, he travels from place to place, and time passes while death hovers relentlessly—as the Christian tries to reconcile competing interests in the material and the spiritual worlds. Yet, through all the uncertainties, Jarman remains optimistic, writing that if and when God's kingdom comes, "We'll greet him as children would have done," with cares absorbed by the worry bird and with innocence, steadfastness, clarity, and purity of heart.

Sources for Further Study

Jarman, Mark. *Body and Soul: Essays on Poetry*. Ann Arbor: University of Michigan Press, 2002. Collection of previously published essays on poetic themes. Contains an autobiography that includes the helpful partial memoir, " Body and Soul, Parts of Life."

_____. "Poetry and Religion." In *Poetry After Modernism*, edited by Robert McDowell. Brownsville, Oreg.: Story Line Press, 1998. An analysis of various religious poetry and the place of religious themes in contemporary American poetry with close readings of T. S. Eliot, John Berryman, Jorie Graham, and others.

Murphy, Jim. "A Conversation with Mark Jarman" *Image* 33 (Winter, 2001-2002): 63-78. An interview in which Jarman covers his composing process, his influences, and his intentions for his poetry.

Opengart, Bea. "God-Wrestling as Postmodern Rhetoric in the Work of Three Contemporary American Poets." *Literature and Belief* 23, no. 1 (2003): 23-37. Applies the theory of sociologist Arthur Waskow, who used the phrase "god-wrestling" to describe the struggle to believe in the poetry of Jarman and two contemporaries and to address their tendency to pose questions about faith without providing answers in the course of their poetry.

Vela, Richard. "The Subject of the Poem: Religion, the Everyday World, and the New Formalism in the Poetry of Mark Jarman." *Pembroke Magazine* 33 (2001): 283-290. Describes how Jarman achieves intimacy through his style, his perception of common events, and reliance on forms of interrogation that fail to resolve the complexities of life and faith, demonstrating that there are no neat endings or easy answers to the provocative questions his verse raises.

Beverly Schneller

QUO VADIS
A Narrative of the Time of Nero

Author: Henryk Sienkiewicz (1846-1916)
First published: 1896 (English translation, 1896)
Edition used: Quo Vadis, translated by W. S. Kuniczak. New York: Maxwell Macmillan International, 1993
Genre: Novel
Subgenres: Catholic fiction; historical fiction (first century); romance
Core issues: Conversion; faith; forgiveness; good vs. evil; love; martyrdom

In Quo Vadis, *Nobel laureate Sienkiewicz paints a picture of the moral and ethical superiority of the Christian faith as its adherents face the persecutions arising from the decadent cruelty of amoral Rome during the days of Nero. Peppered with authentic historical detail, the love story between the brutal, self-centered pagan Roman patrician Vinicius and the self-sacrificing, loving, faithful Christian beauty Lygia parallels and personalizes for the reader the struggle between these two antithetical views of civilization. It is a story of forgiveness and spiritual transformation brought about by Christian love and epitomized by the change in Vinicius among others, as well as a brilliant commentary on why the teachings of the new Christian faith eventually won out over the great Roman Empire.*

Principal characters
Marcus Vinicius, the Roman tribune who desires to have Lygia, unaware she is a Christian
Lygia, a Christian princess of a conquered people and a hostage of Rome; her beauty attracts Marcus Vinicius
Petronius, Vinicius's uncle and Nero's erudite adviser who obtains Lygia from Nero for his nephew and strives to keep the emperor's evil acts in check
Eunice, Petronius's slave girl who deeply loves her master
Nero, a cruel, fickle emperor of Rome who makes decisions based on the advice of sycophants in his court
Tigellinus, the rival of Petronius for Nero's ear and head of the emperor's praetorian guard
Chilon Chilonides, a con artist and traitor hired by Vinicius to find the escaped Lygia, but who has a last-minute conversion and becomes a martyr
Aulus Plautius, the husband of Pomponia and the Roman general who conquered Britain
Pomponia Graecina, Lygia's Christian adoptive mother and Plautius's wife

Ursus, Lygia's massive bodyguard
Acte, a spurned slave lover who still cares for Nero
Poppea Sabina, Nero's evil wife who sees Lygia as a threat
Peter, the apostle sent to convert Rome and leader of the Roman church
Paul, the apostle who befriends and seeks to convert Marcus
Crispus, a legalistic Christian zealot who though faithful sometimes misses the heart of the Gospel

Overview

At the beginning of *Quo Vadis*, after being injured and cared for at the house of the general Plautius, warrior hero and tribune Marcus Vinicius tells his uncle Petronius about his unquenchable desire for a beautiful woman he saw at the general's home and seeks his help in obtaining her. After the pair visit the general, Petronius tells Vinicius he has a plan to obtain the woman.

Petronius tells Nero that Lygia, a hostage of Rome who therefore belongs to Caesar, dwells in the home of Plautius. When Nero sends a centurion to retrieve Lygia from the general's home, Pomponia fears they are coming to kill her husband but is little relieved when she discovers their real mission. Encouraging her adopted daughter to be strong in her Christian faith, she and the general release her to Nero's care, sending with her Christian servants, including the giant Ursus. The angry general rightly suspects Petronius is behind the taking of Lygia and perhaps intends to make her a concubine for himself or Vinicius.

Placed among the concubines, Lygia is directed to the care of Acte, a freedwoman and Nero's former lover, by a letter from Pomponia, who knows Acte has sympathy for the Christians. Acte promises to keep her from the lustful gaze of the emperor. At first believing Petronius betrayed him, Vinicius is delighted to learn that his uncle intends to see that Lygia be given to him. At one of Nero's debauched parties, a drunken Vinicius tries to seduce Lygia, who is saved by Ursus.

Vinicius eagerly anticipates the arrival of Lygia from Nero's palace and is enraged when he learns that someone has spirited her away. In a fit of anger, he smashes the skull of one of the slaves who had failed to prevent her being taken, even though the slave had nursed him from boyhood.

At the recommendation of Petronius's slave girl Eunice, the enraged Vinicius hires the traitorous Chilon to find his displaced property, Lygia. Chilon deduces that Lygia is a Christian, discovers the Christians' secret worship place, and informs Vinicius that he can find her there. Vinicius, accompanied by the gladiator Croton, follows Lygia home from the worship meeting and attempts to forcibly recover her. Ursus intercepts them, kills the giant gladiator, injures Vinicius, and takes the injured man to Lygia, who nurses him back to health. In the company of the Christians and under the influence of the apostles Peter and Paul, Vinicius begins to recognize the inherent moral superiority and spiritual power of the Christian faith. After eventually converting, he is restored to his love, Lygia.

Nero's madness grows, and he torches Rome to create an artistic moment. When the people suspect Nero of starting the fire, his wife and his adviser Tigellinus suggest that the Christians could be blamed instead. Thus begin the horrors of Nero's persecution, in which Christians are dressed in animal skins, placed in an arena, and set on by wild beasts, or used as human torches to light the emperor's garden at parties. In the arena, Lygia is saved from death on the horns of a bull by Ursus and released by Nero at the spectators' demand. Lygia and Vinicius eventually escape to Sicily.

Because Christians in Rome insist that Christianity's chief spokesperson be spared martyrdom, Peter leaves Rome with young Nazarius. On the Appian Way, Peter has a vision in which he sees the Lord walking and queries, "*Quo vadis, Domine?*" or "Where are you going, Lord?" to which Jesus replies he must go to Rome to be crucified a second time if Peter deserts his people. Profoundly moved, Peter returns to Rome where both he and Paul suffer martyrdom, as church tradition has held.

Petronius falls from Nero's favor and comes under a death sentence for his defense of the Christians Vinicius and Lygia. At a party hosted for his friends, Petronius commits suicide along with his beloved slave Eunice, but not before writing a sarcastic and humorous letter to Nero enjoining him to commit any crime he wants but to please stop murdering the arts. Under the threat of being captured by rebellious legions and dying a horrible death at the hands of the people, Nero takes his life with the faithful Acte by his side. In a profound way, the suicides portend the coming death of the empire's nobility (Petronius) as a result of its genocidal cruelty (Nero).

Christian Themes

Sin and evil and its horrifying effects on Roman civilization permeate *Quo Vadis*. From the lust of Vinicius for Lygia that leads to the killing of his faithful servant, to the debauchery of the murderous Nero, sin stains both the individual and the state itself. Even the noblest Roman, Petronius, suffers from it as reflected by his trickery against Aulus Plautius as well as his seeming unconcern, dissolute lifestyle, and ultimate suicide. Sienkiewicz depicts a Rome that was indeed rife with evil and ready to fall.

However, the author also shows that a different kind of Rome was also steadily being created through the Christian conversion and spiritual transformation of its citizenry. The slow but steady change in Vinicius from a murderous man who cares only for himself and his own desires to a kind and caring one concerned about others offers hope that the new Rome will be made up of citizens transformed by the power of a grace and love from beyond this world that stems from a just and compassionate God.

The power of "faith in Christ" and "the faith of Christ" to sustain the characters in difficult circumstances is clear in Sienkiewicz's portrayal. The consummate example is Peter returning to Rome to die with Christ's followers after his vision of the Lord, but the steady resolve of the other believers in the face of martyrdom to stay their course and keep their faith in Christ stands out as well.

The author also examines the theme of forgiveness, which comes to the fore in the struggle of Ursus as a believer to gain forgiveness from Christ after he kills to protect

Lygia. To the amazement of Vinicius, the followers of Christ turn the other cheek even toward the traitorous Chilon. Lygia also embodies the Christian doctrine by offering forgiveness freely to Vinicius in spite of his many sins against her.

The author's Catholicism directs his interpretation of this turbulent time in the early Christian church. Peter heads the church at Rome in keeping with Catholic doctrine while the apostle Paul, the favorite of Protestants and author of the book of Romans, resides in the background, though instrumental in the conversion of Vinicius and bravely quoting Scripture as he faces martyrdom. Finally, Sienkiewicz has the last word on the demise of Rome and the flowering of Catholic Christianity when he triumphantly notes that it is the basilica of Peter that rules the city now, from the Vatican heights—the city and the world.

Sources for Further Study

Gessner, Peter. "Henry Sienkiewicz and *Quo Vadis.*" *Bulletin of the Arts Club of Buffalo,* 1997. An overview that focuses on the portrayal of the early Christians and Petronius.

Giergielewicz, Mieczlav. *Henryk Sienkiewicz: A Biography.* New York: Hippocrene Books, 1991. An authoritative biography of the author who won the Nobel Prize in Literature in 1905.

Hannan, Kevin. Review of *Quo Vadis. The Sarmatian Review* 15, no. 1 (January, 1995). Briefly discusses the author's background research in ancient Rome and Poland in preparation for writing the book.

Mansour, Lawrence. Review of *Quo Vadis. Slavic and E. European Journal* 44, no. 4 (Winter, 2000): 679. Explores the rationale for and analyzes newest English translation of Sienkiewicz's work and finds it wanting in several areas.

Monte, Richard. "Rome in Poland." *History Today* 51, no. 10 (October, 2001): 4-6. Gives insight into the Polish film release of *Quo Vadis* and its significance to the country.

David D. Pettus

THE REASONABLENESS OF CHRISTIANITY AS DELIVERED IN THE SCRIPTURES

Author: John Locke (1632-1704)
First published: 1695
Edition used: The Reasonableness of Christianity as Delivered in the Scriptures, edited with an introduction, notes, critical apparatus, and transcriptions of related manuscripts by John C. Higgins-Biddle. New York: Clarendon Press, 1999
Genre: Nonfiction
Subgenres: Exegesis; hermeneutics; theology
Core issues: Ethics; God; Jesus Christ; religion

By close examination, Locke attempts to show that the Gospels of Christianity are accessible to a reasonable analysis. Confining his interpretations to Christ's words and actions in the first four books and acts, Locke identifies the fundamental beliefs of the Christian faith. Appealing to implicit meanings in the text and piecing together the historical narrative, he explains Christ's words and intentions.

Overview

In *The Reasonableness of Christianity as Delivered in the Scriptures*, John Locke begins by examining the significance of the Fall and its relation to the teachings of Christ as they are given in the New Testament. Quoting biblical text, he concludes that in Eden, Adam and Eve were in a state of righteousness and immortality. The Fall brought death into the world to all of humanity, but Christ restored all humanity to life, potentially. To gain salvation, one must believe that Jesus was the Messiah and obey God's commandments.

Locke notes that numerous instances in the Bible support the idea that Christ was the Son of God. Ancient prophecies had spoken of the coming of a great prophet who would work miracles. Jesus was believed to be that prophet because of the miracles he performed and his teachings. He preached that the kingdom of God had come and that the way to heaven was through repentance and baptism and obedience to God's commandments. He did not immediately declare himself to be the Messiah, however; he left his miracles to speak for his divinity. His trial and crucifixion further proved that Jesus was recognized as the Son of God. Jesus commanded his eleven disciples to go forth after his death and preach that he was the Messiah. Locke concludes that it is therefore reasonable to believe that Jesus was the son of God.

Locke's primary intent is to establish that Jesus was the Messiah, gleaning copious evidence from the Scriptures and quoting the Greek text along with the English version to support his readings. He traces Jesus' every move to explain why Jesus did not proclaim himself the Messiah until just before his crucifixion and why Jesus did and said what he did every step of the way to the cross and after the Resurrection. Locke reasons that Jesus had to die when he did to make way for the Holy Ghost, who could not appear until his death and whose duty was to assist the disciples in their preaching and performing miracles. The Holy Ghost is further proof that Jesus was the Messiah.

The meaning of the law of faith is central to Locke's explanation of Jesus' role and nature, and he explains what is meant by that law, again quoting biblical passages at length: One must believe that Jesus would reward those who seek him diligently, and one must believe that God is merciful to those who obey him. Locke argues that believing that Jesus was the Messiah brought righteousness. Faith alone, however, is insufficient. Baptism admits men into the kingdom of God, but they must thereafter obey the Ten Commandments and the Golden Rule.

As for those who lived before the coming of Christ, Locke reasons that pre-Christians had only to believe what the ancient biblical text promised, that a great prophet was coming. Faith in God's promise of an anointed one was sufficient to save souls, but God's goodness and truth, made manifest by the works of nature, prompted love and faith, as well as God's words. Another difficult question is what becomes of those who never heard of God's message or of Jesus. Locke reasons that humanity is endowed with a natural sense of rightness, which also leads people to intuit the existence of a merciful God.

Turning to the question of why humanity needs Jesus, Locke explains that the ways of God are inscrutable and it would be impertinent to question God's wisdom. A reasonable person would accept without question God's wisdom and goodness; still, the evidence of Christ's usefulness to humanity is too abundant for anyone not to see. Before Christ, humankind suffered from weak reason and was kept in darkness by priests who taught superstition. Polytheism and idolatry ruled. The knowledge of morality came too slowly with the use of natural reason, and the wise men who may have taught the rules of morality were few and widely scattered. Moses was not sufficient because only a few people knew of his teaching. Jesus was necessary to disperse the darkness, to save humanity from the grip of the priests and superstition, and to lead them to the truth. He broke down the walls separating people and sent his disciples out into the world to spread the Word. Christ brought divine authority, and his message was simple: believe in him. Before Christ, humanity had no clear idea of a future state. Christ brought the hope of eternal life, evidenced by his own Resurrection and Ascension into heaven. Before, people had little incentive to be virtuous, for virtue was universally incompatible with earthly happiness. The prospect of salvation and immortality gave them the incentive to obey God's commandments.

According to Locke, the best way to understand God's message is to read the actual words of Jesus and the Apostles. He explains how to read correctly: One must find the principal aim of the writer, what the main idea is, and how it is delivered, and one must look for the author's intent in the discourse, note the coherence, and connect the parts. Finally, one must not pick out certain sayings and make them the whole truth. These few instructions aptly describe his own method.

Christian Themes

Locke argues in *The Reasonableness of Christianity as Delivered in the Scriptures* that biblical text, when examined carefully by a rigorous rationality, provides a clear understanding of Christ's life, teachings, and death. Christ's activities on earth form a historical record that establishes his divinity and primary mission on earth, which was to bring salvation to humanity. The Scriptures, which contain the teachings of Jesus and a record of his life up to and just after his crucifixion, provide all the guidance that is needed for salvation. Paramount among the requirements for life eternal is the belief that Jesus was the Messiah, the Son of God. Faith by itself, however, is insufficient. Salvation cannot be achieved without repentance and a sincere obedience to the laws that God laid down, principally the Ten Commandments.

The teachings of Jesus and his disciples form a canon of law clearly evident from reading the New Testament. Despite the elaborate explanations of the Gospels by learned people, Locke asserts that the individual, to be saved, need only believe that Jesus is the Son of God, is the Messiah, was raised from the dead, delivered humanity from death, and shall come again to pass sentence on them. Learned writers who argue various interpretations of biblical text confuse the meanings of the text and mix in their own ideas. Those who are not as sophisticated as the learned interpreters, are untrained in discourse, or do not have the time, ability, or inclination to reason the mysteries of the Gospel, need not be concerned, for if they adhere to the fundamentals of Christ's teaching with faith and obedience, they will be saved. God's goodness and grace are not intended for only the educated or the wise. Locke's message was that all who believe in God and follow his laws will be saved. God is not only good but also reasonable, and his message is likewise reasonable.

Sources for Further Study

Colman, John. *John Locke's Moral Philosophy*. Edinburgh, Scotland: Edinburgh University Press, 1983. Locke's ideas on morality in general are shown to be consistent with his views of morality in *The Reasonableness of Christianity as Delivered in the Scriptures*.

Higgins-Biddle, John C. Introduction to *The Reasonableness of Christianity as Delivered in the Scriptures*. New York: Clarendon Press, 1999. Examines Locke's text and the controversy it created, together with a scholarly study of variant manuscripts of the work and a lengthy bibliography.

Marshall, John. "Locke, Socinianism, 'Socinianism,' and Unitarianism." In *English Philosophy in the Age of Locke*. Oxford, England: Clarendon Press, 2000. Using *The Reasonableness of Christianity as Delivered in the Scriptures* as evidence, defends Locke against the claims that he was Unitarian and Socinian in his thinking.

Nuovo, Victor, ed. *John Locke and Christianity: Contemporary Responses to "The Reasonableness of Christianity."* Bristol, England: Thoemmes Press, 1997. A collection of original texts that show the extent to which Locke's work stirred much heated debate. The introduction explains the relevance of each excerpt to *The Reasonableness of Christianity as Delivered in the Scriptures*.

The Reasonableness of Christianity / LOCKE   1469

_____. "Locke's Theology, 1694-1704." In *English Philosophy in the Age of Locke*. Oxford, England: Clarendon Press, 2000. Discusses the relation of *The Reasonableness of Christianity as Delivered in the Scriptures* to Locke's theology as a whole.

Bernard E. Morris

RECONCILIATION
Restoring Justice

Author: John W. de Gruchy (1939-   )
First published: Minneapolis, Minn.: Fortress Press, 2002
Genre: Nonfiction
Subgenres: History; theology
Core issues: Africa; confession; forgiveness; Incarnation; justice; reconciliation; social action; truth

De Gruchy considers the meaning of the Christian doctrine of reconciliation and its relevance to political efforts to transform communities and nations, especially after internal strife. His primary case study is the South African Truth and Reconciliation Commission, which involved public hearings where perpetrators of human rights violations during the apartheid regime confessed before victims or family members of victims. The hope was that face-to-face truth telling would lead to forgiveness, reparations for victims, and restoration of justice.

Overview

After slaughter, torture, and organized oppression, how can nations heal? Is the Christian gospel of reconciliation at all relevant in the political arena? Does God's promise of redemption and salvation have any meaning during the messy transition to democracy or during reconstruction of fractured nations? John W. de Gruchy, a political theologian, wrestles with these questions in a study of reconciliation and its relation to restorative as opposed to retributive justice. Personal experience of entrenched racism and institutionalized oppression of non-Europeans during the apartheid regime in South Africa informs his analysis. He contextualizes theological ideas by considering the rationale for and the limitations of hearings conducted by the Truth and Reconciliation Commission (TRC) after the dissolution of apartheid. His ideas are relevant for peacemakers in other countries struggling with reconstruction after periods of atrocities, such as genocide in Rwanda, sectarianism in Northern Ireland, or ethnic cleansing in Serbia.

Reconciliation is organized around three major topics: the language of reconciliation, agency or the role of the church as an instrument of reconciliation, and the process of reconciliation. De Gruchy explains that when people speak of reconciliation, meaning depends on the context. If the context is theological, reconciliation is between fallen humans and God; if personal, it is between people, such as feuding neighbors or spouses; if social, it is among local groups, such as in schools with troubled relations; and if political, it is among larger groups such as victims of apartheid, perpetrators of abuse, and bystanders. In all cases, reconciliation involves a restoration of social relationships by overcoming enmity and abuse.

Ambiguity arises when meaning shifts with context or when the language of victims and perpetrators differs. For example, de Gruchy states, in South Africa, eleven official languages exist. Reconciliation for some black South Africans means restoration of identity, whereas for some white Afrikaners it means restoration of justice or the promise of amnesty. The many meanings of reconciliation for various stakeholders may account for the quasi-religious nature of the TRC. For example, Chairman Desmond Tutu, an Anglican archbishop, opened hearings with prayer and led attendees in a hymn. On the other hand, judges sat on the Amnesty Committee, which resembled a court of law.

Even if meaning is agreed on, people may value some kinds of reconciliation and other kinds not at all. Perceptions of value affect how countries go about rebuilding after internal strife. For example, countries establish truth commissions to document patterns of crimes against humanity and to hold transgressors morally accountable. However, most do not tie truth telling to reconciliation. In fact, it is an open question whether national reconciliation depends on truth. It may depend instead on guarantees of safety, health, economic participation, and social justice. Nevertheless, the South African commission deliberately linked truth to reconciliation. De Gruchy and other South Africans believe that truth telling is essential because meaningful forgiveness—a precursor of reconciliation—depends on the truth.

In South Africa, the nature of justice was debated after apartheid, as were possible governmental responses to gross human rights violations. Although many would have preferred justice to be meted out in courts of law, the cost was prohibitive. An alternative, blanket amnesty for all perpetrators, held no one morally accountable. Thus, blanket amnesty was dismissed as meaningless, inherently unjust, and morally repugnant. As a negotiated compromise, the TRC was charged with granting individual amnesty in exchange for truth. The TRC also provided a means for recognizing personal grief and loss by offering a public place for listening to victim narratives. Public acknowledgment of victims is a form of reparation after grievous harm.

De Gruchy also explores covenantal reconciliation in faith communities, particularly those of the Abrahamic religions of Islam, Judaism, and Christianity. Because he recognizes the plurality of nations worldwide, he emphasizes the necessity of face-to-face conversation among members of different cultural groups. De Gruchy believes that the process of reconciliation is necessarily an imperfect human response to God's intention for a reconciled world in Christ. Hence, his theology of reconciliation is ecumenical rather than merely local or personal.

De Gruchy agrees with Dietrich Bonhoeffer, the German theologian and pastor killed by the Nazis, that grace is costly, inasmuch as being a disciple of Christ means working for social justice in the world. Discipleship entails exchanging one's self for others, thereby suffering vicariously as Christ Incarnate did for humanity. Both de Gruchy and Bonhoeffer see the world as a community in need of repair and, ideally, the church as an agent of reconciliation in the world. This follows from the central narrative of redemption and an understanding of personhood as being social and ethical. The two men echo Saint Paul, who taught that the church is the body of Christ. Interestingly, a parallel notion of personhood exists in South African culture.

Ubuntu, the worldview of indigenous black South Africans, suggests that a person exists because of shared humanity. Consequently, the greatest good is social harmony. Dehumanizing behavior, such as torture, rape, and murder, diminishes everyone because of social relatedness. Thus, one must forgive transgressors to preserve harmony in the community or nation. In reality, forgiveness is painful and costly. It requires moral courage whenever loss is traumatic and grievous. According to de Gruchy, forgiveness is a gift that transforms both victim and perpetrator by righting their imbalanced relationship.

Christian Themes

The Christian doctrine of reconciliation rests on the central "grand narrative" or "metanarrative" of redemption. The story begins with the creation of humans in the "image of God." Humans initially lived in harmony with God and all of nature. De Gruchy writes of this early relationship of trust and companionship as a covenant. However, humans broke the covenant by disobeying God. As a result of the Fall, humans are alienated from God and nature; they long for healing and wholeness. To restore the covenant, God the Creator chose to redeem humanity by offering Jesus of Nazareth as Christ, the anointed mediator. It is through Christ that humans are restored or reconciled to God and to one another.

The symbol of the cross merges the sacred and the secular. It recalls the experience of Christ as a human victim on earth sent to redeem the world through vicarious suffering. This is the model of reconciliation for humans, according to de Gruchy. To heal broken human relationships, one must forgive unconditionally without resentment and without wreaking vengeance.

The injured person who forgives the offender initiates reconciliation. This is a gift inasmuch as true forgiveness cannot be coerced. Forgiveness promotes restoration of social relations by allowing the offender to feel remorse and to offer amends. After the offender confesses and the injured forgives, the two can enter into a covenant to restore harmony. On the other hand, if forgiveness is withheld, reconciliation is unlikely. People who forgive are keeping faith with Jesus' plea to love one's enemies, but others find forgiveness impossible. This is why Christ Incarnate pleads on the cross, "Father, forgive them, for they know not what they do" (Luke 23:34, King James Version). Christ mediates forgiveness and reconciliation when humans fail.

Sources for Further Study

Hayner, Priscilla B. *Unspeakable Truths: Facing the Challenge of Truth Commissions*. New York: Routledge, 2002. Surveys efforts worldwide to rebuild countries by examining patterns of past human rights abuses and by giving voices to victims.

Kelly, Geffrey B., and F. Burton Nelson, eds. *A Testament to Freedom: The Essential Writings of Dietrich Bonhoeffer*. Rev. ed. New York: HarperSanFranciso, 1995. Excerpts from the works of Bonhoeffer, a martyred theologian who resisted the Nazis. He believed that Christians are called to work for social justice as disciples of Christ. Useful essays by the editors introduce each section.

Krog, Antjie. *Country of My Skull: Guilt, Sorrow, and the Limits of Forgiveness in the New South Africa*. New York: Times Books, 1999. A wrenching record of apartheid victims confronting perpetrators in public hearings. Will help readers understand forgiveness as moral courage.

Tutu, Desmond Mpilo. *No Future Without Forgiveness*. New York: Image/Doubleday, 1999. Winner of the 1984 Nobel Peace Prize and former Anglican archbishop, Tutu describes his role as chairperson of the Truth and Reconciliation Commission in South Africa.

Tanja Bekhuis

THE RED AND THE BLACK

Author: Stendhal (Marie-Henri Beyle; 1783-1842)
First published: Le Rouge et le noir, 1830 (English translation, 1898)
Edition used: The Red and the Black: A Chronicle of the Nineteenth Century, translated by Catherine Slater. New York: Oxford University Press, 1991
Genre: Novel
Subgenre: Literary fiction
Core issues: Alienation from God; love

Stendhal's complex, multifaceted novel The Red and the Black *describes Julien Sorel and his attempt to comprehend himself. The author uses this story of love and of the power of passion to control lives to portray the institutions and class struggles of a historical period. He shows how a society was infiltrated by materialism and hypocrisy and yet was dependent on these for survival. From a Christian perspective, the story reveals the meaning of Christianity in a time when the institution of the Catholic Church was deeply corrupted.*

> *Principal characters*
> *Julien Sorel,* the protagonist
> *Madame de Rênal,* the wife of Julien's employer and his first love
> *Monsieur de Rênal,* the mayor of Verrières, Julien's employer
> *Mathilde de La Mole,* the daughter of Julien's second employer and his second love
> *Monsieur de La Mole,* a diplomat, Julien's second employer
> *Abbé Chélan,* the curate of Verrières
> *Abbé Pirard,* a director of a theological seminary in Besançon
> *Fouqué,* a friend of Julien

Overview

The Red and the Black is a fictional depiction of French society in the 1820's, two decades after the French Revolution and its ensuing Terror. The plot was based on Stendhal's personal experiences, on legal documents, and on historical accounts. Specifically, the story was prompted by a real-life case reported in a French newspaper over four days in late December, 1827. The story concerned Antoine Berthier, a twenty-five-year-old tutor and former theological student who a few months before had murdered a woman whose children he had tutored; the murder took place in a church during Mass. This case was the seed for Stendhal's novel.

Stendhal portrays a society fraught with materialism and hypocrisy at all levels. The peasants know how to ingratiate themselves with the rural bourgeoisie in order to profit; the bourgeoisie are in constant competition to outdo each other in status, as is the Parisian aristocracy. Even the Catholic Church is not exempt from this materialism and hypocrisy. Stendhal's protagonist, Julien Sorel, is a young peasant who is ill suited to work in his father's sawmill in the provincial town of Verrières. Julien is an opportunist intent on rising in society. He hates his peasant class and his status as a member of that class; he idolizes Napoleon, but Napoleonic France is dead, and rather than get ahead through the military (the "red"), Julien recognizes the Church (the "black") as the means of rising beyond his station. Having learned Latin from the Abbé Chélan, he finds first opportunity when Abbé Chélan recommends him as a tutor for the children of the Rênals.

Julien impresses the family with his ability to recite Bible verses from memory, but he remains an outsider to the bourgeois society in which he lives. He is a prize about which Monsieur de Rênal enjoys bragging. Julien becomes more and more intent on overcoming his sense of inferiority. Madame de Rênal becomes the means for him to accomplish this goal. Sensitive and susceptible to Julien's youth, she is seduced by him and becomes his mistress. Monsieur de Rênal begins to suspect something, and Madame de Rênal uses an anonymous letter to make her husband believe rumors are being circulated so that he agrees when she asks him to send Julien away. Julien goes to stay with Abbé Chélan, who has been removed as curate through machinations within the Church hierarchy.

Julien's second opportunity to rise in society and make a name for himself comes when he receives a scholarship to the seminary. Here, he meets Abbé Pirard, the director, who is in danger of losing his position because of his Jansenist leanings and his involvement with Monsieur de La Mole. At the seminary, Julien once again feels a sense of alienation, of being different because he is more intelligent than his fellow seminarians. An innately distrusting person, he quickly concludes that everyone is his enemy. Julien sets about developing his skills of deception even further. He realizes he has harmed himself in his efforts to be first in his studies. He discovers that the Church seeks blind obedience, not intellectual brilliance. Abbé Pirard resigns and leaves the seminary. He has become fond of Julien and obtains a post for him as secretary to Monsieur de La Mole.

Julien thus rises to a still higher social class. He is now in the company of the Parisian aristocracy. Although Julien is revolted by the even greater materialism and hypocrisy of this social group, his ambition to be somebody has not lessened. His sense of alienation continues to torment him, however, for once again he finds himself to be different from the individuals with whom he associates. They are members of the aristocracy; he is intelligent and entertaining but is still the son of a peasant.

At this point in the novel, Julien becomes involved in his second love affair. He meets Monsieur de La Mole's daughter Mathilde. This time, it is Mathilde who is the seducer, not Julien. The relationship between Julien and Mathilde is very different from the one he had with Madame de Rênal. Julien and Mathilde seem to take pleasure in humiliating each other, yet the affair continues chaotically and finally results in Mathilde becoming pregnant with his child. Contrary to what the reader would expect, Monsieur de La Mole, although upset at first discovery, not only accepts the situation but also offers Julien an income, a place in the army, and Mathilde in marriage. It would appear that Julien has finally acquired a true place in society. He has received the money and is enjoying his post in the army; Mathilde is very much in love with him and anticipating the marriage.

Then an ironic twist of fate ruins everything for Julien. Monsieur de La Mole, wishing some assurance of Julien's character, has asked him for a reference. Julien tells him to contact Madame de Rênal. Having repented of her sinful affair with Julien and become extremely devout, Madame de Rênal informs Monsieur de La Mole that Julien is a hypocritical opportunist without religious principles who seduces women in an attempt to rise in society. The marriage plans are dashed. Julien, obsessed with the need for vengeance, returns to Verrières and shoots Madame de Rênal. The shooting takes place in, of all places, the church, during Mass. Madame de Rênal is only wounded and does not die, but Julien is arrested, tried, and sentenced to death.

Both Mathilde and Madame de Rênal try unsuccessfully to save Julien. Julien falls in love with Madame de Rênal again, and she with him. Mathilde nevertheless remains faithful to Julien. His confessor comes to him with a scheme to obtain a pardon for him and aid the cause of religion. He wants Julien to undergo a very showy conversion back to Catholicism. He believes that with the Church's influence, a pardon can be obtained. Julien refuses and is guillotined. The novel ends with a macabre description of the two women with Julien's head and his decapitated body.

Christian Themes

Stendhal is often viewed as anticlerical, and in fact *The Red and the Black* may best be described as an anticlerical novel. The main Christian theme concerns the role of the French Catholic Church in society. The Church as portrayed by Stendhal is, like the society in which Julien lives, corrupted by materialism and hypocrisy. The black robe of the cleric privileges him and affords him a cover for his hypocrisy. In his seduction of Madame de Rênal and his affair with Mathilde, Julien brings to mind the play *Tartuffe: Ou, L'Imposteur* (pr. 1664, revised pr. 1667, pb. 1669; *Tartuffe*, 1732), in which Molière exposes the hypocrisy of the resident confessor in the person of Tartuffe. Julien plays much the same role in his position as tutor in Madame de Rênal's house and later as secretary to Monsieur de La Mole.

The young seminarians—who are, for the most part, sons of peasants—see the Church as an avenue toward a career that affords them a full stomach and a way of life that is not as harsh as working in the fields. None of them is inspired with a religious vocation. At the seminary, Julien learns that a priest must be deceptive not only in what he says but also in how he appears. The Jansenist-Jesuit quarrel that split the Church in France appears in the novel as a strong influence in the political machinations within the Church. Julien makes many sarcastic remarks about his vocation when he is at the seminary, including a caustic statement about preparing to spend the rest of his life selling salvation to his parishioners.

Even at the end of the novel, the Church in the person of Julien's confessor is trying to market itself by capitalizing on Julien's predicament. Stendhal thus portrays a

Christianity—or at least the institutions of Christianity—as corrupted by the greed, ambition, human self-interest, and sheer need to survive in the social and political climate of post-Napoleonic France.

Julien's death and the way he regards it have been the object of much discussion by critics: first, because it seems a contrivance (the death sentence is not mandated, as Madame de Rênal does not die), and second, because Julien rejects every opportunity to reverse the death sentence despite the aid of powerful supporters. Instead, Julien seems to rush headlong and almost happily toward his fate, regarding it as "the only honour which cannot be bought." Julien's rejection of life and acceptance of death constitute the ultimate outcome of his pride and corruption.

Sources for Further Study

Haig, Stirling. *Stendhal: "The Red and the Black."* Cambridge, England: Cambridge University Press, 1989. Examines how Stendhal combines personal experience, historical facts, and legal documents with fictional technique to create his novel.

Jones, Colin. *The Cambridge Illustrated History of France.* Cambridge, England: Cambridge University Press, 1999. Chapter 7 provides good historical background for understanding the France of the novel.

Turnell, Martin. *The Art of French Fiction: Prévost, Stendhal, Zola, Maupassant, Gide, Mauriac, Proust.* New York: New Directions, 1959. One of the best critics on nineteenth and twentieth century novelists. Discusses Stendhal's use of language and keywords to elucidate attitudes and situations in his novels.

Unwin, Timothy, ed. *The Cambridge Companion to the French Novel: From 1800 to the Present.* Cambridge, England: Cambridge University Press, 1997. Chapter on reality and its representation in the nineteenth century novel. Places Stendhal's work in relation to that of other novelists of the century. Chronology and guide to further reading.

Shawncey Webb

REDEEMING LOVE

Author: Francine Rivers (1947-   )
First published: 1991
Edition used: Redeeming Love. Sisters, Oreg.: Multnomah, 1997
Genre: Novel
Subgenre: Romance
Core issues: Forgiveness; guilt; love; marriage; redemption; regeneration

In an updated version of the biblical story of Hosea and Gomer set during the California gold rush, Rivers portrays the power of unconditional love to redeem the sinner, heal the wounded, and bring life to the long-dead heart. An illustration of God's pursuit of the individual soul, the story depicts how God reaches into the darkest places to find the foulest sinners and make them whole, enabling them to love as he loves them.

> *Principal characters*
> *Sarah*, renamed Angel, the protagonist, a prostitute
> *Michael Hosea*, Angel's husband
> *Paul*, Michael's brother-in-law, who intends to destroy Angel
> *John Altman*, whom, with his family, Michael and Angel rescue
>   on the road from Sacramento
> *Elizabeth Altman*, John's wife
> *Miriam Altman*, John and Elizabeth's daughter
> *Duke*, who introduced Angel to the world of prostitution
> *Jonathan Axle*, an influential banker
> *Susannah Axle*, Jonathan's daughter

Overview

Redeeming Love is a both a romance novel and a modern retelling of the biblical story of Hosea and Gomer. The story, specifically aimed at a Christian audience, reveals the power of unconditional love to restore, heal, and redeem the wounded heart. As a child growing up in the mid-1800's, Sarah discovers that her father did not want her to be born. Rejected by their family, society, and the church, Sarah and her mother ended up living on the docks, where her mother works as a prostitute until she dies of guilt and a broken heart, clinging tightly to her rosary. Sarah is taken to a wealthy man, called Duke, who names her Angel.

For ten years, Angel first is abused by Duke and then, as a high-priced prostitute, brings him influence and income. Used, unloved, and guilt-ridden, she escapes to California, where she unwillingly returns to prostitution in the gold town Pair-a-Dice. She gains hope when Michael Hosea arrives. Seeing Angel on a walk, Michael hears God whisper to him that he is to marry Angel. Despite his shock at her profession, he obeys and asks her to marry him. She rejects him until, nearly killed by the brothel bodyguard for demanding her freedom, she changes her mind in order to escape her life as a prostitute.

On Michael's farm, Angel begins to heal, but despite Michael's attempts to win her trust, she remains distant. As he begins to break down her barriers, she leaves for Pair-a-Dice but returns, intending to leave for good in the spring. Shortly after she comes back, Paul, Michael's brother-in-law, returns from panning for gold and recognizes Angel. Convinced that she has tricked Michael into marrying her, Paul begins to undermine her new life. He helps her return to Pair-a-Dice, using her along the way, and she returns to prostitution until Michael comes and takes her home by force.

When back on the farm, they try to revive their relationship. Returning from a trip to Sacramento, they come across the Altman family's broken-down wagon. Michael invites the Altmans to spend the winter on their farm before heading to Oregon, and the families become friends. In the spring, Michael talks John into staying in the valley with them. Angel begins to withdraw again and confesses the most sordid details of her past to Michael, but he renews his vows to her and finally breaches her barriers completely.

Afraid to be vulnerable, Angel runs away to Sacramento, where Joseph, a shopkeeper and Michael's friend, gives her work and a place to stay until Michael again comes to get her. They return home, but Paul continues his vendetta against her by hinting that Michael should have married an innocent virgin like Miriam Altman. Angel begins to suspect that Miriam is in love with Michael. After convincing herself that Michael would be better off with Miriam, who could give him children, Angel leaves again when spring returns.

Making her way to San Francisco, Angel at first wanders the streets, facing the temptation to return to prostitution. For the first time, she begins to address God instead of running from him. At her most vulnerable point, God directs her to a small café, where she finds a job and a place to live. However, when a fire destroys the café six months later, she unexpectedly finds herself again face to face with Duke.

Duke takes her to his new establishment, and he offers a choice: manage his girls or be one of them again. Attempting to use her beauty to increase his power and influence, Duke arranges an elaborate introduction for her, but when she comes on stage, Angel undermines his plan by singing "Rock of Ages." Jonathan Axle, an influential banker in the city and a believer who is in the crowd, comes to her aid. When she leaves the stage to face Duke's anger, Axle rescues her, as well as two child prostitutes, freeing them from Duke's power. Angel and the Axle family find new homes for the two rescued children, but Angel stays with them for three years, becoming friends with Susannah Axle, Jonathan's daughter, and beginning to make a new life. As she begins to understand that she is free of her past, Angel grows in her faith and comes, finally, to believe in God and his offer of salvation.

During that time, Miriam finally persuades Paul to marry her, while Michael remains alone. At Miriam's request, Paul unwillingly goes in search of Angel and finds her at the House of Magdelena, the ministry she has started in San Francisco with Susannah, which helps former prostitutes find new and productive lives. Face to face, they finally see the truth about themselves and each other, forgiving each other for all of their past mistakes. Paul reveals that Michael is waiting for her, and at his urging she returns with him to the valley to remain for good. At their reunion, Angel finally tells Michael her real name, Sarah, and they live together, raising five children, for the rest of their lives.

Christian Themes

As the title emphasizes, *Redeeming Love* considers the nature of love, particularly God's unconditional love. The biblical story of the prophet Hosea's difficult marriage to the unfaithful Gomer represented the unfaithfulness that the nation of Israel showed in its covenant relationship with God. Despite the Israelites' sins of idolatry and selfish pride, however, God pursues them repeatedly, just as Hosea pursues Gomer. God works in the same way in the lives of several of the novel's characters, pursuing them as persistently as Michael pursues Angel. God's love, the story demonstrates, follows all people, no matter where they are or how many times they flee God's presence. The novel repeatedly depicts characters stained with sin and surrounded by evil who are saved through God's intervention. Biblical love redeems the sinful and the sick-hearted; it heals the wounded, removing their shame. As a prostitute, Angel knows only a love of shame; through Michael and others, she learns to shed her shame and fear.

The unconditional love of God also brings forgiveness. Though guilt drives both Angel and Paul from Michael and from each other, biblical love enables them to forgive each other and be forgiven, removing guilt and delivering hope and joy. Redeeming love also frees the human heart from the ties that bind it. While everyone else warns Angel to build walls to protect herself, Michael's love, flowing from the love that God has shown him, breaks through her barriers, freeing Angel to live and to love as God intends.

Finally, redeeming love transforms a heart. From a hurting, wounded shadow, the love of God and his people change Angel into a humble, giving, loving servant, rendering her a woman of grace and mercy. Through the story of Michael and Angel, *Redeeming Love* portrays the truth of what happens when God's love breaks through into a person's heart.

Sources for Further Study

Eble, Diane. *Behind the Stories*. Minneapolis, Minn.: Bethany House, 2002. A chapter of this book of essays relates what Francine Rivers has learned through her writing about God, her writing, and herself.

"Finding Faith in Fact and Fiction." *Challenge Newsline*, August, 2003, p. 3. A short article that describes Rivers's development from a writer of romance novels to a writer of faith.

Hudak, Melissa, and Barbara Hoffert. "Book Reviews: Christian Fiction." *Library Journal* 122, no. 18 (1997): 66. Includes a plot synopsis of the book *Redeeming Love* as well as a brief assessment of its quality.

Riggs, Jack R. *Hosea's Heartbreak*. Neptune, N.J.: Loizeaux Brothers, 1983. A commentary on the biblical book of Hosea, providing an explanation and critical analysis of the text as well as lessons for personal application.

Shannah Hogue

RELIGIO MEDICI

Author: Sir Thomas Browne (1605-1682)
First published: wr. 1635, pb. 1642 (unauthorized), 1643 (authorized version)
Edition used: Religio Medici, and Other Works, edited by L. C. Martin. Oxford, England: Oxford University Press, 1964
Genre: Nonfiction
Subgenre: Meditation and contemplation
Core issues: Charity; faith; nature; salvation; scriptures

In this personal meditation, Browne simply states his religious beliefs, which begin with the idea that life on earth is but a prelude to eternal life, and salvation depends on belief in Christ. Belief in Christ is based on knowledge of Christine doctrine revealed in Scripture and on the observation of the ordered and harmonious world God created. Belief necessitates faith as well as the exercise of reason and the senses. Charity is as important as faith, but good works alone do not merit eternal reward. Charity stems from recognition of God in others and acting in accordance with that realization.

Overview

At age thirty, Sir Thomas Browne wrote *Religio Medici*, an explanation and analysis of his religious belief in relationship to his profession as a medical doctor. Intended as a personal meditation, *Religio Medici* circulated in manuscript form for several years, spawning various unauthorized texts. When a critical response to it was published, Browne saw to the publication of a new, authorized edition. Both documents, appearing during an era of social and religious upheaval when men could be executed for expressing their religious beliefs, present a tactful, idiosyncratic expression of a spiritual life shaped by Christian doctrine, medieval and classical thinking, and the explosion of knowledge occurring in the seventeenth century.

The work has two parts: The first explores faith and, implicitly, hope; the second, charity. In the preface, Browne disclaims the thoughts contained in the work as connected to the time in which they were written and not necessarily thoughts he would hold at another, more mature stage of his life. He explains that his meditation is not a scholarly work and asks the reader to read with a mind informed by faith and open to accepting his imaginative self-exploration.

Browne affirms that he has had a happy, serene, long connection with and belief in Christianity as handed down to him through the Church of England and the Reformation. He believes in divine providence. Realizing that some aspects of faith cannot be understood, he eagerly delights in the mystery, stating that he is a man capable of living with uncertainties.

Browne accepts the doctrines of his church but allows himself in the meditation to focus on what would be his ideal relation to God. He appreciates, though now rejects, some of the customs of the Catholic religion, and he advocates tolerance. He would like to subscribe to the heresy that all souls are at last saved and prefers not to judge Turks and Jews who are called heretics. He accepts church doctrine as the practical course and does not wish to promote fragmentation within the church. This easy acceptance of differences sets him apart from many religious zealots of his day and places him in the tradition of moderates such as Richard Hooker, who wrote *Of the Lawes of Ecclesiasticall Politie* (1593, 1597).

In the first part of *Religio Medici*, Browne contemplates and explores several themes. He expresses, as do John Donne and George Herbert, no fear of death and a belief in the witty paradox expressed by Donne that death dies when a person dies, while human beings continue into eternal life. He praises nature, finding nothing ugly there. God, the creator, the great artist of nature, has created a harmonious whole from many related parts. Browne subscribes to the view of life as a great chain of being in which all parts are connected and each part is connected to what is just above and just below it. Thus he reaffirms humankind's spiritual and material nature. He accepts both devils—and their manifestation on earth as witches—and angels. As a seventeenth century thinker accustomed to seeing correspondences, he readily recognizes that within a human being is a microcosm of the macrocosm. He sees in each human the same struggles for harmony that exist in the body politic.

Browne finds in all people the spirit of God, believing that his own spirit existed in the idea of God at the moment of Creation, enabling him to assert and delight in the paradox that although he is a child of Abraham he existed before Abraham. This faith in the spirit of God in humankind is the basis for his conception of charity, which he explores in the second part of *Religio Medicine*.

Browne defines charity by explaining what it is and is not. Charity is not trying to satisfy a benevolent impulse, nor is it giving with the thought that some day this giving will be repaid on earth or in Heaven. It is a real identification with and sympathy for humankind. Here again, he advocates tolerance, reaffirming the similarity of humans, who are all made in the image of God. He recognizes that all people struggle with what he considers an invasion of their thoughts and psyches by the devil, a disrupting spirit that undermines belief in self, God, and right action. Therefore, he values sympathy with, rather than judgment of, others.

Browne explains this impulse to sympathy by likening it to love for a friend. When one truly loves another, the two souls unite and become one. He explores this in an analogy much like one involving souls uniting in Donne's "The Ecstasy." When one has learned to appreciate another in this way, a soul appreciation, one can appreciate the soulfulness of all individuals and feel compassion for all other imperfect human beings. This feeling of compassion motivates charity. Actions—even prayers for others—based on some sympathy, along with an appreciation of God in the other person, are charity.

Browne also explores dreams as they relate to his belief and faith. In dreams, he often feels he is sleeping in God's arms. He then awakens with a sense of well-being and harmony. He sees such sleep as a little death, indicating the joy of the afterlife to come. Sleep is an emblem of death, and life is lived, he says, not in an inn, but a hospital, a place from which all people await release.

Christian Themes

Browne's meditation revolves around faith, hope for salvation, and charity. He describes his faith as an Anglican, explaining that he embraced this Protestant religion that he was born into, guided through by his parents, and later affirmed into by his own conscious choice. Appreciation and acceptance of God and Christ result from reason, observation, and faith. Reason demands study and understanding of Scripture and Church doctrine. It is supported by observation of nature.

Browne's profession, that of a medical doctor, has led him to God by causing him to look closely at nature, discovering the discernible perfection of the created world. Nothing in the world is grotesque or ugly; everything is harmonious and connected. People, whom he calls amphibians, connect to the spiritual angels and material beasts. In addition, people contain the entire world within themselves, perfect microcosms.

In addition to reason and observation, belief requires faith. Faith necessitates acceptance of mystery. Browne delights in mystery, finding his faith the richer for it. Faith is required for salvation, assured only for those who believe in the Incarnation. Browne regrets that so many wise philosophers may be denied salvation and eternal reward, having been born before Christ's coming.

This kind of speculation reflects Browne's atypical tolerance in this era of religious extremism. Although he accepts church doctrine, he does hold hope that God in his mercy will provide for those good people who did not have the opportunity to exercise faith. Knowing the difficulties people face in life, Browne refuses to judge others.

Browne affirms that charity is as important as faith. While doing good works, especially caring for the poor, is essential, true charity for Browne results from totally sympathizing with and appreciating the soul of his fellow human beings. He explains that a true friendship with another, in which two souls become as one, prepares a person to fully apprehend God in each human being. Once this has been accomplished, a person can extend good works, hold good thoughts, and offer prayers for all others.

Sources for Further Study

Bennett, Joan. *Sir Thomas Browne*. Cambridge, England: Cambridge University Press, 1962. Describes and analyzes *Religio Medici*. Bennett's analysis demonstrates the influence of Christian doctrine, medieval and classical thinkers, and seventeenth century philosophers, while noting the particularity of Browne's own style.

Berensmeyer, Ingo. "Rhetoric, Religion, and Politics in Sir Thomas Browne's *Religio Medici*." *Studies in English Literature, 1500-1900* 46 (Winter, 2006): 113-133. Analyzes Browne's text in terms of his discursive stance and the political, religious implications therein.

Huebert, Ronald. "The Private Opinions of Sir Thomas Browne." *Studies in English Literature, 1500-1900* 45 (Winter, 2005): 117-135. Explores the nature of two major attacks on Browne's *Religio Medici*, one when it was circulating in manuscript and the other during the twentieth century, to show that these critics did not evaluate Browne's intentions.

Post, Jonathan F. S. *Sir Thomas Browne*. Boston: Twayne, 1987. Thorough exploration of the life and works of Thomas Browne, placing the *Religio Medici* in the context of the civil and religious strife of its era.

Bernadette Flynn Low

RELIGION
If There Is No God—On God the Devil, Sin, and Other Worries of the So-Called Philosophy of Religion

Author: Leszek Kołakowski (1927-   )
First published: New York: Oxford University Press, 1982
Genre: Nonfiction
Subgenres: Critical analysis; didactic treatise
Core issues: The Deity; God; good vs. evil; morality; problem of evil; sin and sinners; truth

Kołakowski's primary concern in Religion *is God, especially how philosophers and theologians over the centuries have argued for and against God's existence while attempting to reconcile his omnibenevolence and the evils in the world he created. Although Kołakowski's theme is the ultimate irreconcilability of the sacred and the profane, he feels that believers and their critics have helped clarify questions and fostered the spirit of truth in their important inquiries and explications.*

Overview

Czesław Miłosz, the 1980 winner of the Nobel Prize in Literature, once described Poland as a land of "faith in the impossible." Leszek Kołakowski, the 2003 winner of the first John W. Kluge Prize for Lifetime Achievement in the Human Sciences, a million-dollar Nobel-like award, has often tackled impossible ideas in his life and in his many works on history and philosophy. In the Polish phase of his life, as a Marxist, he became convinced of the material and spiritual devastation caused by Stalinist Communism, and during his later career in North America and England, he has emphasized such themes as human freedom, tolerance, and the quest for transcendence in his ardent defense of individual dignity. In *Religion*, his aim is to explore the philosophy of religion, but since neither he nor, in his opinion, anyone else truly understands what religion and philosophy really are, his task is daunting. Nevertheless, because God, if he exists, and the world, if humans can actually comprehend it, are important subjects, Kołakowski thinks that an examination of the ideas of those who sought to justify their belief or disbelief in God will help clarify a pivotal issue of human existence.

After the introduction, *Religion* contains five chapters on the following subjects: theodicy, the God of reasoners, the God of mystics, immortality, and religious language. Though his book is not without humor and irony, Kołakowski, a critic of dogmatic absolutizing in religion and science, seriously tries to understand the philosophical and religious approaches to God before concluding that true communication between rationalists and believers is all but impossible and that both are "illusion hunters." However, the clash between the sacred and profane is real, not illusory, at least in a cultural sense. Kołakowski admits that when people speak about the sacred, they may be saying something about their social context or psychological state, but throughout his book his basic assumption is that religious and rational people mean what they say. This in turn illustrates his "law of the infinite cornucopia": There exists no shortage of arguments to support whatever a person wishes to believe for whatever reason.

From pre-Christian times to the present, various thinkers have tried to reconcile God's goodness with the many evils in the world. Theologians such as Saint Augustine of Hippo and Saint Thomas Aquinas developed privative explanations, asserting that evil is the absence of good rather than a thing in itself. Augustine and Aquinas also attributed evil's entrance into the world to the "Original Sin" of the first humans. Kołakowski is critical of this traditional doctrine because it contradicts a basic moral principle that the innocent should not be punished for the sins of others. Kołakowski also disagrees with Gottfried Wilhelm Leibniz, who introduced the term "theodicy" to describe his defense of God's goodness in the face of the world's evils. Leibniz was forced, by a consideration of God's omniscience and omnipotence, to conclude that God created "the best of all possible worlds." To make human suffering and even the sufferings of animals an inescapable part of the world's harmony is for Kołakowski, as for Voltaire before him, a nefarious trivialization of human pain and anguish. Nevertheless, the sin that brought on all this suffering is called, in traditional Christian theology, "a happy fault" (*felix culpa*) because it led to the redemption of humanity by the God-man Jesus Christ. Though rationalists see the story of redemption as preposterous, Kołakowski thinks that the crucifixion of God's Son to save humankind from its sinfulness is "neither self-contradictory nor inconsistent with empirical knowledge." Rationalists simply cannot understand it, but if people believe, then they can understand it.

In his chapter on the God of reasoners, Kołakowski argues that religious truths never arise from analytical reasoning and require no scientific proofs for their veracity. Indeed, the five proofs of God's existence given by Thomas Aquinas are logically flawed, and even if they were not, they would fail to convince an atheist of God's existence. Nevertheless, these proofs, though invalid, have religious meaning because they help believers discover traces of God's handiwork in the world he created. For Kołakowski, no sound experiential or logical way exists of moving from the finite world to the infinite God. A leap of faith can convince the believer that God exists, but this believer has no way to convert the skeptic.

Mystics claim to have a direct experience of spiritual realities, and Kołakowski, through their writings, has come to admire the extraordinary authenticity of the great Eastern and Western mystics. Historically, religious authorities have been uncomfortable with mystical experience, since mystics, with their direct communication with God, had no real need to use a temporal institution to experience eternal being. Occasionally this led to problems, when mystics felt free to ignore traditional moral norms. Protestant churches in particular have tended to view mystical experience as delusional. Rationalists, too, explain mysticism through self-deception, but Koła-

kowski insists that mystical truths can never properly be squeezed into rational categories. Rationalists can point to contradictions in mystical beliefs, for example, that
God cannot be both absolute being and a loving father, but Christians continue to hold
that God is both, and that God even guides the godless.

In his penultimate chapter, Kołakowski scrutinizes the idea of immortality. He is
critical of attempts to explain immortality as arising from the fear of death, and he is
sympathetic to those who integrate this belief into their quest to find meaning in history. Armed solely with empirical tools, Marxists and other atheist humanists cannot
make sense of "the gigantic rubbish-heap of history" in a way that religious believers,
who hold that God is history's "purpose-giver," would find convincing. The Christian
belief in immortality is rooted in God's promises and Jesus Christ's resurrection, not
on rational arguments or pseudoscientific séances.

Finally, Kołakowski deals with religious language and its struggle to "speak of the
unspeakable." The language of religious belief and moral conviction cannot be
judged by the standards of scientific tests, but the unverifiability of these religious
statements does not deprive them of meaning because no compelling reasons exist for
equating the meaningful solely with the empirical. The language of the Sacred is the
language of worship, of believers who understand the world as members of a community of God. Religious ideas and values can be grasped only from within a group committed to the sacred, and sacred language cannot be translated without distortion into
the language of the profane, whose practitioners have striven to expurgate all value-
and goal-oriented language from empirical science. Kołakowski therefore thinks that
it is highly improbable that a rational ethics will ever be formulated without basing it
in some way on divine authority. As he puts it, moral taboos reside in the kingdom of
the sacred. If God exists, he provides humankind with standards of good and evil; if
God does not exist, humans freely decide on moral standards, whether they are Nazi
thugs or secular saints. Hence Kołakowski's book confronts its readers with a stark
choice: a meaningful world guided by God or an absurd world, originating in emptiness, going nowhere, and ending in nothing.

Christian Themes

Faith in God and commitment to a religious community are central themes of
Christianity. Christians believe first, then they understand. However, Kołakowski ap-
proaches these themes not from the perspective of a personally committed Christian
but from that of a philosopher. Once a Marxist, then a liberal Socialist, Kołakowski
came to see that all secular ways of ordering the world, be they scientific, Marxist, or
Freudian, are not epistemologically superior to religious beliefs in a divine order.
Furthermore, the God of the philosophers—René Descartes, Baruch Spinoza, and
Leibniz—is not the Christian God, who is both absolute being and eternal love.
Granted that paradoxes exist about how providential divine grace and passionless natural laws coexist, Kołakowski still urges faithful Christians to trust their God, whose
existence cannot be scientifically ascertained and whose attributes and relationship to
the world seem contradictory. Christians must also admit that their religion, which

teaches the depravity of humankind, is opposed to Enlightenment humanism, which teaches human self-perfectibility apart from God.

Kołakowski, who has been praised as a preeminent man of reason, nevertheless believes that humankind does not live by reason alone. In his former works he has manifested a profound interest in the Christian foundations of Western civilization, and in this book he expresses his admiration for Christians who are able to overcome the meaninglessness of the world through their belief in an eternal reality who is the source of purpose, who provides principles of good and evil, and who saves humankind from nothingness after death. Although the distance from finite creatures to the infinite God can never be bridged, Christians place their trust in Jesus Christ, who was sent by his Father to span the gap between contingent human existence and the endless fullness of divine love.

Sources for Further Study

Frankenberry, Nancy K., ed. *Radical Interpretation in Religion.* Cambridge, England: Cambridge University Press, 2002. Ten scholars offer several new interpretations of religious belief, which some contrast with Kołakowski's radical separation of religious and rational approaches to God. Index.

Kołakowski, Leszek. *God Owes Us Nothing: A Brief Remark on Pascal's Religion and on the Spirit of Jansenism.* Chicago: University of Chicago Press, 1996. Kołakowski's critical analysis of Pascal's influential attempt to solve the problem of evil. Notes and index.

Pierson, Stanley. *Leaving Marxism: Studies in the Dissolution of an Ideology.* Stanford, Calif.: Stanford University Press, 2001. The author of this work on the decline of Marxism devotes an entire chapter to Kołakowski.

Roberts, Richard. *Religion, Theology, and the Human Sciences.* Cambridge, England: Cambridge University Press, 2002. A collection of essays exploring the religious consequences of the so-called triumph of capitalism and the end of history. Like Kołakowski, Roberts is concerned about Marxism and Christianity. Index.

Robert J. Paradowski

RELIGION IN THE MAKING

Author: Alfred North Whitehead (1861-1947)
First published: 1926
Edition used: Religion in the Making. New York: World, 1960
Genre: Nonfiction
Subgenres: Meditation and contemplation; philosophy; theology
Core issues: Contemplation; God; knowledge; problem of evil; reason; self-knowledge; solitude

Drawing on contemporary accounts of religious experience, such as that of William James, and his own interpretation of metaphysics, Whitehead redefines religion in terms of the private, unique experience of each individual. He regards ritual, emotional expression, dogma, doctrinal theology, and other external trappings of religion as inadequate to the internal life of solitude. His result is not unlike Georg Wilhelm Friedrich Hegel's systematic elevation of philosophical content over religious faith.

Overview

Religion in the Making is a transcription of four short lectures that Alfred North Whitehead gave in Boston in February, 1926: "Religion in History," "Religion and Dogma," "Body and Spirit," and "Truth and Criticism." His intent is philosophical, but his approach is historical. He perceives a sporadic yet inexorable progress through millennia from emotional to rational religion. Moreover, he sees religion as evolving from social and communal to individual and private. The more social, the more barbaric religion is; the more individual, the more civilized; the more communal, the more insipid; and the more private, the more rational. The pinnacle of civilization and rationality is introspective solitariness.

Whitehead begins "Religion in History" by defining religion in several ways, all of which relate to the basic transformation of the believing individual into a contemplative thinker. Above all, religious consciousness is characterized by absolute sincerity. These definitions refer primarily to the private, internal life of the individual, and only in a minor way to the doctrinal or external side of religion. Doctrine is significant only to the extent that it facilitates or promotes the renovation of the sincere individual spirit. Ultimately, religion in its highest development is equivalent to whatever each individual makes of solitariness. Social or shared forms of religion are decadent and often dangerous.

In history, and in every culture, religion proceeds through four universal stages. Whitehead explains that it begins as ritual, which is just the systematic uplifting of daily habit. Ritual gives way to emotion, which creates religion as a cohesive social institution. At this stage the passionate devotion of the believer is seen as the greatest good. Ritual stimulates emotion and emotion intensifies ritual. Neither has any intellectual content. To satisfy the basic human need for such content, the third stage, belief, appears. Belief is manifest as doctrine, which eventually invites philosophical criticism. This criticism appears at the final stage, rationalization, where God appears first as unknown and empty, then as the enemy, and at last as the friend.

At the fourth stage, rational religion approaches philosophy, that is, religious meditation aspires to the level of pure philosophizing. Religious cosmology becomes philosophical metaphysics, and religious morality becomes philosophical ethics. Religion thus alienates itself from its social, ritualistic, and emotional roots, which all seem irrelevant to the philosophical quest for truth. Philosophy is the highest activity of the thinking individual. Philosophical insight is essentially introspective and solitary.

"Religion and Dogma" probes religion's search for metaphysical truth. Solitariness provides insight into universal truth because universality is what the solitary thinker immediately experiences on detachment from all the distractions and annoyances of ordinary life. Among established religions, Whitehead praises Christianity and Buddhism for best encouraging this kind of thought. Their respective dogmas each indicate this priority for their believers. Christianity has the advantage over Buddhism because it has developed naturally from religious consciousness to metaphysical insight, while Buddhism has taken the contrary, unnatural path from metaphysics to religion. Both preach escape from this world as a vital aspect of their dogmas.

Whitehead recommends studying the Old Testament books of Job, Proverbs, and Ecclesiastes, and the lives of Jesus and the Buddha, as excellent preparation for embarking on the philosophical quest for God. Along the way of this quest, dogmas are occasionally formulated to record, codify, or enshrine the truths that have been discerned in religious experience up to that point in history. The book of Psalms is marred by being primarily emotional rather than reflective. For Whitehead, emotional religion is seductive but barren and ultimately contrary to the human spirit.

"Body and Spirit" continues the metaphysical theme of the previous chapter. Whitehead explicitly agrees with the standard Western philosophical tradition that religion, to be intellectually defensible, needs metaphysical underpinning. He summarizes his ontology of a finite God that he expounds in *Science and the Modern World* (1925) and his later work *Process and Reality: An Essay in Cosmology* (1929). According to this ontology, God is in everyone and everything and would not be God without creation. God is the actual, nontemporal entity who transforms abstract, indeterminate creativity into concrete, determinate freedom in time, and thus becomes fulfilled as God.

Whitehead confronts the main problem of any metaphysics of religion, the problem of evil. Both good and evil are real forces. Good is constructive and elevates creation. Evil is destructive and degrades creation. Neither a human nor a hog is naturally evil, but a human acting like a hog is evil, because this degradation is a falling away from the human excellence that could have been. Paradoxically, in some cases, good itself can be evil. For example, good people who become self-righteous, judgmental, or intolerant thereby limit the freedom of others and restrict the continuing process of human moral development.

"Truth and Criticism" emphasizes that religious consciousness is available to any-one who takes the time to think, that religious experience is not different from any other kind of experience, and that religious truth depends on knowledge, not feeling. All that is required to achieve religious and thus metaphysical insight is discipline. The appropriate reasoning process is natural and empirical, from the specific to the general. The final purpose of religion is to overcome evil with good. God is entirely good, and therefore not infinite, since evil is part of the universe. God is the source of true value and the reason why evil must be overcome. As created beings increase their awareness of God and more deliberately involve God in their existence, the less pow-erful evil becomes.

Christian Themes

Whitehead's discussion of his fourth stage of religious development, rationaliza-tion, shows his appreciation of Christianity most clearly. He regards the Bible as the consummate narrative of human progress from ritualistic to rational religion. As such, the Bible inspires its believers to move from communal toward solitary religion. He claims that the sacred texts of Islam and Buddhism perform a similar function, but do not succeed as well as the Bible. He sees Job, the Old Testament prophets, Jesus in the wilderness and on the cross, Saint Paul on the road to Damascus, Muḥammad in exile, and the Buddha under the bodhi tree all as excellent examples of the highest human spiritual achievement, the solitary awakening to the truth. He quotes with approval the famous saying in Amos 5:21-24 that God hates our religious feasts and rituals, but loves our righteousness and justice.

Whitehead claimed not to know much about Georg Wilhem Friedrich Hegel, yet his analysis of the historical development of religion in *Religion in the Making* is re-markably Hegelian. For both Hegel and Whitehead, progress occurs when a certain historical phase finds itself at an impasse and is forced by its own morbidity to rein-vent itself as a new phase. In other words, when any movement becomes incapable of further development in its current trajectory, it must veer in a new direction if it is to preserve itself at all. Both see the world-historical progress from barbaric to rational religion in terms of inexorable historical forces that push the primitive toward the civ-ilized, albeit with a few retrogressive periods of decline. Both also see the ultimate ra-tional religion as Christianity, because it best fosters the refinement of the human spirit.

Sources for Further Study

Ford, Lewis S. *Transforming Process Theism*. Albany: State University of New York Press, 2000. A reinterpretation of Whitehead's philosophy of religion by one of the preeminent Whitehead scholars of the twentieth century.

Franklin, Stephen T. *Speaking from the Depths: Alfred North Whitehead's Herme-neutical Metaphysics of Propositions, Experience, Symbolism, Language, and Re-ligion*. Grand Rapids, Mich.: Wm. B. Eerdmans, 1990. An advanced study of Whitehead's philosophical and theological vocabulary.

Luft, Eric v. d. *God, Evil, and Ethics: A Primer in the Philosophy of Religion*. North Syracuse, N.Y.: Gegensatz, 2004. Sets the historical and philosophical context for Whitehead's meditation on contemplative solitude.

Sia, Santiago. *Religion, Reason, and God: Essays in the Philosophies of Charles Hartshorne and A. N. Whitehead*. New York: Peter Lang, 2004. Attempts to understand from a theological angle the two main exponents of twentieth century process philosophy.

Thompson, Kenneth Frank. *Whitehead's Philosophy of Religion*. The Hague, the Netherlands: Mouton, 1971. A broad consideration of Whitehead's concept of God.

Wilmot, Laurence F. *Whitehead and God: Prolegomena to Theological Reconstruction*. Waterloo, Ont.: Wilfrid Laurier University Press, 1979. The perspective of a retired Anglican minister, dwelling on the relation of Whitehead's metaphysics to Christian salvation.

Eric v. d. Luft

RELIGION WITHIN THE BOUNDS OF MERE REASON

Author: Immanuel Kant (1724-1804)
First published: Die Religion innerhalb der Grenzen der blossen Vernunft, 1793 (English translation, 1838)
Edition used: Religion Within the Limits of Reason Alone, translated by Theodore M. Greene and Hoyt H. Hudson. New York: Harper, 1960
Genre: Nonfiction
Subgenres: Critical analysis; philosophy; theology
Core issues: Church; conscience; ethics; good vs. evil; morality; reason

Kant grounds religion on the absolute moral law, which he sees as the quintessential creation of a perfectly rational God. He argues that the purpose of religion is to promote the ultimate victory of good over evil, reason over emotion, truth over deception, logic over superstition, duty over inclination, personal godliness over communal ritual, and individual freedom over the tyranny of the multitude. Only a thoroughly rational religion can achieve this purpose. Through reason, a moral Kingdom of God can be established on earth.

Overview

In *Grundlegung zur Metaphysik der Sitten* (1785; *Fundamental Principles of the Metaphysics of Ethics*, 1895; better known as *Foundations of the Metaphysics of Morals*, 1950), Immanuel Kant introduced the concept of the categorical imperative, the absolute moral law for his duty-based, or deontological, ethics. Kant presented the categorical imperative in five different but closely related formulations, which are generally referred to as 1, 1A, 2, 3, and 3A: "Act only according to the maxim which you could will to become universal law," "Act only as if, by your will, the maxim of your action would become universal law," "Act only so that you treat humanity as an end and never as a means," "Act only as if your will, by its maxims, were the universal lawgiver," and "Act only according to the maxims of the universal lawgiver in the potential realm of ends."

The premise of Kant's entire ethical philosophy, including his philosophy of religion, is the categorical imperative. It is derived from the principles of individual freedom that he developed in *Kritik der reinen Vernunft* (1781; *Critique of Pure Reason*, 1838), one of the most revolutionary books in the history of philosophy. For Kant, only a free person can be a moral agent, because moral action requires ethical decision making, and only a rational being with free will is capable of that kind of thought. Moral action consists in freely obeying one's duty as known through conscience, without coercion or compromise and regardless of one's personal feeling, inclination to the contrary, or expectation of certain results. Kant seeks to purge emotion from ethical reasoning, moral action, and religion. Conscience, as a gift of God, reveals the categorical imperative to each individual in each problematic ethical situation.

Because Kant reduces not all religion, but true religion, to ethics, so the philosophy of freedom in the *Critique of Pure Reason* and the exposition of the categorical imperative in *Foundations of the Metaphysics of Morals* must be presupposed throughout Kant's philosophy of religion. *Religion Within the Bounds of Mere Reason* is unusually accessible among Kant's works, yet it cannot be fully comprehended unless the reader has first assimilated the basic ideas of the other two works.

Religion Within the Bounds of Mere Reason is divided into four parts, which respectively examine, first, the radical evil inherent in human nature; second, the battle between good and evil principles for dominion over humankind; third, the victory of good over evil and the founding of an earthly Kingdom of God; and finally, the difference between true and false service to God.

Kant immediately sides in part 1 with the school of thought that regards humans as born evil rather than either good or morally neutral. He is particularly opposed to Jean-Jacques Rousseau's optimistic view of human nature that held sway in the Romantic atmosphere of the late eighteenth century. By evil, Kant means inclined toward selfish acts inconsistent with natural moral duty. Evil stems from a Rousseauian prerational or antirational state of innocence. Reason is the remedy for evil. The advent of reason is the beginning of the triumph of goodness.

Part 2 shows Jesus as the personification of the good principle and posits the devil as the evil spirit who holds God-given legal authority over the evil principle. Conflict between good and evil may be regarded as originating from the devil tempting humans to choose him rather than Jesus as lord. God remains in control of evil, yet humans remain free to choose evil and reject God. Kant's model of this familiar conflict is legalistic; humans are caught between God's law and another law that is opposed to God's but that God still allows. God is thus the ultimate lawgiver of both good and evil. Kant admits being unable to explain why God permits evil to exist. He says that natural inclinations, even though they tend toward evil, are good in themselves, insofar as they express human freedom. To use reason to rein in these inclinations is prudent, because to aspire to the moral perfection of Jesus is our duty.

Part 3 emphasizes that godly morality can be achieved only within the church and that the only truly moral people are church members. This is not to say that all church members are moral, as many are pious hypocrites. Part 4 continues this topic and savagely attacks those priests, theologians, and churchgoers who prefer to base their religion on miracles and the supernatural instead of the moral law. For Kant, any belief in any kind of supernatural element is superstition. It is belief without reason, a mockery of faith, and an insult to both the church and God.

Christian Themes

Kant defines God the Father as the author of the categorical imperative and understands Jesus Christ as its teacher on earth. Thus Jesus is the founder of the one true church, not because of his redemptive sacrifice on the cross, but because of his sermons, parables, and exemplary life as the perfect exponent of the moral law. This interpretation is expounded mainly in two sections of part 4 that consider Christianity first as a natural or pretheoretical religion, then as a learned or revealed religion.

Christianity as a Kantian natural religion is tantamount to belief in divinely sanctioned morality. It is spread and maintained by teachers rather than priests and informed by conscience rather than dogma. Its goal is unanimity of moral sentiment and universalizability of the derived maxims of moral action. Kant cites Matthew 5:20-48 to argue that the only people who please God are the morally pure. He uses Matthew 7:13-21 to show that those who act immorally cannot redeem themselves by doing good works for the church. For Kant, duty to the church is unimportant compared with duty to God.

At the more sophisticated stage of revealed religion, Christianity is characterized by theological principles interpreted through historical events such as the life of Jesus, the writing of the New Testament, and the growth of the church. Intellectuals working within the church create a learned faith that can appeal to all people. Faith is not an end in itself. Adherence to simple faith is not sufficient for salvation. The end for Kant is always morality. Kant calls even the most devout service to the church pseudoservice if it consists of obeying priests, believing dogma, or worshiping supernatural beings. True service to the church consists of following the good principle by doing one's duty to the moral law, which Christian theology partially reveals and fully supports.

Kant also differentiates the earthly, historical, or visible church from the heavenly, universal, or invisible church. Both constitute what Kant calls an ethical commonwealth, but the former is temporal, essentially political, and therefore prone to all manner of civil conflict, while the latter is the perfectly harmonious eternal Kingdom of God. The mission of Jesus was to found the Kingdom of God on earth as an ethical commonwealth in which people would obey God's moral law without fail, despite their evil nature.

Sources for Further Study

Daniel, David Mills. *Kant's Religion Within the Bounds of Reason Alone*. London: SCM, 2006. A synopsis aimed at secondary school students and undergraduates.

Di Giovanni, George. *Freedom and Religion in Kant and His Immediate Successors: The Vocation of Humankind, 1774-1800*. New York: Cambridge University Press, 2005. Explains in detail how Kant's contemporary Christian theologians misunderstood and misused his philosophy of religion.

Luft, Eric v. d. *God, Evil, and Ethics: A Primer in the Philosophy of Religion*. North Syracuse, N.Y.: Gegensatz, 2004. Devotes a chapter to Kant's *Reason Within the Bounds of Mere Reason* and offers a new translation of selections from part 4, "On Service and Pseudo-Service Under the Control of the Good Principle, or, on Religion and Clericalism."

Moore, A. W. *Noble in Reason, Infinite in Faculty: Themes and Variations in Kant's Moral and Religious Philosophy*. London: Routledge, 2003. Reinterprets the relations among various kinds of reason, social morality, and Kant's ethical and religious thought.

Reardon, Bernard M. G. *Kant as Philosophical Theologian*. Basingstoke: Macmillan, 1988. Shows how Kant can be a moralizing theist while rejecting both natural and revealed theology.

Eric v. d. Luft

RERUM NOVARUM

Author: Leo XIII (Gioacchino Vincenzo Raffaele Luigi Pecci; 1810-1903)

First published: 1891 (English translation, 1891)

Edition used: The Condition of the Working Classes: The Encyclical "Rerum Novarum." London: Catholic Truth Society, 1951

Genre: Nonfiction

Subgenre: Encyclical

Core issues: Church; justice; poverty; social action

Although Leo XIII was not the first Christian leader to write on social issues, Rerum Novarum *is one of the most important social works of the Christian tradition. His foundational observations have warranted repeated anniversary documents, including Pius XI's* Quadragesimo Anno *(1931) and John Paul II's* Centesimus Annus *(1991). Leo's work has been influential because of his affirmation of four rights: first, of people to attain private property; second, of the church to speak on social issues; third, of employees to form worker associations; and fourth, of workers to receive a just wage.*

Overview

Leo XIII addresses *Rerum Novarum* to the bishops of the Catholic Church. He introduces his reflections by highlighting the social difficulties of the day. With these difficulties in mind, he then discusses five key issues: private property, the right of the Church to speak on social issues, the role of the state, the worker's right to a just wage, and the importance of worker associations. He ends by providing a short conclusion.

Leo explains that the Industrial Revolution has encouraged humankind to ask questions about a variety of social issues, such as the relationship between employers and employees, the just distribution of wealth, the growing isolation of workers, the role of worker associations, and the decline in moral values. More specifically, Leo informs the bishops of the wretched living conditions of the poor; he proposes that Catholic Church leaders must once again refute the errors that have led to such social evils. Leo states that workers are left unprotected because the workers' guilds of old are no longer intact and political institutions have rejected religious teaching. Leo explains that the power of industry is controlled by a few factory owners who are becoming rich from the hard labor of the working class. The lower class suffers from poor working conditions and low wages, and their animosity toward the owning class is escalating.

Leo writes that socialists are seeking to eliminate class division by proposing that possessions be held in common and private property eliminated. In opposition to the socialist response, Leo argues for the right to own private property. He explains that people have the capacity to plan for the future. By possessing land, people can attain the security of owning something with stable value and can enjoy the yearly fruit of the land. Further, the prospect of owning property gives workers hope and a motivation for ingenuity. Without the possibility of owning land, workers often lack the desire to work diligently. As a result, production suffers, and the working class is reduced to a state of poverty even lower than had previously existed.

Leo proposes that the voice of the Church must be heard. He asserts that people should not blame suffering merely on class struggle but should also consider sin and disorder, both of which are never completely eliminated in this world. Leo posits that social classes are natural and ought to work in a complementary manner. Accordingly, he provides a list of duties for both the working and the owning classes. Workers should complete their work, honor the property of their employers, and refrain from rioting. Employers should respect the dignity of their workers by not reducing them to means of production, considering their spiritual well-being, promoting family relations, assigning reasonable work, and providing a living wage.

Leo also posits that the use of wealth is more fundamental than the accumulation of wealth. He writes that possessions on earth do not entail wealth in heaven. Further, he explains that Christ himself demonstrated the dignity of poverty by living with limited material goods. Still, despite his qualification of the condition of poverty, Leo explains that the decrease of poverty is an important goal and he proposes that Christians must continue to assist the poor by discouraging greed and lust and promoting simplicity. Moreover, Leo points to the lives of saintly Christians who have lived unparalleled lives of mercy and charity.

After affirming the right of the church to speak on social issues, Leo discusses the legitimate role of the state. He writes that the state ought to seek the protection of both private and public institutions by the development of good administrative structures. The state ought to promote wholesome morality and ordered family life, protect religion and justice, work toward the equitable distribution of burdens, and protect those who cannot protect themselves, that is, the poor. Further, the state should uphold the right to own private property, allow for the spiritual needs of the community, and establish stable production of material needs by preventing strikes.

Next, Leo discusses the importance of a just wage. He proposes that two things should receive particular attention in the allotment of salaries: personal investment and living necessities. Leo argues that people give themselves in their work and are alienated when they are not compensated for that investment. In addition, employers should be concerned with the living needs of the worker and the worker's family. When business leaders provide their employees with a just wage, they encourage diligence and prevent emigration.

While the state should protect the rights of the working class, Leo posits that these rights ought to receive primary protection from smaller worker organizations. Leo warns against immoral worker associations and encourages those organizations that are concerned with spiritual matters as well as with the provision of assistance when industry is changing or when workers suffer from sickness, old age, or misfortune. Leo concludes by promising that Christians will continue to act according to charity where and when it is needed.

Christian Themes

In the years preceding the papacy of Leo XIII, Church and state relations were often polemical. For his part, Leo engages the state in a manner that affirms the important role of political leadership but still manages to have a critical edge. He is concerned with both the poverty that has resulted from the Industrial Revolution and the socialism that is being proposed as a solution. He explains that humans are tainted with sin and therefore proposes that political theories promising the removal of all suffering can only be misleading. Despite these and other critiques, Leo acknowledges the need for state leadership and therefore encourages reform rather then revolution.

Leo indicates how the Church can contribute to social issues. He writes that the equality of persons comes not from similarity in talent but from redemption in Christ. Different members of society have different talents, all of which should be used for the eternal glory of God. Leo explains that a Christian framework also qualifies the condition of poverty. Because Christians view poverty as a virtue, the focus concerning material goods is on the use rather than the accumulation of goods. Nonetheless, despite the fact that the removal of material poverty is not the final end of Christian faith, Christians are called to assist the poor by living in accordance with the virtues of mercy and charity.

Leo discusses principles that remain central to Christian social ethics, such as the right of workers to associate and the right to private property. He argues that worker organizations can advocate and provide personal assistance for workers in a manner that the state is unable to do. Leo's affirmation of the right to private property is a central claim of his work. If workers have the incentive of private property and the allotment of a just wage, they can live frugally and seek to acquire the stability that comes with owning land. Such a context provides an environment of ingenuity and diligence, which in turn is good for workers, employers, and the state. Leo's reflections provide fundamental principles that still speak to contemporary Christian leaders who can apply Leo's general insights in their own specific diocesan contexts.

Sources for Further Study

Himes, Kenneth R., ed. *Modern Catholic Social Teaching: Commentaries and Interpretations*. Washington, D.C.: Georgetown University Press, 2005. This scholarly collection includes four foundational essays and fourteen commentaries on influential church documents. Each essay includes thorough bibliographical information. Brief index.

Misner, Paul. *Social Catholicism in Europe: From the Onset of Industrialization to the First World War*. New York: Crossroad, 1991. This work provides a history of European social life and reflection spanning from the late eighteenth century to the early twentieth century. Includes a thorough bibliography as well as author and subject indexes.

Pontifical Council for Justice and Peace. *Compendium of the Social Doctrine of the Church*. Translated by Vatican Press. Washington, D.C.: United States Conference of Catholic Bishops, 2005. This reference work provides a comprehensive synthesis of central concepts in Catholic social ethics. Includes thorough reference and analytical indexes.

———————. *The Social Agenda: A Collection of Magisterial Texts*. Città del Vaticano: Libreria Editrice Vaticano, 2000. This work is a concise compilation of official church statements thematically organized to discuss eleven issues central to Christian social ethics.

Kevin Schemenauer

RESTING IN THE BOSOM OF THE LAMB

Author: Augusta Trobaugh (1939-   )
First published: Grand Rapids, Mich.: Baker Books, 1999
Genre: Novel
Subgenre: Evangelical fiction
Core issues: Acceptance; African Americans; forgiveness; friendship; memory; redemption

In rural Georgia, four women—three white women and their black servant, who is more like a family member—are approaching old age. As death nears, they begin to sift through their memories to uncover secrets about their past. These recollections challenge the women to reevaluate their relationships with one another, as tales of deceit, racism, murder, and forgotten family ties are brought to mind.

> Principal characters
>> *Miss Cora*, an elderly white woman who has spells of dementia
>> *Pet*, the narrator and Cora's African American servant
>> *Wynona*, Cora's niece, who lives with Pet and Cora
>> *Lauralee*, Wynona's younger sister, who also lives with Pet and Cora
>> *Mr. Adkins*, Wynona's deceased husband
>> *Hope*, Lauralee's deceased infant daughter
>> *Miss Delia*, Cora's friend
>> *Minnie Louise*, a friend of Pet and servant to Miss Delia
>> *Miss Addie*, Cora's neighbor
>> *Lizzy*, Pet's daughter, given to Minnie Louise at birth
>> *Samantha*, Lizzy's daughter, whom Pet has never met
>> *Maggie Brown*, an elderly woman who accompanies Cora on her search for a grave

Overview

In the beginning of *Resting in the Bosom of the Lamb* by Augusta Trobaugh, Pet addresses a person known only as "baby girl." Pet, an older African American woman, wants to reveal to baby girl all the family secrets that she has kept hidden for most of her life. Unless she has the opportunity to pass them along to a younger generation, they will, she laments, melt away like an ice cube.

Pet's narration gradually reveals the personal histories of four Georgia women—Miss Cora, her nieces Wynona and Lauralee, and Pet herself, who has been a lifelong servant and companion to the three white women. Her narrative moves back and forth between the present and the past, interspersed with interior monologues, italicized in the text.

On a cold November day, Pet remembers the circumstances of each of the women's childhoods, how she and Wynona were born on the same day, how Lauralee came along six years later, and how Pet and Cora as girls would spend the summers together playing with Wynona and Lauralee. As Pet grew older, the intimacy of the relationships lessened because it was not proper for the white girls to play with her as an equal. Pet also remembers her mother telling her that in addition to Patricia (her given name), she also received her great-grandmother's name, an African word that means "Sunrise."

Across the street from the women lives Miss Addie, who is near death. Before she dies, she calls Pet to her bedside and asks her to promise to make Miss Cora remember about someone named Hope. Miss Cora is old enough that she has started to lapse into dementia; she often remembers a grave at Brushy Creek Baptist Cemetery that she wants to find. In one of her rambling stories about family history, Miss Cora says that this grave belongs to an ancestor who fought in the Civil War. Lauralee displays signs of mental or emotional distress. She never speaks and does not attend Miss Addie's funeral.

Through flashbacks, Pet gradually unfolds a pivotal story about Wynona and Lauralee. When Wynona was young, a widower named Mr. Adkins courted her and eventually proposed. Wynona first girlishly laughed at the proposal but then went to Mr. Adkins to apologize and accept. Shortly after their engagement, Mr. Adkins became very religious and, simultaneously, "meaner and meaner for the rest of his life." About two years after the marriage, Wynona's parents both died, and Lauralee came to live with her sister. Mr. Adkins made surreptitious, unwanted sexual advances toward Lauralee and berated her as a harlot. Eventually she became pregnant, clearly raped by Adkins. He told her to get an abortion, but she and Wynona decided that she should keep the baby and that they would move in with Cora and Pet. As they were packing, Mr. Adkins entered the house carrying a shotgun. As the women fought for the gun, it fired, striking Adkins in the face and killing him instantly. Largely through the urging of Pet, the women cleaned up the house and dumped Adkins's body and shotgun next to a creek. The sheriff ruled his death a hunting accident, and apart from Miss Addie, who deduced the truth, no one seemed to suspect the women of murder.

To cover up Lauralee's pregnancy, both Lauralee and Wynona isolated themselves in their house and pretended that Wynona was the expectant mother. When the baby girl was born, they named her Hope and listed Wynona's name as the mother on the birth certificate. Four months later, Hope died after catching scarlet fever from Pet. This death resulted in Lauralee's emotional detachment from society, Pet's guilt over causing Hope's death, and Cora's lifelong disappointment at not having family members to carry on her legacy and stories. A few years later Pet, through an unexplained relationship, gave birth to a baby girl. Fearing that she would kill her daughter just as she had Hope, she gave her baby, Lizzy, to her friend Minnie Louise to rear.

These flashbacks are interspersed into the main narrative, which involves the women's yearly attendance at a camp meeting (a weeklong church revival). During this meeting, Cora, in a state of dementia, searches out the grave she perennially seeks. She takes with her a senile African American woman named Maggie Brown. Cora thinks Maggie is her dead aunt, and Maggie thinks Cora is her mother. The two women trek comically through the countryside and eventually are brought back by a deputy. Along the way Cora confusedly mentions memories of babies (white and black), cribs, and graves.

Toward the end of the book, Pet pieces together these memories for both herself and Cora. She forces Cora to see that Pet's baby Lizzy looks like both Lauralee's child Hope and like Cora's father. This resemblance is due to the fact that Pet and Cora are, in fact, sisters.

The novel ends with Pet's decision to make contact with her granddaughter Samantha, who is about to start college. She is the person addressed at the beginning of the story and will be the one to receive all the family tales and heritage that Cora has been so intent on passing on.

Christian Themes

Although this work was marketed as Christian fiction and published by an evangelical press, it differs greatly from most devotional novels. It has much more in common with regional southern novels such as Olive Ann Burns's *Cold Sassy Tree* (1984). Religious elements certainly lie in the background of the narrative—many hymns are quoted, and the women attend religious gatherings—but the novel rarely engages Christianity directly.

Trobaugh's title highlights a Christian view of love. The book uses John 1:29 ("Behold the lamb of God, which taketh away the sin of the world") as an epigram, but the title also echoes 2 Samuel 12:3 (an allegory in which a man holds a lamb in his bosom) and Isaiah 40:11 ("He shall gather the lambs with his arm, and carry them in his bosom"). In these verses from the Old Testament, the lamb lies in the bosom of another. Trobaugh's title reverses the relationship and has humans resting in the bosom of the lamb, who is Jesus. In a conversation that Pet has with one of Cora's friends, they discuss how Jesus "is like a mama to us," and humans "learn to love ourselves 'cause our mamas loved us." The characters experience the love of God and of Jesus through their communion with one another and their shared maternal experiences. Furthermore, building on the quotation from John, the lamb image conveys a forgiving love, especially soothing to Pet's troubled conscience.

Above all, the novel explores transitions in family relationships. The camp meeting the women attend used to attract a large crowd of families, but now most pews are empty. After Miss Addie dies, her house becomes a funeral parlor. The women, all of whom are approaching their deaths, wrestle with the question of their legacy. By closing with Samantha as the family heir, the novel alludes to the Christian concept of the communion of the saints. Although time will bring an earthly finality to the lives of these women, through God's care, their family will endure, evidenced by the "Family Book" in which Cora adds Pet's stories to those of her own family. Because all the characters will eventually rest in the bosom of the lamb, their communion with one another will be eternal.

Sources for Further Study

Byle, Ann. "For Four Southern Women, Memories Bring Salvation." Review of *Resting in the Bosom of the Lamb. The Grand Rapids Press*, March 28, 1999, p. J6. Contains a summary of the work and places it in the Southern writing tradition.

Flanagan, Margaret. Review of *Resting in the Bosom of the Lamb. Booklist* 95, nos. 9/ 10 (January 1-15, 1999): 835. Provides a description of the work and the reviewer's opinion.

Gray, G. William. Review of *Resting in the Bosom of the Lamb. Tampa Tribune*, March 28, 1999, p. 4. This review focuses on the Southern aspect of Trobaugh's novel.

Hilard, Juli Cragg. "Augusta Trobaugh: Fulfilling Youthful Dreams." *Publishers Weekly* 249, no. 24 (June 17, 2002): 523-524. This profile of Trobaugh discusses her late start in writing and her religious views.

Schliesser, Jill A. Review of *Resting in the Bosom of the Lamb. Southern Living* 34, no. 6 (June, 1999): 128. This review summarizes the plot and praises the author's writing style.

Kyle Keefer

THE RESURRECTION OF GOD INCARNATE

Author: Richard Swinburne (1934-   )
First published: New York: Oxford University Press, 2003
Genre: Nonfiction
Subgenres: Biblical studies; critical analysis; theology
Core issues: Atonement; death; God; Incarnation; Jesus Christ; reason

Swinburne is concerned with the physical aspect of the Resurrection. He assesses the probability of the truth of the claim that Jesus was crucified, dead for thirty-six hours, and then brought back to life by God in his crucified body, which possessed supernatural powers. By examining the life of Jesus and considering the kind of life God would resurrect, Swinburne hopes to show that Jesus was the kind of individual that God would raise from the dead, and he concludes that a consideration of the evidence makes it very probable that Jesus was God Incarnate and rose from the dead.

Overview

The Resurrection of God Incarnate is divided into three parts. In the first part, Richard Swinburne assesses the general background evidence related to the belief that Jesus rose from the dead. One crucial aspect of background evidence is whether the God of classical theism exists. Swinburne assumes that there is a fifty-fifty chance that such a God exists, and he refers the reader to some of his other works that explore this question in more depth. If such a being exists, then the laws of nature depend on that being, and God can suspend those laws if he chooses to do so. This raises the probability that God will raise Jesus from the dead. With respect to the Resurrection, an important source of available historical evidence is the testimony of eyewitnesses to the Resurrection. In Swinburne's view, testimony in general must be taken to be accurate, unless there is evidence to the counter, and therefore the specific testimony to the historicity of the Resurrection should be viewed as accurate.

Swinburne also argues that God would have at least three reasons for becoming incarnate. First, the God of classical theism would want to provide people with a means of atonement. Second, God would do so to identify with people's suffering. Third, God would want to show people a dignified human life and what a perfect human life looks like. Next, Swinburne turns to a consideration of the attributes of God Incarnate and claims that an incarnate God would live a life of supererogatory goodness and would engage in physical, psychological, and social healing. An incarnate God would also teach people how to live and would do so by means of revelation that they could not obtain or discover on their own. God Incarnate must also believe that he is God Incarnate and must ultimately reveal his identity to humanity, teaching that his life provides atonement. He should found a church to carry his message to other generations and cultures. Finally, a super miracle should validate the life of God Incarnate, something like rising from the dead.

In the second part, Swinburne assesses the claim that Jesus satisfies all of the fore-going requirements for God Incarnate, except for the final one, which he considers in the third part. According to Swinburne, the contents of the New Testament appear to be testimony and should be taken as literal historical claims. While some discrepancies exist, this is to be expected and does not undermine his case for the truth of the Resurrection.

Jesus lived a perfect moral life and taught people how to live. For example, he taught that people should love and worship God, love and forgive others, and ask God for good things. Jesus also implied that he was God Incarnate by granting forgiveness of sins and implying his own eternal existence. Also, people are reported to have explicitly acknowledged his divinity in his presence, and Jesus neither corrected them nor disagreed with them. Swinburne also provides textual evidence from the New Testament in support of the claim that Jesus himself was the source of the teaching that he would provide atonement for humanity, and he finally notes that Jesus founded a church that continues to relay his teachings. Swinburne concludes the second part of his work by stating that Jesus is more probably God Incarnate compared with any other prophet in history with respect to the foregoing criteria for being God Incarnate.

In the final part of the book, Swinburne examines the available evidence for the belief that Jesus' life and teachings were validated by a super miracle, namely, raising Jesus from the dead. He first notes that many of the followers of Jesus believed that he appeared to many people after his death and that although there are some differences between the Resurrection accounts, they are not significant enough to undermine the basic elements of the story. Other evidence in support of the Resurrection includes the empty tomb of Jesus as well as the evidence from New Testament texts that the Sunday observance of the Eucharist originated in the post-Resurrection teaching of Jesus. From these two observations, Swinburne infers that people believed they were interacting with Jesus on or soon after Easter Sunday, after he had been crucified, died, and was buried. Next, Swinburne considers five rival theories of what happened—Jesus did not really die on the cross, the disciples misidentified the tomb where Jesus was buried, or the body was stolen by enemies of Jesus, grave robbers, or friends of Jesus—and concludes that all five are incorrect. The Resurrection is what Swinburne calls a super miracle, and he argues that it is God's way of authenticating the life and mission of Jesus. It signifies God's acceptance of the atoning sacrifice of Jesus, as well as the teachings of Jesus.

Christian Themes

Swinburne's strategy is different from that which most scholars adopt when assessing whether Jesus Christ rose from the dead. Only the last third of Swinburne's book focuses on historical evidence from the New Testament and other historical documents regarding the historicity of the Resurrection. Swinburne claims that as long as we have sufficient evidence in favor of the claim that God exists, the need for historical evidence is diminished. Rather than relying solely on historical evidence,

Swinburne holds that by examining the life of Jesus and the kind of life God would resurrect, it is evident that Jesus was the kind of individual whom God would raise from the dead. He argues that there is a significant probability that God would resurrect Jesus. The difficulty in the minds of those who would argue against Swinburne lies in how to assess the a priori probability that God would resurrect Jesus and what kind of life God would see fit to resurrect.

In response, it seems likely that Swinburne's justification for this lies in his view of the unique status of Jesus in history. While many religious prophets were reported to have performed miracles, according to Swinburne two things stand out about Jesus: the large number of miracles attributed to him and their centrality in his ministry, and Jesus' representation of those miracles as the Kingdom of God advancing in a needy world.

Moreover, while someone may charge Swinburne with reading his own theology and religious belief back into his case for Jesus being God Incarnate and a likely candidate for someone whom God would raise from the dead, Swinburne attempts to defend the early followers of Jesus from such a charge. For example, the notion that God would become incarnate was not expected by those followers, and this is a reason against the claim that they were reading their theology back into history. The Resurrection was also unexpected, which in Swinburne's mind goes to show that the disciples did not have to marshal belief in the Resurrection because they expected Jesus to rise bodily from the dead. Rather, they were surprised by this, because it did not fit into their religious expectations of what a Messiah would be and do. Their belief that this event occurred helped spark a worldwide movement that continues to this day.

Sources for Further Study

Hall, Lindsey. *Swinburne's Hell and Hick's Universalism: Are We Free to Reject God?* Burlington, Vt.: Ashgate, 2003. A comparison of the thought on Swinburne and John Hicks on the idea of whether people can reject God. Hicks believes in universal salvation, while Swinburne argues that hell must exist for Christians.

Messer, Richard. *Does God's Existence Need Proof?* New York: Oxford University Press, 1993. Shows the disparity between the thought of Swinburne, who believes that an attempt to prove God's existence is worthwhile, and that of D. Z. Phillips, who does not believe such an attempt is valuable.

Padgett, Alan G., ed. *Reason and the Christian Religion: Essays in Honour of Richard Swinburne.* New York: Oxford University Press, 1994. Two essays in this collection focus on Swinburne's views of the Trinity and Incarnation.

Swinburne, Richard. *The Existence of God.* 2d ed. New York: Clarendon Press, 2004. Contains the arguments that Swinburne refers to several times in *The Resurrection of God Incarnate*, which are intended to show that it is more probable than not that theism is true.

_____. *Faith and Reason.* 2d ed. New York: Clarendon Press, 2005. Explores the relationship between the probability of God's existence and religious faith.

_____. *Providence and the Problem of Evil.* New York: Clarendon Press, 1998. Offers a detailed answer to the question of why a loving God allows so much suffering.

Michael W. Austin

REVELATION AND REASON
The Christian Doctrine of Faith and Knowledge

Author: Emil Brunner (1889-1966)
First published: Offenbarung und Vernunft: Die Lehre von der christlichen Glauben-serkenntnis, 1941 (English translation, 1946)
Edition used: Revelation and Reason: The Christian Doctrine of Faith and Knowledge, translated by Olive Wyon. Philadelphia: Westminster Press, 1946
Genre: Nonfiction
Subgenre: Theology
Core issues: Knowledge; reason; revelation; truth

Brunner states that revelation is God's merciful self-communication in the Word, establishing an "I-Thou" relationship with human beings. Humans are uniquely capable of receiving and obeying the Word, despite the devastating effects of sin, because the formal characteristics of the image of God (reason, language) remain. Brunner stirred controversy by maintaining that a modest general revelation exists in creation, culture, and even other religions, although revelation in the full sense comes only in Christ. Reason, properly used as Logos (meaning), is not antithetical to revelation but serves people's humanity as persons.

Overview

Emil Brunner defines the nature of revelation as a historical encounter. Revelation refers to the mystery of the sovereign God freely and uniquely manifesting himself as the eternal within historical time. Thus revelation is an objective encounter. However, it is also subjective, because revelation must reach its goal through acknowledgment by humans, who are the only beings created with capacity to receive the word of God and who are held responsible to respond and obey. As an "I-Thou" encounter, it is distinctively personal, despite the disparity between the eternal and the temporal. Because God is preeminently a person, we are made persons.

According to Brunner, revelation occurs mainly in the realm of history, through the promise of the Old Covenant, which through Jesus Christ reaches its climax. Jesus did not just "discover" or "convey" revelation, but is himself the word and presence of God. With that foundation established, Brunner can then look backward and forward for witnesses to this historical revelation. In every age, for example, Brunner finds a general revelation in creation, the world of nature. The natural world is not enough to bring salvation, which only Christ can do, but it does hint at God's majesty and, more important, establishes human culpability when people invariably revolt against their Creator. (This meager provision for a natural theology prompted Karl Barth's famous denunciation of Brunner.) To a secondary degree, revelation happens also in historical witnesses to the Word by the church, the Holy Spirit, and the human words of Scripture. However, every avenue to God remains dominated by Christ for Brunner.

What then about the truthfulness of this claim to revelation? Here Brunner defends the validity of human rationality. He argues that human are capable of using and understanding language and thus are able to receive the Word. Reason is a second mode of knowledge and, so long as it observes its proper boundaries, has no inherent conflict with revelation. Together they constitute two conceptions of truth, because humanity, even as grievously fallen sinner, has not been stripped of the formal structures of reasoning, but only of the material contents originally illumining Adam's mind. However, reason yields a very different type of truth than does revelation. Rational knowledge always is impersonal, best suited to the timeless world of physical objects. Because reason reinforces isolation of the human self by holding the created realm at a distance, it cannot comprehend genuine love or self-impartation. Revelation, by contrast, is the truth that "happens" as one encounters the divine, so it is life giving, quintessentially personal, and beyond rational categorizing, and must be received through a surrender of one's will.

If reason and revelation are so distinct, can they cooperate enough to generate a "Christian philosophy"? Brunner answers affirmatively and says that the entire range of human culture constitutes a middle ground between the extremes of formal logic and theology. On this vast continuum of everyday problems and issues, rationality and faith necessarily collaborate—but in each instance proportionate to the degree that wholeness and personhood are involved. Brunner calls this guiding principle his "law of the closeness of relation." That is, "The nearer anything lies to that center of existence where we are concerned with the whole, that is, with man's relation to God and the being of the person, the greater is the disturbance of rational knowledge by sin; the farther away anything lies from this center, the less is the disturbance felt, and the less difference is there between knowing as a believer or as an unbeliever." This determines the proper epistemological mix of faith and reason.

Consequently Christians are freed to pursue or critique secular themes and to help build a humane society, but with the proviso that the more any topic deals with the human self, the more it must be called to respond to the Word. Suspicion is needed only toward autonomous reason, for by glorifying the ego it deepens our isolation by evading awareness of our misery and alienation from God's majesty. However, Brunner welcomes rationality that submits to divine Lordship and thereby finds its proper role as Logos, illuminating new resources and preparing the heart for grace.

The Enlightenment critiqued religion as "mythical," but Brunner insists that symbols remain essential for describing the biblical God who is transcendent yet enters space and time to disclose himself. Myth is cyclical and determined by fate, rather than sequential and consisting of personal decisions. However, truth as encounter between divine and human subjects requires history, not myth, for its framework. Because revelation is anchored in the histories of Israel and Jesus, biblical studies inevitably risk challenges. Brunner denounces any defensiveness against scientific investigation, such as positing an infallible Bible or authoritarian church, and he is confident that historical reason has not undermined any major point of Christian faith. Biblical inspiration does not depend, for example, on demonstrating a uniformity among all apostolic teachings or proving Jesus' miracles, for Jesus himself is the miracle in that "He places us in the presence of the reality of God, as the reality of Him who lays His demand upon us, and who desires to give Himself to us." Thus the living triunal God is himself the final guarantee of both revelation and reason.

Christian Themes

Brunner states that God cannot be objectified or conceived of as an object (even the supreme object) within finite time and space but is utterly transcendent, beyond the reach of human discovery. In his great love for his creation, however, God has chosen to communicate himself through the Word. This entails a merciful condescension and self-impartation to mortals in terms that they can understand. Divine sovereignty over the cosmos exists at the same time as God's tender compassion toward humankind, and therein is exhibited the primordial self-definition of God as person. God's self-giving toward his beloved creation extends partially to the world's religions, but pre-eminently to Israel's history, culminating in Christ, the Word in flesh.

Unlike other mortal life-forms, humanity is distinctively capable of hearing and obeying the word of God. This human capacity for language, including syntax and the formal structures of reason, has been distorted but not erased through humanity's alienation from God, the Fall. It is only the material content of the image of God that has been devastated. The controversy notable in Brunner's later life arose from this modest defense of a residual general revelation and natural theology.

The doctrine of human nature focuses on the will (as Saint Augustine taught), so our humanity is exemplified by the decision whether to attend to and obey the Word. Thus we show ourselves to be persons in this "I-Thou" encounter, responding to and partially reflecting the Creator's personhood. *Imago Dei* (the image of God) is the traditional phrase for our kinship to God's personhood. This includes Logos rationality and language ability, but even more important is humanity's ability to form relationships. Here Brunner shows his indebtedness to Søren Kierkegaard's existentialism by focusing on individual decision and also to the religious socialist movement in the early twentieth century by highlighting the horizontal dimension, our solidarity with fellow humans and with society.

Thus there are two modes of human knowledge, reason and revelation, which need not be antithetical so long as each takes its proper role. Brunner thereby attempts to preserve the Reformation heritage of Christocentrism and revealed grace but also has a pastoral concern for the church's ability to influence the surrounding culture.

Sources for Further Study

Hart, John W. *Karl Barth Versus Emil Brunner: The Formation and Dissolution of a Theological Alliance, 1916-1936*. New York: Peter Lang, 2001. Close examination of the controversy for which Brunner in later generations is best remembered.

Humphrey, J. Edward. *Emil Brunner*. Waco, Tex.: Word Books, 1976. For general audiences the best introduction to Brunner's thought. Sympathetic, fair, with brief biography, selected bibliography.

Kegley, Charles W., and Robert W. Bretall, eds. *The Theology of Emil Brunner.* Vol. 3 in *The Library of Living Theology.* New York: Macmillan, 1962. Definitive collection of essays by seventeen scholars on Brunner's thought and influence, with a reply by Brunner and an autobiography.

Lovin, Robin. *Christian Faith and Public Choices: The Social Ethics of Barth, Brunner, and Bonhoeffer.* Philadelphia: Fortress Press, 1984. A significant work on social ethics that positions Brunner's thought with two other theological giants of his time.

McKim, Mark G. *Emil Brunner: A Bibliography.* ATLA Bibliographies 40. Lanham, Md.: Scarecrow Press, 1996. Excellent brief introduction to Brunner's life and thought, followed by an exhaustive bibliography of everything Brunner ever wrote, edited, coauthored, or reviewed; secondary sources listed.

G. Clarke Chapman

THE RIME OF THE ANCIENT MARINER

Author: Samuel Taylor Coleridge (1772-1834)
First published: 1798
Edition used: The Poems of Samuel Taylor Coleridge: Including Poems and Versions of Poems Now Published for the First Time, edited with textual and bibliographical notes by Ernest Hartley Coleridge. New York: Oxford University Press, 1912
Genre: Poetry
Subgenres: Legends; narrative poetry; parables and fables
Core issues: Atonement; despair; grace; love; nature; wisdom

Perhaps the most memorable of Coleridge's contributions to his and William Words-worth's revolutionary Lyrical Ballads, The Rime of the Ancient Mariner *is a tale of sin, repentance, and atonement. The Mariner's thoughtless, motiveless shooting of the albatross, a bird of "good omen"—whose appearance coincides with the ship's release from ice and the commencement of a needed southern wind—is a sin, he learns, against God, nature, humanity, and the mariner's own soul. The man must atone for that sin by repeating his story to others as a warning against a similar fate.*

> *Principal character*
> *The Ancient Mariner*, the sailor who kills the albatross

Overview

The Rime of the Ancient Mariner begins with one of three wedding guests being accosted by the Ancient Mariner and kept from attending the wedding first by the Mariner's grasp and then by his hypnotic gaze as the Mariner begins to tell the story of his fateful voyage. The Mariner gives no reason for the voyage, saying that they sailed south until they reached the South Pole, where they became icebound and enshrouded in fog. They see and hear nothing but the ice

> The ice was here, the ice was there,
> The ice was all around:
> It cracked and growled, and roared and howled,
> Like noises in a swound

Then an albatross flies into view through the fog. Happy to see another living creature, the men aboard the ship treat it "As if it had been a Christian soul" and they hail it "in God's name." It circles the ship, accepting the crew's hospitable offerings of food, and then the ice splits and a wind begins to blow, allowing the ship to move again.

For nine days the bird follows the ship, coming when the men call and occasionally perching on or near the mast. Then, for no reason, the Mariner shoots it with his crossbow. His shipmates' initial responses are horror and anger. They blame him for killing the creature responsible for the wind that helped free them from the ice and fear that something bad will happen. However, shortly after the bird's death, the fog clears and the shipmates change their mind, claiming now that the bird was responsible for the fog and saying that the Mariner was right to kill the bird. As soon as they have gone around Cape Horn and entered the Pacific Ocean, the wind stops, and the ship comes to a standstill beneath the blazing sun, now at the other extreme from the earlier cold and ice, though parallel in immobility, as highlighted by Samuel Taylor Coleridge's paralleling of word choice and order:

> Water, water every where,
> And all the boards did shrink;
> Water, water, every where,
> Nor any drop to drink.

The crew now again changes its mind and hangs the dead albatross around the Mariner's neck. Shortly thereafter the Mariner spots a ship approaching. In initial joy, the desperate Mariner bites his arm and drinks his own blood to get enough moisture in his mouth to announce what he sees. However, as the ship draws closer it occurs to him to wonder how the other ship can be moving when theirs is not. The ghost ship draws close enough to reveal Life-in-Death and Death gambling for the Mariner. Life-in-Death wins the Mariner and Death takes his consolation prize, the two hundred other men on the ship.

A week passes with the Mariner alone with the dead bodies, whose eyes curse him, and guilty but unable to pray. One night as he watches water snakes swimming in the moonlight, he is so struck by their life and beauty that he loves them and blesses them.

Now that he has repented, the journey homeward begins: The albatross drops from his neck, rain begins to fall, and a strange wind begins to blow above the ship, mysteriously moving it along. The Mariner falls into a trance as the ship speeds faster than mortal endurance, driven by the spirit of the South Pole and manned by spirits who assume the bodies of the fallen crew. While in this trance, the Mariner hears two voices discussing his crime/sin, the fact that he will have to continue to do penance, and the manner by which the ship is moving. When he revives from his trance, he again witnesses the curse on him visible in the dead men's eyes, which prevents him from looking away from them and from praying. Then the spell snaps, "the curse is expiated," Coleridge explains, and the Mariner feels a gentle breeze just as he spies the familiar landscape of home.

As his ship enters the harbor, it is approached by a boat containing a Pilot, the Pilot's boy, and a Hermit. All but the Hermit are afraid of the appearance of the Mariner's ship. As the Pilot's boat draws close, the sea rumbles, and the Mariner's ship suddenly breaks in two and sinks. The Pilot collapses in a fit and the Pilot's boy goes mad, leaving the Hermit to fish the Mariner from the water and the Mariner to row the boat to shore. Once on land, the Mariner begs the Hermit to shrive him, which the Hermit does by having the Mariner answer his question concerning what manner of man the Mariner is. The Mariner responds by feeling a terrible agony that forces him to tell his story; only after he has finished does he feel free. From that point on the Mariner periodically and unexpectedly feels the same agony and travels "from land to land" until he spots the face of the person that he somehow knows must hear his tale.

The poem draws to a close just as the bridal party is leaving the church. The Mariner tells the Wedding Guest that far better for him than any wedding is a walk in good company toward a church to pray and that the best way to pray is to love all things. With that the Mariner bids the Wedding Guest farewell, and the Wedding Guest is left to wake up the following morning a "sadder and a wiser man."

Christian Themes

Although heavily influenced by William Wordsworth and the pantheist tradition, Coleridge diverged from Wordsworth on the source of inspiration for life and poetry: Where Wordsworth believed nature was his source of inspiration, Coleridge believed love was the source of inspiration. Drawing from Christ's instruction that the greatest commandment is love, Coleridge develops a story that illustrates the importance of love not only for the individual soul but also for the balance and harmony among all living things.

The senseless shooting of the albatross, a bird lured to follow the ship by the men's initially friendly treatment, serves as the point of illustration for a parable about right behavior. Even as the hospitality and friendliness toward the albatross and the common sense and decency with which the ship members treated it dried up, the men on the ship are dried to the point that their tongues turn black. Their rottenness causes the sea to rot.

The crew is angry and afraid but unaware of its complicity in the sin, hanging the albatross around the Mariner's neck. For their complicity and unwillingness to take responsibility, they are punished with death. However, the Mariner, because he is directly responsible for killing the bird and showing no mercy, is fated to remain alive like the Wandering Jew who refused Christ the mercy of a cup of water.

Initially, the Mariner does not fully understand his responsibility for what is occurring and blames others: "And never a saint took pity on/ My soul in agony." Because he refuses responsibility, he feels guilt, hearing the departing souls of his shipmates pass by "[l]ike the whizz of [his] crossbow!" and seeing himself as one of the slimy things that lives on, but he cannot repent. Until blessed with an overwhelming sense of love for the beauty of the sea snakes, the "wicked whisper" of both despair and desire to blame others for his predicament prevents him from praying and moving toward atonement, which consists of repeating his story to those who need to hear it that they might learn,

> He prayeth best, who loveth best
> All things both great and small;
> For the dear God who loveth us,
> He made and loveth all.

Sources for Further Study

Barfield, Owen. *What Coleridge Thought*. Middletown, Conn.: Wesleyan University Press, 1971. Focuses on Coleridge's theological and philosophical thought, including his self-proclaimed "passion for Christianity."

Bloom, Harold, ed. *Samuel Taylor Coleridge's "The Rime of the Ancient Mariner."* New York: Chelsea House, 1986. Introduction places the poem in the tradition of Cain and Wandering Jew stories, and essays include studies of the poem's sources and symbolism.

Falke, Cassandra. "The Sin of the Ancient Mariner." *Lamar Journal of the Humanities* 29, no. 1 (Spring, 2004): 5-11. Argues that *The Rime of the Ancient Mariner* can be fully appreciated only within the context of Coleridge's Christianity, particularly his understanding and use of the concepts of Original Sin and the Cain story.

McFarland, Thomas. *Coleridge and the Pantheist Tradition*. Oxford, England: Clarendon Press, 1969. Wide-ranging assessment of Coleridge's coherence of thought, including his literary, theological, and philosophical ideas.

Newlyn, Lucy, ed. *The Cambridge Companion to Coleridge*. Cambridge, England: Cambridge University Press, 2002. Contains commissioned essays by modern critics reassessing Coleridge's poetry and other writing as well as his philosophical and theological ideas.

Daryl Holmes

A RIVER RUNS THROUGH IT

Author: Norman Maclean (1902-1990)
First published: 1976
Edition used: A River Runs Through It, and Other Stories, foreword by Annie Proulx.
   Twenty-fifth Anniversary Edition. Chicago: University of Chicago Press, 2001
Genre: Novella
Subgenre: Literary fiction
Core issues: Beauty; compassion; love; memory; nature

Maclean's story (along with the movie it inspired) greatly popularized fly fishing in American culture, but the deeper significance of the work lies in its critical question of how to help those who refuse help. Fly fishing is compared to religious devotion to reveal the contrasting lifestyles of two brothers. The elder brother, who witnesses the self-destruction of his younger brother, narrates the struggle of the family to make sense of its tragic prodigal.

> *Principal characters*
> *Norman Maclean*, the protagonist/narrator
> *Paul Maclean*, Norman's younger brother
> *The Reverend Maclean*, Norman and Paul's father
> *Neal*, Norman's brother-in-law

Overview

Much of Norman Maclean's *A River Runs Through It* is autobiographical, based on his family experiences as he was raised in a parsonage in western Montana in the early part of the twentieth century. Maclean is the elder son of a Scottish Presbyterian minister. He and his brother, Paul, fish the wild Montana streams as often as possible. Much of the action in this story is set along the Big Blackfoot River. For the Macleans, fly fishing is religion. The Reverend Maclean taught his boys to cast a fly rod with the same discipline that he engendered in them concerning religious studies. The Reverend Maclean believed "man by nature was a mess and had fallen from an original state of grace," but he believed that "only by picking up God's rhythms were we able to regain power and beauty." As far as the Macleans are concerned, fly fishing in the beauty of nature fulfills the call to glorify God and enjoy him forever.

The joyful art of fly fishing is clearly depicted in Maclean's writing. He recounts competitive but friendly experiences with his brother. As the story progresses, however, it becomes clear that Maclean's memory is troubled by a family tragedy. Something is wrong in paradise. Paul has difficulty controlling his drinking and gambling, and his stubborn refusal to be helped contributes to his demise. He also ignores certain hypocritical customs of his region. For example, he dates American Indians, which tends to put him at odds with his society. In one instance, Paul is taken to jail because he took vengeance on someone who had insulted his date. Norman is called to retrieve his drunken brother and Indian girlfriend from jail.

As the elder brother, Maclean conveys a frustrating sense of helplessness concerning Paul. Much of the action of the story details memories of his experiences with Paul and their father. The pleasant memories involve fishing trips where the brothers experienced the pure beauty of the wild rivers and various species of trout and wildlife. In these episodes, Maclean provides something of an Edenic world far removed from the imminent violence of Paul's other world.

Maclean wrote his story nearly forty years after the death of his brother. His writing clearly suggests his attempt to make peace with his apparent inability to help his troubled brother. He writes, "I knew there were others like me who had brothers they did not understand but wanted to help. We are probably those referred to as 'our brother's keepers,' possessed of one of the oldest and possibly one of the most futile and certainly one of the most haunting of instincts. It will not let us go." Later, he again voices this concern: "I still do not understand my brother. He himself always turned aside any offer of help."

Parallel to his own inability to help his brother, Maclean's story also shows Paul and Norman unified, reluctantly trying to help Norman's brother-in-law Neal. Neal has abandoned Montana for the West Coast. His return visit causes comic relief as well as reinforcing the values of home, family, and genuineness. Though raised in Montana, Neal likes to pretend to be a tennis star or talk about fishing when in fact he is good at neither. His artificiality contrasts with the Maclean brothers, who see him for what he really is. They are obligated to try to help him, however. At the request of Norman's wife, Jessie, they take him fishing, even though he does not know how to fly fish and does not want to be out in the wild. Neal eventually deserts the Macleans to spend time with a prostitute. In their drunkenness, Neal and the woman lie naked on a sandbar and are severely sunburned. Norman and Paul, then, have to carry Neal home to his mother to have his burns treated. Neal's presence in the story suggests a weak and ugly artificiality that contrasts notably with Paul's genuine, although flawed, beauty. Also, the teamwork of Paul and Norman is a refreshing respite, but one that does not last because of Paul's looming troubles.

Paul is described as a beautiful artist, especially when handling a fly rod. Norman and his father enjoy Paul's artistry, acknowledging that Paul is the finest fisherman they have known. Paul's ability with a fly rod contrasts with that of his brother and father, and it also illustrates a deeper separation between the Macleans. Neither Norman nor his father can help Paul because he refuses their attempts. It is only in the reconstruction of memory that Norman can make sense of their loss. "You can love completely without complete understanding," he tells his father. This sense of incomplete understanding and the Reverend Maclean's declaration that Paul, despite his tragic life, was "beautiful," form the basic elements from which Maclean tries to reconcile guilt and grace. Despite these fragments of grace, however, Norman remains "haunted by waters."

Christian Themes

Fly fishing is the controlling metaphor in Maclean's *A River Runs Through It*. The beauty and grace involved in this kind of fishing parallels Norman's attempts at achieving the unity he desires with his brother. Fly fishing, for Maclean, is a way of ordering chaos, an attempt to momentarily return to Eden, despite the abundant evidence of a fallen world beyond their rivers. Additionally, it is through fly fishing that the Macleans enjoy and glorify God. For them, there is "no clear line between religion and fly fishing."

A Calvinist, Presbyterian theology is implied in the subtexts of this work, but the Reverend Maclean is somewhat unusual: "Unlike many Presbyterians, he often used the word 'beautiful.'" Most notably, he insists that Paul is beautiful and that his artistry is the means to recover lost grace. In other words, although humanity is a "mess" and "fallen," the concept of beauty functions as Christian grace and counters any implied negative ramifications of the lost child.

A brother's keeper theme is dominant in the book. This theme has haunted the narrator for nearly forty years. Though Norman was unable to protect his brother, his writing may be viewed as an offering of grace to his lost brother. In Christian imagery, Paul is obviously presented as the "prodigal son." Fly fishing is a means of grace to receive the family prodigal.

The Christian notion of Logos also informs the text. Norman and his father discuss the passage in "The Gospel of John" in which Christ is presented as divine Logos and "the Word was in the beginning." The Reverend Maclean believes that "words are underneath the water," which is to say the word precedes water. This distinction is important for the Macleans, who recognize that a river speaks to each one individually. Like grace, understanding may be elusive, but each one may have his unique conversation with the words speaking through water. Further, the narration clarifies that Paul's view of ultimate reality agrees with that of his father. Despite his tragic and perhaps reckless life, Paul's theological and philosophical worldview is comforting to his father and suggests that Paul recognized beauty and reality in a way many may misunderstand.

Sources for Further Study

Browning, Mark. "'Some of the Words Are Theirs': The Elusive Logos in *A River Runs Through It*." *Christianity and Literature* 50, no. 4 (Summer, 2001): 679-688. Difficulty in human communication may be central to understanding Maclean's novella.

Dooley, Patrick. "The Prodigal Son Parable and Maclean's *A River Runs Through It*." *Renascence: Essays on Values in Literature* 58, no. 2 (Winter, 2005): 165-175. Discusses failure within the Maclean family; yet the father, like God, unconditionally loves his wayward son.

Johnson, Don. "The Words Beneath the Stones: Salvation in *A River Runs Through It*." *Aethlon: The Journal of Sport Literature* 14, no. 1 (Fall, 1996): 301-307. Argues that Maclean broadens the Calvinistic view of salvation to consider the role of art. Provides background information and shows how Maclean fictionalized the story.

Weinberger, Theodore. "Religion and Fly Fishing: Taking Norman Maclean Seriously." *Renascence: Essays on Values in Literature* 49, no. 4 (Summer, 1997): 281-289. Contrasts the Maclean family and their society. The prominence of fly fishing is foundational for interpreting the book.

Womack, Kenneth. "'Haunted by Waters': Narrative Reconciliation in Norman Maclean's *A River Runs Through It*." *Critique: Studies in Contemporary Fiction* 42, no. 2 (Winter, 2001): 192-204. Uses interviews of and lectures by Maclean to emphasize that art transcends tragedy.

Kenneth Hada

THE ROBE

Author: Lloyd C. Douglas (1877-1951)
First published: 1942
Edition used: The Robe. Chicago: Houghton Mifflin, 1947
Genre: Novel
Subgenres: Church history; historical fiction (first century)
Core issues: Conversion; discipleship; healing; Jesus Christ; martyrdom; persecution

Marcellus, the Roman tribune charged with overseeing the crucifixion of Jesus, wins the Savior's robe by tossing dice. He puts it on and is overcome with a debilitating depression healed only when he again dons the robe in Athens. Marcellus and his slave, Demetrius, learn about Christianity from a Jewish tailor who mends the robe. Marcellus and Demetrius are sent to Palestine to learn about the new religion, and they become Christians. Back in Rome, when Caligula becomes emperor, their Christianity puts them in danger. Demetrius is attacked and healed by Saint Peter, then departs for Greece. Marcellus is tried for being a Christian and sentenced to death.

Principal characters
> *Marcellus Gallio*, the protagonist, a young Roman tribune from a patrician family
> *Demetrius*, Marcellus's Corinthian slave, who is loyal, intelligent, and athletic
> *Diana*, a beautiful friend of Marcellus's younger sister, a favorite of Emperor Tiberius
> *Theodosia*, the landlord's daughter in Athens who is partial to Demetrius
> *Justus*, a Jewish Christian who teaches Marcellus the Gospel
> *Prince Gaius*, an evil and corrupt Roman who covets Diana
> *Benjamin*, a Jewish tailor in Athens who teaches Aramaic to Marcellus and Demetrius

Overview

Roman senator Marcus Gallio is worried because his son, young tribune Marcellus, has incurred the wrath of the corrupt Prince Gaius. Gaius vindictively orders Marcellus to a remote desert outpost in Minoa (Palestine). Marcellus and his loyal Corinthian slave, Demetrius, must fight to earn the respect of the garrison at Minoa, but eventually they do. During Passover, their detachment goes to Jerusalem to make a show of force, and Demetrius makes eye contact with Jesus while entering the city and is mesmerized. Marcellus, put in charge of the Crucifixion, wins Jesus' robe at dice but becomes so depressed following the event that he can barely function.

Meanwhile, Diana, a beautiful young friend of the Gallio family who is a favorite of Emperor Tiberius and admired by Marcellus, persuades the emperor to recall Marcellus from Minoa. His family, however, is so alarmed by Marcellus's condition that they send him and Demetrius to Athens to recover. In Athens, Marcellus touches the robe again and is healed. Demetrius confides the story to Theodosia, their landlord's daughter. The two men learn about Jewish theology from Benjamin, the Jew who mends the robe for them and also teaches them to speak Aramaic.

Tiberius, interested in the metaphysical, orders Marcellus back to Palestine to learn more about the Jesus movement. Demetrius, who attacks a Roman tribune who has insulted Theodosia, must go into hiding, so the two young men are separated. Marcellus tours Palestine with Justus, a Christian Jew, while pretending to be a textile merchant. He meets many Christians who tell him about Jesus' life and teachings. Demetrius is also in the country and has been baptized into the Christian faith. He is imprisoned, but the jailkeeper recognizes him and gives him back to Marcellus, warning them both to flee the country. The Romans attack the Christians in Jerusalem, and Marcellus sees Peter heal a cripple and witnesses the stoning of Stephen. He too becomes converted to Christianity.

Marcellus and Demetrius return to Rome and to the Gallio family, then head for Cyprus to report to Tiberius. Tiberius, however, orders Marcellus to renounce Christianity, or he will give Diana to the despicable Prince Gaius. Marcellus refuses and is deported, leaving Demetrius on Cyprus in chains.

Marcellus jumps ship and swims to Arpino, where he hires on as clerk on a melon farm. He cheers up the laborers, preaching the Gospel and humanizing the owner and his family. Eventually he feels impelled to return to Rome, where he hears Gaius has been poisoned, and Caligula has succeeded Tiberius as emperor. Caligula has designs on Diana, so Demetrius smuggles her away from Cyprus. They escape to Arpino and stay there with Marcellus's former friends. Meanwhile, Marcellus is meeting with the Christians in the catacombs, where Saint Peter is presiding.

Demetrius returns to Rome but has been wounded. He makes it to the Gallio home, where Sarpedon, the family physician, is unable to help him. However, Peter heals him, then orders him on a mission to spread the Gospel in Greece. Learning that Diana is in Arpino, Marcellus rides there, and he and Diana are married. Sarpedon, envious of Peter's healing powers, betrays Marcellus, Diana, and Demetrius to the authorities. Demetrius has already escaped to Greece, but Marcellus is imprisoned. He is tried for being Christian and is sentenced to death. Diana insists on joining him. As the two walk to their death, they hand the robe to a slave with instructions to give it to Peter.

Christian Themes

The Robe gives readers a feeling for what it must have been like to live in the environs of Jerusalem during the beginning of Christianity. The government of Rome is shown to be riddled with intrigue, corruption, and brutality, the better to contrast with Christian teachings of harmony, love, and peace.

The robe of Christ is not treated as an artifact with miraculous powers. Rather, it serves as a reminder of Christ's life and teachings to those who possess it. Christian believers in the novel are reluctant to share their belief with others who might not accept the idea of a Jewish Messiah arisen from the dead. They prefer to witness their faith by their kindness, acceptance of one another, and willingness to share their belongings with those in need. While Lloyd C. Douglas does not present Christians as morally superior to other characters, exposure to Christ's teachings is shown to lift people from a plane of selfishness and despair to a new level of awareness, compassion, and joy. Menial laborers, when taught Christianity by example and then precept, cease being dissatisfied with their lot and enjoy helping one another. Employers learn to supervise by love and trust rather than by threats and criticism. Tyrannical leaders lose their effectiveness when Christian subjects are unafraid to die.

Spanning a range of localities and countries from Rome to Athens to Cyprus to Jerusalem to Galilee, *The Robe* offers readers a panoramic overview and an action-filled epic drama. They are treated to brief personal sightings of famous historical figures: Jesus Christ, Simon Peter the fisherman, John the Beloved, Stephen the martyr, Herod's daughter Salome, Pontius Pilate, and the Roman caesars Tiberius and Caligula. These cameos dot a sweeping tale that includes romance, humor, pathos, and tragedy, amid an exciting, action-filled journey of adventure and mystery that is meant to provide emotional uplift rather than instruction.

Christian doctrine is not explained in detail; many tenets are ignored in the onrush of plot events. Douglas leaves it up to readers to decide the extent of their belief, preferring instead to show the attractive qualities of discipleship and the world-changing potential of a movement based on love and cooperation rather than competition and force.

Sources for Further Study

Books on Trial. Review of *The Robe. Books on Trial* 3, no. 3 (September, 1944): 568. Brief contemporary book review.

Dawson, Virginia Douglas, and Betty Douglas Wilson. *The Shape of Sunday: An Intimate Biography of Lloyd C. Douglas.* London: P. Davies, 1953. Biographical insights into the author, a former minister turned author in order to reach a "larger congregation."

Frederick, John T. "*The Robe* and *The Apostle*." *English Journal* 33 (January/December, 1944): 281. Frederick, a journalism professor, compares *The Robe* to Sholem Asch's *The Apostle* (1943), finding it lacking in historicity and theological rigor.

Mangan, E. A. Review of *The Robe. Catholic Biblical Quarterly* 5 (1943): 488. Book review from the novel's first publication.

Phy, Allene Stuart. "Retelling the Greatest Story Ever Told: Jesus in Popular Fiction." In *The Bible and Popular Culture in America*, edited by Allene S. Phy. Philadelphia: Fortress Press, 1985. Contextualizes *The Robe* as a popular narrative establishing Douglas's place in religious thought and gives biographical details and anecdotes about the author.

Sally B. Palmer

ROSE

Author: Li-Young Lee (1957-   )
First published: Brockport, N.Y.: BOA Editions, 1986
Genre: Poetry
Subgenres: Lyric poetry; meditation and contemplation; mysticism
Core issues: Beauty; death; love; marriage; mysticism; racism

Rose, a loosely unified book of lyric poems, expresses the sensibility and inner life of its author, meditating on the meaning of his existence in relation to his family and, by extension, his world and God. The family member central to his meditations is his father, an immigrant Chinese minister of a Pennsylvania Presbyterian congregation. This father's death is the traumatic event of the book, and coming to terms with death becomes the central problematic of the book.

Overview

Li-Young Lee, one of the most widely acclaimed American poets at the turn of the twenty-first century, was born in 1957 to Chinese parents in Jakarta, Indonesia; Lee's family emigrated to the United States in 1964. He grew up in Pennsylvania, attended the University of Pittsburgh, and pursued graduate studies at the University of Arizona and the State University of New York, Brockport (which awarded him an honorary doctorate in 1998). Although Lee has taught at prestigious universities (Stanford, Northwestern, University of Iowa), he has preferred to work at a warehouse in Chicago where he, his wife, and their children live with other members of the Lee family.

Family and family members loom large in *Rose*, and no one larger than Lee's father. In fact, this father figure takes on near mythic qualities. He had been physician to Chairman Mao Zedong in Communist China. When he could, he left for Indonesia to become cofounder and vice president of the Christian-oriented University of Gamaliel (Hebrew for "God is my reward"). Unfortunately, Muslim Indonesia was then led by sinophobic president Achmad Sukarno, who unleashed an anti-Chinese pogrom that swept Lee's father into prison in 1959, where he sustained kidney damage. Throughout his year of incarceration, Lee's father proselytized his fellow inmates and his jailers. After bribing his way to freedom, Lee's father became involved in the leadership of an evangelical Christian movement in Hong Kong, preaching to throngs numbering thousands. However, a financial dispute prompted him to migrate to America in 1964, where, in his forties, he enrolled in a Pittsburgh theological seminary. Eventually Lee's father became the Presbyterian pastor of Vandergrift, Pennsylvania. He died in 1980.

Lee's poems show that, in life, his father taught him invaluable lessons in living. He gave his son indelible examples of loving (reflected in "The Gift") and graphically illustrated that true knowledge comes not merely from empirical classroom knowledge. He transcended physical limitations by painting perfect still-life paintings although he had gone blind ("Persimmons"). He showed his son how to savor the jubilance of ripe peaches ("The Weight of Sweetness" and "From Blossoms") as well as the chaste joy in marriage ("Braiding"). In death, the father challenged his son to ask eschatological questions, to confront the mystery of human life, and to seek the wisdom he longs for (the book's first poem, "Epistle") and the truth that he perceives like a dream but cannot understand (the book's last poem, "Visions and Interpretations").

Although the presence of Lee's mother is less frequently felt in *Rose*, she is an important family figure. She was the aristocratic granddaughter of the fifth wife of General Yuan Shikai, the first president of the Republic of China after the fall of the Manchu Dynasty in 1911. In Lee's writings, his mother emerges as a fulfilling wife ("Early in the Morning"), a resourceful helpmate (she engineered their family's escape from Indonesia), a devoted parent capable of being the family head ("Eating Together"), and a person steeped in a Chinese high culture that is unavailable to her Chinese American son ("I Ask My Mother to Sing"). Lee's wife, Donna, is a figure of tender love ("The Gift"), of sensual love ("Persimmons"), through whom he realizes the inevitability of mortality even in the joy of marriage ("Braiding"). Lee has two brothers and a sister who is mentioned with special tenderness ("My Sleeping Loved Ones").

The book *Rose* has three parts. Part 1 comprises thirteen poems largely drawn from the recollected feelings and sensations of their speaker's boyhood; it ends with "Eating Alone," which communicates his sense of loss and loneliness after his father's death. Part 2 is a single poem of 274 lines, "Always a Rose," meditating on the question of death, which opens up the mystery of life. Part 3 opens with "Eating Together" (which counterposes "Eating Alone"); it balances the earlier poem's loneliness with a new sense of community derived from reconstituted commensality. The eleven poems of part 3 also tend to reflect an adult's viewpoint, and they are comparatively more abstract in tone and texture. Although the book is predominantly in free verse, Lee does experiment with poetic form, perhaps more so in part 3 than in part 1. In part 1, for instance, "Epistle" appears to be a nonrhyming terza rima and "Nocturne" an irregularly rhyming sonnet. Part 3, however, contains a tour de force of rhyme in "Between Seasons," where only four words are used repeatedly to end its twenty lines; and in "Visions and Interpretations," stanza lengths are used to create a diminuendo effect as the poem begins with a set of quatrains, continues with triplets, and concludes with couplets.

Christian Themes

When he was growing up, Lee's minister father exhorted him to read the Bible incessantly, and Lee grew to love the book. From it, Exodus, Song of Songs, and Ecclesiastes remain his favorites, and in them one may see the seeds of Lee's major poetic themes: immigration and identity formation, the coupling of sensual and spiritual love, and the attainment of wisdom through pain.

Not surprisingly, biblical echoes and Christian influences abound in *Rose*. Its first poem is entitled "Epistle," an allusion to Saint Paul, and its last poem is "Visions and Interpretations," a reference to mystical religious experiences necessitating exegesis.

At the center of *Rose* is the 274-line poem "Always a Rose." Lee calls this core poem "my meditation." This is more than a casual descriptor, for the poem has the structure of the meditative mystical experience that scholarly studies such as Evelyn Underhill's *Mysticism: A Study in the Nature and Development of Man's Spiritual Consciousness* (1911) extrapolated through analyses of the spiritual experience of such mystics as Saint Francis of Assisi, Saint Catherine of Siena, Saint Ignatius Loyola, Saint Teresa of Ávila, and Saint John of the Cross, among others. Underhill identifies the structure of a meditative mystical experience as passing through five stages: awakening, purgation, illumination, dark night of the soul, and union. Lee's "Always a Rose" progresses precisely through these stages.

The poem is divided into ten sections. Sections 1 and 2 describe the speaker's awakening to the presence of a black rose that is associated with his family and with death—elements he must come to terms with. Sections 3 and 4 deal with purgation. They describe how the speaker had been born with a dreadful birth defect (as a "half girl") and how his physician father had made him eat a medicinal rose that purged him of this defect; the speaker now must "eat" (that is, internalize and overcome) the black rose to deal with his father's death and the problematic of death itself. In sections 5 and 6, the speaker undergoes an illumination lit by his familial experience of knowing love and of loving. By the light of this knowledge (gnosis) and this love (*agape*), the black rose is transformed into a self-generating principle of love and a luminous symbol: "lovely for nothing, lovely for no one/ stunning the afternoon/ with your single flower ablaze." Immediately following the exhilaration of illumination, the meditative subject often falls into despair at the subject's own imperfection, a mood that Saint John of the Cross famously called the dark night of the soul. Thus section 7 of "Always a Rose" begins with the cry "Why do you stay away from me?" and continues with images of death, decay, madness, and night ("O day, come!") through section 8. Only midway through section 9 is "morning" again glimpsed, and love reasserts itself at the end of section 9, leading to section 10 wherein Lee conveys a sense of union through the love that enables him to unite the sweet and the bitter of experience, the living and the dying, and finally "you and I."

Sources for Further Study

Moyers, Bill. *The Language of Life*. New York: Doubleday, 1995. Contains a television interview of Lee, who talks about the influence of his minister father and the Bible on his writing.

Pence, Amy. "Poems from God: A Conversation with Li-Young Lee." *Poets and Writers* 29 (November/December, 2001): 22-27. A serviceable and revealing interview.

Underhill, Evelyn. *Mysticism: A Study in the Nature and Development of Man's Spiritual Consciousness*. 1911. Reprint. London: Methuen, 1967. The authority on this subject; first published in 1911, it has been reprinted more than a dozen times.

Zhou Xiaojing. "Inheritance and Invention in Li-Young Lee's Poetry." *MELUS* 21, no. 1 (Spring, 1996): 113-133. Argues convincingly for a reading of Lee that extends beyond his Chinese identity to include consideration of his Americanized self, Christianity, and so forth.

C. L. Chua

RULE OF ST. BENEDICT

Author: Benedict of Nursia (c. 480-c. 547 C.E.)

First transcribed: Regula sancti Benedicti, c. 540 C.E. (English translation, 1632)

Edition used: RB 1980: The Rule of St. Benedict in Latin and English with Notes, edited by Timothy Fry, O.S.B. Collegeville, Minn.: Liturgical Press, 1981

Genre: Nonfiction

Subgenres: Guidebook; handbook for living

Core issues: Daily living; humility; monasticism; obedience and disobedience; silence

Benedict's rule had an immense influence on the shaping of Western Christianity. Its influence grew slowly as popes sent forth Benedictine monks to evangelize the nations. Then under the influence of Benedict of Aniane, with imperial assistance, it became normative for all monasteries in the West and has remained the dominant monastic rule ever since.

Overview

Benedict was born in the region of Nursia, northeast of Rome; the traditional date of 480 cannot be far from the truth. He went to Rome to study and underwent a religious conversion that led him to renounce the world. He first joined some ascetics at Enfide, east of Rome, and then, for three years, lived in complete solitude at Subiaco. He was later joined by many disciples for whom he established twelve monasteries. Persecution led him to withdraw to Monte Cassino, eighty miles south of Rome, where he established what became a large, flourishing cenobium. He gained a widespread reputation as a holy man, endowed with special charisms. He died around the middle of the century.

The *Rule* is made up of a rather extensive prologue and seventy-three chapters, the last few of which seem to have been added to a completed text and show a somewhat different influence from that of the *Rule of the Master*, which seems to have been the main influence on the *Rule*. The influences of Basil the Great and John Cassian are evident, and they are referred to in the *Rule*, the latter implicitly.

The prologue is a paternal admonition, rich in spiritual teaching. Benedict writes the *Rule* for the one who wishes to return to God by the way of obedience. This calls for repentance and good works. Benedict seeks to establish a school of the Lord's service that is moderate in its demands but that will lead to the heights: "As we progress in this way of life and in faith, we shall run in the path of God's commandments, our hearts overflowing with the inexpressible delight of love." It is through patience that we share in the passion of Christ and merit to share in his kingdom.

In the first chapter the holy legislator speaks of the different kinds of monks: hermits or anchorites, who live alone; sarabites, detestable men who live in small groups and do their own will; gyrovagues, who spend their lives going from one monastery to another; and cenobites, who live in community under a rule and an abbot. These latter are the strongest, and for them Benedict writes his *Rule*.

Therefore, in chapter 2 Benedict immediately speaks about the abbot, the spiritual father who is believed to hold the place of Christ in the monastery and has supreme authority. He is, however, always to remember that he must answer to the Lord, and he is to seek constantly the advice of the brethren: "Everything is to be done with counsel." The abbot is to be elected by the brethren. He, in turn, names his prior—his second in command—and a cellarer, who administers all the temporalities under the direction of the abbot.

Benedict next devotes four chapters to basic monastic spirituality. Chapter 4 is a concise catalog of the "instruments of good work," going from the decalogue to the ultimate piece of advice: If you fail in everything else "never despair of the mercy of God."

Humility is the Benedictine way, and obedience, which is the "first step of humility, which comes naturally to those who cherish Christ above all," is treated extensively in chapter 5 and frequently comes up in the rest of the *Rule*. Silence also merits a chapter, as an expression and safeguard of humility, before Benedict begins his central chapter on the steps of humility. In these twelve steps the whole of Benedictine mysticism is summed up, from conversion, through interior purification and exterior expression, to the perfect love of God where all is now done no longer out of fear but out of love of Christ, good habits, and delight in virtue.

"Nothing is to be preferred to the work of God"—that is, the community prayer, which is drawn from the Church of Rome and unites the monk with the Church. The next eleven chapters (8-18) lay down its order, and then chapter 19 speaks of inner dispositions, giving a simple, all-embracing rule: "Let the mind be in harmony with the voice." A brief but powerful chapter follows on personal prayer: "We must know that God regards our purity of heart and tears of compunction, not our many words." He will return to this when he speaks of the oratory. Provision is made for reading to nourish this prayer, during the work of God, during meals, before the final service of the day, and in private during the day.

Before launching into a penal code, Benedict has a chapter on deans who will assist the abbot in a large monastery, and another on a very important element in the monk's life that profoundly affects all others: his sleep. Eight chapters (23-30) lay down not only the penalties but the great pastoral care the abbot must exert in regard to the erring: "The abbot must exercise the utmost care and concern for the wayward brothers."

After offering a chapter on the cellarer, who is to be like a father to the whole community, Benedict considers the temporalities and temporal services, always bringing in theological principles to ground his very practical provisions: "Regard all utensils and goods of the monastery as sacred vessels of the altar." "Whoever needs less should thank God . . . whoever needs more should feel humble." "To each according to his need." "The brothers should serve one another . . . for such service increases reward and fosters love." "Care of the sick must rank above and before all else, so that they may truly be served as Christ, for he said: 'I was sick and you visited me.'"

As Benedict says in concluding his summary list of monastic works: "The workshop where we are to toil faithfully at all these tasks is the enclosure of the monastery and stability in the community." Benedict has a sense of the monastery as the monks' place; therefore travel is carefully regulated, as is the reception of guests. Christ comes in these latter, especially when they are poor; therefore, they are due great honor and all humane care.

There is a detailed code concerning the admission of new members: "Do not grant newcomers to the monastic life an easy entry . . . test the spirits to see if they are from God." Priests are esteemed, but as monks they are to find their place in the ranks of the brethren: "The monks keep their rank in the monastery according to the date of their entry."

Chapter 72 is one of the most beautiful chapters in the *Rule*: "On Good Zeal": "To their fellow monks they show the pure love of brothers; to God, loving fear; to their abbot, unfeigned and humble love. Let them prefer nothing whatever to Christ, and may he bring us all together to everlasting life."

In a final chapter, Benedict humbly protests that his *Rule* is but for beginners. For those who want to go further, he points to the Scriptures—"What page, what passage of the inspired books of the Old and New Testament is not the truest guide for human life?"—and to John Cassian and Basil the Great.

Christian Themes

With its simple and practical application of Christian virtue to daily living, the *Rule of St. Benedict* became not only the most influential guide to monastic living in the West but also influential as a guide to general principles of Christian living, emphasizing the way of obedience. Obedience is the first step of humility, which comes naturally to those who cherish Christ above all. In the twelve steps of humility the whole of Benedictine mysticism is summed up, from conversion through interior purification and exterior expression to the perfect love of God, where all is now done no longer out of fear but out of love of Christ, good habits, and delight in virtue. It is through patience that we share in the passion of Christ and merit to share in his kingdom.

Sources for Further Study

Benedict of Nursia. *The Rule of the Master*. Translated by Luke Eberle. Cistercian Studies 6. Kalamazoo, Mich.: Cistercian Publications, 1977. This more extensive and less balanced rule is considered to be Benedict's most proximate source. A study of it brings out Benedict's moderating wisdom.

De Vogue, Adalbert. *The Rule of Saint Benedict: A Doctrinal and Spiritual Commentary*. Cistercian Studies 54. Kalamazoo, Mich.: Cistercian Publications, 1983. This concise commentary, written by the foremost scholar in Benedictine studies of his time, bases contemporary interpretations on the most solid scholarship and shares a depth of spiritual wisdom that can come only from a prolonged, serious living of the *Rule*.

McCann, Justin. *Saint Benedict*. New York: Doubleday, 1958. A widely accepted, objective study of the life of Saint Benedict.

Rees, Daniel, et al. *Consider Your Call: A Theology of Monastic Life Today*. Cistercian Studies 18. Kalamazoo, Mich.: Cistercian Publications, 1983. A large group of qualified scholars from the English Benedictine Congregation here collaborate to explore the living of the *Rule*.

Wathen, Ambrose G. *Silence: The Meaning in the Rule of Saint Benedict*. Cistercian Studies 22. Kalamazoo, Mich.: Cistercian Publications, 1983. Beyond its value as a thorough study of a basic element of Benedictine spirituality, Wathen's volume is useful for its comparative introduction to all the Western monastic rules that preceded Benedict's.

M. Basil Pennington

SAINT JOAN
A Chronicle Play in Six Scenes and an Epilogue

Author: George Bernard Shaw (1856-1950)

First produced: pr. 1923, pb. 1924

Edition used: Saint Joan: A Chronicle Play in Six Scenes and an Epilogue, definitive text under the editorial supervision of Dan H. Laurence. New York: Penguin Books, 2001

Genre: Drama

Subgenres: Biography; historical fiction (fifteenth century); legends

Core issues: Catholics and Catholicism; imperialism; justice; martyrdom; Protestants and Protestantism; reason; women

Shaw retells the life of Saint Joan of France, interfacing the views of anthropology and traditional institutional politics and religion. Sixty-seven years old when he wrote his play, Shaw found the personality and ethical example of Jesus Christ admirable but felt his reported claims to divinity were delusional. His Joan is similarly charismatically admirable and delusional. He found church people and politicians mostly intellectually timid and reprehensible. He postulated a "life force" in an evolving universe visible in the lives of "superhumans" such as Joan. Moral order in the universe was something few humans in real history could know.

> *Principal characters*
> *Joan, the Maid*, a French country girl who will become a saint
> *Robert de Baudricourt*, a nobleman who provides Joan with a horse and supplies
> *La Trémouille*, constable of France
> *Archbishop of Rheims*, a political prelate
> *Charles, the Dauphin*, heir to the French throne
> *Dunois*, a French commander
> *Richard de Beauchamp*, the earl of Warwick
> *John Bowyer Spenser Neville de Stogumber*, the chaplain for the earl of Warwick
> *Peter Cauchon*, the bishop of Beauvais
> *Brother John Lemaître*, a Dominican monk and Joan's inquisitor
> *John d'Estivet*, canon of Bayeux, the prosecutor for the Church

Overview

In *Saint Joan: A Chronicle Play in Six Scenes and an Epilogue*, George Bernard Shaw tells a historically faithful version of how Joan of Arc went from being a provincial adolescent, to military hero, to executed heretic, to rehabilitated venerable by the Roman Catholic Church twenty-five years later and to saint in 1920. Shaw's prefaces and postscripts to the play explain his knowledge and admiration of Joan.

In scene 1, in 1429, Robert de Baudricourt, on the River Meuse in France meets Joan of Arc for the first time and sees her extraordinary personality, complete with candidly announced dream visions and messages from saints Catherine, Margaret, and Blessed Michael, who tell her to lead the French army to victory at Orleans. To get the job, she wants an audience with the Dauphin.

In scene 2, March 8, 1429, Joan is in Chinon in Touraine, where she asks the Dauphin to let her lead the French army. She must first go through the rough scrutiny of La Trémouille, the archbishop, Monsieur de Rais (Bluebeard), and Captain La Hire, who has stopped swearing along with the soldiers in the presence of Joan. In realilty, the trial for heresy of Joan begins here. The archbishop's views represent the medieval Roman Catholic Church. "She is not a saint. . . . She does not wear women's clothes." Joan arrives late to meet the Dauphin and other members of the court, who are in disguise to test her. Joan instantly, and with casual humor, picks out the Dauphin.

Ominously, the archbishop says to Joan, "You are in love with religion." Joan asks, "Is there any harm in it?" The archbishop replies, "There is no harm in it, my child. But there is danger." Subsequently, Joan begins to prepare the Dauphin for the military leadership he has to assume and the kingship he will have to receive at Rheims. The scene ends with Charles giving immediate command of the army to Joan.

Scene 3, April 29, 1429, describes the signal victory of the French at Orleans under Joan's command. A short scene, it repeats the story of the charmed change of the wind on the River Loire, filling the sails of the French rafts of soldiers to drive them upriver to overrun the English position. The wind is seen by the troops as a miracle.

Following Orleans are French victories at Jargeau, Meung, Beugeney, and Patny. Scene 4 dramatizes the English side, represented by Richard de Beauchamp, earl of Warwick. The earl converses with the French bishop Cauchon on the political versus the theological merits of the case against Joan that the English, French, and Roman church will conspire to bring.

Scene 5 takes place after the coronation of Charles as king of France in Rheims. Joan and Dunois discuss Joan's cool reception from both secular and church authorities in spite of her spectacular military success for France. The archbishop and Dunois advise against the plan to take Paris. However, Joan takes the army to Paris and is defeated.

Scene 6, May 30, 1431, depicts the arrest and condemnation of Joan to death. First Joan recants her heretical view that her visions are more authoritative to her than the Church, and the Church sentences her to life in prison in solitary confinement. She subsequently retracts her recantation, which is viewed as a relapse into heresy, and is burned at the stake. Shaw's preface to the play states he believed all parties, English, French, and Roman, were sincere in their intentions. Their casuistry was submerged in their sincerity.

The epilogue, a dream of King Charles VII, allows Joan to return alive to the stage, thus complicating the audience's experience of the play as a tragedy. It also locates the play in history by jumping ahead to June, 1456, when the Roman Catholic Church pardoned Joan. A male character from the 1920's appears to report that the Church has canonized Joan.

Christian Themes

In the world of *Saint Joan*, several values collide. The church is jealous of its world-controlling power. England (Warwick) and France (Charles) are jealous of their nationalistic power, and Joan's project is a nationalistic one, though her act is essentially an individualistic or Protestant one. She stands for the liberty of the individual to define God as she chooses. In this historical instance, France is the fortuitous recipient of the caprice of Joan's warrior genius. A subtext of the play is that in the world, that is, Joan's world, there is no hospitality for love or charity. At best, the Roman Catholic Church and the English and French politicians are about slippery abstractions—morality and patriotism, and posturing. The Inquisitor says, "I would go to the stake myself. . . ."

In Shaw's dispensation, Joan is the ultimate Protestant as doomed superwoman. She is a brilliant military leader. He gives her an attractive personality in spite of her being an architect of the violence of warfare. Her nationalistic cause is not a Shavian one. For Shaw, by their natures, neither church nor state can be ethically admirable. He thought the meaning of the Joan story was not optimistic for humanity as it is. A common modern reading of *Saint Joan* is as a report of medieval political chicanery by civil and religious authorities to neutralize or remove individuals who have become inconvenient or expensive obstacles to vested powers. Remarkably, Shaw's treatment of the Joan story is the most faithful to the historical record of the many versions of it that have been written. Shaw's optimism projects beyond history in his hypothesis that for human destiny, a "life force" drives a process of creative evolution ultimately to transcendental consciousness.

Sources for Further Study

Astell, Ann W. "Shaw's *Saint Joan*: Judging Joan and Her Judges." In *Joan of Arc and Sacrificial Authorship*. Notre Dame, Ind.: University of Notre Dame Press, 2003. A reasoned reading of *Saint Joan* in the light of Shaw's Marxism.

Holroyd, Michael. "Collaborating with a Saint." Chapter 2 in *The Lure of Fantasy, 1918-1950*. Vol. 3 in *Bernard Shaw*. New York: Random House, 1991. The authorized biographical account of Shaw's writing and the production history of *Saint Joan*.

Pharand, Michel W. "Part 4: Shaw and Jeanne d'Arc." In *Bernard Shaw and the French*. Gainesville: University Press of Florida, 2000. The reception of Shaw's *Saint Joan* in France, with reference to an inventory of more than a hundred plays about Saint Joan; indispensable for the world reputation of Shaw's play.

Tyson, Brian. *The Story of Shaw's "Saint Joan."* Montreal, Que.: McGill-Queen's University Press, 1982. Examination of Shaw's conception and composition of *Saint Joan* and its first reception and later influence on twentieth century drama.

Weintraub, Stanley, ed. *Saint Joan: Fifty Years After 1923/24-1973/74*. Baton Rouge: Louisiana State University Press, 1973. A treasure trove of positive and negative analyses from twenty-five distinguished writers on *Saint Joan*.

John R. Pfeiffer

SAINT MANUEL BUENO, MARTYR

Author: Miguel de Unamuno y Jugo (1864-1936)

First published: San Manuel Bueno, Mártir, 1931 (English translation, 1954)

Edition used: Abel Sanchez, and Other Stories, translated with an introduction by Anthony Kerrigan. Chicago: H. Regnery, 1956

Genre: Novella

Subgenre: Catholic fiction

Core issues: Death; faith; sacrifice; salvation; service

Unamuno explores his personal crisis of faith and Spain's loss of faith in itself in a story about a village priest who is outwardly devoted to his church and its village congregation, yet lacks their firm faith in the afterlife.

Principal characters

> *Don Manuel*, the protagonist, a Roman Catholic priest
>
> *Angela Carballino*, the narrator, who helps Don Manuel and keeps his secret
>
> *Lazarus Carballino*, Angela's brother, who also helps Don Manuel
>
> *Blasillo*, the mentally disabled villager who adores Don Manuel

Overview

In Miguel de Unamuno's *Saint Manuel Bueno, Martyr* (also known as *Saint Emmanuel the Good, Martyr*), the titular protagonist is a priest who lives an outward life of devotion to church and community while struggling with an inner life filled with doubt about a tenet of his Roman Catholic faith: a belief in life after death. The novella is a story within a story. The narrator, Angela Carballino, more than fifty years old, writes down the secret of Don Manuel's inner life when she hears that the local bishop seeks to canonize him. She never intends the bishop to see the manuscript that she calls a "confession." The epilogue reveals that it was mysteriously given to Unamuno.

Angela first recalls herself at ten and Don Manuel at thirty-seven, the new pastor of the Roman Catholic Church and a newcomer to the village who gave up a brilliant career in the Church to help his widowed sister care for her sons. When Angela returns from a convent school in the city five years later, Don Manuel is as necessary to the village as the mountain and the lake that border it. He tirelessly mends marriages as well as torn clothes and attends the sick and dying as well as the celebrating. He is especially kind to the mentally disabled Blasillo. Don Manuel's voice moves the villagers, especially during Mass on Good Friday, because it sounds as if it were Jesus Christ speaking. As Blasillo wanders the village, he imitates Don Manuel's voice speaking the most moving words of Christ's Passion: "My God, my God, why have you forsaken me?" However, each time the congregation recites the Creed, Don Manuel's voice disappears on the lines about belief in the resurrection.

Angela becomes his "deaconess." She helps him with his pastoral duties in the village. When Angela is twenty-four, her brother Lazarus returns to the village from America. He intends to use his fortune to take Angela and her mother to live in the city, away from the "feudal backwater" of the country. Instead, Angela's mother dies, but not before Don Manuel convinces Lazarus to tell his mother that he would honor her dying wish that he pray for her.

Lazarus becomes Don Manuel's constant companion and finally takes Communion in a public conversion. Alone with Angela, Lazarus confesses that at Don Manuel's request, he converted to the priest's "holy cause," that is, preserving the simple faith of the villagers that keeps their life on earth happy. At first, Lazarus questions this idea as trickery; however, Don Manuel counters, "Dip your fingers in holy water and you will end by believing." Although Don Manuel cannot assent when Lazarus asks him if by celebrating Mass he, too, has come to believe, Lazarus sees him as a martyr who has sacrificed his life for the good of the villagers. During her own confession to Don Manuel, Angela intimates that she, too, knows his secret, and the three become inseparable.

Angela never marries, and for years Lazarus and Don Manuel minister to the villagers. Don Manuel begins to decline during Easter week. When he says good-bye to his friends, he compares himself to Moses, who led his people to the Promised Land but was not allowed by God to enter it himself. He asks Lazarus to be his Joshua and continue his work in the village. He becomes paralyzed and is carried into the church. He holds Blasillo's hand, blesses the congregation, and asks them to pray the Paternoster, Ave Maria, Salve, and Creed. He dies as they reach the line about resurrection and everlasting life. Blasillo also dies.

Lazarus and Angela help the new village priest. Lazarus writes down his conversations with Don Manuel, which Angela draws on for her account, and he dies. Angela concludes that in death Lazarus and Don Manuel's nonbelief turned to belief, yet she continues to question her own belief.

Unamuno's epilogue claims to have transcribed Angela's account and to have created "characters with immortal souls." He comments that the villagers would have believed deeds more than doubts even if Don Manuel's secret had been told. Also, he states that he knows he has written a novel in which nothing happens, but he compares it to the immortality of a mountain.

Christian Themes

Saint Manuel Bueno, Martyr was published at the beginning of the Spanish Republic, the end of Unamuno's six-year exile in France for denouncing Primo de Rivera's dictatorship, and just five years before Unamuno's death. Two of Unamuno's books were listed on the Vatican's Index of Forbidden Books. The themes of life and death, faith, and immortality reverberate on a national as well as a personal level.

The Christological imagery sets up Don Manuel as a martyr for his nation and as a vehicle to present Unamuno's spiritual anguish for himself and Spain. Don Manuel's name suggests "Emmanuel" or "God is with us," a Hebrew name given to Jesus Christ. Similarly, he is the suffering servant who ministers to the poor and loves the children. Lazarus Carballino draws a parallel between the biblical story of Christ calling Lazarus from the tomb by telling his sister that Don Manuel metaphorically raised him from the dead by converting him to the priest's "holy cause."

Lazarus's resurrection resembles the one Unamuno envisioned for Spain: a turning away from the scientific and progressive and a turning inward to "intrahistoria," the soul of Spain, the nation's own Spanishness found within its people, culture, and topography. Don Manuel walks through the village and countryside with Lazarus the way Christ walked with his apostles, and his lectures present thoughts on dealing with the *abulia*, or spiritual paralysis, that gripped his nation as well as his own personal crisis of faith. Unamuno's novels are often termed essays in dialogue form with characters that are personified concepts. Unamuno called them "nivolas," novel-length works that depends on an examination of the characters' spiritual anguish, rather than an action-filled plot. From his earliest nonfiction works, Unamuno, the eldest of the writers called the Generation of 1898 (1890-1905), chastised Spain to regain the faith in itself that it lost in its defeat in the 1898 Spanish-American War. He urged Spain to reject the hidebound ideas of class and race and embrace the spirit of the Spanish Bible, the Castilian Christ, Don Quixote. One of the books that Angela's father urges her to read is *El ingenioso hidalgo don Quixote de la Mancha* (1605, 1615; *The History of the Valorous and Wittie Knight-Errant, Don Quixote of the Mancha*, 1612-1620; better known as *Don Quixote de la Mancha*), and Don Manuel's struggle to preserve the villagers' simple faith is a quixotic quest.

Unamuno's own crisis of faith began when he left the Basque province of his birth for the University of Madrid, where he earned a Ph.D. and culminated in his study of Søren Kierkegaard's idea that the need for God provides proof that God exists. Unamuno terms it *la fe en la fe* or faith in faith itself. Don Quixote's situations are so real because he believes them to be so. Don Manuel urges Lazarus to let his practice of Catholicism bring him to belief, and Angela hopes this worked at the end of life for both men.

Sources for Further Study

Andrachuk, Gregory Peter. "'He That Eateth of This Bread Shall Live Forever' (John 6:58): Lazaro's Communion." *Romance Notes* 31, no. 3 (Spring, 1991): 205-213. Discusses the significance of Lazarus taking communion in his own hand before the practice was allowed in Roman Catholicism and likens it to his becoming a priest in the "new religion" of Valverde de Lucerna.

Biggane, Julia. "Introjection, Loss, and the Politics of Possession in Unamuno's *San Manuel Bueno, Mártir*." *Hispanic Review* (Summer, 2005): 329-349. Discussion of the psychoanalytic, ethical, and political dimensions of mourning as it relates to the state of gender and politics in Spain.

Carey, Douglas M., and Phillip G. Williams. "Religious Confession as Perspective and Mediation in Unamuno's *San Manuel Bueno, Mártir.*" *MLN* 91, no. 2 (March, 1976): 292-310. The themes of absence, replacement, and confession show Don Manuel's struggle to believe. There is a strong discussion of the parallels between Don Manuel and Christ.

Mancing, Howard. "The Lessons of *San Manuel Bueno, Mártir.*" *MLN* 121 (March, 2006): 343-366. Provides a synopsis and a discussion of the characters and the relationships between the novella and Unamuno's life and previous writings.

Yorba-Gray, Galen B. "Don Quixote till Kingdom Come: The (Un)Realized Eschatology of Miguel de Unamuno." *Christianity and Literature* 54, no. 2 (Winter, 2005): 165-182. A description of Unamuno's vision of Don Quixote as spiritual and national savior of Spain because his creativity pushed beyond the apparent limits of the possible.

Cecile Mazzucco-Than

SAINT MAYBE

Author: Anne Tyler (1941-   )
First published: New York: Knopf, 1991
Genre: Novel
Subgenre: Literary fiction
Core issues: Atonement; Communion; forgiveness; redemption; repentance; respon-
  sibility; sainthood

Saint Maybe's prototypal American family confronts issues of guilt and atonement.
Blaming himself for the deaths of his brother and sister-in-law, Ian Bedloe believes
his responsibility is to drop out of college and provide for their three orphans. Mean-
while, Ian explores avenues toward forgiveness and redemption. Making the process
more difficult is the family's refusal to consider the deaths anything but tragic acci-
dents. Ian accepts the Reverend Emmett's arbitrary standard for expiation, but he
must complete his self-appointed task before he finally recognizes that only he can
grant the forgiveness he seeks; thus, eventually his life-affirming marriage and fa-
therhood provide the path to redemption.

> *Principal characters*
> *Ian Bedloe*, the protagonist
> *The Reverend Emmett*, Ian's spiritual adviser
> *Danny Bedloe*, Ian's brother
> *Lucy Bedloe*, Ian's sister-in-law
> *Daphne*,
> *Agatha*, and
> *Thomas Bedloe*, Ian's nieces and nephew
> *Rita de Carlo*, Ian's wife

Overview

The Bedloes in *Saint Maybe* are a typical Anne Tyler family: parents Doug and
Bee, their married daughter Claudia, and their sons Danny (the "golden boy" ex-jock)
and Ian (the typical high school senior). Neighbors consider them an all-American
family, but the Bedloes do not really communicate; thus, they remain detached from
each other. Just as their holiday meals are a collection of hors d'oeuvres, the family
remains a group of individuals whose links to each other are little more intimate than
the family's links to the ever-changing groups of neighborhood exchange students
who temporarily share their lives.

As the novel opens, Danny Bedloe introduces his family to Lucy, "the woman
who's changed my life"; the novel concludes, more than twenty years later, as Ian
Bedloe introduces his family to his infant son, Joshua, and contemplates that life-
changing introductions actually are everyday occurrences. For Ian, most of these life
changes result from what he considers his responsibility for the deaths of Danny and

Lucy. After Ian accuses Lucy of marital infidelity, Danny drives into a wall, perhaps deliberately. Likewise, a few months later, when Lucy dies of a drug overdose, Ian again blames himself, though other members of the Bedloe family frustrate his redemption by insisting these deaths are accidents and thus denying him any role. Nevertheless, Ian feels an overpowering guilt.

Searching for atonement, Ian is drawn to the Reverend Emmett's Church of the Second Chance, an evangelical sect that has discarded traditional forms such as baptism and communion, focusing instead on confession and penance. The Reverend Emmett, a former seminarian, tells Ian that reparations must be concrete and practical, so Ian drops out of college, takes a job as a carpenter (eventually becoming a skilled cabinetmaker), and becomes a surrogate parent to Danny and Lucy's three orphans—Agatha, Thomas, and Daphne. Initially Bee and Doug are reluctant to take responsibility for Agatha and Thomas, who are not Danny's children, so for several years Ian attempts to locate their birth father. Eventually, though, the Bedloes learn that all three children are truly orphans. Ian formally adopts the older children, giving them the Bedloe name. However, he is particularly close to Daphne, whose reckless approach to life is in direct contrast to Ian's caution; she is the one who gives him the nicknames "Saint Maybe" and "Mr. Look Both Ways."

In a series of vignettes, the novel chronicles Ian's struggles toward redemption— and his setbacks—as he tries to compensate for misjudging Lucy and forcing Danny to recognize that Daphne probably is not his child. Although he believes he has accepted responsibility, Ian apparently does not believe that religion alone has expiated his guilt; thus, even though his neighbors and fellow church members regard him as a saint, he is not convinced he should accept the Reverend Emmett's offer to become the church's associate minister. His focus is still his own redemption, which he believes can be accomplished if he successfully raises Agatha, Thomas, and Daphne. In contrast, the Reverend Emmett insists the task that has become his lifelong burden can actually be lifted only when Ian can forgive Danny and Lucy.

Gradually Ian realizes that he cannot force any of the children to accept his religious views. Even before she leaves home, Agatha refuses to attend church, and eventually she and Thomas move away, though they return for holidays. Daphne continues to live at home and attend church, but Ian's attempts to influence her behavior are also unsuccessful; she has a hidden, rebellious side to her life. More than the older children, though, Daphne is concerned that Ian may be lonely. Several times she enlists her siblings in plots to develop a romance between Ian and various teachers or young women at church, but he ignores all such efforts. After Bee's death, however, Agatha insists that Doug and Ian need help in clearing out the house, so she hires Rita de Carlo, the Clutter Counselor. To everyone's surprise, Rita pursues Ian, even ordering a handmade chest so that she will have the occasion to see him again. Still more surprising is the fact Ian is drawn to Rita, no doubt in part because she routinely discards papers and souvenirs, separating herself and her clients from their pasts. He says, however, that he feels safe with her primarily because, unlike other women he has dated, she seems to be "someone who couldn't be harmed."

When they marry, Ian is forty-two and Rita is thirty, so fatherhood is not part of Ian's plan, but during a Sunday morning service, Rita tells him she thinks she is pregnant and that she intends to be happy about that fact. Although initially startled, Ian becomes increasingly enthusiastic about the impending birth. For their son, he builds a cradle, his first work with curved lines that "required eye judgment and personal opinion." Like marriage and fatherhood, this choice reflects his willingness to let go of the past with all its associations of guilt. When he presents his son Joshua to the family, Ian has finally forgiven himself and become focused on the future.

Christian Themes

Two prominent themes are guilt and atonement. Because he articulated his distrust of his sister-in-law Lucy, Ian Bedloe believes he is directly responsible for the death (possible suicide) of his brother, Danny, and the subsequent death of Lucy; however, his parents insist that both deaths are tragic accidents. While no one else blames Ian, there is no one to absolve him of his guilt. The Reverend Emmett's emphasis on concrete reparations appears to suggest a path toward atonement, and his fellow church members come to regard him as saintly, but Ian remains focused on the last few words he exchanged with Danny, even after he has spent years vainly seeking atonement. Only when Rita forces him to discard the doubts and insecurity associated with his past does Ian finally manage to heed the other part of the Reverend Emmett's advice: to forgive himself for his actions and likewise to forgive Danny and Lucy for their reactions.

Although Ian's church, the Church of the Second Chance, does not recognize traditional communion services, the theme of communion is important throughout the novel. For example, the Bedloes create a community on Waverly Street because their holiday meals always include neighbors, including Mrs. Jordan and the Middle Eastern graduate students. At these meals, Bee serves a variety of everyone's favorite hors d'oeuvres rather than a traditional dinner. Meals play an important role throughout the novel. A significant incident involves the various family members' sharing their dreams/nightmares at breakfast on Claudia's thirty-eighth birthday. Ian says nothing, but Claudia's comment that nothing dramatic has ever happened to her contrasts with his inner conflict. Another key symbolic episode occurs at the church's Christian Fellowship Picnic, where Doug Bedloe starts to accept Ian's vocation and his connection with the church as Ian is able to repair damage to a valuable wooden table belonging to the wealthy relative of a church member. Later, Ian begins to regard the Reverend Emmett as an equal in the episode in which he teaches Emmett to make onion dip and the two of them make chips and dip their entire evening meal. The restoration of the Bedloe family is signaled, however, after the marriage of Ian and Rita, when Rita resumes Bee's custom of serving hors d'oeuvres at the family's holiday dinners.

Sources for Further Study

Bail, Paul. *Anne Tyler: A Critical Companion*. Westport, Conn.: Greenwood Press, 1998. Detailed critical analysis of individual novels with a separate chapter devoted to the place of each novel in the Tyler canon.

Croft, Robert W. *Anne Tyler: A Bio-Bibliography.* Westport, Conn.: Greenwood Press, 1995. Thematic critical biography combined with a comprehensive bibliography of primary and secondary sources, including source materials from the Anne Tyler Papers at Duke University.

Stephens, C. Ralph, ed. *The Fiction of Anne Tyler.* Jackson: University Press of Mississippi, 1990. Collection of critical essays analyzing typical Tyler themes and evaluating Tyler's place in contemporary American writing.

Tyler, Anne. *Dinner at the Homesick Restaurant.* New York: Knopf, 1982. Tyler's portrayal of the communication failures within the Tull family as they attempt to create family cohesiveness.

Charmaine Allmon Mosby

SAPPHICS AND UNCERTAINTIES
Poems, 1970-1986

Author: Timothy Steele (1948-   )
First published: Fayetteville: University of Arkansas Press, 1995
Genre: Poetry
Subgenre: Epigrams; lyric poetry
Core issues: The Beatitudes; beauty; Creation; humility

Through his poetry, Steele conveys the idea that the ability to perceive God in creation enhances faith. A fulfilling relationship with God does not require much more than individual piety. People who experience God around them in their daily lives manifest their faith through humility, love, and trust. Such attitudes, according to Steele, underscore harmony and beauty in the ordinary course of life.

Overview

Sapphics and Uncertainties is a single-volume reissue of Timothy Steele's *Uncertainties and Rest* (1979) and his *Sapphics Against Anger, and Other Poems* (1986). Steele's reputation as a poet rests on his facility with formal elements of lyric verse writing such as meter, rhyme, and styles; his clear and powerful poetic diction; and his expertise as a literary critic. In addition to ten books of poetry, Steele has published two books on prosody, a critical edition of the poetry of J. V. Cunningham, and numerous reviews and essays on individual poets and of poetry. Steele's doctoral thesis, completed at Brandeis University in 1977, was directed by J. V. Cunningham, who took an interest in Steele's poetry as well. In 1979, Steele published *Uncertainties and Rest*. In 2006, Steele published his tenth book of poetry, *Toward the Winter Solstice*, which continues the exploration of Christian thought found in his earlier books.

In *Sapphics and Uncertainties*, four poems deal directly with religious topics. "The Wartburg, 1521-22" describes Martin Luther's exile from his teaching position, and "In the King's Rooms" is spoken by the persona of King David, the great Israeli leader of the Old Testament. "Of Faith," the middle section of "Three Notes Toward Definitions," explores manifestations of faith in daily life. "Devotional Sonnet" is an expression of the merits of individual piety.

Other poems in the collection ("Angel") show nostalgia for Christmas as an important setting from childhood. "The Messenger" may be interpreted as the Holy Spirit in a piece on inspiration in springtime; and the enigmatic "One Morning," about a beginning and an end, is open to a resurrection-theme reading. "With a Copy of Ronald Firbank" is a tribute to a Catholic satirical novelist. Here the speaker assesses Firbank's career as a minor novelist obsessed with the rituals of the Catholic Church and who, like Martin Luther, was not afraid to criticize the clergy for veniality.

Matthew chapter 5, which contains the Sermon on the Mount and the Beatitudes, has particular resonance in Steele's poetry. "Nightpiece" and "Epigram 5: Matthew 5:15" both rely on parts of this scriptural text. In his 1994 poetry collection, *The Color Wheel*, Steele crafts "Beatitudes While Setting Out the Trash" around the verse "Blessed are the meek" and "Decisions, Decisions" in which the speaker says, "In God alone, intention/ And execution are simultaneous./ In God alone can choice be sure it *is* choice." These poems reveal a certitude resulting from the explorations of faith in *Sapphics and Uncertainties.*

"The Wartburg, 1521-22" describes the exile of Martin Luther, an Augustinian priest, who taught explication of the Bible at Wittenberg University from 1512 to 1546. His 1520 attack on Catholic doctrine and on Pope Leo X forced Luther to go into hiding, where he continued to write pamphlets on abuses in the Roman Catholic Church and to translate the Bible. This poem is composed of six sestets (six-line stanzas) rhyming *ababcc*. Spoken in the third person, the text shows Luther enclosed in the garden and by his beliefs. When he leaves for Wittenberg after the ten months of exile are over on "one gray dawn in early March," he enters "the modern world" that he helped create.

"In the King's Rooms" is spoken in the persona of King David in exile in Mahanaim, a city located somewhere along the Jordan River. Mahanaim is first mentioned in Genesis 32:2, and the name translates as either "two camps" or "two armies," either definition befitting this poem. The poem is based in 2 Samuel 17 and 18, which describes how King David (whose name means "Beloved") was forced to go to Mahanaim when his son, Absalom, tried to overthrow him. The British poet John Dryden made this incident the subject of his lyric satire *Absalom and Achitophel* (1681-1862). Steele's poem in four stanzas of five lines (cinquains) rhymes *abaab*. The first stanza speaks to King David's aspiration to "forever dwell in quiet" and to write his Psalms of praise to God. In the second stanza, he reviews his past successes, including how he killed Goliath and earned his reputation with King Saul, who gave David his daughter, Michal, as a reward for his bravery. Soon, though, Saul became jealous of David, and David formed an army to overthrow him. The third stanza captures the irony of David's situation, as Absalom has rebelled against his father. The fourth stanza captures David's resignation about Absalom's certain death, which came at the hands of Joab (Samuel 18), causing David genuine distress. To gain and retain his throne, King David had to revolt, turn loyal men against their king, and continually live on guard against assassination and invasion. In Steele's poem, the old king is tired and does not appeal to God to aid him, but rather the strength of his own character, demonstrating faith in himself.

Both these poems show the importance of choice, a theme that Steele shared with Cunningham, while "Of Faith" and "Devotional Sonnet" reflect another side of Steele's appreciation of Cunningham's verse. Though Cunningham lost his Catholic faith, Steele, in commenting on this in his edition of *The Poems of J. V. Cunningham* (1997), presents a contrasting idea: "The fact that God can be everything frees us to realize our particular selves" and as his poems show, to see God in all things.

"Of Faith," in five seven-line stanzas, opens with the elided line "A puzzling topic this." Framed by "Of Culture" and "Of Friendship," faith is the center of this three-part poem "Three Notes Toward Definitions." Here the speaker considers how language is used to describe faith, especially its names, and how it is known or experienced. In the third stanza, the speaker supports a definition of faith as truth, referring parenthetically to a major doctrinal passage from Hebrews 11:1-33 in which faith is defined as "the substance of things to be hoped for, the evidence of things that appear not." He moves on to cite Saint Augustine's *Confessiones* (397-400; *Confessions*, 1620), a major conversion autobiography; Blaise Pascal's *Pensées* (1670; *Monsieur Pascal's Thoughts, Meditations, and Prayers*, 1688; best known as *Pensées*), the work of the seventeenth century mathematician; and Charles Darwin's *The Autobiography of Charles Darwin, 1809-1882, with Original Omissions Restored* (1958), intended to invoke the evolution and creationism debates. In the fourth stanza, the speaker considers the French poet Rimbaud and the Italian religious painter Duccio as secularized examples of faith in one's art.

Finally, "A Devotional Sonnet" presents a speaker separated from those he loves, but not alone, because he has God. The poem describes his room, which is like a monastic cell, but instead of religious objects, it holds books, a bottle of wine, and broken pieces of china. The moment captured in the poem is a meditation as the speaker admits to sin and shows hope in the idea that God "will restrain me if I stray/ Too far from love I both reject and want." The speaker feels he must ask God to be compassionate toward him. Written as an Elizabethan sonnet, the poem harks to the devotional sonnets of John Donne, Gerard Manley Hopkins, and the modern poet Mark Jarman.

Christian Themes

Steele's realism balances images of life and death and of home and exile. For all the riches and richness the world offers, abandonment, loss, and waste lurk in its corners. As he writes in the poem "Golden Age," "Even in fortunate times,/ The nectar is spiked with woe." If people fail, nature seems more stable, as "At the Summit" indicates. In this poem, the hikers ascend to the edge of a gorge and are awestruck by the ancient beauty. This is anticipated, whereas the "poppies" and the "deer's tracks" are unanticipated evidence of the Creator. Although Steele's poetry makes use of the Christian tradition, particularly Catholicism, his is not primarily religious verse. Instead Steele calls on dogma, doctrines, and sacred language to explore the idea of faith as a dimension of society. Additionally, Steele's speakers are aware of God as part of the fabric of the universe, available to be seen and experienced as each individual desires in everyday life.

Sources for Further Study

Jarman, Mark. "Poetry and Religion." In *Poetry After Modernism*, edited by Robert McDowell. Rev. ed. Brownsville, Oreg.: Story Line Press, 1998. An essay assessing the contemporary poetry community's interest in writing on religious themes with examples of modern poets whose work addresses matters of faith.

Steele, Timothy. Interview by Cynthia Haven. *The Cortland Review* (June, 2000). An interview in which Steele discusses his writing style and his interests as a poet-critic.

_____, ed. *The Poems of J. V. Cunningham.* Athens, Ohio: Swallow Press, 1997. Contains Steele's critical appraisal of Cunningham's verse and annotated poetry texts. Close reading of Cunningham and Steele shows similarities between Steele's "Epigram 5" and Cunningham's "1 Corinthians 13," as both are epigrams, and between Cunningham's "With a Copy of Swift's Works" and Steele's "With a Copy of Ronald Firbank."

Walzer, Kevin. *The Ghost of Tradition. Expansive Poetry and Modernism.* Ashland, Oreg.: Story Line Press, 1998. Chapter 5 includes an analysis of Steele's formalism and reworks part of Walzer's article "The Poetry of Timothy Steele" previously published in the *Tennessee Quarterly.*

Beverly Schneller

THE SCARLET LETTER

Author: Nathaniel Hawthorne (1804-1864)
First published: 1850
Edition used: The Scarlet Letter. New York: Bantam Books, 1986
Genre: Novel
Subgenre: Romance
Core issues: Guilt; Puritans and Puritanism; redemption; sin and sinners; solitude; suffering; women

Hawthorne's classic novel examines the tension between the law as the basis for society and the need for human sympathy within the framework of an ideal Christian community. It suggests that while humans must submit to the law and not merely follow romantic impulses, the law itself must be rooted in Christian compassion.

> *Principal characters*
> *Hester Prynne*, the protagonist
> *Arthur Dimmesdale*, Hester's lover
> *Roger Chillingworth*, Hester's estranged husband
> *Pearl*, the daughter of Hester Prynne and Arthur Dimmesdale
> *Mistress Hibbins*, a witch
> *Governor Bellingham*, the governor of the Puritan colony
> *John Wilson*, a local magistrate

Overview

Nathaniel Hawthorne's first novel, *The Scarlet Letter*, is introduced by a long chapter entitled "The Custom House," which chronicles the author's recent politically motivated dismissal from his position at the Salem Custom House. In this introduction Hawthorne describes both his short-lived experiences as a political appointee as well as his recent re-emergence as a novelist. Hawthorne creates a historical and artistic connection to his own Puritan ancestors by presenting a fictionalized account of his discovery of an old cloth scarlet letter bound with ancient legal documents.

The novel proper opens with Hester Prynne, the protagonist, emerging from the depths of an ancient-looking prison, which the narrator calls the "black flower" of the Puritan community's imagined utopia. As she mounts the scaffold for public display with her infant daughter Pearl in her arms and an elaborately embroidered scarlet letter *A* on her breast, scornful women call for worse, more violent punishments. From the beginning then, the stern law of the aged Puritan magistrates and the jeering townsfolk are juxtaposed with the reader's own sense of compassion for the suffering woman and her newborn child. It is at this point, as well, that the reader is made aware of the complex structure of the character relations. While on the scaffold, Hester sees her estranged husband, Roger Chillingworth, who has been, for a time, learning medicinal arts from the Indians. The first few chapters of the novel after the initial scaffold scene establish the triangular relationship connecting Hester Prynne, Arthur Dimmesdale, and Roger Chillingworth.

The central issue of the novel is how Hester's punishment affects her relationships with others and how it changes her and Pearl. Hester, who takes up residence in a small cottage on the edge of town, is described as a living ghost, unable to find sympathy in the community in which she lives. She becomes an allegorical type in the Puritan symbolic imagination and is often reduced to a symbol within the sermons of church services. Hawthorne suggests that the scarlet letter, as a disciplinary measure, is ultimately a failure because Hester's own elaborate artistic rendering of it—and the other meanings besides "Adultery" that can be assigned to it—makes it more an expression of individual resistance to the law than an enactment of the law's force. Furthermore, the scarlet letter serves to isolate Hester and Pearl from the rest of the society. The narrator insists on numerous occasions that the real effect of the punishment is to drive both Hester and Pearl beyond the scope of the law and the bonds of sympathy. Shunned by society, Hester and Pearl become more metaphorically associated with the wilderness that surrounds them.

A second main issue that structures the novel is the consequence of Hester's apparently ethical decision to conceal Dimmesdale's identity as the father. By preserving her lover's anonymity, Hester unwittingly assists in his destruction by both his own gnawing guilt and by the manipulative machinations of Chillingworth, who takes up residence as the Reverend Dimmesdale's private doctor. Through his close proximity to the reverend, and as a consequence of their growing intimacy, Chillingworth is able to take advantage of the reverend's increasing psychic vulnerability. The narrator observes that Chillingworth himself is transformed, through the obsessive probing into Dimmesdale's symptoms, into a satanic figure for whom cruelty is elevated to an art form.

It is only with the revelation of Chillingworth's identity that Dimmesdale is able to confront his own sin and take any sort of action. Perhaps the most memorable scene in the novel is the central one in which Dimmesdale's guilt drives him to the scaffold at night, where he meets Hester and Pearl. It is here that Dimmesdale fails himself by refusing to honor Pearl's wish that he hold her hand in the light of day. However, it is the forest meeting between Hester and Dimmesdale that transforms the latter and urges him to act. Under Hester's "lawless" influence, Dimmesdale begins to contemplate and finally accepts the formerly unthinkable notion of leaving the Puritan settlement of which he is a spiritual leader. After the meeting with Hester in the forest, Dimmesdale is aflame with new hope for their future life together. However, as the narrator makes clear, Dimmesdale's romantic conversion is a form of madness, a kind of lawlessness that has been chiefly represented, up to this point, by Hester and Pearl. It is this madness, the narrator says, that allows Dimmesdale to gain new insights into his condition of sin and accept the possibility of action. This transformation ultimately leads to the climax of the novel, the public revelation of his guilt. In the conclusion of the novel, the narrator states that while Hester would not be the prophetess of the new truth of the relation between the sexes, she would take up both her scarlet letter (which is no longer a stigma) and a place in the community, assuming a role as the counselor and friend to other women.

Christian Themes

The Scarlet Letter raised complex and often uncomfortable questions about the relationship between sin and sympathy for Hawthorne's nineteenth century audience. At the time of its publication in 1850, several Christian editorial writers, in fact, criticized Hawthorne's novel for not adequately emphasizing Hester's renunciation of her sin and the process of her atonement. Some argued that because Hawthorne's story was not clearly enough an example designed for moral instruction, it should not be told at all. Earlier American seduction novels such as *Charlotte Temple* (1791) and *The Coquette: Or, The History of Eliza Wharton; A Novel Founded on Fact* (1797) invited the reader not only to witness the female protagonist's moral struggle and downfall, but also to forgive her transgressions as they were repented, typically in death. *The Scarlet Letter*, in contrast, invites the reader to sympathize with the sinner as she struggles, often rebelliously, to work out her relationship to her sin and the punishment for that sin.

The point of Hawthorne's text, like several of his earlier short stories, is to question if not outright criticize the severity of the Puritan law and the self-righteous intolerance of the Puritan community. Like other authors of his day, Hawthorne uses seventeenth century Puritanism as a point of departure for reflecting on what a Christian community should strive for in the nineteenth century. By emphasizing the figure of Hester Prynne as a sister of mercy throughout the novel, Hawthorne suggests that the ideal Christian community should be one based on charity, compassion, and mercy rather than rigid dogmatism and harsh judgment. Within the framework of Puritanism, however, Hester's good works are not and should not be viewed as a means for her redemption or salvation, since under Puritan doctrine this would amount to a form of religious heresy (Puritans rejected the belief, known as Arminianism, that an individual can achieve his or her own salvation through righteous action). Under the Five Points of Calvinism, election (that is, salvation) is considered "unconditional," and grace is likewise "irresistible." According to Calvinistic belief, with the gift of God's son Jesus Christ, humans entered into a new covenant based on grace, not works. Through the representation of Hester's isolation, rebellion, and final reemergence as a fixture of understanding and sympathy in her community, Hawthorne seems to argue that the Puritan law divides individuals from one another, making them vulnerable to self-righteousness rather than cultivating a sense of caring and forgiveness.

Hawthorne suggests that sin, the *sine qua non* of humanity, is also the condition for the possibility of sympathy. It is through the fall into sin and consequently the experience of suffering (through guilt, self-reflection, and redemption) that individuals learn to truly identify with and love their neighbor.

Sources for Further Study

Boudreau, Kristin. "Hawthorne's Model of Christian Charity." In *Sympathy in American Literature: American Sentiments from Jefferson to the Jameses*. Gainesville: University Press of Florida, 2002. This chapter relates Hawthorne's novel to the question of Christian charity in the writings of Puritan governor John Winthrop.

Durst Johnson, Claudia. *Understanding the Scarlet Letter: A Student Casebook to Issues, Sources, and Historical Documents*. Westport, Conn.: Greenwood Press, 1995. This volume is an excellent source book for historical and critical texts relating to Hawthorne's novel.

Thomas, Brook. "Love and Politics, Sympathy and Justice in *The Scarlet Letter*." In *The Cambridge Companion to Nathaniel Hawthorne*, edited by Richard H. Millington. Cambridge, England: Cambridge University Press, 2004. This essay examines the question of marriage as it relates to the Puritan tradition and to Hawthorne's novel.

Sean J. Kelly

SCENES OF CLERICAL LIFE

Author: George Eliot (1819-1880)
First published: 1858
Edition used: Scenes of Clerical Life, edited by David Lodge. Baltimore: Penguin
   Books, 1973
Genre: Short fiction
Subgenres: Literary fiction; stories
Core issues: Clerical life; grace; Incarnation; love; redemption

The three novellas in Scenes of Clerical Life *reveal the major themes that run through
all of Eliot's novels. In these short works, she dramatically captures the political, social, and religious tensions of a rural England confronting its industrial future. Her
three sketches of provincial clergy not only offer glimpses into the theological debates
of the mid-nineteenth century but also provide brilliant portraits of the foibles and the
heroism of ordinary individuals seeking to discover the meaning of religion.*

> *Principal characters*
> *Amos Barton*, the protagonist in "The Sad Fortunes of the
>   Reverend Amos Barton"
> *Amelia "Milly" Barton*, Amos's wife
> *Countess Czerlaski*, the Bartons' neighbor
> *Maynard Gilfil*, the protagonist in "Mr. Gilfil's Love Story"
> *Caterina*, Maynard's beloved
> *Sir Christopher Cheverel*, Maynard's patron
> *Captain Anthony Wybrow*, Sir Christopher's nephew
> *Janet Dempster*, the protagonist in "Janet's Repentance"
> *Robert Dempster*, Janet's husband
> *Mr. Tryan*, an Evangelical curate

Overview

George Eliot's first fiction, *Scenes of Clerical Life*, comprises three scenes, or
sketches, of individual clergy in the late eighteenth and early nineteenth century English Midlands: "The Sad Fortunes of the Reverend Amos Barton," "Mr. Gilfil's
Love Story," and "Janet's Repentance." Each story explores one clergyman's struggles with the hypocrisy of society, the demands of institutional religion, the challenges of provincial life, the nature of true love, and the meaning of true religion.

"The Sad Fortunes of the Reverend Amos Barton" opens twenty-five years before
Amos Barton appears in the village of Milby at Shepperton Church. In that earlier
time, the church itself was stately and beautiful, and the Sabbath services were conducted according to an older liturgy and hymns sung to the accompaniment of
stringed instruments rather than an organ. By the time Amos Barton arrives, the

church building and the liturgy have become more modern, reflecting the struggles between the various reform movements of the Anglican Church in the mid-nineteenth century.

Amos Barton is a circuit rider—serving three churches—who barely makes enough money from his work to feed and clothe his wife and six children. Not a handsome man, he is the subject of gossip because he is a bad dresser, a deficient speaker, and a thoughtless husband and father. In contrast, his wife Milly (Amelia), a beautiful and graceful soul, holds the household together and is greatly admired—and often pitied—by her neighbors. She works so hard performing the daily chores and keeping the creditors at bay that her health suffers. So concerned with the spiritual health of his parishioners, Barton fails to notice his wife's ill health until it is too late.

Milly's health and Barton's reputation suffer when a wealthy neighbor, Countess Czerlaski, moves into their already crowded household after losing her own. She treats the Bartons, especially Milly, like servants, and her stay with the family causes a great scandal in the village. Both his neighbors and his fellow clergy lose respect for Barton, who welcomes the countess into his home out of kindness and pastoral compassion. Pregnant with their seventh child, Milly falls ill from the extra work. Although she bears the baby prematurely, she eventually dies, and Barton is forlorn, recognizing that he had not loved Milly enough. Not long after Milly's death, Barton loses his position, and he and his children must move to a parish in a manufacturing town.

"Mr. Gilfil's Love Story" deals with the life and love of Maynard Gilfil, the parish priest who preceded Amos Barton in Milby. More respected and liked than Barton, Gilfil seldom asked his parishioners for money or about the eternal state of their souls. He performed his spiritual tasks with brevity, preaching short sermons without much reference to the religious topics of his day.

Before coming to Milby, Gilfil had served as a chaplain for Sir Christopher Cheverel at Cheverel Manor. A few years earlier in Italy, the childless Cheverels adopted Caterina, a young Italian orphan whom they were raising as their own daughter. The Cheverels' nephew, Captain Anthony Wybrow, and Gilfil grew up like brothers with Caterina. As Caterina blossoms into a young woman, Gilfil falls in love with her, and she falls in love with Anthony.

Anthony, however, is engaged to Lady Assher, a wealthy and impetuous socialite in his own social class. At the same time, Anthony has been making love to Caterina. Angry, hurt, and jealous, Caterina confronts Anthony about his plans, and he unfeelingly declares his intention to marry Lady Assher. Searching for a way out of his dilemma and knowing Gilfil's affections for Caterina, Anthony suggests that Sir Christopher orchestrate Gilfil and Caterina's marriage. When Sir Christopher proposes this plan to Gilfil, the chaplain exposes Anthony's deceptions and refuses to marry Caterina under such conditions. Meanwhile, Caterina, angered at Anthony's deceptions, plots to kill him. Before she can murder him, Anthony succumbs to a heart attack, and Caterina becomes physically ill and spiritually bereft. After Gilfil nurtures her back to spiritual and physical health, Caterina falls in love with him. They marry, but Caterina dies several months after their wedding, leaving Mr. Gilfil once more alone in his vicarage.

Like the previous two scenes, "Janet's Repentance" is set in Milby and deals with the conflict between Anglicanism and Evangelicalism. Tryan, the new vicar in the chapel on Paddiford Common, preaches extemporaneously, has religious meetings in people's cottages, and fills the aisles of his church with Dissenters. Tryan lives a life of self-sacrifice, bringing mercy to the poor.

Local lawyer Robert Dempster opposes Tryan and his kind of religion. Dempster hatches an anti-Tryan plan at the Red Lion pub, where he drinks steadily and heavily every night. Janet Dempster, Robert's wife, supports her husband in his crusade until she meets Tryan one day. When they exchange glances, Janet recognizes the soul of a fellow sufferer.

Because Janet does not live up to his ideal as a wife, Robert frequently beats her. When Robert throws Janet out of the house in a drunken rage one night, she seeks refuge with a neighbor, who eventually calls Tryan. Tryan's story of suffering emboldens Janet to live a life of self-sacrifice rather than self-despair. After Tryan dies, Janet, like many of Eliot's heroines, undertakes a life of love, mercy, and service.

Christian Themes

Although *Scenes of Clerical Life* is Eliot's first fiction about religion, she had been thinking about religion for at least a decade prior to the publication of *Scenes of Clerical Life*. In 1846, she translated D. F. Strauss's groundbreaking *Das Leben Jesu* (1835) as *The Life of Jesus Christ Critically Examined*; eight years later, she translated Ludwig Feuerbach's *Das Wesen des Christentums* (1841; *The Essence of Christianity*, 1854). Both of these works, critical of the foundations of traditional Christianity, influenced Eliot's portrait of the bankruptcy of traditional religion in *Scenes of Clerical Life*.

Moreover, by the time Eliot published *Scenes of Clerical Life*, the Anglican Church was facing challenges on all sides. The Tractarian, or Oxford, movement of the 1830's sought to reform the Anglican Church along Catholic lines. This High Church movement emphasized the power and authority of the bishops. The Low Church, or Evangelical, movement, on the other hand, tried to move the Anglican Church in a more Protestant direction, challenging the power of the bishops and asserting the authority of individual believers.

In each of the novellas in *Scenes of Clerical Life*, the village of Milby struggles with these issues, most starkly in "Janet's Repentance." The Evangelical clergymen Amos Barton, Maynard Gilfil, and Tryan represent the freedom from stifling liturgy and corrupt episcopal power of the Anglican Church. Although Eliot portrays each cleric as less than heroic, each of them brings new perspectives on the meaning of true religion to Milby. True religion, in these novellas, is the religion of kindness and humanity.

Sources for Further Study

Hardy, Barbara. *The Novels of George Eliot*. London: Athlone Press, 1963. Hardy's splendid critical work remains the best introduction to Eliot's fiction.

Hertz, Neil. *George Eliot's Pulse*. Stanford, Calif.: Stanford University Press, 2003. Hertz offers a brilliant reading of the ways that Eliot uses particular narrative techniques to develop specific themes.

Karl, Frederick R. *George Eliot*. New York: Norton, 1995. Still the best critical and intellectual biography of Eliot.

Noble, Thomas A. *George Eliot's "Scenes of Clerical Life."* New Haven, Conn.: Yale University Press, 1965. The only full-length treatment of Eliot's first fictions, Noble's book examines the reception of the work and the book's impact on Eliot's later work.

Oldfield, Derek, and Sybil Oldfield. *"Scenes of Clerical Life*: The Diagram and the Picture." In *Critical Essays on George Eliot*, edited by Barbara Hardy. London: Routledge & Kegan Paul, 1969. Shows how Eliot uses the German philosopher Feuerbach's ideas about religion to structure *Scenes of Clerical Life*.

Henry L. Carrigan, Jr.

SCIENCE AND HEALTH WITH KEY TO THE SCRIPTURES

Author: Mary Baker Eddy (1821-1910)
First published: 1875
Edition used: Science and Health with Key to the Scriptures. Boston: First Church of
   Christ, Scientist, 1991
Genre: Nonfiction
Subgenres: Biblical studies; handbook for living; sermons
Core issues: Atonement; God; healing; prayer; religion; scriptures

*Using the Bible as her primary reference, Eddy discusses her philosophy about the
true nature of healing. She explains that the source of healing comes from the power
of God and is invoked by attuning one's spiritual nature with God through faith,
prayer, and meditation. Eddy believes that humankind must follow the example of
Christ and practice his method of healing.* Science and Health with Key to the Scriptures *was written as a guidebook for changing lives by increasing faith in God, encouraging Scripture study, and promoting healing through implementation of spiritual law.*

Overview

During her bouts with chronic illness in the 1850's and 1860's, Mary Baker Eddy
became interested in the accounts of healing performed by Jesus Christ that are recorded in the Bible. Through prayer and careful study, she became convinced that the
true source of healing is a spiritual gift that comes from God. She referred to the spiritual way in which Christ healed as Christian Science. In 1875, she published *Science
and Health* as the textbook for Christian Science. Her main goal in writing the book
was not to present a new form of theology but to provide a guidebook for religious
practice. The phrase "with key to the Scriptures" was added to the title in 1883. Eddy
believed that her book provided the key for others to better understand the teachings
in the Bible.

Science and Health with Key to the Scriptures is composed of three sections. The
largest section is devoted to the main topics that are at the center of the Christian Science religion founded by Eddy in 1879. These include prayer, the Atonement, love,
spiritual development, and healing based on spiritual laws. The second section focuses on Scriptures from the Bible and an examination of portions of the books of
Genesis and Revelations. The second section also contains a glossary of 125 common
terms used in the Bible, defined by Eddy in terms of her metaphysical, spiritual interpretations. The last section of the book, added by Eddy in 1902, contains the testimonials of numerous individuals who claim to have been healed or relieved of severe illnesses and adversities by application of the healing principles explained by Eddy in
Science and Health with Key to the Scriptures.

In her book, Eddy proclaims that the life and works of Jesus Christ, from his working of miracles, particularly healing, to his resurrection, to his final ascension above
all materialism, represent conclusive evidence for the spiritual nature of human be-

ings. She views his life as exemplifying the potential for humans to act above and beyond the finite limits of a temporal, material existence. She portrays Christ's healing power as the operation of divine power through an understanding of spiritual laws. Although she does not deify Christ, Eddy declares that his life was the defining event in the history of the world, making the salvation of humanity from the mortal state possible. Christ's atoning sacrifice in Gethsemane and his yielding to death on the cross at Calvary enabled him to become the mediator between God and human beings. A central theme in *Science and Health with Key to the Scriptures* is that each person can follow the example of Jesus Christ, find spiritual identity, better understand the spiritual nature of healing, and live more like Jesus did.

After careful study of the Bible, Eddy concluded that it was Christ's commission to preach the Gospel and heal the sick. The former had been done to some extent but little had been accomplished with the latter. In *Science and Health with Key to the Scriptures*, Eddy unveils her fundamental idea that physical healing can be realized through the operation of spiritual laws. If people live their lives in accordance with revealed spiritual principles in the Scriptures, they will be in harmony with God and his divine Gospel plan. Eddy asserts her belief that the concept of matter is shaped by the limitations of the human mind. Through prayer and meditation, the power of God can heal individuals of physical, emotional, and mental illnesses by bringing human nature into conformity with the spiritual nature of humanity. Healing involves not only human bodily change but also spiritual change invoked by divine intervention outside mortality. Eddy explains that natural phenomena are governed by God, and therefore, the true medicine for healing disease and overcoming adversity must also come from God. She advocates relying on him for healing and good health.

Eddy emphasizes that studying the Bible brings people closer to God by filling them with the light of Christ. She declares the love of God for every human being and that he is always available if one seeks him. The book contains more than seven hundred quotations from the Bible and numerous references to scriptural teachings, events, and individuals in the Bible. In her 1902 revision of *Science and Health with Key to the Scriptures*, Eddy placed the chapters on prayer and the Atonement as the first two chapters in the book to emphasize the essential role that the Atonement and prayer play in healing and helping individuals reach their maximum potential. The content of the book is meant to build faith in God, provide purpose in life, and promote peace and healing, both physically and spiritually. *Science and Health with Key to the Scriptures* has been named as one of the seventy-five books written by women that have most changed the world.

Christian Themes

A cornerstone topic that permeates the pages of *Science and Health with Key to the Scriptures* is the existence of a supreme, infinite God. Eddy characterizes God with qualities of being all-loving, omnipotent, and possessing infinite goodness. As a result, he can be accessed by demonstrating active faith in him and sincerely praying to him. Eddy believes that humans are the likeness and image of God. By drawing closer to God, individuals move to a higher plane of living and develop inner peace and comfort. God's divine laws are applicable to each person every day.

Eddy pleas for people to follow the example of Jesus Christ and strive to live as he did every day. She promotes the principle of treating others the way we would like to be treated. Jesus Christ is the Son of God who carried out the Atonement, which was necessary to overcome sin and reconcile humankind with God. Eddy reminds the reader that this supreme act is evidence of God's divine, efficacious love. Through the crucifixion and resurrection of Christ, death is overcome. Each individual can rise again and live eternally.

Science and Health with Key to the Scriptures emphasizes the necessity for individuals to study the Bible on a daily basis. Because the true nature of each individual is spiritual, spiritual nourishment must be provided from divine sources, which include sincere prayer to God, faithful study of the Bible, and living by God's words. Eddy explains the application of biblical teachings to the practice of everyday Christian living and to working out one's eternal salvation. Reading the Bible strengthens one's trust in the power of prayer and the power of God and makes Christ's teachings practical in the world today.

Sources for Further Study

Gardner, Martin. *The Healing Revelations of Mary Baker Eddy: The Rise and Fall of Christian Science.* Buffalo, N.Y.: Prometheus Books, 1993. Gardner analyzes the ideas and concepts promoted by Eddy in *Science and Health with Key to the Scriptures,* how they led to the establishment and growth of the Christian Science religion, and the factors that caused the decline of that religion.

Gottschalk, Stephen. *Rolling Away the Stone: Mary Baker Eddy's Challenge to Materialism.* Bloomington: Indiana University Press, 2006. Contains an account of the founding of the Christian Science religion centered around the theme of spiritual healing that was promoted by Mary Baker Eddy.

Piepmeier, Alison. *Out in Public: Configurations of Women's Bodies in Nineteenth-Century America.* Chapel Hill: University of North Carolina Press, 2004. In discussing the lives of a few exemplary women, Piepmeier extols the life of Mary Baker Eddy as an example of faith, hope, and courage in speaking out in a predominantly man's world about key issues associated with medicine and healing.

Schoepflin, Rennie B. *Christian Science on Trial: Religious Healing in America.* Baltimore: Johns Hopkins University Press, 2003. By examining the messages presented by Eddy in *Science and Health with Key to the Scriptures,* Schoepflin highlights the contributions of Eddy as a teacher, healer, and religious leader.

Thomas, Robert David. *With Bleeding Footsteps: Mary Baker Eddy's Path to Religious Leadership.* New York: Knopf, 1994. This work explores the life of Mary Baker Eddy, her philosophy about healing as promoted by the Scriptures, her rise to religious leadership, and the themes contained in *Science and Health with Key to the Scriptures.*

Alvin K. Benson

THE SCREWTAPE LETTERS

Author: C. S. Lewis (1898-1963)

First published: 1941, installments in *The Guardian*; in book form, 1942; revised edition published as *The Screwtape Letters and Screwtape Proposes a Toast*, 1961

Edition used: The Screwtape Letters, with Screwtape Proposes a Toast. San Francisco: HarperSanFrancisco, 2001

Genre: Novel

Subgenres: Humor; letters

Core issues: Conversion; daily living; God; love; salvation; sin and sinners; spiritual warfare

God has given every human being the power to choose freely between God and Satan, salvation and damnation. Lewis presents this drama through the eyes of a senior devil who is advising a less experienced satanic spirit on how to win over the young man to whom he has been assigned.

> *Principal characters*
> *The Devil*, ruler of hell, referred to by his subordinates as Our Father
> *Screwtape*, a senior devil, author of the letters
> *Wormwood*, his nephew, a less experienced devil
> *God*, referred to by the devils as the Enemy
> *The patient*, the young man whom Wormwood tempts
> *The patient's mother*, with whom the patient lives
> *Glubose*, her devil
> *The patient's girl friend*, a dedicated Christian
> *Slumtrimpet*, her devil

Overview

The Screwtape Letters is made up of thirty-one undated letters from a senior devil called Screwtape to his nephew Wormwood. In these letters, Screwtape offers advice to the younger demon as he attempts to secure the soul of a human being, referred to as "the patient." The book, then, is the account of a young man's journey to the heavenly city, though in this case the narrator is his enemy, a demon who hopes to block his salvation.

In his first letter, Screwtape makes it clear that the surest way to lose the patient is to encourage him to use his reason, for inevitably, his reason will take him to God, whom the devils call the Enemy. Wormwood must find his opportunities by getting his patient to reason falsely or to be governed by his emotions. Screwtape is not discouraged when the patient becomes a Christian, for he explains to Wormwood that new converts often experience an emotional letdown. Wormwood should direct the patient's attention to the irritating habits or the hypocrisy of the other people in his church. Screwtape also suggests that the patient be encouraged to notice his mother's annoying habits to the point that he will have difficulty praying for her. Screwtape is delighted when the patient falls in with a wealthy group of skeptics. The patient is so proud of his new friends that Screwtape believes the struggle for his soul is over. However, God again manifests himself to the patient, and the result is a second conversion.

In his fifth letter, Screwtape reprimands Wormwood for his assumption that the outbreak of World War II would make it easier to capture souls. Unfortunately, war provides occasions for selfless deeds, and the Enemy judges such deeds on their own merits, not on his approval of the cause. However, as Screwtape points out later, anxiety is a good climate for demonic activity. Meanwhile, Wormwood is urged to make the patient a connoisseur of churches, then a partisan of a single point of view. Wormwood can also make sure the patient sees his mother as the glutton that her own demon, Glubose, encourages her to be. Wormwood should also attack through the patient's sexual nature. As Screwtape explains, his being a Christian is no impediment, for when a Christian marries because he is "in love," he sets himself up for disappointment, thus providing marvelous opportunities for the demons pursuing his soul.

Screwtape begins his twenty-second letter with a sarcastic reference to Wormwood's attempt to get his uncle in trouble with the satanic secret police by repeating some unguarded comments that were made in the letters. Wormwood will pay the price for his action, Screwtape promises, as well as for all his other mistakes. The most serious of them is Wormwood's allowing his charge to fall in love with a virtuous young woman from a loving, Christian family. To Screwtape's horror, the girl is also witty; indeed, he muses, she might well laugh even at him. The idea puts Screwtape into such a state that he turns into a centipede and has to dictate the rest of that letter to his secretary, Toadpipe.

However, Screwtape has not given up. He now suggests that Wormwood attack on two fronts, one intellectual and one emotional. Wormwood is to urge the patient's Christian friends, and thus the patient himself, to reduce Christ to the status of a mere historical figure, useful for promoting social justice or some other cause. Meanwhile, Screwtape has learned from Slimtrimpet, the demon assigned to the young woman, that she has a habit of laughing at nonbelievers. Now Wormwood can use her flaw to persuade the patient that he is, and indeed deserves to be, a member of a small, select group; such feelings, of course, will result in pride. Wormwood is also told to encourage the two lovers to compete in exhibiting unselfishness, thus establishing resentments that can persist for years.

The last three letters are prompted by German air raids on the town where the patient lives. As Screwtape points out, it is to the Enemy's advantage to have the patient die, for up to that point he has resisted all temptations and if he remains true, he will become God's forever. As long as he is alive, however, Screwtape and Wormwood still have a chance to seduce him. To Screwtape's disappointment, although the first raid frightens the patient, he does his duty. Then he is mortally wounded. The patient recognizes Wormwood for what he is, sees angelic spirits, and then finds himself in Christ's presence. Screwtape is left with just one consolation: that he will be allowed to make a meal of Wormwood or at least to snack on him.

Christian Themes

C. S. Lewis accepts the traditional doctrine that each person on earth is a central figure in a great drama that ends only with that person's death. Every individual, no matter how humble, is a prize for which God and Satan are always struggling. At times, God seems to withdraw from the battle; however, when he appears to be absent, he expects human beings to avoid evil by using their reason, the power he gave humans at the time of creation. For centuries, Christian thinkers have held that reason inevitably leads both to belief and to its corollary, Christian conduct. Satan's only hope, then, is to persuade one to reason falsely or to permit the emotions and the appetites to take the place of reason. The seven deadly sins—wrath, avarice, sloth, pride, lechery or lust, envy, and gluttony—all involve the emotions. False reasoning can lead to such errors as the reduction of Christ to a historical figure, the assumption that Christian doctrine needs to be reworked so as to apply to contemporary life, and the insistence that the real value of religion is the support it gives to another cause, such as social justice.

Although reason can help a person avoid evil in thought and deed, reason alone cannot save a person. Unlike Satan, who wants to acquire people so that he can consume them, God loves human beings, as is evident in the fact that he sent his Son to live among them, to teach them, and to die for their sins. Whenever a human being is in greatest need, God makes his presence felt, as he does when the patient has his second conversion and also at the time of his death.

This focus on salvation accounts for a crucial difference between the way the two forces view time. The satanic powers appeal to human greed, trying to convince their prey that their time is their own, to be spent as they wish, and encouraging them to live not in the present, but in some imagined future time, when all their vicious impulses will be satisfied. By contrast, there are only two times of importance to Christians: the present, when they must do their duty, and eternity, when they will be with God.

Sources for Further Study

Holmer, Paul. *C. S. Lewis: The Shape of His Faith and Thought*. New York: Harper and Row, 1976. A lucid, succinct overview of Lewis's theology.

Hooper, Walter, ed. *C. S. Lewis: A Companion and Guide*. San Francisco: Harper-SanFrancisco, 1996. Includes a chronological biography of Lewis, short biographies of his associates, definitions and place descriptions, a "Key Ideas" section, and critical analyses of the works.

Lewis, C. S. *Mere Christianity*. New York: Macmillan, 1952. The author identifies the views common to Christians of all denominations. One of his best-known works.

Sims, John A. *Missionaries to the Skeptics: Christian Apologists for the Twentieth*

Century—C. S. Lewis, Edward John Carnell, and Reinhold Niebuhr. Macon, Ga.: Mercer University Press, 1995. Places the beliefs of three major Christian theologians within the context of their personal experiences. Bibliography and index.

Walker, Andrew, and James Patrick, eds. *Rumours of Heaven: Essays in Celebration of C. S. Lewis.* Guildford, Surrey, England: Eagle, 1998. Originally published as *A Christian for All Christians: Essays in Honour of C. S. Lewis* in 1990. Essays on subjects such as Lewis's debt to historic Christianity, his attention to narrative, and his use of myth. Notes and selected bibliography.

Rosemary M. Canfield Reisman

THE SEAL OF GAIA
A Novel of the Antichrist

Author: Marlin Maddoux (1933-2004)
First published: Nashville, Tenn.: Word, 1998
Genre: Novel
Subgenres: Apocalyptic fiction; evangelical fiction; science fiction
Core issues: Apocalypse; conversion; good vs. evil; imperialism; morality; persecution; religion

In Maddoux's evangelical, apocalyptic novel The Seal of Gaia, *the new Social Order wants to establish peace and ecological balance. As rising media star Steve Weston soon learns, this is merely a cover for a Satanic plot to destroy all life on Earth.*

> *Principal characters*
> *Steve Weston*, a reporter and director of Sky News Network
> *Wilhelm Wallenberg*, Steve's mentor
> *Audrey Montaigne*, Steve's cohost and future love interest
> *Secretary-General of the New Earth Federation*, the Antichrist
> *Lori Weston*, Steve's wife
> *Sheila Harper*, Lori's coworker, a Christian
> *Bernard Mueller*, the creator of Omega, the world computer
> *Dwight Pennington*, Lori's father, who has been studying
>   Christian end-time beliefs
> *Martha Pennington*, Lori's mother, who is taken in the Rapture
> *The Principals*, a group of wealthy families who have been
>   controlling and guiding humanity for centuries
> *Amos Dorian*, a sadistic general in the New Earth Federation
> *Samuel Wilson*, a Christian doctor who reveals the truth about the
>   Kavrinski Institute for Human Life

Overview

The Seal of Gaia takes place in 2033, when the world is being quickly unified under the New Earth Federation (NEF) in the name of peace and a balanced earth ecology, now personified as a deity named Gaia. Under its Social Order program, for years the NEF has been indoctrinating children, including Steve Weston, who has grown up to become the head reporter and new director of the Sky News Network. Steve's loyalty to the new world and its mysterious yet frightening leader is tested in the first half of the novel.

While Steve works his way into the higher levels of the NEF and learns about their future plans to cleanse the world, his wife, Lori, works on indoctrinating children at a local school. Indoctrination includes having children play violent video games and participate in guided meditations to find a Wise Counselor as well as removing them to boarding schools if their families do not follow the Social Order. Lori's work brings her into direct conflict with another teacher, Sheila Harper, who refuses to let go of her outdated Christian beliefs. When Sheila interferes with Lori's class to save her own daughter, Lori has her fired and her child taken to a far-away school.

Lori's career is hampered by her young child, so she, urged by her Satanic Wise Counselors, arranges for his murder right before his third birthday. Luckily for the child, Steve becomes further involved with the NEF to secure the child's release. Turning to Sheila, Lori fights off the demonic spirits in her by converting to Christianity a few months before the believers are taken in the Rapture and spared the increased attacks from the NEF.

Maddoux reveals a Social Order supported through a network of other institutions. The new Gaian religion draws heavily on Eastern traditions, claiming that all previous saviors and religious figures are merely Ascended Masters trying to lead people toward their new level of spirituality. A series of laws has allowed governments greater control over and the ability to exploit humans, and the NEF gains control over all weapons, commerce, and media services via a biochip that it offers to implant in people in exchange for greater protection in a world ravaged for decades by disease and war. The Principals seem to have planned and created most of the conflict and death in the world to set up the NEF.

Steve's journey up the ranks of the NEF is facilitated by his mentor, Wilhelm Wallenberg, who has discovered a horrible plan called the Gaia Project that is scheduled to reduce the world population from seven billion to two billion within a short amount of time. When Wallenberg's doubts are discovered, he is cleverly eliminated, and Steve finds himself having to hide his own doubts as he rises higher in the NEF in his attempt to either prove or disprove Wallenberg's and others' fears about the Secretary-General and the Principals who control him.

His primary job as a reporter allows Steve to gain the confidence of people and access information unknown to the rest of the world. He uncovers a vicious human organ harvesting program, routine reductions of benefits for the elderly and ill to force them into suicide, and medical experimentation on those considered too "negative" for the Social Order. Steve learns a bit more about the Principals, but their identities are never revealed beyond the basic fact that they are wealthy families who have been exercising ultimate control over the planet for centuries. He also meets Christians and those studying them, including his in-laws, and hears about the Antichrist and Jesus, though none of this makes much of a difference until the final solution is revealed.

Omega is a computer system designed to administer the NEF and promote the Social Order, and it has gained sentience, according to its creator, Bernard Mueller, who contacts Steve. The problem with Omega is that she has decided that the earth is at the breaking point, and she is about to start a countdown to destroy all human life with the most powerful bombs available. Steve tries to reason with her, but he soon sees that she too is possessed by Satan, and only the intervention of the Archangel Michael saves the world at the last moment.

Satan and the Secretary-General of the NEF have other plans of attack and begin the final promotion of the Gaian religion and the cleansing of the world. Finally realizing just who controls the NEF and designed the Social Order (Satan), Steve calls in some big favors and makes a plea on his newscast for people to resist the biochip implant, now called the seal of Gaia.

Steve and his coworker Audrey Montaigne join up with disillusioned NEF forces and other freedom lovers, including non-Christians. While they plan their own attack, they must fend off both supernatural and military assaults, protected by their growing faith in Jesus and their quick martial training. The novel ends without a resolution, suggesting that Maddoux planned a sequel before his death.

Christian Themes

Maddoux's vision of the Apocalypse is one of a world unified by new religion and imperialism working hand in hand to promote evil through the persecution of anyone classified as "subhuman" or "negative." The evil in this future world of 2033 is played out on several moral levels, including the direct threat toward anyone rejecting the new Gaia religion, the legal right to commit suicide or murder dependents, and the misuse of science to kill entire towns.

The forces of good work through faith and quiet outreach at first until they are faced with having to choose a biochip called the seal of Gaia or lose civil and economic rights. In the first two-thirds of the novel. the Christians convert through living their faithful life and witnessing to those loved ones whom they think they can reach. Once the seal is promoted, they turn to military resistance and even join forces with non-Christians to oppose the new Social Order.

The battle between good and evil, the dominant theme of *The Seal of Gaia*, is then fought on every level. While this battle plays out on a grand scale as towns are destroyed, people are poisoned, and religion is forced on the masses, the real struggle is in the individual. Time and again, Maddoux offers his characters choices between moral and immoral actions and opportunities to accept Jesus and witness to others.

Sources for Further Study

Frykholm, Amy Johnson. *Rapture Culture: Left Behind in Evangelical America*. Oxford, England: Oxford University Press, 2004. Examines the rising popularity of evangelical fiction and uses Maddoux's novel as an example of common themes in the genre.

Maddoux, Marlin, and Christopher Corbett. *A Christian Agenda: Game Plan for a New Era*. Kingsburg, Calif.: International Christian Media, 1993. An articulation of Maddoux's religious and political beliefs, which play out well in *The Seal of Gaia*.

Mort, John. *Christian Fiction: A Guide to the Genre*. Greenwood, Conn.: Libraries Unlimited, 2002. Discusses several trends in Christian literature and cites examples of several popular fantasy and science fiction books.

Seed, David, ed. *Imagining Apocalypse: Studies in Cultural Crisis.* New York: St. Martin's Press, 2000. Several articles focus on different aspects of Christian science fiction and examine modern attitudes toward sex, science, and government.

TammyJo Eckhart

THE SECOND COMING

Author: Walker Percy (1916-1990)
First published: New York: Farrar, Straus and Giroux, 1980
Genre: Novel
Subgenres: Catholic fiction; literary fiction; romance
Core issues: Death; doubt; hope; love; memory; self-knowledge

Will Barrett, a wealthy middle-aged widower reconsidering his life and considering suicide, and Allie Huger, an escaped mental patient in her early twenties, experience separation from society and doubt in the divine separately, but they find a hopeful way to face the future together. Though many religious convictions are represented and pushed by other characters in the book, it is through communion with the earth and with each other that the unlikely couple hope to find meaning and peace.

> *Principal characters*
> *Will Barrett*, the protagonist
> *Marion Barrett*, Will's deceased wife
> *Ed Barrett*, Will's deceased father
> *Leslie Barrett*, Will's daughter
> *Lewis Peckham*, Will's friend
> *Allison Huger*, Will's lover, an escaped mental patient
> *Kitty Vaught Huger*, Allison's mother
> *Jack Curl*, a chaplain

Overview

Walker Percy told the first part of the story of Will Barrett in *The Last Gentleman* (1966) and continues it in *The Second Coming.* In this novel, something is wrong with Will Barrett, a retired Wall Street lawyer in his mid-forties. His golf game, usually excellent, is suffering; he keeps falling down; he is obsessed with the movement of the Jews, which he interprets as a possible sign; and he is haunted by long-suppressed memories. Will has returned to the Carolina mountains where he grew up and is consumed with thoughts of suicide. His wife, Marion, a disabled, fat Christian philanthropist, has been dead less than a year, and his born-again daughter, Leslie, is getting married in a few weeks. Will cannot find solace in either woman's faith. He finds no help in Jack Curl, the chaplain who runs the nursing home funded by the Barretts, or in Lewis Peckham, his atheist friend.

Will considers the extent of his deceased father's legacy: two guns and a lust for suicide. Will recalls what was referred to as the "hunting accident" in his family and realizes that on that day, his father not only attempted suicide but also attempted homicide. Ed Barrett, tortured by living a "death-in-life" and believing he was bequeathing it to his son, tried to end it for both of them. He failed at both that day but did manage to kill himself not long after (Percy's own father committed suicide). Will decides to devise a test that will solve his problem. He dispatches the proper letters to cover his tracks however the experiment works out, then climbs into a cave in the Carolina mountains and waits. Will believes that if there is a God, he will receive a sign that will allow him to live renewed; if not, there will be no sign and he will die.

Meanwhile, Allison Huger, a young adult, finds herself on a bench. She cannot remember who she is or how she got there. In her hand she holds a notebook in which she has apparently written some notes to herself. She discovers that she has spent the last few years of her life in a mental institution her parents committed her to. She does not think, communicate, or interact the way others do, and her parents feel she can never live completely on her own. In the institution, she was regularly subjected to electromagnetic shock therapy. The information in the notebook is written in her own hand, telling her how to escape from the hospital; that she will remember very little, as is typical for a few days after getting "buzzed"; and why she has chosen now to escape. By spying on a meeting between her parents and her doctor, she has learned that she has just inherited some property. She gathers the supplies the notebook tells her she will need and heads up the mountain to the greenhouse on her property. In the following days, she takes great pleasure in cleaning the greenhouse and making it habitable; in particular, she enjoys the mental and physical exertions required for hoisting things. A dog decides to live with her, Will happens on her when he loses a golf ball, and an occasional hiker stops for water, but in general she is alone and not upset about that, except at four o'clock in the afternoon.

Will has to call his test off. After a week in the cave, he develops an awful toothache that takes precedence over questions regarding God's existence. Weak and sick, he tries to climb out of the mountain the way he came in but loses his way, comes tumbling out of the wrong cave exit, and smashes through the ceiling of Allie's greenhouse. She bathes and feeds him, runs his errands, and hoists him up when he falls. She realizes she is in love with him, not knowing that her mother, Kitty, was his girlfriend many years ago or that Will knows who she is. Will leaves, promising to come back, but is detained by his illness. After falling down again, he is diagnosed with a rare disease affecting the pH balance in his body. His pH levels must be maintained constantly, and he is admitted as a patient into his own nursing home. When his pH levels are back to normal, he is no longer concerned about God or with the movement of the Jews and its possible meaning; however, he still thinks of the girl.

Eventually, after learning that Kitty has found out where Allie is and is going to retrieve her, largely to have her deemed incompetent and sell her property, Will leaves the home. Will and Allie check into a motel, where they make love, a renewing and sacred experience for both, and plan for the future. They will marry, ending all property claims by the Hugers, and they will begin a new life. Will plans to use skills learned from men in the nursing home, who were put out to pasture by society but still had valuable skills and knowledge, to build homes on the property and grow produce; they will make love in the afternoons to fill the four o'clock void. As he prepares for his nuptials, Will wonders if he is crazy to want both God and Allie. He rephrases the question to himself: "No, not want, must have. And will have."

Christian Themes

The title of this novel is, of course, a reference to the prophesied second coming of Jesus Christ; Will wonders if the last days are on him as he considers whether the movement of the Jews is a possible sign. Part of the theme of salvation are the changes both major characters undergo. Will spends the majority of the book contemplating Christianity. He cannot decide whether he finds it more difficult to relate to the faithful or the unfaithful, but he certainly cannot place himself in either camp. The answers he receives, whether from his traditionally Christian wife, his evangelical daughter, his atheist friend, his death-loving father, or his chaplain, seemingly embarrassed by religion, are not good enough.

Though Will sees his test as a failure, one he never gets to complete, Percy seems to be suggesting that Will does get an answer. It is not as black and white, perhaps, as the manifestation of God Will may have hoped for in the cave or the personal relationship with Christ attested to by his daughter, but it is his climbing into the cave, his testing, his timely toothache, and his inability to find his way that bring him literally crashing into his salvation. It is through Allie that he is, in a very real way, reborn. His final divesting himself of his father's legacy, both the guns and the urge for suicide, are the signs that he has in fact chosen life. For Allie, as well, the story is one of rebirth. It is literally her second coming into the world, as she finds herself relearning, or learning in some cases, how to communicate, how to work, how to love, and how to live.

Will is, like many of Percy's characters, a searcher who has not yet found what he is looking for. At the end of *The Second Coming*, however, Will has actually found something. Although he did not have a personal encounter with God, the end of the novel is filled with a sense of hope that through working on the land, loving truly, and searching without cynicism, he will find meaning, peace, and possibly even religion.

Sources for Further Study

Ciuba, Gary M. *Walker Percy: Books of Revelations*. Athens: University of Georgia Press, 1991. Study focused on the apocalyptic elements of Percy's fiction, with a chapter devoted to *The Second Coming*.

Moore, Benita A. "Language as Sacrament in Walker Percy's *The Second Coming*." *Journal of the American Academy of Religion* 60, no. 2 (Summer, 1992): 281-299. Considers the addition of the female Heideggerian search to the expected male Kierkegaardian search and its relation to language in *The Second Coming*.

Pridgen, Allen. *Walker Percy's Sacramental Landscapes: The Search in the Desert*. Selinsgrove, Pa.: Susquehanna University Press, 2000. Argues that Percy's protagonists can find sacramental signs toward meaning amid their affluent but empty cultural landscapes. Will Barrett is considered extensively.

Quinlan, Kieran. *Walker Percy: The Last Catholic Novelist*. Baton Rouge: Louisiana State University Press, 1996. This study argues that Percy's Catholicism is his defining characteristic and attempts to present his theology.

Lily Corwin

SECRETS IN THE DARK
A Life in Sermons

Author: Frederick Buechner (1926-   )
First published: San Francisco: HarperSanFrancisco, 2006
Genre: Nonfiction
Subgenre: Sermons
Core issues: Christmas; church; faith; hope; memory

Buechner's talents as a novelist inform this collection of sermons and talks, culled from his entire career. His central concerns are the meaning of faith, the human longing for a true home, and the necessity of being open to God's message.

Overview

A *Life in Sermons*, the subtitle of Frederick Buechner's collection *Secrets in the Dark*, is not strictly accurate. To begin with, not all the pieces collected in it are sermons. Some of the pieces were originally given as talks, such as "Adolescence and the Stewardship of Pain," delivered at St. Paul's School; "The Newness of Things," given at the installation of Buechner's friend Douglas Hale as headmaster at Mercersburg Academy; and "Faith and Fiction," given at the New York Public Library. Some are essays: "The Good Book as a Good Book," which appeared in *A Complete Literary Guide to the Bible* (1993), edited by Leland Ryken and Tremper Longman, is on the relationship of fiction and religion; and "Paul Sends His Love," which first appeared in *Incarnation: Contemporary Writers on the New Testament* (1991), edited by Alfred Corn, is on Paul's First Letter to the Corinthians. However, the rest of the collection consists of sermons delivered over the course of Buechner's life, ranging from those he delivered at Philips Exeter Academy beginning in 1959 ("The Magnificent Defeat") to one given at Princeton University's anniversary celebration, "A 250th Birthday Prayer." Many of them have appeared in earlier Buechner collections—*The Magnificent Defeat* (1966), *The Hungering Dark* (1969), *A Room Called Remember* (1984), *The Clown in the Belfry: Writings on Faith and Fiction* (1991), *The Longing for Home: Recollections and Reflections* (1996)—and their republication here indicates that Buechner considers them to be his best work in this genre. Also included are a few sermons that have not been published before.

Also, while many of these sermons contain autobiographical elements, they do not form a quasi-autobiography; they are more the sermons of a lifetime than a life in sermons. The portrait that they paint of Buechner's life, aside from the richness given to observations that result from his life as a parent and his career as a writer, is a remarkably consistent one. Like many reflective minds, Buechner's is always open to the possibility of revelation and epiphany, but the pilgrimage charted throughout these sermons is grounded in a few basic concepts that Buechner returns to again and again. The first sermons in this collection were delivered to a group of students who were resolutely resistant to any religious message, and this sense of preaching to the un-willing underlies many of Buechner's messages. His ministerial vocation is indeed a calling: he calls his listeners to come with him on a search for God and Jesus in their lives, on a journey to what he sees as their true home.

One must remember, however, that most of these pieces are sermons, not essays, and were written to be delivered and heard, not read. As such, they have a particular struc-ture: title; introductory text(s), the vast majority of which are from the Bible; the sermon itself; and a concluding prayer in italics (although the italics soon disappear, and the conclusion transforms itself into the substance of a prayer). Because they are sermons, and Buechner is a novelist, the sermons' organizational pattern is often more associa-tional than logical; in a way, the movement of thought toward the central kernel of the message within reproduces the pattern of the journey the soul takes toward faith. For example, "A Room Called Remember," one of the early sermons, begins with quota-tions from the Old Testament (from Chronicles about David's worship of God before the ark) and the New (Jesus' words on the cross to the good thief). Buechner begins by talking about dreams in general and how they sometimes reveal a profound truth about the dreamer, then recalls one such dream in which he tries to return to a hotel room where he was extraordinarily happy: The name of the room is Remember. Buechner then goes on to discuss different types of remembrance; the type of remembrance he thinks the room stands for is the type in which we remember our entire lives, and dis-cover in that remembrance how God has touched our lives. A bald summary like this cannot transmit the flavor of the entire sermon: how the theme is introduced, modu-lated, and recapitulated; how the texts are interwoven into the fabric of the message, amplifying it and transforming it; and how the filaments of its development tie it to-gether. The journey to the message is the message. In remembrance is belief.

Also adding to the sermons' effectiveness is Buechner's use of fictional strategies to bring his examples vividly before his listeners. He often describes a biblical scene as if it were a passage in a novel. In "The Magnificent Defeat," he re-creates Jacob's pretending to be his brother Esau; in "Birth," he writes three dramatic monologues about the birth of Jesus (delivered by the Innkeeper, a Wise Man, and a Shepherd); in "A Sprig of Hope," he describes Noah's summoning by God and the release of the dove to find land; in "Air for Two Voices," he shows what the Annunciation might have looked like; and in "The Truth of Stories," he presents the parable of the prodigal son as a modern first-person narrative. Buechner meticulously analyzes the miracle of resurrection in "Jairus's Daughter," not only because of its religious meaning, but also because Mark's narrative of it is so detailed, almost an eyewitness account, that it ap-proaches the density of a scene in a novel. Buechner also analyzes his own fiction not only to discuss his own religious subjects (such as his portrayal of saints and sanctity) but also to show that an author's receptivity to his characters is like the receptivity that people should have in their lives to God. Buechner points out that in a way that tran-scends symbolism and metaphor, the Gospels and indeed the whole Bible are based on an identification of the Word and God— in the Hebrew word *dabhar*, which means "word" and "deed" at the same time, and in the beginning of John's Gospel: "The Word was God." To read the story of Jesus is not the entire message; that Jesus is the story is equally important.

Christian Themes

Buechner's concerns as a Presbyterian minister are not confined to one denomination; indeed, several times he bemoans the fact that like the early Church, Christianity has splintered into factions. The central thread that runs through these sermons and talks is Buechner's conception of faith. Faith is not dogmatic, static, and blinkered: It is both dynamic—"a movement towards" as he calls it—and subject to doubts and hesitation. It is not something that remains unwavering, full of certitude; it is a constant struggle to realize that even though we may seem to be in a world bereft of God's voice and presence, he is actually present and communicating with us, if we can only learn to be open and remember. Faith requires us to "pay attention," to be receptive to the workings of God in the world, according to Buechner. Two epiphanic moments for Buechner (although he does not call them that) occur when a minister, in giving Buechner communion, calls him by his first name, and when a woman he passes by on the street tells him, "Jesus loves you." These moments make Buechner understand that God speaks to everyone personally and that he calls us by our names.

An equally strong theme in *Secrets in the Dark* is the realization that the world is not our home; we are all longing for our true home with God. In "The Great Dance," Buechner finds himself in tears at a performance of killer whales at Sea World. After learning he was not alone in his reaction, he comes to the conclusion that he was overjoyed because the show was a foreshadowing of the Peaceable Kingdom, the home we should have had and will come into one day. All human homes, no matter how dear, are only reminders of the hunger we have for our final home. With his literary bent, Buechner encapsulates salvation history as a version of the hoary plot summary "boy meets girl, boy loses girl, boy gets girl." God creates the world, the world loses God, God saves the world. Buechner says that salvation story is our story too.

Sources for Further Study

Buechner, Frederick. "Ordained to Write: An Interview with Frederick Buechner." Interview by Richard Kauffman. *Christian Century* 119 (September 11-24, 2002): 26-33. A valuable retrospective interview in which Buechner discusses his ministry as a novelist and minister and his use of autobiography in his writing.

McCoy, Marjorie, with Charles S. McCoy. *Frederick Buechner: Novelist and Theologian of the Lost and Found*. San Francisco: Harper & Row, 1988. A persuasive attempt to connect Buechner's vocations as novelist and religious thinker by analyzing his themes and concerns: In his works, theology is transfigured into storytelling.

Wriglesworth, Chad. "George A. Buttrick and Frederick Buechner: Messengers of Reconciling Laughter." *Christianity and Literature* 53 (Autumn, 2002): 59-75. Convincingly shows how Buttrick's religious thinking in his sermons affected Buechner not only in his conversion but also in his art.

William Laskowski

THE SECRETS OF BARNEVELD CALVARY

Author: James C. Schaap (1948-   )
First published: Grand Rapids, Mich.: Baker Books, 1997
Genre: Short fiction
Subgenre: Literary fiction
Core issues: African Americans; hope; redemption; self-knowledge

In eight short stories, the fictional pastor of a church in the small town of Barneveld, Iowa, reveals the secrets of church members and town residents. The narrator relates the circumstances surrounding these stories—told to him in confidence—of decades-old grudges, deaths, extramarital affairs and sex, disappointed parents, and consuming guilt. Through his sensitive telling, the pastor intimates the hope he holds for those involved, despite their tragic circumstances and personal frailties.

> *Principal characters*
> *An unnamed pastor,* head of Calvary Church in Barneveld, Iowa, who narrates all eight short stories
> *Crystal te Lindert,* a young pregnant woman
> *Duane Foxhoven,* a landscaper with a grudge
> *The Reverend Cecil Meekhof,* a popular retired pastor in Barneveld
> *Sarah Esselink,* the church pianist
> *Chris Esselink,* Sarah's homosexual son
> *Mindy Brink,* a seventeen-year-old girl who feels guilt for her boyfriend's accident
> *Lenny Bolstad,* Mindy's boyfriend
> *Holly Eidemiller,* a homeowner and town saint
> *Russ Ruiter,* vice president of the local bank
> *Adrianna Meekhof,* a woman who develops a relationship with her boss
> *Les Meekhof,* Adrianna's husband
> *Stuart Mackey,* Adrianna's lover
> *Ted Bennink,* a father who was a soldier liberating Dachau
> *Mins de Boom,* the school janitor

Overview

In *The Secrets of Barneveld Calvary,* James C. Schaap presents eight short stories in which the narrator, a pastor in a small Iowa town, describes personal secrets told to him by residents of the town and expresses his hope for redemption for those whose secrets are here revealed.

In "The Profession of Crystal te Lindert," the title character is a young pregnant woman unsure if the father of her baby is her gruff husband, Butch, white like his wife and the rest of Barneveld, or Cedrick Myles, a star African American college basketball player from across the state. In the midst of her pregnancy, Crystal confesses her Christian faith to the church council, and from there the narrator recounts her story, demonstrating both questionable moral decisions from Crystal's past and his confidence in the truth of her more recent experience of faith.

A decades-long grudge, passed from deceased father to his now-adult son, is the centerpiece of "Duane Foxhoven's Trees for Tomorrow." The Reverend Cecil Meekhof, the popular, retired pastor of another church in Barneveld, hires Duane's company to landscape his home, unaware that Duane is the son of a man Meekhof angrily confronted and effectively excommunicated because of black-market business dealings during World War II, when Duane was a young boy and Meekhof was a zealous young preacher. After Meekhof dies, the narrator examines how Duane may or may not be passing the grudge down to his own son.

In "The Temptations of Sarah Esselink," the church pianist has two secrets: a penchant for supermarket tabloids and a mostly closeted homosexual son, Chris, in California, with whom she has an ongoing but uncertain relationship. Chris calls when Sarah is suddenly admitted to the hospital for angioplasty, and the two reach an uneasy truce over Chris's sexuality and faith and Sarah's past parenting. Sarah later makes good on a hospital-room bargain with God to give up the tabloids, one she rescinds after a chance visit to one newspaper's office in Florida, an event that provides a picture of her trust in God in dealing with her relationship with Chris.

Guilt and penance that far outweigh any possible offense plague "Mindy Brink at River Bend." After Mindy, seventeen and shy, has dated factory worker Lenny Bolstad, twenty-one and reckless, a few times, Lenny arranges a late-night fishing expedition for the couple at a secluded riverside spot, complete with sleeping bag. When she refuses his sexual advances, an enraged Lenny speeds away on his motorcycle and crashes, his injuries leaving him without use of his arms and part of his mind. Blaming herself for the accident, Mindy offers vigilant pledges of love and devotion that are thought excessive by those around her. Only another visit to the river, this time with her twin brother, Alan, helps Mindy, along with her brother, to see the true responsibility for the tragedy.

Town saint Holly Eidemiller fights the local bank's proposed purchase of her childhood home in "The Wester Homeplace," and the narrator slowly learns the reasons behind Holly's uncharacteristic resistance. Holly's brother Herbie was killed forty years earlier playing chicken at a train crossing with other teenagers, including Russ Ruiter, now vice president of the bank. Most believe that Herbie simply jumped too late, but Holly alone remains silently convinced that Russ pushed Herbie to his death, a conviction so bitter that the narrator abandons his pursuit of healing.

In "Adrianna Meekhof, Stuart Mackey, and Mutual Sin," sensitive Adrianna, married to cold and unsuccessful Les, works for Stuart, five years a grieving widower, and the needy pair form a brief and loving relationship of conversations and embraces, but nothing more. Convinced of her sin, Adrianna resigns, and when Les learns why, he confronts Stuart, drives to his own business, and takes his own life. Stuart and Adrianna discover the body and move it to suggest a natural death, unbeknown to any besides Adrianna's son, Mark, informed by his father's posthumously received letter. Years later, with Adrianna and Stuart happily married, Mark reveals his knowledge of their secret.

A father and teenage son visit Little Bighorn in "Ted Bennink and the King of the Jews," and on hearing his son Mark's account of some of the more gruesome details of Custer's last stand, Ted flashes back to World War II, when he was an American soldier helping liberate the Nazi concentration camp at Dachau. Mark, now a history professor, discovers shortly after his father's death that Ted was relieved of his command after allowing his men and camp prisoners to slaughter guards in that hellish German camp, a memory Ted is comforted in through his conviction that Christ himself descended into hell before his resurrection.

"Mins the Scavenger" is Mins de Boom, the simple, devout school janitor, an immigrant from the Netherlands who married later in life, not for love but for mutual convenience, and who on retirement becomes known for collecting cans from rural roadsides. When Mins one day discovers a viola along his route, he finds he can inexplicably play it, perhaps recalling his mother's playing from his youth. The night before returning the instrument to its owner, Mins secretly and beautifully plays it at a cemetery, heard only by a patrolling police officer.

Christian Themes

Despite all the secrets harbored by these stories' characters, many of them dark and painful to the characters or to others, and despite their sins, shortcomings, or unfortunate circumstances, the narrator maintains an undaunted hope for each of them, even in cases, as with Duane Foxhoven or Holly Eidemiller, where neither he nor anyone else has been able to help the people overcome the secrets.

The hope the narrator holds is for each individual's redemption, a hope provided by his—and their—belief in the redemptive power of Christ. In Schaap's stories, his characters' need for redemption is made plain by the sins some have committed and the secrets they continue to keep, but the narrator's confidence in the possibility, or even likelihood, of their redemption is made just as plain by the narrator's frequent codas in the stories, where he expresses his belief not only in these people's ability to change their lives but also in the power of Christ to help them make those transformations.

As a pastor, the narrator sees all the members of the flock—the people of his church and of the town of Barneveld—not as his subjects but as individuals whose spiritual care he has been entrusted with. More important, he views them each worthy of hope and of having their stories told. Though aware he is breaking confidences, the narrator tells the stories with pastoral sensitivity, not gossipy sensationalism, as if now far enough away in time or distance to feel safe in exposing the confessions he presents.

Sources for Further Study

Horstman, Joey Earl. "Our Town." Review of *The Secrets of Barneveld Calvary*. *Mars Hill Review* 10 (Winter/Spring, 1998): 141-143. An extensive review of the book, highlighting the role of the narrator and characterization.

Schaap, James Calvin. "On Truth, Fiction, and Being a Christian Writer." *Christian Century* 114, no. 36 (December 17, 1997): 1188-1193. Schaap's essay on the meaning of being both a Christian and a writer of fiction, though not necessarily of Christian fiction, cites Flannery O'Connor as a primary influence.

_____. "Writing and Knowing." In *Shouts and Whispers: Twenty-one Writers Speak About Their Writing*. Grand Rapids, Mich.: Wm. B. Eerdmans, 2006. The author's philosophical essay (accompanied by an illustrative short story) characterizes fiction writing as a combination of experience and imagination.

Clint Wrede

THE SENSE OF THE PRESENCE OF GOD

Author: John Baillie (1886-1960)
First published: New York: Charles Scribner's Sons, 1962
Genre: Nonfiction
Subgenres: Essays; history; theology
Core issues: Faith; God; knowledge; revelation; trust in God

Often considered Scotland's pre-eminent twentieth century theologian, Baillie died in 1960 after he had written but before he could deliver the 1961-1962 Gifford lectures. The manuscript, left in a finished state, was published in 1962 as The Sense of the Presence of God. *The Gifford lectures, traditionally concerned with how natural theology is affected by developments in science and other areas of contemporary culture, provided an appropriate forum for Baillie's lifelong interest in the conversation between traditional religious ideas and modern doubts.*

Overview

Trained in philosophy and theology, John Baillie taught at universities in Scotland, the United States, and Canada, and was a significant figure in the ecumenical church developments of the second third of the twentieth century. His views represent a middle position between the extremes of theological liberalism (Rudolf Bultmann, Paul Tillich) and theological conservatism (Karl Barth).

In *The Sense of the Presence of God*, Baillie states that human experience (construed broadly enough to include "the sense of the presence of God") provides a basis for knowledge sufficient for practical action, though it does not support claims to theoretical comprehension: "There can be no apprehension of the divine presence that is not at the same time a summons to a divinely-appointed task." He insists that "we can see to do the work we were meant to do. . . . [And] if our end is the love and service of God, we cannot justly demand more light until we have better used the light we already have." Baillie thus sides with those who think that God wants us to embrace religious belief and action despite (or even, in a sense, because of) "the very limitation of our possible knowledge." He explicitly compares, but also contrasts, his view with Immanuel Kant's attempt to limit knowledge to make room for faith. Religious knowledge is practical rather than speculative, but nonetheless knowledge.

Baillie rejects a narrow, positivist conception of experience, which he sees as philosophically inadequate in its own terms and as unrealistically divorced from the lessons of life. He believes that he, like others, has sensed the presence of God, though he grants that someone else might explain the experience away—just as someone insensitive to aesthetics might describe the sunset in a way that is complete, naturalistically speaking, while still missing the crucial element of beauty. Baillie thus resists the liberal impulse to explain away religious experience in psychological, social, or other terms.

However, Baillie also views this foundational religious and moral experience as a basis for critical reflection on the culturally and historically contingent forms of religious expression. The limits of any human understanding of the divine imply a willingness to re-examine and renew the forms of religious doctrine. He says that "the only exclusive claim which Christians are justified in making is not for what we call 'Christianity,' not for their own brand of pious practices . . . but in the revelation . . . of God in Jesus Christ our Lord—a very necessary distinction which . . . Dr Barth exaggerated into a complete disjunction." He looks forward to a theological liberalism that has learned from Barth's conservative challenge.

In sum, Baillie asserts the presence of God even as he rejects the presumption of those who claim to know what God would have in mind—either to argue against God's existence (as in the problem of evil), or to argue for certitude about God's will.

> We cannot pretend to know in advance how God *ought* to act for the enlightenment and salvation of the human race. . . . The only question which—shall I say, as a good empiricist?—I have a right to ask is: Do I in fact find God coming to meet me in Jesus Christ as nowhere else, or do I not? . . . To this question the Christian can do no other than return an affirmative answer. So when the German philosopher . . . tells me that "The Godhead loves not to pour His whole fulness into a single instance," I cannot but wonder how he knew this.

This encounter with God in Christ is the foundational experience that is the basis for practical religious knowledge.

This insistence on the limitations of religious convictions, when these are viewed as theoretical or speculative claims, implies an antifundamentalist caution about questions of exactness and literalness. Baillie emphasizes the historical dimension of religious reflection, noting the dependency of its formulations on the "thought-forms" and languages of human cultures. On the other hand, a seemly intellectual modesty should not be allowed to devolve into the incoherence of relativism or the inadequacy of emotivism; he repeatedly rejects "reductive naturalism." Baillie sees religious language as making meaningful, if imprecise, claims about the nature of reality—claims best understood in terms of the practical relationships individuals have both with God and with one another, and in terms of the Gospel narrative.

Christian Themes

To the liberal, the conservative's desire to preserve the forms of the past buries the spirit of belief in the dead letter of dogma. To the conservative, the liberal's desire to tell the truth by making it new is an open invitation to self-delusion and revisionism. In theology, as in politics and elsewhere in culture, this struggle is constantly replayed. In his attempt to occupy the middle ground, Baillie touches on many traditional Christian themes.

There are, for example, discussions of the doctrine of the Trinity, the "fatherhood" of God, miracles, the good news of the Incarnation, the humility and humiliation of

Christ, the priority of the personality of Christ to that of human beings, and the central importance of the Gospel narratives. He examines the incomprehensibility of God, the impossibility of "demythologizing," the priority of our knowledge of divine perfection to our knowledge of finite creatures, the nature of God's kingdom, and the fear of the Lord. Baillie also discusses the naturally Christian soul, the nature of faith and works, salvation, trust, the overcoming of personal doubt, providence, the importance of gratitude, and the unity of humankind. Other topics include the relevance of the categories of Greek metaphysics to Christian thought, the connection between doctrine and heresy, the inadequacy of natural theology, the comparison of science and faith, the priority of value to science, and the "existential" significance of Christianity.

Of special interest, given Baillie's mediating approach, is his discussion of the conflict of different faiths. While he firmly rejects the idea that religions other than Christianity contain no truth, he also insists that our ability to distinguish their elements of God-given truth from humanly inspired error is possible only on the basis of the essential Christian revelation. However, he believes that the encounter with other religions can help clarify what that essential revelation—in contrast with accidental historical and cultural accretions—really is, thereby returning faith to its foundation in experience.

Sources for Further Study

Baillie, John. *And the Life Everlasting*. New York: Charles Scribner's Sons, 1933. Baillie discusses Christian and other views about human immortality.

_____. *Our Knowledge of God*. New York: Charles Scribner's Sons, 1939. Often regarded as Baillie's best book, this volume presents the state of his thinking on the question of religious knowledge two decades before the Gifford lectures.

Fergusson, David, ed. *Christ, Church and Society: Essays on John Baillie and Donald Baillie*. New York: T. and T. Clark International, 2000. A collection of sixteen essays covering the lives, theological views, and church work of Baillie and his theologian brother, including a bibliography of their publications.

Hood, Adam. *Baillie, Oman, and Macmurray: Experience and Religious Belief*. Burlington, Vt.: Ashgate, 2003. A comparison of Baillie's ideas about the experiential grounds of religious belief with those of two other twentieth century Scottish theologians; two chapters are devoted specifically to Baillie.

Newlands, George. *John and Donald Baillie: Transatlantic Theology*. New York: Peter Lang, 2002. An intellectual and cultural biography of the Baillie brothers, examining their influence on each other and on international ecumenical theology and church work.

Edward Johnson